Tolley's Guide to t
Act 2006

by
Jean-Paul da Costa and Helen Harvie

Members of the LexisNexis Group worldwide

United Kingdom	LexisNexis Butterworths, a Division of Reed Elsevier (UK) Ltd, Halsbury House, 35 Chancery Lane, London, WC2A 1EL, and London House, 20–22 East London Street, Edinburgh EH7 4BQ
Argentina	LexisNexis Argentina, Buenos Aires
Australia	LexisNexis Butterworths, Chatswood, New South Wales
Austria	LexisNexis Verlag ARD Orac GmbH & Co KG, Vienna
Benelux	LexisNexis Benelux, Amsterdam
Canada	LexisNexis Canada, Markham, Ontario
Chile	LexisNexis Chile Ltda, Santiago
China	LexisNexis China, Beijing and Shanghai
France	LexisNexis SA, Paris
Germany	LexisNexis Deutschland GmbH, Munster
Hong Kong	LexisNexis Hong Kong, Hong Kong
India	LexisNexis India, New Delhi
Italy	Giuffrè Editore, Milan
Japan	LexisNexis Japan, Tokyo
Malaysia	Malayan Law Journal Sdn Bhd, Kuala Lumpur
Mexico	LexisNexis Mexico, Mexico
New Zealand	LexisNexis NZ Ltd, Wellington
Poland	Wydawnictwo Prawnicze LexisNexis Sp, Warsaw
Singapore	LexisNexis Singapore, Singapore
South Africa	LexisNexis Butterworths, Durban
USA	LexisNexis, Dayton, Ohio

First published in 2007

Published by LexisNexis Butterworths

A CIP Catalogue record for this book is available from the British Library.

ISBN 978 0 7545 2746 6

Typeset by Columns Design Ltd, Reading, England
Printed and bound in Great Britain by Hobbs the Printers Ltd, Totton, Hampshire

Visit LexisNexis Butterworths at www.lexisnexis.co.uk

Foreword

The Charities Act 2006 is legislation which promises to change the face of charity, above all by its encouragement of an innovatory approach to the need for all charities to do all they can to serve the public good. Many of us regard this as a golden opportunity for the whole world of charity to show that it does not merely mean well (which thankfully is not open to very great doubt) but is determined to do its best. If so then the one thing which no charity advisor can afford to do is to lag behind in his understanding both of the new legislation and of how it is going to work in practice. Best practice is going, one might say, to need above all else the understanding of best practices. Many of us in Lincoln's Inn will indeed be only too alive to the fact that theoretical answers are no longer going to be much help to the charity which knows it needs a practical answer to the basic question 'how then shall we serve'?

It is therefore a privilege to have been asked to pave the way for those who open this book, intended as it is to be a practical guide. Who knows which of us can ever hope to claim that practice will make perfect? But that the true test of charity in the future will be in the world of practice and not of theory is plain beyond doubt, and I have equally no doubt that many a practitioner is going to be deeply indebted to the authors for helping us in our search for ways of getting on with the job that matters and wasting as little time as possible on the obscurities of a statute which, when all is said and done (and despite the admirable attempts of various members of the House of Lords to improve it while the Bill was in committee), follows a pattern which can hardly be said to be user-friendly. Guides such as this should speed us all on our way to the hard question of how can the public get most value for what is, after all, the public's own money as soon as it has been dedicated to charity?

Charity could perhaps now be summed up in terms of a new commitment to the rules revealed by close study of the parable of the talents. Those of us who have the good fortune to be involved in the vastly rewarding field of law that is the domain of charity will know that most of the time our hearts should be committed more to results than our intellects to legal niceties. That way the talents should multiply and esoteric questions about what is a talent and what in law its origins can be left to those who have the time and the inclination to debate them. In the best traditions of the Tolley Guides we can take this book safe in the knowledge that the authors start with their hearts in the right place, determined to end up with their readers feeling that they have had a proper and practical education.

And that would seem to be one case where no-one could doubt the assumption that education will be for the public benefit.

Christopher McCall QC

Lincoln's Inn

April 2007

Preface

When we first came to write this book in 2004 it looked as if the new Charities Bill would enter Parliament and have a swift passage through, like almost every other piece of legislation introduced by the Government. Work leading up to the Bill had started back in 2001 with the commissioning of a review of the law affecting charities and the not-for-profit sector. This led to the publication in 2002 of the Prime Minister's Strategy Unit report entitled 'Private Action, Public Benefit', which laid the ground for the Bill that would eventually follow.

While there were certain areas of reform that generated some controversy – in particular the new 'public benefit' test, which appeared to be targeted at the tax relief enjoyed by private schools and hospitals – the vast majority of the changes proposed were welcomed by the 'third sector', and everyone expected that the new legislation would move quickly onto the statute books. What nobody had anticipated was the impact which the Iraq war, a General Election and a determined House of Lords would have on the progress of the Bill through Parliament.

Two years after the Bill's introduction, and after extensive revision during its Committee stages in both the Lords and the Commons, one afternoon in early November 2006 the Bill received Royal Assent along with dozens of other pieces of legislation, just when everyone (including the Charity Commission) had given up hope of seeing the new legislation enacted until 2007.

It must be said that although few Acts take so long to pass through Parliament, the Charities Act 2006 certainly benefited from its slower than normal maturation, with most of the concerns raised against the original Bill being ironed out by the time Royal Assent was finally granted. All credit must be given to the Parliamentary Committees who put in so much work. There were, however, two surprising aspects of the new legislation that were not addressed during its long passage. The first was that although the Bill was heralded as a major reform of charity law, rather than introducing an entirely new statute, the 2006 Act simply amended the Charities Act 2003, making the legislation far less accessible to charity trustees and workers than one would have wished for.

The second surprise was that when the Bill was eventually enacted the Government immediately announced that the Act would be phased in over an eighteen month period, with many of the more complex provisions of the Act being introduced last. Whilst it might have been understandable that the Charity Commission would need time to prepare for the implementation of the Act had its progress been swifter, the reasons are less apparent given the considerable amount of time which elapsed from inception to enactment.

However protracted its gestation, the Charities Act 2006 in its final form offers benefits for almost every charity, and we hope that this book will help guide you through the legislation to find those aspects of the new Act that can help your charity or client.

No publication so long in preparation would have been possible without the unstinting support of our partners and families and the hard work of our PAs, Claire Burns and Sally Franks, and we would like to thank them and also Christopher McCall QC, who wrote the foreword to this book.

Jean-Paul da Costa and Helen Harvie

Thomas Eggar, Solicitors

April 2007

Contents

Chapter 1

Introduction

Introduction

1.1 It may be unfair to describe the development of charity law in England and Wales as glacial, but it is true to say that significant changes in charity law are relatively rare and slow-paced, and much of the framework of English charity law has continued to be based on principles dating back over 400 years. The intervention of a General Election, the impact of domestic and international terrorism, and extensive amendment at the Committee stages of its passage through Parliament all played a part in the remarkably slow progress of the Charities Act 2006 on to the statute books.

While the law may be slow to evolve, charities themselves are quick to respond to the ever accelerating pace of change in society and the needs which this creates. Far from the philanthropic trusts which formed the basis for many charities established in the Victorian and Edwardian periods, many of today's charities have become large national and international organisations operating at the forefront of society. It is impossible to turn on the television or pick up a newspaper without seeing the work of British charities, whether in leading relief projects in war torn states, helping the victims of natural disasters or pioneering the latest advances in medicine. Rather than charities being challenged by society's ever changing needs, it is often the case that it is the State that finds itself playing catch up to voluntary organisations that have already identified and begun to address new charitable causes.

Just as charities continue to grow so the appetite of the British public to provide support for charitable organisations increases. According to figures published by the National Council for Voluntary Organisations ('NCVO') in 2006 the UK voluntary sector in 2003/04 had a total income of £26.3 billion and assets of £66.8 billion (*The UK Voluntary Almanac 2006: The State of the Sector* (February 2006) NCVO). The Charity Commission estimates that by 2006 this income figure had grown to £36 billion for registered charities alone. The social benefits of the work undertaken by these charities go far beyond their direct charitable objects, with the sector employing over 608,000 people and estimated to make a contribution of over £7 billion a year to the UK gross domestic product.

Statistics show that the number of registered charities continues to rise, having grown from around 98,000 active charities in 1991 to well over 190,000 in 2006. Tellingly though, over a third of the voluntary sector's income comes from statutory sources (*The UK Voluntary Almanac 2006: The State of the Sector* (February 2006) NCVO).

Given their inclination to modernise almost every key social area, it is not surprising that the Government's attention turned to the charity sector. In July 2001 Tony Blair commissioned a review of the law and regulation of charities and other not-for-profit organisations, which was carried out by the Prime Minister's Strategy Unit. The results of the review were published in September 2002 in a document entitled 'Private Action, Public Benefit'. The report identified the strengths and weakness of the existing legal and regulatory framework, and made a series of recommendations for reform. As a result of the review the Government initiated a public consultation from September 2002 to January 2003 to invite the public, and in particular interested organisations, to comment on the recommendations contained within the review. The results of this consultation were published by the Home Office in July 2003 in a paper entitled 'Charities and Not-for-Profits: A Modern Legal Framework', in which the Government confirmed its acceptance of most of the recommendations contained within the original review and their proposals on implementation.

In this report the Government set out its intention to create a modern legal framework to support and encourage a vibrant and diverse voluntary sector, which would continue to enjoy a high level of public confidence. The key areas for reform identified were:

- to update and expand the list of charitable purposes and place a clear emphasis on the requirement to deliver public benefit;
- to introduce a range of measures designed to enable charities to administer themselves more efficiently and to be more effective in their work;
- to develop a new legal form specifically for charities;
- to provide for a greater degree of accountability for charities currently excepted or exempt from the requirement to register with the Charity Commission;
- to improve the regulation of charity fundraising; and
- to modernise the Charity Commission's functions and powers as a regulator and to increase its accountability.

The Charities Act 2006 delivers on all of these objectives with, it may be said, varying degrees of success. However, there is no doubt that the overall thrust and purpose of the new legislation has been strongly welcomed by the charity sector, notwithstanding the inevitable criticism of certain provisions contained within it.

However, disappointingly the Charities Act 2006 is not a consolidating statute, but simply augments and amends the Charities Act 1993.

Charitable purposes and public benefit

1.2 The most hotly debated element of the new legislation has been the provisions dealing with new classes of charitable purposes, and the requirement for all charities to demonstrate 'public benefit'. Previously, most charities falling within one of the so called 'four heads of charity' were able to rely on the presumption that as a result of being educational, religeous or welfare charities they automatically satisfied the requirement for public benefit, notwithstanding that in many instances the public at large were unlikely to be able to benefit from their charitable activities. In the run up to the introduction of the new legislation the Government made it clear that in future it expected 'fee-based' charities, such as private schools and hospitals, to do far more to meet the public benefit test than simply accepting fee-paying customers, if they wished to retain their charitable status.

Introduction of a new legal form for charities

1.3 One of the most eagerly awaited developments introduced by the Charities Act 2006 (by charity advisors, if not charities themselves), is a new form of legal entity designed specifically for charities. Until now charities have had to 'borrow' one of a number of existing legal structures in order to establish themselves under English Law. The Charities Act 2006 introduces an entirely new legal entity, the 'Charitable Incorporated Organisation', which is a form of legal structure exclusively available to registered charities. Charities will be able to continue to use the other existing legal structures; however, it is anticipated that most new charities will wish to use the new legal structure and many existing charities will wish to convert, as the new structure offers many of the benefits of limited liability protection without some of the problems of dual regulation faced by charities that adopt a company structure.

Modernisation of the Charity Commission

1.4 While a number of the areas touched on by the new legislation were seen as requiring reform, it is probably fair to say that an overhaul of the legal structure of the Charity Commission was not one of them. Nevertheless, the Commission has found itself the subject of the Government's reforming hand in a move which brings the Charity Commission's previously anomalous status in line with the mainstream Civil Service structure, and arguably creates scope for greater ministerial control over the Commission.

Chapter 2

Registration and Charitable Status

Introduction to registration

2.1 Since the introduction of the Charities Act 1993 ('CA 1993') the trustees of a charity have been under a statutory duty to register their charity with the Charity Commission once the annual income of that charity reached a certain level, or it benefited from the use of land or a permanent endowment. This position has been revised under the Charities Act 2006 ('ChaA 2006'), although the statutory duty still applies.

Historic position on registration

2.2 CA 1993 s 3(5) specified that the following were required to be registered:

- Any charity whose income from all sources in aggregate exceeded £1,000 a year.
- Any charity which had:
  - — the use or occupation of land; or
  - — any permanent endowment.

Below the £1,000 gross annual income threshold charities could opt to register if they wished.

Certain charities were not required to register as they were exempt or excepted (CA 1993 s 3(5)(a), (b)). The exempt charities were listed in CA 1993 Sch 2. Higher and Further Education corporations were included by later amendments (Teaching and Higher Education Act 1988 s 44(1), Sch 3 para 9 and the School Standards and Framework Act 1988 s 140, Sch 30 para 48). Registered places of worship were also not required to register (CA 1993 s 3(5)).

Excepted charities were not expressly listed in CA 1993 but their status derived from orders and regulations. They included some voluntary schools, Scout and Guide organisations, certain religious charities and armed forces charities. The Government have estimated that exempt and excepted charities number at least 110,000 ('Draft Regulatory Impact Assessment' (27 May 2004)) (see **2.5** to **2.11** below for further information on exempt and excepted charities).

The Charity Commission has operated a somewhat controversial 'gateway' procedure whereby at the point of registration it considered not just the legality of the objects of the proposed charity, but also its proposed activities, when determining whether or not it should be entered on the register. There is no reason to assume that this will change under ChaA 2006; in fact this is fully in line with the Charity Commission's new objectives and regulatory powers.

Registration under ChaA 2006

2.3 The new provisions relating to registration are to be found in ChaA 2006 s 9. These amend CA 1993 by completely replacing the whole of s 3 and substituting new ss 3, 3A and 3B. Section 3 relates to the register itself, s 3A to the registration threshold and s 3B to the duties of charity trustees.

The duties of trustees have not changed in respect of registration. In principle all charities must be registered unless they are exempt or below the thresholds for excepted and non-excepted charities.

General registration

2.4 The threshold for compulsory registration has increased from £1,000 to £5,000 gross annual income for all non-exempt and non-excepted charities (CA 1993 s 3A(2)(d)).

The reason for this is that the Government wishes to ensure that smaller charities do not have to enter the bureaucratic net until they have sufficient resources to meet the regulatory demands. The Government had recommended increasing the threshold to £10,000 (see the Cabinet Office's Strategy Unit report 'Private Action, Public Benefit' (September 2002)), but this was opposed by many charities on the basis that charitable registration gives them credibility with funders. In any event the Charity Commission does not regularly scrutinise those charities with an annual income under £10,000, and small (unincorporated) charities are able to submit a reduced annual return and accounts. Interestingly, CA 1993 s 3A(10) states that 'gross income' shall be deemed to mean the gross income in the charity's previous financial year or, at the discretion of the Charity Commission, an estimate of the gross annual income at the date in question.

The one exception to the above is the new Charitable Incorporated Organisation ('CIO'), which has to be registered with the Charity Commission regardless of income (for further details on CIOs see CHAPTER 3).

The requirement that a charity has to register simply because it has permanent endowment or the use or occupation of any land, regardless of its annual income, has been removed. This is a significant change.

Charities that hold land but have very little income will no longer need to register, although they may choose to do so (see below).

It is still possible to register voluntarily if the charity's gross annual income is below £5,000 (CA 1993 s 3A(6)), though past experience suggests that the Charity Commission may discourage this. Indeed, it has already issued guidance that states that it will only register charities below the threshold in 'exceptional circumstances'. This cannot be legally enforced as the wording of s 3A(6) states that they 'must' be registered if they request it. As before, those charities that have voluntarily registered can ask to be removed from the register (CA 1993 s 3(6)), although presumably only if their gross annual income remains below £5,000 at the time that they make the request.

The Secretary of State has the power to amend the thresholds for registration (CA 1993 s 3A(7)–(8)). For the general threshold this is in the same terms as under the old CA 1993 s 3(12) and allows him to alter the threshold in consequence of changes in the value of money or to extend the scope of the exception. For excepted charities he only has the power to *reduce* the scope of the exception. Exempt charities are not affected as there is no threshold for registration that applies to them. The Secretary of State is provided with an interim power to vary the threshold (ChaA 2006 s 10). This power ceases to have effect as soon as the new CA 1993 s 3A(1)–(5) come into force. This is so that the changes can be effected even before the commencement of that provision.

The threshold may only be amended by order after a report on the operation of ChaA 2006 has been laid before Parliament (CA 1993 s 3A(8)), as required under the provisions of the new legislation (ChaA 2006 s 73). This report should be prepared no later than five years from the date of Royal Assent (ChaA 2006 s 73(1)). In other words, Ministers will appoint someone to report to Parliament on the impact of the Act by 8 November 2011. However, they have indicated that they will review the various financial thresholds within a year of Royal Assent, with a view to raising or simplifying them.

Exempt and excepted charities

2.5 Under CA 1993, certain charities are exempt or excepted from registration with the Charity Commission. Excepted charities are not registered but may still be regulated by the Charity Commission. Exempt charities are neither registered nor fully regulated, although the Charity Commission has had available to it some limited powers for use with exempt charities. These powers are extended in ChaA 2006 (see **2.9**)

Exempt charities

2.6 The list of previously exempt charities was contained in CA 1993 Sch 2. The list comprised institutions and includes several national museums, universities (including those of Oxford, Cambridge, London, Durham and Newcastle), colleges of further and higher education, Winchester College and Eton, housing associations and provident societies. Schedule 2 did not confer charitable status on these institutions but ensured that any that were charitable were treated as exempt.

Neither the Government nor the Charity Commission know exactly how many exempt charities there are, but they have estimated that there are around 10,000 ('Draft Regulatory Impact Assessment' (27 May 2004)).

In the original draft Charities Bill, published 27 May 2004, it was envisaged that exempt charities would be required to register if their gross annual income was over £100,000, in the same way as excepted charities, or if they had no principal regulator. However, the Home Office estimated that 7,800 of the 10,000 exempt charities would be required to register. Most of these would be voluntary schools. Because of the cost of registration and the added regulatory burden for these schools, it was recommended by the Joint Parliamentary Committee in its report dated 30 September 2004 that it would be better to designate a principal regulator for voluntary schools and remove the requirement that exempt charities should register.

Reduction in exempt charities

2.7 Whilst exempt charities are not required to register (expressly excluded in CA 1993 s 3A(2)) and may not voluntarily register (not included in CA 1993 s 3A(6)), many of those previously exempt will now be required to register as they no longer qualify as exempt, although the Secretary of State does have the power to make them excepted charities as long as their gross annual income is below £100,000 (CA 1993 s 3A(4)).

The list of exempt charities has been amended and reduced (ChaA 2006 s 11, amending CA 1993 Sch 2), although the Secretary of State has the power to add particular institutions or categories of institutions to CA 1993 Sch 2 (ChaA 2006 s 11(11), referring to CA 1993 Sch 2).

The following have now been expressly removed from the list and will lose their exempt charity status:

- Winchester and Eton Colleges (ChaA 2006 s 11(3)(b)).
- The Church Commissioners and any institutions administered by them (ChaA 2006 s 11(7)).
- The Welsh Church or property administered by it (ChaA 2006 s 11(2), (9)).
- Certain church investment funds and deposit funds (ChaA 2006 s 11(2), (9)).
- Students' unions (ChaA 2006 s 11(6), (9)).

- Common investment funds that only admit exempt charities (ChaA 2006 s 11(10)).

The following have been added to the list:

- Higher education corporations (ChaA 2006 s 11(4)).
- Further education corporations (ChaA 2006 s 11(5)).

Although these latter bodies had already been incorporated into CA 1993 by later amendments.

The list has also been amended to delete those societies registered as Friendly Societies and to restrict Industrial and Provident Societies to those registered as social landlords (ChaA 2006 s 11(8)).

The Secretary of State has the power to amend this or other legislation (ChaA 2006 s 11(13)) in order to add more exempt charities to the list or delete those existing exempt charities. However, he can only do this if the reason is to ensure appropriate or effective regulation of those charities and compliance by the charity trustees with their legal obligations (ChaA 2006 s 11(12)).

Exempt charities and their principal regulators

2.8 The rationale behind exempting certain charities is that some charities do not require Charity Commission regulation because they already have a principal regulator of their own, for example, government departments or public authorities. Often these regulators are also the funding body. However, the concern is that many of these regulators are not aware of their role and there is no mechanism for ensuring compliance with charity law. This means that there is no way of ensuring that these charities justify their tax reliefs, and this could reflect badly on the charity sector.

One of the key concerns raised during the consultation period was how the Charity Commission would work with principal regulators and who would take precedence, given that the Charity Commission is able to exercise regulatory power over exempt charities. This has been addressed to some extent with a provision that states that the Charity Commission will always consult with the relevant regulator before taking enforcement action (ChaA 2006 s 14, introducing CA 1993 s 86A). How this will work in practice remains to be seen, especially as principal regulators are unlikely to welcome the intervention of the Charity Commission. However, any government body or Minister of the Crown who is a principal regulator now has a statutory duty to promote compliance by charity trustees with their legal obligations in exercising control and management of the administration of their charity (ChaA 2006 s 13). The Secretary of State may make regulations to provide principal regulators with any statutory powers they need to achieve this objective (ChaA 2006 s 13(5)). Principal regulators will not, however, have available to them the raft of powers available to the Charity Commission.

The Draft Regulatory Impact Assessment, dated 27 May 2004, accompanying the original draft Charities Bill, contained a list of proposed principal regulators (see **Appendix 4**). The Secretary of State also has power to prescribe a body or Minister as the principal regulator (ChaA 2006 s 13(4)(b)).

Increased regulation of exempt charities

2.9 CA 1993 holds that exempt charities are not registrable. There is no statutory threshold for their registration (CA 1993 s 3A(2)) and they cannot voluntarily register (expressly excluded from CA 1993 s 3A(6)).

ChaA 2006 Sch 5 enhances the existing regulation of exempt charities. The Schedule includes a list of amendments to CA 1993, ensuring that exempt charities are subject to the mainstream regulation of the Charity Commission. These provide the Charity Commission with the following powers, which previously applied to all charities except exempt charities:

- The power to require a charity to change its name (ChaA 2006 Sch 5 para 1, amending CA 1993 s 6).
- The power to institute a section 8 inquiry (although this power is limited and may only be used at the request of the principal regulator) (ChaA 2006 Sch 5 para 2, amending CA 1993 s 8).
- The power to call for documents and to search records (ChaA 2006 Sch 5 para 3, amending CA 1993 s 9).
- The power to give directions about dormant bank accounts (ChaA 2006 Sch 5 para 7, amending CA 1993 s 28).
- The power to order any disqualified trustee to repay sums received from charity funds for acting whilst disqualified (ChaA 2006 Sch 5 para 9, amending CA 1993 s 73).

Other changes include the following:

- Restrictions on when the Charity Commission may exercise its jurisdiction in charity proceedings are removed for exempt charities (ChaA 2006 Sch 5 para 4, amending CA 1993 s 16).
- Expenditure incurred when an exempt charity is involved in promoting a Bill in Parliament must now be approved by the Charity Commission or the courts (ChaA 2006 Sch 5 para 5, amending CA 1993 s 17).
- Section 8 inquiries now apply to exempt charities, although the compulsory removal and/or appointment of trustees can only take place after a section 8 inquiry has been initiated (ChaA 2006 Sch 5 para 6, amending CA 1993 s 18).
- Charity Commission approval is now required for court proceedings,

and the Attorney General may now take action against an exempt charity (ChaA 2006 Sch 5 para 8, amending CA 1993 s 33).

The overall result of these amendments is to ensure that exempt charities are subject to increased scrutiny and regulation, despite not being required to register.

Excepted charities

2.10 In a similar way to exempt charities, excepted charities were not previously required to register with the Charity Commission. This is because they are already registered with their own umbrella or support groups. Excepted charities include armed forces charities, Guide and Scout groups and certain religious denominations. Not all religious charities are excepted, however, and certain denominations are subject to the regulations. For example, mosques are required to register. Excepted charities have been excepted either by order of the Charity Commission or of the Secretary of State.

The registration rules now apply, however, to charities that are excepted either by the Charity Commission or by regulations and where their gross annual income exceeds £100,000 (CA 1993 s 3A(2)(b), (c)). Excepted charities below this level of income can voluntarily register (s 3A(6)).

The Government estimates that there are more than 100,000 excepted charities, of which at least 5,000 will be required to register ('Draft Regulatory Impact Assessment' (27 May 2004)). These include armed forces charities, Church of England parishes and Methodist and Baptist churches. The Charity Commission anticipates that the cost of registering this initial phase of excepted charities will be up to £650,000, with an extra £250,000 per annum for regulation (Joint Parliamentary Committee Report (15 September 2004)).

Future for excepted charities

2.11 Existing excepted charities will continue to be classified as excepted. However, neither the Charity Commission nor the Secretary of State will have the power in future to make orders for new excepted charities (CA 1993 s 3A(3), (4), as inserted by ChaA 2006 s 9).

It is the Government's stated intention to continue to lower the registration threshold for excepted charities to ensure that more charities are subject to Charity Commission regulation. Indeed the Secretary of State only has the power to reduce the scope of the exception (CA 1993 s 3A(8)(a), as inserted by ChaA 2006 s 9). Obviously this objective needs to be weighed against the cost and resources necessary to practically process the level of new registrations.

Duties of trustees

2.12 CA 1993 s 3B, as inserted by ChaA 2006 s 9, outlines and expands upon the duties of trustees that already exist (CA 1993 s 3(7)). These include the duties to register, to supply documents to the Charity Commission, to notify it of any changes to the objects of the charity or to notify it if a charity ceases to exist.

The meaning of charity

2.13 The three essential components in establishing charitable status are:

(1) that the purposes of the organisation shall be charitable as recognised by law;

(2) that those purposes shall be exclusively charitable and have no element of private benefit; and

(3) that there must be public benefit.

ChaA 2006 s 1 provides a definition of the meaning of charity. This states that a charity is an institution which:

> '(a) is established for charitable purposes only; and
>
> (b) falls to be subject to the control of the High Court in the exercise of its jurisdiction with respect to charities.'

This confirms the established position; namely, that an organisation that has both charitable and non-charitable purposes is not considered to be charitable.

This definition, based largely on the interpretation section of CA 1993 (CA 1993 s 96), is to apply except where a different definition is used in a particular statute. Any reference to the preamble or to the Statute of Elizabeth I (Charitable Uses Act 1601) is to be construed as referring to a charity.

Institution can include 'a trust or undertaking, whether incorporated or not'. A charitable association is classified as an undertaking.

The definition only applies to charities in England and Wales as this is where the jurisdiction of the High Court ends.

Introduction to charitable purposes

2.14 One of the key changes in ChaA 2006 is the introduction of a list of charitable purposes. The aim is to codify the charitable purposes that have developed under common law. However, it is not intended to be exhaustive and there still remains sufficient flexibility for the list of charitable purposes to continue to develop in the future.

History of charitable purposes

2.15 Before ChaA 2006 there was no statutory definition of charitable purposes. The list of purposes accepted under law derived from ancient case law. The preamble to the Statute of Elizabeth I (Charitable Uses Act 1601) contained many of the basic concepts of current charity law. However, because they were in the preamble to the statute, rather than in the statute itself, this was not actually a statutory definition. Instead it was an indication of purposes or activities that the State considered to be of benefit to the public.

It was in an ancient tax case, *Comrs for Special Purposes of the Income Tax v Pemsel [1891] AC 531, 3 TC 53, HL*, that charitable purposes were defined as falling under the four main heads of:

- the relief of poverty;
- the advancement of education;
- the advancement of religion; and
- other purposes beneficial to the community.

As charity law developed, largely by analogy, many of the accepted charitable purposes fell within the fourth category and as such were not explicit.

The one exception to the lack of statutory definition was that of 'recreational' charities that were defined in the Recreational Charities Act 1958 (for further details see **2.31**).

New charitable purposes

2.16 In its report on the voluntary sector, 'Private Action, Public Benefit', published in September 2002, the Government's stated intention was to provide a more modern definition of charity, ensuring that the public had greater confidence in what was charitable in the eyes of the law. Their intention was not necessarily to expand the definition of what was charitable but to ensure that it was clearly defined. In line with their desire to make charities more open to the public and more accountable, the list of charitable purposes needed to be defined in Statute.

ChaA 2006 s 2(2) introduces the first statutory list of charitable purposes. However, more fundamentally, it introduces a dual requirement. A purpose is charitable if it (a) falls within the new list of 13 purposes *and* (b) is for the public benefit (ChaA 2006 s 2(1)) (see **2.32–2.34**).

It is assumed that the common law position on other aspects of charitable status such as class of beneficiaries (see **2.37**), exclusively charitable nature (see **2.38**) and the treatment of charities whose beneficiaries are largely based overseas, will continue to apply.

List of charitable purposes

2.17 The new legislation contains the following list of 13 charitable purposes (ChaA 2006 s 2(2)). These are not just individual purposes but heads of charity that can comprise a range of purposes:

(a) The prevention or relief of poverty.

(b) The advancement of education.

(c) The advancement of religion.

(d) The advancement of health or the saving of lives.

(e) The advancement of citizenship or community development.

(f) The advancement of the arts, culture, heritage or science.

(g) The advancement of amateur sport.

(h) The advancement of human rights, conflict resolution or reconciliation or the promotion of religious or racial harmony or equality and diversity.

(i) The advancement of environmental protection or improvement.

(j) The relief of those in need by reason of youth, age, ill-health, disability, financial hardship or other disadvantage.

(k) The advancement of animal welfare.

(l) The promotion of the efficiency of the armed forces of the Crown, or of the efficiency of the police, fire and rescue services or ambulance services.

(m) Any other purposes that are recognised as charitable under subsection (4) (ChaA 2006 s 2(4)).

The effect of item (m) is to ensure that any purposes that are charitable under existing charity law, or are analogous to, or within the spirit of, any purposes listed above or recognised as charitable under existing charity law, may be included. This is also the mechanism by which future development of the list of charitable purposes can take place.

The prevention or relief of poverty

2.18 This is one of the fundamental charitable purposes recognised in the preamble to the Statute of Elizabeth I (Charitable Uses Act 1601) and in *Comrs for Special Purposes of the Income Tax v Pemsel [1891] AC 531, 3 TC 53, HL.*

Poverty does not necessarily mean destitution, it can be temporary or permanent, and it does not necessarily depend upon eligibility for state benefits. It can also include preventing someone falling into poverty.

The advancement of education

2.19 The advancement of education is a purpose which is believed to be self-evident in its scope and is generally construed quite widely. It not only includes formal education, but also the development of skills, training and research. Indeed this purpose is used as the foundation for very many UK and overseas charities.

The advancement of religion

2.20 This is one of the original charitable purposes. A definition of 'religion' (ChaA 2006 s 2(3)(a)) that included non-deity and multi-deity groups was incorporated at committee stage (recommended by the Joint Parliamentary Committee in its report dated 30 September 2004). This is to address the concern that some religions, such as Buddhism and Jainism, do not worship a god.

The common law position and the Charity Commission's interpretation of the law is revealed very clearly in their decision to reject the Church of Scientology's application to register as a charity (Charity Commission decision, dated 9 December 1999).

In the opinion of the Charity Commission the key elements of the advancement of religion are:

- a belief in a supreme being;
- an expression of belief in that supreme being revealed through worship (which could manifest itself in acts of submission, veneration, praise, thanksgiving or intercession); and
- the promotion of moral or spiritual welfare and improvement of the community or general public benefit.

The Charity Commission considered that the Church of Scientology did believe in a supreme being. However, it decided that the Church's activities of auditing and training did not constitute worship. Nor could it be described as promoting the spiritual welfare of the whole community, given that access or participation in its doctrines require membership and are not generally available to the public at large. The Commission did state that membership itself would not necessarily preclude charitable status, as long as the beliefs and practices were accessible to the public and were capable of being applied and adopted by them according to their individual judgement.

This is likely to be a charitable purpose that will continue to give rise to much debate in the future, particularly given the removal of the presumption of public benefit (see **2.34**).

The advancement of health or the saving of lives

2.21 This is not one of the original charitable purposes but it has been recognised as fundamentally charitable for a long time. The advancement of health includes the prevention or relief of sickness, disease or human suffering (ChaA 2006 s 2(3)(b)).

The scope of this purpose can extend beyond treatment to the provision of services and facilities to assist the recovery of people who are sick, convalescent, disabled or infirm or to provide comfort to patients. It can also include complementary and alternative methods and medicines. However, there is a focus on the efficacy of the various treatments and whether or not they achieve the results that they claim. Equally, there is more scrutiny of therapies that purport to replace conventional medicine rather than act in a genuinely complementary way. A House of Lords report provides some guidance in this area (The Sixth Report of the House of Lords Select Committee on Science and Technology, Session 1999–2000). Also to be considered is the Charity Commission decision on NFSH Charitable Trust Limited (decision dated 10 August 2002, registered no: 211133), where the application was to register a charity dealing with spiritual healing. The application was successful.

The saving of lives element was introduced during the Parliamentary Committee stage, largely as a result of the lobbying of major charities working in this area.

The advancement of citizenship or community development

2.22 This is one of the most radical new charitable purposes. It was not fully defined early on in the development of this legislation (see the Cabinet Office's Strategy Unit report 'Private Action, Public Benefit' (September 2002)), being described then as 'social and community advancement' It is not clear how this will be applied in practice.

This purpose includes rural or urban regeneration and the promotion of civic responsibility, volunteering, the voluntary sector or the effectiveness or efficiency of charities (ChaA 2006 s 2(3)(c)). This allows for the increasing development of community enterprises, support for social and community infrastructure and charities concerned with social investment.

The concept of rural or urban regeneration as charitable is relatively recent. The Charity Commission issued guidance that stated that the promotion of rural or urban regeneration in areas of social and economic deprivation should be charitable (Guidance Note RR2 'Promotion of Urban and Rural Regneration' (March 1999, updated June 2006)). It then developed the theme in Guidance Note RR5 (dated November 2000) to community capacity building. This provides that the development of a physical community facility or other benefit for a geographical community should be charitable. Example objects are available on the Charity Commission website.

The advancement of the arts, culture, heritage or science

2.23 The advancement of art can include abstract, conceptual, representational, figurative and performance art. It can include computer, video and multimedia art. It can be both professional and amateur and can also include the provision of arts facilities.

There is a criterion of merit which must be satisfied. For example, museums and art galleries must demonstrate that their collections and exhibits meet the following criteria:

- They must be set up for the benefit of the public. They must provide sufficient public access and ensure that any private benefit gained by individuals is incidental. Exhibits or collections must not be used for any non-charitable purposes, such as trading.
- They must satisfy a criterion of merit. The collections or exhibits need to at least be capable of educating the minds of the public, the museum or art gallery intends to serve. The experience gained by the public must be capable of being of value to them.

Heritage includes preserving land and buildings, as well as preserving traditions and local or national history.

Culture was introduced during the legislative process (see the Joint Parliamentary Committee Report (30 September 2004)) to bring it in line with Scottish legislation (Charities and Trustee Investment (Scotland) Act 2005), although many have argued that it does not add much to the advancement of arts and of heritage.

The advancement of science includes both scientific research and learned societies and institutions.

The advancement of amateur sport

2.24 The key point to note about this charitable purpose is that the sport needs to promote health by involving physical or mental skill and exertion (ChaA 2006 s 2(3)(d)). Originally the 'mental skill' element was not included and activities such as chess would have been excluded. However, this was amended. It also includes the promotion of community participation in healthy recreation.

However, sports clubs that are already 'registered' for the purposes of tax relief under FA 2002 Sch 18 and known as Community Amateur Sports Clubs (CASCs) will not be eligible for charitable status (ChaA 2006 s 5(4), (5)), despite the fact that their constitutions are akin to a charity, including a charitable dissolution clause. They can elect to apply for charitable status, but this will result in a loss of CASC status and those associated tax reliefs.

The advancement of human rights, conflict resolution or reconciliation or the promotion of religious or racial harmony or equality and diversity

2.25 The advancement of human rights has been one of the most difficult areas for the Charity Commission to deal with. When this legislation was under consideration, the Charity Commission published the 'Guide to Human Rights' (January 2005). The main concern involved reconciling its approach to human rights with charities that operate in countries with poor human rights records, and with the problem of when the promotion of human rights becomes a purely political purpose. It had been recommended by the Joint Parliamentary Committee Report (30 September 2004), that the Charity Commission should take a more lenient approach to political campaigning. There was evidence of some relaxation of the Charity Commission approach in the guidance it issued at that time (Guidance Note CC9 'Campaigning and Political Activities' (September 2004).

Conflict resolution has a clearly stated purpose. It can include national and international conflicts, as well as groups involved in mediation, conciliation or reconciliation.

The final element, the promotion of religious or racial harmony or equality and diversity, is intended to actively lessen conflict between different races and religions and to eliminate discrimination.

The advancement of environmental protection or improvement

2.26 This includes the conservation of the natural environment and the promotion of sustainable development. Conservation may include individual species, habitat or the environment generally. In a similar way to the promotion of the arts, this is subject to evaluation against a criterion of merit.

The relief of those in need by reason of youth, age, ill-health, disability, financial hardship or other disadvantage

2.27 This can include relief given by the provision of accommodation and care to such persons. See also the Recreational Charities Act 1958, discussed at 2.31.

The advancement of animal welfare

2.28 Again this is a charitable purpose that was not included in the original draft of the legislation (draft Charities Bill, published 27 May 2004), although it had been recognised as a charitable purpose for some time. Substantial pressure was exerted by the major animal charities to ensure its inclusion in the list of purposes.

This purpose can include the prevention of cruelty, the relief of suffering of animals, animal sanctuaries, the re-homing of animals, feral animal control and the provision of veterinary care and treatment.

The promotion of the efficiency of the armed forces and the rescue services

2.29 This charitable purpose was missing in the original list of purposes but was included at Committee stage as a result of concern expressed about armed forces charities and the fact that their charitable nature is not fully understood by the public. These charities have not been required to register with the Charity Commission previously and indeed, with the regular change of personnel, may find it hard to comply with statutory requirements. However, the Charity Commission has been actively consulting on this point.

A late amendment also included the emergency and rescue services.

Other purposes

2.30 There were several surprising omissions in the list of thirteen charitable purposes. These include the prevention of crime, the provision of social housing and the relief of unemployment. It is assumed that these and others will continue to fall within the final category.

Recreational Charities Act 1958

2.31 Charities registered under the Recreational Charities Act 1958 fall into a different category. The Government and the Charity Commission have long been unhappy about this area of the law, as they have had difficulty reconciling the specific wording of the statute with current social circumstances. There is also the difficulty that it provides for 'female members of the public at large'. This could give rise to many conflicts with current UK legislation and the European Convention on Human Rights.

Charities in this category must provide facilities for recreation or other leisure time occupation. They must provide those facilities in the interests of social welfare and with a view to improving the conditions of life for the beneficiaries. The beneficiaries must fall within a given list, including those who require the facilities by reason of their youth, age, infirmity or disablement, poverty or social and economic circumstances. Alternatively, the facilities must be available to the public at large.

This aspect of the law is now incorporated into the tenth charitable purpose and the Government has taken the opportunity to iron out some of the difficulties (ChaA 2006 s 5). The wording has now been amended to clarify the social welfare criterion and to ensure that both male and female members of the public at large are included (ChaA 2006 s 5(2)).

Miners' welfare trusts will not retain their charitable status unless they satisfy the general criteria in ChaA 2006 ss 1–3 (ChaA 2006 s 5(3)). Other than miners' welfare trusts, the charitable status of charities already registered under the Recreational Charities Act 1958 will not be affected (although see the notes on ongoing checks for public benefit at **2.34**).

Public benefit – historic position

2.32 Before the introduction of ChaA 2006 there was much debate about the introduction of a public benefit test, and the Government wished to demonstrate to the public that organisations that have charitable status are genuinely operating for the public good. This is not a new concept. Charities have always been expected to provide public benefit. However, there was previously a legal presumption that the first three categories of charitable purposes – advancement of education, advancement of religion and relief of poverty – automatically provided a public benefit. It was therefore only necessary to address this issue if a charity were to fall under the fourth category of 'other purposes beneficial to the community'. Even within the fourth category, this issue would only be addressed on the registration of a new charity. Assessment of the public benefit requirement would take place during the registration process, but not thereafter.

Definition of 'public benefit'

2.33 There has never been a statutory definition of 'public benefit' and indeed one is not included in ChaA 2006. The Government report 'Private Action, Public Benefit' (September 2002) stated that public benefit meant that a charity's purposes must (i) confer benefit as opposed to harm, (ii) benefit either the whole community or a significant section of it and (iii) confer only incidental private benefit.

During the legislative process a definition of public benefit was commissioned. This definition stated that the public benefit requirement would be satisfied if:

- the purpose was intended to provide benefit (in the sense of common good or social value);
- the purpose was directed at the public at large or a sufficient section of it; and
- any private benefit was incidental to the purpose and reasonable.

However, it was subsequently rejected on the basis that it was not sufficiently flexible. It was therefore concluded that the common law basis for public benefit would continue to apply.

Public benefit test

2.34 The legislative process included much debate about how and to what extent a public benefit test should be introduced. A joint statement or concordat was prepared by the Home Office and the Charity Commission and submitted to the Joint Parliamentary Committee. It stated that they had agreed on the following approach:

- Public benefit should be determined on a case-by-case basis.
- The Charity Commission should take account of social and economic context when assessing public benefit.
- Different standards should apply for different purposes.
- The law should evolve.
- The principles in *Re Resch's Will Trusts [1969] 1 AC 514, [1967] 3 All ER 915* should apply.

Re Resch's Will Trusts was a Privy Council case that involved a fee charging hospital and whether or not it could be considered to provide sufficient public benefit, despite the element of charging fees. The case laid out a number of principles as follows:

- Direct and indirect benefits should be taken into account.
- The fact that fees were charged would not necessarily preclude public benefit.
- Poor people should not be excluded from receiving benefit.

The presumption of public benefit referred to above at **2.32** has now been removed by ChaA 2006. Charities with objects for the advancement of education, the advancement of religion and the relief of poverty now need to prove public benefit in the same way as other charities. This does not affect historic registrations, but will affect new registrations (however, see below for comments on checks for public benefit in existing charities).

It was recommended in the Joint Parliamentary Committee Report that the concordat should be incorporated into ChaA 2006 or in statutory guidance issued by the Secretary of State. However, the Government preferred to leave it to the Charity Commission to issue non-binding guidance. Many commentators are relieved at this outcome as they feel that it is less vulnerable to political influence. With no statutory definition, it will be left to the courts to provide interpretation through case law.

Charity Commission guidance

2.35 It is for the Charity Commission to inform charities of the public benefit requirement. Indeed it is included as one of the objectives of the Charity Commission (CA 1993 s 1B, as inserted by ChaA 2006 s 7). The Commission's 'public benefit objective' is to 'promote awareness and understanding of the operation of the public benefit requirement' (CA 1993 s 1B(3), as inserted by ChaA 2006 s 7) (for further details on the Charity Commission's objectives see **11.3**). The Charity Commission must develop and issue guidance, following public or other consultation, in whatever form it thinks appropriate (ChaA 2006 s 4(5)). The Commission can subsequently revise this guidance with or without consultation, at its discretion (ChaA 2006 s 4(3), (4)). Although this guidance is not legally binding on trustees, it 'must have regard to any such guidance when exercising any powers or duties to which the guidance is relevant' (ChaA 2006 s 4(6)).

In the Joint Parliamentary Committee Report, the Charity Commission indicated the kind of criteria it would be using in assessing public benefit. These included the following:

- Whether any individuals or other organisations (other than those who should properly benefit from the charitable services) are significantly benefiting or profiting from the charity.
- Where the charitable services are available only to a charity's members, any restrictions on who can be a member which are inconsistent with the charitable purposes.
- Physical access to buildings and land, where that is relevant to delivery of the charitable purpose.
- Where the level of fees charged for services may have the effect of excluding the less well off, whether there is alternative provision for access to services for those unable to pay.
- Whether the charity confers any indirect public benefit (eg relief of the public sector).

Although the definition of public benefit may not have changed, the basis of implementation has changed dramatically. In future *all* charities need to show that they provide sufficient public benefit, not only at the point of registration, but on an ongoing basis. The Charity Commission is committed to an ongoing programme of reviews and public character checks of existing charities.

On 7 March 2007 the Charity Commission issued its first consultation paper on public benefit, comprising the following:

- An analysis of the law.
- The public perceptions of public benefit (the results of a marketing poll).
- Draft public benefit guidance.
- A partial regulatory impact assessment.

The marketing poll stated that the key standards emerging from the research were that charities should respond to need, enhance lives, educate and develop, foster a sense of community and provide for future generations.

Initial proposals put forward by the Commission included the use of the existing reporting framework for charity trustees to comment on whether of not they are meeting public benefit requirements.

The Charity Commission indicated that its initial focus would be on those charities:

- advancing education;
- advancing religion;
- relieving poverty; and
- charging fees.

At the time of writing, the public benefit requirement is due to come into force in early 2008.

Fee charging charities

2.36 Fee charging charities were clearly the target of the Government in its introduction of the public benefit requirement, particularly the independent school sector. It is estimated that there are around 1,000 independent schools (Joint Parliamentary Committee Report (30 September 2004)). Indeed, Ministers were explicit in expressing the view that these types of charities would have to produce strong evidence of a sufficiently wide public benefit in order to retain their charitable status. In this regard the third element of the *Re Resch's Will Trusts* requirements (see 2.34) is highly significant in that the poor cannot be excluded. The Charity Commission has increasingly talked of the need for people on a low income to be able to benefit.

Independent schools have already been making changes to open up access to their facilities and scholarships. One Government salvo even indicated that they might need to consider providing scholarships and bursaries up to the level of their tax reliefs. The balance between the benefits they provide and the benefits they receive is clearly something that will be looked at for sometime. Ideas to demonstrate public benefit that have been discussed by the independent school sector include:

- means-tested scholarships and bursaries;
- making facilities, educational materials and know-how available to local communities, schools and further education colleges;
- providing adult learning programmes, long-distance and internet learning, holiday courses and exchange programmes open to the local community;
- partnerships with local schools and colleges, including sponsoring awards and competitions; and
- careers fairs open to the public.

It will be interesting to see how the criteria for public benefit will be implemented in the future, and is something which fee charging charities in particular will be following very intently.

Class of beneficiaries

2.37 One of the key elements of the public benefit test under common law is that a sufficient size of beneficiary class must fall within the range of potential benefit in order for the prospective charity's objects to qualify as providing 'public' benefit. This means that, for example, a closed order of nuns cannot be charitable if they are completely inward-looking and therefore will not benefit the public (see *Gilmour v Coats [1949] AC 426, [1949] 1 All ER 848*). If the nuns, however, are involved with the local community in any way, the position may well be different (see the Charity Commission decision on Society of the Precious Blood, Report 1989 paras 56–62, Decisions Vol 3, pp 11–17).

There are certain exceptions to this principle. For charities involved in the relief of poverty it is possible to benefit a narrow class of beneficiaries, as evidenced in the 'poor relations' and 'poor employees' cases (see *Re Scarisbrick [1951] Ch 622, [1951] 1 All ER 822, CA* and *Dingle v Turner [1972] AC 601, [1972] 1 All ER 878, HL*). Equally there are the 'founder's kin' cases for advancement of education (see *Re Compton [1945] Ch 123, [1945] All ER 198* and *Spencer v All Soul's College (1762) Wilm 163*). While it is not possible to set up a charity exclusively for the benefit of the relatives of the founder, it is possible to do so for a wider class of beneficiaries, but to stipulate that preference be given to those relatives. These cases are well established in common law and it is assumed that they will not be affected by the new public benefit requirement. However, it will be interesting to see whether the implementation of the guidance will result in such cases becoming non-charitable. The Charity Commission has indicated that it will view such cases with extreme caution. The Commission considers that on a general survey of the circumstances and considerations regarded as relevant, it must be possible to describe the class of beneficiaries in objective and impersonal terms, otherwise it is likely that it will consider the charity as having been established for private benefit.

Exclusively charitable

2.38 Closely linked to the above is the question of whether or not the range of beneficiaries is exclusively charitable. If it is possible to benefit someone outside the scope of the charitable purpose, it will not be exclusively charitable and will therefore not qualify for registration. One example of this is a charity that provides housing for the working classes. It has been determined that this does not qualify as charitable on the basis that not every member of the working class is necessarily poor (see *Re Sanders' Will Trusts, Public Trustee v McLaren [1954] Ch 265*).

Loss of charitable status

2.39 The logical implication of the public benefit review is that certain charities will be found not to provide sufficient public benefit, and will suffer a loss of charitable status as a consequence.

ChaA 2006 does not make it clear what happens in these cases. There is an argument that if an organisation is found not to be charitable, then it has never been charitable and should simply continue to operate but without the tax reliefs associated with charitable status and the registered charity regime. This was the approach taken by the Charity Commission in the rifle club cases, where the clubs were reclassified as non-charitable and simply removed from the register. It was suggested that independent schools and private hospitals should be removed from the register but should continue to receive favourable tax treatment (in the Joint Parliamentay Committee Report (30 September 2004)). There was also a suggestion in the same report that a charity should be able to elect to be removed.

However, where an organisation has ceased to be charitable, the Charity Commission already has the power to apply those funds, by way of a cy-pres scheme, for similar exclusively charitable purposes (CA 1993 s 13). It has available to it wider powers that are usually used in the event of mismanagement of charity funds (CA 1993 s 18). The powers are also available 'if it is necessary or desirable to act for the purpose of protecting the property of the charity'. A section 8 inquiry must have been instituted. No reason needs to be given for initiating a section 8 inquiry, although a report must be produced. The powers available include the appointment of additional trustees or the appointment of a receiver or manager, the freezing of assets and the vesting of property in the Official Custodian. If there has been misconduct or mismanagement, the Charity Commission may remove a trustee or order a scheme to be established.

It was recommended, in the Joint Parliamentary Committee Report, that ChaA 2006 should make it clear what happens in the event that a charity loses its charitable status. However, this was not incorporated into the Act. It seems that it was felt that the Charity Commission already had sufficient powers to deal with such situations. The Charity Commission has been at pains to point out that a loss of charitable status will be a last resort if a charity fails or refuses to co-operate. If the trustees refuse to co-operate they will be replaced.

There has been uncertainty in the past as to whether the Charity Commission has the power to deal with the assets of a charitable company or whether these are protected by the corporate structure. It is certainly the case that the Charity Commission can present a petition to the court to wind up an incorporated charity and to re-apply the company's assets. With the increased use of corporate vehicles, this question will have important ramifications.

Charities should not consider voluntarily de-registering without seeking professional advice. Even if they can continue to operate without the tax reliefs, they need to be wary of hidden tax liabilities. Certain taxes, including capital gains tax (the three-year claw-back in TCGA 1992 s 256), inheritance tax (IHTA 1984 s 70 on exit from a trust) and stamp duty land tax (the three-year claw-back in FA 2003 Sch 8), may be subject to a claw-back or one-off charge where a charity loses its charitable status.

Chapter 3

Charitable Companies and CIOs

Introduction

3.1 When reviewing the regulation of the voluntary sector, the Cabinet Office's Strategy Unit recognised the increasing popularity of using limited liability companies (particularly companies limited by guarantee) as a vehicle for creating new charities (Cabinet Office's Strategy Unit report 'Private Action, Public Benefit' (September 2002)). This trend reflects not only an increased awareness amongst charity trustees of the personal financial risks associated with acting as the trustee of a charity, but also the fact that more and more charities are structuring their operations in a way akin to that of commercial enterprises, with many large charities employing hundreds or thousands of staff and with incomes running into tens of millions of pounds.

The legal framework within which limited companies operate was not designed for charitable organisations, and it has been argued for some time that the dual regulatory burden faced by charities operating as limited companies needed to be examined. Charities operating in this way are subject to regulation under both the Charities Acts and the Companies Acts. Under the two legal regimes they are required to file separate annual returns and accounts with both the Charity Commission and the Registrar of Companies.

The Charities Act 2006 ('ChaA 2006') addresses this issue, firstly by simplifying some of the rules governing charities established as companies, and more importantly by introducing a new corporate vehicle especially for charities called the Charitable Incorporated Organisation ('CIO'). The concept of the CIO was first recommended by the DTI in a company law review in 2001, and met with considerable support both from the Charity Commission and subsequently the Strategy Unit.

Altering the constitution of existing charitable companies

3.2 The Charities Act 1993 ('CA 1993') s 64 contained provisions governing the alteration by charitable companies of their objects. Where the constitution of a charitable company allowed it to alter its objects then any exercise of that power which had the effect of causing the company to cease to be a charity would not affect any income or property which had accrued to the charity before the change was made, nor would it affect any property acquired other than at full value (CA 1993 s 64(1)).

Likewise, any attempt by a charitable company to alter the objects in its memorandum of association or change any other provisions in its memorandum or articles of association which directed or restricted the way in which assets could be used or applied was ineffective unless the written consent of the Charity Commission had previously been obtained (CA 1993 s 64(2)).

Alterations under ChaA 2006

3.3 ChaA 2006 s 31 substitutes for CA 1993 s 64(2) a new regime under which the prior written consent of the Charity Commission is required for 'regulated alterations' to the constitution of a charitable company. As was already the case under CA 1993 s 64(2)(a), any alteration to the objects of a charitable company contained in its memorandum of association still requires the prior consent of the Charity Commission (CA 1993 s 64(2A)(a)). In future, however, any other changes to the constitution do not require the Charity Commission's approval unless either:

- they relate to an alteration to a provision dealing with the application of charity property on dissolution (CA 1993 s 62(2A)(b)); or
- the alteration is one which would allow for any benefits to be obtained by a trustee or member of the charity or a person connected with them (CA 1993 s 62(2A)(c)).

The word 'benefit' has its ordinary wide meaning and can include indirect, as well as any direct, benefit but it does not include any remuneration that has been properly authorised under the provisions contained in CA 1993 s 73A (CA 1993 s 64(2B)(a)).

This means that other types of change to the memorandum and articles of association of a charitable company which affect the way in which a charity's assets are restricted or applied no longer require the Charity Commission's prior approval. This does not mean that assets which are given for a specific purpose can be used by the trustees of a charitable company in any way they wish simply by making an alteration or addition to the charity's constitution. It does however work in harmony with the relaxation on applying charity funds given in ChaA 2006 s 43.

Introduction to Charitable Incorporated Organisations

3.4 One of the most interesting and eagerly awaited aspects of ChaA 2006 is the introduction of a new type of legal entity designed exclusively for registered charities, the Charitable Incorporated Organisation ('CIO'). In order to steer CIOs well clear of the legislation governing companies (including the Companies Acts 1985 and 1989) ChaA 2006 makes CIOs a creature of the Charity Commission, which becomes responsible for dealing with the registration and administration of CIOs in a way not dissimilar to the responsibility which the Registrar of Companies has for companies. ChaA 2006 does this by introducing a new CA 1993 Part 8A and Sch 5B. However, these new sections only set out the basic framework for CIOs, with the more detailed technical provisions being reserved for secondary legislation.

The nature of a CIO

3.5 Like a limited company, a CIO is a corporate body (CA 1993 s 69A(2)). That is to say it has a legal identity which is quite separate from its trustees or members. This is in contrast to an unincorporated association, for example, which has no independent legal identity of its own. It is important to understand however that a CIO is not a company, although the legislation has clearly been crafted in a way which closely mimics the law governing limited liability companies.

Another important distinction between a CIO and charitable company arises from the process of registration. For a charitable company, registration of the company with the Registrar of Companies is quite separate from registration with the Charity Commission as a charity. For a small charitable company with a turnover below £5,000 per annum, it is therefore possible to obtain the benefit of limited liability protection without the need to register as a charity with the Charity Commission. If a charity chooses to establish itself as a CIO then it is the process of registering with the Charity Commission as a charity which gives the CIO its status. This means that any charity which wishes to establish itself as a CIO is compelled to register, even if it would otherwise have fallen below the annual income threshold for registration for smaller charities, or otherwise have been exempt or excepted.

The constitution of a CIO

3.6 Every CIO must have a governing instrument, which is called its 'constitution' (CA 1993 s 69A(3)), and its principal office must be situated in England or Wales (CA 1993 s 69A(4)). Charities whose activities are focused exclusively outside of England or Wales are therefore obliged to have their principal office in England or Wales. ChaA 2006 gives no guidance as to what is meant by principal office. However, it is suggested that it means the place from which ultimate control is exercised and through which the English courts and the Charity Commission can exercise dominion over the CIO. The Charities and Trustees Investment (Scotland) Act 2005 provides for the creation of CIOs whose principal offices are situated in Scotland.

One requirement of CIOs that came in for particular criticism during the consultation phase is the requirement of CIOs to have at least one member (CA 1993 s 69A(5)). This mimics the requirement of companies to have at least one member, which is a requirement that owes its origin in part to European Community law, which introduced the concept of the single member company at a time when in the UK companies were required to have a minimum of two members.

In some senses the requirement that a CIO have at least one member appears a strange one, since the constitution of the CIO can provide that any members that do exist can be allowed to have no liability to contribute to the assets of the CIO on a winding up (CA 1993 s 69B(5)(b)). From a creditor's point of view the existence of one or more members is therefore of very little comfort. From a legal perspective it makes more sense, since the concept of 'incorporation' is tied up with the notion of incorporating the members who make the application for incorporation. It may be that the legislators also wanted to emulate the law applying to companies as closely as possible. Such considerations, if they were taken into account, may have been misleading, since it can be argued that the reason for creating CIOs was to establish a limited liability entity which was not subject to the requirements (and perceived shortcomings) applicable to companies. To simply recreate a company under the control of the Charity Commission, as opposed to the Registrar of Companies, would be pointless. At the outset of the review it had been mooted that CIOs should be available in both a 'foundation' form, without members, as well as a 'membership' form, with members. This proposal was never adopted, which seems to be somewhat at odds with the rational that CIOs are intended to simplify unnecessary regulation.

Liability

3.7 The constitution of a CIO can either provide for its members to have some liability to contribute to the assets of the CIO on a winding up (as is currently the case with a company limited by guarantee) (CA 1993 s 69A(6)(b)), or can provide for the members to have no such liability (CA 1993 s 69A(6)(a)). The members of a CIO are not, however, automatically given limited liability protection. It is important therefore to make sure that if the members are to have no liability (or only limited liability) this is expressly set out in the constitution of the CIO.

As we shall see at **3.15**, if the CIO is being formed as part of the process of converting an existing charity established as a company into a CIO then it is not permitted for the members to have a lower limit of liability under the CIO than they had as members of the company.

If the constitution of a CIO provides for its members to be liable to contribute to its assets in the event of a winding up then this will be treated in law as if a contract existed between the CIO and each member creating this obligation, and requiring each member to observe all of the provisions of the constitution (CA 1993 Sch 5B para 3). This provision appears to be intended to prevent a member of a CIO from arguing that no consideration was given by the CIO for his financial obligation, thereby closing off any potential loophole that might exist to enable the member to escape liability in the event of insolvency. Any money which is payable by a member to a CIO under its constitution will be treated in law as being 'a specialty debt', which means that the obligation to pay arises where the charity is constituted, rather than where the member resides (which could be abroad).

Constitution contents

3.8 The constitution of a guaranteed company is comprised of two parts: the memorandum of association (containing the objects of the company) and the articles of association (which contain the internal rules governing its administration). With a CIO the objects and the administrative provisions are all contained within a single document called its 'constitution'. The constitution must state (CA 1993 s 69B(1), (2)):

- the name of the charity;
- its purposes (ie objects);
- whether its principal office is in England or Wales;
- the liability (if any) of members to contribute on a winding up;
- who is eligible for membership and how a person becomes a member;
- how persons who are to be the charity's trustees are appointed and any conditions of eligibility for becoming a trustee; and
- provisions dealing with the application of the assets of the CIO on dissolution.

As with all charities, a CIO is required to apply its assets in furtherance of its objects and in accordance with the provisions of its constitution (CA 1993 Sch 5B para 2).

Other provisions to be contained within the constitution document can be specified by the Secretary of State through secondary legislation.

Trustees of CIOs

3.9 The constitution of a CIO can be drafted to require that the trustees be members in order to be eligible to stand as trustees, or that the members are the trustees, but this need not be the case and it is equally permissible for the trustees and the members to be entirely unrelated (CA 1993 s 69B(6)). Since the legislation only requires a minimum of one member and a minimum of one trustee, and since a trustee may be a member, it would appear that it is possible to establish a CIO with only a single trustee, who is also its sole member. The Charity Commission has, however, indicated that it would not be inclined to register a CIO on such a basis and would wish to see a minimum of two trustees unless a very good reason could be shown, such as the existence of a trust corporation as the sole trustee.

Language of the constitution

3.10 If a CIO's principal office is situated in England the constitution must be in English. However, if the principal office is in Wales then the constitution may be in English or Welsh (CA 1993 s 69B(4)).

Amendments to the constitution of a CIO

3.11 The members of a CIO can amend its constitution either by passing a resolution at a general meeting, with a 75% majority of those voting at the meeting (whether in person, by proxy or post, depending what is permitted by the CIO's constitution), or by unanimous written resolution from all of its members (CA 1993 Sch 5B para 14(2)). This power to amend the constitution is not exercisable if the amendment would result in the CIO ceasing to be a charity (CA 1993 Sch 5B para 14(4)).

Any amendments to the constitution of a CIO will not be effective unless and until the prior written consent of the Charity Commission has been obtained if the amendment involves:

- an alteration to the CIO's objects;
- an alteration to the CIO's constitution affecting how the assets of the charity are applied on its dissolution; or
- any alternation to the constitution which would result in a trustee or member or anyone connected with them obtaining a benefit in relation to the charity (CA 1993 Sch 5B para 14(5), (6)).

Similar to the obligation on a limited company to provide a copy of any resolution altering its memorandum or articles of association (together with an updated copy of its memorandum and articles of association), CA 1993 Sch 5B para 15 requires a CIO to supply to the Charity Commission a copy of any resolution amending its constitution, together with a copy of the revised constitution, within 15 days of the date on which the resolution to alter the constitution was passed. Any amendments that are passed will not be effective until they have been registered by the Charity Commission.

If the Charity Commission's consent is required for a constitutional change and this is not obtained beforehand, the Charity Commission is entitled to refuse to register the change (CA 1993 Sch 5B para 15(4)), and is required not to register a change if it considers the CIO had no power to make the change, for example if it would cause the CIO to cease to be a charity or would in some other way violate the regulations (CA 1993 Sch 5B para 15(3)).

Naming a CIO

3.12 CA 1993 s 69C, introduced by ChaA 2006, contains various requirements relating to the use and display of a CIO's name which are similar to the provisions in the Companies Act 1985 and Business Names Act 1985 applicable to companies.

The name of the CIO must appear legibly in all (CA 1993 s 69C(1)):

- business letters;
- notices and other official publications;
- cheques, invoices, receipts and other similar documents; and
- instruments creating, transferring, varying or extinguishing any interest in land or buildings.

If the charity's name does not include the words 'charitably incorporated organisation' or 'CIO' (or their Welsh equivalent) then this needs to be clearly stated on any of the documents referred to in the list above (CA 1993 s 69C(3), (5)).

For CIO's whose principal offices are situated in Wales they may choose to include the words 'Sefydliad Corfforedig Elusennol' or 'SCE' in their title (CA 1993 s 69C(4)).

Any charity trustee of a CIO or any other person (which could include an employee or volunteer) of a CIO on whose behalf any of the documents listed above are issued which fail to comply with the requirements of CA 1993 s 69C will be guilty of a criminal offence and may be liable to a fine (CA 1993 s 69D(1)). If they sign or authorise the signing of a cheque or similar instrument that does not meet these criteria then in addition they will be personally liable to the holder of any cheque or similar financial instrument which they were responsible for issuing in the name of the CIO, unless the relevant financial obligation is met by the CIO (CA 1993 s 69D(2)).

It is also an offence under ChaA 2006 for someone to hold out an organisation as being a CIO when it is not, unless the person who does so can show that they had reasonable grounds for believing that it was a CIO (CA 1993 s 69D(3), (4)).

Registering a CIO

3.13 The process of registering a CIO involves two separate but interrelated steps. The first is a request to the Charity Commission to establish the CIO, and the second is to register the CIO as a charity. In practice these steps are dealt with simultaneously.

The reference in the CA 1993 s 69F to registration as a charity as part of the registration process means that the process of registration of a CIO automatically results in a CIO becoming a registered charity. The Charity Commission has clarified that if a CIO that has been registered subsequently finds that its annual income has fallen below the threshold for registration as a charity of £5,000 per annum, the charity will need to satisfy the Commission that it expects its income to rise again above the threshold if it is to remain in existence.

Anyone (known as 'the applicants') wishing to apply to register a CIO must submit to the Charity Commission (CA 1993 s 69E(2)):

- a copy of the proposed constitution of the CIO;
- the prescribed registration documents; and
- any other documents or information which the Charity Commission may require for the purposes of processing the application.

The Charity Commission *must* refuse an application if either (CA 1993 s 69E(3)):

- it is not satisfied that the CIO would qualify as a charity if registered; or
- the proposed constitution does not contain any of the required information.

The Charity Commission also has discretion to refuse an application if the name of the proposed CIO is the same as or similar to the name of another charity (whether registered or not), or if the Charity Commission is of the opinion under their powers contained in CA 1993 s 6(2)(b)–(e) that the proposed name (CA 1993 s 69E(4)):

- is likely to mislead the public as to the true nature or purpose of the charity or the activities which it carries on;
- includes any word or expression which is restricted or prohibited by any regulations;
- is likely to give the impression that the charity is connected with the Government or any local authority or other body or individual to which it is not connected; or
- in the Charity Commission's opinion the name is offensive.

If the Charity Commission is satisfied that the application should proceed, then registration of the CIO on the Register of Charities will not only constitute it as a corporate body, but will also establish the CIO as a registered charity. This is in contrast to other types of charitable body (such as guaranteed companies, trusts or unincorporated associations) where the body needs to have been established *before* the application for registration as a charity is made.

Any property or assets held in trust by the applicants setting up a charity as a CIO pending its formation are automatically vested in the CIO on its registration by virtue of CA 1993 s 69F(3). This helps to simplify the process of incorporation, and means that the ownership of assets donated prior to the formal registration of a CIO should never be in doubt. In the case of assets such as land or shares, where a formal process of registration is necessary to convey the legal title, s 69F(3) does not dispense with the formality of registering the change of ownership.

Conversion of an existing charity to a CIO

3.14 In order to encourage existing charities to adopt the new CIO structure, ChaA 2006 provides an express mechanism for the conversion of an existing charity into a CIO. Unfortunately, this conversion mechanism is only available to existing charitable companies and charities which are registered societies under the Industrial and Provident Societies Act 1965. This is presumably because these entities are already corporate bodies in law and therefore it was felt that it would be straightforward for these entities to transfer from being registered with Companies House or the Financial Services Authority ('FSA') to being registered with the Charity Commission. Charities that are established as trusts or unincorporated associations will first of all need to apply to establish a new CIO and then transfer their assets across to the CIO once it has been established. This is similar to the process of converting a charity established as an unincorporated association into a guaranteed company.

Interestingly ChaA 2006 also allows the Secretary of State to provide for the conversion of Community Interest Companies ('CICs') into CIOs, and for these to be registered as charities. At the time of publication these regulations have not yet been produced, but what is notable is that CICs are not charities and therefore they may need to undergo a number of changes to their memorandum and articles of association in order to successfully convert, while existing non-corporate registered charities are given no path for conversion. This seems to confirm the analysis that the prime consideration in offering an easy route for conversion was whether the body was already corporate or not, rather than whether it was a charity, which on the face of it appears rather odd.

Although relatively few charitable companies and registered societies have a share capital, if they do have one then all of the issued shares will need to be fully paid up if an application to covert to a CIO is to be permitted

(CA 1993 s 69G(2)(a)). Conversion is not available for charities that are exempt from registration (CA 1993 s 69G(2)(b)).

The process of conversion

3.15 The process for converting an existing charitable company or registered society to a CIO is very similar to the process of registering a new CIO. In addition to submitting the documents and information required to register a new CIO, the charitable company or registered society must also supply the Charity Commission with a copy of a resolution of the charity (a) approving its conversion to a CIO, and (b) adopting the proposed new constitution of the CIO (CA 1993 s 69G(5)).

Typically these resolutions will be dealt with together, and it is advisable that they are passed on a conditional basis so that if the Charity Commission's approval for the conversion process is declined for any reason the existing organisation can continue unaffected. The requirements applicable to the contents of the constitution of a new CIO also apply to the proposed constitution of a CIO created by conversion.

These two resolutions need to be passed by either a 75% majority of members present and voting at a general meeting (including those voting by proxy or post, if this is permitted) or through a unanimous written resolution signed by (or on behalf of) all of the members of the charitable company or registered society who are entitled to vote on a special resolution at a general meeting (CA 1993 s 69G(6)).

Where the charity seeking conversion is an existing company limited by guarantee, the constitution of the new CIO must provide for the members of the CIO to be liable to contribute to the assets of the CIO on a winding up to an extent not less than the amount which they are liable to contribute to the assets of the guarantee company of which they are currently a member if it were to be wound up. However, if the amount of the members' guarantee is for £10 or less, this requirement is dropped, and conversion to a CIO can be used to reduce the pre-existing liability of members to creditors down to zero if the members wish (CA 1993 s 69G(8)–(10)).

This means that a charity currently operating as a guarantee company that converts to a CIO may no longer need to explain a member's liability to contribute on a winding up in its membership form.

Consideration of applications for conversion

3.16 ChaA 2006 requires that the Charity Commission consults with the relevant registrar with whom a charity applying for conversion is currently registered (presumably to ensure that it is in good standing, and to avoid the potentially embarrassing scenario of a charity simply applying for conversion because it is about to be struck off another register), and *must* consult with anyone else the Charity Commission considers it appropriate to notify about the application (CA 1993 s 69H(1)).

The Charity Commission *must* refuse an application for conversion if (CA 1993 s 69H(2)):

- it is not satisfied that the CIO would qualify as a charity if registered; or
- the proposed constitution does not contain the information required in CA 1993 s 69B (see **3.8**); or
- if the restrictions on limiting members' liability in CA 1993 s 69G(8) and (9) are not compiled with (see **3.14**).

The Charity Commission also has discretion to refuse an application if:

- the name of the proposed CIO is the same as or similar to the name of another charity (whether registered or not);
- the Charity Commission is of the opinion, under the powers contained in CA 1993 s 6(2)(b)–(e), that the proposed name:
  - — is likely to mislead the public as to the true nature or purpose of the charity or the activities which it carries on;
  - — includes any word or expression which is restricted or prohibited by any regulations;
  - — is likely to give the impression that the charity is connected with the Government or any local authority or other body or individual with which it is not connected; or
  - — in the Charity Commission's opinion the name is offensive; or
- as a result of its consultation process the Charity Commission considers it would not be appropriate to allow conversion to proceed (CA 1993 s 69H(3)).

If the Charity Commission decides to approve an application for conversion, then not only will it register the CIO on the Register of Charities, it will also send notification to Companies House or the FSA as appropriate, advising them of the conversion (CA 1993 s 69I(1)). It is important to note that conversion does not take place until Companies House (in the case of a charitable company) or the FSA (in the case of a registered society) removes the organisation applying for conversion from their register (CA 1993 s 69I(2)). Until that point registration with the Charity Commission is considered to be provisional only. Care therefore needs to be taken to ensure that the trustees of the charity do not commit the CIO to any liabilities until registration has become effective.

Practicalities of conversion

3.17 The first members of a CIO that is formed through the conversion of an existing charitable company or registered society will be the existing members of the charitable company or registered society at the time of conversion (CA 1993 s 69I(4)(c)). This means that there is no necessity to take special steps to transfer the membership of the charitable company or registered society to the CIO, as the transfer will take place automatically.

If the converting charitable company or registered society happens to have a share capital then the process of conversion will automatically cancel any shares that have been issued, and no former shareholders will have any rights with respect to those shares following cancellation (CA 1993 s 69I(5)). If shares have been issued for any special purpose it may be necessary to review this and to take professional advice before converting to a CIO to make sure that shareholders are not prejudiced, although any rights which have accrued before conversion will not be lost (CA 1993 s 69I(6)).

Merging CIOs

By amalgamation

3.18 Having provided a straightforward mechanism for certain types of charity and registered society to convert to CIO status it is no surprise to find that ChaA 2006 also introduces an equally straightforward mechanism for two or more CIOs to amalgamate. The provisions contained in CA 1993 s 69K envisage that CIOs that wish to merge can do so through the incorporation of a new successor CIO.

The application process and requirements for amalgamation are very similar to those that apply for the conversion of an existing charitable company to a CIO. One difference is that each CIO involved in the merger must submit copies of the resolutions approving the amalgamation and adopting the constitution of the new CIO (CA 1993 s 69K(4)). The same 75% majority or unanimous written resolution applies (CA 1993 s 69K(5)).

The proposed amalgamation needs to be advertised in a way which, in the opinion of each of the existing CIOs' trustees, will most likely ensure that the proposed amalgamation comes to the attention of those who will be affected by it. This notice needs to inform people who may be affected by the amalgamation that they are entitled to make written representations to the Charity Commission within the timeframe stipulated by the Charity Commission, and a copy of this notice needs to be sent to the Charity Commission at the same time (CA 1993 s 69K(7)).

When contemplating the amalgamation of two CIOs the trustees and the advisors to the charities need to consider carefully whether the constitution of the new CIO reflects the constitutions of the merging CIOs with regard to:

- their charitable objects;
- the provisions dealing with the application of charitable property on dissolution; and
- the rules governing the basis on which charity trustees or members (or people connected with them) can benefit from the charity (CA 1993 s 69K(10)–(12));

since if the Charity Commission is not satisfied on any of these points it may decide to decline the application for amalgamation.

As well as maintaining a record of the new CIO, the Charity Commission is also required to keep a note of the names of the CIOs which amalgamated to form the new charity (CA 1993 s 69L(5)(c)). This will be useful in tracing old CIOs that have dissolved through merger.

The registration of the new CIO automatically leads to the deregistration and dissolution of the old CIOs and the assignment of all of their prior rights, assets and liabilities to the new charity (CA 1993 s 69L(3)). There is therefore an automatic legal novation of everything associated with the old CIOs to the new entity, which makes the process much more straightforward than the merger of other sorts of charitable organisation, where individual assets and liabilities normally need to be assigned or novated. Notwithstanding the automatic legal novation provisions contained in ChaA 2006, it is recommended that the trustees and their advisors ensure that every third party with whom the old CIOs had a relationship are notified of the change, especially the likes of landlords, banks and local authorities. Title to assets such as land and shares will also still need to be re-registered into the name of the new CIO.

Very helpfully, ChaA 2006 ensures that if gifts are made to any of the pre-amalgamation CIOs these are automatically treated as having been made to the new body (CA 1993 s 69L(4)). This is of particular importance to charities that are the beneficiaries of legacies, and who might otherwise be concerned about the legal impact of amalgamation on their entitlement to benefit from testamentary bequests.

By transfer

3.19 The amalgamation process described in CA 1993 s 69K envisages that two or more CIOs can merge through the creation of a new successor CIO. A more common scenario is that one CIO wishes to merge into another CIO by transferring its rights, assets and liabilities across, and this is catered for by CA 1993 s 69M.

The process of transfer is very similar to that for amalgamation, except that both the transferring and receiving CIOs must each send the Charity Commission copies of resolutions agreeing to the transfer (CA 1993 s 69M(2)). Having received copies of the resolutions the Charity Commission may require the transferring CIO to give public notice of the intended transfer in a comparable manner to a CIO wishing to amalgamate, except that the giving of such notice is at the discretion of the Charity Commission and is subject to a period of 28 day's notice, beginning with the date when public notice of the resolution to transfer is given by the CIO (CA 1993 s 69M(4)). If the Charity Commission does not notify the charity applying to transfer its assets as to whether the application has been approved or not within six months of the resolution approving the transfer being received by the Charity Commission (or if public notice is required, then six months from the date the public notice is given), approval is deemed to have been given by the Commission (CA 1993 s 69M(8), (9)). The Charity Commission does, however, have the right to extend the six month period by up to a further six months, provided it hasn't already lapsed (CA 1993 s 69M(10)).

If the Charity Commission requires public notice to be given, then it is required to take into account any representations that are made by interested parties if these are submitted within the 28 day period (CA 1993 s 69M(4)(b)). The transfer will not take affect until the Charity Commission confirms that the transfer has been approved.

In a similar way to amalgamation, the trustees and advisors to a charity looking at a potential transfer under CA 1993 s 69M need to consider carefully whether the constitution of the receiving CIO sufficiently accommodates the objects of the transferring CIO with regard to matters such as charitable objects and provisions dealing with the application of charitable property on dissolution, as the Charity Commission has the power to reject an application for transfer if it is not satisfied that these are sufficiently aligned (CA 1993 s 69M(7)). Likewise, provision is made for the automatic transfer of gifts made to the transferring charity to pass to the receiving charity (CA 1993 s 69M(13)).

Winding up, insolvency and dissolution of CIOs

3.20 CA 1993 s 69 already contains provisions dealing with the winding up and dissolution of charitable companies. CA 1993 s 69N recognises that special provisions are needed to deal with the winding up, insolvency, dissolution and restoration of CIOs, since they are a new type of incorporated entity that falls outside existing Companies Act legislation. ChaA 2006 does not, however, contain any express provisions dealing with the winding up of CIOs and this is dealt with in secondary legislation.

Additional provisions covering CIOs

3.21 CA 1993 s 74 gives certain powers to the trustees of small charities to transfer their property to other charities. CA 1993 s 69O introduced by ChaA 2006 extends the scope of s 74 to the transfer of property to one or more CIOs.

ChaA 2006 also inserts CA 1993 Sch 5A, which contains further provisions applicable to CIOs concerning the constitution and operation of CIOs. Subject to any provisions in a CIO's constitution to the contrary, a CIO is deemed to have the power to do anything which is necessary to further its objects or is conducive or incidental to doing so (CA 1993 Sch 5B para 1(2)).

Third parties dealing with CIOs

3.22 To ensure that any third parties dealing with a CIO are not prejudiced by its novel legal structure, ChaA 2006 confirms that third parties that deal with CIOs are in much the same position as those dealing with limited companies. So, for example, if the trustees of a CIO intend for a CIO to enter into a commercial arrangement with a third party then any lack of constitutional power to act in that way cannot be raised as an argument to try and avoid a commitment that has been entered into by the CIO (CA 1993 Sch 5B para 5(2)). This only applies, however, where the third party has given full value in money or money's worth in relation to the transaction in question, and where the third party was not aware that the transaction was beyond the constitutional capacity of the CIO or the powers of its trustees, and dealt with the CIO in good faith. A third party dealing with a CIO is not, however, expected to make enquiries regarding the CIO's constitutional capacity or the powers of its trustees. CA 1993 Sch 5B para 5(6) extends these principles to the transfer or grant of an interest in land.

While CA 1993 Sch 5B para 5 ensures that third parties dealing in good faith with a charity established as a CIO do not need to concern themselves with whether the CIO's constitution gives it or its trustees power to act in a particular way, it does not excuse the trustees of the CIO from personal liability for acting beyond their constitutional powers. It also does not prevent anyone from taking legal action to stop a CIO or its trustees from acting beyond their constitutional powers (CA 1993 Sch 5B para 6(1)).

Duties of trustees and members of CIOs

3.23 One aspect of the new law relating to CIOs which is of particular interest is that, unlike other charitable structures, in the case of a CIO not only are the trustees liable to exercise their powers and perform their functions in good faith to further the objects of the CIO, but so also are the members (CA 1993 Sch 5B para 9). This means that a charity with a membership that has converted to being a CIO, where previously the members were able to make decisions from a purely personal (and possibly selfish) point of view, as members of a CIO each member will need to ensure that he exercises his powers in a way which is most likely to further the aims of the charity. This is a subtle but potentially important change which may have interesting consequences, particularly for those charities that have a large and active membership.

The trustees of CIOs are obliged to exercise skill and care in performing their duties to a level which is reasonable, taking into account their particular knowledge or experience. Trustees with professional expertise, such as lawyers, accountants or surveyors, will therefore need to ensure that they conduct their duties with the requisite level of skill and knowledge attributable to their profession (CA 1993 Sch 5B para 10).

The rules governing the payment of trustees of the CIO are identical to those for any other type of charity. ChaA 2006 makes it clear that the trustees of a CIO may not personally benefit from any arrangements entered into by the CIO unless they disclose to all of the other trustees any material interest which they have in the transaction or with any other person or body entering into the transaction with the CIO.

Chapter 4

Information, Accounting and Reporting

Introduction

4.1 One of the key themes behind the reforms leading to the Charities Act 2006 ('ChaA 2006') was the desire to create 'greater accountability and transparency to build public trust and confidence ... by improving information available to the public ... and regulating fundraising more effectively' (see the Cabinet Office's Strategy Unit report 'Private Action, Public Benefit' (September 2002)). This drive towards greater transparency and accountability in the voluntary sector reflects a similar move in both the public and commercial sectors over recent years, as illustrated by the introduction of the Freedom of Information Act 2000 and the rules on corporate governance affecting public companies.

While ChaA 2006 itself contains only limited provisions dealing with the extension of this philosophy of accountability, the Act was preceded in 2005 by the Charities (Accounts and Reports) Regulations 2005, SI 2005/572, and a review of the system for Annual Returns, which together directly implemented the philosophy of greater openness and transparency for larger charities whilst reducing 'red tape' for smaller charities.

Annual Returns and Summary Information Returns

4.2 Over the last two years a new system for Annual Returns has been developed and refined. Different Returns have to be made depending upon the annual income of the charity in question. These can be summarised as follows:

Annual income	*Return*
Below £10,000 per annum (pa)	Annual Information Update only. No Accounts required.
Between £10,000 and £100,000 pa	Annual Return, but only Part A.
Between £100,000 and £250,000 pa	Annual Return, but only Part A. May be invited to submit Return online.

Annual income	*Return*
Between £250,000 and £1 million pa	Annual Return including Part B. May submit online.
Over £1 million pa	Annual Return including SIR. May submit online.

Charities are only issued with the relevant Return for their income, based on the income for the previous year. The Returns must be submitted within 10 months of the end of the charity's financial year.

The Summary Information Return ('SIR') was introduced because of concerns raised in the Cabinet Office's Strategy Unit report 'Private Action, Public Benefit' (September 2002), that there was a lack of accessible and relevant information available on charities. The idea behind the SIR is that it will help the public to understand what a charity does and how it has performed.

When the SIR was originally piloted in 2004/05 concerns were expressed that the return duplicated existing information which larger charities were already supplying, but asked for this information in a different way. The SIR has been adapted and now forms Part C of the Annual Return.

The SIR should enable charities to provide details of their key aims, activities and achievements for the year, along with information about any factors that affected performance. The summary can direct readers to more detailed information contained in the Trustees' Annual Report and Accounts (and these will need to be much more detailed with the introduction of SORP 2005 – see **4.4**), in annual reviews, charity websites and any other published information, such as business plans. Charities are now encouraged to include SIRs on their own websites. All completed SIRs are available to view on the Charity Commission website (www.charitycommission.gov.uk).

GuideStar UK

4.3 In 2003 a new charity called GuideStar UK was established with the support of the Institute for Philanthropy. The new charity, which was based on a similar model operating in the United States, was set up to create a comprehensive and easily accessible database of information on the activities of UK charities with the aim of providing the general public with more information on the activities of UK charities. This is intended to help donors, grant makers, researchers, policy makers and the general public to understand the work of charities, and to be able to identify particular charities servicing particular areas of interest.

In March 2004 GuideStar UK was awarded a grant of £2.9 million over three years from the 'Invest to Save' budget, a joint Treasury and Cabinet Office initiative aimed at encouraging innovation and partnership to improve quality and cost effectiveness in the public sector. GuideStar UK also received support from several other charitable and philanthropic bodies.

After two years of development and consultation, GuideStar UK was launched on 12 December 2005. It currently holds details of over 160,000 registered charities in England and Wales. It also aims to include information about charities in Scotland and Northern Ireland, and about social enterprises and informal voluntary bodies.

Unlike the Charity Commission's publicly accessible entries, which only cover basic information concerning the charities that are recorded on the register, the aim of GuideStar is to provide additional information which is extracted from the documents and reports submitted by charities to the Commission each year. In addition, charities are invited to add extra information to their entries on the website. GuideStar has committed itself not to evaluate or comment on the performance of individual charities or to compile league tables, but simply to provide factual information to the public concerning the charities that are represented on the database.

More information is available at http://www.guidestar.org.uk.

The Charities (Accounts and Reports) Regulations 2005

4.4 The Charities Act 1992 ('CA 1992') ss 19–27 (subsequently incorporated into CA 1993) together with the Charities (Accounts and Reports) Regulations 1995, SI 1995/2724, and the Statement of Recommended Practice for Accounting by Charities ('SORP'), October 1995, introduced a new system of accounting, auditing and reporting for charities for financial years commencing after 1 March 1996. These arrangements were updated with effect from 1 January 2001 by the Charities (Accounts and Reports) Regulations 2000, SI 2000/2868, and an updated SORP 2000. From 31 March 2005 the 1995 and 2000 Regulations and SORP were replaced by the Charities (Accounts and Reports) Regulations 2005, SI 2005/572, and the Statement of Recommended Practice for Accounting by Charities (SORP 2005), published in March 2005.

A detailed examination of SORP 2005 and SI 2005/572 is beyond the scope of this publication. The main aims of the Regulations are to ensure that within a charity's statement of account there is

- an enhanced annual report by the trustees of the performance of the charity against its objectives;
- greater detail on the activities, services and projects which the charity has undertaken during the relevant period; and
- a change to the statement of financial affairs which will hopefully

ensure that it becomes easier to fully understand and appreciate the charity's financial position and how its income and expenditure relate to its charitable objects,

with the intention of making it easier to see how effectively a charity is operating against its stated aims.

SORP 2005 builds on SORP 2000 and includes the financial reporting standards and urgent issue task force abstracts issued or withdrawn up to 30 April 2004, as well as the contents of the Cabinet Office's Strategy Unit report 'Private Action, Public Benefit'. One objective of SORP 2005 is to ensure that the trustees' annual report provides a clearer link between the strategies, objectives and activities of a charity and its financial performance over the relevant period.

SORP 2005 applies to all charities generally, unless they are covered by particular SORP provisions, and is relevant to all charities preparing accounts on an accrual basis, but not to charities that prepare receipts and payment accounts. SORP 2005 applies to accounting periods beginning on or after 1 April 2005.

Annual audit or examination of accounts of unincorporated charities

4.5 CA 1992 s 21 and subsequently CA 1993 s 43 introduced the requirement for charities that were not companies either to have their accounts audited or independently examined, depending on their level of income. A requirement for every charity to have its accounts professionally audited would have been an unreasonable financial burden and therefore CA 1993 provided that the audit requirement only applied to charities:

- whose gross income or expenditure exceeded £250,000 in the current financial year; or
- whose gross income or expenditure exceeded £250,000 in either of the two preceding financial years.

In recognition of the increasing size of charities over the past 12 years, ChaA 2006 s 28 amends CA 1993 s 43 by removing the reference to a charity's expenditure as one of the tests for requiring an audit, and by increasing the income threshold to £500,000. ChaA 2006 also introduces an additional aggregate asset value test of £2.8 million (before deduction of liabilities). At the time of writing this test only applies to charities whose gross income exceeds the accounts threshold of £100,000, below which charities can prepare the simpler form of accounts permitted by CA 1993 s 42(3).

An amendment to CA 1993 s 43(2) has been introduced to ensure that where a charity's accounts are required to be audited the rules on ineligibility of an auditor for reasons of lack of independence previously contained in Companies Act 1989 Part 2 now apply to the auditing of all charity accounts that are required to be audited.

CA 1993 s 43(3) has also been amended to remove the consideration of expenditure as a relevant factor when determining whether a charity's accounts need to have an independent examination. Previously, CA 1993 s 43(3), as amended by Deregulation and Contracting Out Act 1994 s 28, required a charity to have an independent examination of its accounts where either its income or its total expenditure in a relevant year exceeded £10,000. In future an independent examination is only required by charities whose income exceeds £10,000 but falls below the new audit limit.

ChaA 2006 s 28(5) introduces a new CA 1993 s 43(3A) so that charities that previously had to have their accounts audited as a result of having an income above £250,000 but are no longer required to do so because their income falls below the new increased audit threshold of £500,000, are required to have their accounts independently examined by someone with a relevant qualification should they elect not to have their accounts audited by a qualified auditor. For these purposes, someone will be considered to have the 'relevant qualification' if they are either a member of the Chartered Institute of Public Finance and Accountancy or are a member of a recognised body under Companies Act 1985 s 249D(3) which would mean:

- a member of the Institute of Chartered Accountants in England and Wales;
- a member of the Institute of Chartered Accountants of Scotland;
- a member of the Institute of Chartered Accountants in Ireland;
- a member of the Association of Chartered Certified Accountants;
- a member of the Association of International Accountants;
- a member of the Association of Accounting Technicians;
- a member of the Chartered Institute of Management Accountants; or
- a member of the Institute of Chartered Secretaries and Administrators.

Whistle blowing

4.6 Perhaps one of the most significant changes in terms of charity accounting arises as a result of the introduction of CA 1993 ss 44A and 68A. These two sections reflect a substantially similar purpose in that they place on an auditor or independent examiner involved in reviewing a charity's accounts an obligation to immediately report to the Charity Commission in writing if they become aware of any matter relating to the activities or affairs of the charity (or any connected body) which they have reasonable cause to believe would have a material significance with regard to the exercise by the Charity Commission of its powers under CA 1993 s 8 (general power to institute enquires) or s 19 (power to act for protection of charities) (CA 1993 s 44A(2)).

If the auditor or independent examiner considers that a matter could be relevant to the Charity Commission or the exercise of its powers, but the matter does not fall within the mandatory reporting requirements referred to previously, ChaA 2006 gives the accountant the power to decide to report the matter to the Charity Commission in any event. It must be presumed that the reason for enshrining this statutory power is to ensure that the exercise of such a power by an accountant will override any common law duty of confidentiality which an accountant owes to his client. This duty continues to exist, notwithstanding that the accountant's retainer may have ended (CA 1993 s 44A(4)).

Group accounting

4.7 As well as reforming the rules governing the requirement for the audit and examination of charity accounts, ChaA 2006 also introduces new rules affecting the preparation and auditing of accounts for groups where the parent body is a charity. The new provisions contained in ChaA 2006 s 30 and Sch 6 introduce new CA 1993 s 49A and Sch 5A, which require almost all charities with subsidiaries, other than exempt charities, to prepare annual accounts for the whole group in future.

For charities established as limited companies with incorporated subsidiaries Companies Act 1985 already requires such groups to prepare consolidated accounts. For non-corporate charities, however, no such requirement previously existed.

Under CA 1993 Sch 5A para 1 a charity will be treated as a 'parent charity' if (a) it falls to be treated as the parent of a group under the Companies Act 1985 s 258, and (b) it is not a company. Not surprisingly the subordinate undertakings of such a parent charity are known as its 'subsidiary undertakings', though certain types of entity, such as special trusts, are excluded from this definition (CA 1993 Sch 5A para 1(4)).

The new group accounting rules cover not just subsidiaries that are companies but any 'undertaking', as defined by Companies Act 1985 s 259(1), and any charity (whether covered by s 259 or not). This means that an undertaking will include a corporate body, partnership or unincorporated association carrying on a trade or business. The parent charity and its relevant subsidiary undertakings are know as the 'group' for the purposes of the new rules.

Where a charitable 'group' exists, the trustees will need to ensure that proper accounting records are maintained not just for each undertaking within the group, but also for the group as a whole (CA 1993 Sch 5A para 2(1)). These records need to comply with the existing requirements contained in CA 1993 s 41(1). Even if a subsidiary undertaking is not required to keep accounts to the standard required by CA 1993 the parent charity will still need to ensure that sufficient records are kept so as to ensure that the consolidated group accounts prepared under the new rules meet the requisite standard.

The new rules apply if a charity finds that it is the parent of a group at the end of its financial year. In those circumstances the parent charity must prepare consolidated group accounts unless:

- at the time the charity is itself the subsidiary of another charity;
- the income for the group does not exceed the group accounting threshold; or
- any regulations require or permit a subsidiary undertaking to be excluded.

If the aggregate gross group income or aggregate value of assets of a charitable group exceed a certain threshold, or the parent charity is required to have its accounts audited, then the accounts for the group must also be audited (CA 1993 Sch 5A para 6(3)) and similar audit provisions will apply to the consolidated group accounts. There are also similar provisions applying to the examination of group accounts where the threshold requirements for a full audit have not been met.

CA 1993 Sch 5A ensures that the duty on auditors to bring certain matters to the attention of the Charity Commission (see **4.6**) applies equally to audited group accounts.

Chapter 5

Charity Trustees and Auditors

Introduction

5.1 The Government's initial report on the voluntary sector focused on, amongst other things, good governance and the need to attract good quality skilled trustees (see the Cabinet Office's Strategy Unit report 'Private Action, Public Benefit' (September 2002)).

The Charities Act 2006 ('ChaA 2006') introduces a series of reforming provisions that directly affect charity trustees. These include a new statutory power to remunerate trustees, as well as a useful extension of the relief from liability. However, to counter these positive provisions, a number of additional duties have been imposed. These are all included in ChaA 2006 Part 2 Ch 9.

Trustees' powers

5.2 The new range of powers available to trustees includes the power for smaller charities to amend their governing documents (see **10.7** and **10.10**) and to release certain permanent endowment funds (see **6.2**). However, one of the most significant changes in ChaA 2006 is the introduction of a statutory power to remunerate trustees, although this is not as exciting as it may at first seem.

Trustees' remuneration – historic position

5.3 The historic position was that charity trustees were not supposed to derive a personal benefit from acting as a trustee unless authority was provided by the governing document, by the Charity Commission (under the Charities Act 1993 ('CA 1993') s 26), by the court or, very rarely, by statute (the Housing Act 1996 Sch 1 Part 1 applies to the trustees of some charitable housing associations). This was to ensure that there was no conflict between the best interests of a charity and the personal interests of a trustee, and the propositions applied equally to incorporated and unincorporated charities. Personal benefits included direct benefits, such as remuneration, and indirect benefits, such as the occupation of property or subsidised rates for the use of charity facilities.

The Charity Commission provides a comprehensive guide (Guidance Note CC11) to payment of trustees, including a useful checklist of points for trustees to consider before employing and remunerating a trustee. These include conflict of interest procedures, reporting in the accounts, consultation with all interested parties, independent advice on the level of payment or alternative quotes, the need for formal contracts, whether the same services could be provided by a volunteer and whether paid trustees are in the minority in the trustee group.

Even if an existing charity had the power to amend its constitution, the payment of trustees was one of the amendments that required the prior approval of the Charity Commission. This was also the case for incorporated charities. Theoretically, Companies House should have asked to see a copy of the pre-approved draft resolution, endorsed with the necessary prescribed wording (prescribed by CA 1993 s 64) before amending their records. In practice, amendments may often have been put through without notification to Companies House. However, any amendments that were implemented without this prior approval would not be valid from a charity law perspective and charity trustees would be acting in breach of trust if they paid one of their number without the amendment having received Charity Commission approval. In the worst case scenario the trustee who received payment could be required to reimburse the charity to the full extent of the payments made. The remaining trustees could also be personally liable for any unauthorised diminution of charity funds.

It has always been possible to apply to the Charity Commission for the power to remunerate a trustee, but the Commission has been reluctant to provide a blanket power. The Commission was more likely to approve the payment of an individual trustee, assuming that the necessary case had been made. The Charity Commission would require evidence that the payment was both reasonable and necessary and that any conflict of interest would be disclosed and properly managed. Theoretically the Commission had more lenient procedures for small charities.

The problem with this historical approach is that although the underlying principle may have been a sound one it did not provide sufficient flexibility to meet the needs of today's voluntary sector. Many of the largest incorporated charities operate in the same way as commercial organisations in their management structure. They have managing directors and other executives who are salaried employees of the charity. If they are also to be trustees, it will be necessary to justify their remuneration. If they are simply considered to be employees with a completely separate non-executive trustee body, this may result in an unwieldy decision-making structure or may not be truly representative of the way that the organisation operates.

The original definition of 'connected persons'

5.4 The restrictions described above also extended to remunerating 'connected persons'. The Charity Commission has stated that when carrying out its regular reviews of charities on the register, one of the most common findings is that there is a trustee who is receiving an indirect benefit via a member of his family. Quite often this is because a family member is being remunerated by the charity for their particular services or skills. Another common situation is where the firm in which a professional trustee is a partner is paid professional fees without there being a charging clause in the constitution. It is not even necessary for the partner to be an equity partner within the firm.

The original definition of a 'connected person' (CA 1993 Sch 5) extended to relatives of a trustee, including children, grandchildren, parents, grandparents, brothers or sisters, or any spouse of the trustee or of any of the named relatives. It also included an institution which was controlled by the trustee, either alone or in combination with any of the above relatives, or a body corporate in which the trustee had a substantial interest, again either alone or in combination with relatives.

New statutory power of remuneration

5.5 For the reasons given above, the introduction of a new statutory power of remuneration of trustees was widely welcomed by the voluntary sector. Provision had been made in previous legislation (Trustee Act 2000 s 30) for the Secretary of State to introduce a statutory power of remuneration for charity trustees by way of statutory instrument. However, such regulations had never been introduced and in any event they would only have related to trust corporations and professional trustees.

CA 1993 ss 73A and 73B, as inserted by ChaA 2006 s 36, allow a trustee to be remunerated for services provided to a charity. The word 'services' can include goods that are supplied in connection with the provision of services, but not goods unconnected with services. As has always been the case however, a trustee can still not be paid simply for acting as a trustee. Nor can he or she receive a benefit from connected persons (see **5.4**) unless the statutory procedure is also followed for their remuneration. 'Benefits' can mean direct or indirect benefits (CA 1993 s 73B(4), as inserted by ChaA 2006 s 36). ChaA 2006 makes it expressly clear that 'remuneration' includes any benefit in kind (CA 1993 s 73B(4), as inserted by ChaA 2006 s 36).

Conditions

5.6 In order to provide the necessary safeguards to prevent abuse of the new statutory power to remunerate trustees there are conditions that must be met. These are as follows:

(1) There must be a written agreement between the charity (or, in the case of an unincorporated charity, the charity trustees) and the trustee being paid. This agreement must set out the amount or maximum

amount of remuneration which will be paid (Condition A, see CA 1993 s 73A(3)(a), as inserted by ChaA 2006 s 36). As a further safeguard, any guidance issued by the Charity Commission must be followed when entering into this agreement (CA 1993 s 73B(1), as inserted by ChaA 2006 s 36).

(2) The amount of remuneration, as set out in the agreement, must be reasonable in the circumstances (Condition A, see CA 1993 s 73A(3)(b), as inserted by ChaA 2006 s 36). This means that written agreement is more likely to apply to individual transactions rather than ongoing situations, given the requirement to consider each individual set of circumstances.

(3) Before entering into a written agreement the charity trustees must be satisfied that it will be in the best interests of the charity for the services to be provided by the relevant trustee for the amount set out in the agreement (Condition B, see CA 1993 s 73A(4), as inserted by ChaA 2006 s 36).

When reaching this decision the charity trustees (whether of an unincorporated or incorporated charity) must comply with the statutory duty of care (CA 1993 s 73B(2), referring to Trustee Act 2000 s 1(1)). This states that a trustee must exercise such care and skill as is reasonable in the circumstances, having regard in particular (a) to any special knowledge or experience that he has or holds himself out as having, and (b) if he acts as trustee in the course of a business or profession, to any special knowledge or experience that it is reasonable to expect of a person acting in the course of that kind of business or profession. This applies equally to incorporated charities, even though they are strictly not subject to the Trustee Act 2000.

This does mean that a record will need to be kept of the decision-making process and of any alternative quotes considered. This is already recommended as good practice (see Charity Commission Guidance Note CC11), but it will now be a statutory condition.

(4) Where one or more trustees are to be paid under the new provisions, the total number of trustees who are entitled to receive payment (whether under this type of agreement or through any other means, such as under a charging clause in the charity's constitution or as a result of a Charity Commission order) or who are connected with a trustee who is entitled to receive payment, must constitute a minority of the trustees (Condition C, see CA 1993 s 73A(5), as inserted by ChaA 2006 s 36). Agreements may be considered to remain in force for as long as there are any obligations that have not been fully discharged (CA 1993 s 73B(3), as inserted by ChaA 2006 s 36).

(5) The objects of the charity must not contain any express provision that prohibits a trustee from receiving remuneration (Condition D, see CA

1993 s 73A(6), as inserted by ChaA 2006 s 36). This is a surprisingly common provision in older constitutions.

These conditions will not apply to remuneration already approved by the governing document, by statute, by the court or by the Charity Commission (CA 1993 s 73A(7), (8), as inserted by ChaA 2006 s 36) but they clearly show what is expected by way of good practice in any event. Interestingly, the conditions do not require that a paid trustee is appointed using a fair and open procedure.

The new definition of 'connected persons'

5.7 The concept of 'connected persons' is as described above (see 5.4). However, the new legislation specifies the list of connected persons for the purpose of the new statutory power to remunerate trustees (CA 1993 s 73B(5), as inserted by ChaA 2006 s 36). This is more limited in scope than for other matters (CA 1993 Sch 5), as it does not include officers, agents or employees of the charity, donors of land or their relatives.

The list in CA 1993 s 73B(5) is comprehensive and includes the child, parent, grandchild, grandparent, brother or sister of a trustee, as well as the spouse or civil partner of any of these relatives. It also includes the spouse or civil partner of a trustee. The term 'child' includes stepchild or illegitimate child, and 'spouse' includes anyone living with another as if they were a spouse (incorporated by CA 1993 s 73B(6), as inserted by ChaA 2006 s 36). The inclusion of civil partners reflects the introduction of the Civil Partnership Act 2004, which came into force on 5 December 2005.

The list in s 73B(5) also includes any institution which is controlled by the trustee, either alone or in combination with any of the above relatives, or a body corporate in which the trustee has a substantial interest, again either alone or in combination with any of those relatives. It also catches a person carrying on business in partnership with the trustee or any of the above relatives.

Conflict of interest

5.8 As an additional safeguard, a trustee who is to benefit from remuneration under an agreement, for example a contract for services, is technically 'disqualified' from acting in relation to that decision or to any other matter connected with the agreement (CA 1993 s 73C, as inserted by ChaA 2006 s 37). This is a stronger measure than simply noting the conflict in a conflicts register. This applies equally to the remuneration of any connected person (CA 1993 s 73C(1)(b)). The trustee certainly must not vote or be counted in any quorum. He may be well advised to leave the room when the contract is being discussed and the fact that this has happened should be recorded in the meeting minutes. If this process is not followed, although the decision itself will not be invalid (CA 1993 s 73C(3)), the Charity Commission may make an order in relation to the payment (CA 1993 s 73C(4)).

If the payment or benefit has not been paid or received, the Charity Commission may direct that the whole or part of the payment should not be paid (CA 1993 s 73C(6)). If the payment or benefit has been received, the Charity Commission may require the trustee to repay the remuneration either in whole or in part, or the whole or part of the value of any benefit in kind (CA 1993 s 73C(5)). This value would be determined by the Charity Commission. Failure to follow proper procedures may result in a Charity Commission order, which would mean that the trustee would lose his entitlement to that payment at any time now or in the future. This may appear draconian but it is much more lenient than the original provision (included in the draft Charity Bill, published on 27 May 2004), which provided that a trustee infringing these provisions could find himself subject to criminal prosecution leading to a prison term or fine, or both.

Charity Commission orders under this section may be the subject of an appeal to the new Charity Tribunal (included in the list at ChaA 2006 Sch 4) (for further details see CHAPTER 12).

Trustee indemnity insurance

5.9 The new legislation addresses the long standing issue of trustee indemnity insurance and provides a statutory power for charity trustees to avail themselves of trustee indemnity insurance (CA 1993 s 73F, as inserted by ChaA 2006 s 39). This provision is linked to remuneration of trustees because it has always been viewed by the Charity Commission as a trustee benefit, given that the insurance protects the trustees personally although the premiums are paid out of charity funds.

Historic position

5.10 In a similar way to trustee remuneration, charity trustees have previously only been able to take out trustee indemnity insurance if they were legally authorised to do so. This authority could derive from an express charging clause in the governing document of the charity, from the Charity Commission or occasionally from the court.

The Charity Commission had relaxed its position on trustee indemnity insurance in recent years. Although the Commission still consider it to be a trustee benefit, it recognises that trustees were increasingly concerned about their personal liability and reluctant to take on the onerous role of trustee without the reassurance of indemnity insurance. The Charity Commission was generally willing to authorise trustee indemnity insurance as long as it only covered claims made against trustees for acts either properly undertaken in the administration of the charity or undertaken in breach of trust but made as a result of an honest mistake.

Where the governing constitution of a charity did not contain the power to take out trustee indemnity insurance, it was possible to make an application to the Charity Commission to amend the constitution in this respect. A 'fast-track' procedure had been introduced and forms were available from the Charity Commission that could be used by the trustees to apply for the incorporation of the relevant amendment.

The new statutory power

5.11 The new statutory power cannot be used if there is an express prohibition on taking out trustee indemnity insurance in the governing constitution. This will still require a scheme. However, it will be available if the constitution only contains a blanket prohibition relating to trustee remuneration (CA 1993 s 73F(8), as inserted by ChaA 2006 s 39), or where the power is conditional on Charity Commission approval. In the latter case the Charity Commission has confirmed that trustees can assume that the requirement for Commission approval has been deleted.

Before taking out trustee indemnity insurance the trustees must give careful consideration to whether or not exercising this power is in the best interests of the charity (CA 1993 s 73F(4)). The statutory duty of care also applies (CA 1993 s 73F(5), referring to Trustee Act 2000 s 1(1)) (see **5.6**). However, the conditions applying to remuneration are not applicable here. Trustees can simply arrange the insurance or can amend their constitution without the prior approval of the Charity Commission.

The new statutory provisions reflect those that have been included in the Charity Commission model constitutional documents for some time. These provisions ensure that any policy taken out will specifically exclude cover for any liability incurred by a trustee in defending criminal proceedings where he has been convicted ('convicted' means a final conviction with no appeal outstanding, see CA 1993 s 73F(3)) of fraud, dishonesty or wilful or reckless misconduct, or for the payment of a criminal fine or statutory penalty, or for any liability incurred as a result of the trustee not considering, or not caring about, the best interests of the charity (CA 1993 s 73F(2)). These exclusions may be varied by the Secretary of State as long as the variations are approved by both Houses of Parliament (CA 1993 s 73F(6), (7)).

Given these statutory exclusions, as well as the exclusions imposed by insurance companies, trustees are well advised to consider carefully the extent to which they are protected by the policy they wish to take out, particularly in light of the size of the premium. This is particularly appropriate where incorporated charities are concerned, given that they inherently enjoy no personal liability in most cases where a trustee has acted lawfully. Trustees may also be affected in their decision by the further provision considered at **5.14** below, which gives the Charity Commission the power to relieve trustees from liability.

Trustees' liability

5.12 One of the greatest concerns for charity trustees is the issue of personal liability. It has always been the case that charity trustees are personally liable for the way in which they administer the affairs of a charity, but in these days of substantial awards in courts and tribunals, the magnitude of the risk has changed. This liability is limited to some extent by using an incorporated charity structure. However, it is not possible to eliminate it altogether.

Although it is generally possible to reimburse a trustee from charity funds for any liability he has incurred if he has acted in good faith, there remains the risk that he may act in breach of trust, either through ignorance or because it cannot be avoided. In such a situation he may not be protected, particularly if the liability exceeds the extent of the charity's assets.

One apparently small measure in ChaA 2006 will offer some comfort to charity trustees who are concerned about their personal position.

Relief from liability

Historic position

5.13 Before the introduction of ChaA 2006, a trustee could already apply to the court for relief from personal liability. This applied to directors of incorporated charities as well as to trustees of unincorporated charities. Although incorporated charities have their own legal identity, providing trustees with some personal protection, it is still possible for trustees to incur personal liabilities.

Applications to the court for relief could be made under two separate provisions, depending on whether the charity was incorporated or unincorporated (Companies Act 1985 s 727(1) and Trustee Act 1925 s 61). Both provisions required the trustee or director to establish that he acted honestly and reasonably and, having regard to all the circumstances, ought fairly to be excused. It was also possible to apply to the High Court for equitable relief, again assuming that the trustee had acted honestly and made a genuine mistake.

However, these provisions were little used, partly because many trustees were not aware of their existence, but also because they involved a court application, with all the associated procedural requirements and costs.

The Charity Commission previously had no power to grant relief, although it could choose not to enforce restitution.

The new position

5.14 It is now possible to apply direct to the Charity Commission for relief from personal liability (CA 1993 s 73D, as inserted by ChaA 2006 s 38). The Charity Commission will be able to make an order relieving a trustee wholly or partly from personal liability where he has acted honestly, reasonably and ought fairly to be excused for the breach (CA 1993 s 73D(2)). This applies equally to holding and custodian trustees. The order for relief may be on such terms as the Charity Commission thinks fit (CA 1993 s 73D(3)).

The new provision has some obvious advantages, such as speed and much lower costs. However, one additional advantage is that, unlike a court application, it will be possible to apply to the Charity Commission for relief even where the trustee is not absolutely certain that he is actually liable (CA 1993 s 73D(2)(a)). It is not necessary to prove that an actual breach has occurred. However, this will not necessarily provide blanket protection against any future breaches.

This new provision will provide a great measure of relief to trustees who are not only concerned about the extent of their personal liability, but who may find it difficult to determine when they are or are not likely to be liable. When you add to this measure the increased power of the Charity Commission to provide trustees with advice (see **7.6**), charity trustees can now be further reassured when considering issues of personal liability.

However, a note of caution needs to be included. The onus of proving that he has acted honestly and reasonably will fall on the trustee. It may be hard to predict what would be considered to be reasonable in a particular set of circumstances. Courts have been reluctant to provide relief from liability where a trustee is paid or is a professional trustee. Merely taking professional advice in a matter will not satisfy the reasonableness test. The trustee will need to show that he acted prudently in relation to that advice. In addition a trustee may not necessarily be relieved where he has entered into a personal contractual liability, for example where the trustees of an unincorporated charity have taken out a lease on behalf of the charity. This remains a significant problem.

Auditors

5.15 The new legislation also allows the Charity Commission to grant relief from liability to auditors, independent examiners or anyone else appointed to examine a charity's accounts (CA 1993 s 73D, as inserted by ChaA 2006 s 38). The same provisions apply as in the paragraph above. In addition, a new CA 1993 s 73E, as inserted by ChaA 2006 s 38, extends the power of the courts to grant relief to auditors and independent examiners or anyone else examining the accounts of incorporated charities or Charitable Incorporated Organisations (see **Chapter 3**) who would not previously have qualified for court relief (under Companies Act 1985 s 727).

In combination with the new whistle-blowing obligations (see **4.6**) this is likely to mean that auditors and independent examiners will become much more active in the regulation of charities' activities, as is no doubt envisaged by the legislation.

Waiver of disqualification

5.16 ChaA 2006 makes certain subtle but important changes to the rules governing the waiver of a trustee's disqualification (CA 1993 s 72(4A), as inserted by ChaA 2006 s 35). The existing CA 1993 s 72 contains the list of circumstances in which a trustee may be disqualified from acting as a charity trustee. These include having been convicted of an offence of dishonesty or deception, being an undischarged bankrupt, having been disqualified from acting as a company director or having been removed from office by the Charity Commission or by the court for misconduct or mismanagement of the charity's affairs. Previously the Charity Commission had the discretion to waive this disqualification in respect of the trusteeship of a particular charity or class of charities, as long as it was not prohibited by company law for directors. However, the onus was on the charity trustee to convince the Charity Commission that a waiver would be in the best interests of the charity (CA 1993 s 72(4)).

The new provisions provide that a trustee who has been removed from office by the Charity Commission or by the court for misconduct or mismanagement of a charity can now apply after five years for the disqualification to be waived. The Charity Commission will be obliged to approve the waiver unless there are special circumstances for not granting the waiver (CA 1993 s 72(4A)) or the waiver is prohibited under company law. This does not apply to a trustee who has been convicted of a relevant offence or is an undischarged bankrupt.

Chapter 6

Endowments and Mergers

Endowments

Introduction

6.1 The Charities Act 1993 ('CA 1993') already contained provisions which allowed charity trustees to access the capital of a permanent endowment if they were of the opinion that the assets of the charity were too small, in relation to its objects, for the charity to be able to usefully achieve its aims through the expenditure of income alone. This power was, however, subject to some very serious restrictions that limited its potential application.

Firstly, the permanent endowment could not consist of or include any land or buildings, and secondly, the charity (which could not be a charitable company or exempt charity) had to have an income of less than £1,000 in its last financial year (CA 1993 s 75(1)(b)). The power to access the capital of a permanent endowment under CA 1993 s 75 was therefore restricted only to very small charities. Even then the trustees needed to satisfy themselves whether the objects of the charity would have been better served by transferring or dividing the assets with another charity or charities under CA 1993 s 74 (ignoring any transfer or division which would impose an unacceptable burden of cost on the charity) (CA 1993 s 75(4)).

Assuming that such a transfer was rejected by the trustees, the trustees would need to pass a resolution with at least a two thirds majority (CA 1993 s 75(3)) determining to free the charity's permanent endowment from restrictions to expend capital. The trustees were then required to go through a process of giving public notice of the resolution (CA 1993 s 75(5)(a)), as well as sending a copy to the Charity Commission (CA 1993 s 75(5)(b)), who then had three months to decide whether to agree or not with the resolution (old CA 1993 s 75(7)).

This was clearly a cumbersome and lengthy process. The Charities Act 2006 ('ChaA 2006') introduces a major overhaul of this area, extending its application from small charities to charities of all sizes, as well as to capital that is the subject of a special trust.

Power to spend capital for small charities

6.2 ChaA 2006 s 43 introduces a new CA 1993 s 75, which replaces the old s 75 entirely.

Under the new s 75, a small charity is defined as a charity to which the provisions applicable to larger charities covered by the new s 75A do not apply. A larger charity is defined as one whose gross income in its last financial year exceeded £1,000 and where the market value of its endowment fund exceeds £10,000 (CA 1993 s 75A(2)). A small charity would therefore need to fall below this threshold.

Like the old s 75, the new provisions continue not to be available to charities that are established as companies or corporate bodies themselves (including Charitiable Incorporated Organisations ('CIOs')) (CA 1993 s 75(1)), although s 75 should apply if the assets are simply administered by another charity which is a company, CIO or registered society. Unlike the old s 75, which excluded the power to spend capital if the permanent endowment included any land (old CA 1993 s 75(1)(b)), the new s 75 imposes no such restriction any longer.

In order for the trustees to be able to access the capital of the permanent endowment it was previously necessary for them to conclude that the property of the charity was too small in relation to its aims for any useful purpose to be achievable through the expenditure of the income alone. It was felt that at times this test could be hard to apply, and so the new s 75(4) introduces a test of whether the purposes applicable to the permanent endowment 'could be carried out more effectively' if both capital, as well as income, could be spent.

For smaller charities there is no longer a need to give consideration as to whether assets should be transferred or shared with another charity, nor do they have to go through the process of giving notice to the public and the Charity Commission and then waiting for the Charity Commission's response. Instead, they are able to start accessing the capital as soon as they have passed a resolution that it is appropriate for them to do so, and such a resolution only requires a simple majority (CA 1993 s 75(3)).

Power to spend capital for larger charities

6.3 ChaA 2006 introduces a new CA 1993 s 75A which extends the power to spend capital to larger charities. In doing so, it uses many of the concepts described above for smaller charities whilst retaining many of the safeguards that previously existed under the old s 75 because of the larger amounts that may be involved.

Again, the power is available only to unincorporated charities where the trustees consider that the objects applicable to the endowment fund will be able to more effectively carry on if the capital, as well as the income, of the endowment can be spent (CA 1993 s 75A(4)). In this respect the power is exactly the same as it is for smaller charities. Section 75A does not, however, apply to all endowments, but only to those where the property in question was given by:

- a particular individual or institution; or
- two or more individuals or institutions for a common purpose (CA 1993 s 75A(1)(a)).

Unlike small charities, where the trustees can access the capital as soon as they have passed the necessary resolution, for larger charities the trustees are first required to send a copy of their resolution and the reasons for passing it to the Charity Commission (CA 1993 s 75A(5)(a)). The Commission can then require the trustees to give public notice of their resolution to access the capital, as well as also directing the trustees to provide the Commission with any additional information which it may require (CA 1993 s 75A(6), (7)). The Charity Commission is required to take into account any representations which are made to it by interested parties within 28 days of the date that any public notice is given, and the Commission must also take into account any evidence which exists as to the wishes of the donor of the gift as well as any change in the circumstances of the charity since the gift was made (CA 1993 s 75A(8)).

The Charity Commission is prohibited from agreeing with the resolution unless the proposal to utilise the capital is consistent with the spirit of the gift under which it was originally given to the charity, and provided the trustees have complied with all of the requirements of s 75A (CA 1993 s 75A(9)). The Commission is required to give notice to the trustees within three months of the date of receiving a copy of the resolution from the trustees whether the Commission concurs or disagrees with the proposal (CA 1993 s 75A(10)).

Power to spend capital which is the subject of a special trust

6.4 Where, pursuant to its powers under CA 1993 s 96(5), the Charity Commission has decided that all or part of an institution (typically a trust) which has been set up in connection with a charity is to be treated as a separate charity the trustees of that charitable body (referred to in the Act as the 'relevant charity') are given special powers under a new CA 1993 s 75B to be able to access the capital of the permanent endowment in a way which is virtually identical to that for larger charities under CA 1993 s 75A, described above.

Where the market value of the fund exceeds £10,000 and the capital consists of property which has been given by a particular individual or institution, or two or more individuals or institutions for a common purpose, the trustees must go through the same process of submitting a resolution to the Commission as they would if the fund belonged to a larger charity.

Charity mergers

Introduction

6.5 As we saw in CHAPTER 3, ChaA 2006 introduced specific provisions designed to facilitate the merger of CIOs. In recognition of the growing number of charity mergers and takeovers that are occurring, and the difficulties which this can sometimes create for gifts and legacies that have been made to charities that have been merged, ChaA 2006 s 44 introduces new CA 1993 ss 75C and 75D, which are specifically aimed at addressing this.

Register of mergers

6.6 The Charity Commission is now required to establish and maintain a specific register of charity mergers (CA 1993 s 75C(1)). This register records all mergers where:

- two or more charities are merged in such a way that the property of one or more charity is transferred to the other and the charity or charities transferring their assets cease to exist;
- two or more charities transfer their assets into a new charity and where all of the transferring charities used to exist (CA 1993 s 75C(4));
- a charity which has both a permanent endowment and unrestricted assets has transferred all of its unrestricted property to another charity, in circumstances where this does not give rise to it ceasing to exist (CA 1993 s 75C(5)); and
- a vesting declaration is made in connection with a charity merger (CA 1993 s 75C(7)).

It is the trustees of the receiving charity who are required to notify the Charity Commission that the transfer has taken place. They can do this either when the transfer has occurred or, if there are a number of assets to be transferred, when the last of these has been transferred (CA 1993 s 75C(6)). When notifying the Commission of a transfer the trustees need to specify not only the property that was transferred and when it took place, but also certify that arrangements have been made to ensure that any liabilities of the transferring charity will be discharged. If the transfer in question arises as a result of a vesting declaration, then certain details of the declaration also need to be included in the notification to the Commission (CA 1993 s 75C(8), (9)).

The new register of charity mergers is available to the public for inspection and contains details of when the transfer or transfers of charity property took place, details of any vesting declaration and any other information which the Charity Commission considers appropriate (CA 1993 s 75D(3)).

Vesting declarations

6.7 In order to facilitate the process of transferring legal title of charity assets from one charity to another as part of the merger process ChaA 2006 introduces the mechanism of a pre-merger vesting declaration. This is a declaration that is executed as a deed by the trustees of the charity wishing to transfer its assets, in which they must specify that as part of a charity merger they wish all of the charity's assets (apart from certain excluded categories of property) to belong to the receiving charity from a particular date (CA 1993 s 75E(1)). The effect of the vesting declaration is to pass the legal title of the assets in question to the receiving charity without any further action being necessary, and is similar to the mechanism for merging CIOs.

A vesting declaration cannot, however, be used to transfer title to certain types of assets (CA 1993 s 75E(3)). These are:

- land held as security for money subject to the trusts of the charity wishing to transfer it (except where the land is held as security for a debenture or debenture stock);
- land which is held under lease or some other agreement which contains a prohibition on assignment without the prior consent of a third party (unless that consent has already been given); and
- shares, annuities and other types of property whose transfer is dependent on registration in the books or records of a third party, or in some other manner prescribed by law.

So far as registered land is concerned, a vesting declaration will be effective subject to the transfer being registered by the Land Registry (CA 1993 s 75E(4)).

It is notable that the recognition in CA 1993 s 75E that a charity cannot transfer certain types of assets without the approval or involvement of a third party is something that is notably missing in the section dealing with CIO mergers. Nevertheless, it would be safe to assume that such third party approval or involvement will be required just as much when CIOs merge as for other types of charity transactions.

Consequences of registering a charity merger

6.8 The introduction of a register of charity mergers and the requirement for applicable charities to register any mergers with the Charity Commission have an important and valuable benefit, which is made clear in the new CA 1993 s 75F.

In future if a gift is made to a charity which has gone through a merger, and the gift takes effect on or after the date that the merger has been registered with the Commission, the gift will automatically be deemed to be a gift to the charity which received the assets of the transferring charity. This is particularly useful for gifts that are made by way of legacies and wills, and means that a charity which takes over the property of another charity through a merger will automatically benefit from any legacies that were made to the transferring charity, providing the trustees of the receiving charity have registered the merger with the Charity Commission.

Chapter 7

Assistance and Supervision of Charities

Introduction

7.1 In line with the recommendations contained in the Cabinet Office's Strategy Unit report, the Charities Act 2006 ('ChaA 2006') provides the Charity Commission with a series of powers to help and assist charities, as well as to strengthen the Commission's increased regulatory role. Many of these new provisions were introduced by the Joint Parliamentary Committee when reviewing the draft Charities Bill.

These powers include the power to suspend trustees as members of a charity (and indeed to determine the overall membership), the power to provide enhanced advice to trustees, the power to give directions for the application or protection of charity property and the power to enter charity premises to seize documents.

At the same time there are signs of slight relaxation in certain areas, such as the publicity requirements relating to schemes (see CHAPTER 8) and the ability for Scottish and Northern Irish charities to participate in common investment schemes.

Finally, a useful amendment to the conveyancing regime for charities was introduced at the House of Lords stage. This allows the CA 1993 s 36 procedure to apply to charges over property.

Power to enter premises

7.2 Probably the most draconian of the new powers granted to the Charity Commission in ChaA 2006 is the power to enter premises (Charities Act 1993 ('CA 1993') s 31A, as inserted by ChA 2006 s 26). The Charity Commission previously had the power to call for documents or information (CA 1993 s 9); however, it did not have the power to enter charity premises to obtain that information if it was not provided voluntarily.

The new power is only to be used in furtherance of a section 8 inquiry, which is an investigation that can be instigated by the Charity Commission where it suspects an abuse of charity assets. Under the new CA 1993 s 31A the Charity Commission can apply for a warrant issued by a Justice of the Peace to enter charity premises. The warrant will only be issued if a member of the Charity Commission's staff swears under oath that the Commission has 'reasonable grounds for believing' that certain conditions are satisfied. These conditions are:

- that a section 8 inquiry has been instituted;
- that information or documentation vital to the enquiry are located on the premises and that it is information that could be required under CA 1993 s 9(1);
- that if an order were made by the Charity Commission requesting that information it would not be complied with, or that the information would be removed, tampered with, hidden or destroyed.

It is clear from this that the power is only intended for extreme circumstances, not for everyday investigating.

If a warrant is issued, the member of Charity Commission staff named in the warrant is entitled to:

- enter and search the premises specified;
- take any other persons with them which they consider are required to assist them;
- take possession of any documents, computer disks or other electronic storage devices which they consider contain information relevant to the inquiry and which are considered to be at risk of being removed, altered or destroyed;
- take copies of any information contained in the above; and
- require anyone on the premises to provide an explanation or the location of any such documents or information, or assistance in taking copies or extracts.

When the draft Charities Bill was published there was some concern that this new power would provide any agent of the Charity Commission with the ability to enter any charity premises. This was particularly pertinent given that section 8 inquiries are often carried out by third parties, and not by staff of the Charity Commission. The final version of ChaA 2006, however, restricts this power to employees of the Charity Commission, although they may be accompanied by any third party or parties they choose.

The legislation does place some limits on this power. The entry and search must be made at a reasonable hour, and must be carried out within one month of the date of issue of the warrant (CA 1993 s 31A(4)). The warrant must be produced for inspection if required.

Careful records need to be kept by the person entering the premises. They must record the date and time of entry, the length of time they stay on the premises, details of who has accompanied them, what actions are carried out and what documents or other property are removed (CA 1993 s 31A(6)). A copy of these records must be provided to the occupier of the premises (CA 1993 s 31A(7)) if requested. This can be requested before the inspectors leave.

The Charity Commission is permitted to retain any seized documents or property for as long as it considers necessary for the inquiry (CA 1993 s 31A(9)). The documents and property should be returned as soon as it ceases to be necessary to retain them (CA 1993 s 31A(10)). In practice this means that copies should be taken and originals returned as soon as practicable. Originals may be returned to the person from whom they were seized or to the charity trustees. This could result in the return of charity property to the trustees.

ChaA 2006 s 26(2) gives effect to the Criminal Justice and Police Act 2001 s 50, which means that the Charity Commission can seize records if either it believes the records contain relevant information but cannot determine that at the time, or it knows that the records contain the information but it cannot access them on the premises.

This new power to enter charity property and seize records is a wide-ranging power. It is not clear how 'reasonable grounds' for belief will be interpreted but it is certain that this provides the Charity Commission with substantial new power to enforce its inquiry powers.

Anyone who obstructs the Charity Commission in the exercise of its power under a warrant will be subject to criminal prosecution and may receive up to a level 5 fine or up to 51 weeks in prison (CA 1993 s 31A(11)) or both.

Power to suspend trustees as members

7.3 The Charity Commission already had power under CA 1993 ss 16 and 18 to remove or suspend trustees and other officers or employees of a charity under certain circumstances. However, this power is quite restricted. It either relates only to specific circumstances, such as where there has been loss of mental capacity, bankruptcy, liquidation or absence or it may be used if the Charity Commission believes that a trustee or other officer has been responsible for, or privy to, the misconduct or mismanagement of the charity, and has by his conduct contributed to it or facilitated it, in which case a section 8 inquiry had to be instigated.

There was, however, an anomaly in the fact that an individual removed or suspended in this way could still continue to be involved in the affairs of the charity, even in the decision-making processes, as long as he was a member of the charity. He could conceivably even be involved in voting himself back into office or reacquiring his previous status. This problem had become more relevant with the increase in membership of charities and incorporated charities (charities established as limited companies). In an incorporated charity many key decisions lie with the membership, rather than with the board of trustees, although these are frequently one and the same.

ChaA 2006 removes this anomaly with a new CA 1993 s 18A, introduced by ChaA 2006 s 19. This enables the Charity Commission to suspend or remove trustees, officers, agents or employees from membership of a charity, in the event that an order has been made under CA 1993 s 18(1) or 18(2).

In the case of suspension, if a trustee, officer, agent or employee is to be suspended from office, they may also be suspended from membership, in which case the period of suspension will be the same for both office and membership (CA 1993 s 18A(2)).

Where a trustee, officer, agent or employee has been removed from office under CA 1993 s 18A(1)(b), the Charity Commission can also terminate the individual's membership with the charity until such time as the Charity Commission decides to reinstate them (CA 1993 s 18A(3)). If a request for reinstatement is made after five years from the date of the order removing an individual from membership CA 1993 s 18A(4) states that the Commission's consent should be given to their reinstatement unless there are special circumstances that dictate otherwise.

Power to determine membership

7.4 For a large number of charities, membership of the charity plays an important part in attracting and retaining volunteers and supporters who help the charity to achieve its aims. Although one might think that the question of whether someone is a member of a charity should be a straightforward one, this is not always the case. Records of membership are often incomplete, and where membership is not tied to the payment of an annual subscription, membership can appear to continue long after a person has in fact ceased to consider themselves interested in a charity, simply because they never communicate this to the charity in question.

Charitable trusts do not need to have members. However, for incorporated charities and unincorporated associations members play an important legal role in the operation of the charity.

In incorporated charities most of the key decisions will involve recourse to the membership, with obligations laid down in either the charity's memorandum and articles of association or the Companies Acts. These decisions include amending the constitution, appointing trustees, merging with another charity or winding up the charity. Usually such decisions need to be taken at a general meeting, where strict procedures for calling meetings, time limits and quorums must be observed for a resolution to be valid.

It is clear therefore that in some charities the membership will have important decision-making powers, and in order for those powers to be properly exercised the procedures laid down in the charity's governing instrument must be followed. If the trustees cannot be certain who the members are it may be impossible to exercise these constitutional powers. If the correct procedures are not followed it may result in the validity of decisions being brought into question. In the case of the appointment of trustees, it may result in casting doubt on decisions of the trustee body.

ChaA 2006 s 25 inserts a new CA 1993 s 29A, which now gives the Charity Commission (or someone appointed by them) the authority to determine who the members of a charity are in one of two circumstances:

- in the context of a section 8 inquiry; or
- at the request of the charity.

Trustees who therefore find themselves unable to determine who their members are, or whether certain persons are members or not can now turn to the Charity Commission for an authoritative decision. However, the Charity Commission will not enter into trustee disputes.

Power to give directions

7.5 CA 1993 s 18 provided the Charity Commission with power to act in relation to charity assets when it had instituted a section 8 inquiry and was satisfied that there had either been misconduct or mismanagement, or it was necessary to act to protect charity property. However, the power was limited to appointing a receiver, dealing with the trustees and essentially freezing the assets, although the Commission could compel the transfer of the legal title to property.

ChaA 2006 s 20 extends this power by introducing a new CA 1993 s 19A. Again, a section 8 inquiry has to have been launched on the basis of the same suspicions. The Charity Commission now has the power to give directions dealing with any aspect of the charity's affairs. It is able to give these directions not only to the trustees of the charity, but to any officer or employee of the charity, or if the charity is a legal 'person' in its own right, then to the charity itself (CA 1993 s 19A(2)). The Commission can even give directions to a trustee who is not a charity trustee (for example a custodian trustee of charity property). The specified action must be taken whether or not the directed party would normally have the power to carry out this action and is absolved from any responsibility in this (CA 1993 s 19A(4)) whilst still preserving the contractual and other rights of other parties. The only limit on the Charity Commission's power is that any direction given by it must not require action to be taken that will conflict with the aims of the charity, with its constitution or with any statute (CA 1993 s 19A(5)).

Significantly, s 19A does not give the Charity Commission the power to direct people who are not directly connected with a charity but who control charity property, in how they should deal with that property.

Instead a new CA 1993 s 19B, introduced by ChaA 2006 s 21, deals with similar powers in circumstances where a section 8 inquiry has not been launched but where the Charity Commission believes that charity funds are being misapplied. This is a significant extension of the Charity Commission's power as it steps outside the constraints of a section 8 inquiry, and can be used by the Charity Commission at any time.

In order to exercise its power under s 19B the Charity Commission has to be satisfied that:

- a person in possession or control of charity property is unwilling to apply it for proper purposes; and
- it is necessary or desirable for an order to be made to ensure that this proper application is secured.

The Charity Commission is able to direct the person in question to deal with the charity property in any way the Commission considers appropriate. As before, any direction given by the Charity Commission under s 19B must not require someone to take steps that would conflict with the objects of the charity in question, with its constitution or with any statute.

Power to give advice

7.6 The Charity Commission has always advised trustees on the way in which it could exercise its duties as charity trustees. ChaA 2006 s 24 completely replaces CA 1993 s 29 and, while retaining the key provisions of the old s 29, goes on to broaden this out so that advice can be given on the proper administration of charities, as well as trustees' duties.

In reality this is a statutory enactment of what is already current practice for the Charity Commission. It is already possible to write to the Charity Commission direct and request a view on a proposed course of action or on the duty or liability of a trustee. The Commission will normally give concrete advice on the fundamental trusts of a charity, the existing powers of trustees, restrictions on any particular assets of the charity and any proposed restructuring or merging of a charity. The Commission is, however, reluctant to give an opinion on internal trustee disputes.

The new CA 1993 s 29 allows any or all of the charity trustees to make a written application to the Charity Commission for advice. The draft Bill had contemplated that this advice could be sought by employees or officers of the charity as well as trustees, but the final version of ChaA 2006 only authorises trustees to seek advice.

The advice can relate to the performance of a trustee's duties or to the general administration of the charity. Indeed the Charity Commission now has as one of its objectives the encouragement and facilitatation of better charity administration (see CHAPTER 11). The Commission can also provide generic advice to a particular charity, to a class of charities or to all charities in any form it chooses and it has complete discretion over the form that this advice should take (CA 1993 s 29(5)).

The great comfort for charity trustees is that, having received this advice and acted upon it, the trustees are then protected from any accusation of breach of trust (CA 1993 s 29(2)). This is a form of indemnity that many trustees will find valuable in the context of potential personal liability. Care must be taken to remember that this protection is ineffective if the trustees have failed to provide all of the 'material facts', or the decision of a court has been given or court proceedings are pending in respect of the same matter. If the Charity Commission is therefore duped into giving a favourable opinion, that opinion cannot be relied on.

Publicity requirements relating to schemes and orders

7.7 The existing CA 1993 s 20 required the Charity Commission to follow certain procedures to publicise particular schemes and orders, and stipulated the timescales that had to be followed. At times this was felt to be unduly lengthy and cumbersome, and could frustrate the whole purpose of making a scheme or order if rapid action was required.

ChaA 2006 s 22 therefore overhauls CA 1993 s 20 and, while retaining the basic requirement to give publicity to a proposed scheme to administer a charity, allows the Charity Commission to decide how long the period of notice should be, or whether the circumstances are such that it would be appropriate to dispense with a period of publicity altogether, although it must still make a copy available for one month after the scheme is sealed. This discretion to dispense with public notice of a proposed scheme can be exercised by the Charity Commission where it is satisfied that it is appropriate to do so:

- by reason of the nature of the scheme; or
- for any other reason.

This is a very wide discretion indeed. Even if the Charity Commission decides to publicise a scheme, although it remains duty bound to take account of any representations received, it can move ahead with the scheme with or without amendment. Some may argue that this means that publicity of a scheme will in future be nothing more than window dressing. However, only time will tell to what extent the Charity Commission chooses to exercise this new power.

Publicity requirements relating to appointments or removals

7.8 ChaA 2006 s 22 also introduces similar changes to the publicity requirements applicable to Charity Commission orders dealing with the appointment, discharge or removal of charity trustees, officers, employees and agents in a new CA 1993 s 20A.

Usually the Charity Commission needs to give public notice of the proposed exercise of its power under CA 1993 s 20A, including a timetable for responses (CA 1993 s 20A(2)). If a trustee, officer or employee is to be removed against his will he must receive at least one month's notice and be given a period within which to make representations. If the individual cannot be located or has no address in the UK, the Charity Commission is not required to give notice.

CA 1993 s 20A(4) allows the Charity Commission to dispense with giving public notice *if it is satisfied that for any reason compliance with the requirement is unnecessary*. This wording is deliberately vague and gives the Charity Commission a very wide discretion. Although the affected person must receive one month's notice there is no compulsory public notice and no need to make amendments based on representations.

Common investment schemes

7.9 ChaA 2006 s 23 amends CA 1993 ss 24 and 25. Section 24 deals with Common Investment Funds ('CIFs'), which are similar to unit trusts, and s 25 deals with Common Deposit Funds ('CDFs'), which act like deposit accounts for cash.

A CIF is established by a scheme of the court or of the Charity Commission on the application of two or more charities pursuant to CA 1993 s 24(2). It may also be established by statute (CA 1993 s 24(9)). A CIF is only open to charities and is deemed to be a charity itself. A CIF will be an exempt charity if participation is limited to exempt charities, but otherwise it will be subject to registration as a charity in its own right. CIFs provide diversification of investment to reduce risk, they are tax efficient, administratively simple and cost effective. They enjoy the same tax status as other charities and are able to pay dividends gross.

In principle, the Charity Commission is prepared to establish a CIF where investment restrictions are justified by the objectives of a particular group of charities, although the investment restrictions cannot be permanent and must be subject to regular review.

It is also possible to have a pooling scheme whereby a body of trustees establish a common pool of investments for some or all of a group of charities that they administer. This is useful where charities are administering a wide range of restricted and unrestricted funds that can benefit from a common investment.

CA 1993 s 24 provides that only charities in England and Wales are eligible to participate in common investment schemes. ChaA 2006 s 23 amends CA 1993 ss 24 and 25, allowing Scottish and Northern Irish charities which are eligible for UK tax reliefs to now participate in common investment schemes, so that it is possible to accept investments from charities located throughout the UK and Northern Ireland.

Restrictions on mortgaging

7.10 One anomaly in CA 1993 meant that while a charity was able to mortgage charity property without the prior approval of the court or the Charity Commission as security for the repayment of a specific loan (provided that certain procedures were followed), the charity was still required to obtain court or Charity Commission consent if it wished to charge charity property for any other purpose, such as, for example, giving a legal charge over property to guarantee the use of a grant. This is a quite common requirement, for example, for the Big Lottery Fund, and has created many problems for charities.

ChaA 2006 s 27 relaxes the restrictions on mortgaging by amending s 38(2) and (3). Provided that the trustees have first obtained proper written advice, a legal charge may now be granted for the repayment of a loan or grant or the discharge of any other proposed obligation of the charity giving the security.

Where the security relates to a loan or grant, the advice obtained should comment on:

- whether the loan or grant is necessary to further the course of action in question;
- whether the terms are reasonable; and
- whether the charity has the ability to repay the loan or grant in the cirumstances in which they may become repayable.

Where the security is to be given for any other obligation of the charity, the advice the trustees receive must address whether it is reasonable for the charity to undertake to discharge the obligation given the purposes of the charity.

New CA 1993 s 38(3B)–(3D) also make provision for any future loans which the same lender may make to the charity. This ensures that any future loans are subject to identical requirements for professional advice as above.

Chapter 8

Scheme Making

Introduction

8.1 The Charities Act 2006 ('ChaA 2006') ss 15–18 deal with the application of charity property cy-pres and the ability of the Charity Commission or the court to make cy-pres schemes.

ChaA 2006 s 15, amending the Charities Act 1993 ('CA 1993') s 13, updates the principle of cy-pres to make it more relevant to current social and economic circumstances. ChaA 2006 s 16, amending CA 1993 s 14, extends certain powers of the court to the Charity Commission. ChaA 2006 s 17, inserting CA 1993 s 14A, deals with the application of funds that have been raised by public appeal where the appeal has failed, while ChaA 2006 s 18, inserting CA 1993 s 14B, regulates cy-pres schemes themselves.

Doctrine of cy-pres

8.2 Cy-pres is an ancient principle of charity law. It regulates the way in which the court or the Charity Commission can amend the objects of a charity or apply charity funds according to the spirit and intention of the original gift. This is particularly important where a charity has ceased to be workable or funds have been raised for a particular purpose that has subsequently failed. It also deals with legacies in wills where a particular charity has not been clearly identified or has ceased to exist.

CA 1993 s 13

8.3 The existing legislation (CA 1993 s 13) lists the circumstances in which the objects of a charity may be altered to allow the property of the charity to be applied cy-pres. This list of circumstances (CA 1993 s 13(1)) is exhaustive and is as follows:

'(a) where the original purposes, in whole or in part

(i) have been as far as may be fulfilled; or

(ii) cannot be carried out, or not according to the directions given and to the spirit of the gift; or

(b) where the original purposes provide a use for part only of the property available by virtue of the gift; or

(c) where the property available by virtue of the gift and other property applicable for similar purposes can be more effectively used in conjunction, and to that end can suitably, regard being had to the spirit of the gift, be made applicable to common purposes; or

(d) where the original purposes were laid down by reference to an area which then was but has since ceased to be a unit for some other purpose, or by reference to a class of persons or to an area which has for any reason since ceased to be suitable, regard being had to the spirit of the gift, or to be practical in administering the gift; or

(e) where the original purposes, in whole or in part, have, since they were laid down

(i) been adequately provided for by other means; or

(ii) ceased, as being useless or harmful to the community or for other reasons, to be in law charitable; or

(iii) ceased in any other way to provide a suitable and effective method of using the property available by virtue of the gift, regard being had to the spirit of the gift.'

The court and the Charity Commission have always strictly followed the list of circumstances. They also refer scrupulously to the original spirit of the gift. This means that there is a limit to the extent to which they can allow for changes in social circumstances since the date of the gift.

Amendments in ChaA 2006

8.4 The main thrust of the amendments introduced by ChaA 2006 is to redefine 'the spirit of the gift' wherever it is referred to in the existing legislation (CA 1993 s 13, as amended by ChaA 2006 s 15(2)). The phrase 'the spirit of the gift' will now be replaced by the phrase 'the appropriate considerations'.

The appropriate considerations are now defined in CA 1993 s 13(1A) as:

'(a) (on the one hand) the spirit of the gift concerned, and

(b) (on the other) the social and economic circumstances prevailing at the time of the proposed alteration of the original purposes.'

This is a clear attempt to ensure that, although the spirit of the gift should remain an important consideration, it should not automatically take precedence over practical current methods for dealing with that property in the most appropriate manner.

Unknown donors

8.5 If property is given for a particular purpose that fails, it is possible to use those funds for general charitable purposes if (a) the trustees have followed the prescribed publicity procedure (CA 1993 s 14(1), (2)), or (b) the property derives from a certain type of fund-raising, mainly from collection boxes (CA 1993 s 14(3)), or (c) the court has determined that it is unreasonable to trace the donor because of the size of the donation or the length of time that has elapsed (CA 1993 s 14(4)). The court's power to direct that such property be applied for general charitable purposes is now extended to the Charity Commission (CA 1993 s 14(4), as amended by ChaA 2006 s 16).

Application of specific appeal funds

8.6 CA 1993 s 14A, as inserted by ChaA 2006 s 17, deals with the situation where a charity launches an appeal for funds or property for a specific charitable purpose and then the appeal fails. As long as the appeal contains the necessary statement from the charity, any donor will now have to make it clear at the outset if he wishes funds or property to be returned to him in these circumstances. The wording of the appeal should make clear that, in the event that the appeal fails, the funds raised will be applied cy-pres for the general purposes of the charity unless the donor signs a 'relevant declaration' at the time of making the gift. The relevant declaration states that, if the appeal fails, the donor wishes the trustees holding the property to contact him and give him the opportunity to request the return of his gift or an equivalent sum to the value of the gift at the time the gift was made (CA 1993 s 14A(3)).

If the appeal does fail and the donor has signed the relevant declaration, the trustees must contact the original donor and follow a particular procedure (CA 1993 s 14A(5)), which is to be prescribed by the Charity Commission (CA 1993 s 14A(9)). The trustees must ask if he wishes to take back his donation. If the donor has not replied within the given period for response, again to be prescribed by the Charity Commission, or if the trustees have been unable to locate the donor, they may apply those funds for the general charitable purposes of the charity (CA 1993 s 14A(6)). This is also the case if the charity has been unable to locate the donor, despite following the proper procedure.

If the donor does not make a relevant declaration, despite this being requested in the appeal literature, the funds may be applied for the charity's general purposes should the particular project fail without any further obligation on the part of the charity (CA 1993 s 14A(7)).

These new rules apply whether or not the donor receives anything of value in return for his donation (CA 1993 s 14A(8)(b)). If an appeal contains some elements that request a relevant declaration and some that do not, a donor will be considered to have been requested to sign a relevant declaration unless he can prove otherwise (CA 1993 s 14A(8)(c)).

Cy-pres schemes

8.7 CA 1993 s 14B, as inserted by ChaA 2006 s 18, outlines the way in which cy-pres schemes are to be dealt with in future.

Either the Charity Commission or the court can make a cy-pres scheme allowing charity property to be applied for such charitable purposes or held on trust for such other charity as they think fit (CA 1993 s 14B(2)). This section applies where either the property is to be transferred to another charity, or where there is to be a change of objects for the original charity.

When considering the options, the Charity Commission or the court must take account of (CA 1993 s 14B(3)):

- the spirit of the original gift;
- the desirability of ensuring that the property is applied for charitable purposes which are close to the original purposes; and
- the need for the relevant charity (ie the donor charity) to have purposes which are suitable and effective in the light of current social and economic circumstances.

All of the above should be given equal weight, and the 'spirit' of the gift is no longer of paramount consideration. This applies not only to the original property but to any property derived from it (CA 1993 s 14B(5)).

The Charity Commission or the court may impose a duty on any recipient charity to apply the funds or the property so far as is reasonably practicable for purposes 'similar in character' to the original purposes (CA 1993 s 14B(4)). This is important where the original purposes are still useful but can be better used in conjunction with other charity property.

Publicity requirements

8.8 See 7.7 for amended publicity requirements for Charity Commission schemes.

Chapter 9

Fundraising

Introduction

9.1 The complex world of charity fundraising has been the subject of review for some time. The Charities Act 2006 ('ChaA 2006') provides a new statutory licensing scheme for public charitable collections and an update to the statements to be included in fundraising literature. It also assumes that the self-regulation of the sector, which was the subject of the Buse Commission, will continue, but it reserves the right for the Secretary of State to intervene (for further details see **9.3**). The Government has also been concerned about the aggressive fundraising techniques used by certain charities, and the need to maintain public confidence in charities.

Self-regulation

9.2 The Government has made it clear that the charity sector must develop and implement a scheme of self-regulation for fundraising. This is because of significant levels of abuse, resulting in the charity sector as a whole finding its reputation tarnished.

The Buse Commission undertook an 18-month review starting in 2003. A steering committee appointed by the Commission proposed a final structure in January 2005. The self-regulatory scheme will be made up of the following components:

- A code of conduct.
- A donor's charter.
- A fundraising promise.
- Codes of Fundraising Practice (there are now 26 Codes of Fundraising Practice).

The Home Office has provided funding, along with the Scottish executive, for a period of five years. The scheme is being promoted by the Institute of Fundraising (see www.institute-of-fundraising.org.uk). The Fundraising Standards Board ('FSB') (www.fsboard.org.uk) has been created to introduce a new self-regulatory scheme in the UK. It formally launched the scheme on 12 February 2007. It will work closely with the Institute of Fundraising. On 16 March 2007 a Memorandum of Understanding was published jointly by the FSB and the Charity Commission explaining how they would co-operate on the regulation of fundraising for charities.

There is also the Public Fundraising Regulatory Association ('PFRA') (see www.pfra.org.uk), which deals with best practice for face-to-face fundraising. This is the fastest growing method of fundraising, and the PFRA estimate that £210 million will be raised using direct debits and standing orders over the next five years. PFRA also has a Code of Practice, largely based on the Institute of Fundraising Codes of Practice.

Government intervention

9.3 ChaA 2006 s 69 introduces a new Charities Act 1992 ('CA 1992') s 64A.

CA 1992 s 64 already allowed the Secretary of State to make regulations to prescribe the form and content of agreements with fundraisers and commercial participators, to enforce those agreements and to prevent unauthorised fundraising. Section 64(2)(e) also gave a general power to regulate funds raised for charitable, benevolent or philanthropic purposes. The new s 64A reinforces this power and extends it to cover good practice generally. It applies to charities, their trustees and managers, trading companies, fundraisers and even volunteers (s 64A(7)(d)).

Section 64A(1) states that the Secretary of State 'may make such regulations as appear to him to be necessary or desirable for or in connection with regulating charity fund-raising'. This covers charities, persons or companies connected with charities and anyone promoting benevolent or philanthropic purposes.

The Government can make such regulations as ensure good practice in fundraising. Section 64A(4) states that good practice means that fundraising is carried out in such a way that:

- it does not unreasonably intrude on the privacy of those from whom funds are being solicited or procured;
- it does not involve the making of unreasonably persistent approaches to persons to donate funds;
- it does not result in undue pressure being placed on persons to donate funds; and
- it does not involve the making of any false or misleading representation about the extent or urgency of the need for the funds raised, the use to which they will be put or the activities, achievements or finances of the organisation in question.

In addition ChaA 2006 s 63 allows the Secretary of State to make regulations regulating the conduct of public charitable collections (s 63(1)(b)). This could include the keeping and publication of accounts, prevention of annoyance to the public, prescribing forms of badges or certificates for collectors, ensuring that collectors show their badge or certificate when requested, and the introduction of an age limit for collectors (s 63(3)).

The good practice requirement expressly does not extend to primary purpose trading on the part of charities themselves (CA 1992 s 64A(2)). This is defined in CA 1992 s 64A(8) as where:

'(a) the trade is carried on in the course of the actual carrying out of a primary purpose; or

(b) the work in connection with the trade is mainly carried out by beneficiaries of the charity.'

There is no requirement for consultation with any interested organisations before such regulations are introduced. Any breach of the regulations would result in a fine not exceeding level 2 on the standard scale (CA 1992 s 64A(6)), although the statute does state that a person has to 'persistently fail' and do so 'without reasonable excuse' before liability arises. Enforcement remains an issue.

Regulation of public charitable collections

9.4 ChaA 2006 ss 45–62 set out a new unified statutory licensing scheme for public collections. This harmonises the previously fragmented system that was subject to differing interpretations in different areas of the country. These sections deal with public charitable collections, whether they are collections in a public place or door-to-door collections. They encompass all public collections, including the previously grey area of direct debit collectors, and even cover collections for non-charitable organisations. These have been expressly included to attempt to deal with bogus collectors raising funds for non-charities.

Definition of public charitable collections

9.5 The definitions section is to be found in ChaA 2006 s 45. Public charitable collections include collections in any public place or by means of visits to houses and/or business premises. Collections may not just be for registered charities, but for 'charitable, benevolent or philanthropic purposes'. The donations solicited may be of money or of other property. The giving of money can be by any means and it does not matter if the donations are given for any form of consideration (s 45(3)). The appeal itself must involve a representation to the public that the proceeds of the collection will be applied for charitable, benevolent or philanthropic purposes (s 45(2)(b)).

ChaA 2006 s 46 defines charitable appeals that are *not* public charitable collections and so *not* subject to the new licensing regime. The list of appeals is as follows:

- Those made in the course of a public meeting (s 46(1)(a)).
- Those made on enclosed land associated with and next to a church or place of public worship (s 46(1)(b)).
- Those made on land where the public have access only with the express or implied permission of the occupier of the land (s 46(1)(c)(i)).
- Those made on land where the public have access only by virtue of an enactment (s 46(1)(c)(ii)).
- Those made by leaving an unattended receptacle available for collections (s 46(1)(d)). This does not include receptacles that are temporarily unattended but are actually in the custody of an individual.

Historic regulation of street collections

9.6 Historically, street collections were regulated by Police, Factories, etc (Miscellaneous Provisions) Act 1916 s 5, as amended by Local Government Act 1972 s 251. This provided that local authorities could make regulations specifying the conditions for charitable collections in public places. Some local authorities required licences, others did not.

However, this rather ancient statute did not envisage modern social practices (for example collecting by direct debit), and individual local authorities all applied different criteria. Many did not consider direct debit collections as public collections, and indeed they were not strictly covered by the existing legislation. Many local authorities interpreted 'public places' in such a way that privately owned properties, such as shopping centres, were not included.

Definition of public place

9.7 As indicated above, the definition of 'public place' has been subject to varying interpretations. However, ChaA 2006 defines this in some detail. Public place is defined as including any highway or any other place to which members of the public have access. It does not include the interior of buildings unless there is a public area within that building. Stations, airports and shopping precincts are specifically listed, but it also includes 'any other similar public area' (ChaA 2006 s 45(5)).

It does not include anywhere to which the public has ticketed access. Nor does it include anywhere to which the public has been admitted solely for the purpose of the appeal in question (ChaA 2006 s 45(6)).

The historic licensing regime

9.8 Previously, charities had to obtain a licence from the appropriate licensing authority. This could be the local authority or, in the case of the

City of London, thc Common Council or the Chief Commissioner of Police in the Metropolitan Police District.

Larger charities involved in national fundraising campaigns could apply to the Home Office for a national exemption order. There were 40 holders of national exemption orders.

The new licensing regime

9.9 The new licensing regime introduced by ChaA 2006 has two elements:

- A public collections certificate issued by the Charity Commission.
- A permit for individual collections issued by the local authority in the area of the collection.

All those involved in public charitable collections must have both a certificate and a permit, unless they are able to qualify for one of the exemptions. However, in order to ensure that the new regulations are focused on the risk areas and also proportionate, there are specific exemptions for small local collections (see **9.17**) and door-to-door collections of goods (see **9.18**). A public collections certificate may still be required for door-to-door collections if it does not qualify as a small local collection. However, small local collections are exempt from the requirement to obtain either a certificate or a permit.

Anyone not complying with the new licensing requirements is guilty of a criminal offence and will be subject to a fine not exceeding level 5 on the standard scale (ChaA 2006 s 48(3)).

For further details on public collections certificates see **9.10–9.16**.

For further details of local authority permits see **9.19–9.26**.

Public collections certificates

9.10 Anyone who is proposing to promote a public charitable collection must apply to the Charity Commission for a public collections certificate, unless the collection is exempt (see **9.17**).

This is a new role for the Charity Commission. In the original draft Bill it was proposed that local authorities should carry out this function. However, it was felt that the Charity Commission was in a better position to assess the fitness of a charity.

Application for a public collections certificate

9.11 ChaA 2006 s 51 deals with the procedure for application to the Charity Commission.

The Charity Commission will issue regulations specifying the form in which the application should be made, the contents and the latest date by which the application may be made for an individual collection (s 51(5)).

The application will need to contain basic information about the proposed collection or collections. It will also need to specify the period for which the certificate is sought. The maximum period is set at five years (s 51(3)).

On receiving an application, the Charity Commission can make such enquiries as it thinks fit (ChaA 2006 s 52(1)). It can then either issue a public collections certificate or refuse the application on one or more of the specified grounds (see **9.12**). It may also issue a certificate for a reduced period (s 52(3)(b)), or with conditions attached (s 52(4)), as yet to be specified.

In the case of a rejection or where conditions are attached, the Charity Commission must notify the applicant of its decision and the reasons for the decision (s 52(7)). The Commission must also notify the applicant of their right to appeal the decision and the time limit within which an appeal can be brought (see **9.16**).

Grounds for refusing a certificate

9.12 ChaA 2006 s 53 lists the grounds on which the Charity Commission can refuse an application for a public collections certificate. These are as follows:

- That the applicant has been convicted of a relevant offence relating to public collections and misleading the public.
- That the applicant is purporting to collect funds on behalf of a charity or a benevolent or philanthropic institution and the Charity Commission is not satisfied that they are authorised to do so.
- That the applicant has previously carried out a similar collection and did not exercise the required due diligence.
- Linked to the above, the Charity Commission is not convinced that the applicant will exercise due diligence in the future.
- That the percentage of the proceeds going to the charitable cause is inadequate in relation to the total.
- That the applicant would be likely to receive too excessive a level of remuneration.
- That the applicant did not provide sufficient information, either in the original application or as a result of enquiries from the Charity Commission.
- That the information provided is false or misleading in the view of the Charity Commission.

- That the applicant has previously breached any conditions attached to a public collections certificate or to a permit or to any regulations issued by the Secretary of State.

The question of 'due diligence' is defined in ChaA 2006 s 53(2)(b). This states that due diligence is required in ensuring that any individual collectors are fit and proper persons, that they comply with any statements required by law (see **9.28–9.30** below) and that the applicant should ensure that any badges or certificates of authority are only available to authorised collectors, and not open to abuse.

Ongoing administration of certificates

9.13 Because public collections certificates can be issued for a maximum period of five years, ChaA 2006 ss 54–56 deal with the powers of the Charity Commission in relation to the certificates during the period that they are in force.

ChaA 2006 s 54 provides the Charity Commission with the power to ask for further information from the original applicant, not just at the point of submitting the application but also during the period of validity of the certificate (s 54(1)). This is in addition to the Charity Commission's existing powers to call for information, particularly in relation to a section 8 inquiry (CA 1993 s 8).

Transfer of certificates

9.14 ChaA 2006 s 55 deals with the transfer of the benefit of a public collections certificate from the original holders to other individuals. This requires the approval of the Charity Commission (s 55(1)).

Section 55(3) states that the certificate may only be transferred from the trustees of an unincorporated charity to other trustees of the same charity, subject not only to the consent of the recipient trustees, but also to the consent of the whole trustee body (s 55(3)). Presumably this also means that certificates cannot be transferred between other types of organisations and between professional fundraisers. Incorporated charities are not referred to in s 55. Section 55(7) states quite explicitly that this is the only way that a certificate may be transferred.

The Charity Commission must serve notice of its decision and the reasons (s 55(4)). The decision is subject to appeal (s 55(5)).

Withdrawal or variation of certificate

9.15 ChaA 2006 s 56 allows the Charity Commission to revisit the question of a public collections certificate after it has been issued.

The Charity Commission may avail itself of the power in this section where (ChaA 2006 s 56(2)–(4)):

- it has reason to believe that there has been a change in circumstances since the original application;
- it is of the opinion that, had the application been made at this time, it would have been refused or issued with different or additional conditions;
- the holder of a certificate has unreasonably refused to provide information or documentation;
- it has reason to believe that information provided with the original application or in response to subsequent enquiries is false or misleading; or
- it has reason to believe that there has been a breach of any condition or certificate, or that such a breach is continuing.

In the above circumstances, the Charity Commission has the power to (s 56(1)):

- withdraw the certificate;
- suspend the certificate;
- attach any condition to the certificate, providing that it would have been appropriate to attach such a condition at the time of the original application (s 56(5)); or
- vary an existing condition.

The above power may be used by the Charity Commission on more than one occasion.

In exercising the above power, the Charity Commission must notify the holder of its decision and the reasons behind the decision (s 56(7)). Again the decision is subject to appeal (s 56(8)) and the variations do not come into effect until the appeal period or process is complete (s 56(10)), unless the Charity Commission considers that it is in the public interest to effect the variations immediately (s 56(9)). Any suspension may only last a maximum of six months from the date the decision is implemented (s 56(11)).

Appeals against decisions

9.16 ChaA 2006 s 57 provides applicants with a right to appeal decisions relating to the issuing of a public collections certificate. This provides that an applicant may have recourse to the Charity Tribunal (see further in CHAPTER 12) on the following aspects (s 57(1)–(3)):

- The refusal to issue a public collections certificate.
- Any conditions attached to a certificate, including the variation of an existing condition.
- The withdrawal or suspension of a certificate.
- The refusal to transfer a certificate.

Not only does the original applicant have a right of appeal, but also the Attorney General may appeal a decision taken or refused on any of the above (s 57(4)).

The Charity Tribunal must consider afresh the decision reached and, if necessary, seek further evidence not necessarily available to the Charity Commission (s 57(5)). It may dismiss the appeal, quash the decision or substitute a new decision (s 57(6)). If it quashes the decision, it will return the issue to the Charity Commission either for fresh consideration or to implement a decision of the Tribunal (s 57(7)).

Local short-term collections

9.17 These are governed by ChaA 2006 s 50. The duration of a short-term collection is yet to be prescribed in regulations. However, it is certain that there will be a given time period. The other criteria for these collections is that they should be local in character (s 50(2)).

'Local in character' is not defined in ChaA 2006 but is a concept recognised under the previous regime, except that it was administered by the local police force rather than the local authority. The Secretary of State may also prescribe the matters that a local authority must take into account when reaching its decision (ChaA 2006 s 63(1)(a)).

Assuming that the appeal in question falls within the criteria for a local, short-term collection, the promoters must notify the local authority within the prescribed period before the collection of the basic details of the appeal. They should state the purpose of the appeal, the date or dates on which the collections will be conducted and the location. Other matters may be included in regulations (s 50(3)).

The collection will be exempt from any requirement to obtain a public collections certificate or a permit, unless the local authority serves the promoters with a notice stating that either they do not qualify for the exemption, or they have previously been guilty of breaching the regulations for local collections, or have been convicted of a relevant offence (s 50(4)). This differs from the previous law, where a licence had to be obtained from the chief officer of police for the relevant area.

Any decision of the local authority must include an explanation of the reasons behind the decision. Any decision would be subject to appeal to a magistrate's court under ChaA 2006 s 62(1) (see **9.26**).

Any breach of the requirement to notify the local authority of the details of a local short-term collection could result in prosecution and a fine not exceeding level 3 on the standard scale (ChaA 2006 s 50(6)).

Door-to-door collections

9.18 Until ChaA 2006 this area of the law was regulated by the House-to-House Collections Act 1939 and associated regulations (for example the House-to-House Collections Regulations 1947, SI 1947/2662, as amended).

Door-to-door collections are now governed by ChaA 2006 s 49. If a door-to-door collection is also a local, short-term collection, the criteria in **9.17** apply. However, if it does not qualify, it may still be relieved from the need to apply for a local authority permit. However, it will still require a public collections certificate from the Charity Commission (s 49(1)(a)).

As above, the promoters must notify the local authority within the prescribed period before the collection of the basic details of the appeal. They should state the purpose of the appeal, the date or dates on which the collections will be conducted and the location (s 49(3)). Other matters may be included in regulations. There is no difference drawn between the collection of goods and other items, except in the area of sanctions (see below).

Any breach of the requirement to notify the local authority of the details of the appeal could result in prosecution and a fine. There is a two-tier structure. If the promoters fail to obtain the public collections certificate and/or notify the local authority, they may receive a fine not exceeding level 5 on the standard scale (s 49(4)). However, if the above is the case but the collection is for goods only, the fine will not exceed level 3 on the standard scale (section 49(5)). This is presumably on the basis that collections of goods are likely to be organised by local charity shops. If the door-to-door collection also happens to qualify as a local short-term collection, the lesser sanction in s 50(6) may apply (see **9.17**).

Local authority permits

9.19 In addition to obtaining a public collections certificate, anyone who is proposing to promote a public charitable collection in a public place in the area of a local authority must apply to the authority for a permit (ChaA 2006 s 58(1)), unless the collection is exempt (see **9.17** and **9.18**).

This is the equivalent of the licence under the previous regime, where promoters had to apply to the relevant licensing authority (see **9.8**).

Key issues are whether local authorities will have the resources to deal with these applications, what the timetable for response will be and, for example, whether applicants in London will need to apply separately to all 32 London boroughs.

Application for a permit

9.20 ChaA 2006 s 58 deals with the procedure for application. Regulations will be issued prescribing the content of the application and the deadline for making the application before the date of the collection.

The application will need to contain basic information about the proposed collection or collections and the date or dates for which the permit should be issued. In the case of two or more dates, the maximum period for the permit to span is 12 months (s 58(3)(a)). The application should also be accompanied by the public collections certificate obtained from the Charity Commission. In the event that an application has been made to the Charity Commission and no decision has been reached before the date of the collection itself, an application for a permit should be submitted before the date in any event (s 58(4)).

Having considered the application, the local authority may either issue a permit or refuse the application on the only ground available to it (see **9.22**). It may also attach conditions (see **9.21**).

In the case of refusal or attached conditions, the local authority must notify the applicant of its decision and the reasons for the decision. It must also notify the applicant of their right to appeal the decision (s 59(5), (6)).

Conditions attaching to a permit

9.21 When issuing a permit, the local authority may attach one or more of the following conditions (ChaA 2006 s 59(3)):

- Conditions specifying day, date, time or frequency of collections.
- Conditions relating to locality.
- Conditions relating to the manner in which the collection is conducted.
- Any other conditions prescribed in regulations.

The local authority will have regard to the local circumstances of the proposed collection.

Grounds for refusing a permit

9.22 There is only one ground for a local authority to refuse a permit and that is that the proposed collection would cause undue inconvenience to members of the public (ChaA 2006 s 60(1)). This may be because of the date or day of the week, the proposed time, the frequency of the collections or the locality.

They may also take into account other collections authorised for the same day or place, or even for the day before or after the proposed date (s 60(2)). However, this is not relevant if the collection is to take place at a venue which is only available for the particular charitable appeal (s 60(3)).

Despite the desire to institute a unified licensing system, it is possible that local authorities will differ in the way they interpret these provisions.

Withdrawal or variation of permit

9.23 ChaA 2006 s 61 allows the local authority to revisit the question of a permit after it has been issued.

The local authority may avail itself of the powers in this section where:

- it has reason to believe that there has been a change in circumstances since the original permit was issued;
- it is of the opinion that, had the application been made at this time, it would have been refused or issued with different or additional conditions;
- it has reason to believe that information provided by the holder or holders of the permit was false or misleading; or
- it has reason to believe that there has been a breach of any condition or permit, or that such a breach is continuing.

In the above circumstances, the local authority has the power to:

- withdraw the permit;
- attach any condition to the permit, providing that it would have been appropriate to attach such a condition at the time of the original application (ChaA 2006 s 61(5)); or
- vary an existing condition.

There appears to be no equivalent of the suspension of a public collections certificate. There is no inclusion of a notice period when these powers are exercised by the local authority.

The above powers may be used by the local authority on more than one occasion, and the subsequent change in circumstances will relate to the previous exercise of any of its powers (s 61(6)).

In exercising any of the above powers, the local authority must notify the permit holder of its decision and the reasons behind the decision (s 61(7)).

It must also send a copy of its decision and reasons to the Charity Commission (s 61(9)) where a permit has been withdrawn.

Appeals against decisions

9.24 ChaA 2006 s 62 provides applicants with a right to appeal decisions of the local authority relating to the issuing of a permit. An applicant may have recourse to a magistrates' court on the following aspects:

- The refusal to issue a permit.
- Any conditions attached to a permit, including the variation of an existing permit.
- The withdrawal of a permit.
- The determination that a collection is not a local, short-term collection (for further details see **9.17**) or that a promoter has breached any fundraising provisions or been convicted of a relevant offence.

An appeal will be by way of complaint for an order and will follow the usual civil court procedure (s 62(4)).

Where a local authority has withdrawn a permit, or attached a condition or varied a condition, this shall not be effective until the appeal period or process is complete (s 61(10)).

Any decision of the magistrates' court may be appealed to the Crown Court. The court may confirm, vary or reverse a local authority decision (s 62(7)). The local authority does not have to implement any ruling until the time for bringing an appeal has expired (s 62(9)).

Conclusions on the new licensing regime

9.25 The new licensing regime is an improvement on the old regime because it is more coherent and unified. However, it remains complex to administer, particularly with regard to the relationship between the public collections certificate and the permit, given that these are issued by two different bodies. Questions of resource and time limits are not yet clear.

Charities will undoubtedly need to be careful to keep records of all collections, regardless of the size of the appeal or of the charity.

Fundraising statements

9.26 CA 1992 was largely repealed by CA 1993 but the main provision that remains in force relates to statements made by professional fundraisers and commercial participators.

CA 1992 s 60 required that in any statement made in the course of an appeal that money would be paid to a charity, the statement had to include clear details of the charity and, if there was more than one, the split and in general terms the proportion or amount to be paid to each charity, or the way in which this was to be calculated.

The regime applied to both commercial participators and professional fundraisers and any breach of the provisions could result in a fine. However, enforcement of these provisions was not consistent by all local authorities, particularly in relation to commercial participators.

Commercial participators and professional fundraisers

9.27 CA 1992 s 58(1) defines 'a commercial participator' as anyone who:

> '(a) carries on for gain a business other than a fund-raising business, but
>
> (b) in the course of that business, engages in any promotional venture in the course of which it is represented that charitable contributions are to be given to or applied for the benefit of the institution.'

'Professional fundraiser' is defined as:

> '(a) any person (apart from a charitable institution or a company connected with such an institution) who carries on a fundraising business, or
>
> (b) any other person (apart from a person excluded by virtue of subsection (2) or (3)) who for reward solicits money or other property for the benefit of a charitable institution, if he does so otherwise than in the course of any fundraising venture undertaken by a person falling within paragraph (a) above.'

CA 1992 s 58(2)–(3) lists those bodies or individuals who are not professional fundraisers. These include connected companies, trustees, officers or employees, lower-paid collectors, commercial participators and radio or TV presenters.

Revised statements

9.28 ChaA 2006 s 67 amends CA 1992 s 60 to require more information about the proportion of the appeal fund that is payable to the professional fundraiser or the commercial particpator. ChaA 2006 s 67 introduces the idea of a 'notifiable amount' and the definition is contained in s 67(5) as a reference:

> '(a) to the actual amount of the remuneration or sum, if that is known at the time when the statement is made; and
>
> (b) otherwise to the estimated amount of the remuneration or sum, calculated as accurately as is reasonably possible in the circumstances.'

ChaA 2006 s 68 introduces a new CA 1992 s 60A. This deals with those persons who raise money for a charity but are not professional fundraisers or commercial participators. Rather than informing the public of a notifiable amount, these persons must state that they are officers of the charity and are receiving payment as such (new s 60A(4)). Presumably, if they are volunteers this does not apply to them.

The same section introduces an exemption in a new CA 1992 s 60B for lower-paid collectors. Lower-paid collectors are defined as those who earn less than £5 per day or £500 per year. These figures may by varied by the Minister (new s 60B(6)).

Conclusions on revised fundraising statements

9.29 The new provisions relating to fundraising statements do little to clarify the current position. The method of calculating the notifiable amount is complex. For commercial participators in particular it might be better if the amount was stated as a percentage of the profits.

The new provisions attempt to deal with fundraising by employees of a charity but do not appear to cover volunteers.

Of more of a problem is that while CA 1992 s 60 provides that any breach may result in a conviction and fine, in practice there is little evidence that such sanctions will be imposed except in the most extreme circumstances.

Chapter 10

Powers of Unincorporated Charities

Introduction

10.1 The Charities Act 2006 ('ChaA 2006') ss 40–42 amend and extend the provisions in the Charities Act 1993 ('CA 1993') s 74, replacing s 74 and adding ss 74A, 74B and 74C. These provide unincorporated charities with the power to make alterations to their objects, to amend the administrative provisions in their constitution and even to wind up their charity and transfer its assets. This is assuming that these powers are not expressly contained within their constitution. If they do not have these powers available to them, their only recourse otherwise would be to apply to the Charity Commission for a scheme, even for straightforward administrative updates.

ChaA 2006 ss 40 and 41 limit these powers to unincorporated charities (trusts and associations) that have an annual gross income of below £10,000 and have no 'designated' land (land that is held on trusts that stipulate that it be used for the purposes of the charity). The figure of £10,000 may be amended by the Secretary of State. The annual income limit is raised from £5,000 to £10,000 so that more unincorporated charities will fall within the remit.

ChaA 2006 s 42 applies to *all* unincorporated charities.

It also relaxes the public notice provision. Rather than having to give public notice, this is at the discretion of the Charity Commission, having received a copy of the relevant resolution. The time for consideration is reduced from 3 months to 60 days. The old CA 1993 s 74 expressly excluded exempt charities. These are no longer excluded and may therefore avail themselves of these powers. The amendment of administrative provisions does not require the approval of the Charity Commission.

In addition to the above, there is a general relaxation of the regime applicable to permanent endowment funds and this may well benefit certain unincorporated charities (see CHAPTER 6).

Power to transfer property

10.2 ChaA 2006 s 40 replaces completely the existing CA 1993 s 74. It applies to unincorporated charities with an annual gross income of below £10,000 and no designated land.

When a charity is no longer able to fulfil its purpose, or it has insufficient assets to further its objects, the charity trustees may well be forced to consider the possibility of winding up the charity. The basic premise is that a charitable trust may continue into perpetuity and, unless the governing document provides a mechanism for winding up the charity (which many old constitutions do not) or a power to vary the constitution in this respect, it may not be possible to wind up the charity. It is likely that the constitution will provide for all assets to be transferred to another charity on winding up, otherwise it would not have been registrable in the first place. However, it might not provide the mechanism by which the winding up may be carried out. It is clear that the wording in the new CA 1993 s 74 states that *all* property of the charity is to be transferred. This cannot be used for simply transferring some of the charity's assets to a linked charity where it is not able to do so under its constitution.

Considerations for the trustees

10.3 Before passing the resolution, the charity trustees must be completely satisfied that they have considered and determined:

- that it is 'expedient' in furthering the charity's original purpose that its assets be transferred to another charity; and
- that the objects of the receiving charity are wide enough to include the objects of the transferring charity.

The trustees should minute their conclusions. (It is worth noting that, even after winding up, the records of the dissolving charity have to be kept for at least six years, and that this is part of the winding up requirement.)

The transferee charity will need to ensure that the donated assets continue to be used for the original objects and, if necessary, may need to treat them as restricted funds for this purpose. However, interestingly ChaA 2006 provides some relaxation of this requirement in the new CA 1993 s 74(11). This states that trustees of the receiving charity do not need to treat the funds in this way if they 'consider that complying with it would not result in a suitable and effective method of applying the property'. This does appear to leave the way open for such funds to become unrestricted for logistical reasons.

Procedure for transferring property

10.4 CA 1993 s 74(2) provides that charity trustees may pass a resolution to transfer all of their charity's assets to one or more other charities, in proportions to be specified in the resolution. The recipient charity or charities need not be registered, but could be exempt or excepted or simply below the threshold for registration (s 74(3)). This power is provided to the trustees and does not require a resolution of the membership. This is a prerequisite to winding up and requesting that the charity be removed from the Charity Commission Register.

The resolution must be passed by a majority of not less than two-thirds of the charity trustees who vote on the resolution (s 74(5)). A quorum will still be necessary for the meeting at which this resolution will be taken, although obviously this is the quorum for trustee meetings and not for general meetings of the membership.

Having passed the resolution, a copy will then need to be sent to the Charity Commission with a statement of the reasons for passing it (s 74(6)). The Charity Commission can ask for further information (s 74(8)) or request that the trustees give public notice of the resolution (s 74(7)), ensuring that at least 28 days is allowed for representations from the public.

Timing of the resolution to transfer

10.5 The resolution will come into effect 60 days from the date that the resolution is received by the Charity Commission (CA 1993 s 74(9)), unless the Charity Commission objects on procedural grounds or on the merits of the proposal (s 74A(2)), in which case the resolution will not take effect.

If the charity trustees are required to give public notice of the resolution, the 60-day period stops running from the date that the direction is given to the charity trustees and does not start running again until 42 days after the date on which the trustees give public notice (s 74A(3)).

If the Charity Commission requests further information from the trustees, the 60-day period is suspended between the date of the request for information and the date on which that information is provided (s 74A(4)).

Should the 60-day period be suspended for more than 120 days, then the resolution will automatically become ineffective (s 74A(6)).

Once the resolution takes effect, the property should be transferred in accordance with the resolution. Where property is held by the Official Custodian, the trustees can request that the Charity Commission makes a vesting order.

Transfer where charity has permanent endowment

10.6 CA 1993 s 74B deals with the transfer of assets which include a permanent endowment (property which is subject to a restriction on capital expenditure). Again, this is for the benefit of unincorporated charities with an income below £10,000. The procedure is as above, but the resolution must contain separate resolutions dealing with the permanent endowment and with the unrestricted property. Where a permanent endowment is concerned, the trustees must ensure that the receiving charity has purposes which are 'substantially similar' to the purposes of the transferring charity (s 74B(6)). In the case of more than one recipient, each charity must have purposes which are substantially similar to at least one of the transferor's purposes and taken together they must have purposes that are substantially similar to all of the transferor's purposes (s 74B(7)).

Amending the charitable purposes

10.7 ChaA 2006 s 41 contains a completely new provision which will be very useful for small charities. It applies to unincorporated charities with an annual gross income of below £10,000 and no designated land. It introduces a new CA 1993 s 74C.

This new section gives charity trustees the power to modify or replace all or any of the existing objects of their charity. Interestingly this power lies solely with the trustees and does not require a resolution of the members, as might be expected.

The resolution must be passed by a majority of not less than two-thirds of the charity trustees who vote on the resolution (s 74C(5)). A quorum will still be necessary for the meeting at which this resolution will be taken, although obviously this is the quorum for trustee meetings and not for general meetings of the membership.

Having passed the resolution, a copy will need to be sent to the Charity Commission with a statement of the reasons for passing it (s 74C(6)). The Charity Commission can ask for further information (s 74C(8)) or request that the trustees give public notice of the resolution (s 74C(7)), ensuring that at least 28 days is allowed for representations from the public.

Considerations for the trustees

10.8 Before passing a CA 1993 s 74C resolution, the trustees must be completely satisfied that they have considered and determined:

- that it is 'expedient' in the interests of the charity for the purposes in question to be replaced; and
- that the new purposes consist of or include purposes that are similar in character to the original purposes. However, there is a slight relaxation in the wording that states 'so far as is reasonably practicable'. This does mean that trustees will need to take care in framing the wording of the new purposes.

The trustees should minute their conclusions. CA 1993 s 74B(3) emphasises the fact that the new objects must be charitable.

Timing of the resolution to amend purposes

10.9 A resolution passed under CA 1993 s 74C will come into effect 60 days from the date that the resolution is received by the Charity Commission (s 74C(9)), unless the Charity Commission objects on procedural grounds or on the merits of the proposal (s 74A(2)), in which case the resolution will not take effect.

If the charity trustees are required to give public notice of the resolution, the 60-day period stops running from the date that the direction was given to the trustees and does not start running again until 42 days after the date on which the trustees gave public notice (s 74A(3)).

If the Charity Commission requests further information from the trustees, again the 60-day period is suspended between the date of the request for information and the date on which that information is provided.

Should the 60-day period be suspended for more than 120 days, then the resolution becomes automatically ineffective (s 74A(6)).

Amending powers or procedures

10.10 ChaA 2006 s 42 contains the equivalent of the power to amend the purposes, but provides charities with the power to amend their powers and procedures. Unlike the above sections, this provision applies to *all* unincorporated charities, regardless of annual income. It introduces a new CA 1993 s 74D.

This section provides the charity trustees with the power to modify or replace the existing powers or administrative provisions of the charity. The trustees may resolve to make these amendments. However, unlike the powers in ChaA 2006 ss 40 and 41, there is a requirement that the resolution be ratified by the membership. If there is no membership separate from the trustee body, the resolution of the trustees will be sufficient. There is no requirement that the resolution be passed by a minimum number of trustees. It would therefore appear that the resolution can be passed by a simple majority decision.

If, however, there is a separate membership, the resolution must be passed at a general meeting by no less than two-thirds of the members attending the meeting. The quorum for general meetings will apply. The alternative is for a decision to be taken without a vote, but the decision in this case must be unanimous (CA 1993 s 74C(4)(b)). This would cover the situation where a written resolution is used.

Unlike with ChaA 2006 ss 40 and 41, there is no requirement that the resolution be sent to the Charity Commission (although it would need to be notified in any event of any amendments to the constitution). There is no statutory list of considerations for the trustees to take into account when reaching their decision. There is no provision for the Charity Commission to challenge the resolution or for there to be a public notice period.

The resolution becomes effective from the date contained within the resolution itself or, where this date is later, from the date that the resolution is ratified by the members in general meeting (s 74C(6)). There is no 60-day waiting period.

Chapter 11

The Charity Commission

History of the Charity Commission

11.1 While charity law may trace its origins back to the preamble to the Statute of Charitable Uses 1601, for most of the time since then charities have only been accountable to the courts. It was not until 1853 that the Charity Commissioners were brought into being, and for the past 150 years very little has happened to substantially change the way in which the Charity Commission is constituted and operates. As in so many other areas however, the present Government has found the urge to alter the organs of government through legislation irresistible, and therefore not only does the Charities Act 2006 ('ChaA 2006') make significant changes to the administration and operation of charities, but also to the constitution and administration of the Charity Commission itself.

It may come as a surprise to many who have had dealings with the Charity Commission on a regular basis to discover that legally, prior to ChaA 2006 there was no such body as the Charity Commission. Instead, all of the functions and powers of the Commission were held personally by a group of Charity Commissioners who were appointed by the Home Secretary (Charities Act 1993 ('CA 1993') Sch 1 para 1(3)) and who, under the supervision of the Treasury, appointed such Assistant Commissioners and other staff as were necessary to enable the Charity Commissioners to carry out their statutory duties (CA 1993 Sch 1 para 2(1)).

ChaA 2006 abolishes the Charity Commissioners for England and Wales (CA 1993 s 1A(3)) and in their place creates a new corporate body known as the 'Charity Commission for England and Wales' (CA 1993 s 1A(1)). All of the functions of the Charity Commissioners and all of their rights and liabilities and assets are transferred to the new Charity Commission (CA 1993 s 1A(4)) and rather neatly and logically the Chief Charity Commissioner automatically becomes chair of the new Commission (CA 1993 Sch 2 para 2(1)) and the remaining Charity Commissioners become members of the Charity Commission (CA 1993 Sch 2 para 2(2)). Likewise, ChaA 2006 ensures that anything done by the Charity Commissioners or which was in the process of being dealt with by them immediately before ChaA 2006 comes into affect (including any legal proceedings) is to be treated as having been done or continued by the new Charity Commission (CA 1993 Sch 2 para 3(1), (2)).

Composition of the Charity Commission

11.2 To complement the conversion of the Charity Commissioners into an incorporated body, ChaA 2006 establishes a new Board of the

Commission which consists of a chairman and between four and eight other members (CA 1993 Sch 1A para 1(1)) appointed by the Secretary of State (Sch 1A para 1(2)), whereas previously there were only three Charity Commissioners (although these three were able to appoint a number of assistant commissioners to assist them).

The Board must still include at least two members who have been legally qualified for at least seven years (Sch 1A para 1(3)(b)). There is also now an additional requirement that at least one member represents the interests of Wales. This Welsh representative is appointed in consultation with the Welsh National Assembly (Sch 1A para 1(3)(c)). Appointment to the Board is for a maximum three-year term (Sch 1A para 3(1)). A Board member may be reappointed at the end of their term but may not hold office for more than a total of ten years (Sch 1A para 3(4)).

The Board of the Commission have responsibility for appointing the chief executive (Sch 1A para 5(1)(a)) and the rest of the Charity Commission staff (Sch 1A para 5(1)(b)). The Commission can also establish any committees and sub-committees (and these can include people who are not on the Commission itself) (Sch 1A para 6(1)).

Whereas CA 1993 specified that where the Commissioners sat as a Board, depending upon the number of Commissioners, there was a specific number of Commissioners required to make a meeting quorate (Sch 1 para 3(4)), under ChaA 2006, the Act no longer specifies a quorum and leaves it to the Commission to regulate its own procedures as it feels is appropriate (Sch 1A para 7(1)).

In order to avoid any uncertainty that could arise from the incorporation process, ChaA 2006, as previously mentioned, expressly appoints the existing Commissioners as the first members of the new Commission, and even goes so far as to ensure that it is clear that from an employment standpoint there is no break in their continuity of employment (CA 1993 Sch 2 para 2). ChaA 2006 also ensures that there is complete legal continuity with anything that was being done by the Charity Commission immediately prior to incorporation, so as to avoid the possibility of anything falling into a legal void as a result of the change of status of the Commission (CA 1993 Sch 2 para 3).

Duties and responsibilities of the Charity Commission

11.3 If there was one area in which CA 1993 was extraordinarily brief, it was with regard to setting out what the basic objectives of the Charity Commission were. The extent of the guidance given was contained in CA 1993 s 1(3) and (4), which provided that the general function of the Commissioners was to promote the effective use of charitable resources through better administration and information for trustees and to encourage charities to meet their stated objects. In keeping with modern business practice, ChaA 2006 provides a much clearer picture of what the new Commission should see its role as being and what its objectives and duties are.

The Charity Commission's regulatory objectives may be summarised as being:

- to promote and maintain public confidence in charities;
- to ensure that all charities meet the public benefit test in carrying on their aims;
- to increase compliance with legal obligations by charity trustees;
- to encourage charities to maximise their social and economic impact through the effective use of their assets; and
- to improve the accountability of charities to their beneficiaries, donors and the general public.

Having established the objectives for the new Charity Commission, ChaA 2006 goes on to state that its general functions are:

- to determine whether or not an organisation is a charity;
- to encourage and facilitate better charity administration;
- to identify and investigate potential mismanagement or misconduct in the administration of the charity and take appropriate action;
- to issue and review public collection certificates;
- to gather, evaluate and publish information relating to the Charity Commission's operations, which include amongst other things, operating the Register of Charities; and
- to advise the Government on matters relating to the Charity Commission's objectives and functions.

In addition to its various roles, the legislation also imposes on the Charity Commission the duty to:

- perform its functions in a way which is compatible with and appropriate for achieving its regulatory objectives;
- facilitate innovation by charities;
- ensure that it uses its resources in the most efficient, effective and economic way;
- ensure that they perform its functions in a way that encourages charitable giving and volunteering; and
- manage its affairs having regard to the principles of good regulatory practice and corporate governance.

11.4 In addition to the various express powers which are contained within CA 1993 and ChaA 2006, the Act makes it expressly clear that the Charity Commission has the power to do anything which facilitates or supports its general functions and duties (CA 1993 s 1E). This will limit the ability to challenge the conduct of the Commission on grounds of *ultra vires*. The Act does, however, make it clear that this does not entitle the Commission to act as a charity trustee or to be directly involved in the administration of charities (CA 1993 s 1E(2)). Given the extensive powers which the Charity Commission now has, it is arguable that the Commission can just as effectively control the administration of charities indirectly, as if it were to do so directly.

Chapter 12

Charity Tribunal

Introduction

12.1 For many people the introduction of the Charity Tribunal ('the Tribunal') as a court of first instance to hear appeals against decisions of the Charity Commission will be one of the most important and welcome developments of the new legislation. Under the Charities Act 1993 ('CA 1993'), a party that was dissatisfied with a decision or order made by the Charity Commission was forced to bring an action through the High Court pursuant to a right given under CA 1993 s 92 (which re-enacted Charities Act 1960 s 42). If a party was unable to challenge the Charity Commission under s 92 then the only alternative was a costly and potentially complex petition for judicial review, which, not surprisingly, few charities or charity trustees were keen to contemplate.

Matters that can be appealed

12.2 When the draft Charities Bill was first introduced the scope of the matters which the Tribunal could consider was tightly circumscribed by the legislation. Thankfully, during the passage of the Bill through Parliament the Tribunal's remit was significantly increased. The table at CA 1993 Sch 1C (reproduced below) contains a detailed list of the Charity Commission decisions from which a right of appeal exists to the Tribunal, who has the right to bring such an appeal and what powers the Tribunal has to deal with a successful appeal in relation to each matter.

Commission decision that may be appealed to the Tribunal	*Persons entitled to bring appeal*	*Powers of Tribunal to deal with particular appeal*
Decision of the Commission under section 3 or 3A of this Act— (a) to enter or not to enter an institution in the register of charities, or (b) to remove or not to remove an institution from the register.	The persons are— (a) the persons who are or claim to be the charity trustees of the institution, (b) (if a body corporate) the institution itself, and (c) any other person who is or may be affected by the decision.	Power to quash the decision and (if appropriate)— (a) remit the matter to the Commission, (b) direct the Commission to rectify the register.
Decision of the Commission not to make a determination under section 3(9) of this Act in relation to particular information contained in the register.	The persons are— (a) the charity trustees of the charity to which the information relates, (b) (if a body corporate) the charity itself, and (c) any other person who is or may be affected by the decision.	Power to quash the decision and (if appropriate) remit the matter to the Commission.
Direction given by the Commission under section 6 of this Act requiring the name of a charity to be changed.	The persons are— (a) the charity trustees of the charity to which the direction relates, (b) (if a body corporate) the charity itself, and (c) any other person who is or may be affected by the direction.	Power to— (a) quash the direction and (if appropriate) remit the matter to the Commission, (b) substitute for the direction any other direction which could have been given by the Commission.

Commission decision that may be appealed to the Tribunal	*Persons entitled to bring appeal*	*Powers of Tribunal to deal with particular appeal*
Decision of the Commission to institute an inquiry under section 8 of this Act with regard to a particular institution.	The persons are— (a) the persons who have control or management of the institution, and (b) (if a body corporate) the institution itself.	Power to direct the Commission to end the inquiry.
Decision of the Commission to institute an inquiry under section 8 of this Act with regard to a class of institutions.	The persons are— (a) the persons who have control or management of any institution which is a member of the class of institutions, and (b) (if a body corporate) any such institution.	Power to— (a) direct the Commission that the inquiry should not consider a particular institution, (b) direct the Commission to end the inquiry.
Order made by the Commission under section 9 of this Act requiring a person to supply information or a document.	The persons are any person who is required to supply the information or document.	Power to— (a) quash the order, (b) substitute for all or part of the order any other order which could have been made by the Commission.
Order made by the Commission under section 16(1) of this Act (including such an order made by virtue of section 23(1)).	The persons are— (a) in a section 16(1)(a) case, the charity trustees of the charity to which the order relates or (if a body corporate) the charity itself, (b) in a section 16(1)(b) case, any person discharged or removed by the order, and (c) any other person who is or may be affected by the order.	Power to— (a) quash the order in whole or in part and (if appropriate) remit the matter to the Commission, (b) substitute for all or part of the order any other order which could have been made by the Commission, (c) add to the order anything which could have been contained in an order made by the Commission.

Commission decision that may be appealed to the Tribunal	*Persons entitled to bring appeal*	*Powers of Tribunal to deal with particular appeal*
Order made by the Commission under section 18(1) of this Act in relation to a charity.	The persons are— (a) the charity trustees of the charity, (b) (if a body corporate) the charity itself, (c) in a section 18(1)(i) case, any person suspended by the order, and (d) any other person who is or may be affected by the order.	Power to— (a) quash the order in whole or in part and (if appropriate) remit the matter to the Commission, (b) substitute for all or part of the order any other order which could have been made by the Commission, (c) add to the order anything which could have been contained in an order made by the Commission.
Order made by the Commission under section 18(2) of this Act in relation to a charity.	The persons are— (a) the charity trustees of the charity, (b) (if a body corporate) the charity itself, (c) in a section 18(2)(i) case, any person removed by the order, and (d) any other person who is or may be affected by the order.	Power to— (a) quash the order in whole or in part and (if appropriate) remit the matter to the Commission, (b) substitute for all or part of the order any other order which could have been made by the Commission, (c) add to the order anything which could have been contained in an order made by the Commission.

Commission decision that may be appealed to the Tribunal	*Persons entitled to bring appeal*	*Powers of Tribunal to deal with particular appeal*
Order made by the Commission under section 18(4) of this Act removing a charity trustee.	The persons are— (a) the charity trustee, (b) the remaining charity trustees of the charity of which he was a charity trustee, (c) (if a body corporate) the charity itself, and (d) any other person who is or may be affected by the order.	Power to— (a) quash the order in whole or in part and (if appropriate) remit the matter to the Commission, (b) substitute for all or part of the order any other order which could have been made by the Commission, (c) add to the order anything which could have been contained in an order made by the Commission.
Order made by the Commission under section 18(5) of this Act appointing a charity trustee.	The persons are— (a) the other charity trustees of the charity, (b) (if a body corporate) the charity itself, and (c) any other person who is or may be affected by the order.	Power to— (a) quash the order in whole or in part and (if appropriate) remit the matter to the Commission, (b) substitute for all or part of the order any other order which could have been made by the Commission, (c) add to the order anything which could have been contained in an order made by the Commission.

Commission decision that may be appealed to the Tribunal	*Persons entitled to bring appeal*	*Powers of Tribunal to deal with particular appeal*
Decision of the Commission— (a) to discharge an order following a review under section 18(13) of this Act, or (b) not to discharge an order following such a review.	The persons are— (a) the charity trustees of the charity to which the order relates, (b) (if a body corporate) the charity itself, (c) if the order in question was made under section 18(1)(i), any person suspended by it, and (d) any other person who is or may be affected by the order.	Power to— (a) quash the decision and (if appropriate) remit the matter to the Commission, (b) make the discharge of the order subject to savings or other transitional provisions, (c) remove any savings or other transitional provisions to which the discharge of the order was subject, (d) discharge the order in whole or in part (whether subject to any savings or other transitional provisions or not).
Order made by the Commission under section 18A(2) of this Act which suspends a person's membership of a charity.	The persons are— (a) the person whose membership is suspended by the order, and (b) any other person who is or may be affected by the order.	Power to quash the order and (if appropriate) remit the matter to the Commission.
Order made by the Commission under section 19A(2) of this Act which directs a person to take action specified in the order.	The persons are any person who is directed by the order to take the specified action.	Power to quash the order and (if appropriate) remit the matter to the Commission.

Commission decision that may be appealed to the Tribunal	*Persons entitled to bring appeal*	*Powers of Tribunal to deal with particular appeal*
Order made by the Commission under section 19B(2) of this Act which directs a person to apply property in a specified manner.	The persons are any person who is directed by the order to apply the property in the specified manner.	Power to quash the order and (if appropriate) remit the matter to the Commission.
Order made by the Commission under section 23(2) of this Act in relation to any land vested in the official custodian in trust for a charity.	The persons are— (a) the charity trustees of the charity, (b) (if a body corporate) the charity itself, and (c) any other person who is or may be affected by the order.	Power to— (a) quash the order and (if appropriate) remit the matter to the Commission, (b) substitute for the order any other order which could have been made by the Commission, (c) add to the order anything which could have been contained in an order made by the Commission.
Decision of the Commission not to make a common investment scheme under section 24 of this Act.	The persons are— (a) the charity trustees of a charity which applied to the Commission for the scheme, (b) (if a body corporate) the charity itself, and (c) any other person who is or may be affected by the decision.	Power to quash the decision and (if appropriate) remit the matter to the Commission.

Commission decision that may be appealed to the Tribunal	*Persons entitled to bring appeal*	*Powers of Tribunal to deal with particular appeal*
Decision of the Commission not to make a common deposit scheme under section 25 of this Act.	The persons are— (a) the charity trustees of a charity which applied to the Commission for the scheme, (b) (if a body corporate) the charity itself, and (c) any other person who is or may be affected by the decision.	Power to quash the decision and (if appropriate) remit the matter to the Commission.
Decision by the Commission not to make an order under section 26 of this Act in relation to a charity.	The persons are— (a) the charity trustees of the charity, and (b) (if a body corporate) the charity itself.	Power to quash the decision and (if appropriate) remit the matter to the Commission.
Direction given by the Commission under section 28 of this Act in relation to an account held in the name of or on behalf of a charity.	The persons are— (a) the charity trustees of the charity, (b) (if a body corporate) the charity itself, and (c) any other person who is or may be affected by the order.	Power to— (a) quash the direction and (if appropriate) remit the matter to the Commission, (b) substitute for the direction any other direction which could have been given by the Commission, (c) add to the direction anything which could have been contained in a direction given by the Commission.

Commission decision that may be appealed to the Tribunal	*Persons entitled to bring appeal*	*Powers of Tribunal to deal with particular appeal*
Order made by the Commission under section 31 of this Act for the taxation of a solicitor's bill.	The persons are— (a) the solicitor, (b) any person for whom the work was done by the solicitor, and (c) any other person who is or may be affected by the order.	Power to— (a) quash the order, (b) substitute for the order any other order which could have been made by the Commission, (c) add to the order anything which could have been contained in an order made by the Commission.
Decision of the Commission not to make an order under section 36 of this Act in relation to land held by or in trust for a charity.	The persons are— (a) the charity trustees of the charity, (b) (if a body corporate) the charity itself, and (c) any other person who is or may be affected by the decision.	Power to quash the decision and (if appropriate) remit the matter to the Commission.
Decision of the Commission not to make an order under section 38 of this Act in relation to a mortgage of land held by or in trust for a charity.	The persons are— (a) the charity trustees of the charity, (b) (if a body corporate) the charity itself, and (c) any other person who is or may be affected by the decision.	Power to quash the decision and (if appropriate) remit the matter to the Commission.

Commission decision that may be appealed to the Tribunal	*Persons entitled to bring appeal*	*Powers of Tribunal to deal with particular appeal*
Order made by the Commission under section 43(4) of this Act requiring the accounts of a charity to be audited.	The persons are— (a) the charity trustees of the charity, (b) (if a body corporate) the charity itself, and (c) any other person who is or may be affected by the order.	Power to— (a) quash the order, (b) substitute for the order any other order which could have been made by the Commission, (c) add to the order anything which could have been contained in an order made by the Commission.
Order made by the Commission under section 44(2) of this Act in relation to a charity, or a decision of the Commission not to make such an order in relation to a charity.	The persons are— (a) the charity trustees of the charity, (b) (if a body corporate) the charity itself, (c) in the case of a decision not to make an order, the auditor, independent examiner or examiner, and (d) any other person who is or may be affected by the order or the decision.	Power to— (a) quash the order or decision and (if appropriate) remit the matter to the Commission, (b) substitute for the order any other order of a kind the Commission could have made, (c) make any order which the Commission could have made.
Decision of the Commission under section 46(5) of this Act to request charity trustees to prepare an annual report for a charity.	The persons are— (a) the charity trustees, and (b) (if a body corporate) the charity itself.	Power to quash the decision and (if appropriate) remit the matter to the Commission.

Commission decision that may be appealed to the Tribunal	*Persons entitled to bring appeal*	*Powers of Tribunal to deal with particular appeal*
Decision of the Commission not to dispense with the requirements of section 48(1) in relation to a charity or class of charities.	The persons are the charity trustees of any charity affected by the decision.	Power to quash the decision and (if appropriate) remit the matter to the Commission.
Decision of the Commission— (a) to grant a certificate of incorporation under section 50(1) of this Act to the trustees of a charity, or (b) not to grant such a certificate.	The persons are— (a) the trustees of the charity, and (b) any other person who is or may be affected by the decision.	Power to quash— (a) the decision, (b) any conditions or directions inserted in the certificate, and (if appropriate) remit the matter to the Commission.
Decision of the Commission to amend a certificate of incorporation of a charity under section 56(4) of this Act.	The persons are— (a) the trustees of the charity, and (b) any other person who is or may be affected by the amended certificate of incorporation.	Power to quash the decision and (if appropriate) remit the matter to the Commission.
Decision of the Commission not to amend a certificate of incorporation under section 56(4) of this Act.	The persons are— (a) the trustees of the charity, and (b) any other person who is or may be affected by the decision not to amend the certificate of incorporation.	Power to— (a) quash the decision and (if appropriate) remit the matter to the Commission, (b) make any order the Commission could have made under section 56(4).

Commission decision that may be appealed to the Tribunal	*Persons entitled to bring appeal*	*Powers of Tribunal to deal with particular appeal*
Order of the Commission under section 61(1) or (2) of this Act which dissolves a charity which is an incorporated body.	The persons are— (a) the trustees of the charity, (b) the charity itself, and (c) any other person who is or may be affected by the order.	Power to— (a) quash the order and (if appropriate) remit the matter to the Commission, (b) substitute for the order any other order which could have been made by the Commission, (c) add to the order anything which could have been contained in an order made by the Commission.
Decision of the Commission to give, or withhold, consent under section 64(2), 65(4) or 66(1) of this Act in relation to a body corporate which is a charity.	The persons are— (a) the charity trustees of the charity, (b) the body corporate itself, and (c) any other person who is or may be affected by the decision.	Power to quash the order and (if appropriate) remit the matter to the Commission.
Order made by the Commission under section 69(1) of this Act in relation to a company which is a charity.	The persons are— (a) the directors of the company, (b) the company itself, and (c) any other person who is or may be affected by the order.	Power to— (a) quash the order and (if appropriate) remit the matter to the Commission, (b) substitute for the order any other order which could have been made by the Commission, (c) add to the order anything which could have been contained in an order made by the Commission.

Commission decision that may be appealed to the Tribunal	*Persons entitled to bring appeal*	*Powers of Tribunal to deal with particular appeal*
Order made by the Commission under section 69(4) of this Act which gives directions to a person or to charity trustees.	The persons are— (a) in the case of directions given to a person, that person, (b) in the case of directions given to charity trustees, those charity trustees and (if a body corporate) the charity of which they are charity trustees, and (c) any other person who is or may be affected by the directions.	Power to— (a) quash the order, (b) substitute for the order any other order which could have been made by the Commission, (c) add to the order anything which could have been contained in an order made by the Commission.
Decision of the Commission under section 69E of this Act to grant an application for the constitution of a CIO and its registration as a charity.	The persons are any person (other than the persons who made the application) who is or may be affected by the decision.	Power to quash the decision and (if appropriate)— (a) remit the matter to the Commission, (b) direct the Commission to rectify the register of charities.
Decision of the Commission under section 69E of this Act not to grant an application for the constitution of a CIO and its registration as a charity.	The persons are— (a) the persons who made the application, and (b) any other person who is or may be affected by the decision.	Power to— (a) quash the decision and (if appropriate) remit the matter to the Commission, (b) direct the Commission to grant the application.

Commission decision that may be appealed to the Tribunal	*Persons entitled to bring appeal*	*Powers of Tribunal to deal with particular appeal*
Decision of the Commission under section 69H of this Act not to grant an application for the conversion of a charitable company or a registered society into a CIO and the CIO's registration as a charity.	The persons are— (a) the charity which made the application, (b) the charity trustees of the charity, and (c) any other person who is or may be affected by the decision.	Power to— (a) quash the decision and (if appropriate) remit the matter to the Commission, (b) direct the Commission to grant the application.
Decision of the Commission under section 69K of this Act to grant an application for the amalgamation of two or more CIOs and the incorporation and registration as a charity of a new CIO as their successor.	The persons are any creditor of any of the CIOs being amalgamated.	Power to quash the decision and (if appropriate) remit the matter to the Commission.
Decision of the Commission under section 69K of this Act not to grant an application for the amalgamation of two or more CIOs and the incorporation and registration as a charity of a new CIO as their successor.	The persons are— (a) the CIOs which applied for the amalgamation, (b) the charity trustees of the CIOs, and (c) any other person who is or may be affected by the decision.	Power to— (a) quash the decision and (if appropriate) remit the matter to the Commission, (b) direct the Commission to grant the application.

Commission decision that may be appealed to the Tribunal	*Persons entitled to bring appeal*	*Powers of Tribunal to deal with particular appeal*
Decision of the Commission to confirm a resolution passed by a CIO under section 69M(1) of this Act.	The persons are any creditor of the CIO.	Power to quash the decision and (if appropriate) remit the matter to the Commission.
Decision of the Commission not to confirm a resolution passed by a CIO under section 69M(1) of this Act.	The persons are— (a) the CIO, (b) the charity trustees of the CIO, and (c) any other person who is or may be affected by the decision.	Power to— (a) quash the decision and (if appropriate) remit the matter to the Commission, (b) direct the Commission to confirm the resolution.
Decision of the Commission under section 72(4) of this Act to waive, or not to waive, a person's disqualification.	The persons are— (a) the person who applied for the waiver, and (b) any other person who is or may be affected by the decision.	Power to— (a) quash the decision and (if appropriate) remit the matter to the Commission, (b) substitute for the decision any other decision of a kind which could have been made by the Commission.
Order made by the Commission under section 73(4) of this Act in relation to a person who has acted as charity trustee or trustee for a charity.	The persons are— (a) the person subject to the order, and (b) any other person who is or may be affected by the order.	Power to— (a) quash the order and (if appropriate) remit the matter to the Commission, (b) substitute for the order any other order which could have been made by the Commission.

Commission decision that may be appealed to the Tribunal	*Persons entitled to bring appeal*	*Powers of Tribunal to deal with particular appeal*
Order made by the Commission under section 73C(5) or (6) of this Act requiring a trustee or connected person to repay, or not to receive, remuneration.	The persons are— (a) the trustee or connected person, (b) the other charity trustees of the charity concerned, and (c) any other person who is or may be affected by the order.	Power to— (a) quash the order and (if appropriate) remit the matter to the Commission, (b) substitute for the order any other order which could have been made by the Commission.
Decision of the Commission to notify charity trustees under section 74A(2) of this Act that it objects to a resolution of the charity trustees under section 74(2) or 74C(2).	The persons are— (a) the charity trustees, and (b) any other person who is or may be affected by the decision.	Power to quash the decision.
Decision of the Commission not to concur under section 75A of this Act with a resolution of charity trustees under section 75A(3) or 75B(2).	The persons are— (a) the charity trustees, (b) (if a body corporate) the charity itself, and (c) any other person who is or may be affected by the decision.	Power to quash the decision and (if appropriate) remit the matter to the Commission.
Decision of the Commission to withhold approval for the transfer of property from trustees to a parish council under section 79(1) of this Act.	The persons are— (a) the trustees, (b) the parish council, and (c) any other person who is or may be affected by the decision.	Power to quash the decision and (if appropriate) remit the matter to the Commission.

Commission decision that may be appealed to the Tribunal	*Persons entitled to bring appeal*	*Powers of Tribunal to deal with particular appeal*
Order made by the Commission under section 80(2) of this Act in relation to a person holding property on behalf of a recognised body or of any person concerned in its management or control.	The persons are— (a) the person holding the property in question, and (b) any other person who is or may be affected by the order.	Power to quash the order and (if appropriate) remit the matter to the Commission.
Decision of the Commission not to give a direction under section 96(5) or (6) of this Act in relation to an institution or a charity.	The persons are the trustees of the institution or charity concerned.	Power to quash the decision and (if appropriate) remit the matter to the Commission.
Decision of the Commission under paragraph 15 of Schedule 5B to this Act to refuse to register an amendment to the constitution of a CIO.	The persons are— (a) the CIO, (b) the charity trustees of the CIO, and (c) any other person who is or may be affected by the decision.	Power to quash the decision and (if appropriate)— (a) remit the matter to the Commission, (b) direct the Commission to register the amendment.

In addition to the persons mentioned in the centre column of the table above, the Attorney General is also entitled to bring such an appeal to the Tribunal (CA 1993 Sch 1C para 1(2)), and in each instance the Charity Commission will be the respondent.

When hearing an appeal the Tribunal will consider afresh the decision, direction or order that the Commission was involved in making and, very helpfully for anyone bringing such an appeal, the Tribunal is allowed to take into account evidence which was not available to the Commission at the time of its original deliberations. This means that an applicant bringing an appeal potentially has a chance not only to challenge a Commission decision but to get the right outcome for their charity.

Reviewable matters

12.3 As well as hearing appeals against Charity Commission decisions, directions and orders mentioned in the table above, the Tribunal can also consider applications to review certain matters that might otherwise have been the subject of an application to the High Court for judicial review. These so called 'reviewable matters', detailed in CA 1993 Sch 1C para 3(2), relate to decisions of the Commission:

(a) to institute an inquiry under CA 1993 s 8 with regard to a particular institution;

(b) to institute an inquiry under s 8 with regard to a class of institutions;

(c) not to make a common investment scheme under s 24;

(d) not to make a common deposit scheme under s 25;

(e) not to make an order under s 26 in relation to a charity (power to authorise dealings in charity property);

(f) not to make an order under s 36 in relation to land held by or in trust for a charity; and

(g) not to make an order under s 38 in relation to a mortgage of land held by or in trust for a charity.

An application for the Tribunal to consider a reviewable matter can be brought either by the persons mentioned in the table above corresponding with the relevant matter or by the Attorney General.

Composition of the Tribunal

12.4 Charities Act 2006 ('ChaA 2006') s 8 introduces a new CA 1993 Part 1A and new Schs 1B, 1C and 1D, which deal with matters such as the composition of the new Charity Tribunal. The Tribunal comprises both legally qualified and non-legally qualified members who, together with a president, are appointed by the Lord Chancellor (CA 1993 Sch 1B para 1(2)). The president and legal members are required to have at least seven years' legal qualification (Sch 1B para 1(3), and see also Courts and Legal Services Act 1919 s 71), while non-legal members are required to have such appropriate knowledge or experience relating to charities as the Lord Chancellor deems appropriate (Sch 1B para 1(4)). The president of the Tribunal may be assisted by a deputy, to be appointed from amongst one of the legally qualified members.

For the purposes of undertaking the day-to-day functions of the Tribunal, the Tribunal sits as a panel which can consist either of the president, or a legally qualified member sitting alone, or the president or a legally qualified member sitting with two other members, or with the consent of the parties to the appeal the president or a legal member sitting with one other member (Sch 1B para 8(2)). Normally, decisions of the Tribunal will be based on a majority vote. However, if the president or a legally qualified member is sitting with just one other member then they will have the casting vote. The consequence of this is that, effectively, where the panel consists of one legally qualified member and one non-legally qualified member, if there is a deadlock in the voting the legally qualified member's decision will carry sway, although if both members are legally qualified then the president can set guidelines as to who will have the casting vote (Sch 1A para 9(2)–(4)).

Procedures at the Tribunal

12.5 Under ChaA 2006 the Lord Chancellor determines the rules governing the right to bring appeals to the Tribunal and how proceedings are to be conducted before it. This power extends to specifying such things as the rules of evidence that will apply at Tribunal hearings, steps that must be taken before an appeal is brought, how appeal decisions are to be recorded and publicised and the awarding of costs (CA 1993 s 2B(1)–(3)).

When the draft Charities Bill was originally introduced it was noted that there were no proper provisions dealing with costs. During the Bill's passage the issue of costs was addressed through the introduction of the new provisions contained in CA 1993 s 2B(5)–(7). These provide that if the Tribunal considers that (a) a party before it has acted vexatiously, frivolously or unreasonably, or (b) that a decision, direction or order of the Charity Commission was unreasonable it can order the offending party to pay some or all of the other party's costs in connection with the proceedings. These provisions can be criticised on two grounds. Firstly, the intent of the first costs provision is clearly to try and dissuade charity trustees from bringing appeals through the Tribunal unless they have good grounds to do so. While the economic sense of this is undeniable, it is possible that it will discourage poorer charities from utilising the Tribunal route to challenge a Commission decision for fear of the potential economic consequences. Secondly, since a charity has little chance of recovering its costs, even if it succeeds in its appeal, unless it can show that the Commission decision was unreasonable, again this will act to discourage all but those charities who feel they can afford the full legal cost of bringing an appeal. Arguably, these better off charities are the same ones that would have had the means previously to bring an appeal through the High Court. We will therefore have to wait and see if a consequence of these costs provisions is to deprive access to the Tribunal for the very charities for whom the appeals process was intended.

References to the Tribunal

12.6 As well as allowing the interested parties listed in the table above to bring appeals to the Tribunal, under CA 1993 Sch 1D the Charity

Commission is also given the right to refer questions of charity law or its application in a particular set of circumstances to the Tribunal for a ruling. In order to do so, however, the Commission requires the consent of the Attorney General. The Attorney General is also given a similar right to refer matters to the Tribunal. In either case any charity or other person who may be affected by the outcome of the issue may, with the Tribunal's permission, participate in the proceedings.

Where the Commission does decide to refer an issue of law to the Tribunal for a ruling under the rights contained in CA 1993 Sch 1D, the Commission must not rely on any previous view as to the operation of charity law concerning the facts at hand until the proceedings (including any appeal) have been concluded and any time in which to bring an appeal has expired (CA 1993 Sch 1D para 3(2)). This restriction will not, however, apply if any steps taken by the Commission in relation to the subject of the proceedings are taken with the consent of (a) the other party to the proceedings, or (b) a charity that although not a party to the proceedings would potentially be affected by their outcome (CA 1993 Sch 1D para 5(1)).

Appeals from the Tribunal

12.7 Where a party to proceedings before the Tribunal considers that there is a point of law on which it wishes to appeal, then it can bring an appeal to the High Court with either the consent of the Tribunal or the High Court (CA 1993 s 2C). As with the Tribunal itself, the High Court is entitled to consider the issue that was brought before the Tribunal and take into account any new evidence that was not previously available (CA 1993 s 2C(3)).

Appendix 1

Charities Act 1992

Charities Act 1992

1992 Chapter 41

An Act to amend the Charities Act 1960 and make other provision with respect to charities; to regulate fund-raising activities carried on in connection with charities and other institutions; to make fresh provision with respect to public charitable collections; and for connected purposes.

[16th March 1992]

BE IT ENACTED by the Queen's most Excellent Majesty, by and with the advice and consent of the Lords Spiritual and Temporal, and Commons, in this present Parliament assembled, and by the authority of the same, as follows:

Arrangement

Part I
Charities

(Notes: Repealed by the Charities Act 2006, s 75(2), Sch 9. Date in force: to be appointed: see the Charities Act 2006, s 79(2).)

Preliminary

(Notes: Repealed by the Charities Act 2006, s 75(2), Sch 9. Date in force: to be appointed: see the Charities Act 2006, s 79(2).)

1 *Interpretation of Part I, etc*

(Notes: Repealed by the Charities Act 2006, s 75(2), Sch 9. Date in force: to be appointed: see the Charities Act 2006, s 79(2).)

...

2–28 ...

Charity property

(Notes: Repealed by the Charities Act 2006, s 75(2), Sch 9. Date in force: to be appointed: see the Charities Act 2006, s 79(2).)

29 *Divestment of charity property held by official custodian for charities*

(Notes: Repealed by the Charities Act 2006, s 75(2), Sch 9. Date in force: to be appointed: see the Charities Act 2006, s 79(2).)

30 *Provisions supplementary to s 29*

(Notes: Repealed by the Charities Act 2006, s 75(2), Sch 9. Date in force: to be appointed: see the Charities Act 2006, s 79(2).)

31–35...
36 *Removal of requirements under statutory provisions for consent to dealings with charity land*

(Notes: Repealed by the Charities Act 2006, s 75(2), Sch 9; for savings see 75(2), Sch 9, para 29(1), (2)(b). Date in force: to be appointed: see the Charities Act 2006, s 79(2).)

37–46...

Miscellaneous and supplementary

(Notes: Repealed by the Charities Act 2006, s 75(2), Sch 9. Date in force: to be appointed: see the Charities Act 2006, s 79(2).)

47–48...

49 Amendment of Redundant Churches and Other Religious Buildings Act 1969

(Notes: Repealed by the Charities Act 2006, s 75(2), Sch 9; for savings see 75(2), Sch 9, para 28. Date in force: to be appointed: see the Charities Act 2006, s 79(2).)

50 Contributions towards maintenance etc of almshouses

(Notes: Repealed by the Charities Act 2006, s 75(2), Sch 9; for savings see 75(2), Sch 9, para 29(1), (2)(c). Date in force: to be appointed: see the Charities Act 2006, s 79(2).)

51–57...

Part II
Control of Fund-raising for Charitable Institutions

Preliminary

58 Interpretation of Part II

Control of fund-raising

59 Prohibition on professional fund-raiser etc raising funds for charitable institution without an agreement in prescribed form
60 Professional fund-raisers etc required to indicate institutions benefiting and arrangements for remuneration
[60A Other persons making appeals required to indicate institutions benefiting and arrangements for remuneration]

(Notes: Inserted by the Charities Act 2006, s 68. Date in force: to be appointed: see the Charities Act 2006, s 79(2).)

[60B Exclusion of lower-paid collectors from provisions of section 60A]

(Notes: Inserted by the Charities Act 2006, s 68. Date in force (for certain purposes): 27 February 2007: see SI 2007/309, art 2, Schedule.) Date in force (for remaining purposes): to be appointed: see the Charities Act 2006, s 79(2).)

61 Cancellation of payments and agreements made in response to appeals
62 Right of charitable institution to prevent unauthorised fund-raising
63 False statements relating to institutions which are not registered charities

Supplementary

64 Regulations about fund-raising
[64A Reserve power to control fund-raising by charitable institutions]

(Notes: Inserted by the Charities Act 2006, s 69. Date in force: 27 February 2007: see SI 2007/309, art 2, Schedule.)

Part III
Public Charitable Collections

(Notes: Repealed by the Charities Act 2006, s 75(1), (2), Sch 8, paras 89, 91, Sch 9. Date in force: 27 February 2007: see SI 2007/309, art 2, Schedule.)

Preliminary

(Notes: Repealed by the Charities Act 2006, s 75(1), (2), Sch 8, paras 89, 91, Sch 9. Date in force: 27 February 2007: see SI 2007/309, art 2, Schedule.)

65 *Interpretation of Part III*

(Notes: Repealed by the Charities Act 2006, s 75(1), (2), Sch 8, paras 89, 91, Sch 9. Date in force: 27 February 2007: see SI 2007/309, art 2, Schedule.)

Prohibition on conducting unauthorised collections

(Notes: Repealed by the Charities Act 2006, s 75(1), (2), Sch 8, paras 89, 91, Sch 9. Date in force: 27 February 2007: see SI 2007/309, art 2, Schedule.)

66 *Prohibition on conducting public charitable collections without authorisation*

(Notes: Repealed by the Charities Act 2006, s 75(1), (2), Sch 8, paras 89, 91, Sch 9. Date in force: 27 February 2007: see SI 2007/309, art 2, Schedule.)

Permits

(Notes: Repealed by the Charities Act 2006, s 75(1), (2), Sch 8, paras 89, 91, Sch 9. Date in force: 27 February 2007: see SI 2007/309, art 2, Schedule.)

67 *Applications for permits to conduct public charitable collections*

(Notes: Repealed by the Charities Act 2006, s 75(1), (2), Sch 8, paras 89, 91, Sch 9. Date in force: 27 February 2007: see SI 2007/309, art 2, Schedule.)

68 *Determination of applications and issue of permits*

(Notes: Repealed by the Charities Act 2006, s 75(1), (2), Sch 8, paras 89, 91, Sch 9. Date in force: 27 February 2007: see SI 2007/309, art 2, Schedule.)

69 *Refusal of permits*

(Notes: Repealed by the Charities Act 2006, s 75(1), (2), Sch 8, paras 89, 91, Sch 9. Date in force: 27 February 2007: see SI 2007/309, art 2, Schedule.)

70 *Withdrawal etc of permits*

(Notes: Repealed by the Charities Act 2006, s 75(1), (2), Sch 8, paras 89, 91, Sch 9. Date in force: 27 February 2007: see SI 2007/309, art 2, Schedule.)

71 *Appeals*

(Notes: Repealed by the Charities Act 2006, s 75(1), (2), Sch 8, paras 89, 91, Sch 9. Date in force: 27 February 2007: see SI 2007/309, art 2, Schedule.)

Orders made by Charity Commissioners

(Notes: Repealed by the Charities Act 2006, s 75(1), (2), Sch 8, paras 89, 91, Sch 9. Date in force: 27 February 2007: see SI 2007/309, art 2, Schedule.)

72 *Orders made by Charity Commissioners*

(Notes: Repealed by the Charities Act 2006, s 75(1), (2), Sch 8, paras 89, 91, Sch 9. Date in force: 27 February 2007: see SI 2007/309, art 2, Schedule.)

Supplementary

(Notes: Repealed by the Charities Act 2006, s 75(1), (2), Sch 8, paras 89, 91, Sch 9. Date in force: 27 February 2007: see SI 2007/309, art 2, Schedule.)

73 *Regulations*

(Notes: Repealed by the Charities Act 2006, s 75(1), (2), Sch 8, paras 89, 91, Sch 9. Date in force: 27 February 2007: see SI 2007/309, art 2, Schedule.)

Part I
Charities

NOTES

Amendment

Repealed by the Charities Act 2006, s 75(2), Sch 9.

Date in force: to be appointed: see the Charities Act 2006, s 79(2).

Preliminary

NOTES

Amendment

Repealed by the Charities Act 2006, s 75(2), Sch 9.

Date in force: to be appointed: see the Charities Act 2006, s 79(2).

1 Interpretation of Part I, etc

(1) In this Part—

'the 1960 Act' means the Charities Act 1960;
'financial year'—
- *(a) in relation to a charity which is a company, shall be construed in accordance with section 223 of the Companies Act 1985; and*
- *(b) in relation to any other charity, shall be construed in accordance with regulations made by virtue of section 20(2);*

'gross income', in relation to a charity, means its gross recorded income from all sources, including special trusts;
'independent examiner', in relation to a charity, means such a person as is mentioned in section 21(3)(a);
'the official custodian' means the official custodian for charities;
'the register' (unless the context otherwise requires) means the register of charities kept under section 4 of the 1960 Act, and 'registered' shall be construed accordingly;
'special trust' means property which is held and administered by or on behalf of a charity for any special purposes of the charity, and is so held and administered on separate trusts relating only to that property.

(2), (3) < . . . >

(4) No vesting or transfer of any property in pursuance of any provision of this Part, or of any provision of the 1960 Act as amended by this Part, shall operate as a breach of a covenant or condition against alienation or give rise to a forfeiture.

NOTES

Initial Commencement

To be appointed: see s 79(2).

Appointment

Sub-s (1): Appointment (in part): 1 September 1992: see SI 1992/1900, art 2, Sch 1.

Sub-s (3): Appointment: 1 September 1992: see SI 1992/1900, art 2, Sch 1.

Extent

This Act does not extend to Scotland: see s 79(3).

Amendment

Repealed by the Charities Act 2006, s 75(2), Sch 9.

Date in force: to be appointed: see the Charities Act 2006, s 79(2).

Sub-ss (2), (3): repealed by the Charities Act 1993, s 98(2), Sch 7.

...

2–28 ...

...

NOTES

Amendment

Repealed by the Charities Act 1993, s 98(2), Sch 7.

Charity property

NOTES

Amendment

Repealed by the Charities Act 2006, s 75(2), Sch 9.

Date in force: to be appointed: see the Charities Act 2006, s 79(2).

29 Divestment of charity property held by official custodian for charities

(1) The official custodian shall, in accordance with this section, divest himself of all property to which this subsection applies.

(2) Subsection (1) applies to any property held by the official custodian in his capacity as such, with the exception of—

- *(a) any land; and*
- *(b) any property (other than land) which is vested in him by virtue of an order of the Commissioners under section 20 of the 1960 Act [or section 18 of the Charities Act 1993] (power to act for protection of charities).*

(3) Where property to which subsection (1) applies is held by the official custodian in trust for particular charities, he shall (subject to subsection (7)) divest himself of that property in such manner as the Commissioners may direct.

(4) Without prejudice to the generality of subsection (3), directions given by the Commissioners under that subsection may make different provision in relation to different property held by the official custodian or in relation to different classes or descriptions of property held by him, including (in particular)—

- *(a) provision designed to secure that the divestment required by subsection (1) is effected in stages or by means of transfers or other disposals taking place at different times;*
- *(b) provision requiring the official custodian to transfer any specified investments, or any specified class or description of investments, held by him in trust for a charity—*
  - *(i) to the charity trustees or any trustee for the charity, or*
  - *(ii) to a person nominated by the charity trustees to hold any such investments in trust for the charity;*
- *(c) provision requiring the official custodian to sell or call in any specified investments, or any specified class or description of investments, so held by him and to pay any proceeds of sale or other money accruing therefrom—*
  - *(i) to the charity trustees or any trustee for the charity, or*
  - *(ii) into any bank account kept in its name.*

(5) The charity trustees of a charity may, in the case of any property falling to be transferred by the official custodian in accordance with a direction under subsection (3), nominate a person to hold any such property in trust for the charity; but a person shall not be so nominated unless—

- *(a) if an individual, he resides in England and Wales; or*
- *(b) if a body corporate, it has a place of business there.*

(6) Directions under subsection (3) shall, in the case of any property vested in the official custodian by virtue of section 22(6) of the 1960 Act (common investment funds), provide for any such property to be transferred—

- *(a) to the trustees appointed to manage the common investment fund concerned; or*
- *(b) to any person nominated by those trustees who is authorised by or under the common investment scheme concerned to hold that fund or any part of it.*

(7) Where the official custodian—

(a) *holds any relevant property in trust for a charity, but*
(b) *after making reasonable inquiries is unable to locate the charity or any of its trustees,*

he shall—

(i) *unless the relevant property is money, sell the property and hold the proceeds of sale pending the giving by the Commissioners of a direction under subsection (8);*
(ii) *if the relevant property is money, hold it pending the giving of any such direction;*

and for this purpose 'relevant property' means any property to which subsection (1) applies or any proceeds of sale or other money accruing to the official custodian in consequence of a direction under subsection (3).

(8) Where subsection (7) applies in relation to a charity ('the dormant charity'), the Commissioners may direct the official custodian—

(a) *to pay such amount as is held by him in accordance with that subsection to such other charity as is specified in the direction in accordance with subsection (9), or*
(b) *to pay to each of two or more other charities so specified in the direction such part of that amount as is there specified in relation to that charity.*

(9) The Commissioners may specify in a direction under subsection (8) such charity or charities as they consider appropriate, being in each case a charity whose purposes are, in the opinion of the Commissioners, as similar in character to those of the dormant charity as is reasonably practicable; but the Commissioners shall not so specify any charity unless they have received from the charity trustees written confirmation that they are willing to accept the amount proposed to be paid to the charity.

(10) Any amount received by a charity by virtue of subsection (8) shall be received by the charity on terms that—

(a) *it shall be held and applied by the charity for the purposes of the charity, but*
(b) *it shall, as property of the charity, nevertheless be subject to any restrictions on expenditure to which it, or (as the case may be) the property which it represents, was subject as property of the dormant charity.*

(11) At such time as the Commissioners are satisfied that the official custodian has divested himself of all property held by him in trust for particular charities, all remaining funds held by him as official custodian shall be paid by him into the Consolidated Fund.

(12) Nothing in subsection (11) applies in relation to any property held by the official custodian which falls within subsection (2)(a) or (b).

(13) In this section 'land' does not include any interest in land by way of mortgage or other security.

NOTES

Initial Commencement

To be appointed: see s 79(2).

Appointment

Appointment: 1 September 1992: see SI 1992/1900, art 2, Sch 1.

Extent

This Act does not extend to Scotland: see s 79(3).

Amendment

Repealed by the Charities Act 2006, s 75(2), Sch 9.

Date in force: to be appointed: see the Charities Act 2006, s 79(2).

Sub-s (2): in para (b) words in square brackets inserted by the Charities Act 1993, s 98(1), Sch 6, para 29(2).

30 Provisions supplementary to s 29

(1) Any directions of the Commissioners under section 29 above shall have effect notwithstanding anything—

(a) in the trusts of a charity, or
(b) in section 17(1) of the 1960 Act [or section 22(1) of the Charities Act 1993] (supplementary provisions as to property vested in official custodian).

(2) Subject to subsection (3), any provision—

(a) of the trusts of a charity, or
(b) of any directions given by an order of the Commissioners made in connection with a transaction requiring the sanction of an order under section 29(1) of the 1960 Act (restrictions on dealing with charity property),

shall cease to have effect if and to the extent that it requires or authorises personal property of the charity to be transferred to or held by the official custodian; and for this purpose 'personal property' extends to any mortgage or other real security, but does not include any interest in land other than such an interest by way of mortgage or other security.

(3) Subsection (2) does not apply to—

(a) any provision of an order made under section 20 of the 1960 Act [or section 18 of the Charities Act 1993] (power to act for protection of charities); or
(b) any provision of any other order, or of any scheme, of the Commissioners if the provision requires trustees of a charity to make payments into an account maintained by the official custodian with a view to the accumulation of a sum as capital of the charity (whether or not by way of recoupment of a sum expended out of the charity's permanent endowment);

but any such provision as is mentioned in paragraph (b) shall have effect as if, instead of requiring the trustees to make such payments into an account maintained by the official custodian, it required the trustees to make such payments into an account maintained by them or by any other person (apart from the official custodian) who is either a trustee for the charity or a person nominated by them to hold such payments in trust for the charity.

(4) The disposal of any property by the official custodian in accordance with section 29 above shall operate to discharge him from his trusteeship of that property.

(5) Where any instrument issued by the official custodian in connection with any such disposal contains a printed reproduction of his official seal, that instrument shall have the same effect as if it were duly sealed with his official seal.

NOTES

Initial Commencement

To be appointed: see s 79(2).

Appointment

Appointment: 1 September 1992: see SI 1992/1900, art 2, Sch 1.

Extent

This Act does not extend to Scotland: see s 79(3).

Amendment

Repealed by the Charities Act 2006, s 75(2), Sch 9.

Date in force: to be appointed: see the Charities Act 2006, s 79(2).

Sub-ss (1), (3): words in square brackets inserted by the Charities Act 1993, s 98(1), Sch 6, para 29(3), (4).

31–35 ...

...

NOTES

Amendment

Repealed by the Charities Act 1993, s 98(2), Sch 7.

36 Removal of requirements under statutory provisions for consent to dealings with charity land

(1) Any provision—

(a) establishing or regulating a particular charity and contained in, or having effect under, any Act of Parliament, or
(b) contained in the trusts of a charity,

shall cease to have effect if and to the extent that it provides for dispositions of, or other dealings with, land held by or in trust for the charity to require the consent of the Commissioners (whether signified by order or otherwise).

(2) Any provision of an order or scheme under the Education Act 1944 or the Education Act 1973 relating to a charity shall cease to have effect if and to the extent that it requires, in relation to any sale, lease or other disposition of land held by or in trust for the charity, approval by the Commissioners or the Secretary of State of the amount for which the land is to be sold, leased or otherwise disposed of.

(3) In this section 'land' means land in England or Wales.

NOTES

Initial Commencement

To be appointed: see s 79(2).

Appointment

Appointment: 1 January 1993: see SI 1992/1900, art 4, Sch 3.

Extent

This Act does not extend to Scotland: see s 79(3).

Amendment

Repealed by the Charities Act 2006, s 75(2), Sch 9; for savings see 75(2), Sch 9, para 29(1), (2)(b).

Date in force: to be appointed: see the Charities Act 2006, s 79(2).

37–46 ...

...

NOTES

Amendment

Repealed by the Charities Act 1993, s 98(2), Sch 7.

Miscellaneous and supplementary

NOTES

Amendment

Repealed by the Charities Act 2006, s 75(2), Sch 9.

Date in force: to be appointed: see the Charities Act 2006, s 79(2).

47–48 ...

...

NOTES

Amendment

Repealed by the Charities Act 1993, s 98(2), Sch 7.

49 Amendment of Redundant Churches and Other Religious Buildings Act 1969

The Redundant Churches and Other Religious Buildings Act 1969 shall have effect subject to the amendments specified in Schedule 5 to this Act.

NOTES

Initial Commencement

To be appointed: see s 79(2).

Appointment

Appointment: 1 September 1992: see SI 1992/1900, art 2, Sch 1.

Extent

This Act does not extend to Scotland: see s 79(3).

Amendment

Repealed by the Charities Act 2006, s 75(2), Sch 9; for savings see 75(2), Sch 9, para 28.

Date in force: to be appointed: see the Charities Act 2006, s 79(2).

50 Contributions towards maintenance etc of almshouses

(1) Any provision in the trusts of an almshouse charity which relates to the payment by persons resident in the charity's almshouses of contributions towards the cost of maintaining those almshouses and essential services in them shall cease to have effect if and to the extent that it provides for the amount, or the maximum amount, of such contributions to be a sum specified, approved or authorised by the Commissioners.

(2) In subsection (1)—

'almshouse' means any premises maintained as an almshouse, whether they are called an almshouse or not; and
'almshouse charity' means a charity which is authorised under its trusts to maintain almshouses.

NOTES

Initial Commencement

To be appointed: see s 79(2).

Appointment

Appointment: 1 September 1992: see SI 1992/1900, art 2, Sch 1.

Extent

This Act does not extend to Scotland: see s 79(3).

Amendment

Repealed by the Charities Act 2006, s 75(2), Sch 9; for savings see 75(2), Sch 9, para 29(1), (2)(c).

Date in force: to be appointed: see the Charities Act 2006, s 79(2).

51–57 ...

...

NOTES

Amendment

Repealed by the Charities Act 1993, s 98(2), Sch 7.

Part II
Control of Fund-raising for Charitable Institutions

Preliminary

58 Interpretation of Part II

(1) In this Part—

'charitable contributions', in relation to any representation made by any commercial participator or other person, means—
- (a) the whole or part of—
  - (i) the consideration given for goods or services sold or supplied by him, or
  - (ii) any proceeds (other than such consideration) of a promotional venture undertaken by him, or
- (b) sums given by him by way of donation in connection with the sale or supply of any such goods or services (whether the amount of such sums is determined by reference to the value of any such goods or services or otherwise);

'charitable institution' means a charity or an institution (other than a charity) which is established for charitable, benevolent or philanthropic purposes;
'charity' means a charity within the meaning of [the Charities Act 1993];
'commercial participator', in relation to any charitable institution, means any person [(apart from a company connected with the institution)] who—
- (a) carries on for gain a business other than a fund-raising business, but
- (b) in the course of that business, engages in any promotional venture in the course of which it is represented that charitable contributions are to be given to or applied for the benefit of the institution;

'company' has the meaning given by section [97 of the Charities Act 1993];
'the court' means the High Court or a county court;
'credit card' means a card which is a credit-token within the meaning of the Consumer Credit Act 1974;

'debit card' means a card the use of which by its holder to make a payment results in a current account of his at a bank, or at any other institution providing banking services, being debited with the payment;
'fund-raising business' means any business carried on for gain and wholly or primarily engaged in soliciting or otherwise procuring money or other property for charitable, benevolent or philanthropic purposes;
'institution' includes any trust or undertaking;
['the Minister' means the Minister for the Cabinet Office;]
'professional fund-raiser' means—

(a) any person (apart from a charitable institution [or a company connected with such an institution]) who carries on a fund-raising business, or
(b) any other person (apart from a person excluded by virtue of subsection (2) or (3)) who for reward solicits money or other property for the benefit of a charitable institution, if he does so otherwise than in the course of any fund-raising venture undertaken by a person falling within paragraph (a) above;

'promotional venture' means any advertising or sales campaign or any other venture undertaken for promotional purposes;
'radio or television programme' includes any item included in a programme service within the meaning of the Broadcasting Act 1990.

(2) In subsection (1), paragraph (b) of the definition of 'professional fund-raiser' does not apply to any of the following, namely—

(a) any charitable institution or any company connected with any such institution;
(b) any officer or employee of any such institution or company, or any trustee of any such institution, acting (in each case) in his capacity as such;
(c) any person acting as a collector in respect of a public charitable collection (apart from a person who is *to be treated as a promoter of such a collection by virtue of section 65(3)* [a promoter of such a collection as defined in section 47(1) of the Charities Act 2006]);
(d) any person who in the course of a relevant programme, that is to say a radio or television programme in the course of which a fund-raising venture is undertaken by—
  (i) a charitable institution, or
  (ii) a company connected with such an institution,
  makes any solicitation at the instance of that institution or company; or
(e) any commercial participator;

and for this purpose 'collector' and 'public charitable collection' have the same meaning as in *Part III of this Act* [Chapter 1 of Part 3 of the Charities Act 2006].

(3) In addition, paragraph (b) of the definition of 'professional fund-raiser' does not apply to a person if he does not receive—

(a) more than—
  (i) £5 per day, or
  (ii) £500 per year,
  by way of remuneration in connection with soliciting money or other property for the benefit of the charitable institution referred to in that paragraph; or
(b) more than £500 by way of remuneration in connection with any fund-raising venture in the course of which he solicits money or other property for the benefit of that institution.

(4) In this Part any reference to charitable purposes, where occurring in the context of a reference to charitable, benevolent or philanthropic purposes, is a reference to charitable purposes *whether or not the purposes are charitable within the meaning of any rule of law* [as defined by section 2(1) of the Charities Act 2006].

(5) For the purposes of this Part a company is connected with a charitable institution if—

(a) the institution, or
(b) the institution and one or more other charitable institutions, taken together,

is or are entitled (whether directly or through one or more nominees) to exercise, or control the exercise of, the whole of the voting power at any general meeting of the company.

(6) In this Part—

(a) 'represent' and 'solicit' mean respectively represent and solicit in any manner whatever, whether expressly or impliedly and whether done—
   (i) by speaking directly to the person or persons to whom the representation or solicitation is addressed (whether when in his or their presence or not), or
   (ii) by means of a statement published in any newspaper, film or radio or television programme,

   or otherwise, and references to a representation or solicitation shall be construed accordingly; and
(b) any reference to soliciting or otherwise procuring money or other property is a reference to soliciting or otherwise procuring money or other property whether any consideration is, or is to be, given in return for the money or other property or not.

(7) Where—

(a) any solicitation of money or other property for the benefit of a charitable institution is made in accordance with arrangements between any person and that institution, and
(b) under those arrangements that person will be responsible for receiving on behalf of the institution money or other property given in response to the solicitation,

then (if he would not be so regarded apart from this subsection) that person shall be regarded for the purposes of this Part as soliciting money or other property for the benefit of the institution.

(8) Where any fund-raising venture is undertaken by a professional fund-raiser in the course of a radio or television programme, any solicitation which is made by a person in the course of the programme at the instance of the fund-raiser shall be regarded for the purposes of this Part as made by the fund-raiser and not by that person (and shall be so regarded whether or not the solicitation is made by that person for any reward).

(9) In this Part 'services' includes facilities, and in particular—

(a) access to any premises or event;
(b) membership of any organisation;
(c) the provision of advertising space; and
(d) the provision of any financial facilities;

and references to the supply of services shall be construed accordingly.

(10) The [Minister] may by order amend subsection (3) by substituting a different sum for any sum for the time being specified there.

NOTES

Initial Commencement

To be appointed: see s 79(2).

Appointment

Appointment: 1 March 1995: see SI 1994/3023, art 2.

Extent

This Act does not extend to Scotland: see s 79(3).

Amendment

Sub-s (1): in definitions 'charity' words 'the Charities Act 1993' in square brackets substituted by the Charities Act 1993, s 98(1), Sch 6, para 29(5).

Sub-s (1): in definition 'commercial participator' words '(apart from a company connected with the institution' in square brackets inserted by the Deregulation and Contracting Out Act 1994, s 25.

Sub-s (1): in definitions 'company' words '97 of the Charities Act 1993' in square brackets substituted by the Charities Act 1993, s 98(1), Sch 6, para 29(5).

Sub-s (1): definition 'the Minister' inserted by the Charities Act 2006, s 75(1), Sch 8, paras 89, 90(1), (2).

Date in force: 8 November 2006: see the Charities Act 2006, s 79(1)(g).

Sub-s (1): in definition 'professional fund-raiser' words 'or a company connected with such an institution' in square brackets inserted by the Deregulation and Contracting Out Act 1994, s 25.

Sub-s (2): words 'to be treated as a promoter of such a collection by virtue of section 65(3)' in italics repealed and subsequent words in square brackets substituted by the Charities Act 2006, s 75(1), Sch 8, paras 89, 90(1), (3)(a).

Date in force: to be appointed: see the Charities Act 2006, s 79(2).

Sub-s (2): words 'Part III of this Act' in italics repealed and subsequent words in square brackets substituted by the Charities Act 2006, s 75(1), Sch 8, paras 89, 90(1), (3)(b).

Date in force: to be appointed: see the Charities Act 2006, s 79(2).

Sub-s (4): words 'whether or not the purposes are charitable within the meaning of any rule of law' in italics repealed and subsequent words in square brackets substituted by the Charities Act 2006, s 75(1), Sch 8, paras 89, 90(1), (4).

Date in force: to be appointed: see the Charities Act 2006, s 79(2).

Sub-s (10): word 'Minister' in square brackets substituted by SI 2006/2951, art 6, Schedule, para 3(a).

Date in force: 13 December 2006: see SI 2006/2951, art 1(2).

Control of fund-raising

59 Prohibition on professional fund-raiser etc raising funds for charitable institution without an agreement in prescribed form

(1) It shall be unlawful for a professional fund-raiser to solicit money or other property for the benefit of a charitable institution unless he does so in accordance with an agreement with the institution satisfying the prescribed requirements.

(2) It shall be unlawful for a commercial participator to represent that charitable contributions are to be given to or applied for the benefit of a charitable institution unless he does so in accordance with an agreement with the institution satisfying the prescribed requirements.

(3) Where on the application of a charitable institution the court is satisfied—

(a) that any person has contravened or is contravening subsection (1) or (2) in relation to the institution, and
(b) that, unless restrained, any such contravention is likely to continue or be repeated,

the court may grant an injunction restraining the contravention; and compliance with subsection (1) or (2) shall not be enforceable otherwise than in accordance with this subsection.

(4) Where—

(a) a charitable institution makes any agreement with a professional fund-raiser or a commercial participator by virtue of which—

(i) the professional fund-raiser is authorised to solicit money or other property for the benefit of the institution, or

(ii) the commercial participator is authorised to represent that charitable contributions are to be given to or applied for the benefit of the institution,

as the case may be, but

(b) the agreement does not satisfy the prescribed requirements in any respect,

the agreement shall not be enforceable against the institution except to such extent (if any) as may be provided by an order of the court.

(5) A professional fund-raiser or commercial participator who is a party to such an agreement as is mentioned in subsection (4)(a) shall not be entitled to receive any amount by way of remuneration or expenses in respect of anything done by him in pursuance of the agreement unless—

(a) he is so entitled under any provision of the agreement, and

(b) either—

(i) the agreement satisfies the prescribed requirements, or

(ii) any such provision has effect by virtue of an order of the court under subsection (4).

(6) In this section 'the prescribed requirements' means such requirements as are prescribed by regulations made by virtue of section 64(2)(a).

NOTES

Initial Commencement

To be appointed: see s 79(2).

Appointment

Appointment (for the purpose of exercising the power to make regulations): 28 November 1994: see SI 1994/3023, art 2.

Appointment (for remaining purposes): 1 March 1995: see SI 1994/3023, art 2.

Extent

This Act does not extend to Scotland: see s 79(3).

60 Professional fund-raisers etc required to indicate institutions benefiting and arrangements for remuneration

(1) Where a professional fund-raiser solicits money or other property for the benefit of one or more particular charitable institutions, the solicitation shall be accompanied by a statement clearly indicating—

(a) the name or names of the institution or institutions concerned;

(b) if there is more than one institution concerned, the proportions in which the institutions are respectively to benefit; and

(c) (in general terms) the method by which the fund-raiser's remuneration in connection with the appeal is to be determined

[(c) the method by which the fund-raiser's remuneration in connection with the appeal is to be determined and the notifiable amount of that remuneration].

(2) Where a professional fund-raiser solicits money or other property for charitable, benevolent or philanthropic purposes of any description (rather than for the benefit of one or more particular charitable institutions), the solicitation shall be accompanied by a statement clearly indicating—

(a) the fact that he is soliciting money or other property for those purposes and not for the benefit of any particular charitable institution or institutions;

(b) the method by which it is to be determined how the proceeds of the appeal are to be distributed between different charitable institutions; and

(c) (in general terms) the method by which his remuneration in connection with the appeal is to be determined

[(c) the method by which his remuneration in connection with the appeal is to be determined and the notifiable amount of that remuneration].

(3) Where any representation is made by a commercial participator to the effect that charitable contributions are to be given to or applied for the benefit of one or more particular charitable institutions, the representation shall be accompanied by a statement clearly indicating—

(a) the name or names of the institution or institutions concerned;

(b) if there is more than one institution concerned, the proportions in which the institutions are respectively to benefit; and

(c) (in general terms) the method by which it is to be determined—

(i) what proportion of the consideration given for goods or services sold or supplied by him, or of any other proceeds of a promotional venture undertaken by him, is to be given to or applied for the benefit of the institution or institutions concerned, or

(ii) what sums by way of donations by him in connection with the sale or supply of any such goods or services are to be so given or applied,

as the case may require

[(c) the notifiable amount of whichever of the following sums is applicable in the circumstances—

(i) the sum representing so much of the consideration given for goods or services sold or supplied by him as is to be given to or applied for the benefit of the institution or institutions concerned,

(ii) the sum representing so much of any other proceeds of a promotional venture undertaken by him as is to be so given or applied, or

(iii) the sum of the donations by him in connection with the sale or supply of any such goods or services which are to be so given or supplied].

[(3A) In subsections (1) to (3) a reference to the 'notifiable amount' of any remuneration or other sum is a reference—

(a) to the actual amount of the remuneration or sum, if that is known at the time when the statement is made; and

(b) otherwise to the estimated amount of the remuneration or sum, calculated as accurately as is reasonably possible in the circumstances.]

(4) If any such solicitation or representation as is mentioned in any of subsections (1) to (3) is made—

(a) in the course of a radio or television programme, and

(b) in association with an announcement to the effect that payment may be made, in response to the solicitation or representation, by means of a credit or debit card,

the statement required by virtue of subsection (1), (2) or (3) (as the case may be) shall include full details of the right to have refunded under section 61(1) any payment of £50 or more which is so made.

(5) If any such solicitation or representation as is mentioned in any of subsections (1) to (3) is made orally but is not made—

(a) by speaking directly to the particular person or persons to whom it is addressed and in his or their presence, or

(b) in the course of any radio or television programme,

the professional fund-raiser or commercial participator concerned shall, within seven days of any payment of £50 or more being made to him in response to the solicitation or representation, give to the person making the payment a written statement—

(i) of the matters specified in paragraphs (a) to (c) of that subsection; and
(ii) including full details of the right to cancel under section 61(2) an agreement made in response to the solicitation or representation, and the right to have refunded under section 61(2) or (3) any payment of £50 or more made in response thereto.

(6) In subsection (5) above the reference to the making of a payment is a reference to the making of a payment of whatever nature and by whatever means, including a payment made by means of a credit card or a debit card; and for the purposes of that subsection—

(a) where the person making any such payment makes it in person, it shall be regarded as made at the time when it is so made;
(b) where the person making any such payment sends it by post, it shall be regarded as made at the time when it is posted; and
(c) where the person making any such payment makes it by giving, by telephone or by means of any other [electronic communications apparatus], authority for an account to be debited with the payment, it shall be regarded as made at the time when any such authority is given.

(7) Where any requirement of subsections (1) to (5) is not complied with in relation to any solicitation or representation, the professional fund-raiser or commercial participator concerned shall be guilty of an offence and liable on summary conviction to a fine not exceeding the fifth level on the standard scale.

(8) It shall be a defence for a person charged with any such offence to prove that he took all reasonable precautions and exercised all due diligence to avoid the commission of the offence.

(9) Where the commission by any person of an offence under subsection (7) is due to the act or default of some other person, that other person shall be guilty of the offence; and a person may be charged with and convicted of the offence by virtue of this subsection whether or not proceedings are taken against the first-mentioned person.

(10) In this section—

'the appeal', in relation to any solicitation by a professional fund- raiser, means the campaign or other fund-raising venture in the course of which the solicitation is made;

...

NOTES

Initial Commencement

To be appointed: see s 79(2).

Appointment

Appointment: 1 March 1995: see SI 1994/3023, art 2.

Extent

This Act does not extend to Scotland: see s 79(3).

Amendment

Sub-s (1): para (c) substituted by the Charities Act 2006, s 67(1), (2); for transitional provisions and savings see s 75(3), Sch 10, para 15 thereto.

Date in force: to be appointed: see the Charities Act 2006, s 79(2).

Sub-s (2): para (c) substituted by the Charities Act 2006, s 67(1), (3); for transitional provisions and savings see s 75(3), Sch 10, para 15 thereto.

Date in force: to be appointed: see the Charities Act 2006, s 79(2).

Sub-s (3): para (c) substituted by the Charities Act 2006, s 67(1), (4); for transitional provisions and savings see s 75(3), Sch 10, para 15 thereto.

Date in force: to be appointed: see the Charities Act 2006, s 79(2).

Sub-s (3A): inserted by the Charities Act 2006, s 67(1), (5); for transitional provisions and savings see s 75(3), Sch 10, para 15 thereto.

Date in force: to be appointed: see the Charities Act 2006, s 79(2).

Sub-s (6): in para (c) words 'electronic communications apparatus' in square brackets substituted by the Communications Act 2003, s 406(1), Sch 17, para 118.

Date in force (for the purpose only of enabling the networks and services functions and the spectrum functions to be carried out by the Director General of Telecommunications and the Secretary of State respectively, during the transitional period (as provided for by the Communications Act 2003, s 408(6)): 25 July 2003–29 December 2003: see SI 2003/1900, arts 2(1), 3(1), Sch 1 and the Communications Act 2003, ss 406(6), 408, Sch 18, para 2.

Date in force (for the purpose of conferring the networks and services functions and the spectrum functions on OFCOM): 29 December 2003: by virtue of SI 2003/3142, art 3(2).

Sub-s (10): definition 'telecommunication apparatus' (omitted) repealed by the Communications Act 2003, s 406(7), Sch 19(1).

Date in force (for the purpose only of enabling the networks and services functions and the spectrum functions to be carried out by the Director General of Telecommunications and the Secretary of State respectively, during the transitional period (as provided for by the Communications Act 2003, s 408(6)): 25 July 2003–29 December 2003: see SI 2003/1900, arts 2(1), 3(1), Sch 1 and the Communications Act 2003, ss 406(6), 408, Sch 18, para 2.

Date in force (for the purpose of conferring the networks and services functions and the spectrum functions on OFCOM): 29 December 2003: by virtue of SI 2003/3142, art 3(2).

[60A Other persons making appeals required to indicate institutions benefiting and arrangements for remuneration]

[(1) Subsections (1) and (2) of section 60 apply to a person acting for reward as a collector in respect of a public charitable collection as they apply to a professional fund-raiser.

(2) But those subsections do not so apply to a person excluded by virtue of—

(a) subsection (3) below, or
(b) section 60B(1) (exclusion of lower-paid collectors).

(3) Those subsections do not so apply to a person if—

(a) section 60(1) or (2) applies apart from subsection (1) (by virtue of the exception in section 58(2)(c) for persons treated as promoters), or
(b) subsection (4) or (5) applies,

in relation to his acting for reward as a collector in respect of the collection mentioned in subsection (1) above.

(4) Where a person within subsection (6) solicits money or other property for the benefit of one or more particular charitable institutions, the solicitation shall be accompanied by a statement clearly indicating—

(a) the name or names of the institution or institutions for whose benefit the solicitation is being made;
(b) if there is more than one such institution, the proportions in which the institutions are respectively to benefit;
(c) the fact that he is an officer, employee or trustee of the institution or company mentioned in subsection (6); and
(d) the fact that he is receiving remuneration as an officer, employee or trustee or (as the case may be) for acting as a collector.

(5) Where a person within subsection (6) solicits money or other property for charitable, benevolent or philanthropic purposes of any description (rather than for the benefit of one or more particular charitable institutions), the solicitation shall be accompanied by a statement clearly indicating—

(a) the fact that he is soliciting money or other property for those purposes and not for the benefit of any particular charitable institution or institutions;
(b) the method by which it is to be determined how the proceeds of the appeal are to be distributed between different charitable institutions;
(c) the fact that he is an officer, employee or trustee of the institution or company mentioned in subsection (6); and
(d) the fact that he is receiving remuneration as an officer, employee or trustee or (as the case may be) for acting as a collector.

(6) A person is within this subsection if—

(a) he is an officer or employee of a charitable institution or a company connected with any such institution, or a trustee of any such institution,
(b) he is acting as a collector in that capacity, and
(c) he receives remuneration either in his capacity as officer, employee or trustee or for acting as a collector.

(7) But a person is not within subsection (6) if he is excluded by virtue of section 60B(4).

(8) Where any requirement of—

(a) subsection (1) or (2) of section 60, as it applies by virtue of subsection (1) above, or
(b) subsection (4) or (5) above,

is not complied with in relation to any solicitation, the collector concerned shall be guilty of an offence and liable on summary conviction to a fine not exceeding level 5 on the standard scale.

(9) Section 60(8) and (9) apply in relation to an offence under subsection (8) above as they apply in relation to an offence under section 60(7).

(10) In this section—

'the appeal', in relation to any solicitation by a collector, means the campaign or other fund-raising venture in the course of which the solicitation is made;
'collector' has the meaning given by section 47(1) of the Charities Act 2006;
'public charitable collection' has the meaning given by section 45 of that Act.]

NOTES

Amendment

Inserted by the Charities Act 2006, s 68.

Date in force: to be appointed: see the Charities Act 2006, s 79(2).

[60B Exclusion of lower-paid collectors from provisions of section 60A]

[(1) Section 60(1) and (2) do not apply (by virtue of section 60A(1)) to a person who is under the earnings limit in subsection (2) below.

(2) A person is under the earnings limit in this subsection if he does not receive—

(a) more than—
 (i) £5 per day, or
 (ii) £500 per year,
 by way of remuneration for acting as a collector in relation to relevant collections, or
(b) more than £500 by way of remuneration for acting as a collector in relation to the collection mentioned in section 60A(1).

(3) In subsection (2) 'relevant collections' means public charitable collections conducted for the benefit of—

(a) the charitable institution or institutions, or
(b) the charitable, benevolent or philanthropic purposes,

for whose benefit the collection mentioned in section 60A(1) is conducted.

(4) A person is not within section 60A(6) if he is under the earnings limit in subsection (5) below.

(5) A person is under the earnings limit in this subsection if the remuneration received by him as mentioned in section 60A(6)(c)—

(a) is not more than—
 (i) £5 per day, or
 (ii) £500 per year, or
(b) if a lump sum, is not more than £500.

(6) The Minister may by order amend subsections (2) and (5) by substituting a different sum for any sum for the time being specified there.]

NOTES

Amendment

Inserted by the Charities Act 2006, s 68.

Date in force (for remaining purposes): to be appointed: see the Charities Act 2006, s 79(2).

61 Cancellation of payments and agreements made in response to appeals

(1) Where—

(a) a person ('the donor'), in response to any such solicitation or representation as is mentioned in any of subsections (1) to (3) of section 60 which is made in the course of a radio or television programme, makes any payment of £50 or more to the relevant fund-raiser by means of a credit card or a debit card, but
(b) before the end of the period of seven days beginning with the date of the solicitation or representation, the donor serves on the relevant fund-raiser a notice in writing which, however expressed, indicates the donor's intention to cancel the payment,

the donor shall (subject to subsection (4) below) be entitled to have the payment refunded to him forthwith by the relevant fund-raiser.

(2) Where—

(a) a person ('the donor'), in response to any solicitation or representation falling within subsection (5) of section 60, enters into an agreement with the relevant fund-raiser under which the donor is, or may be, liable to make any payment or payments to the relevant fund-raiser, and the amount or aggregate amount which the donor is, or may be, liable to pay to him under the agreement is £50 or more, but
(b) before the end of the period of seven days beginning with the date when he is given any such written statement as is referred to in that subsection, the donor serves on the relevant fund-raiser a notice in writing which, however expressed, indicates the donor's intention to cancel the agreement,

the notice shall operate, as from the time when it is so served, to cancel the agreement and any liability of any person other than the donor in connection with the making of any such payment or payments, and the donor shall (subject to subsection (4) below) be entitled to have any payment of £50 or more made by him under the agreement refunded to him forthwith by the relevant fund-raiser.

(3) Where, in response to any solicitation or representation falling within subsection (5) of section 60, a person ('the donor')—

(a) makes any payment of £50 or more to the relevant fund-raiser, but
(b) does not enter into any such agreement as is mentioned in subsection (2) above,

then, if before the end of the period of seven days beginning with the date when the donor is given any such written statement as is referred to in subsection (5) of that section, the donor serves on the relevant fund-raiser a notice in writing which, however expressed, indicates the donor's intention to cancel the payment, the donor shall (subject to subsection (4) below) be entitled to have the payment refunded to him forthwith by the relevant fund-raiser.

(4) The right of any person to have a payment refunded to him under any of subsections (1) to (3) above—

(a) is a right to have refunded to him the amount of the payment less any administrative expenses reasonably incurred by the relevant fund-raiser in connection with—
  (i) the making of the refund, or
  (ii) (in the case of a refund under subsection (2)) dealing with the notice of cancellation served by that person; and
(b) shall, in the case of a payment for goods already received, be conditional upon restitution being made by him of the goods in question.

(5) Nothing in subsections (1) to (3) above has effect in relation to any payment made or to be made in respect of services which have been supplied at the time when the relevant notice is served.

(6) In this section any reference to the making of a payment is a reference to the making of a payment of whatever nature and (in the case of subsection (2) or (3)) a payment made by whatever means, including a payment made by means of a credit card or a debit card; and subsection (6) of section 60 shall have effect for determining when a payment is made for the purposes of this section as it has effect for determining when a payment is made for the purposes of subsection (5) of that section.

(7) In this section 'the relevant fund-raiser', in relation to any solicitation or representation, means the professional fund-raiser or commercial participator by whom it is made.

(8) The [Minister] may by order—

(a) amend any provision of this section by substituting a different sum for the sum for the time being specified there; and
(b) make such consequential amendments in section 60 as he considers appropriate.

NOTES

Initial Commencement

To be appointed: see s 79(2).

Appointment

Appointment: 1 March 1995: see SI 1994/3023, art 2.

Extent

This Act does not extend to Scotland: see s 79(3).

Amendment

Sub-s (8): word 'Minister' in square brackets substituted by SI 2006/2951, art 6, Schedule, para 3(b).

Date in force: 13 December 2006: see SI 2006/2951, art 1(2).

62 Right of charitable institution to prevent unauthorised fund-raising

(1) Where on the application of any charitable institution—

(a) the court is satisfied that any person has done or is doing either of the following, namely—
  (i) soliciting money or other property for the benefit of the institution, or
  (ii) representing that charitable contributions are to be given to or applied for the benefit of the institution,

  and that, unless restrained, he is likely to do further acts of that nature, and

(b) the court is also satisfied as to one or more of the matters specified in subsection (2),

then (subject to subsection (3)) the court may grant an injunction restraining the doing of any such acts.

(2) The matters referred to in subsection (1)(b) are—

(a) that the person in question is using methods of fund-raising to which the institution objects;

(b) that that person is not a fit and proper person to raise funds for the institution; and

(c) where the conduct complained of is the making of such representations as are mentioned in subsection (1)(a)(ii), that the institution does not wish to be associated with the particular promotional or other fund-raising venture in which that person is engaged.

(3) The power to grant an injunction under subsection (1) shall not be exercisable on the application of a charitable institution unless the institution has, not less than 28 days before making the application, served on the person in question a notice in writing—

(a) requesting him to cease forthwith—
  (i) soliciting money or other property for the benefit of the institution, or
  (ii) representing that charitable contributions are to be given to or applied for the benefit of the institution,

  as the case may be; and

(b) stating that, if he does not comply with the notice, the institution will make an application under this section for an injunction.

(4) Where—

(a) a charitable institution has served on any person a notice under subsection (3) ('the relevant notice') and that person has complied with the notice, but

(b) that person has subsequently begun to carry on activities which are the same, or substantially the same, as those in respect of which the relevant notice was served,

the institution shall not, in connection with an application made by it under this section in respect of the activities carried on by that person, be required by virtue of that subsection to serve a further notice on him, if the application is made not more than 12 months after the date of service of the relevant notice.

(5) This section shall not have the effect of authorising a charitable institution to make an application under this section in respect of anything done by a professional fund-raiser or commercial participator in relation to the institution.

NOTES

Initial Commencement

To be appointed: see s 79(2).

Appointment

Appointment: 1 March 1995: see SI 1994/3023, art 2.

Extent

This Act does not extend to Scotland: see s 79(3).

See Further

See further, in relation to additional requirements for the purposes of sub-s (3) above: the Charitable Institutions (Fund-Raising) Regulations 1994, SI 1994/3024, reg 4.

63 False statements relating to institutions which are not registered charities

(1) Where—

(a) a person solicits money or other property for the benefit of an institution in association with a representation that the institution is a registered charity, and
(b) the institution is not such a charity,

he shall be guilty of an offence and liable on summary conviction to a fine not exceeding the fifth level on the standard scale.

[(1A) In any proceedings for an offence under subsection (1), it shall be a defence for the accused to prove that he believed on reasonable grounds that the institution was a registered charity.]

(2) In [this section] 'registered charity' means a charity which is for the time being registered in the register of charities kept under [section 3 of the Charities Act 1993].

NOTES

Initial Commencement

To be appointed: see s 79(2).

Appointment

Appointment: 1 March 1995: see SI 1994/3023, art 2.

Extent

This Act does not extend to Scotland: see s 79(3).

Amendment

Sub-s (1A): inserted by the Deregulation and Contracting Out Act 1994, s 26(2).

Sub-s (2): first words in square brackets substituted by the Deregulation and Contracting Out Act 1994, s 26(3); second words in square brackets substituted by the Charities Act 1993, s 98(1), Sch 6, para 29(6).

Supplementary

64 Regulations about fund-raising

(1) The [Minister] may make such regulations as appear to him to be necessary or desirable for any purposes connected with any of the preceding provisions of this Part.

(2) Without prejudice to the generality of subsection (1), any such regulations may—

(a) prescribe the form and content of—
  (i) agreements made for the purposes of section 59, and
  (ii) notices served under section 62(3);
(b) require professional fund-raisers or commercial participators who are parties to such agreements with charitable institutions to make available to the institutions books, documents or other records (however kept) which relate to the institutions;

(c) specify the manner in which money or other property acquired by professional fund-raisers or commercial participators for the benefit of, or otherwise falling to be given to or applied by such persons for the benefit of, charitable institutions is to be transmitted to such institutions;

(d) provide for any provisions of section 60 or 61 having effect in relation to solicitations or representations made in the course of radio or television programmes to have effect, subject to any modifications specified in the regulations, in relation to solicitations or representations made in the course of such programmes—
   (i) by charitable institutions, or
   (ii) by companies connected with such institutions,
   and, in that connection, provide for any other provisions of this Part to have effect for the purposes of the regulations subject to any modifications so specified;

(e) make other provision regulating the raising of funds for charitable, benevolent or philanthropic purposes (whether by professional fund-raisers or commercial participators or otherwise).

(3) In subsection (2)(c) the reference to such money or other property as is there mentioned includes a reference to money or other property which, in the case of a professional fund-raiser or commercial participator—

(a) has been acquired by him otherwise than in accordance with an agreement with a charitable institution, but

(b) by reason of any solicitation or representation in consequence of which it has been acquired, is held by him on trust for such an institution.

(4) Regulations under this section may provide that any failure to comply with a specified provision of the regulations shall be an offence punishable on summary conviction by a fine not exceeding the second level on the standard scale.

NOTES

Initial Commencement

To be appointed: see s 79(2).

Appointment

Appointment (for the purpose of exercising the power to make regulations): 28 November 1994: see SI 1994/3023, art 2.

Appointment (for remaining purposes): 1 March 1995: see SI 1994/3023, art 2.

Extent

This Act does not extend to Scotland: see s 79(3).

Amendment

Sub-s (1): word 'Minister' in square brackets substituted by SI 2006/2951, art 6, Schedule, para 3(c).

Date in force: 13 December 2006: see SI 2006/2951, art 1(2).

Subordinate Legislation

Charitable Institutions (Fund-Raising) Regulations 1994, SI 1994/3024.

[64A Reserve power to control fund-raising by charitable institutions]

[(1) The Minister may make such regulations as appear to him to be necessary or desirable for or in connection with regulating charity fund-raising.

(2) In this section 'charity fund-raising' means activities which are carried on by—

(a) charitable institutions,
(b) persons managing charitable institutions, or
(c) persons or companies connected with such institutions,

and involve soliciting or otherwise procuring funds for the benefit of such institutions or companies connected with them, or for general charitable, benevolent or philanthropic purposes.

But 'activities' does not include primary purpose trading.

(3) Regulations under this section may, in particular, impose a good practice requirement on the persons managing charitable institutions in circumstances where—

(a) those institutions,
(b) the persons managing them, or
(c) persons or companies connected with such institutions,

are engaged in charity fund-raising.

(4) A 'good practice requirement' is a requirement to take all reasonable steps to ensure that the fund-raising is carried out in such a way that—

(a) it does not unreasonably intrude on the privacy of those from whom funds are being solicited or procured;
(b) it does not involve the making of unreasonably persistent approaches to persons to donate funds;
(c) it does not result in undue pressure being placed on persons to donate funds;
(d) it does not involve the making of any false or misleading representation about any of the matters mentioned in subsection (5).

(5) The matters are—

(a) the extent or urgency of any need for funds on the part of any charitable institution or company connected with such an institution;
(b) any use to which funds donated in response to the fund-raising are to be put by such an institution or company;
(c) the activities, achievements or finances of such an institution or company.

(6) Regulations under this section may provide that a person who persistently fails, without reasonable excuse, to comply with any specified requirement of the regulations is to be guilty of an offence and liable on summary conviction to a fine not exceeding level 2 on the standard scale.

(7) For the purposes of this section—

(a) 'funds' means money or other property;
(b) 'general charitable, benevolent or philanthropic purposes' means charitable, benevolent or philanthropic purposes other than those associated with one or more particular institutions;
(c) the persons 'managing' a charitable institution are the charity trustees or other persons having the general control and management of the administration of the institution; and
(d) a person is 'connected' with a charitable institution if he is an employee or agent of—
   (i) the institution,
   (ii) the persons managing it, or
   (iii) a company connected with it,
   or he is a volunteer acting on behalf of the institution or such a company.

(8) In this section 'primary purpose trading', in relation to a charitable institution, means any trade carried on by the institution or a company connected with it where—

(a) the trade is carried on in the course of the actual carrying out of a primary purpose of the institution; or

(b) the work in connection with the trade is mainly carried out by beneficiaries of the institution.]

NOTES

Amendment

Inserted by the Charities Act 2006, s 69.

Part III Public Charitable Collections

NOTES

Amendment

Repealed by the Charities Act 2006, s 75(1), (2), Sch 8, paras 89, 91, Sch 9.

Preliminary

NOTES

Amendment

Repealed by the Charities Act 2006, s 75(1), (2), Sch 8, paras 89, 91, Sch 9.

65 Interpretation of Part III

(1) In this Part—

(a) 'public charitable collection' means (subject to subsection (2)) a charitable appeal which is made—
 (i) in any public place, or
 (ii) by means of visits from house to house; and
(b) 'charitable appeal' means an appeal to members of the public to give money or other property (whether for consideration or otherwise) which is made in association with a representation that the whole or any part of its proceeds is to be applied for charitable, benevolent or philanthropic purposes.

(2) Subsection (1)(a) does not apply to a charitable appeal which—

(a) is made in the course of a public meeting; or
(b) is made—
 (i) on land within a churchyard or burial ground contiguous or adjacent to a place of public worship, or
 (ii) on other land occupied for the purposes of a place of public worship and contiguous or adjacent to it,
 being (in each case) land which is enclosed or substantially enclosed (whether by any wall or building or otherwise); or
(c) is an appeal to members of the public to give money or other property by placing it in an unattended receptacle;

and for the purposes of paragraph (c) above a receptacle is unattended if it is not in the possession or custody of a person acting as a collector.

(3) In this Part, in relation to a public charitable collection—

(a) 'promoter' means a person who (whether alone or with others and whether for remuneration or otherwise) organises or controls the conduct of the charitable appeal in question, and associated expressions shall be construed accordingly; and
(b) 'collector' means any person by whom that appeal is made (whether made by him alone or with others and whether made by him for remuneration or otherwise);

but where no person acts in the manner mentioned in paragraph (a) above in respect of a public charitable collection, any person who acts as a collector in respect of it shall for the purposes of this Part be treated as a promoter of it as well.

(4) In this Part—

'local authority' means the council of a [Welsh county or county borough, of a] district or of a London borough, the Common Council of the City of London, or the Council of the Isles of Scilly; and
'proceeds', in relation to a public charitable collection, means all money or other property given (whether for consideration or otherwise) in response to the charitable appeal in question.

(5) In this Part any reference to charitable purposes, where occurring in the context of a reference to charitable, benevolent or philanthropic purposes, is a reference to charitable purposes whether or not the purposes are charitable within the meaning of any rule of law.

(6) The functions exercisable under this Part by a local authority shall be exercisable—

(a) as respects the Inner Temple, by its Sub-Treasurer, and
(b) as respects the Middle Temple, by its Under Treasurer;

and references in this Part to a local authority or to the area of a local authority shall be construed accordingly.

(7) It is hereby declared that an appeal to members of the public (other than one falling within subsection (2)) is a public charitable collection for the purposes of this Part if—

(a) it consists in or includes the making of an offer to sell goods or to supply services, or the exposing of goods for sale, to members of the public, and
(b) it is made as mentioned in sub-paragraph (i) or (ii) of subsection (1)(a) and in association with a representation that the whole or any part of its proceeds is to be applied for charitable, benevolent or philanthropic purposes.

This subsection shall not be taken as prejudicing the generality of subsection (1)(b).

(8) In this section—

'house' includes any part of a building constituting a separate dwelling;
'public place', in relation to a charitable appeal, means—
- *(a) any highway, and*
- *(b) (subject to subsection (9)) any other place to which, at any time when the appeal is made, members of the public have or are permitted to have access and which either—*
  - *(i) is not within a building, or*
  - *(ii) if within a building, is a public area within any station, airport or shopping precinct or any other similar public area.*

(9) In subsection (8), paragraph (b) of the definition of 'public place' does not apply to—

(a) any place to which members of the public are permitted to have access only if any payment or ticket required as a condition of access has been made or purchased; or
(b) any place to which members of the public are permitted to have access only by virtue of permission given for the purposes of the appeal in question.

NOTES

Initial Commencement

To be appointed: see s.79(2).

Amendment

Repealed by the Charities Act 2006, s 75(1), (2), Sch 8, paras 89, 91, Sch 9.

Prohibition on conducting unauthorised collections

NOTES

Amendment

Repealed by the Charities Act 2006, s 75(1), (2), Sch 8, paras 89, 91, Sch 9.

66 Prohibition on conducting public charitable collections without authorisation

(1) No public charitable collection shall be conducted in the area of any local authority except in accordance with—

(a) a permit issued by the authority under section 68; or
(b) an order made by the Charity Commissioners under section 72.

(2) Where a public charitable collection is conducted in contravention of subsection (1), any promoter of that collection shall be guilty of an offence and liable on summary conviction to a fine not exceeding the fourth level on the standard scale.

NOTES

Initial Commencement

To be appointed: see s 79(2).

Amendment

Repealed by the Charities Act 2006, s 75(1), (2), Sch 8, paras 89, 91, Sch 9.

Permits

NOTES

Amendment

Repealed by the Charities Act 2006, s 75(1), (2), Sch 8, paras 89, 91, Sch 9.

67 Applications for permits to conduct public charitable collections

(1) An application for a permit to conduct a public charitable collection in the area of a local authority shall be made to the authority by the person or persons proposing to promote that collection.

(2) Any such application—

(a) shall specify the period for which it is desired that the permit, if issued, should have effect, being a period not exceeding 12 months; and
(b) shall contain such information as may be prescribed by regulations under section 73.

(3) Any such application—

(a) shall be made at least one month before the relevant day or before such later date as the local authority may in the case of that application allow, . . .
(b) . . .

and for this purpose 'the relevant day' means the day on which the collection is to be conducted or, where it is to be conducted on more than one day, the first of those days.

(4) Before determining any application duly made to them under this section, a local authority shall consult the chief officer of police for the police area which comprises or includes their area and may make such other inquiries as they think fit.

NOTES

Initial Commencement

To be appointed: see s 79(2).

Amendment

Repealed by the Charities Act 2006, s 75(1), (2), Sch 8, paras 89, 91, Sch 9.

68 Determination of applications and issue of permits

(1) Where an application for a permit is duly made to a local authority under section 67 in respect of a public charitable collection, the authority shall either—

(a) issue a permit in respect of the collection, or
(b) refuse the application on one or more of the grounds specified in section 69,

and, where they issue such a permit, it shall (subject to section 70) have effect for the period specified in the application in accordance with section 67(2)(a).

(2) A local authority may, at the time of issuing a permit under this section, attach to it such conditions as they think fit, having regard to the local circumstances of the collection; but the authority shall secure that the terms of any such conditions are consistent with the provisions of any regulations under section 73.

(3) Without prejudice to the generality of subsection (2), a local authority may attach conditions—

(a) specifying the day of the week, date, time or frequency of the collection;
(b) specifying the locality or localities within their area in which the collection may be conducted;
(c) regulating the manner in which the collection is to be conducted.

(4) Where a local authority—

(a) refuse to issue a permit, or
(b) attach any condition to a permit under subsection (2),

they shall serve on the applicant written notice of their decision to do so and of the reasons for their decision; and that notice shall also state the right of appeal conferred by section 71(1) or (as the case may be) section 71(2), and the time within which such an appeal must be brought.

NOTES

Initial Commencement

To be appointed: see s 79(2).

Amendment

Repealed by the Charities Act 2006, s 75(1), (2), Sch 8, paras 89, 91, Sch 9.

69 Refusal of permits

(1) A local authority may refuse to issue a permit to conduct a public charitable collection on any of the following grounds, namely—

(a) that it appears to them that the collection would cause undue inconvenience to members of the public by reason of—
   (i) the day of the week or date on which,
   (ii) the time at which,
   (iii) the frequency with which, or
   (iv) the locality or localities in which,

it is proposed to be conducted;

(b) *that the collection is proposed to be conducted on a day on which another public charitable collection is already authorised (whether under section 68 or otherwise) to be conducted in the authority's area, or on the day falling immediately before, or immediately after, any such day;*

(c) *that it appears to them that the amount likely to be applied for charitable, benevolent or philanthropic purposes in consequence of the collection would be inadequate, having regard to the likely amount of the proceeds of the collection;*

(d) *that it appears to them that the applicant or any other person would be likely to receive an excessive amount by way of remuneration in connection with the collection;*

(e) *that the applicant has been convicted—*

(i) *of an offence under section 5 of the 1916 Act, under the 1939 Act, under section 119 of the 1982 Act or regulations made under it, or under this Part or regulations made under section 73 below, or*

(ii) *of any offence involving dishonesty or of a kind the commission of which would in their opinion be likely to be facilitated by the issuing to him of a permit under section 68 above;*

(f) *where the applicant is a person other than a charitable, benevolent or philanthropic institution for whose benefit the collection is proposed to be conducted, that they are not satisfied that the applicant is authorised (whether by any such institution or by any person acting on behalf of any such institution) to promote the collection; or*

(g) *that it appears to them that the applicant, in promoting any other collection authorised under this Part or under section 119 of the 1982 Act, failed to exercise due diligence—*

(i) *to secure that persons authorised by him to act as collectors for the purposes of the collection were fit and proper persons;*

(ii) *to secure that such persons complied with the provisions of regulations under section 73 below or (as the case may be) section 119 of the 1982 Act; or*

(iii) *to prevent badges or certificates of authority being obtained by persons other than those he had so authorised.*

(2) A local authority shall not, however, refuse to issue such a permit on the ground mentioned in subsection (1)(b) if it appears to them—

(a) *that the collection would be conducted only in one location, which is on land to which members of the public would have access only by virtue of the express or implied permission of the occupier of the land; and*

(b) *that the occupier of the land consents to the collection being conducted there;*

and for this purpose 'the occupier', in relation to unoccupied land, means the person entitled to occupy it.

(3) In subsection (1)—

(a) *in the case of a collection in relation to which there is more than one applicant, any reference to the applicant shall be construed as a reference to any of the applicants; and*

(b) *(subject to subsection (4)) the reference in paragraph (g)(iii) to badges or certificates of authority is a reference to badges or certificates of authority in a form prescribed by regulations under section 73 below or (as the case may be) under section 119 of the 1982 Act.*

(4) Subsection (1)(g) applies to the conduct of the applicant (or any of the applicants) in relation to any public charitable collection authorised under regulations made under section 5 of the 1916 Act (collection of money or sale of articles in a street or other public place), or authorised under the 1939 Act (collection of money or other property by means of visits from house to house), as it applies to his conduct in relation to a collection authorised under this Part, subject to the following modifications, namely—

(a) *in the case of a collection authorised under regulations made under the 1916 Act—*

(i) the reference in sub-paragraph (ii) to regulations under section 73 below shall be construed as a reference to the regulations under which the collection in question was authorised, and

(ii) the reference in sub-paragraph (iii) to badges or certificates of authority shall be construed as a reference to any written authority provided to a collector pursuant to those regulations; and

(b) in the case of a collection authorised under the 1939 Act—

(i) the reference in sub-paragraph (ii) to regulations under section 73 below shall be construed as a reference to regulations under section 4 of that Act, and

(ii) the reference in sub-paragraph (iii) to badges or certificates of authority shall be construed as a reference to badges or certificates of authority in a form prescribed by such regulations.

(5) In this section—

'the 1916 Act' means the Police, Factories, &c (Miscellaneous Provisions) Act 1916;
'the 1939 Act' means the House to House Collections Act 1939; and
'the 1982 Act' means the Civic Government (Scotland) Act 1982.

NOTES

Initial Commencement

To be appointed: see s 79(2).

Amendment

Repealed by the Charities Act 2006, s 75(1), (2), Sch 8, paras 89, 91, Sch 9.

70 Withdrawal etc of permits

(1) Where a local authority who have issued a permit under section 68—

(a) have reason to believe that there has been a change in the circumstances which prevailed at the time when they issued the permit, and are of the opinion that, if the application for the permit had been made in the new circumstances of the case, the permit would not have been issued by them, or

(b) have reason to believe that any information furnished to them by the promoter (or, in the case of a collection in relation to which there is more than one promoter, by any of them) for the purposes of the application for the permit was false in a material particular,

then (subject to subsection (2)) they may—

(i) withdraw the permit;
(ii) attach any condition to the permit; or
(iii) vary any existing condition of the permit.

(2) Any condition imposed by the local authority under subsection (1) (whether by attaching a new condition to the permit or by varying an existing condition) must be one that could have been attached to the permit under section 68(2) at the time when it was issued, assuming for this purpose—

(a) that the new circumstances of the case had prevailed at that time, or
(b) (in a case falling within paragraph (b) of subsection (1) above) that the authority had been aware of the true circumstances of the case at that time.

(3) Where a local authority who have issued a permit under section 68 have reason to believe that there has been or is likely to be a breach of any condition of it, or that a breach of such a condition is continuing, they may withdraw the permit.

(4) Where under this section a local authority withdraw, attach any condition to, or vary an existing condition of, a permit, they shall serve on the promoter written notice of their

decision to do so and of the reasons for their decision; and that notice shall also state the right of appeal conferred by section 71(2) and the time within which such an appeal must be brought.

(5) Where a local authority so withdraw, attach any condition to, or vary an existing condition of, a permit, the permit shall nevertheless continue to have effect as if it had not been withdrawn or (as the case may be) as if the condition had not been attached or the variation had not been made—

(a) until the time for bringing an appeal under section 71(2) has expired, or
(b) if such an appeal is duly brought, until the determination or abandonment of the appeal.

NOTES

Initial Commencement

To be appointed: see s 79(2).

Amendment

Repealed by the Charities Act 2006, s 75(1), (2), Sch 8, paras 89, 91, Sch 9.

71 Appeals

(1) A person who has duly applied to a local authority under section 67 for a permit to conduct a public charitable collection in the authority's area may appeal to a magistrates' court against a decision of the authority to refuse to issue a permit to him.

(2) A person to whom a permit has been issued under section 68 may appeal to a magistrates' court against—

(a) a decision of the local authority under that section or section 70 to attach any condition to the permit; or
(b) a decision of the local authority under section 70 to vary any condition so attached or to withdraw the permit.

(3) An appeal under subsection (1) or (2) shall be by way of complaint for an order, and the Magistrates' Courts Act 1980 shall apply to the proceedings; ....

(4) Any such appeal shall be brought within 14 days of the date of service on the person in question of the relevant notice under section 68(4) or (as the case may be) section 70(4); and for the purposes of this subsection an appeal shall be taken to be brought when the complaint is made.

(5) An appeal against the decision of a magistrates' court on an appeal under subsection (1) or (2) may be brought to the Crown Court.

(6) On an appeal to a magistrates' court or the Crown Court under this section, the court may confirm, vary or reverse the local authority's decision and generally give such directions as it thinks fit, having regard to the provisions of this Part and of regulations under section 73.

(7) It shall be the duty of the local authority to comply with any directions given by the court under subsection (6); but the authority need not comply with any directions given by a magistrates' court—

(a) until the time for bringing an appeal under subsection (5) has expired, or
(b) if such an appeal is duly brought, until the determination or abandonment of the appeal.

NOTES

Initial Commencement

To be appointed: see s 79(2).

Amendment

Repealed by the Charities Act 2006, s 75(1), (2), Sch 8, paras 89, 91, Sch 9.

Sub-s (3): words omitted repealed by the Courts Act 2003, s 109(1), (3), Sch 8, para 358, Sch 10.

Date in force: 1 April 2005: see SI 2005/910, art 3(y), (aa); for transitional provisions see SI 2005/911, arts 2–5.

Orders made by Charity Commissioners

NOTES

Amendment

Repealed by the Charities Act 2006, s 75(1), (2), Sch 8, paras 89, 91, Sch 9.

72 Orders made by Charity Commissioners

(1) Where the Charity Commissioners are satisfied, on the application of any charity, that that charity proposes—

(a) to promote public charitable collections—
(i) throughout England and Wales, or
(ii) throughout a substantial part of England and Wales,
in connection with any charitable purposes pursued by the charity, or
(b) to authorise other persons to promote public charitable collections as mentioned in paragraph (a),

the Commissioners may make an order under this subsection in respect of the charity.

(2) Such an order shall have the effect of authorising public charitable collections which—

(a) are promoted by the charity in respect of which the order is made, or by persons authorised by the charity, and
(b) are so promoted in connection with the charitable purposes mentioned in subsection (1),

to be conducted in such area or areas as may be specified in the order.

(3) An order under subsection (1) may—

(a) include such conditions as the Commissioners think fit;
(b) be expressed (without prejudice to paragraph (c)) to have effect without limit of time, or for a specified period only;
(c) be revoked or varied by a further order of the Commissioners.

(4) Where the Commissioners, having made an order under subsection (1) in respect of a charity, make any further order revoking or varying that order, they shall serve on the charity written notice of their reasons for making the further order, unless it appears to them that the interests of the charity would not be prejudiced by the further order.

[(5) Section 89(1), (2) and (4) of the Charities Act 1993 (provisions as to orders made by the Commissioners) shall apply to an order made by them under this section as it applies to an order made by them under that Act.

(6) In this section 'charity' and 'charitable purposes' have the same meaning as in that Act.]

NOTES

Initial Commencement

To be appointed: see s 79(2).

Amendment

Repealed by the Charities Act 2006, s 75(1), (2), Sch 8, paras 89, 91, Sch 9.

Supplementary

NOTES

Amendment

Repealed by the Charities Act 2006, s 75(1), (2), Sch 8, paras 89, 91, Sch 9.

73 Regulations

(1) The [Minister] may make regulations—

(a) prescribing the information which is to be contained in applications made under section 67;

(b) for the purpose of regulating the conduct of public charitable collections authorised under—

- *(i) permits issued under section 68; or*
- *(ii) orders made by the Charity Commissioners under section 72.*

(2) Regulations under subsection (1)(b) may, without prejudice to the generality of that provision, make provision—

(a) about the keeping and publication of accounts;

(b) for the prevention of annoyance to members of the public;

(c) with respect to the use by collectors of badges and certificates of authority, or badges incorporating such certificates, and to other matters relating to such badges and certificates, including, in particular, provision—

- *(i) prescribing the form of such badges and certificates;*
- *(ii) requiring a collector, on request, to permit his badge, or any certificate of authority held by him for the purposes of the collection, to be inspected by a constable or a duly authorised officer of a local authority, or by an occupier of any premises visited by him in the course of the collection;*

(d) for prohibiting persons under a prescribed age from acting as collectors, and prohibiting others from causing them so to act.

(3) Regulations under this section may provide that any failure to comply with a specified provision of the regulations shall be an offence punishable on summary conviction by a fine not exceeding the second level on the standard scale.

NOTES

Initial Commencement

To be appointed: see s 79(2).

Amendment

Repealed by the Charities Act 2006, s 75(1), (2), Sch 8, paras 89, 91, Sch 9.

Sub-s (1): word 'Minister' in square brackets substituted by SI 2006/2951, art 6, Schedule, para 3(d).

Date in force: 13 December 2006: see SI 2006/2951, art 1(2).

74 Offences

(1) A person shall be guilty of an offence if, in connection with any charitable appeal, he displays or uses—

(a) *a prescribed badge or a prescribed certificate of authority which is not for the time being held by him for the purposes of the appeal pursuant to regulations under section 73, or*

(b) *any badge or article, or any certificate or other document, so nearly resembling a prescribed badge or (as the case may be) a prescribed certificate of authority as to be likely to deceive a member of the public.*

(2) A person guilty of an offence under subsection (1) shall be liable on summary conviction to a fine not exceeding the fourth level on the standard scale.

(3) Any person who, for the purposes of an application made under section 67, knowingly or recklessly furnishes any information which is false in a material particular shall be guilty of an offence and liable on summary conviction to a fine not exceeding the fourth level on the standard scale.

[(3A) Any person who knowingly or recklessly provides the Commissioners with information which is false or misleading in a material particular shall be guilty of an offence if the information is provided in circumstances in which he intends, or could reasonably be expected to know, that it would be used by them for the purpose of discharging their functions under section 72.

(3B) A person guilty of an offence under subsection (3A) shall be liable—

(a) *on summary conviction, to a fine not exceeding the statutory maximum;*

(b) *on conviction or indictment, to imprisonment for a term not exceeding two years or to a fine, or both.]*

(4) In subsection (1) 'prescribed badge' and 'prescribed certificate of authority' mean respectively a badge and a certificate of authority in such form as may be prescribed by regulations under section 73.

NOTES

Initial Commencement

To be appointed: see s 79(2).

Amendment

Repealed by the Charities Act 2006, s 75(1), (2), Sch 8, paras 89, 91, Sch 9.

Part IV
General

75 Offences by bodies corporate

Where any offence—

(a) under this Act or any regulations made under it, or

(b) ...

is committed by a body corporate and is proved to have been committed with the consent or connivance of, or to be attributable to any neglect on the part of, any director, manager, secretary or other similar officer of the body corporate, or any person who was purporting to act in any such capacity, he as well as the body corporate shall be guilty of that offence and shall be liable to be proceeded against and punished accordingly.

In relation to a body corporate whose affairs are managed by its members, 'director' means a member of the body corporate.

NOTES

Initial Commencement

To be appointed: see s 79(2).

Appointment

Appointment: 1 September 1992: see SI 1992/1900, art 2, Sch 1.

Extent

This Act does not extend to Scotland: see s 79(3).

Amendment

Words omitted repealed by the Charities Act 1993, s 98(2), Sch 7.

76 Service of documents

(1) This section applies to—

(a) …
(b) any notice or other document required or authorised to be given or served under Part II of this Act; *and*
(c) *any notice required to be served under Part III of this Act.*

(2) A document to which this section applies may be served on or given to a person (other than a body corporate)—

(a) by delivering it to that person;
(b) by leaving it at his last known address in the United Kingdom; or
(c) by sending it by post to him at that address.

(3) A document to which this section applies may be served on or given to a body corporate by delivering it or sending it by post—

(a) to the registered or principal office of the body in the United Kingdom, or
(b) if it has no such office in the United Kingdom, to any place in the United Kingdom where it carries on business or conducts its activities (as the case may be).

(4) Any such document may also be served on or given to a person (including a body corporate) by sending it by post to that person at an address notified by that person for the purposes of this subsection to the person or persons by whom it is required or authorised to be served or given.

NOTES

Initial Commencement

To be appointed: see s 79(2).

Appointment

Appointment: 1 September 1992: see SI 1992/1900, art 2, Sch 1.

Extent

This Act does not extend to Scotland: see s 79(3).

Amendment

Sub-s (1): para (a) repealed by the Charities Act 1993, s 98(2), Sch 7.

Sub-s (1): para (c) and word 'and' in italics immediately preceding it repealed by the Charities Act 2006, s 75(1), (2), Sch 8, paras 89, 92, Sch 9.

77 Regulations and orders

(1) Any regulations or order of the [Minister] under this Act—

(a) shall be made by statutory instrument; and
(b) (subject to *subsection (2)* [subsections (2) and (2A)]) shall be subject to annulment in pursuance of a resolution of either House of Parliament.

(2) Subsection (1)(b) does not apply—

(a)–(c)< ... > ; or
(d) to an order under section 79(2).

[(2A) Subsection (1)(b) does not apply to regulations under section 64A, and no such regulations may be made unless a draft of the statutory instrument containing the regulations has been laid before, and approved by a resolution of, each House of Parliament.]

(3) Any regulations or order of the [Minister] under this Act may make—

(a) different provision for different cases; and
(b) such supplemental, incidental, consequential or transitional provision or savings as the [Minister] considers appropriate.

(4) Before making any regulations under section < ... > 64 [or 64A] *or 73* the [Minister] shall consult such persons or bodies of persons as he considers appropriate.

NOTES

Initial Commencement

To be appointed: see s 79(2).

Appointment

Appointment: 1 September 1992: see SI 1992/1900, art 2, Sch 1.

Extent

This Act does not extend to Scotland: see s 79(3).

Amendment

Sub-s (1): word 'Minister' in square brackets substituted by SI 2006/2951, art 6, Schedule, para 3(e).

Date in force: 13 December 2006: see SI 2006/2951, art 1(2).

Sub-s (1): in para (b) words 'subsection (2)' in italics repealed and subsequent words in square brackets substituted by the Charities Act 2006, s 75(1), Sch 8, paras 89, 93(1), (2).

Sub-s (2): words omitted repealed by the Charities Act 1993, s 98(2), Sch 7.

Sub-s (2A): inserted by the Charities Act 2006, s 75(1), Sch 8, paras 89, 93(1), (3).

Sub-s (3): word 'Minister' in square brackets in both places it occurs substituted by SI 2006/2951, art 6, Schedule, para 3(e).

Date in force: 13 December 2006: see SI 2006/2951, art 1(2).

Sub-s (4): words omitted repealed by the Charities Act 1993, s 98(2), Sch 7.

Sub-s (4): words 'or 64A' in square brackets inserted by the Charities Act 2006, s 75(1), Sch 8, paras 89, 93(1), (4)(a).

Sub-s (4): words 'or 73' in italics repealed by the Charities Act 2006, s 75(1), (2), Sch 8, paras 89, 93(1), (4)(b), Sch 9.

Sub-s (4): word 'Minister' in square brackets substituted by SI 2006/2951, art 6, Schedule, para 3(e).

Date in force: 13 December 2006: see SI 2006/2951, art 1(2).

Subordinate Legislation

Charities (Qualified Surveyors' Reports) Regulations 1992, SI 1992/2980 (made under sub-s (3)).

Charity Commissioners' Fees (Copies and Extracts) Regulations 1992, SI 1992/2986 (made under sub-s (3)).

Charities Act 1992 (Commencement No 2) Order 1994, SI 1994/3023 (made under sub-s (3)).

Charitable Institutions (Fund-Raising) Regulations 1994, SI 1994/3024 (made under sub-s (3)).

78 Minor and consequential amendments and repeals

(1) The enactments mentioned in Schedule 6 to this Act shall have effect subject to the amendments there specified (which are either minor amendments or amendments consequential on the provisions of this Act).

(2) The enactments mentioned in Schedule 7 to this Act (which include some that are already spent or are no longer of practical utility) are hereby repealed to the extent specified in the third column of that Schedule.

NOTES

Initial Commencement

To be appointed: see s 79(2).

Appointment

Appointment: 1 September 1992: see SI 1992/1900, art 2, Sch 1.

Extent

This Act does not extend to Scotland: see s 79(3).

79 Short title, commencement and extent

(1) This Act may be cited as the Charities Act 1992.

(2) This Act shall come into force on such day as the [Minister] may by order appoint; and different days may be so appointed for different provisions or for different purposes.

(3) Subject to subsections (4) to (6) below, this Act extends only to England and Wales.

(4), (5) ...

(6) The amendments in Schedule 6, and *(subject to subsection (7))* the repeals in Schedule 7, have the same extent as the enactments to which they refer, and section 78 extends accordingly.

(7) The repeal in Schedule 7 of the Police, Factories, &c (Miscellaneous Provisions) Act 1916 does not extend to Northern Ireland.

NOTES

Initial Commencement

To be appointed: see sub-s (2) above.

Appointment

Appointment: 1 September 1992: see SI 1992/1900, art 2, Sch 1.

Extent

This Act does not extend to Scotland: see sub-s (3) above.

Amendment

Sub-s (2): word 'Minister' in square brackets substituted by SI 2006/2951, art 6, Schedule, para 3(f).

Date in force: 13 December 2006: see SI 2006/2951, art 1(2).

Sub-ss (4), (5): repealed by the Charities Act 1993, s 98(2), Sch 7.

Sub-s (6): words '(subject to subsection (7))' in italics repealed by the Charities Act 2006, s 75(1), (2), Sch 8, paras 89, 94(a), Sch 9.

Date in force: to be appointed: see the Charities Act 2006, s 79(2).

Sub-s (7): repealed by the Charities Act 2006, s 75(1), (2), Sch 8, paras 89, 94(b), Sch 9.

Date in force: to be appointed: see the Charities Act 2006, s 79(2).

Subordinate Legislation

Charities Act 1992 (Commencement No 1 and Transitional Provisions) Order 1992, SI 1992/1900 (made under sub-s (2)).

Charities Act 1992 (Commencement No 2) Order 1994, SI 1994/3023 (made under sub-s (2)).

Schedule 1

...

...

NOTES

Amendment

Repealed by the Charities Act 1993, s 98(2), Sch 7.

Schedule 2

...

...

NOTES

Amendment

Repealed by the Charities Act 1993, s 98(2), Sch 7.

Schedule 3

...

...

NOTES

Amendment

Repealed by the Charities Act 1993, s 98(2), Sch 7.

Schedule 4

...

...

NOTES

Amendment

Repealed by the Charities Act 1993, s 98(2), Sch 7.

Schedule 5
Amendments of Redundant Churches and Other Religious Buildings Act 1969

. . .

NOTES

Initial Commencement

To be appointed: see s 79(2).

Appointment

Appointment: 1 September 1992: see SI 1992/1900, art 2, Sch 1.

Extent

This Act does not extend to Scotland: see s 79(3).

Amendment

Repealed by the Charities Act 2006, s 75(2), Sch 9; for savings see 75(2), Sch 9, para 28.

Date in force: to be appointed: see the Charities Act 2006, s 79(2).

This Schedule substitutes the Redundant Churches and Other Religious Buildings Act 1969, ss 4, 5.

Schedule 6
Minor and Consequential Amendments

< ... >

NOTES

Initial Commencement

To be appointed: see s 79(2).

Appointment

Paras 1, 3–8, 13(1), (3): 1 January 1993: see SI 1992/1900, art 4, Sch 3.

Paras 2, 10(a), 11, 12, 14–17: 1 September 1992: see SI 1992/1900, art 2, Sch 1.

Extent

This Act does not extend to Scotland: see s 79(3).

Amendment

This Schedule contains amendments only.

Repealed in part by the Charities Act 1993, s 98(2), Sch 7.

Repealed in part by the Finance Act 1999, s 139, Sch 20, Pt V(5).

Date in force: this repeal has effect in relation to instruments executed on or after 6 February 2000: see the Finance Act 1999, Sch 20, Pt V(5).

Repealed in part by the Charities and Trustee Investment (Scotland) Act 2005, s 104, Sch 4, Pt 1, para 8.

Date in force: to be appointed: see the Charities and Trustee Investment (Scotland) Act 2005, s 107(2).

Repealed in part by the Charities Act 2006, s 75(2), Sch 9.

Repealed in part by the Companies Act 2006, s 1295, Sch 16.

Date in force: to be appointed: see the Companies Act 2006, s 1300(2).

Schedule 7
Repeals

Chapter	*Short title*	*Extent of repeal*
1872 c 24	Charitable Trustees Incorporation Act 1872	In section 2, the words from 'and all' onwards.
		In section 4, the words from '; and the appointment' onwards.
		In section 5, the words from '; and nothing' onwards.
		In section 7, the words from '; and there' onwards.
		The Schedule.
1916 c 31	*Police, Factories, &c (Miscellaneous Provisions) Act 1916*	*The whole Act.*
1939 c 44	House to House Collections Act 1939	The whole Act.
1940 c 31	War Charities Act 1940	The whole Act.
1948 c 29	National Assistance Act 1948	Section 41.
1958 c 49	Trading Representations (Disabled Persons) Act 1958	Section 1(2)(b).
1959 c 72	Mental Health Act 1959	Section 8(3).
1960 c 58	Charities Act 1960	In section 4(6), the words from 'and any person' onwards.
		Section 6(6) and (9).
		Section 7(4).

Chapter	*Short title*	*Extent of repeal*
		…
		Section 16(2).
		In section 19(6), the words 'or the like reference from the Secretary of State'.
		In section 22, subsection (6) and, in subsection (9), the words from ', and the' to 'endowment' (where last occurring).
		Section 27.
		Section 29.
		In section 30C(1)(c), the words 'by or'.
		Section 31.
		Section 44.
		In section 45(3), the words 'Subject to subsection (9) of section twenty-two of this Act,'.
		In section 46, the words ', subject to subsection (9) of section twenty-two of this Act,'.
		In Schedule 1, in paragraph 1(3), the words 'Subject to sub-paragraph (6) below,'.
		In Schedule 6, the entry relating to the War Charities Act 1940.
1966 c 42	Local Government Act 1966	In Schedule 3, in column 1 of Part II, paragraph 20.
1968 c 60	Theft Act 1968	In Schedule 2, in Part III, the entry relating to the House to House Collections Act 1939.
1970 c 42	Local Authority Social Services Act 1970	In Schedule 1, the entry relating to section 41 of the National Assistance Act 1948.
1972 c 70	Local Government Act 1972	Section 210(8).
		In Schedule 29, paragraphs 22 and 23.
1983 c 41	Health and Social Services and Social Security Adjudications Act 1983	Section 30(3).
1983 c 47	National Heritage Act 1983	In Schedule 4, paragraphs 13 and 14.
1985 c 9	Companies Consolidation (Consequential Provisions) Act 1985	In Schedule 2, the entry relating to section 30(1) of the Charities Act 1960.
…	…	…
1986 c 41	Finance Act 1986	Section 33.

NOTES

Initial Commencement

To be appointed: see s 79(2).

Appointment

Appointment (in part): 1 September 1992: see SI 1992/1900, art 2, Sch 1.

Appointment (remainder): 1 January 1993: see SI 1992/1900, art 4, Sch 3.

Extent

This Act does not extend to Scotland: see s 79(3).

Amendment

Entry relating to the Police, Factories, &c (Miscellaneous Provisions) Act 1916: repealed by the Charities Act 2006, s 75(1), (2), Sch 8, paras 89, 95, Sch 9.

Date in force: to be appointed: see the Charities Act 2006, s 79(2).

Words omitted from entry relating to the Charities Act 1960 repealed, and entry relating to the Charities Act 1985 repealed so far as not in force on 1 August 1993, by the Charities Act 1993, s 98(2), Sch 7.

Appendix 2

Charities Act 1993

Charities Act 1993

1993 Chapter 10

An Act to consolidate the Charitable Trustees Incorporation Act 1872 and, except for certain spent or transitional provisions, the Charities Act 1960 and Part I of the Charities Act 1992.

[27th May 1993]

BE IT ENACTED by the Queen's most Excellent Majesty, by and with the advice and consent of the Lords Spiritual and Temporal, and Commons, in this present Parliament assembled, and by the authority of the same, as follows:

Arrangement

Part I
The *Charity Commissioners* [Charity Commission] and the Official Custodian for Charities

(Notes: Words 'Charity Commissioners' in italics repealed and subsequent words in square brackets substituted by the Charities Act 2006, s 75(1), Sch 8, paras 96, 97. Date in force: to be appointed: see the Charities Act 2006, s 79(2).)

1 ...

(Notes: Repealed by the Charities Act 2006, ss 6(6), 75(2), Sch 9. Date in force: 27 February 2007: see SI 2007/309, art 2, Schedule.)

[1A The Charity Commission]

(Notes: Inserted by the Charities Act 2006, s 6(1). Date in force: 27 February 2007: see SI 2007/309, art 2, Schedule.)

[1B The Commission's objectives]

(Notes: Inserted by the Charities Act 2006, s 7. Date in force: 27 February 2007: see SI 2007/309, art 2, Schedule; for transitional provisions and savings see the Charities Act 2006, ss 4(2), (4)(a), 75(3), Sch 10, para 1.)

[1C The Commission's general functions]

(Notes: Inserted by the Charities Act 2006, s 7. Date in force (for certain purposes): 27 February 2007: see SI 2007/309, art 2, Schedule. Date in force (for remaining purposes): to be appointed: see the Charities Act 2006, s 79(2).)

[1D The Commission's general duties]

(Notes: Inserted by the Charities Act 2006, s 7. Date in force: 27 February 2007: see SI 2007/309, art 2, Schedule.)

[1E The Commission's incidental powers]

(Notes: Inserted by the Charities Act 2006, s 7. Date in force (for certain purposes): 27 February 2007: see SI 2007/309, art 2, Schedule. Date in force (for remaining purposes): to be appointed: see the Charities Act 2006, s 79(2).)

2 The official custodian for charities

[Part IA
The Charity Tribunal]

(Notes: Inserted by the Charities Act 2006, s 8(1). Date in force (for certain purposes): 27 February 2007: see SI 2007/309, art 2, Schedule. Date in force (for remaining purposes): to be appointed: see the Charities Act 2006, s 79(2).)

[2A The Charity Tribunal]

(Notes: Inserted by the Charities Act 2006, s 8(1). Date in force: to be appointed: see the Charities Act 2006, s 79(2).)

[2B Practice and procedure]

(Notes: Inserted by the Charities Act 2006, s 8(1). Date in force (for certain purposes): 27 February 2007: see SI 2007/309, art 2, Schedule. Date in force (for remaining purposes): to be appointed: see the Charities Act 2006, s 79(2).)

[2C Appeal from Tribunal]

(Notes: Inserted by the Charities Act 2006, s 8(1). Date in force (for certain purposes): 27 February 2007: see SI 2007/309, art 2, Schedule. Date in force (for remaining purposes): to be appointed: see the Charities Act 2006, s 79(2).)

[2D Intervention by Attorney General]

(Notes: Inserted by the Charities Act 2006, s 8(1). Date in force: to be appointed: see the Charities Act 2006, s 79(2).)

Part II
Registration and Names of Charities

Registration of charities

3 The register of charities [3 Register of charities]

(Notes: Substituted, together with ss 3A, 3B, for this section as originally enacted, by the Charities Act 2006, s 9. Date in force: to be appointed: see the Charities Act 2006, s 79(2).)

[3A Registration of charities]

(Notes: Substituted, together with ss 3, 3B, for s 3 as originally enacted, by the Charities Act 2006, s 9. Date in force (for certain purposes): 27 February 2007: see SI 2007/309, art 2, Schedule. Date in force (for remaining purposes): to be appointed: see the Charities Act 2006, s 79(2).)

[3B Duties of trustees in connection with registration]

(Notes: Substituted, together with ss 3, 3A, for s 3 as originally enacted, by the Charities Act 2006, s 9. Date in force (for certain purposes): 27 February 2007: see SI 2007/309, art 2, Schedule. Date in force (for remaining purposes): to be appointed: see the Charities Act 2006, s 79(2).)

4 Effect of, and claims and objections to, registration
5 Status of registered charity (other than small charity) to appear on official publications etc

Charity names

6 Power of *Commissioners* [Commission] to require charity's name to be changed

(Notes: Section heading: word 'Commissioners' in italics repealed and subsequent word in square brackets substituted by the Charities Act 2006, s 75(1), Sch 8, paras 96, 100(1), (2). Date in force: to be appointed: see the Charities Act 2006, s 79(2).)

7 Effect of direction under s 6 where charity is a company

Part III
Commissioners' Information Powers **[Information Powers]**

(Notes: Words 'Commissioners' Information Powers' in italics repealed and subsequent words in square brackets substituted by the Charities Act 2006, s 75(1), Sch 8, paras 96, 101. Date in force: to be appointed: see the Charities Act 2006, s 79(2).)

8 General power to institute inquiries
9 Power to call for documents and search records
[10 Disclosure of information to Commission]

(Notes: Substituted, together with ss 10A–10C for this section as originally enacted, by the Charities Act 2006, s 75(1), Sch 8, paras 96, 104. Date in force: 8 November 2006: see the Charities Act 2006, s 79(1)(g).)

[10A Disclosure of information by Commission]

(Notes: Substituted, together with ss 10, 10B, 10C for s 10 as originally enacted, by the Charities Act 2006, s 75(1), Sch 8, paras 96, 104. Date in force: 8 November 2006: see the Charities Act 2006, s 79(1)(g).)

[10B Disclosure to and by principal regulators of exempt charities]

(Notes: Substituted, together with ss 10, 10A, 10C for s 10 as originally enacted, by the Charities Act 2006, s 75(1), Sch 8, paras 96, 104. Date in force: 8 November 2006: see the Charities Act 2006, s 79(1)(g).)

[10C Disclosure of information: supplementary]

(Notes: Substituted, together with ss 10, 10A, 10B for s 10 as originally enacted, by the Charities Act 2006, s 75(1), Sch 8, paras 96, 104. Date in force: 8 November 2006: see the Charities Act 2006, s 79(1)(g).)

11 Supply of false or misleading information to *Commissioners* [Commission], etc

(Notes: Section heading: word 'Commissioners' in italics repealed and subsequent word in square brackets substituted by the Charities Act 2006, s 75(1), Sch 8, paras 96, 105(1), (2). Date in force: to be appointed: see the Charities Act 2006, s 79(2).)

12 ...

(Notes: Repealed by the Data Protection Act 1998, s 74(2), Sch 16, Pt I. Date in force: 1 March 2000: see SI 2000/183, art 2(1).)

Part IV
Application of Property Cy-près and Assistance and Supervision of Charities by Court *and Commissioners* [and Commission]

(Notes: Words 'and Commissioners' in italics repealed and subsequent words in square brackets substituted by the Charities Act 2006, s 75(1), Sch 8, paras 96, 106. Date in force: to be appointed: see the Charities Act 2006, s 79(2).)

Extended powers of court and variation of charters

13 Occasions for applying property cy-près
14 Application cy-près of gifts of donors unknown or disclaiming
[14A Application cy-près of gifts made in response to certain solicitations]

(Notes: Inserted by the Charities Act 2006, s 17. Date in force (for certain purposes): 27 February 2007: see SI 2007/309, art 2, Schedule. Date in force (for remaining purposes): to be appointed: see the Charities Act 2006, s 79(2).)

[14B Cy-près schemes]

(Notes: Inserted by the Charities Act 2006, s 18; for transitional provisions and savings see s 75(3), Sch 10, para 3 thereto. Date in force: to be appointed: see the Charities Act 2006, s 79(2).)

15 Charities governed by charter, or by or under statute

Powers of Commissioners [Powers of Commission] to make schemes and act for protection of charities etc

(Notes: Words 'Powers of Commissioners' repealed and subsequent words in square brackets substituted by the Charities Act 2006, s 75(1), Sch 8, paras 96, 108. Date in force: to be appointed: see the Charities Act 2006, s 79(2).)

16 Concurrent jurisdiction with High Court for certain purposes
17 Further powers to make schemes or alter application of charitable property
18 Power to act for protection of charities
[18A Power to suspend or remove trustees etc from membership of charity]

(Notes: Inserted by the Charities Act 2006, s 19; for transitional provisions and savings see s 75(3), Sh 10, para 4 thereto. Date in force: to be appointed: see the Charities Act 2006, s 79(2).)

19 Supplementary provisions relating to *receiver and manager* [interim manager] appointed for a charity

(Notes: Section heading: words 'receiver and manager' in italics repealed and subsequent words in square brackets substituted by the Charities Act 2006, s 75(1), Sch 8, paras 96, 112(1), (7). Date in force: to be appointed: see the Charities Act 2006, s 79(2).)

[19A Power to give specific directions for protection of charity]

(Notes: Inserted by the Charities Act 2006, s 20; for transitional provisions and savings see s 75(3), Sch 10, para 5 thereto. Date in force: to be appointed: see the Charities Act 2006, s 79(2).)

[19B Power to direct application of charity property]

(Notes: Inserted by the Charities Act 2006, s 21. Date in force: to be appointed: see the Charities Act 2006, s 79(2).)

[19C Copy of order under section 18, 18A, 19A or 19B, and Commission's reasons, to be sent to charity]

(Notes: Inserted by the Charities Act 2006, s 75(1), Sch 8, paras 96, 113. Date in force: to be appointed: see the Charities Act 2006, s 79(2).)

[20 Publicity relating to schemes]

(Notes: Substituted, together with s 20A, for this section as originally enacted, by the Charities Act 2006, s 22. Date in force: 27 February 2007: see SI 2007/309, art 2, Schedule.)

[20A Publicity for orders relating to trustees or other individuals]

(Notes: Substituted, together with s 20, for s 20 as originally enacted, by the Charities Act 2006, s 22. Date in force: 27 February 2007: see SI 2007/309, art 2, Schedule.)

Property vested in official custodian

21 Entrusting charity property to official custodian, and termination of trust
22 Supplementary provisions as to property vested in official custodian
23 Divestment in the case of land subject to Reverter of Sites Act 1987

Establishment of common investment or deposit funds

24 Schemes to establish common investment funds
25 Schemes to establish common deposit funds
[25A Meaning of 'Scottish recognised body' and 'Northern Ireland charity' in sections 24 and 25]

(Notes: Inserted by the Charities Act 2006, s 23(4). Date in force: 27 February 2007: see SI 2007/309, art 2, Schedule.)

Additional powers of Commissioners [Additional powers of Commission]

(Notes: Substituted by the Charities Act 2006, s 75(1), Sch 8, paras 96, 118. Date in force: to be appointed: see the Charities Act 2006, s 79(2).)

26 Power to authorise dealings with charity property etc
27 Power to authorise ex gratia payments etc
28 Power to give directions about dormant bank accounts of charities
[29 Power to give advice and guidance]

(Notes: Substituted by the Charities Act 2006, s 24. Date in force: 27 February 2007: see SI 2007/309, art 2, Schedule.)

[29A Power to determine membership of charity]

(Notes: Inserted by the Charities Act 2006, s 25. Date in force: 27 February 2007: see SI 2007/309, art 2, Schedule.)

30 Powers for preservation of charity documents
31 Power to order taxation of solicitor's bill
[31A Power to enter premises]

(Notes: Inserted by the Charities Act 2006, s 26(1). Date in force: 27 February 2007: see SI 2007/309, art 2, Schedule; for transitional provisions and savings see the Charities Act 2006, s 75(3), Sch 10, para 6.)

Legal proceedings relating to charities

32 Proceedings by *Commissioners* [Commission]

(Notes: Section heading: word 'Commissioners' in italics repealed and subsequent word in square brackets substituted by the Charities Act 2006, s 75(1), Sch 8, paras 96, 124(1), (4). Date in force: to be appointed: see the Charities Act 2006, s 79(2).)

33 Proceedings by other persons
34 Report of s 8 inquiry to be evidence in certain proceedings

Meaning of 'trust corporation'

35 Application of provisions to trust corporations appointed under s 16 or 18

Part V
Charity Land

36 Restrictions on dispositions
37 Supplementary provisions relating to dispositions
38 Restrictions on mortgaging
39 Supplementary provisions relating to mortgaging
40 Release of charity rentcharges

Part VI
Charity Accounts, Reports and Returns

41 Duty to keep accounting records
42 Annual statements of accounts
43 Annual audit or examination of charity accounts

[43A Annual audit or examination of English National Health Service charity accounts]

(Notes: Inserted by SI 2005/1074, art 3(1), (3). Date in force: this amendment has effect in relation to the financial year of a trust starting on or after 1 April 2004: see SI 2005/1074, art 1(2).)

[43B Annual audit or examination of Welsh National Health Service charity accounts]

(Notes: Inserted by SI 2005/1074, art 3(1), (3). Date in force: this amendment has effect in relation to the financial year of a trust starting on or after 1 April 2004: see SI 2005/1074, art 1(2).)

44 Supplementary provisions relating to audits etc
[44A Duty of auditors etc to report matters to Commission]

(Notes: Inserted by the Charities Act 2006, s 29(1); for transitional provisions and savings see s 75(3), Sch 10, para 8 thereto. Date in force: to be appointed: see the Charities Act 2006, s 79(2).)

45 Annual reports
46 Special provision as respects accounts and annual reports of exempt and other excepted charities
47 Public inspection of annual reports etc
48 Annual returns by registered charities
49 *Offences* [49 Offences]

(Notes: Substituted by the Charities Act 2006, s 75(1), Sch 8, paras 96, 142. Date in force: to be appointed: see the Charities Act 2006, s 79(2).)

[49A Group accounts]

(Notes: Inserted by the Charities Act 2006, s 30(1). Date in force: to be appointed: see the Charities Act 2006, s 79(2).)

Part VII
Incorporation of Charity Trustees

50 Incorporation of trustees of a charity
51 Estate to vest in body corporate
52 Applications for incorporation
53 Nomination of trustees, and filling up vacancies
54 Liability of trustees and others, notwithstanding incorporation
55 Certificate to be evidence of compliance with requirements for incorporation
56 Power of *Commissioners* [Commission] to amend certificate of incorporation

(Notes: Section heading: word 'Commissioners' in italics repealed and subsequent word in square brackets substituted by the Charities Act 2006, s 75(1), Sch 8, paras 96, 146(1), (6). Date in force: to be appointed: see the Charities Act 2006, s 79(2).)

57 Records of applications and certificates
58 Enforcement of orders and directions
59 Gifts to charity before incorporation to have same effect afterwards
60 Execution of documents by incorporated body
61 Power of *Commissioners* [Commission] to dissolve incorporated body

(Notes: Section heading: word 'Commissioners' in italics repealed and subsequent words in square brackets substituted by the Charities Act 2006, s 75(1), Sch 8, paras 96, 149(1), (6). Date in force: to be appointed: see the Charities Act 2006, s 79(2).)

62 Interpretation of Part VII

Part VIII
Charitable Companies

63 Winding up
64 Alteration of objects clause
65 Invalidity of certain transactions
66 *Requirement of consent of Commissioners* [*Commission*] *to certain acts* [66 Consent of Commission required for approval etc by members of charitable companies]

(Notes: Substituted, together with s 66A, for this section as originally enacted, by the Companies Act 2006, s 226. Date in force: to be appointed: see the Companies Act 2006, s 1300(2). Section heading: word 'Commissioners' repealed and subsequent word in square brackets substituted by the Charities Act 2006, s 75(1), Sch 8, paras 96, 153. Date in force: to be appointed: see the Charities Act 2006, s 79(2).)

[66A Consent of Commission required for certain acts of charitable company]

(Notes: Substituted, together with s 66, for s 66 as originally enacted, by the Companies Act 2006, s 226. Date in force: to be appointed: see the Companies Act 2006, s 1300(2).)

67 Name to appear on correspondence etc
68 Status to appear on correspondence etc
[68A Duty of charity's auditors etc to report matters to Commission]

(Notes: Inserted by the Charities Act 2006, s 33; for transitional provisions and savings see s 75(3), Sch 10, para 10 thereto. Date in force: to be appointed: see the Charities Act 2006, s 79(2).)

69 Investigation of accounts

[Part VIIIA
Charitable Incorporated Organisations]

(Notes: Inserted by the Charities Act 2006, s 34, Sch 7, Pt 1, para 1. Date in force (for certain purposes): 27 February 2007: see SI 2007/309, art 2, Schedule. Date in force (for remaining purposes): to be appointed: see the Charities Act 2006, s 79(2).)

[Nature and constitution]

(Notes: Inserted by the Charities Act 2006, s 34, Sch 7, Pt 1, para 1. Date in force (for certain purposes): 27 February 2007: see SI 2007/309, art 2, Schedule. Date in force (for remaining purposes): to be appointed: see the Charities Act 2006, s 79(2).)

[69A Charitable incorporated organisations]

(Notes: Inserted by the Charities Act 2006, s 34, Sch 7, Pt 1, para 1. Date in force: to be appointed: see the Charities Act 2006, s 79(2).)

[69B Constitution]

(Notes: Inserted by the Charities Act 2006, s 34, Sch 7, Pt 1, para 1. Date in force (for certain purposes): 27 February 2007: see SI 2007/309, art 2, Schedule. Date in force (for remaining purposes): to be appointed: see the Charities Act 2006, s 79(2).)

[69C Name and status]

(Notes: Inserted by the Charities Act 2006, s 34, Sch 7, Pt 1, para 1. Date in force: to be appointed: see the Charities Act 2006, s 79(2).)

[69D Offences connected with name and status]

(Notes: Inserted by the Charities Act 2006, s 34, Sch 7, Pt 1, para 1. Date in force: to be appointed: see the Charities Act 2006, s 79(2).)

[Registration]

(Notes: Inserted by the Charities Act 2006, s 34, Sch 7, Pt 1, para 1. Date in force (for certain purposes): 27 February 2007: see SI 2007/309, art 2, Schedule. Date in force (for remaining purposes): to be appointed: see the Charities Act 2006, s 79(2).)

[69E Application for registration]

(Notes: Inserted by the Charities Act 2006, s 34, Sch 7, Pt 1, para 1. Date in force (for certain purposes): 27 February 2007: see SI 2007/309, art 2, Schedule. Date in force (for remaining purposes): to be appointed: see the Charities Act 2006, s 79(2).)

[69F Effect of registration]

(Notes: Inserted by the Charities Act 2006, s 34, Sch 7, Pt 1, para 1. Date in force: to be appointed: see the Charities Act 2006, s 79(2).)

[Conversion, amalgamation and transfer]

(Notes: Inserted by the Charities Act 2006, s 34, Sch 7, Pt 1, para 1. Date in force (for certain purposes): 27 February 2007: see SI 2007/309, art 2, Schedule. Date in force (for remaining purposes): to be appointed: see the Charities Act 2006, s 79(2).)

[69G Conversion of charitable company or registered industrial and provident society]

(Notes: Inserted by the Charities Act 2006, s 34, Sch 7, Pt 1, para 1. Date in force (for certain purposes): 27 February 2007: see SI 2007/309, art 2, Schedule. Date in force (for remaining purposes): to be appointed: see the Charities Act 2006, s 79(2).)

[69H Conversion: consideration of application]

(Notes: Inserted by the Charities Act 2006, s 34, Sch 7, Pt 1, para 1. Date in force (for certain purposes): 27 February 2007: see SI 2007/309, art 2, Schedule. Date in force (for remaining purposes): to be appointed: see the Charities Act 2006, s 79(2).)

[69I Conversion: supplementary]

(Notes: Inserted by the Charities Act 2006, s 34, Sch 7, Pt 1, para 1. Date in force: to be appointed: see the Charities Act 2006, s 79(2).)

[69J Conversion of community interest company]

(Notes: Inserted by the Charities Act 2006, s 34, Sch 7, Pt 1, para 1. Date in force (for the purposes of exercising the power to make subordinate legislation): 27 February 2007: see SI 2007/309, art 2, Schedule. Date in force (for remaining purposes): to be appointed: see the Charities Act 2006, s 79(2).)

[69K Amalgamation of CIOs]

(Notes: Inserted by the Charities Act 2006, s 34, Sch 7, Pt 1, para 1. Date in force: to be appointed: see the Charities Act 2006, s 79(2).)

[69L Amalgamation: supplementary]

(Notes: Inserted by the Charities Act 2006, s 34, Sch 7, Pt 1, para 1. Date in force: to be appointed: see the Charities Act 2006, s 79(2).)

[69M Transfer of CIO's undertaking]

(Notes: Inserted by the Charities Act 2006, s 34, Sch 7, Pt 1, para 1. Date in force: to be appointed: see the Charities Act 2006, s 79(2).)

[Winding up, insolvency and dissolution]

(Notes: Inserted by the Charities Act 2006, s 34, Sch 7, Pt 1, para 1. Date in force (for the purposes of exercising the power to make subordinate legislation): 27 February 2007: see SI 2007/309, art 2, Schedule. Date in force (for remaining purposes): to be appointed: see the Charities Act 2006, s 79(2).)

[69N Regulations about winding up, insolvency and dissolution]

(Notes: Inserted by the Charities Act 2006, s 34, Sch 7, Pt 1, para 1. Date in force (for the purposes of exercising the power to make subordinate legislation): 27 February 2007: see SI 2007/309, art 2, Schedule. Date in force (for remaining purposes): to be appointed: see the Charities Act 2006, s 79(2).)

[Miscellaneous]

(Notes: Inserted by the Charities Act 2006, s 34, Sch 7, Pt 1, para 1. Date in force (for certain purposes): 27 February 2007: see SI 2007/309, art 2, Schedule. Date in force (for remaining purposes): to be appointed: see the Charities Act 2006, s 79(2).)

[69O Power to transfer all property of unincorporated charity to one or more CIOs]

(Notes: Inserted by the Charities Act 2006, s 34, Sch 7, Pt 1, para 1. Date in force: to be appointed: see the Charities Act 2006, s 79(2).)

[69P Further provision about CIOs]

(Notes: Inserted by the Charities Act 2006, s 34, Sch 7, Pt 1, para 1. Date in force: to be appointed: see the Charities Act 2006, s 79(2).)

[69Q Regulations]

(Notes: Inserted by the Charities Act 2006, s 34, Sch 7, Pt 1, para 1. Date in force (for the purposes of exercising the power to make subordinate legislation): 27 February 2007: see SI 2007/309, art 2, Schedule. Date in force (for remaining purposes): to be appointed: see the Charities Act 2006, s 79(2).)

Part IX
Miscellaneous

...

(Notes: Repealed by virtue of the Trustee Act 2000, s 40(1), (3), Sch 2, Pt I, para 2, Sch 4, Pt I and by the Charities and Trustee Investment (Scotland) Act 2005, s 95, Sch 3, para 9. Date in force (in relation to England and Wales): 1 February 2001: see SI 2001/49, art 2. Date in force (in relation to Scotland): 1 January 2006: see SSI 2005/644, art 2(1), Schedule.)

70 ...

(Notes: Repealed by virtue of the Trustee Act 2000, s 40(1), (3), Sch 2, Pt I, para 2, Sch 4, Pt I and by the Charities and Trustee Investment (Scotland) Act 2005, s 95, Sch 3, para 9. Date in force (in relation to England and Wales): 1 February 2001: see SI 2001/49, art 2. Date in force (in relation to Scotland): 1 January 2006: see SSI 2005/644, art 2(1), Schedule.)

71 ...

(Notes: Repealed by virtue of the Trustee Act 2000, s 40(1), (3), Sch 2, Pt I, para 2, Sch 4, Pt I and by the Charities and Trustee Investment (Scotland) Act 2005, s 95, Sch 3, para 9. Date in force (in relation to England and Wales): 1 February 2001: see SI 2001/49, art 2. Date in force (in relation to Scotland): 1 January 2006: see SSI 2005/644, art 2(1), Schedule.)

Disqualification for acting as charity trustee [Charity trustees]

(Notes: Substituted by the Charities Act 2006, s 75(1), Sch 8, paras 96, 155. Date in force: to be appointed: see the Charities Act 2006, s 79(2).)

72 Persons disqualified for being trustees of a charity
73 Persons acting as charity trustee while disqualified

[73A Remuneration of trustees etc providing services to charity]

(Notes: Inserted by the Charities Act 2006, s 36; for transitional provisions and savings see s 75(3), Sch 10, para 12 thereto. Date in force: to be appointed: see the Charities Act 2006, s 79(2).)

[73B Supplementary provisions for purposes of section 73A]

(Notes: Inserted by the Charities Act 2006, s 36; for transitional provisions and savings see s 75(3), Sch 10, para 12 thereto. Date in force: to be appointed: see the Charities Act 2006, s 79(2).)

[73C Disqualification of trustee receiving remuneration under section 73A]

(Notes: Inserted by the Charities Act 2006, s 37. Date in force: to be appointed: see the Charities Act 2006, s 79(2).)

[73D Power to relieve trustees, auditors etc from liability for breach of trust or duty]

(Notes: Inserted by the Charities Act 2006, s 38; for transitional provisions and savings see s 75(3), Sch 10, para 13 thereto. Date in force (for certain purposes): 27 February 2007: see SI 2007/309, art 2, Schedule. Date in force (for remaining purposes): to be appointed: see the Charities Act 2006, s 79(2).)

[73E Court's power to grant relief to apply to all auditors etc of charities which are not companies]

(Notes: Inserted by the Charities Act 2006, s 38; for transitional provisions and savings see s 75(3), Sch 10, para 13 thereto. Date in force (for certain purposes): 27 February 2007: see SI 2007/309, art 2, Schedule. Date in force (for remaining purposes): to be appointed: see the Charities Act 2006, s 79(2).)

[73F Trustees' indemnity insurance]

(Notes: Inserted by the Charities Act 2006, s 39. Date in force: 27 February 2007: see SI 2007/309, art 2, Schedule.)

Small charities [Miscellaneous powers of charities]

(Notes: Substituted by the Charities Act 2006, s 75(1), Sch 8, paras 96, 158. Date in force: to be appointed: see the Charities Act 2006, s 79(2).)

74 Power to transfer all property, modify objects etc [74 Power to transfer all property of unincorporated charity]

(Notes: Substituted, together with ss 74A, 74B for this section as originally enacted, by the Charities Act 2006, s 40. Date in force: to be appointed: see the Charities Act 2006, s 79(2).)

[74A Resolution not to take effect or to take effect at later date]

(Notes: Substituted, together with ss 74, 74B for s 74 as originally enacted, by the Charities Act 2006, s 40. Date in force: to be appointed: see the Charities Act 2006, s 79(2).)

[74B Transfer where charity has permanent endowment]

(Notes: Substituted, together with ss 74, 74A for s 74 as originally enacted, by the Charities Act 2006, s 40. Date in force: to be appointed: see the Charities Act 2006, s 79(2).)

[74C Power to replace purposes of unincorporated charity]

(Notes: Inserted by the Charities Act 2006, s 41. Date in force: to be appointed: see the Charities Act 2006, s 79(2).)

[74D Power to modify powers or procedures of unincorporated charity]

(Notes: Inserted by the Charities Act 2006, s 42. Date in force: 27 February 2007: see SI 2007/309, art 2, Schedule.)

75 *Power to spend capital* [75 Power of unincorporated charities to spend capital: general]

(Notes: Substituted, together with ss 75A, 75B for this section as originally enacted, by the Charities Act 2006, s 43. Date in force: to be appointed: see the Charities Act 2006, s 79(2).)

[75A Power of larger unincorporated charities to spend capital given for particular purpose]

(Notes: Substituted, together with ss 75, 75B for s 75 as originally enacted, by the Charities Act 2006, s 43. Date in force: to be appointed: see the Charities Act 2006, s 79(2).)

[75B Power to spend capital subject to special trusts]

(Notes: Substituted, together with ss 75, 75A for s 75 as originally enacted, by the Charities Act 2006, s 43. Date in force: to be appointed: see the Charities Act 2006, s 79(2).)

[Mergers]

(Notes: Inserted by the Charities Act 2006, ss 44, 75(3), Sch 10, para 14. Date in force: to be appointed: see the Charities Act 2006, s 79(2).)

[75C Register of charity mergers]

(Notes: Inserted by the Charities Act 2006, s 44; for transitional provisions and savings see s 75(3), Sch 10, para 14 thereto. Date in force: to be appointed: see the Charities Act 2006, s 79(2).)

[75D Register of charity mergers: supplementary]

(Notes: Inserted by the Charities Act 2006, s 44. Date in force: to be appointed: see the Charities Act 2006, s 79(2).)

[75E Pre-merger vesting declarations]

(Notes: Inserted by the Charities Act 2006, s 44. Date in force: to be appointed: see the Charities Act 2006, s 79(2).)

[75F Effect of registering charity merger on gifts to transferor]

(Notes: Inserted by the Charities Act 2006, s 44. Date in force: to be appointed: see the Charities Act 2006, s 79(2).)

Local charities

76 Local authority's index of local charities
77 Reviews of local charities by local authority
78 Co-operation between charities, and between charities and local authorities
79 Parochial charities

Scottish charities

80 Supervision by *Commissioners* [Commission] of certain Scottish charities

(Notes: Section heading: word 'Commissioners' in italics repealed and subsequent word in square brackets substituted by the Charities Act 2006, s 75(1), Sch 8, paras 96, 162(1), (7). Date in force: to be appointed: see the Charities Act 2006, s 79(2).)

Administrative provisions about charities

81 Manner of giving notice of charity meetings, etc
82 Manner of executing instruments
83 Transfer and evidence of title to property vested in trustees

Part X
Supplementary

84 Supply by *Commissioners* [Commission] of copies of documents open to public inspection

(Notes: Section heading: word 'Commissioners' in italics repealed and subsequent words in square brackets substituted by the Charities Act 2006, s 75(1), Sch 8, paras 96, 163(1), (5). Date in force: to be appointed: see the Charities Act 2006, s 79(2).)

85 Fees and other amounts payable to *Commissioners* [Commission]

(Notes: Section heading: word 'Commissioners' in italics repealed and subsequent word in square brackets substituted by the Charities Act 2006, s 75(1), Sch 8, paras 96, 164(1), (5). Date in force: to be appointed: see the Charities Act 2006, s 79(2).)

86 Regulations and orders
[86A Consultation by Commission before exercising powers in relation to exempt charity]

(Notes: Inserted by the Charities Act 2006, s 14. Date in force: to be appointed: see the Charities Act 2006, s 79(2).)

87 Enforcement of requirements by order of *Commissioners* [Commission]

(Notes: Section heading: word 'Commissioners' in italics repealed and subsequent word in square brackets substituted by the Charities Act 2006, s 75(1), Sch 8, paras 96, 166(1), (4). Date in force: to be appointed: see the Charities Act 2006, s 79(2).)

88 Enforcement of orders of *Commissioners* [Commission]

(Notes: Section heading: word 'Commissioners' in italics repealed and subsequent word in square brackets substituted by the Charities Act 2006, s 75(1), Sch 8, paras 96, 167(1), (5). Date in force: to be appointed: see the Charities Act 2006, s 79(2).)

89 Other provisions as to orders of *Commissioners* [Commission]

(Notes: Section heading: word 'Commissioners' in italics repealed and subsequent words in square brackets substituted by the Charities Act 2006, s 75(1), Sch 8, paras 96, 168(1), (7). Date in force: to be appointed: see the Charities Act 2006, s 79(2).)

90 Directions of *the Commissioners* [the Commission]

(Notes: Section Heading: words 'the Commissioners' in italics repealed and subsequent words in square brackets substituted by the Charities Act 2006, s 75(1), Sch 8, paras 96, 169. Date in force: to be appointed: see the Charities Act 2006, s 79(2).)

91 Service of orders and directions
92 *Appeals from Commissioners*

(Notes: Repealed by the Charities Act 2006, s 75(1), (2), Sch 8, paras 96, 171, Sch 9; for transitional provisions and savings see s 75(3), Sch 10, para 18. Date in force: to be appointed: see the Charities Act 2006, s 79(2).)

93 Miscellaneous provisions as to evidence
94 Restriction on institution of proceedings for certain offences
95 Offences by bodies corporate
96 Construction of references to a 'charity' or to particular classes of charity
97 General interpretation
98 Consequential amendments and repeals
99 …

(Notes: Repealed by the Statute Law (Repeals) Act 2004. Date in force: 22 July 2004: (no specific commencement provision).)

100 Short title and extent

Schedule 1

…

(Notes: Repealed by the Charities Act 2006, ss 6(6), 75(2), Sch 9. Date in force: 27 February 2007: see SI 2007/309, art 2, Schedule.)

[Schedule 1A
The Charity Commission]

(Notes: Inserted by the Charities Act 2006, s 6(2), Sch 1; for effect see s 6(7), Sch 2, para 2(6) thereto. Date in force: 27 February 2007: see SI 2007/309, art 2, Schedule.)

[Schedule 1B
The Charity Tribunal]

(Notes: Inserted by the Charities Act 2006, s 8(2), Sch 3. Date in force: to be appointed: see the Charities Act 2006, s 79(2).)

[Schedule 1C
Appeals and Applications to Charity Tribunal]

(Notes: Inserted by the Charities Act 2006, s 8(3), Sch 4. Date in force (for certain purposes): 27 February 2007: see SI 2007/309, art 2, Schedule. Date in force (for remaining purposes): to be appointed: see the Charities Act 2006, s 79(2).)

[Schedule 1D
References to Charity Tribunal]

(Notes: Inserted by the Charities Act 2006, s 8(3), Sch 4. Date in force: to be appointed: see the Charities Act 2006, s 79(2).)

Schedule 2
Exempt Charities

Schedule 3
Enlargement of Areas of Local Charities

Schedule 4
Court's Jurisdiction Over Certain Charities Governed by or Under Statute

Schedule 5
Meaning of 'Connected Person' for Purposes of Section 36(2)

[Schedule 5A
Group Accounts]

(Notes: Inserted by the Charities Act 2006, s 30(2); for transitional provisions and savings see s 75(1), Sch 6, Sch 10, para 17 thereto. Date in force (for certain purposes): 27 February 2007: see SI 2007/309, art 2, Schedule. Date in force (for remaining purposes): to be appointed: see the Charities Act 2006, s 79(2).)

[Schedule 5B
Further Provision about Charitable Incorporated Organisations]

(Notes: Inserted by the Charities Act 2006, s 34, Sch 7, Pt 1, para 2. Date in force (for certain purposes): 27 February 2007: see SI 2007/309, art 2, Schedule. Date in force (for remaining purposes): to be appointed: see the Charities Act 2006, s 79(2).)

Schedule 6
Consequential Amendments

Schedule 7
Repeals

Schedule 8
...

(Notes: Repealed by the Statute Law (Repeals) Act 2004. Date in force: 22 July 2004: (no specific commencement provision).)

Part I
The Charity Commissioners [Charity Commission] and the Official Custodian for Charities

NOTES

Amendment

Words 'Charity Commissioners' repealed and subsequent words in square brackets substituted by the Charities Act 2006, s 75(1), Sch 8, paras 96, 97.

Date in force: to be appointed: see the Charities Act 2006, s 79(2).

1 The Charity Commissioners

(1) There shall continue to be a body of Charity Commissioners for England and Wales, and they shall have such functions as are conferred on them by this Act in addition to any functions under any other enactment for the time being in force.

(2) The provisions of Schedule 1 to this Act shall have effect with respect to the constitution and proceedings of the Commissioners and other matters relating to the Commissioners and their officers and employees.

(3) The Commissioners shall (without prejudice to their specific powers and duties under other enactments) have the general function of promoting the effective use of charitable resources by encouraging the development of better methods of administration, by giving charity trustees information or advice on any matter affecting the charity and by investigating and checking abuses.

(4) It shall be the general object of the Commissioners so to act in the case of any charity (unless it is a matter of altering its purposes) as best to promote and make effective the work of the charity in meeting the needs designated by its trusts; but the Commissioners shall not themselves have power to act in the administration of a charity.

(5) The Commissioners shall, as soon as possible after the end of every year, make to the [Minister] a report on their operations during that year, and he shall lay a copy of the report before each House of Parliament.

NOTES

Initial Commencement

Specified date: 1 August 1993: see s 99(1).

Amendment

Repealed by the Charities Act 2006, ss 6(6), 75(2), Sch 9.

Sub-s (5): word 'Minister' in square brackets substituted by SI 2006/2951, art 6, Schedule, para 4(a).

Date in force: 13 December 2006: see SI 2006/2951, art 1(2).

[1A The Charity Commission]

[(1) There shall be a body corporate to be known as the Charity Commission for England and Wales (in this Act referred to as 'the Commission').

(2) In Welsh the Commission shall be known as 'Comisiwn Elusennau Cymru a Lloegr'.

(3) The functions of the Commission shall be performed on behalf of the Crown.

(4) In the exercise of its functions the Commission shall not be subject to the direction or control of any Minister of the Crown or other government department.

(5) But subsection (4) above does not affect—

(a) any provision made by or under any enactment;
(b) any administrative controls exercised over the Commission's expenditure by the Treasury.

(6) The provisions of Schedule 1A to this Act shall have effect with respect to the Commission.]

NOTES

Amendment

Inserted by the Charities Act 2006, s 6(1).

[1B The Commission's objectives]

[(1) The Commission has the objectives set out in subsection (2).

(2) The objectives are—

1 The public confidence objective.
2 The public benefit objective.
3 The compliance objective.
4 The charitable resources objective.
5 The accountability objective.

(3) Those objectives are defined as follows—

1 The public confidence objective is to increase public trust and confidence in charities.
2 The public benefit objective is to promote awareness and understanding of the operation of the public benefit requirement.
3 The compliance objective is to promote compliance by charity trustees with their legal obligations in exercising control and management of the administration of their charities.
4 The charitable resources objective is to promote the effective use of charitable resources.
5 The accountability objective is to enhance the accountability of charities to donors, beneficiaries and the general public.

(4) In this section 'the public benefit requirement' means the requirement in section 2(1)(b) of the Charities Act 2006 that a purpose falling within section 2(2) of that Act must be for the public benefit if it is to be a charitable purpose.]

NOTES

Amendment

Inserted by the Charities Act 2006, s 7.

[1C The Commission's general functions]

[(1) The Commission has the general functions set out in subsection (2).

(2) The general functions are—

1 Determining whether institutions are or are not charities.
2 Encouraging and facilitating the better administration of charities.

3 Identifying and investigating apparent misconduct or mismanagement in the administration of charities and taking remedial or protective action in connection with misconduct or mismanagement therein.

4 Determining whether public collections certificates should be issued, and remain in force, in respect of public charitable collections.

5 Obtaining, evaluating and disseminating information in connection with the performance of any of the Commission's functions or meeting any of its objectives.

6 Giving information or advice, or making proposals, to any Minister of the Crown on matters relating to any of the Commission's functions or meeting any of its objectives.

(3) The Commission's fifth general function includes (among other things) the maintenance of an accurate and up-to-date register of charities under section 3 below.

(4) The Commission's sixth general function includes (among other things) complying, so far as is reasonably practicable, with any request made by a Minister of the Crown for information or advice on any matter relating to any of its functions.

(5) In this section 'public charitable collection' and 'public collections certificate' have the same meanings as in Chapter 1 of Part 3 of the Charities Act 2006.]

NOTES

Amendment

Inserted by the Charities Act 2006, s 7.

Date in force (for remaining purposes): to be appointed: see the Charities Act 2006, s 79(2).

[1D The Commission's general duties]

[(1) The Commission has the general duties set out in subsection (2).

(2) The general duties are—

1 So far as is reasonably practicable the Commission must, in performing its functions, act in a way—
   (a) which is compatible with its objectives, and
   (b) which it considers most appropriate for the purpose of meeting those objectives.

2 So far as is reasonably practicable the Commission must, in performing its functions, act in a way which is compatible with the encouragement of—
   (a) all forms of charitable giving, and
   (b) voluntary participation in charity work.

3 In performing its functions the Commission must have regard to the need to use its resources in the most efficient, effective and economic way.

4 In performing its functions the Commission must, so far as relevant, have regard to the principles of best regulatory practice (including the principles under which regulatory activities should be proportionate, accountable, consistent, transparent and targeted only at cases in which action is needed).

5 In performing its functions the Commission must, in appropriate cases, have regard to the desirability of facilitating innovation by or on behalf of charities.

6 In managing its affairs the Commission must have regard to such generally accepted principles of good corporate governance as it is reasonable to regard as applicable to it.]

NOTES

Amendment

Inserted by the Charities Act 2006, s 7.

[1E The Commission's incidental powers]

[(1) The Commission has power to do anything which is calculated to facilitate, or is conducive or incidental to, the performance of any of its functions or general duties.

(2) However, nothing in this Act authorises the Commission—

(a) to exercise functions corresponding to those of a charity trustee in relation to a charity, or

(b) otherwise to be directly involved in the administration of a charity.

(3) Subsection (2) does not affect the operation of section 19A or 19B below (power of Commission to give directions as to action to be taken or as to application of charity property).]

NOTES

Amendment

Inserted by the Charities Act 2006, s 7.

Date in force (for remaining purposes): to be appointed: see the Charities Act 2006, s 79(2).

2 The official custodian for charities

(1) There shall continue to be an officer known as the official custodian for charities (in this Act referred to as 'the official custodian') whose function it shall be to act as trustee for charities in the cases provided for by this Act; and the official custodian shall be by that name a corporation sole having perpetual succession and using an official seal which shall be officially and judicially noticed.

(2) Such officer of the Commissioners as they may from time to time designate shall be the official custodian.

[(2) Such individual as the Commission may from time to time designate shall be the official custodian.]

(3) The official custodian shall perform his duties in accordance with such general or special directions as may be given him by the *Commissioners* [Commission], and his expenses (except those re-imbursed to him or recovered by him as trustee for any charity) shall be defrayed by the *Commissioners* [Commission].

(4) Anything which is required to or may be done by, to or before the official custodian may be done by, to or before any *officer of the Commissioners* [member of the staff of the Commission] generally or specially authorised *by them* [by it] to act for him during a vacancy in his office or otherwise.

(5) The official custodian shall not be liable as trustee for any charity in respect of any loss or of the mis-application of any property unless it is occasioned by or through the wilful neglect or default of the custodian or of any person acting for him; but the Consolidated Fund shall be liable to make good to a charity any sums for which the custodian may be liable by reason of any such neglect or default.

(6) The official custodian shall keep such books of account and such records in relation thereto as may be directed by the Treasury and shall prepare accounts in such form, in such manner and at such times as may be so directed.

(7) The accounts so prepared shall be examined and certified by the Comptroller and Auditor General, *and the report to be made by the Commissioners to the Secretary of State for any year shall include a copy of the accounts so prepared for any period ending in or with the year and of the certificate and report of the Comptroller and Auditor General with respect to those accounts.*

[(8) The Comptroller and Auditor General shall send to the Commission a copy of the accounts as certified by him together with his report on them.

(9) The Commission shall publish and lay before Parliament a copy of the documents sent to it under subsection (8) above.]

NOTES

Derivation

This section derived from the Charities Act 1960, s 3(1)–(7).

Initial Commencement

Specified date: 1 August 1993: see s 99(1).

Extent

This section does not extend to Scotland.

Amendment

Sub-s (2): substituted by the Charities Act 2006, s 75(1), Sch 8, paras 96, 98(1), (2).

Sub-s (3): word 'Commission' in square brackets in both places they occur substituted by the Charities Act 2006, s 75(1), Sch 8, paras 96, 98(1), (3).

Sub-s (4): words 'member of the staff of the Commission' in square brackets substituted by the Charities Act 2006, s 75(1), Sch 8, paras 96, 98(1), (4)(a).

Sub-s (4): words 'by it' in square brackets substituted by the Charities Act 2006, s 75(1), Sch 8, paras 96, 98(1), (4)(b).

Sub-s (7): words omitted repealed by the Charities Act 2006, s 75(1), (2), Sch 8, paras 96, 98(1), (5), Sch 9.

Sub-ss (8), (9): inserted by the Charities Act 2006, s 75(1), Sch 8, paras 96, 98(1), (6).

[Part IA The Charity Tribunal]

NOTES

Amendment

Inserted by the Charities Act 2006, s 8(1).

Date in force (for remaining purposes): to be appointed: see the Charities Act 2006, s 79(2).

[2A The Charity Tribunal]

[(1) There shall be a tribunal to be known as the Charity Tribunal (in this Act referred to as 'the Tribunal').

(2) In Welsh the Tribunal shall be known as 'Tribiwnlys Elusennau'.

(3) The provisions of Schedule 1B to this Act shall have effect with respect to the constitution of the Tribunal and other matters relating to it.

(4) The Tribunal shall have jurisdiction to hear and determine—

(a) such appeals and applications as may be made to the Tribunal in accordance with Schedule 1C to this Act, or any other enactment, in respect of decisions, orders or directions of the Commission, and

(b) such matters as may be referred to the Tribunal in accordance with Schedule 1D to this Act by the Commission or the Attorney General.

(5) Such appeals, applications and matters shall be heard and determined by the Tribunal in accordance with those Schedules, or any such enactment, taken with section 2B below and rules made under that section.]

NOTES

Amendment

Inserted by the Charities Act 2006, s 8(1).

Date in force: to be appointed: see the Charities Act 2006, s 79(2).

[2B Practice and procedure]

[(1) The Lord Chancellor may make rules—

(a) regulating the exercise of rights to appeal or to apply to the Tribunal and matters relating to the making of references to it;
(b) about the practice and procedure to be followed in relation to proceedings before the Tribunal.

(2) Rules under subsection (1)(a) above may, in particular, make provision—

(a) specifying steps which must be taken before appeals, applications or references are made to the Tribunal (and the period within which any such steps must be taken);
(b) specifying the period following the Commission's final decision, direction or order within which such appeals or applications may be made;
(c) requiring the Commission to inform persons of their right to appeal or apply to the Tribunal following a final decision, direction or order of the Commission;
(d) specifying the manner in which appeals, applications or references to the Tribunal are to be made.

(3) Rules under subsection (1)(b) above may, in particular, make provision—

(a) for the President or a legal member of the Tribunal (see paragraph 1(2)(b) of Schedule 1B to this Act) to determine preliminary, interlocutory or ancillary matters;
(b) for matters to be determined without an oral hearing in specified circumstances;
(c) for the Tribunal to deal with urgent cases expeditiously;
(d) about the disclosure of documents;
(e) about evidence;
(f) about the admission of members of the public to proceedings;
(g) about the representation of parties to proceedings;
(h) about the withdrawal of appeals, applications or references;
(i) about the recording and promulgation of decisions;
(j) about the award of costs.

(4) Rules under subsection (1)(a) or (b) above may confer a discretion on—

(a) the Tribunal,
(b) a member of the Tribunal, or
(c) any other person.

(5) The Tribunal may award costs only in accordance with subsections (6) and (7) below.

(6) If the Tribunal considers that any party to proceedings before it has acted vexatiously, frivolously or unreasonably, the Tribunal may order that party to pay to any other party to the proceedings the whole or part of the costs incurred by that other party in connection with the proceedings.

(7) If the Tribunal considers that a decision, direction or order of the Commission which is the subject of proceedings before it was unreasonable, the Tribunal may order the Commission to pay to any other party to the proceedings the whole or part of the costs incurred by that other party in connection with the proceedings.

(8) Rules of the Lord Chancellor under this section—

(a) shall be made by statutory instrument, and
(b) shall be subject to annulment in pursuance of a resolution of either House of Parliament.

(9) Section 86(3) below applies in relation to rules of the Lord Chancellor under this section as it applies in relation to regulations and orders of the Minister under this Act.]

NOTES

Amendment

Inserted by the Charities Act 2006, s 8(1).

Date in force (for remaining purposes): to be appointed: see the Charities Act 2006, s 79(2).

[2C Appeal from Tribunal]

[(1) A party to proceedings before the Tribunal may appeal to the High Court against a decision of the Tribunal.

(2) Subject to subsection (3) below, an appeal may be brought under this section against a decision of the Tribunal only on a point of law.

(3) In the case of an appeal under this section against a decision of the Tribunal which determines a question referred to it by the Commission or the Attorney General, the High Court—

(a) shall consider afresh the question referred to the Tribunal, and
(b) may take into account evidence which was not available to the Tribunal.

(4) An appeal under this section may be brought only with the permission of—

(a) the Tribunal, or
(b) if the Tribunal refuses permission, the High Court.

(5) For the purposes of subsection (1) above—

(a) the Commission and the Attorney General are to be treated as parties to all proceedings before the Tribunal, and
(b) rules under section 2B(1) above may include provision as to who else is to be treated as being (or not being) a party to proceedings before the Tribunal.]

NOTES

Amendment

Inserted by the Charities Act 2006, s 8(1).

Date in force (for remaining purposes): to be appointed: see the Charities Act 2006, s 79(2).

[2D Intervention by Attorney General]

[(1) This section applies to any proceedings—

(a) before the Tribunal, or
(b) on an appeal from the Tribunal,

to which the Attorney General is not a party.

(2) The Tribunal or, in the case of an appeal from the Tribunal, the court may at any stage of the proceedings direct that all the necessary papers in the proceedings be sent to the Attorney General.

(3) A direction under subsection (2) may be made by the Tribunal or court—

(a) of its own motion, or
(b) on the application of any party to the proceedings.

(4) The Attorney General may—

(a) intervene in the proceedings in such manner as he thinks necessary or expedient, and
(b) argue before the Tribunal or court any question in relation to the proceedings which the Tribunal or court considers it necessary to have fully argued.

(5) Subsection (4) applies whether or not the Tribunal or court has given a direction under subsection (2).]

NOTES

Amendment

Inserted by the Charities Act 2006, s 8(1).

Date in force: to be appointed: see the Charities Act 2006, s 79(2).

Part II
Registration and Names of Charities

Registration of charities

3 The register of charities [3 Register of charities]

(1) The Commissioners shall continue to keep a register of charities, which shall be kept by them in such manner as they think fit.

(2) There shall be entered in the register every charity not excepted by subsection (5) below; and a charity so excepted (other than one excepted by paragraph (a) of that subsection) may be entered in the register at the request of the charity, but (whether or not it was excepted at the time of registration) may at any time, and shall at the request of the charity, be removed from the register.

(3) The register shall contain—

(a) the name of every registered charity; and
(b) such other particulars of, and such other information relating to, every such charity as the Commissioners think fit.

(4) Any institution which no longer appears to the Commissioners to be a charity shall be removed from the register, with effect, where the removal is due to any change in its purposes or trusts, from the date of that change; and there shall also be removed from the register any charity which ceases to exist or does not operate.

(5) The following charities are not required to be registered—

(a) any charity comprised in Schedule 2 to this Act (in this Act referred to as an 'exempt charity');
(b) any charity which is excepted by order or regulations;
(c) any charity which has neither—
 (i) any permanent endowment, nor
 (ii) the use or occupation of any land,
 and whose income from all sources does not in aggregate amount to more than £1,000 a year;
[*(c) any charity whose gross income does not exceed £5,000;*]

and no charity is required to be registered in respect of any registered place of worship.

[*(5A) In subsection (5) above, paragraph (a) shall be read as referring also to—*

(a) any higher education corporation within the meaning of the Education Reform Act 1988, and
(b) any further education corporation within the meaning of the Further and Higher Education Act 1992]

[*(5B) In addition, in subsection (5) above—*

(a) paragraph (a) shall be read as referring also to—
 (i) any body to which section 23(1)(a) or (b) of the School Standards and Framework Act 1998 applies, and
 (ii) any Education Action Forum established by virtue of section 10(1) of that Act; and
(b) paragraph (b) shall be read as referring also to any foundation to which section 23(3) of that Act applies;

but an order of the Commissioners, or regulations made by the [*Minister*], *may provide that section 23(3) of that Act shall cease to apply to any such foundation as is mentioned in that provision or to any such foundation of a description specified in the order or regulations.*]

(6) With any application for a charity to be registered there shall be supplied to the Commissioners copies of its trusts (or, if they are not set out in any extant document, particulars of them), and such other documents or information as may be prescribed by regulations made by the [*Minister*] *or as the Commissioners may require for the purpose of the application.*

(7) It shall be the duty—

(a) of the charity trustees of any charity which is not registered nor excepted from registration to apply for it to be registered, and to supply the documents and information required by subsection (6) above; and
(b) of the charity trustees (or last charity trustees) of any institution which is for the time being registered to notify the Commissioners if it ceases to exist, or if there is any change in its trusts or in the particulars of it entered in the register, and to supply to the Commissioners particulars of any such change and copies of any new trusts or alterations of the trusts.

(8) The register (including the entries cancelled when institutions are removed from the register) shall be open to public inspection at all reasonable times; and copies (or particulars) of the trusts of any registered charity as supplied to the Commissioners under this section shall, so long as it remains on the register, be kept by them and be open to public inspection at all reasonable times, except in so far as regulations made by the [*Minister*] *otherwise provide.*

(9) Where any information contained in the register is not in documentary form, subsection (8) above shall be construed as requiring the information to be available for public inspection in legible form at all reasonable times.

(10) If the Commissioners so determine, subsection (8) above shall not apply to any particular information contained in the register and specified in their determination.

(11) Nothing in the foregoing subsections shall require any person to supply the Commissioners with copies of schemes for the administration of a charity made otherwise than by the court, or to notify the Commissioners of any change made with respect to a registered charity by such a scheme, or require a person, if he refers the Commissioners to a document or copy already in the possession of the Commissioners, to supply a further copy of the document; but where by virtue of this subsection a copy of any document need not be supplied to the Commissioners, a copy of it, if it relates to a registered charity, shall be open to inspection under subsection (8) above as if supplied to the Commissioners under this section.

(12) If the [*Minister*] *thinks it expedient to do so—*

(a) in consequence of changes in the value of money, or
(b) with a view to extending the scope of the exception provided for by subsection (5)(c) above,

he may by order amend subsection (5)(c) by substituting a different sum for the sum for the time being specified there.

(13) The reference in subsection (5)(b) above to a charity which is excepted by order or regulations is to a charity which—

(a) *is for the time being permanently or temporarily excepted by order of the Commissioners; or*

(b) *is of a description permanently or temporarily excepted by regulations made by the [Minister],*

and which complies with any conditions of the exception.

[*(13A)In this section any reference to a charity's 'gross income' shall be construed, in relation to a particular time—*

(a) *as a reference to the charity's gross income in its financial year immediately preceding that time, or*

(b) *if the Commission so determines, as a reference to the amount which the Commission estimates to be the likely amount of the charity's gross income in such financial year of the charity as is specified in the determination.*]

(14) In this section 'registered place of worship' means any land or building falling within section 9 of the Places of Worship Registration Act 1855 (that is to say, the land and buildings which if the Charities Act 1960 had not been passed, would by virtue of that section as amended by subsequent enactments be partially exempted from the operation of the Charitable Trusts Act 1853), and for the purposes of this subsection 'building' includes part of a building.

[(1) There shall continue to be a register of charities, which shall be kept by the Commission.

(2) The register shall be kept by the Commission in such manner as it thinks fit.

(3) The register shall contain—

(a) the name of every charity registered in accordance with section 3A below (registration), and

(b) such other particulars of, and such other information relating to, every such charity as the Commission thinks fit.

(4) The Commission shall remove from the register—

(a) any institution which it no longer considers is a charity, and

(b) any charity which has ceased to exist or does not operate.

(5) If the removal of an institution under subsection (4)(a) above is due to any change in its trusts, the removal shall take effect from the date of that change.

(6) A charity which is for the time being registered under section 3A(6) below (voluntary registration) shall be removed from the register if it so requests.

(7) The register (including the entries cancelled when institutions are removed from the register) shall be open to public inspection at all reasonable times.

(8) Where any information contained in the register is not in documentary form, subsection (7) above shall be construed as requiring the information to be available for public inspection in legible form at all reasonable times.

(9) If the Commission so determines, subsection (7) shall not apply to any particular information contained in the register that is specified in the determination.

(10) Copies (or particulars) of the trusts of any registered charity as supplied to the Commission under section 3B below (applications for registration etc) shall, so long as the charity remains on the register—

(a) be kept by the Commission, and
(b) be open to public inspection at all reasonable times.]

NOTES

Derivation

Sub-s (1) derived from the Charities Act 1960, s 4(1), as substituted by the Charities Act 1992, s 2(1), (2); sub-ss (2), (3), (5) derived from the Charities Act 1960, s 4(2), (2A), (4), as amended by the Charities Act 1992, s 2(1), (3)–(5); sub-ss (4), (14) derived from the Charities Act 1960, s 4(3), (9); sub-ss (6), (8) derived from the Charities Act 1960, ss 4(5), (7), as read with s 43(1) thereof, as substituted by the Education Act 1973, s 1(3), Sch 1, para 1(1), (7); sub-s (7) derived from the Charities Act 1960, s 4(6), as amended by the Charities Act 1992, s 78(2), Sch 7; sub-ss (9), (10), (12) derived from the Charities Act 1960, s 4(7A), (7B), (8A), as added by the Charities Act 1992, s 2(1), (6), (7); sub-s (11) derived from the Charities Act 1960, s 4(8), as amended by the Education Act 1973, s 1(4), (5), Sch 2, Part III; sub-s (13) derived from the Charities Act 1960, s 45(6).

Initial Commencement

Specified date: 1 August 1993: see s 99(1).

Extent

This section does not extend to Scotland.

Amendment

Substituted, together with ss 3A, 3B, for this section as originally enacted, by the Charities Act 2006, s 9.

Date in force: to be appointed: see the Charities Act 2006, s 79(2).

Sub-s (5): sub-para (c) substituted by SI 2007/789, art 2(1), (2).

Date in force: 23 April 2007: see SI 2007/789, art 1.

Sub-s (5A): inserted by the Teaching and Higher Education Act 1998, s 44(1), Sch 3, para 9.

Date in force: 1 October 1998: see SI 1998/2215, art 2.

Sub-s (5B): inserted by the School Standards and Framework Act 1998, s 140(1), Sch 30, para 48.

Date in force: 1 February 1999: see SI 1999/120, art 2(1), Sch 1.

Sub-s (5B): word 'Minister' in square brackets substituted by SI 2006/2951, art 6, Schedule, para 4(c).

Date in force: 13 December 2006: see SI 2006/2951, art 1(2).

Sub-s (6): word 'Minister' in square brackets substituted by SI 2006/2951, art 6, Schedule, para 4(c).

Date in force: 13 December 2006: see SI 2006/2951, art 1(2).

Sub-s (8): word 'Minister' in square brackets substituted by SI 2006/2951, art 6, Schedule, para 4(c).

Date in force: 13 December 2006: see SI 2006/2951, art 1(2).

Sub-s (12): word 'Minister' in square brackets substituted by SI 2006/2951, art 6, Schedule, para 4(c).

Date in force: 13 December 2006: see SI 2006/2951, art 1(2).

Sub-s (13): in para (b) word 'Minister' in square brackets substituted by SI 2006/2951, art 6, Schedule, para 4(c).

Date in force: 13 December 2006: see SI 2006/2951, art 1(2).

Sub-s (13A): inserted by SI 2007/789, art 2(1), (3).

Date in force: 23 April 2007: see SI 2007/789, art 1.

Subordinate Legislation

Charities (Exception from Registration) Regulations 1996, SI 1996/180 (made under sub-ss (5), (13)).

Charities (Exception From Registration) (Amendment) Regulations 2002, SI 2002/1598 (made under sub-ss (5), (13)).

[3A Registration of charities]

[(1) Every charity must be registered in the register of charities unless subsection (2) below applies to it.

(2) The following are not required to be registered—

[(a) any exempt charity (see Schedule 2 to this Act);
(b) any charity which for the time being—
  (i) is permanently or temporarily excepted by order of the Commission, and
  (ii) complies with any conditions of the exception,
  and whose gross income does not exceed £100,000;
(c) any charity which for the time being—
  (i) is, or is of a description, permanently or temporarily excepted by regulations made by the [Minister], and
  (ii) complies with any conditions of the exception,
  and whose gross income does not exceed £100,000; and]
(d) any charity whose gross income does not exceed £5,000.

(3) For the purposes of subsection (2)(b) above—

(a) any order made or having effect as if made under section 3(5)(b) of this Act (as originally enacted) and in force immediately before the appointed day has effect as from that day as if made under subsection (2)(b) (and may be varied or revoked accordingly); and
(b) no order may be made under subsection (2)(b) so as to except on or after the appointed day any charity that was not excepted immediately before that day.

(4) For the purposes of subsection (2)(c) above—

(a) any regulations made or having effect as if made under section 3(5)(b) of this Act (as originally enacted) and in force immediately before the appointed day have effect as from that day as if made under subsection (2)(c) (and may be varied or revoked accordingly);
(b) such regulations shall be made under subsection (2)(c) as are necessary to secure that all of the formerly specified institutions are excepted under that provision (subject to compliance with any conditions of the exception and the financial limit mentioned in that provision); but
(c) otherwise no regulations may be made under subsection (2)(c) so as to except on or after the appointed day any description of charities that was not excepted immediately before that day.

(5) In subsection (4)(b) above 'formerly specified institutions' means—

(a) any institution falling within section 3(5B)(a) or (b) of this Act as in force immediately before the appointed day (certain educational institutions); or
(b) any institution ceasing to be an exempt charity by virtue of section 11 of the Charities Act 2006 or any order made under that section.

(6) A charity within—

(a) subsection (2)(b) or (c) above, or
(b) subsection (2)(d) above,

must, if it so requests, be registered in the register of charities.

(7) The Minister may by order amend—

(a) subsection (2)(b) and (c) above, or
(b) subsection (2)(d) above,

by substituting a different sum for the sum for the time being specified there.

(8) The Minister may only make an order under subsection (7) above—

(a) so far as it amends subsection (2)(b) and (c), if he considers it expedient to so with a view to reducing the scope of the exception provided by those provisions;
(b) so far as it amends subsection (2)(d), if he considers it expedient to do so in consequence of changes in the value of money or with a view to extending the scope of the exception provided by that provision,

and no order may be made by him under subsection (7)(a) unless a copy of a report under section 73 of the Charities Act 2006 (report on operation of that Act) has been laid before Parliament in accordance with that section.

(9) In this section 'the appointed day' means the day on which subsections (1) to (5) above come into force by virtue of an order under section 79 of the Charities Act 2006 relating to section 9 of that Act (registration of charities).

(10) In this section any reference to a charity's 'gross income' shall be construed, in relation to a particular time—

(a) as a reference to the charity's gross income in its financial year immediately preceding that time, or
(b) if the Commission so determines, as a reference to the amount which the Commission estimates to be the likely amount of the charity's gross income in such financial year of the charity as is specified in the determination.

(11) The following provisions of this section—

(a) subsection (2)(b) and (c),
(b) subsections (3) to (5), and
(c) subsections (6)(a), (7)(a), (8)(a) and (9),

shall cease to have effect on such day as the Minister may by order appoint for the purposes of this subsection.]

NOTES

Amendment

Substituted, together with ss 3, 3B for s 3, as originally enacted, by the Charities Act 2006, s 9.

Date in force (for remaining purposes): to be appointed: see the Charities Act 2006, s 79(2).

Sub-s (2): in para (c)(i) word 'Minister' in square brackets substituted by SI 2006/2951, art 6, Schedule, para 4(d).

Date in force: 13 December 2006: see SI 2006/2951, art 1(2).

[3B Duties of trustees in connection with registration]

[(1) Where a charity required to be registered by virtue of section 3A(1) above is not registered, it is the duty of the charity trustees—

(a) to apply to the Commission for the charity to be registered, and
[(b) to supply the Commission with the required documents and information.

(2) The 'required documents and information' are—

(a) copies of the charity's trusts or (if they are not set out in any extant document) particulars of them,
(b) such other documents or information as may be prescribed by regulations made by the Minister, and
(c) such other documents or information as the Commission may require for the purposes of the application.

(3) Where an institution is for the time being registered, it is the duty of the charity trustees (or the last charity trustees)—

(a) to notify the Commission if the institution ceases to exist, or if there is any change in its trusts or in the particulars of it entered in the register, and
(b) (so far as appropriate), to supply the Commission with particulars of any such change and copies of any new trusts or alterations of the trusts.

(4) Nothing in subsection (3) above requires a person—]

(a) to supply the Commission with copies of schemes for the administration of a charity made otherwise than by the court,
(b) to notify the Commission of any change made with respect to a registered charity by such a scheme, or
(c) if he refers the Commission to a document or copy already in the possession of the Commission, to supply a further copy of the document.

(5) Where a copy of a document relating to a registered charity—

(a) is not required to be supplied to the Commission as the result of subsection (4) above, but
(b) is in the possession of the Commission,

a copy of the document shall be open to inspection under section 3(10) above as if supplied to the Commission under this section.]

NOTES

Amendment

Substituted, together with ss 3, 3A for s 3, as originally enacted, by the Charities Act 2006, s 9.

Date in force (for remaining purposes): to be appointed: see the Charities Act 2006, s 79(2).

4 Effect of, and claims and objections to, registration

(1) An institution shall for all purposes other than rectification of the register be conclusively presumed to be or to have been a charity at any time when it is or was on the register of charities.

(2) Any person who is or may be affected by the registration of an institution as a charity may, on the ground that it is not a charity, object to its being entered by *the Commissioners* [the Commission] in the register, or apply [to the Commission] for it to be removed from the register; and provision may be made by regulations made by the Secretary of State as to the manner in which any such objection or application is to be made, prosecuted or dealt with.

(3) *An appeal against any decision of the Commissioners to enter or not to enter an institution in the register of charities, or to remove or not to remove an institution from the register, may be brought in the High Court by the Attorney General, or by the persons who are or claim to be the charity trustees of the institution, or by any person whose objection or application under subsection (2) above is disallowed by the decision.*

(4) If there is an appeal to the *High Court* [Tribunal] against any decision of *the Commissioners* [the Commission] to enter an institution in the register, or not to remove an institution from the register, then until *the Commissioners are* [the Commission is] satisfied whether the decision of *the Commissioners* [the Commission] is or is not to stand, the entry in the register shall be maintained, but shall be in suspense and marked to indicate that it is in suspense; and for the purposes of subsection (1) above an institution shall be deemed not to be on the register during any period when the entry relating to it is in suspense under this subsection.

(5) Any question affecting the registration or removal from the register of an institution may, notwithstanding that it has been determined by a decision on appeal under *subsection (3) above* [Schedule 1C to this Act], be considered afresh by *the Commissioners* [the Commission] and shall not be concluded by that decision, if it appears to *the Commissioners* [the Commission] that there has been a change of circumstances or that the decision is inconsistent with a later judicial decision, *whether given on such an appeal or not.*

NOTES

Derivation

Sub-ss (1), (3)–(5) derived from the Charities Act 1960, s 5(1), (3)–(5); sub-s (2) derived from the Charities Act 1960, s 5(2), as read with 43(1) thereof, as substituted by the Education Act 1973, s 1(3), Sch 1, para 1(1), (7).

Initial Commencement

Specified date: 1 August 1993: see s 99(1).

Extent

This section does not extend to Scotland.

Amendment

Sub-s (2): words 'the Commission' in square brackets substituted by the Charities Act 2006, s 75(1), Sch 8, paras 96, 99(1), (2)(a).

Sub-s (2): words 'to the Commission' in square brackets inserted by the Charities Act 2006, s 75(1), Sch 8, paras 96, 99(1), (2)(b).

Sub-s (3): repealed by the Charities Act 2006, s 75(1), (2), Sch 8, paras 96, 99(1), (3), Sch 9; for transitional provisions and savings see s 75(3), Sch 10, para 18 thereto.

Date in force: to be appointed: see the Charities Act 2006, s 79(2).

Sub-s (4): words 'High Court' in italics repealed and subsequent word in square brackets substituted by the Charities Act 2006, s 75(1), Sch 8, paras 96, 99(1), (4)(a); for transitional provisions and savings see s 75(3), Sch 10, para 18 thereto.

Date in force: to be appointed: see the Charities Act 2006, s 79(2).

Sub-s (4): words 'the Commission' in square brackets in both places they occur substituted by the Charities Act 2006, s 75(1), Sch 8, paras 96, 99(1), (4)(b).

Sub-s (4): words 'the Commission is' in square brackets substituted by the Charities Act 2006, s 75(1), Sch 8, paras 96, 99(1), (4)(c).

Sub-s (5): words 'subsection (3) above' in italics repealed and subsequent words in square brackets substituted by the Charities Act 2006, s 75(1), Sch 8, paras 96, 99(1), (5)(a); for transitional provisions and savings see s 75(3), Sch 10, para 18 thereto.

Date in force: to be appointed: see the Charities Act 2006, s 79(2).

Sub-s (5): words 'the Commission' in square brackets in both places they occur substituted by the Charities Act 2006, s 75(1), Sch 8, paras 96, 99(1), (5)(b).

Sub-s (5): words ', whether given on such an appeal or not' in italics repealed by the Charities Act 2006, s 75(1), (2), Sch 8, paras 96, 99(1), (5)(c), Sch 9; for transitional provisions and savings see s 75(3), Sch 10, para 18 thereto.

Date in force: to be appointed: see the Charities Act 2006, s 79(2).

5 Status of registered charity (other than small charity) to appear on official publications etc

(1) This section applies to a registered charity if its gross income in its last financial year exceeded [£10,000].

(2) Where this section applies to a registered charity, the fact that it is a registered charity shall be stated ... in legible characters—

(a) in all notices, advertisements and other documents issued by or on behalf of the charity and soliciting money or other property for the benefit of the charity;
(b) in all bills of exchange, promissory notes, endorsements, cheques and orders for money or goods purporting to be signed on behalf of the charity; and
(c) in all bills rendered by it and in all its invoices, receipts and letters of credit.

[(2A) The statement required by subsection (2) above shall be in English, except that, in the case of a document which is otherwise wholly in Welsh, the statement may be in Welsh if it consists of or includes the words 'elusen cofrestredig' (the Welsh equivalent of 'registered charity').]

(3) Subsection (2)(a) above has effect whether the solicitation is express or implied, and whether the money or other property is to be given for any consideration or not.

(4) If, in the case of a registered charity to which this section applies, any person issues or authorises the issue of any document falling within paragraph (a) or (c) of subsection (2) above [which does not contain the statement] required by that subsection, he shall be guilty of an offence and liable on summary conviction to a fine not exceeding level 3 on the standard scale.

(5) If, in the case of any such registered charity, any person signs any document falling within paragraph (b) of subsection (2) above [which does not contain the statement] required by that subsection, he shall be guilty of an offence and liable on summary conviction to a fine not exceeding level 3 on the standard scale.

(6) The [Minister] may by order amend subsection (1) above by substituting a different sum for the sum for the time being specified there.

NOTES

Derivation

This section derived from the Charities Act 1992, s 3.

Initial Commencement

Specified date: 1 August 1993: see s 99(1).

Extent

This section does not extend to Scotland.

Amendment

Sub-s (1): sum in square brackets substituted by SI 1995/2696, art 2(2).

Sub-s (2): words omitted repealed by the Welsh Language Act 1993, ss 32(2), 35, Sch 2.

Sub-s (2A): inserted by the Welsh Language Act 1993, s 32(3).

Sub-ss (4), (5): words in square brackets substituted by the Welsh Language Act 1993, s 32(4), (5).

Sub-s (6): word 'Minister' in square brackets substituted by SI 2006/2951, art 6, Schedule, para 4(f).

Date in force: 13 December 2006: see SI 2006/2951, art 1(2).

Subordinate Legislation

Charities Act 1993 (Substitution of Sums) Order 1995, SI 1995/2696 (made under sub-s (1)).

Charity names

6 Power of Commissioners [Commission] to require charity's name to be changed

(1) Where this subsection applies to a charity, the *Commissioners* [Commission] may give a direction requiring the name of the charity to be changed, within such period as is specified in the direction, to such other name as the charity trustees may determine with the approval of the *Commissioners* [Commission].

(2) Subsection (1) above applies to a charity if—

(a) it is a registered charity and its name ('the registered name')—
  (i) is the same as, or
  (ii) is in the opinion of the *Commissioners* [Commission] too like,
  the name, at the time when the registered name was entered in the register in respect of the charity, of any other charity (whether registered or not);
(b) the name of the charity is in the opinion of the *Commissioners* [Commission] likely to mislead the public as to the true nature—
  (i) of the purposes of the charity as set out in its trusts, or
  (ii) of the activities which the charity carries on under its trusts in pursuit of those purposes;
(c) the name of the charity includes any word or expression for the time being specified in regulations made by the [Minister] and the inclusion in its name of that word or expression is in the opinion of the *Commissioners* [Commission] likely to mislead the public in any respect as to the status of the charity;
(d) the name of the charity is in the opinion of the *Commissioners* [Commission] likely to give the impression that the charity is connected in some way with Her Majesty's Government or any local authority, or with any other body of persons or any individual, when it is not so connected; or
(e) the name of the charity is in the opinion of the *Commissioners* [Commission] offensive;

and in this subsection any reference to the name of a charity is, in relation to a registered charity, a reference to the name by which it is registered.

(3) Any direction given by virtue of subsection (2)(a) above must be given within twelve months of the time when the registered name was entered in the register in respect of the charity.

(4) Any direction given under this section with respect to a charity shall be given to the charity trustees; and on receiving any such direction the charity trustees shall give effect to it notwithstanding anything in the trusts of the charity.

(5) Where the name of any charity is changed under this section, then (without prejudice to *section 3(7)(b) above* [section 3B(3)]) it shall be the duty of the charity trustees forthwith to notify the *Commissioners* [Commission] of the charity's new name and of the date on which the change occurred.

(6) A change of name by a charity under this section does not affect any rights or obligations of the charity; and any legal proceedings that might have been continued or commenced by or against it in its former name may be continued or commenced by or against it in its new name.

(7) Section 26(3) of the Companies Act 1985 (minor variations in names to be disregarded) shall apply for the purposes of this section as if the reference to section 26(1)(c) of that Act were a reference to subsection (2)(a) above.

(8) Any reference in this section to the charity trustees of a charity shall, in relation to a charity which is a company, be read as a reference to the directors of the company.

(9) *Nothing in this section applies to an exempt charity.*

NOTES

Derivation

This section derived from the Charities Act 1992, s 4.

Initial Commencement

Specified date: 1 August 1993: see s 99(1).

Extent

This section does not extend to Scotland.

Amendment

Section heading: word 'Commissioners' repealed and subsequent word in square brackets substituted by the Charities Act 2006, s 75(1), Sch 8, paras 96, 100(1), (2).

Date in force: to be appointed: see the Charities Act 2006, s 79(2).

Word 'Commission' in square brackets in each place it occurs substituted by the Charities Act 2006, s 75(1), Sch 8, paras 96, 100(1), (2).

Sub-s (2): in para (c) word 'Minister' in square brackets substituted by SI 2006/2951, art 6, Schedule, para 4(g).

Date in force: 13 December 2006: see SI 2006/2951, art 1(2).

Sub-s (5): words 'section 3(7)(b) above' in italics repealed and subsequent words in square brackets substituted by the Charities Act 2006, s 75(1), Sch 8, paras 96, 100(1), (3).

Date in force: to be appointed: see the Charities Act 2006, s 79(2).

Sub-s (9): repealed by the Charities Act 2006, ss 12, 75(2), Sch 5, para 1, Sch 9.

Date in force: to be appointed: see the Charities Act 2006, s 79(2).

7 Effect of direction under s 6 where charity is a company

(1) Where any direction is given under section 6 above with respect to a charity which is a company, the direction shall be taken to require the name of the charity to be changed by resolution of the directors of the company.

(2) Section 380 of the Companies Act 1985 (registration etc of resolutions and agreements) shall apply to any resolution passed by the directors in compliance with any such direction.

(3) Where the name of such a charity is changed in compliance with any such direction, the registrar of companies—

(a) shall, subject to section 26 of the Companies Act 1985 (prohibition on registration of certain names), enter the new name on the register of companies in place of the former name, and

(b) shall issue a certificate of incorporation altered to meet the circumstances of the case;

and the change of name has effect from the date on which the altered certificate is issued.

NOTES

Derivation

This section derived from the Charities Act 1992, s 5.

Initial Commencement

Specified date: 1 August 1993: see s 99(1).

Extent

This section does not extend to Scotland.

Part III
Commissioners' Information Powers [Information Powers]

NOTES

Amendment

Words 'Commissioners' Information Powers' repealed and subsequent words in square brackets substituted by the Charities Act 2006, s 75(1), Sch 8, paras 96, 101.

Date in force: to be appointed: see the Charities Act 2006, s 79(2).

8 General power to institute inquiries

(1) *The Commissioners* [The Commission] may from time to time institute inquiries with regard to charities or a particular charity or class of charities, either generally or for particular purposes, but no such inquiry shall extend to any exempt charity [except where this has been requested by its principal regulator].

(2) *The Commissioners* [The Commission] may either conduct such an inquiry *themselves* [itself] or appoint a person to conduct it and make a report *to them* [to the Commission].

(3) For the purposes of any such inquiry *the Commissioners, or a person appointed by them* [the Commission, or a person appointed by the Commission] to conduct it, may direct any person (subject to the provisions of this section)—

(a) to furnish accounts and statements in writing with respect to any matter in question at the inquiry, being a matter on which he has or can reasonably obtain information, or to return answers in writing to any questions or inquiries addressed to him on any such matter, and to verify any such accounts, statements or answers by statutory declaration;
(b) to furnish copies of documents in his custody or under his control which relate to any matter in question at the inquiry, and to verify any such copies by statutory declaration;
(c) to attend at a specified time and place and give evidence or produce any such documents.

(4) For the purposes of any such inquiry evidence may be taken on oath, and the person conducting the inquiry may for that purpose administer oaths, or may instead of administering an oath require the person examined to make and subscribe a declaration of the truth of the matters about which he is examined.

(5) *The Commissioners* [The Commission] may pay to any person the necessary expenses of his attendance to give evidence or produce documents for the purpose of an inquiry under this section, and a person shall not be required in obedience to a direction under

paragraph (c) of subsection (3) above to go more than ten miles from his place of residence unless those expenses are paid or tendered to him.

(6) Where an inquiry has been held under this section, *the Commissioners* [the Commission] may either—

(a) cause the report of the person conducting the inquiry, or such other statement of the results of the inquiry as *they think* [the Commission thinks] fit, to be printed and published, or
(b) publish any such report or statement in some other way which is calculated in *their opinion* [the Commission's opinion] to bring it to the attention of persons who may wish to make representations *to them* [to the Commission] about the action to be taken.

(7) The council of a county or district, the Common Council of the City of London and the council of a London borough may contribute to the expenses of *the Commissioners* [the Commission] in connection with inquiries under this section into local charities in the council's area.

NOTES

Derivation

Sub-ss (1), (2), (4) derived from the Charities Act 1960, s 6(1), (2), (4); sub-s (3) derived from the Charities Act 1960, s 6(3), as amended by the Charities Act 1992, s 6(1), (2); sub-s (5) derived from the Charities Act 1960, s 6(5), as amended by the Charities Act 1992, s 6(1), (3); sub-s (6) derived from the Charities Act 1960, s 6(7), as substituted by the Charities Act 1992, s 6(1), (5); sub-s (7) derived from the Charities Act 1960, s 6(8), as amended by the Local Government Act 1963, s 93(1), Sch 18, Part II, and the Local Government Act 1972, s 272(1), Sch 30.

Initial Commencement

Specified date: 1 August 1993: see s 99(1).

Extent

This section does not extend to Scotland.

Amendment

Sub-s (1): words 'The Commission' in square brackets substituted by the Charities Act 2006, s 75(1), Sch 8, paras 96, 102(1), (2).

Sub-s (1): words 'except where this has been requested by its principal regulator' in square brackets inserted by the Charities Act 2006, s 12, Sch 5, para 2.

Date in force: to be appointed: see the Charities Act 2006, s 79(2).

Sub-s (2): words 'The Commission' in square brackets substituted by the Charities Act 2006, s 75(1), Sch 8, paras 96, 102(1), (3)(a).

Sub-s (2): word 'itself' in square brackets substituted by the Charities Act 2006, s 75(1), Sch 8, paras 96, 102(1), (3)(b).

Sub-s (2): words 'to the Commission' in square brackets substituted by the Charities Act 2006, s 75(1), Sch 8, paras 96, 102(1), (3)(c).

Sub-s (3): words 'the Commission, or a person appointed by the Commission' in square brackets substituted by the Charities Act 2006, s 75(1), Sch 8, paras 96, 102(1), (4).

Sub-s (5): words 'The Commission' in square brackets substituted by the Charities Act 2006, s 75(1), Sch 8, paras 96, 102(1), (5).

Sub-s (6): words 'the Commission' in square brackets substituted by the Charities Act 2006, s 75(1), Sch 8, paras 96, 102(1), (6)(a).

Sub-s (6): in para (a) words 'the Commission thinks' in square brackets substituted by the Charities Act 2006, s 75(1), Sch 8, paras 96, 102(1), (6)(b).

Sub-s (6): in para (b) words 'the Commission's opinion' in square brackets substituted by the Charities Act 2006, s 75(1), Sch 8, paras 96, 102(1), (6)(c).

Sub-s (6): in para (b) words 'to the Commission' in square brackets substituted by the Charities Act 2006, s 75(1), Sch 8, paras 96, 102(1), (6)(d).

Sub-s (7): words 'the Commission' in square brackets substituted by the Charities Act 2006, s 75(1), Sch 8, paras 96, 102(1), (7).

9 Power to call for documents and search records

(1) *The Commissioners* [The Commission] may by order—

(a) require any person to *furnish them* [furnish the Commission] with any information in his possession which relates to any charity and is relevant to the discharge of *their functions* [the Commission's functions] or of the functions of the official custodian;

(b) require any person who has in his custody or under his control any document which relates to any charity and is relevant to the discharge of *their functions* [the Commission's functions] or of the functions of the official custodian—

  (i) to *furnish them* [furnish the Commission] with a copy of or extract from the document, or

  (ii) (unless the document forms part of the records or other documents of a court or of a public or local authority) to transmit the document itself to *them for their* [the Commission for its] inspection.

(2) Any *officer of the Commissioners, if so authorised by them* [member of the staff of the Commission, if so authorised by it], shall be entitled without payment to inspect and take copies of or extracts from the records or other documents of any court, or of any public registry or office of records, for any purpose connected with the discharge of the functions of *the Commissioners* [the Commission] or of the official custodian.

(3) *The Commissioners* [The Commission] shall be entitled without payment to keep any copy or extract furnished *to them* [to it] under subsection (1) above; and where a document transmitted *to them* [to the Commission] under that subsection for *their inspection* [it to inspect] relates only to one or more charities and is not held by any person entitled as trustee or otherwise to the custody of it, *the Commissioners* [the Commission] may keep it or may deliver it to the charity trustees or to any other person who may be so entitled.

(4) *No person properly having the custody of documents relating only to an exempt charity shall be required under subsection (1) above to transmit to the Commissioners any of those documents, or to furnish any copy of or extract from any of them.*

(5) The rights conferred by subsection (2) above shall, in relation to information recorded otherwise than in legible form, include the right to require the information to be made available in legible form for inspection or for a copy or extract to be made of or from it.

[(6) In subsection (2) the reference to a member of the staff of the Commission includes the official custodian even if he is not a member of the staff of the Commission.]

NOTES

Derivation

Sub-s (1) derived from the Charities Act 1960, s 7(1), as substituted by the Charities Act 1992, s 7(1), (2); sub-ss (2)–(4) derived from the Charities Act 1960, s 7(2), (3), (5); sub-s (5) derived from the Charities Act 1960, s 7(6), as added by the Charities Act 1992, s 7(1), (4).

Initial Commencement

Specified date: 1 August 1993: see s 99(1).

Extent

This section does not extend to Scotland.

Amendment

Sub-s (1): words 'The Commission' in square brackets substituted by the Charities Act 2006, s 75(1), Sch 8, paras 96, 103(1), (2)(a).

Sub-s (1): in para (a) words 'furnish the Commission' in square brackets substituted by the Charities Act 2006, s 75(1), Sch 8, paras 96, 103(1), (2)(b).

Sub-s (1): in para (a) words 'the Commission's functions' in square brackets substituted by the Charities Act 2006, s 75(1), Sch 8, paras 96, 103(1), (2)(c).

Sub-s (1): in para (b) words 'the Commission's functions' in square brackets substituted by the Charities Act 2006, s 75(1), Sch 8, paras 96, 103(1), (2)(c).

Sub-s (1): in para (b)(i) words 'furnish the Commission' in square brackets substituted by the Charities Act 2006, s 75(1), Sch 8, paras 96, 103(1), (2)(b).

Sub-s (1): in para (b)(ii) words 'the Commission for its' in square brackets substituted by the Charities Act 2006, s 75(1), Sch 8, paras 96, 103(1), (2)(d).

Sub-s (2): words 'member of the staff of the Commission, if so authorised by it' in square brackets substituted by the Charities Act 2006, s 75(1), Sch 8, paras 96, 103(1), (3)(a).

Sub-s (2): words 'the Commission' in square brackets substituted by the Charities Act 2006, s 75(1), Sch 8, paras 96, 103(1), (3)(b).

Sub-s (3): words 'The Commission' and 'the Commission' in square brackets substituted by the Charities Act 2006, s 75(1), Sch 8, paras 96, 103(1), (4)(a), (e).

Sub-s (3): words 'to it' and 'to the Commission' in square brackets substituted by the Charities Act 2006, s 75(1), Sch 8, paras 96, 103(1), (4)(b), (c).

Sub-s (3): words 'it to inspect' in square brackets substituted by the Charities Act 2006, s 75(1), Sch 8, paras 96, 103(1), (4)(d).

Sub-s (4): repealed by the Charities Act 2006, ss 12, 75(2), Sch 5, para 3, Sch 9.

Date in force: to be appointed: see the Charities Act 2006, s 79(2).

Sub-s (6): inserted by the Charities Act 2006, s 75(1), Sch 8, paras 96, 103(1), (5).

[10 Disclosure of information to Commission]

[(1) Any relevant public authority may disclose information to the Commission if the disclosure is made for the purpose of enabling or assisting the Commission to discharge any of its functions.

(2) But Revenue and Customs information may be disclosed under subsection (1) only if it relates to an institution, undertaking or body falling within one (or more) of the following paragraphs—

(a) a charity;
(b) an institution which is established for charitable, benevolent or philanthropic purposes;
(c) an institution by or in respect of which a claim for exemption has at any time been made under section 505(1) of the Income and Corporation Taxes Act 1988;
(d) a subsidiary undertaking of a charity;
(e) a body entered in the Scottish Charity Register which is managed or controlled wholly or mainly in or from England or Wales.

(3) In subsection (2)(d) above 'subsidiary undertaking of a charity' means an undertaking (as defined by section 259(1) of the Companies Act 1985) in relation to which—

(a) a charity is (or is to be treated as) a parent undertaking in accordance with the provisions of section 258 of, and Schedule 10A to, the Companies Act 1985, or
(b) two or more charities would, if they were a single charity, be (or be treated as) a parent undertaking in accordance with those provisions.

(4) For the purposes of the references to a parent undertaking—

(a) in subsection (3) above, and
(b) in section 258 of, and Schedule 10A to, the Companies Act 1985 as they apply for the purposes of that subsection,

'undertaking' includes a charity which is not an undertaking as defined by section 259(1) of that Act.]

NOTES

Derivation

This section derived from the Charities Act 1992, s 52.

Amendment

Substituted, together with ss 10A–10C for this section as originally enacted, by the Charities Act 2006, s 75(1), Sch 8, paras 96, 104.

Date in force: 8 November 2006: see the Charities Act 2006, s 79(1)(g).

[10A Disclosure of information by Commission]

[(1) Subject to subsections (2) and (3) below, the Commission may disclose to any relevant public authority any information received by the Commission in connection with any of the Commission's functions—

(a) if the disclosure is made for the purpose of enabling or assisting the relevant public authority to discharge any of its functions, or
(b) if the information so disclosed is otherwise relevant to the discharge of any of the functions of the relevant public authority.

(2) In the case of information disclosed to the Commission under section 10(1) above, the Commission's power to disclose the information under subsection (1) above is exercisable subject to any express restriction subject to which the information was disclosed to the Commission.

(3) Subsection (2) above does not apply in relation to Revenue and Customs information disclosed to the Commission under section 10(1) above; but any such information may not be further disclosed (whether under subsection (1) above or otherwise) except with the consent of the Commissioners for Her Majesty's Revenue and Customs.

(4) Any responsible person who discloses information in contravention of subsection (3) above is guilty of an offence and liable—

(a) on summary conviction, to imprisonment for a term not exceeding 12 months or to a fine not exceeding the statutory maximum, or both;
(b) on conviction on indictment, to imprisonment for a term not exceeding two years or to a fine, or both.

(5) It is a defence for a responsible person charged with an offence under subsection (4) above of disclosing information to prove that he reasonably believed—

(a) that the disclosure was lawful, or
(b) that the information had already and lawfully been made available to the public.

(6) In the application of this section to Scotland or Northern Ireland, the reference to 12 months in subsection (4) is to be read as a reference to 6 months.

(7) In this section 'responsible person' means a person who is or was—

(a) a member of the Commission,
(b) a member of the staff of the Commission,
(c) a person acting on behalf of the Commission or a member of the staff of the Commission, or
(d) a member of a committee established by the Commission.]

NOTES

Amendment

Substituted, together with ss 10, 10B, 10C for s 10 as originally enacted, by the Charities Act 2006, s 75(1), Sch 8, paras 96, 104.

Date in force: 8 November 2006: see the Charities Act 2006, s 79(1)(g).

[10B Disclosure to and by principal regulators of exempt charities]

[(1) Sections 10 and 10A above apply with the modifications in subsections (2) to (4) below in relation to the disclosure of information to or by the principal regulator of an exempt charity.

(2) References in those sections to the Commission or to any of its functions are to be read as references to the principal regulator of an exempt charity or to any of the functions of that body or person as principal regulator in relation to the charity.

(3) Section 10 above has effect as if for subsections (2) and (3) there were substituted—

'(2) But Revenue and Customs information may be disclosed under subsection (1) only if it relates to—

(a) the exempt charity in relation to which the principal regulator has functions as such, or
(b) a subsidiary undertaking of the exempt charity.

(3) In subsection (2)(b) above 'subsidiary undertaking of the exempt charity' means an undertaking (as defined by section 259(1) of the Companies Act 1985) in relation to which—

(a) the exempt charity is (or is to be treated as) a parent undertaking in accordance with the provisions of section 258 of, and Schedule 10A to, the Companies Act 1985, or
(b) the exempt charity and one or more other charities would, if they were a single charity, be (or be treated as) a parent undertaking in accordance with those provisions.'

(4) Section 10A above has effect as if for the definition of 'responsible person' in subsection (7) there were substituted a definition specified by regulations under section 13(4)(b) of the Charities Act 2006 (regulations prescribing principal regulators).

(5) Regulations under section 13(4)(b) of that Act may also make such amendments or other modifications of any enactment as the Secretary of State considers appropriate for securing that any disclosure provisions that would otherwise apply in relation to the principal regulator of an exempt charity do not apply in relation to that body or person in its or his capacity as principal regulator.

(6) In subsection (5) above 'disclosure provisions' means provisions having effect for authorising, or otherwise in connection with, the disclosure of information by or to the principal regulator concerned.]

NOTES

Amendment

Substituted, together with ss 10, 10A, 10C for s 10 as originally enacted, by the Charities Act 2006, s 75(1), Sch 8, paras 96, 104.

Date in force: to be appointed: see the Charities Act 2006, s 79(2).

[10C Disclosure of information: supplementary]

[(1) In sections 10 and 10A above 'relevant public authority' means—

(a) any government department (including a Northern Ireland department),
(b) any local authority,
(c) any constable, and
(d) any other body or person discharging functions of a public nature (including a body or person discharging regulatory functions in relation to any description of activities).

(2) In section 10A above 'relevant public authority' also includes any body or person within subsection (1)(d) above in a country or territory outside the United Kingdom.

(3) In sections 10 to 10B above and this section—

'enactment' has the same meaning as in the Charities Act 2006;
'Revenue and Customs information' means information held as mentioned in section 18(1) of the Commissioners for Revenue and Customs Act 2005.

(4) Nothing in sections 10 and 10A above (or in those sections as applied by section 10B(1) to (4) above) authorises the making of a disclosure which—

(a) contravenes the Data Protection Act 1998, or
(b) is prohibited by Part 1 of the Regulation of Investigatory Powers Act 2000.]

NOTES

Amendment

Substituted, together with ss 10, 10A, 10B for s 10 as originally enacted, by the Charities Act 2006, s 75(1), Sch 8, paras 96, 104.

Date in force: 8 November 2006: see the Charities Act 2006, s 79(1)(g).

11 Supply of false or misleading information to Commissioners [Commission], etc

(1) Any person who knowingly or recklessly provides the *Commissioners* [Commission] with information which is false or misleading in a material particular shall be guilty of an offence if the information—

(a) is provided in purported compliance with a requirement imposed by or under this Act; or
(b) is provided otherwise than as mentioned in paragraph (a) above but in circumstances in which the person providing the information intends, or could reasonably be expected to know, that it would be used by the *Commissioners* [Commission] for the purpose of discharging *their functions* [its functions] under this Act.

(2) Any person who wilfully alters, suppresses, conceals or destroys any document which he is or is liable to be required, by or under this Act, to produce to the *Commissioners* [Commission] shall be guilty of an offence.

(3) Any person guilty of an offence under this section shall be liable—

(a) on summary conviction, to a fine not exceeding the statutory maximum;
(b) on conviction on indictment, to imprisonment for a term not exceeding two years or to a fine, or both.

(4) In this section references to the *Commissioners* [Commission] include references to any person conducting an inquiry under section 8 above.

NOTES

Derivation

This section derived from the Charities Act 1992, s 54.

Initial Commencement

Specified date: 1 August 1993: see s 99(1).

Extent

This section does not extend to Scotland.

Amendment

Section heading: word 'Commissioners' repealed and subsequent word in square brackets substituted by the Charities Act 2006, s 75(1), Sch 8, paras 96, 105(1), (2).

Date in force: to be appointed: see the Charities Act 2006, s 79(2).

Word 'Commission' in square brackets in each place it occurs substituted by the Charities Act 2006, s 75(1), Sch 8, paras 96, 105(1), (2).

Sub-s (1): in para (b) words 'its functions' in square brackets substituted by the Charities Act 2006, s 75(1), Sch 8, paras 96, 105(1), (3).

12 ...

...

NOTES

Amendment

Repealed by the Data Protection Act 1998, s 74(2), Sch 16, Pt I.

Date in force: 1 March 2000: see SI 2000/183, art 2(1).

Part IV
Application of Property Cy-près and Assistance and Supervision of Charities by Court and Commissioners [and Commission]

NOTES

Amendment

Words 'and Commissioners' repealed and subsequent words in square brackets substituted by the Charities Act 2006, s 75(1), Sch 8, paras 96, 106.

Date in force: to be appointed: see the Charities Act 2006, s 79(2).

Extended powers of court and variation of charters

13 Occasions for applying property cy-près

(1) Subject to subsection (2) below, the circumstances in which the original purposes of a charitable gift can be altered to allow the property given or part of it to be applied cy-près shall be as follows—

(a) where the original purposes, in whole or in part—
  (i) have been as far as may be fulfilled; or

(ii) cannot be carried out, or not according to the directions given and to the spirit of the gift; or

(b) where the original purposes provide a use for part only of the property available by virtue of the gift; or

(c) where the property available by virtue of the gift and other property applicable for similar purposes can be more effectively used in conjunction, and to that end can suitably, regard being had to *the spirit of the gift* [the appropriate considerations], be made applicable to common purposes; or

(d) where the original purposes were laid down by reference to an area which then was but has since ceased to be a unit for some other purpose, or by reference to a class of persons or to an area which has for any reason since ceased to be suitable, regard being had to *the spirit of the gift* [the appropriate considerations], or to be practical in administering the gift; or

(e) where the original purposes, in whole or in part, have, since they were laid down,—

(i) been adequately provided for by other means; or

(ii) ceased, as being useless or harmful to the community or for other reasons, to be in law charitable; or

(iii) ceased in any other way to provide a suitable and effective method of using the property available by virtue of the gift, regard being had to *the spirit of the gift* [the appropriate considerations].

[(1A) In subsection (1) above 'the appropriate considerations' means—

(a) (on the one hand) the spirit of the gift concerned, and

(b) (on the other) the social and economic circumstances prevailing at the time of the proposed alteration of the original purposes.]

(2) Subsection (1) above shall not affect the conditions which must be satisfied in order that property given for charitable purposes may be applied cy-près except in so far as those conditions require a failure of the original purposes.

(3) References in the foregoing subsections to the original purposes of a gift shall be construed, where the application of the property given has been altered or regulated by a scheme or otherwise, as referring to the purposes for which the property is for the time being applicable.

(4) Without prejudice to the power to make schemes in circumstances falling within subsection (1) above, the court may by scheme made under the court's jurisdiction with respect to charities, in any case where the purposes for which the property is held are laid down by reference to any such area as is mentioned in the first column in Schedule 3 to this Act, provide for enlarging the area to any such area as is mentioned in the second column in the same entry in that Schedule.

(5) It is hereby declared that a trust for charitable purposes places a trustee under a duty, where the case permits and requires the property or some part of it to be applied cy-près, to secure its effective use for charity by taking steps to enable it to be so applied.

NOTES

Derivation

This section derived from the Charities Act 1960, s 13.

Initial Commencement

Specified date: 1 August 1993: see s 99(1).

Extent

This section does not extend to Scotland.

Amendment

Sub-s (1): in para (c) words 'the spirit of the gift' in italics repealed and subsequent words in square brackets substituted by the Charities Act 2006, s 15(1), (2).

Date in force: to be appointed: see the Charities Act 2006, s 79(2).

Sub-s (1): in para (d) words 'the spirit of the gift' in italics repealed and subsequent words in square brackets substituted by the Charities Act 2006, s 15(1), (2).

Date in force: to be appointed: see the Charities Act 2006, s 79(2).

Sub-s (1): in para (e)(iii) words 'the spirit of the gift' in italics repealed and subsequent words in square brackets substituted by the Charities Act 2006, s 15(1), (2).

Date in force: to be appointed: see the Charities Act 2006, s 79(2).

Sub-s (1A): inserted by the Charities Act 2006, s 15(3).

Date in force: to be appointed: see the Charities Act 2006, s 79(2).

14 Application cy-près of gifts of donors unknown or disclaiming

(1) Property given for specific charitable purposes which fail shall be applicable cy-près as if given for charitable purposes generally, where it belongs—

(a) to a donor who after—
   (i) the prescribed advertisements and inquiries have been published and made, and
   (ii) the prescribed period beginning with the publication of those advertisements has expired,

   cannot be identified or cannot be found; or

(b) to a donor who has executed a disclaimer in the prescribed form of his right to have the property returned.

(2) Where the prescribed advertisements and inquiries have been published and made by or on behalf of trustees with respect to any such property, the trustees shall not be liable to any person in respect of the property if no claim by him to be interested in it is received by them before the expiry of the period mentioned in subsection (1)(a)(ii) above.

(3) For the purposes of this section property shall be conclusively presumed (without any advertisement or inquiry) to belong to donors who cannot be identified, in so far as it consists—

(a) of the proceeds of cash collections made by means of collecting boxes or by other means not adapted for distinguishing one gift from another; or
(b) of the proceeds of any lottery, competition, entertainment, sale or similar money-raising activity, after allowing for property given to provide prizes or articles for sale or otherwise to enable the activity to be undertaken.

(4) The court [or the Commission] may by order direct that property not falling within subsection (3) above shall for the purposes of this section be treated (without any advertisement or inquiry) as belonging to donors who cannot be identified where it appears to the court [or the Commission] either—

(a) that it would be unreasonable, having regard to the amounts likely to be returned to the donors, to incur expense with a view to returning the property; or
(b) that it would be unreasonable, having regard to the nature, circumstances and amounts of the gifts, and to the lapse of time since the gifts were made, for the donors to expect the property to be returned.

(5) Where property is applied cy-près by virtue of this section, the donor shall be deemed to have parted with all his interest at the time when the gift was made; but where property is so applied as belonging to donors who cannot be identified or cannot be found, and is not so applied by virtue of subsection (3) or (4) above—

(a) the scheme shall specify the total amount of that property; and
(b) the donor of any part of that amount shall be entitled, if he makes a claim not later than six months after the date on which the scheme is made, to recover from the

charity for which the property is applied a sum equal to that part, less any expenses properly incurred by the charity trustees after that date in connection with claims relating to his gift; and

(c) the scheme may include directions as to the provision to be made for meeting any such claim.

(6) Where—

(a) any sum is, in accordance with any such directions, set aside for meeting any such claims, but

(b) the aggregate amount of any such claims actually made exceeds the relevant amount,

then, if *the Commissioners so direct* [the Commission so directs], each of the donors in question shall be entitled only to such proportion of the relevant amount as the amount of his claim bears to the aggregate amount referred to in paragraph (b) above; and for this purpose 'the relevant amount' means the amount of the sum so set aside after deduction of any expenses properly incurred by the charity trustees in connection with claims relating to the donors' gifts.

(7) For the purposes of this section, charitable purposes shall be deemed to 'fail' where any difficulty in applying property to those purposes makes that property or the part not applicable cy-près available to be returned to the donors.

(8) In this section 'prescribed' means prescribed by regulations made by *the Commissioners* [the Commission]; and such regulations may, as respects the advertisements which are to be published for the purposes of subsection (1)(a) above, make provision as to the form and content of such advertisements as well as the manner in which they are to be published.

(9) Any regulations made by *the Commissioners* [the Commission] under this section shall be published by *the Commissioners* [the Commission] in such manner as *they think fit* [it thinks fit].

(10) In this section, except in so far as the context otherwise requires, references to a donor include persons claiming through or under the original donor, and references to property given include the property for the time being representing the property originally given or property derived from it.

(11) This section shall apply to property given for charitable purposes, notwithstanding that it was so given before the commencement of this Act.

NOTES

Derivation

Sub-ss (1), (5) derived from the Charities Act 1960, s 14(1), (4) as amended by the Charities Act 1992, s 15(1), (2), (4); sub-ss (2), (6), (8), (9) derived from the Charities Act 1960, s 14(1A), (4A), (5A), (5B), as added by the Charities Act 1992, s 15(1), (3), (5), (6); sub-ss (3), (4), (7), (10), (11) derived from the Charities Act 1960, s 14(2), (3), (5), (6), (7).

Initial Commencement

Specified date: 1 August 1993: see s 99(1).

Extent

This section does not extend to Scotland.

Amendment

Sub-s (4): words 'or the Commission' in square brackets in both places they occur inserted by the Charities Act 2006, s 16.

Date in force: to be appointed: see the Charities Act 2006, s 79(2).

Sub-s (6): words 'the Commission so direct' in square brackets substituted by the Charities Act 2006, s 75(1), Sch 8, paras 96, 107(1), (2).

Sub-s (8): words 'the Commission' in square brackets substituted by the Charities Act 2006, s 75(1), Sch 8, paras 96, 107(1), (3).

Sub-s (9): words 'the Commission' in square brackets in both places they occur substituted by the Charities Act 2006, s 75(1), Sch 8, paras 96, 107(1), (4)(a).

Sub-s (9): words 'it thinks fit' in square brackets substituted by the Charities Act 2006, s 75(1), Sch 8, paras 96, 107(1), (4)(b).

[14A Application cy-près of gifts made in response to certain solicitations]

[(1) This section applies to property given—

(a) for specific charitable purposes, and
(b) in response to a solicitation within subsection (2) below.

(2) A solicitation is within this subsection if—

(a) it is made for specific charitable purposes, and
(b) it is accompanied by a statement to the effect that property given in response to it will, in the event of those purposes failing, be applicable cy-près as if given for charitable purposes generally, unless the donor makes a relevant declaration at the time of making the gift.

(3) A 'relevant declaration' is a declaration in writing by the donor to the effect that, in the event of the specific charitable purposes failing, he wishes the trustees holding the property to give him the opportunity to request the return of the property in question (or a sum equal to its value at the time of the making of the gift).

(4) Subsections (5) and (6) below apply if—

(a) a person has given property as mentioned in subsection (1) above,
(b) the specific charitable purposes fail, and
(c) the donor has made a relevant declaration.

(5) The trustees holding the property must take the prescribed steps for the purpose of—

(a) informing the donor of the failure of the purposes,
(b) enquiring whether he wishes to request the return of the property (or a sum equal to its value), and
(c) if within the prescribed period he makes such a request, returning the property (or such a sum) to him.

(6) If those trustees have taken all appropriate prescribed steps but—

(a) they have failed to find the donor, or
(b) the donor does not within the prescribed period request the return of the property (or a sum equal to its value),

section 14(1) above shall apply to the property as if it belonged to a donor within paragraph (b) of that subsection (application of property where donor has disclaimed right to return of property).

(7) If—

(a) a person has given property as mentioned in subsection (1) above,
(b) the specific charitable purposes fail, and
(c) the donor has not made a relevant declaration,

section 14(1) above shall similarly apply to the property as if it belonged to a donor within paragraph (b) of that subsection.

(8) For the purposes of this section—

(a) 'solicitation' means a solicitation made in any manner and however communicated to the persons to whom it is addressed,
(b) it is irrelevant whether any consideration is or is to be given in return for the property in question, and
(c) where any appeal consists of both solicitations that are accompanied by statements within subsection (2)(b) and solicitations that are not so accompanied, a person giving property as a result of the appeal is to be taken to have responded to the former solicitations and not the latter, unless he proves otherwise.

(9) In this section 'prescribed' means prescribed by regulations made by the Commission, and any such regulations shall be published by the Commission in such manner as it thinks fit.

(10) Subsections (7) and (10) of section 14 shall apply for the purposes of this section as they apply for the purposes of section 14.]

NOTES

Amendment

Inserted by the Charities Act 2006, s 17.

Date in force (for remaining purposes): to be appointed: see the Charities Act 2006, s 79(2).

[14B Cy-près schemes]

[(1) The power of the court or the Commission to make schemes for the application of property cy-près shall be exercised in accordance with this section.

(2) Where any property given for charitable purposes is applicable cy-près, the court or the Commission may make a scheme providing for the property to be applied—

(a) for such charitable purposes, and
(b) (if the scheme provides for the property to be transferred to another charity) by or on trust for such other charity,

as it considers appropriate, having regard to the matters set out in subsection (3).

(3) The matters are—

(a) the spirit of the original gift,
(b) the desirability of securing that the property is applied for charitable purposes which are close to the original purposes, and
(c) the need for the relevant charity to have purposes which are suitable and effective in the light of current social and economic circumstances.

The 'relevant charity' means the charity by or on behalf of which the property is to be applied under the scheme.

(4) If a scheme provides for the property to be transferred to another charity, the scheme may impose on the charity trustees of that charity a duty to secure that the property is applied for purposes which are, so far as is reasonably practicable, similar in character to the original purposes.

(5) In this section references to property given include the property for the time being representing the property originally given or property derived from it.

(6) In this section references to the transfer of property to a charity are references to its transfer—

(a) to the charity, or
(b) to the charity trustees, or
(c) to any trustee for the charity, or
(d) to a person nominated by the charity trustees to hold it in trust for the charity,

as the scheme may provide.]

NOTES

Amendment

Inserted by the Charities Act 2006, s 18; for transitional provisions and savings see s 75(3), Sch 10, para 3 thereto.

Date in force: to be appointed: see the Charities Act 2006, s 79(2).

15 Charities governed by charter, or by or under statute

(1) Where a Royal charter establishing or regulating a body corporate is amendable by the grant and acceptance of a further charter, a scheme relating to the body corporate or to the administration of property held by the body (including a scheme for the cy-près application of any such property) may be made by the court under the court's jurisdiction with respect to charities notwithstanding that the scheme cannot take effect without the alteration of the charter, but shall be so framed that the scheme, or such part of it as cannot take effect without the alteration of the charter, does not purport to come into operation unless or until Her Majesty thinks fit to amend the charter in such manner as will permit the scheme or that part of it to have effect.

(2) Where under the court's jurisdiction with respect to charities or the corresponding jurisdiction of a court in Northern Ireland, or under powers conferred by this Act or by any Northern Ireland legislation relating to charities, a scheme is made with respect to a body corporate, and it appears to Her Majesty expedient, having regard to the scheme, to amend any Royal charter relating to that body, Her Majesty may, on the application of that body, amend the charter accordingly by Order in Council in any way in which the charter could be amended by the grant and acceptance of a further charter; and any such Order in Council may be revoked or varied in like manner as the charter it amends.

(3) The jurisdiction of the court with respect to charities shall not be excluded or restricted in the case of a charity of any description mentioned in Schedule 4 to this Act by the operation of the enactments or instruments there mentioned in relation to that description, and a scheme established for any such charity may modify or supersede in relation to it the provision made by any such enactment or instrument as if made by a scheme of the court, and may also make any such provision as is authorised by that Schedule.

NOTES

Derivation

Sub-ss (1), (3) derived from the Charities Act 1960, s 15(1), (3); sub-s (2) derived from the Charities Act 1960, s 15(2), as read with the Interpretation Act 1978, s 24(4).

Initial Commencement

Specified date: 1 August 1993: see s 99(1).

Extent

This section does not extend to Scotland.

Modification

The Northern Ireland Act 1998 makes new provision for the government of Northern Ireland for the purpose of implementing the Belfast Agreement (the agreement reached at multi-party talks on Northern Ireland and set out in Command Paper 3883). As a consequence of that Act, any reference in this section to the Parliament of Northern Ireland or the Assembly established under the Northern Ireland Assembly Act 1973, s 1, certain office-holders and Ministers, and any legislative act and certain financial dealings thereof, shall, for the period specified, be construed in accordance with Sch 12, paras 1–11 to the 1998 Act.

Subordinate Legislation

Royal College of Ophthalmologists (Charter Amendment) Order 1998, SI 1998/2252 (made under sub-s (2)).

Corporation of the Cranleigh and Bramley Schools (Charter Amendments) Order 1999, SI 1999/656 (made under sub-s (2)).

Royal College of Physicians of London (Charter Amendment) Order 1999, SI 1999/667 (made under sub-s (2)).

Licensed Victuallers' National Homes (Charter Amendment) Order 2000, SI 2000/1348 (made under sub-s (2)).

Institution of Chemical Engineers (Charter Amendment) Order 2004, SI 2004/1986 (made under sub-s (2)).

Powers of Commissioners [Powers of Commission] to make schemes and act for protection of charities etc

NOTES

Amendment

Words 'Powers of Commissioners' repealed and subsequent words in square brackets substituted by the Charities Act 2006, s 75(1), Sch 8, paras 96, 108.

Date in force: to be appointed: see the Charities Act 2006, s 79(2).

16 Concurrent jurisdiction with High Court for certain purposes

(1) Subject to the provisions of this Act, *the Commissioners* [the Commission] may by order exercise the same jurisdiction and powers as are exercisable by the High Court in charity proceedings for the following purposes—

(a) establishing a scheme for the administration of a charity;
(b) appointing, discharging or removing a charity trustee or trustee for a charity, or removing an officer or employee;
(c) vesting or transferring property, or requiring or entitling any person to call for or make any transfer of property or any payment.

(2) Where the court directs a scheme for the administration of a charity to be established, the court may by order refer the matter to *the Commissioners for them* [the Commission for it] to prepare or settle a scheme in accordance with such directions (if any) as the court sees fit to give, and any such order may provide for the scheme to be put into effect by order of *the Commissioners* [the Commission] as if prepared under subsection (1) above and without any further order of the court.

(3) *The Commissioners* [The Commission] shall not have jurisdiction under this section to try or determine the title at law or in equity to any property as between a charity or trustee for a charity and a person holding or claiming the property or an interest in it adversely to the charity, or to try or determine any question as to the existence or extent of any charge or trust.

(4) Subject to the following subsections, *the Commissioners shall not exercise their* [the Commission shall not exercise its] jurisdiction under this section as respects any charity, except—

(a) on the application of the charity; or
(b) on an order of the court under subsection (2) above; or
(c) *in the case of a charity other than an exempt charity,* on the application of the Attorney General.

(5) In the case of a charity *which is not an exempt charity and* whose *income from all sources does not in aggregate* [gross income does not] exceed £500 a year, *the Commissioners may exercise their* [the Commission may exercise its] jurisdiction under this section on the application—

(a) of any one or more of the charity trustees; or
(b) of any person interested in the charity; or
(c) of any two or more inhabitants of the area of the charity if it is a local charity.

(6) Where in the case of a charity, other than an exempt charity, *the Commissioners are* [the Commission is] satisfied that the charity trustees ought in the interests of the charity to apply for a scheme, but have unreasonably refused or neglected to do so and *the Commissioners have* [the Commission has] given the charity trustees an opportunity to make representations to them, *the Commissioners* [the Commission] may proceed as if an application for a scheme had been made by the charity but *the Commissioners* [the Commission] shall not have power in a case where *they act* [it acts] by virtue of this subsection to alter the purposes of a charity, unless forty years have elapsed from the date of its foundation.

(7) Where—

(a) a charity cannot apply to *the Commissioners* [the Commission] for a scheme by reason of any vacancy among the charity trustees or the absence or incapacity of any of them, but
(b) such an application is made by such number of the charity trustees as *the Commissioners consider* [the Commission considers] appropriate in the circumstances of the case,

the Commissioners [the Commission] may nevertheless proceed as if the application were an application made by the charity.

(8) *The Commissioners* [The Commission] may on the application of any charity trustee or trustee for a charity exercise *their jurisdiction* [its jurisdiction] under this section for the purpose of discharging him from his trusteeship.

(9) Before exercising any jurisdiction under this section otherwise than on an order of the court, *the Commissioners shall give notice of their* [the Commission shall give notice of its] intention to do so to each of the charity trustees, except any that cannot be found or has no known address in the United Kingdom or who is party or privy to an application for the exercise of the jurisdiction; and any such notice may be given by post, and, if given by post, may be addressed to the recipient's last known address in the United Kingdom.

(10) *The Commissioners shall not exercise their* [The Commission shall not exercise its] jurisdiction under this section in any case (not referred to them by order of the court) which, by reason of its contentious character, or of any special question of law or of fact which it may involve, or for other reasons, *the Commissioners* [the Commission] may consider more fit to be adjudicated on by the court.

(11) *An appeal against any order of the Commissioners under this section may be brought in the High Court by the Attorney General.*

(12) *An appeal against any order of the Commissioners under this section may also, at any time within the three months beginning with the day following that on which the order is published, be brought in the High Court by the charity or any of the charity trustees, or by any person removed from any office or employment by the order (unless he is removed with the concurrence of the charity trustees or with the approval of the special visitor, if any, of the charity).*

(13) No *appeal shall be brought under subsection (12) above except with a certificate of the Commissioners that it is a proper case for an appeal or with the leave of one of the judges of the High Court attached to the Chancery Division.*

(14) *Where an order of the Commissioners under this section establishes a scheme for the administration of a charity, any person interested in the charity shall have the like right of appeal under subsection (12) above as a charity trustee, and so also, in the case of a charity*

which is a local charity in any area, shall any two or more inhabitants of the area and the council of any parish or (in Wales) any community comprising the area or any part of it.

(15) If the [Minister] thinks it expedient to do so—

(a) in consequence of changes in the value of money, or
(b) with a view to increasing the number of charities in respect of which *the Commissioners may exercise their* [the Commission may exercise its] jurisdiction under this section in accordance with subsection (5) above,

he may by order amend that subsection by substituting a different sum for the sum for the time being specified there.

NOTES

Derivation

Sub-s (1) derived from the Charities Act 1960, s 18(1), as amended by the Charities Act 1992, s 47, Sch 3, para 6; sub-ss (2), (3), (8)–(11) derived from the Charities Act 1960, s 18(2), (3), (7)–(10); sub-ss (4), (6) derived from the Charities Act 1960, s 18(4), (6), as amended by the Charities Act 1992, s 13(1), (2), (4); sub-s (5) derived from the Charities Act 1960, s 18(5), as substituted by the Charities Act 1992, s 13(1), (3); sub-ss (7), (15) derived from the Charities Act 1960, s 18(6A), (13), as added by the Charities Act 1992, s 13(1), (5), (6); sub-ss (12), (13) derived from the Charities Act 1960, s 18(11); sub-s (14) derived from the Charities Act 1960, s 18(12), as amended by the Local Government Act 1972, ss 210(9)(d), (10), 272(1), Sch 30, and as read with s 179(1), (4) thereof.

Initial Commencement

Specified date: 1 August 1993: see s 99(1).

Extent

This section does not extend to Scotland.

Amendment

Sub-s (1): words 'the Commission' in square brackets substituted by the Charities Act 2006, s 75(1), Sch 8, paras 96, 109(1), (2).

Sub-s (2): words 'the Commission for it' in square brackets substituted by the Charities Act 2006, s 75(1), Sch 8, paras 96, 109(1), (3)(a).

Sub-s (2): words 'the Commission' in square brackets substituted by the Charities Act 2006, s 75(1), Sch 8, paras 96, 109(1), (3)(b).

Sub-s (3): words 'The Commission' in square brackets substituted by the Charities Act 2006, s 75(1), Sch 8, paras 96, 109(1), (4).

Sub-s (4): words 'the Commission shall not exercise its' in square brackets substituted by the Charities Act 2006, s 75(1), Sch 8, paras 96, 109(1), (5).

Sub-s (4)(c): words 'in the case of a charity other than an exempt charity,' in italics repealed by the Charities Act 2006, ss 12, 75(2), Sch 5, para 4(1), (2), Sch 9.

Date in force: to be appointed: see the Charities Act 2006, s 79(2).

Sub-s (5): words 'which is not an exempt charity and' in italics repealed by the Charities Act 2006, ss 12, 75(2), Sch 5, para 4(1), (3), Sch 9.

Date in force: to be appointed: see the Charities Act 2006, s 79(2).

Sub-s (5): words 'gross income does not' in square brackets substituted by the Charities Act 2006, s 75(1), Sch 8, paras 96, 109(1), (6)(a).

Sub-s (5): words 'the Commission may exercise its' in square brackets substituted by the Charities Act 2006, s 75(1), Sch 8, paras 96, 109(1), (6)(b).

Sub-s (6): words 'the Commission is' in square brackets substituted by the Charities Act 2006, s 75(1), Sch 8, paras 96, 109(1), (7)(a).

Sub-s (6): words 'the Commission has' in square brackets substituted by the Charities Act 2006, s 75(1), Sch 8, paras 96, 109(1), (7)(b).

Sub-s (6): words 'the Commission' in square brackets in both places they occur substituted by the Charities Act 2006, s 75(1), Sch 8, paras 96, 109(1), (7)(c).

Sub-s (6): words 'it acts' in square brackets substituted by the Charities Act 2006, s 75(1), Sch 8, paras 96, 109(1), (7)(d).

Sub-s (7): in para (a) words 'the Commission' in square brackets substituted by the Charities Act 2006, s 75(1), Sch 8, paras 96, 109(1), (8)(a).

Sub-s (7): in para (b) words 'the Commission considers' in square brackets substituted by the Charities Act 2006, s 75(1), Sch 8, paras 96, 109(1), (8)(b).

Sub-s (7): words 'the Commission' in square brackets substituted by the Charities Act 2006, s 75(1), Sch 8, paras 96, 109(1), (8)(a).

Sub-s (8): words 'The Commission' in square brackets substituted by the Charities Act 2006, s 75(1), Sch 8, paras 96, 109(1), (9)(a).

Sub-s (8): words 'its jurisdiction' in square brackets substituted by the Charities Act 2006, s 75(1), Sch 8, paras 96, 109(1), (9)(b).

Sub-s (9): words 'the Commission shall give notice of its' in square brackets substituted by the Charities Act 2006, s 75(1), Sch 8, paras 96, 109(1), (10).

Sub-s (10): words 'The Commission shall not exercise its' in square brackets substituted by the Charities Act 2006, s 75(1), Sch 8, paras 96, 109(1), (11)(a).

Sub-s (10): words 'the Commission' in square brackets substituted by the Charities Act 2006, s 75(1), Sch 8, paras 96, 109(1), (11)(b).

Sub-ss (11)–(14): repealed by the Charities Act 2006, s 75(1), (2), Sch 8, paras 96, 109(1), (12), Sch 9; for transitional provisions and savings see s 75(3), Sch 10, para 18 thereto.

Date in force: to be appointed: see the Charities Act 2006, s 79(2).

Sub-s (15): word 'Minister' in square brackets substituted by SI 2006/2951, art 6, Schedule, para 4(i).

Date in force: 13 December 2006: see SI 2006/2951, art 1(2).

Sub-s (15): in para (b) words 'the Commission may exercise its' in square brackets substituted by the Charities Act 2006, s 75(1), Sch 8, paras 96, 109(1), (13).

17 Further powers to make schemes or alter application of charitable property

(1) Where it appears to *the Commissioners* [the Commission] that a scheme should be established for the administration of a charity, but also that it is necessary or desirable for the scheme to alter the provision made by an Act of Parliament establishing or regulating the charity or to make any other provision which goes or might go beyond the powers exercisable *by them* [by the Commission] apart from this section, or that it is for any reason proper for the scheme to be subject to parliamentary review, then (subject to subsection (6) below) *the Commissioners* [the Commission] may settle a scheme accordingly with a view to its being given effect under this section.

(2) A scheme settled by *the Commissioners* [the Commission] under this section may be given effect by order of the [Minister], and a draft of the order shall be laid before Parliament.

(3) Without prejudice to the operation of section 6 of the Statutory Instruments Act 1946 in other cases, in the case of a scheme which goes beyond the powers exercisable apart from this section in altering a statutory provision contained in or having effect under any public general Act of Parliament, the order shall not be made unless the draft has been approved by resolution of each House of Parliament.

(4) Subject to subsection (5) below, any provision of a scheme brought into effect under this section may be modified or superseded by the court or *the Commissioners* [the Commission] as if it were a scheme brought into effect by order of *the Commissioners* [the Commission] under section 16 above.

(5) Where subsection (3) above applies to a scheme, the order giving effect to it may direct that the scheme shall not be modified or superseded by a scheme brought into effect otherwise than under this section, and may also direct that that subsection shall apply to any scheme modifying or superseding the scheme to which the order gives effect.

(6) The *Commissioners* [Commission] shall not proceed under this section without the like application and the like notice to the charity trustees, as would be required *if they were* [if the Commission was] proceeding (without an order of the court) under section 16 above; but on any application for a scheme, or in a case where *they act* [it acts] by virtue of subsection (6) or (7) of that section, the *Commissioners* [Commission] may proceed under this section or that section as appears *to them* [to it] appropriate.

(7) Notwithstanding anything in the trusts of a charity, no expenditure incurred in preparing or promoting a Bill in Parliament shall without the consent of the court or *the Commissioners* [the Commission] be defrayed out of any moneys applicable for the purposes of a charity *but this subsection shall not apply in the case of an exempt charity.*

(8) Where *the Commissioners are* [the Commission is] satisfied—

(a) that the whole of the income of a charity cannot in existing circumstances be effectively applied for the purposes of the charity; and
(b) that, if those circumstances continue, a scheme might be made for applying the surplus cy-près; and
(c) that it is for any reason not yet desirable to make such a scheme;

then *the Commissioners* [the Commission] may by order authorise the charity trustees at their discretion (but subject to any conditions imposed by the order) to apply any accrued or accruing income for any purposes for which it might be made applicable by such a scheme, and any application authorised by the order shall be deemed to be within the purposes of the charity.

(9) An order under subsection (8) above shall not extend to more than £300 out of income accrued before the date of the order, nor to income accruing more than three years after that date, nor to more than £100 out of the income accruing in any of those three years.

NOTES

Derivation

Sub-ss (1)–(5), (7) derived from the Charities Act 1960, s 19(1)–(5), (7); sub-s (6) derived from the Charities Act 1960, s 19(6), as amended by the Charities Act 1992, ss 47, 78(2), Sch 3, para 7, Sch 7; sub-ss (8), (9) derived from the Charities Act 1960, s 19(8).

Initial Commencement

Specified date: 1 August 1993: see s 99(1).

Extent

This section does not extend to Scotland.

Amendment

Sub-s (1): words 'the Commission' in square brackets in both places they occur substituted by the Charities Act 2006, s 75(1), Sch 8, paras 96, 110(1), (2)(a).

Sub-s (1): words 'by the Commission' in square brackets substituted by the Charities Act 2006, s 75(1), Sch 8, paras 96, 110(1), (2)(b).

Sub-s (2): words 'the Commission' in square brackets substituted by the Charities Act 2006, s 75(1), Sch 8, paras 96, 110(1), (3).

Sub-s (2): word 'Minister' in square brackets substituted by SI 2006/2951, art 6, Schedule, para 4(j).

Date in force: 13 December 2006: see SI 2006/2951, art 1(2).

Sub-s (4): words 'the Commission' in square brackets in both places they occur substituted by the Charities Act 2006, s 75(1), Sch 8, paras 96, 110(1), (4).

Sub-s (6): word 'Commission' in square brackets in both places it occurs substituted by the Charities Act 2006, s 75(1), Sch 8, paras 96, 110(1), (5)(a).

Sub-s (6): words 'if the Commission was' in square brackets substituted by the Charities Act 2006, s 75(1), Sch 8, paras 96, 110(1), (5)(b).

Sub-s (6): words 'it acts' in square brackets substituted by the Charities Act 2006, s 75(1), Sch 8, paras 96, 110(1), (5)(c).

Sub-s (6): words 'to it' in square brackets substituted by the Charities Act 2006, s 75(1), Sch 8, paras 96, 110(1), (5)(d).

Sub-s (7): words 'the Commission' in square brackets substituted by the Charities Act 2006, s 75(1), Sch 8, paras 96, 110(1), (6).

Sub-s (7): words 'but this subsection shall not apply in the case of an exempt charity' in italics repealed by the Charities Act 2006, ss 12, 75(2), Sch 5, para 5, Sch 9.

Date in force: to be appointed: see the Charities Act 2006, s 79(2).

Sub-s (8): words 'the Commission is' in square brackets substituted by the Charities Act 2006, s 75(1), Sch 8, paras 96, 110(1), (7)(a).

Sub-s (8): words 'the Commission' in square brackets substituted by the Charities Act 2006, s 75(1), Sch 8, paras 96, 110(1), (7)(b).

Subordinate Legislation

Charities (The Royal Philanthropic Society) Order 1994, SI 1994/1235 (made under sub-s (2)).

Charities (The Bridge House Estates) Order 1995, SI 1995/1047 (made under sub-s (2)).

Charities (The Royal School for the Blind) Order 1996, SI 1996/1667 (made under sub-s (2)).

Charities (The Shrubbery) Order 2003, SI 2003/1688 (made under sub-s (2)).

Charities (Alexandra Park and Palace) Order 2004, SI 2004/160 (made under sub-s (2)).

Charities (National Trust) Order 2005, SI 2005/712 (made under sub-s (1)).

Charities (Bridge House Estates) Order 2007, SI 2007/550 (made under sub-s (1)).

18 Power to act for protection of charities

(1) Where, at any time *after they have* [after it has] instituted an inquiry under section 8 above with respect to any charity, *the Commissioners are* [the Commission is] satisfied—

(a) that there is or has been any misconduct or mismanagement in the administration of the charity; or
(b) that it is necessary or desirable to act for the purpose of protecting the property of the charity or securing a proper application for the purposes of the charity of that property or of property coming to the charity,

the Commissioners may of their [the Commission may of its] own motion do one or more of the following things—

(i) by order suspend any trustee, charity trustee, officer, agent or employee of the charity from the exercise of his office or employment pending consideration being given to his removal (whether under this section or otherwise);
(ii) by order appoint such number of additional charity trustees *as they consider* [as it considers] necessary for the proper administration of the charity;
(iii) by order vest any property held by or in trust for the charity in the official custodian, or require the persons in whom any such property is vested to transfer it to him, or appoint any person to transfer any such property to him;
(iv) order any person who holds any property on behalf of the charity, or of any trustee for it, not to part with the property without the approval of *the Commissioners* [the Commission];
(v) order any debtor of the charity not to make any payment in or towards the discharge of his liability to the charity without the approval of *the Commissioners* [the Commission];
(vi) by order restrict (notwithstanding anything in the trusts of the charity) the transactions which may be entered into, or the nature or amount of the payments which may be made, in the administration of the charity without the approval of *the Commissioners* [the Commission];
(vii) by order

appoint (in accordance with section 19 below) *a receiver* [an interim manager, who shall act as receiver] and manager in respect of the property and affairs of the charity.

(2) Where, at any time after *they have* [it has] instituted an inquiry under section 8 above with respect to any charity, *the Commissioners are* [the Commission is] satisfied—

(a) that there is or has been any misconduct or mismanagement in the administration of the charity; and
(b) that it is necessary or desirable to act for the purpose of protecting the property of the charity or securing a proper application for the purposes of the charity of that property or of property coming to the charity,

the Commissioners may of their [the Commission may of its] own motion do either or both of the following things—

(i) by order remove any trustee, charity trustee, officer, agent or employee of the charity who has been responsible for or privy to the misconduct or mismanagement or has by his conduct contributed to it or facilitated it;
(ii) by order establish a scheme for the administration of the charity.

(3) The references in subsection (1) or (2) above to misconduct or mismanagement shall (notwithstanding anything in the trusts of the charity) extend to the employment for the remuneration or reward of persons acting in the affairs of the charity, or for other administrative purposes, of sums which are excessive in relation to the property which is or is likely to be applied or applicable for the purposes of the charity.

(4) *The Commissioners* [The Commission] may also remove a charity trustee by order made of *their own motion* [its own motion]—

(a) where, within the last five years, the trustee—
  (i) having previously been adjudged bankrupt or had his estate sequestrated, has been discharged, or
  (ii) having previously made a composition or arrangement with, or granted a trust deed for, his creditors, has been discharged in respect of it;
(b) where the trustee is a corporation in liquidation;

(c) where the trustee is incapable of acting by reason of mental disorder within the meaning of the Mental Health Act 1983;
(d) where the trustee has not acted, and will not declare his willingness or unwillingness to act;
(e) where the trustee is outside England and Wales or cannot be found or does not act, and his absence or failure to act impedes the proper administration of the charity.

(5) *The Commissioners may by order made of their* [The Commission may by order made of its] own motion appoint a person to be a charity trustee—

(a) in place of a charity trustee *removed by them* [removed by the Commission] under this section or otherwise;
(b) where there are no charity trustees, or where by reason of vacancies in their number or the absence or incapacity of any of their number the charity cannot apply for the appointment;
(c) where there is a single charity trustee, not being a corporation aggregate, and *the Commissioners are of* [the Commission is of] opinion that it is necessary to increase the number for the proper administration of the charity;
(d) where *the Commissioners are of* [the Commission is of] opinion that it is necessary for the proper administration of the charity to have an additional charity trustee because one of the existing charity trustees who ought nevertheless to remain a charity trustee either cannot be found or does not act or is outside England and Wales.

(6) The powers of *the Commissioners* [the Commission] under this section to remove or appoint charity trustees of *their own motion* [its own motion] shall include power to make any such order with respect to the vesting in or transfer to the charity trustees of any property as *the Commissioners* [the Commission] could make on the removal or appointment of a charity trustee *by them* [by it] under section 16 above.

(7) Any order under this section for the removal or appointment of a charity trustee or trustee for a charity, or for the vesting or transfer of any property, shall be of the like effect as an order made under section 16 above.

(8) *Subject to subsection (9) below, subsections (11) to (13) of section 16 above shall apply to orders under this section as they apply to orders under that section.*

(9) *The requirement to obtain any such certificate or leave as is mentioned in section 16(13) above shall not apply to—*

(a) an appeal by a charity or any of the charity trustees of a charity against an order under subsection (1)(vii) above appointing a receiver and manager in respect of the charity's property and affairs, or
(b) an appeal by a person against an order under subsection (2)(i) or (4)(a) above removing him from his office or employment.

(10) *Subsection (14) of section 16 above shall apply to an order under this section which establishes a scheme for the administration of a charity as it applies to such an order under that section.*

(11) The power of *the Commissioners* [the Commission] to make an order under subsection (1)(i) above shall not be exercisable so as to suspend any person from the exercise of his office or employment for a period of more than twelve months; but (without prejudice to the generality of section 89(1) below), any such order made in the case of any person may make provision as respects the period of his suspension for matters arising out of it, and in particular for enabling any person to execute any instrument in his name or otherwise act for him and, in the case of a charity trustee, for adjusting any rules governing the proceedings of the charity trustees to take account of the reduction in the number capable of acting.

(12) Before exercising any jurisdiction under this section otherwise than by virtue of subsection (1) above, *the Commissioners* [the Commission] shall give notice of *their intention* [its intention] to do so to each of the charity trustees, except any that cannot be

found or has no known address in the United Kingdom; and any such notice may be given by post and, if given by post, may be addressed to the recipient's last known address in the United Kingdom.

(13) *The Commissioners* [The Commission] shall, at such intervals as *they think fit* [it thinks fit], review any order made *by them* [by it] under paragraph (i), or any of paragraphs (iii) to (vii), of subsection (1) above; and, if on any such review it appears *to them* [to the Commission] that it would be appropriate to discharge the order in whole or in part, *they shall* [the Commission shall] so discharge it (whether subject to any savings or other transitional provisions or not).

(14) If any person contravenes an order under subsection (1)(iv), (v) or (vi) above, he shall be guilty of an offence and liable on summary conviction to a fine not exceeding level 5 on the standard scale.

(15) Subsection (14) above shall not be taken to preclude the bringing of proceedings for breach of trust against any charity trustee or trustee for a charity in respect of a contravention of an order under subsection (1)(iv) or (vi) above (whether proceedings in respect of the contravention are brought against him under subsection (14) above or not).

(16) This section shall not apply to an exempt charity.

[(16) In this section—

(a) subsections (1) to (3) apply in relation to an exempt charity, and
(b) subsections (4) to (6) apply in relation to such a charity at any time after the Commission have instituted an inquiry under section 8 with respect to it,

and the other provisions of this section apply accordingly.]

NOTES

Derivation

Sub-ss (1), (2), (8)–(10), (14), (15) derived from the Charities Act 1960, s 20(1), (1A), (7), (7A), (7B), (10), (10A), as substituted by the Charities Act 1992, s 8(1), (2), (5), (9); sub-ss (3), (4), (11), (12) derived from the Charities Act 1960, s 20(2), (3), (8), (9), as amended by the Charities Act 1992, s 8(1), (3), (4), (6), (7); sub-ss (5)–(7), (16) derived from the Charities Act 1960, s 20(4)–(6), (12); sub-s (13) derived from the Charities Act 1960, s 20(9A). as added by the Charities Act 1992, s 8(1), (8).

Initial Commencement

Specified date: 1 August 1993: see s 99(1).

Extent

This section does not extend to Scotland.

Amendment

Sub-s (1): words 'after it has' in square brackets substituted by the Charities Act 2006, s 75(1), Sch 8, paras 96, 111(1), (2)(a).

Sub-s (1): words 'the Commission is' in square brackets substituted by the Charities Act 2006, s 75(1), Sch 8, paras 96, 111(1), (2)(b).

Sub-s (1): words 'the Commission may of its' in square brackets substituted by the Charities Act 2006, s 75(1), Sch 8, paras 96, 111(1), (2)(c).

Sub-s (1): in para (b)(ii) words 'as it considers' in square brackets substituted by the Charities Act 2006, s 75(1), Sch 8, paras 96, 111(1), (2)(d).

Sub-s (1): in para (b)(iv) words 'the Commission' in square brackets substituted by the Charities Act 2006, s 75(1), Sch 8, paras 96, 111(1), (2)(e).

Sub-s (1): in para (b)(v) words 'the Commission' in square brackets substituted by the Charities Act 2006, s 75(1), Sch 8, paras 96, 111(1), (2)(e).

Sub-s (1): in para (b)(vi) words 'the Commission' in square brackets substituted by the Charities Act 2006, s 75(1), Sch 8, paras 96, 111(1), (2)(e).

Sub-s (1): in para (b)(vii) words 'an interim manager, who shall act as receiver' in square brackets substituted by the Charities Act 2006, s 75(1), Sch 8, paras 96, 111(1), (2)(f).

Sub-s (2): words 'it has' in square brackets substituted by the Charities Act 2006, s 75(1), Sch 8, paras 96, 111(1), (3)(a).

Sub-s (2): words 'the Commission is' in square brackets substituted by the Charities Act 2006, s 75(1), Sch 8, paras 96, 111(1), (3)(b).

Sub-s (2): words 'the Commission may of its' in square brackets substituted by the Charities Act 2006, s 75(1), Sch 8, paras 96, 111(1), (3)(c).

Sub-s (4): words 'The Commission' in square brackets substituted by the Charities Act 2006, s 75(1), Sch 8, paras 96, 111(1), (4)(a).

Sub-s (4): words 'its own motion' in square brackets substituted by the Charities Act 2006, s 75(1), Sch 8, paras 96, 111(1), (4)(b).

Sub-s (5): words 'The Commission may by order made of its' in square brackets substituted by the Charities Act 2006, s 75(1), Sch 8, paras 96, 111(1), (5)(a).

Sub-s (5): in para (a) words 'removed by the Commission' in square brackets substituted by the Charities Act 2006, s 75(1), Sch 8, paras 96, 111(1), (5)(b).

Sub-s (5): in paras (c), (d) words 'the Commission is of' in square brackets substituted by the Charities Act 2006, s 75(1), Sch 8, paras 96, 111(1), (5)(c).

Sub-s (6): words 'the Commission' in square brackets in both places they occur substituted by the Charities Act 2006, s 75(1), Sch 8, paras 96, 111(1), (6)(a).

Sub-s (6): words 'its own motion' in square brackets substituted by the Charities Act 2006, s 75(1), Sch 8, paras 96, 111(1), (6)(b).

Sub-s (6): words 'by it' in square brackets substituted by the Charities Act 2006, s 75(1), Sch 8, paras 96, 111(1), (6)(c).

Sub-ss (8)–(10): repealed by the Charities Act 2006, s 75(1), (2), Sch 8, paras 96, 111(1), (7), Sch 9; for transitional provisions and savings see s 75(3), Sch 10, para 18 thereto.

Date in force: to be appointed: see the Charities Act 2006, s 79(2).

Sub-s (11): words 'the Commission' in square brackets substituted by the Charities Act 2006, s 75(1), Sch 8, paras 96, 111(1), (8).

Sub-s (12): words 'the Commission' in square brackets substituted by the Charities Act 2006, s 75(1), Sch 8, paras 96, 111(1), (9)(a).

Sub-s (12): words 'its intention' in square brackets substituted by the Charities Act 2006, s 75(1), Sch 8, paras 96, 111(1), (9)(b).

Sub-s (13): words 'The Commission' in square brackets substituted by the Charities Act 2006, s 75(1), Sch 8, paras 96, 111(1), (10)(a).

Sub-s (13): words 'it think fit' in square brackets substituted by the Charities Act 2006, s 75(1), Sch 8, paras 96, 111(1), (10)(b).

Sub-s (13): words 'by it' in square brackets substituted by the Charities Act 2006, s 75(1), Sch 8, paras 96, 111(1), (10)(c).

Sub-s (13): words 'to the Commission' in square brackets substituted by the Charities Act 2006, s 75(1), Sch 8, paras 96, 111(1), (10)(d).

Sub-s (13): words 'the Commission shall' in square brackets substituted by the Charities Act 2006, s 75(1), Sch 8, paras 96, 111(1), (10)(e).

Sub-s (16): substituted by the Charities Act 2006, s 12, Sch 5, para 6.

Date in force: to be appointed: see the Charities Act 2006, s 79(2).

[18A Power to suspend or remove trustees etc from membership of charity]

[(1) This section applies where the Commission makes—

(a) an order under section 18(1) above suspending from his office or employment any trustee, charity trustee, officer, agent or employee of a charity, or
(b) an order under section 18(2) above removing from his office or employment any officer, agent or employee of a charity,

and the trustee, charity trustee, officer, agent or employee (as the case may be) is a member of the charity.

(2) If the order suspends the person in question from his office or employment, the Commission may also make an order suspending his membership of the charity for the period for which he is suspended from his office or employment.

(3) If the order removes the person in question from his office or employment, the Commission may also make an order—

(a) terminating his membership of the charity, and
(b) prohibiting him from resuming his membership of the charity without the Commission's consent.

(4) If an application for the Commission's consent under subsection (3)(b) above is made five years or more after the order was made, the Commission must grant the application unless satisfied that, by reason of any special circumstances, it should be refused.]

NOTES

Amendment

Inserted by the Charities Act 2006, s 19; for transitional provisions and savings see s 75(3), Sch 10, para 4 thereto.

Date in force: to be appointed: see the Charities Act 2006, s 79(2).

19 Supplementary provisions relating to receiver and manager [interim manager] appointed for a charity

(1) The Commissioners may under section 18(1)(vii) above appoint to be receiver and manager in respect of the property and affairs of a charity such person (other than an officer or employee of theirs) as they think fit.

[(1) The Commission may under section 18(1)(vii) above appoint to be interim manager in respect of a charity such person (other than a member of its staff) as it thinks fit.]

(2) Without prejudice to the generality of section 89(1) below, any order made by *the Commissioners* [the Commission] under section 18(1)(vii) above may make provision with respect to the functions to be discharged by the *receiver and manager* [interim manager] appointed by the order; and those functions shall be discharged by him under the supervision of *the Commissioners* [the Commission].

(3) In connection with the discharge of those functions any such order may provide—

(a) for the *receiver and manager* [interim manager] appointed by the order to have such powers and duties of the charity trustees of the charity concerned (whether arising under this Act or otherwise) as are specified in the order;

(b) for any powers or duties exercisable or falling to be performed by the *receiver and manager* [interim manager] by virtue of paragraph (a) above to be exercisable or performed by him to the exclusion of those trustees.

(4) Where a person has been appointed *receiver and manager* [interim manager] by any such order—

(a) section 29 below shall apply to him and to his functions as a person so appointed as it applies to a charity trustee of the charity concerned and to his duties as such; and

(b) *the Commissioners* [the Commission] may apply to the High Court for directions in relation to any particular matter arising in connection with the discharge of those functions.

(5) The High Court may on an application under subsection (4)(b) above—

(a) give such directions, or

(b) make such orders declaring the rights of any persons (whether before the court or not),

as it thinks just; and the costs of any such application shall be paid by the charity concerned.

(6) Regulations made by the [Minister] may make provision with respect to—

(a) the appointment and removal of persons appointed in accordance with this section;

(b) the remuneration of such persons out of the income of the charities concerned;

(c) the making of reports to *the Commissioners* [the Commission] by such persons.

(7) Regulations under subsection (6) above may, in particular, authorise *the Commissioners* [the Commission]—

(a) to require security for the due discharge of his functions to be given by a person so appointed;

(b) to determine the amount of such a person's remuneration;

(c) to disallow any amount of remuneration in such circumstances as are prescribed by the regulations.

NOTES

Derivation

Sub-ss (1)–(5), (7) derived from the Charities Act 1960, s 20A(1)–(5), (7), as added by the Charities Act 1992, s 9; sub-s (6) derived from the Charities Act 1960, s 20A(6), as added by the Charities Act 1992, s 9, and as read with the Charities Act 1960, s 43(1), as substituted by the Education Act 1973, s 1(3), Sch 1, para 1(1), (7).

Initial Commencement

Specified date: 1 August 1993: see s 99(1).

Extent

This section does not extend to Scotland.

Amendment

Section heading: words 'receiver and manager' repealed and subsequent words in square brackets substituted by the Charities Act 2006, s 75(1), Sch 8, paras 96, 112(1), (7).

Date in force: to be appointed: see the Charities Act 2006, s 79(2).

Sub-s (1): substituted by the Charities Act 2006, s 75(1), Sch 8, paras 96, 112(1), (2).

Sub-s (2): words 'the Commission' in square brackets in both places they occur substituted by the Charities Act 2006, s 75(1), Sch 8, paras 96, 112(1), (3)(a).

Sub-s (2): words 'interim manager' in square brackets substituted by the Charities Act 2006, s 75(1), Sch 8, paras 96, 112(1), (3)(b).

Sub-s (3): words 'interim manager' in square brackets in both places they occur substituted by the Charities Act 2006, s 75(1), Sch 8, paras 96, 112(1), (4).

Sub-s (4): words 'interim manager' in square brackets substituted by the Charities Act 2006, s 75(1), Sch 8, paras 96, 112(1), (5)(a).

Sub-s (4): in para (b) words 'the Commission' in square brackets substituted by the Charities Act 2006, s 75(1), Sch 8, paras 96, 112(1), (5)(b).

Sub-s (6): word 'Minister' in square brackets substituted by SI 2006/2951, art 6, Schedule, para 4(k).

Date in force: 13 December 2006: see SI 2006/2951, art 1(2).

Sub-s (6): in para (c) words 'the Commission' in square brackets substituted by the Charities Act 2006, s 75(1), Sch 8, paras 96, 112(1), (6).

Sub-s (7): words 'the Commission' in square brackets substituted by the Charities Act 2006, s 75(1), Sch 8, paras 96, 112(1), (6).

[19A Power to give specific directions for protection of charity]

[(1) This section applies where, at any time after the Commission has instituted an inquiry under section 8 above with respect to any charity, it is satisfied as mentioned in section 18(1)(a) or (b) above.

(2) The Commission may by order direct—

(a) the charity trustees,
(b) any trustee for the charity,
(c) any officer or employee of the charity, or
(d) (if a body corporate) the charity itself,

to take any action specified in the order which the Commission considers to be expedient in the interests of the charity.

(3) An order under this section—

(a) may require action to be taken whether or not it would otherwise be within the powers exercisable by the person or persons concerned, or by the charity, in relation to the administration of the charity or to its property, but
(b) may not require any action to be taken which is prohibited by any Act of Parliament or expressly prohibited by the trusts of the charity or is inconsistent with its purposes.

(4) Anything done by a person or body under the authority of an order under this section shall be deemed to be properly done in the exercise of the powers mentioned in subsection (3)(a) above.

(5) Subsection (4) does not affect any contractual or other rights arising in connection with anything which has been done under the authority of such an order.]

NOTES

Amendment

Inserted by the Charities Act 2006, s 20; for transitional provisions and savings see s 75(3), Sch 10, para 5 thereto.

Date in force: to be appointed: see the Charities Act 2006, s 79(2).

[19B Power to direct application of charity property]

[(1) This section applies where the Commission is satisfied—

(a) that a person or persons in possession or control of any property held by or on trust for a charity is or are unwilling to apply it properly for the purposes of the charity, and
(b) that it is necessary or desirable to make an order under this section for the purpose of securing a proper application of that property for the purposes of the charity.

(2) The Commission may by order direct the person or persons concerned to apply the property in such manner as is specified in the order.

(3) An order under this section—

(a) may require action to be taken whether or not it would otherwise be within the powers exercisable by the person or persons concerned in relation to the property, but
(b) may not require any action to be taken which is prohibited by any Act of Parliament or expressly prohibited by the trusts of the charity.

(4) Anything done by a person under the authority of an order under this section shall be deemed to be properly done in the exercise of the powers mentioned in subsection (3)(a) above.

(5) Subsection (4) does not affect any contractual or other rights arising in connection with anything which has been done under the authority of such an order.]

NOTES

Amendment

Inserted by the Charities Act 2006, s 21.

Date in force: to be appointed: see the Charities Act 2006, s 79(2).

[19C Copy of order under section 18, 18A, 19A or 19B, and Commission's reasons, to be sent to charity]

[(1) Where the Commission makes an order under section 18, 18A, 19A or 19B, it must send the documents mentioned in subsection (2) below—

(a) to the charity concerned (if a body corporate), or
(b) (if not) to each of the charity trustees.

(2) The documents are—

(a) a copy of the order, and
(b) a statement of the Commission's reasons for making it.

(3) The documents must be sent to the charity or charity trustees as soon as practicable after the making of the order.

(4) The Commission need not, however, comply with subsection (3) above in relation to the documents, or (as the case may be) the statement of its reasons, if it considers that to do so—

(a) would prejudice any inquiry or investigation, or
(b) would not be in the interests of the charity;

but, once the Commission considers that this is no longer the case, it must send the documents, or (as the case may be) the statement, to the charity or charity trustees as soon as practicable.

(5) Nothing in this section requires any document to be sent to a person who cannot be found or who has no known address in the United Kingdom.

(6) Any documents required to be sent to a person under this section may be sent to, or otherwise served on, that person in the same way as an order made by the Commission under this Act could be served on him in accordance with section 91 below.]

NOTES

Amendment

Inserted by the Charities Act 2006, s 75(1), Sch 8, paras 96, 113.

Date in force: to be appointed: see the Charities Act 2006, s 79(2).

20 Publicity for proceedings under ss 16 to 18 [20 Publicity relating to schemes]

(1) The Commissioners shall not make any order under this Act to establish a scheme for the administration of a charity, or submit such a scheme to the court or the [Minister] for an order giving it effect, unless not less than one month previously there has been given public notice of their proposals, inviting representations to be made to them within a time specified in the notice, being not less than one month from the date of such notice, and, in the case of a scheme relating to a local charity, other than on ecclesiastical charity, in a parish or (in Wales) a community, a draft of the scheme has been communicated to the parish or community council or, in the case of a parish not having a council, to the chairman of the parish meeting.

(2) The Commissioners shall not make any order under this Act to appoint, discharge or remove a charity trustee or trustee for a charity (other than the official custodian), unless not less than one month previously there has been given the like public notice as is required by subsection (1) above for an order establishing a scheme but this subsection shall not apply in the case of—

(a) an order under section 18(1)(ii) above; or
(b) an order discharging or removing a trustee if the Commissioners are of opinion that it is unnecessary and not in his interest to give publicity to the proposal to discharge or remove him.

(3) Before the Commissioners make an order under this Act to remove without his consent a charity trustee or trustee for a charity, or an officer, agent or employee of a charity, the Commissioners shall, unless he cannot be found or has no known address in the United Kingdom, give him not less than one month's notice of their proposal, inviting representations to be made to them within a time specified in the notice.

(4) Where notice is given of any proposals as required by subsections (1) to (3) above, the Commissioners shall take into consideration any representations made to them about the proposals within the time specified in the notice, and may (without further notice) proceed with the proposals either without modification or with such modifications as appear to them to be desirable.

(5) Where the Commissioners make an order which is subject to appeal under subsection (12) of section 16 above the order shall be published either by giving public notice of it or by giving notice of it to all persons entitled to appeal against it under that subsection, as the Commissioners think fit.

(6) Where the Commissioners make an order under this Act to establish a scheme for the administration of a charity, a copy of the order shall, for not less than one month after the order is published, be available for public inspection at all reasonable times at the Commissioners' office and also at some convenient place in the area of the charity, if it is a local charity.

(7) Any notice to be given under this section of any proposals or order shall give such particulars of the proposals or order, or such directions for obtaining information about them, as the Commissioners think sufficient and appropriate, and any public notice shall be given in such manner as they think sufficient and appropriate.

(8) Any notice to be given under this section, other than a public notice, may be given by post and, if given by post, may be addressed to the recipient's last known address in the United Kingdom.

[(1) The Commission may not—

(a) make any order under this Act to establish a scheme for the administration of a charity, or
(b) submit such a scheme to the court or the Minister for an order giving it effect,

unless, before doing so, the Commission has complied with the publicity requirements in subsection (2) below.

This is subject to any disapplication of those requirements under subsection (4) below.

(2) The publicity requirements are—

(a) that the Commission must give public notice of its proposals, inviting representations to be made to it within a period specified in the notice; and
(b) that, in the case of a scheme relating to a local charity (other than an ecclesiastical charity) in a parish or in a community in Wales, the Commission must communicate a draft of the scheme to the parish or community council (or, where a parish has no council, to the chairman of the parish meeting).

(3) The time when any such notice is given or any such communication takes place is to be decided by the Commission.

(4) The Commission may determine that either or both of the publicity requirements is or are not to apply in relation to a particular scheme if it is satisfied that—

(a) by reason of the nature of the scheme, or
(b) for any other reason,

compliance with the requirement or requirements is unnecessary.

(5) Where the Commission gives public notice of any proposals under this section, the Commission—

(a) must take into account any representations made to it within the period specified in the notice, and
(b) may (without further notice) proceed with the proposals either without modifications or with such modifications as it thinks desirable.

(6) Where the Commission makes an order under this Act to establish a scheme for the administration of a charity, a copy of the order must be available, for at least a month after the order is published, for public inspection at all reasonable times—

(a) at the Commission's office, and
(b) if the charity is a local charity, at some convenient place in the area of the charity.

Paragraph (b) does not apply if the Commission is satisfied that for any reason it is unnecessary for a copy of the scheme to be available locally.

(7) Any public notice of any proposals which is to be given under this section—

(a) is to contain such particulars of the proposals, or such directions for obtaining information about them, as the Commission thinks sufficient and appropriate, and
(b) is to be given in such manner as the Commission thinks sufficient and appropriate.]

NOTES

Derivation

Sub-s (1) derived from the Charities Act 1960, s 21(1), as read with the Local Government Act 1972, s 179(1), (4); sub-ss (2), (3) derived from the Charities Act 1960, s 21(2), (3), as amended by the Charities Act 1992, s 47, Sch 3, para 8; sub-ss (4)–(8) derived from the Charities Act 1960, s 21(4)–(8).

Initial Commencement

Specified date: 1 August 1993: see s 99(1).

Extent

This section does not extend to Scotland.

Amendment

Substituted, together with s 20A, for this section as originally enacted, by the Charities Act 2006, s 22.

Sub-s (1): word 'Minister' in square brackets substituted by SI 2006/2951, art 6, Schedule, para 4(l).

Date in force: 13 December 2006: see SI 2006/2951, art 1(2).

[20A Publicity for orders relating to trustees or other individuals]

[(1) The Commission may not make any order under this Act to appoint, discharge or remove a charity trustee or trustee for a charity, other than—

(a) an order relating to the official custodian, or
(b) an order under section 18(1)(ii) above,

unless, before doing so, the Commission has complied with the publicity requirement in subsection (2) below.

This is subject to any disapplication of that requirement under subsection (4) below.

(2) The publicity requirement is that the Commission must give public notice of its proposals, inviting representations to be made to it within a period specified in the notice.

(3) The time when any such notice is given is to be decided by the Commission.

(4) The Commission may determine that the publicity requirement is not to apply in relation to a particular order if it is satisfied that for any reason compliance with the requirement is unnecessary.

(5) Before the Commission makes an order under this Act to remove without his consent—

(a) a charity trustee or trustee for a charity, or
(b) an officer, agent or employee of a charity,

the Commission must give him not less than one month's notice of its proposals, inviting representations to be made to it within a period specified in the notice.

This does not apply if the person cannot be found or has no known address in the United Kingdom.

(6) Where the Commission gives notice of any proposals under this section, the Commission—

(a) must take into account any representations made to it within the period specified in the notice, and
(b) may (without further notice) proceed with the proposals either without modifications or with such modifications as it thinks desirable.

(7) Any notice of any proposals which is to be given under this section—

(a) is to contain such particulars of the proposals, or such directions for obtaining information about them, as the Commission thinks sufficient and appropriate, and

(b) (in the case of a public notice) is to be given in such manner as the Commission thinks sufficient and appropriate.

(8) Any notice to be given under subsection (5)—

(a) may be given by post, and
(b) if given by post, may be addressed to the recipient's last known address in the United Kingdom.]

NOTES

Amendment

Substituted, together with s 20, for s 20 as originally enacted, by the Charities Act 2006, s 22.

Property vested in official custodian

21 Entrusting charity property to official custodian, and termination of trust

(1) The court may by order—

(a) vest in the official custodian any land held by or in trust for a charity;
(b) authorise or require the persons in whom any such land is vested to transfer it to him; or
(c) appoint any person to transfer any such land to him;

but this subsection does not apply to any interest in land by way of mortgage or other security.

(2) Where property is vested in the official custodian in trust for a charity, the court may make an order discharging him from the trusteeship as respects all or any of that property.

(3) Where the official custodian is discharged from his trusteeship of any property, or the trusts on which he holds any property come to an end, the court may make such vesting orders and give such directions as may seem to the court to be necessary or expedient in consequence.

(4) No person shall be liable for any loss occasioned by his acting in conformity with an order under this section or by his giving effect to anything done in pursuance of such an order, or be excused from so doing by reason of the order having been in any respect improperly obtained.

NOTES

Derivation

Sub-s (1) derived from the Charities Act 1960, s 16(1), as substituted by the Charities Act 1992, s 47, Sch 3, para 4(a); sub-ss (2)–(4) derived from the Charities Act 1960, s 16(3)–(5).

Initial Commencement

Specified date: 1 August 1993: see s 99(1).

Extent

This section does not extend to Scotland.

22 Supplementary provisions as to property vested in official custodian

(1) Subject to the provisions of this Act, where property is vested in the official custodian in trust for a charity, he shall not exercise any powers of management, but he shall as trustee of

any property have all the same powers, duties and liabilities, and be entitled to the same rights and immunities, and be subject to the control and orders of the court, as a corporation appointed custodian trustee under section 4 of the Public Trustee Act 1906 except that he shall have no power to charge fees.

(2) Subject to subsection (3) below, where any land is vested in the official custodian in trust for a charity, the charity trustees shall have power in his name and on his behalf to execute and do all assurances and things which they could properly execute or do in their own name and on their own behalf if the land were vested in them.

(3) If any land is so vested in the official custodian by virtue of an order under section 18 above, the power conferred on the charity trustees by subsection (2) above shall not be exercisable by them in relation to any transaction affecting the land, unless the transaction is authorised by order of the court or of *the Commissioners* [the Commission].

(4) Where any land is vested in the official custodian in trust for a charity, the charity trustees shall have the like power to make obligations entered into by them binding on the land as if it were vested in them; and any covenant, agreement or condition which is enforceable by or against the custodian by reason of the land being vested in him shall be enforceable by or against the charity trustees as if the land were vested in them.

(5) In relation to a corporate charity, subsections (2), (3) and (4) above shall apply with the substitution of references to the charity for references to the charity trustees.

(6) Subsections (2), (3) and (4) above shall not authorise any charity trustees or charity to impose any personal liability on the official custodian.

(7) Where the official custodian is entitled as trustee for a charity to the custody of securities or documents of title relating to the trust property, he may permit them to be in the possession or under the control of the charity trustees without thereby incurring any liability.

NOTES

Derivation

Sub-ss (1), (4), (7) derived from the Charities Act 1960, s 17(1), (3), (6); sub-ss (2), (5), (6) derived from the Charities Act 1960, s 17(2), (4), (5), as amended by the Charities Act 1992, s 47, Sch 3, para 5(a), (c); sub-s (3) derived from the Charities Act 1960, s 17(2A), as added by the Charities Act 1992, s 47, Sch 3, para 5(b).

Initial Commencement

Specified date: 1 August 1993: see s 99(1).

Extent

This section does not extend to Scotland.

Amendment

Sub-s (3): words 'the Commissioners' in italics repealed and subsequent words in square brackets substituted by the Charities Act 2006, s 75(1), Sch 8, paras 96, 114.

Date in force: to be appointed: see the Charities Act 2006, s 79(2).

23 Divestment in the case of land subject to Reverter of Sites Act 1987

(1) Where—

(a) any land is vested in the official custodian in trust for a charity, and
(b) it appears to *the Commissioners* [the Commission] that section 1 of the Reverter of Sites Act 1987 (right of reverter replaced by [trust]) will, or is likely to, operate in relation to the land at a particular time or in particular circumstances,

the jurisdiction which, under section 16 above, is exercisable by *the Commissioners* [the Commission] for the purpose of discharging a trustee for a charity may, at any time before section 1 of that Act ('the 1987 Act') operates in relation to the land, be exercised *by them of their own* [by the Commission of its own] motion for the purpose of—

(i) making an order discharging the official custodian from his trusteeship of the land, and
(ii) making such vesting orders and giving such directions as *appear to them* [appear to the Commission] to be necessary or expedient in consequence.

(2) Where—

(a) section 1 of the 1987 Act has operated in relation to any land which, immediately before the time when that section so operated, was vested in the official custodian in trust for a charity, and
(b) the land remains vested in him but on the trust arising under that section,

the court or *the Commissioners (of their own motion)* [the Commission (of its own motion)] may—

(i) make an order discharging the official custodian from his trusteeship of the land, and
(ii) (subject to the following provisions of this section) make such vesting orders and give such directions as appear to it *or them* to be necessary or expedient in consequence.

(3) Where any order discharging the official custodian from his trusteeship of any land—

(a) is made by the court under section 21(2) above, or by *the Commissioners* [the Commission] under section 16 above, on the grounds that section 1 of the 1987 Act will, or is likely to, operate in relation to the land, or
(b) is made by the court or *the Commissioners* [the Commission] under subsection (2) above,

the persons in whom the land is to be vested on the discharge of the official custodian shall be the relevant charity trustees (as defined in subsection (4) below), unless the court or (as the case may be) *the Commissioners is or are* [the Commission is] satisfied that it would be appropriate for it to be vested in some other persons.

(4) In subsection (3) above 'the relevant charity trustees' means—

(a) in relation to an order made as mentioned in paragraph (a) of that subsection, the charity trustees of the charity in trust for which the land is vested in the official custodian immediately before the time when the order takes effect, or
(b) in relation to an order made under subsection (2) above, the charity trustees of the charity in trust for which the land was vested in the official custodian immediately before the time when section 1 of the 1987 Act operated in relation to the land.

(5) Where—

(a) section 1 of the 1987 Act has operated in relation to any such land as is mentioned in subsection (2)(a) above, and
(b) the land remains vested in the official custodian as mentioned in subsection (2)(b) above,

then (subject to subsection (6) below), all the powers, duties and liabilities that would, apart from this section, be those of the official custodian as [trustee] of the land shall instead be those of the charity trustees of the charity concerned; and those trustees shall have power in his name and on his behalf to execute and do all assurances and things which they could properly execute or do in their own name and on their own behalf if the land were vested in them.

(6) Subsection (5) above shall not be taken to require or authorise those trustees to sell the land at a time when it remains vested in the official custodian.

(7) Where—

(a) the official custodian has been discharged from his trusteeship of any land by an order under subsection (2) above, and
(b) the land has, in accordance with subsection (3) above, been vested in the charity trustees concerned or (as the case may be) in any persons other than those trustees,

the land shall be held by those trustees, or (as the case may be) by those persons, as [trustees] on the terms of the trust arising under section 1 of the 1987 Act.

(8) The official custodian shall not be liable to any person in respect of any loss or misapplication of any land vested in him in accordance with that section unless it is occasioned by or through any wilful neglect or default of his or of any person acting for him; but the Consolidated Fund shall be liable to make good to any person any sums for which the official custodian may be liable by reason of any such neglect or default.

(9) In this section any reference to section 1 of the 1987 Act operating in relation to any land is a reference to a [trust] arising in relation to the land under that section.

NOTES

Derivation

This section derived from the Charities Act 1992, s 31.

Initial Commencement

Specified date: 1 August 1993: see s 99(1).

Extent

This section does not extend to Scotland.

Amendment

Sub-s (1): in para (b) word 'trust' in square brackets substituted by the Trusts of Land and Appointment of Trustees Act 1996, s 25(1), Sch 3, para 26; for savings in relation to entailed interests created before the commencement of that Act, and savings consequential upon the abolition of the doctrine of conversion, see s 25(4), (5) thereof.

Sub-s (1): words 'the Commissioners' in italics in both places they occur repealed and subsequent words in square brackets substituted by the Charities Act 2006, s 75(1), Sch 8, paras 96, 115(1), (2)(a).

Date in force: to be appointed: see the Charities Act 2006, s 79(2).

Sub-s (1): words 'by them of their own' in italics repealed and subsequent words in square brackets substituted by the Charities Act 2006, s 75(1), Sch 8, paras 96, 115(1), (2)(b).

Date in force: to be appointed: see the Charities Act 2006, s 79(2).

Sub-s (1): in para (ii) words 'appear to them' in italics repealed and subsequent words in square brackets substituted by the Charities Act 2006, s 75(1), Sch 8, paras 96, 115(1), (2)(c).

Date in force: to be appointed: see the Charities Act 2006, s 79(2).

Sub-s (2): words 'the Commissioners (of their own motion)' in italics repealed and subsequent words in square brackets substituted by the Charities Act 2006, s 75(1), Sch 8, paras 96, 115(1), (3)(a).

Date in force: to be appointed: see the Charities Act 2006, s 79(2).

Sub-s (2): in para (ii) words 'or them' in italics repealed by the Charities Act 2006, s 75(1), (2), Sch 8, paras 96, 115(1), (3)(b), Sch 9.

Date in force: to be appointed: see the Charities Act 2006, s 79(2).

Sub-s (3): in paras (a), (b) words 'the Commissioners' in italics repealed and subsequent words in square brackets substituted by the Charities Act 2006, s 75(1), Sch 8, paras 96, 115(1), (4)(a).

Date in force: to be appointed: see the Charities Act 2006, s 79(2).

Sub-s (3): words 'the Commissioners is or are' in italics repealed and subsequent words in square brackets substituted by the Charities Act 2006, s 75(1), Sch 8, paras 96, 115(1), (4)(b).

Date in force: to be appointed: see the Charities Act 2006, s 79(2).

Sub-s (5): word 'trustee' in square brackets substituted by the Trusts of Land and Appointment of Trustees Act 1996, s 25(1), Sch 3, para 26; for savings in relation to entailed interests created before the commencement of that Act, and savings consequential upon the abolition of the doctrine of conversion, see s 25(4), (5) thereof.

Sub-s (7): word 'trustees' in square brackets substituted by the Trusts of Land and Appointment of Trustees Act 1996, s 25(1), Sch 3, para 26; for savings in relation to entailed interests created before the commencement of that Act, and savings consequential upon the abolition of the doctrine of conversion, see s 25(4), (5) thereof.

Sub-s (9): word 'trust' in square brackets substituted by the Trusts of Land and Appointment of Trustees Act 1996, s 25(1), Sch 3, para 26; for savings in relation to entailed interests created before the commencement of that Act, and savings consequential upon the abolition of the doctrine of conversion, see s 25(4), (5) thereof.

Establishment of common investment or deposit funds

24 Schemes to establish common investment funds

(1) The court or *the Commissioners* [the Commission] may by order make and bring into effect schemes (in this section referred to as 'common investment schemes') for the establishment of common investment funds under trusts which provide—

(a) for property transferred to the fund by or on behalf of a charity participating in the scheme to be invested under the control of trustees appointed to manage the fund; and
(b) for the participating charities to be entitled (subject to the provisions of the scheme) to the capital and income of the fund in shares determined by reference to the amount or value of the property transferred to it by or on behalf of each of them and to the value of the fund at the time of the transfers.

(2) The court or *the Commissioners* [the Commission] may make a common investment scheme on the application of any two or more charities.

(3) A common investment scheme may be made in terms admitting any charity to participate, or the scheme may restrict the right to participate in any manner.

[(3A) A common investment scheme may provide for appropriate bodies to be admitted to participate in the scheme (in addition to the participating charities) to such extent as the trustees appointed to manage the fund may determine.

(3B) In this section 'appropriate body' means—

(a) a Scottish recognised body, or
(b) a Northern Ireland charity,

and, in the application of the relevant provisions in relation to a scheme which contains provisions authorised by subsection (3A) above, 'charity' includes an appropriate body.

'The relevant provisions' are subsections (1) and (4) to (6) and (in relation only to a charity within paragraph (b)) subsection (7).]

(4) A common investment scheme may make provision for, and for all matters connected with, the establishment, investment, management and winding up of the common investment fund, and may in particular include provision—

(a) for remunerating persons appointed trustees to hold or manage the fund or any part of it, with or without provision authorising a person to receive the remuneration notwithstanding that he is also a charity trustee of or trustee for a participating charity;
(b) for restricting the size of the fund, and for regulating as to time, amount or otherwise the right to transfer property to or withdraw it from the fund, and for enabling sums to be advanced out of the fund by way of loan to a participating charity pending the withdrawal of property from the fund by the charity;
(c) for enabling income to be withheld from distribution with a view to avoiding fluctuations in the amounts distributed, and generally for regulating distributions of income;
(d) for enabling money to be borrowed temporarily for the purpose of meeting payments to be made out of the funds;
(e) for enabling questions arising under the scheme as to the right of a charity to participate, or as to the rights of participating charities, or as to any other matter, to be conclusively determined by the decision of the trustees managing the fund or in any other manner;
(f) for regulating the accounts and information to be supplied to participating charities.

(5) A common investment scheme, in addition to the provision for property to be transferred to the fund on the basis that the charity shall be entitled to a share in the capital and income of the fund, may include provision for enabling sums to be deposited by or on behalf of a charity on the basis that (subject to the provisions of the scheme) the charity shall be entitled to repayment of the sums deposited and to interest thereon at a rate determined by or under the scheme; and where a scheme makes any such provision it shall also provide for excluding from the amount of capital and income to be shared between charities participating otherwise than by way of deposit such amounts (not exceeding the amounts properly attributable to the making of deposits) as are from time to time reasonably required in respect of the liabilities of the fund for the repayment of deposits and for the interest on deposits, including amounts required by way of reserve.

(6) Except in so far as a common investment scheme provides to the contrary, the rights under it of a participating charity shall not be capable of being assigned or charged, nor shall any trustee or other person concerned in the management of the common investment fund be required or entitled to take account of any trust or other equity affecting a participating charity or its property or rights.

(7) The powers of investment of every charity shall include power to participate in common investment schemes unless the power is excluded by a provision specifically referring to common investment schemes in the trusts of the charity.

(8) A common investment fund shall be deemed for all purposes to be a charity*; and if the scheme admits only exempt charities, the fund shall be an exempt charity for the purposes of this Act.*

(9) Subsection (8) above shall apply not only to common investment funds established under the powers of this section, but also to any similar fund established for the exclusive benefit of charities by or under any enactment relating to any particular charities or class of charity.

NOTES

Derivation

Sub-ss (1)–(7) derived from the Charities Act 1960, s 22(1)–(5), (7), (8); sub-s (8) derived from the Charities Act 1960, s 22(9), as amended by the Charities Act 1992, ss 47, 78(2), Sch 3, para 9(b), Sch 7; sub-s (9) derived from the Charities Act 1960, s 22(11), as amended by the Financial Services Act 1986, s 212(2), Sch 16, para 1(b).

Initial Commencement

Specified date: 1 August 1993: see s 99(1).

Extent

This section does not extend to Scotland.

Amendment

Sub-s (1): words 'the Commissioners' in italics repealed and subsequent words in square brackets substituted by the Charities Act 2006, s 75(1), Sch 8, paras 96, 116.

Date in force: to be appointed: see the Charities Act 2006, s 79(2).

Sub-s (2): words 'the Commissioners' in italics repealed and subsequent words in square brackets substituted by the Charities Act 2006, s 75(1), Sch 8, paras 96, 116.

Date in force: to be appointed: see the Charities Act 2006, s 79(2).

Sub-ss (3A), (3B): inserted by the Charities Act 2006, s 23(1).

Sub-s (8): words from '; and if the' to the end repealed by the Charities Act 2006, s 11(10).

Date in force: to be appointed: see the Charities Act 2006, s 79(2).

25 Schemes to establish common deposit funds

(1) The court or *the Commissioners* [the Commission] may by order make and bring into effect schemes (in this section referred to as 'common deposit schemes') for the establishment of common deposit funds under trusts which provide—

(a) for sums to be deposited by or on behalf of a charity participating in the scheme and invested under the control of trustees appointed to manage the fund; and
(b) for any such charity to be entitled (subject to the provisions of the scheme) to repayment of any sums so deposited and to interest thereon at a rate determined under the scheme.

(2) Subject to subsection (3) below, the following provisions of section 24 above, namely—

(a) *subsections (2) to (4)* [subsections (2), (3) and (4)], and
(b) subsections (6) to (9),

shall have effect in relation to common deposit schemes and common deposit funds as they have effect in relation to common investment schemes and common investment funds.

(3) In its application in accordance with subsection (2) above, subsection (4) of that section shall have effect with the substitution for paragraphs (b) and (c) of the following paragraphs—

'(b) for regulating as to time, amount or otherwise the right to repayment of sums deposited in the fund;
(c) for authorising a part of the income for any year to be credited to a reserve account maintained for the purpose of counteracting any losses accruing to the fund, and generally for regulating the manner in which the rate of interest on deposits is to be determined from time to time;'.

[(4) A common deposit scheme may provide for appropriate bodies to be admitted to participate in the scheme (in addition to the participating charities) to such extent as the trustees appointed to manage the fund may determine.

(5) In this section 'appropriate body' means—

(a) a Scottish recognised body, or
(b) a Northern Ireland charity,

and, in the application of the relevant provisions in relation to a scheme which contains provisions authorised by subsection (4) above, 'charity' includes an appropriate body.

(6) 'The relevant provisions' are—

(a) subsection (1) above, and
(b) subsections (4) and (6) of section 24 above, as they apply in accordance with subsections (2) and (3) above, and
(c) (in relation only to a charity within subsection (5)(b) above) subsection (7) of that section, as it so applies.]

NOTES

Derivation

This section derived from the Charities Act 1960, s 22A, as added by the Charities Act 1992, s 16.

Initial Commencement

Specified date: 1 August 1993: see s 99(1).

Extent

This section does not extend to Scotland.

Amendment

Sub-s (1): words 'the Commissioners' in italics repealed and subsequent words in square brackets substituted by the Charities Act 2006, s 75(1), Sch 8, paras 96, 117.

Date in force: to be appointed: see the Charities Act 2006, s 79(2).

Sub-s (2): in para (a) words 'subsections (2), (3) and (4)' in square brackets substituted by the Charities Act 2006, s 23(2).

Sub-ss (4)–(6): inserted by the Charities Act 2006, s 23(3).

[25A Meaning of 'Scottish recognised body' and 'Northern Ireland charity' in sections 24 and 25]

[(1) In sections 24 and 25 above 'Scottish recognised body' means a body—

(a) established under the law of Scotland, or
(b) managed or controlled wholly or mainly in or from Scotland,

to which the Commissioners for Her Majesty's Revenue and Customs have given intimation, which has not subsequently been withdrawn, that relief is due under section 505 of the Income and Corporation Taxes Act 1988 in respect of income of the body which is applicable and applied to charitable purposes only.

(2) In those sections 'Northern Ireland charity' means an institution—

(a) which is a charity under the law of Northern Ireland, and
(b) to which the Commissioners for Her Majesty's Revenue and Customs have given intimation, which has not subsequently been withdrawn, that relief is due under section 505 of the Income and Corporation Taxes Act 1988 in respect of income of the institution which is applicable and applied to charitable purposes only.]

NOTES

Amendment

Inserted by the Charities Act 2006, s 23(4).

Additional powers of Commissioners [Additional powers of Commission]

NOTES

Amendment

Substituted by the Charities Act 2006, s 75(1), Sch 8, paras 96, 118.

Date in force: to be appointed: see the Charities Act 2006, s 79(2).

26 Power to authorise dealings with charity property etc

(1) Subject to the provisions of this section, where it appears to *the Commissioners* [the Commission] that any action proposed or contemplated in the administration of a charity is expedient in the interests of the charity, *they may* [the Commission may] by order sanction that action, whether or not it would otherwise be within the powers exercisable by the charity trustees in the administration of the charity; and anything done under the authority of such an order shall be deemed to be properly done in the exercise of those powers.

(2) An order under this section may be made so as to authorise a particular transaction, compromise or the like, or a particular application of property, or so as to give a more general authority, and (without prejudice to the generality of subsection (1) above) may authorise a charity to use common premises, or employ a common staff, or otherwise combine for any purpose of administration, with any other charity.

(3) An order under this section may give directions as to the manner in which any expenditure is to be borne and as to other matters connected with or arising out of the action thereby authorised; and where anything is done in pursuance of an authority given by any such order, any directions given in connection therewith shall be binding on the charity trustees for the time being as if contained in the trusts of the charity; but any such directions may on the application of the charity be modified or superseded by a further order.

(4) Without prejudice to the generality of subsection (3) above, the directions which may be given by an order under this section shall in particular include directions for meeting any expenditure out of a specified fund, for charging any expenditure to capital or to income, for requiring expenditure charged to capital to be recouped out of income within a specified period, for restricting the costs to be incurred at the expense of the charity, or for the investment of moneys arising from any transaction.

(5) An order under this section may authorise any act notwithstanding that it is prohibited by any of the disabling Acts mentioned in subsection (6) below or that the trusts of the charity provide for the act to be done by or under the authority of the court; but no such order shall authorise the doing of any act expressly prohibited by Act of Parliament other than the disabling Acts or by the trusts of the charity or shall extend or alter the purposes of the charity.

[(5A) In the case of a charity that is a company, an order under this section may authorise an act notwithstanding that it involves the breach of a duty imposed on a director of the company under Chapter 2 of Part 10 of the Companies Act 2006 (general duties of directors).]

(6) The Acts referred to in subsection (5) above as the disabling Acts are the Ecclesiastical Leases Act 1571, the Ecclesiastical Leases Act 1572, the Ecclesiastical Leases Act 1575 and the Ecclesiastical Leases Act 1836.

(7) An order under this section shall not confer any authority in relation to a building which has been consecrated and of which the use or disposal is regulated, and can be further regulated, by a scheme having effect under the Union of Benefices Measures 1923 to 1952, the Reorganisation Areas Measures 1944 and 1954, the Pastoral Measure 1968 or the Pastoral Measure 1983, the reference to a building being taken to include part of a building and any land which under such a scheme is to be used or disposed of with a building to which the scheme applies.

NOTES

Derivation

Sub-ss (1)–(4) derived from the Charities Act 1960, s 23(1)–(4); sub-ss (5)–(7) derived from the Charities Act 1960, s 23(5), (6), as read with the Interpretation Act 1978, s 17(2)(a).

Initial Commencement

Specified date: 1 August 1993: see s 99(1).

Extent

This section does not extend to Scotland.

Amendment

Sub-s (1): words 'the Commissioners' in italics repealed and subsequent words in square brackets substituted by the Charities Act 2006, s 75(1), Sch 8, paras 96, 119(a).

Date in force: to be appointed: see the Charities Act 2006, s 79(2).

Sub-s (1): words 'they may' in italics repealed and subsequent words in square brackets substituted by the Charities Act 2006, s 75(1), Sch 8, paras 96, 119(b).

Date in force: to be appointed: see the Charities Act 2006, s 79(2).

Sub-s (5A): inserted by the Companies Act 2006, s 181(4).

Date in force: to be appointed: see the Companies Act 2006, s 1300(2).

27 Power to authorise ex gratia payments etc

(1) Subject to subsection (3) below, *the Commissioners* [the Commission] may by order exercise the same power as is exercisable by the Attorney General to authorise the charity trustees of a charity—

(a) to make any application of property of the charity, or
(b) to waive to any extent, on behalf of the charity, its entitlement to receive any property,

in a case where the charity trustees—

(i) (apart from this section) have no power to do so, but
(ii) in all the circumstances regard themselves as being under a moral obligation to do so.

(2) The power conferred on *the Commissioners* [the Commission] by subsection (1) above shall be exercisable *by them* [by the Commission] under the supervision of, and in accordance with such directions as may be given by, the Attorney General; and any such directions may in particular require *the Commissioners* [the Commission], in such circumstances as are specified in the directions—

(a) to refrain from exercising that power; or
(b) to consult the Attorney General before exercising it.

(3) Where—

(a) an application is made to *the Commissioners for them* [the Commission for it] to exercise that power in a case where *they are not* [it is not] precluded from doing so by any such directions, but
(b) *they consider* [the Commission considers] that it would nevertheless be desirable for the application to be entertained by the Attorney General rather than *by them* [by the Commission],

they shall [the Commission shall] refer the application to the Attorney General.

(4) It is hereby declared that where, in the case of any application made *to them* [to the Commission] as mentioned in subsection (3)(a) above, *the Commissioners determine* [the

Commission determines] the application by refusing to authorise charity trustees to take any action falling within subsection (1)(a) or (b) above, that refusal shall not preclude the Attorney General, on an application subsequently made to him by the trustees, from authorising the trustees to take that action.

NOTES

Derivation

This section derived from the Charities Act 1960, s 23A, as added by the Charities Act 1992, s 17.

Initial Commencement

Specified date: 1 August 1993: see s 99(1).

Extent

This section does not extend to Scotland.

Amendment

Sub-s (1): words 'the Commissioners' in italics repealed and subsequent words in square brackets substituted by the Charities Act 2006, s 75(1), Sch 8, paras 96, 120(1), (2).

Date in force: to be appointed: see the Charities Act 2006, s 79(2).

Sub-s (2): words 'the Commissioners' in italics in both places they occur repealed and subsequent words in square brackets substituted by the Charities Act 2006, s 75(1), Sch 8, paras 96, 120(1), (3)(a).

Date in force: to be appointed: see the Charities Act 2006, s 79(2).

Sub-s (2): words 'by them' in italics repealed and subsequent words in square brackets substituted by the Charities Act 2006, s 75(1), Sch 8, paras 96, 120(1), (3)(b).

Date in force: to be appointed: see the Charities Act 2006, s 79(2).

Sub-s (3): in para (a) words 'the Commissioners for them' in italics repealed and subsequent words in square brackets substituted by the Charities Act 2006, s 75(1), Sch 8, paras 96, 120(1), (4)(a).

Date in force: to be appointed: see the Charities Act 2006, s 79(2).

Sub-s (3): in para (a) words 'they are not' in italics repealed and subsequent words in square brackets substituted by the Charities Act 2006, s 75(1), Sch 8, paras 96, 120(1), (4)(b).

Date in force: to be appointed: see the Charities Act 2006, s 79(2).

Sub-s (3): in para (b) words 'they consider' in italics repealed and subsequent words in square brackets substituted by the Charities Act 2006, s 75(1), Sch 8, paras 96, 120(1), (4)(c).

Date in force: to be appointed: see the Charities Act 2006, s 79(2).

Sub-s (3): in para (b) words 'by them' in italics repealed and subsequent words in square brackets substituted by the Charities Act 2006, s 75(1), Sch 8, paras 96, 120(1), (4)(d).

Date in force: to be appointed: see the Charities Act 2006, s 79(2).

Sub-s (3): words 'they shall' in italics repealed and subsequent words in square brackets substituted by the Charities Act 2006, s 75(1), Sch 8, paras 96, 120(1), (4)(e).

Date in force: to be appointed: see the Charities Act 2006, s 79(2).

Sub-s (4): words 'to them' in italics repealed and subsequent words in square brackets substituted by the Charities Act 2006, s 75(1), Sch 8, paras 96, 120(1), (5)(a).

Date in force: to be appointed: see the Charities Act 2006, s 79(2).

Sub-s (4): words 'the Commissioners determine' in italics repealed and subsequent words in square brackets substituted by the Charities Act 2006, s 75(1), Sch 8, paras 96, 120(1), (5)(b).

Date in force: to be appointed: see the Charities Act 2006, s 79(2).

28 Power to give directions about dormant bank accounts of charities

(1) Where *the Commissioners* [the Commission]—

(a) *are informed* [is informed] by a relevant institution—
  (i) that it holds one or more accounts in the name of or on behalf of a particular charity ('the relevant charity'), and
  (ii) that the account, or (if it so holds two or more accounts) each of the accounts, is dormant, and

(b) *are unable* [is unable], after making reasonable inquiries, to locate that charity or any of its trustees,

they may give [it may give] a direction under subsection (2) below.

(2) A direction under this subsection is a direction which—

(a) requires the institution concerned to transfer the amount, or (as the case may be) the aggregate amount, standing to the credit of the relevant charity in the account or accounts in question to such other charity as is specified in the direction in accordance with subsection (3) below; or

(b) requires the institution concerned to transfer to each of two or more other charities so specified in the direction such part of that amount or aggregate amount as is there specified in relation to that charity.

(3) The *Commissioners* [Commission] may specify in a direction under subsection (2) above such other charity or charities as *they consider* [it considers] appropriate, having regard, in a case where the purposes of the relevant charity are known *to them* [to the Commission], to those purposes and to the purposes of the other charity or charities; but the *Commissioners* [Commission] shall not so specify any charity unless *they have received* [it has received] from the charity trustees written confirmation that those trustees are willing to accept the amount proposed to be transferred to the charity.

(4) Any amount received by a charity by virtue of this section shall be received by the charity on terms that—

(a) it shall be held and applied by the charity for the purposes of the charity, but

(b) it shall, as property of the charity, nevertheless be subject to any restrictions on expenditure to which it was subject as property of the relevant charity.

(5) Where—

(a) *the Commissioners have been* [the Commission has been] informed as mentioned in subsection (1)(a) above by any relevant institution, and

(b) before any transfer is made by the institution in pursuance of a direction under subsection (2) above, the institution has, by reason of any circumstances, cause to believe that the account, or (as the case may be) any of the accounts, held by it in the name of or on behalf of the relevant charity is no longer dormant,

the institution shall forthwith notify those circumstances in writing to *the Commissioners* [the Commission]; and, if it appears to *the Commissioners* [the Commission] that the account or accounts in question is or are no longer dormant, *they shall revoke* [it shall revoke] any direction under subsection (2) above which has previously been given *by them* [by it] to the institution with respect to the relevant charity.

(6) The receipt of any charity trustees or trustee for a charity in respect of any amount received from a relevant institution by virtue of this section shall be a complete discharge of the institution in respect of that amount.

(7) No obligation as to secrecy or other restriction on disclosure (however imposed) shall preclude a relevant institution from disclosing any information to *the Commissioners* [the Commission] for the purpose of enabling *them to discharge their functions* [the Commission to discharge its functions] under this section.

(8) For the purposes of this section—

(a) an account is dormant if no transaction, other than—
  (i) a transaction consisting in a payment into the account, or
  (ii) a transaction which the institution holding the account has itself caused to be effected,
  has been effected in relation to the account within the period of five years immediately preceding the date when *the Commissioners are informed* [the Commission is informed] as mentioned in paragraph (a) of subsection (1) above;
(b) a 'relevant institution' means—
  (i) the Bank of England;
  [(ii) a person who has permission under Part 4 of the Financial Services and Markets Act 2000 to accept deposits;
  (iii) an EEA firm of the kind mentioned in paragraph 5(b) of Schedule 3 to that Act which has permission under paragraph 15 of that Schedule (as a result of qualifying for authorisation under paragraph 12(1) of that Schedule) to accept deposits; or
  (iv) such other person who may lawfully accept deposits in the United Kingdom as may be prescribed by the [Minister];] and
(c) references to the transfer of any amount to a charity are references to its transfer—
  (i) to the charity trustees, or
  (ii) to any trustee for the charity,
  as the charity trustees may determine (and any reference to any amount received by a charity shall be construed accordingly).

[(8A) Sub-paragraphs (ii) to (iv) of the definition of 'relevant institution' in subsection (8)(b) must be read with—

(a) section 22 of the Financial Services and Markets Act 2000;
(b) any relevant order under that section; and
(c) Schedule 2 to that Act.]

(9) For the purpose of determining the matters in respect of which any of the powers conferred by section 8 or 9 above may be exercised it shall be assumed that *the Commissioners have* [the Commission has] no functions under this section in relation to accounts to which this subsection applies (with the result that, for example, a relevant institution shall not, in connection with the functions of *the Commissioners* [the Commission] under this section, be required under section 8(3)(a) above to furnish any statements, or answer any questions or inquiries, with respect to any such accounts held by the institution).

This subsection applies to accounts which are dormant accounts by virtue of subsection (8)(a) above but would not be such accounts if sub-paragraph (i) of that provision were omitted.

(10) *Subsection (1) above shall not apply to any account held in the name of or on behalf of an exempt charity.*

NOTES

Derivation

Sub-ss (1)–(7), (9), (10) derived from the Charities Act 1992, s 18(1)–(7), (9), (10); sub-s (8) derived from the Charities Act 1992, s 18(8), as modified by the Banking Coordination (Second Council Directive) Regulations 1992, SI 1992/3218, reg 82(1), Sch 10, Part I, para 33.

Initial Commencement

Specified date: 1 August 1993: see s 99(1).

Extent

This section does not extend to Scotland.

Amendment

Sub-s (1): words 'the Commissioners' in italics repealed and subsequent words in square brackets substituted by the Charities Act 2006, s 75(1), Sch 8, paras 96, 121(1), (2)(a).

Date in force: to be appointed: see the Charities Act 2006, s 79(2).

Sub-s (1): in para (a) words 'are informed' in italics repealed and subsequent words in square brackets substituted by the Charities Act 2006, s 75(1), Sch 8, paras 96, 121(1), (2)(b).

Date in force: to be appointed: see the Charities Act 2006, s 79(2).

Sub-s (1): in para (b) words 'are unable' in italics repealed and subsequent words in square brackets substituted by the Charities Act 2006, s 75(1), Sch 8, paras 96, 121(1), (2)(c).

Date in force: to be appointed: see the Charities Act 2006, s 79(2).

Sub-s (1): words 'they may give' in italics repealed and subsequent words in square brackets substituted by the Charities Act 2006, s 75(1), Sch 8, paras 96, 121(1), (2)(d).

Date in force: to be appointed: see the Charities Act 2006, s 79(2).

Sub-s (3): word 'Commissioners' in italics in both places it occurs repealed and subsequent word in square brackets substituted by the Charities Act 2006, s 75(1), Sch 8, paras 96, 121(1), (3)(a).

Date in force: to be appointed: see the Charities Act 2006, s 79(2).

Sub-s (3): words 'they consider' in italics repealed and subsequent words in square brackets substituted by the Charities Act 2006, s 75(1), Sch 8, paras 96, 121(1), (3)(b).

Date in force: to be appointed: see the Charities Act 2006, s 79(2).

Sub-s (3): words 'to them' in italics repealed and subsequent words in square brackets substituted by the Charities Act 2006, s 75(1), Sch 8, paras 96, 121(1), (3)(c).

Date in force: to be appointed: see the Charities Act 2006, s 79(2).

Sub-s (3): words 'they have received' in italics repealed and subsequent words in square brackets substituted by the Charities Act 2006, s 75(1), Sch 8, paras 96, 121(1), (3)(d).

Date in force: to be appointed: see the Charities Act 2006, s 79(2).

Sub-s (5): in para (a) words 'the Commissioners have been' in italics repealed and subsequent words in square brackets substituted by the Charities Act 2006, s 75(1), Sch 8, paras 96, 121(1), (4)(a).

Date in force: to be appointed: see the Charities Act 2006, s 79(2).

Sub-s (5): words 'the Commissioners' in italics in both places they occur repealed and subsequent words in square brackets substituted by the Charities Act 2006, s 75(1), Sch 8, paras 96, 121(1), (4)(b).

Date in force: to be appointed: see the Charities Act 2006, s 79(2).

Sub-s (5): words 'they shall revoke' in italics repealed and subsequent words in square brackets substituted by the Charities Act 2006, s 75(1), Sch 8, paras 96, 121(1), (4)(c).

Date in force: to be appointed: see the Charities Act 2006, s 79(2).

Sub-s (5): words 'by them' in italics repealed and subsequent words in square brackets substituted by the Charities Act 2006, s 75(1), Sch 8, paras 96, 121(1), (4)(d).

Date in force: to be appointed: see the Charities Act 2006, s 79(2).

Sub-s (7): words 'the Commissioners' in italics repealed and subsequent words in square brackets substituted by the Charities Act 2006, s 75(1), Sch 8, paras 96, 121(1), (5)(a).

Date in force: to be appointed: see the Charities Act 2006, s 79(2).

Sub-s (7): words 'them to discharge their functions' in italics repealed and subsequent words in square brackets substituted by the Charities Act 2006, s 75(1), Sch 8, paras 96, 121(1), (5)(b).

Date in force: to be appointed: see the Charities Act 2006, s 79(2).

Sub-s (8): in para (a) words 'the Commissioners are informed' in italics repealed and subsequent words in square brackets substituted by the Charities Act 2006, s 75(1), Sch 8, paras 96, 121(1), (6).

Date in force: to be appointed: see the Charities Act 2006, s 79(2).

Sub-s (8): para (b)(ii)–(iv) substituted, for para (b)(ii)–(v) as originally enacted, by SI 2001/3649, art 339(1), (2).

Date in force: 1 December 2001: see SI 2001/3649, art 1.

Sub-s (8): in para (b)(iv) word 'Minister' in square brackets substituted by SI 2006/2951, art 6, Schedule, para 4(m).

Date in force: 13 December 2006: see SI 2006/2951, art 1(2).

Sub-s (8A): inserted by SI 2001/3649, art 339(1), (3).

Date in force: 1 December 2001: see SI 2001/3649, art 1.

Sub-s (9): words 'the Commissioners have' in italics repealed and subsequent words in square brackets substituted by the Charities Act 2006, s 75(1), Sch 8, paras 96, 121(1), (7)(a).

Date in force: to be appointed: see the Charities Act 2006, s 79(2).

Sub-s (9): words 'the Commissioners' in italics repealed and subsequent words in square brackets substituted by the Charities Act 2006, s 75(1), Sch 8, paras 96, 121(1), (7)(b).

Date in force: to be appointed: see the Charities Act 2006, s 79(2).

Sub-s (10): repealed by the Charities Act 2006, ss 12, 75(2), Sch 5, para 7, Sch 9.

Date in force: to be appointed: see the Charities Act 2006, s 79(2).

29 Power to advise charity trustees [29 Power to give advice and guidance]

(1) The Commissioners may on the written application of any charity trustee give him their opinion or advice on any matter affecting the performance of his duties as such.

(2) A charity trustee or trustee for a charity acting in accordance with the opinion or advice of the Commissioners given under this section with respect to the charity shall be deemed, as regards his responsibility for so acting, to have acted in accordance with his trust, unless, when he does so, either—

(a) *he knows or has reasonable cause to suspect that the opinion or advice was given in ignorance of material facts; or*
(b) *the decision of the court has been obtained on the matter or proceedings are pending to obtain one.*

[(1) The Commission may, on the written application of any charity trustee or trustee for a charity, give that person its opinion or advice in relation to any matter—

(a) relating to the performance of any duties of his, as such a trustee, in relation to the charity concerned, or

(b) otherwise relating to the proper administration of the charity.

(2) A charity trustee or trustee for a charity who acts in accordance with any opinion or advice given by the Commission under subsection (1) above (whether to him or to another trustee) is to be taken, as regards his responsibility for so acting, to have acted in accordance with his trust.

(3) But subsection (2) above does not apply to a person if, when so acting, either—

(a) he knows or has reasonable cause to suspect that the opinion or advice was given in ignorance of material facts, or
(b) a decision of the court or the Tribunal has been obtained on the matter or proceedings are pending to obtain one.

(4) The Commission may, in connection with its second general function mentioned in section 1C(2) above, give such advice or guidance with respect to the administration of charities as it considers appropriate.

(5) Any advice or guidance so given may relate to—

(a) charities generally,
(b) any class of charities, or
(c) any particular charity,

and may take such form, and be given in such manner, as the Commission considers appropriate.]

NOTES

Derivation

This section derived from the Charities Act 1960, s 24.

Initial Commencement

Specified date: 1 August 1993: see s 99(1).

Extent

This section does not extend to Scotland.

Amendment

Substituted by the Charities Act 2006, s 24.

[29A Power to determine membership of charity]

[(1) The Commission may—

(a) on the application of a charity, or
(b) at any time after the institution of an inquiry under section 8 above with respect to a charity,

determine who are the members of the charity.

(2) The Commission's power under subsection (1) may also be exercised by a person appointed by the Commission for the purpose.

(3) In a case within subsection (1)(b) the Commission may, if it thinks fit, so appoint the person appointed to conduct the inquiry.]

NOTES

Amendment

Inserted by the Charities Act 2006, s 25.

30 Powers for preservation of charity documents

(1) *The Commissioners* [The Commission] may provide books in which any deed, will or other document relating to a charity may be enrolled.

(2) The *Commissioners* [Commission] may accept for safe keeping any document of or relating to a charity, and the charity trustees or other persons having the custody of documents of or relating to a charity (including a charity which has ceased to exist) may with the consent of the *Commissioners* [Commission] deposit them with the *Commissioners* [Commission] for safe keeping, except in the case of documents required by some other enactment to be kept elsewhere.

(3) Where a document is enrolled by *the Commissioners* [the Commission] or is for the time being deposited *with them* [with the Commission] under this section, evidence of its contents may be given by means of a copy certified by any *officer of the Commissioners generally or specially authorised by them* [member of the staff of the Commission generally or specially authorised by the Commission] to act for this purpose; and a document purporting to be such a copy shall be received in evidence without proof of the official position, authority or handwriting of the person certifying it or of the original document being enrolled or deposited as aforesaid.

(4) Regulations made by the [Minister] may make provision for such documents deposited with *the Commissioners* [the Commission] under this section as may be prescribed by the regulations to be destroyed or otherwise disposed of after such period or in such circumstances as may be so prescribed.

(5) Subsections (3) and (4) above shall apply to any document transmitted to *the Commissioners* [the Commission] under section 9 above and kept *by them* [by the Commission] under subsection (3) of that section, as if the document had been deposited *with them* [with the Commission] for safe keeping under this section.

NOTES

Derivation

Sub-ss (1)–(3), (5) derived from the Charities Act 1960, s 25(1)–(3), (5); sub-s (4) derived from the Charities Act 1960, s 25(4), as read with s 43(1) thereof, as substituted by the Education Act 1973, s 1(3), Sch 1, para 1(1), (7).

Initial Commencement

Specified date: 1 August 1993: see s 99(1).

Extent

This section does not extend to Scotland.

Amendment

Sub-s (1): words 'The Commissioners' in italics repealed and subsequent words in square brackets substituted by the Charities Act 2006, s 75(1), Sch 8, paras 96, 122(1), (2).

Date in force: to be appointed: see the Charities Act 2006, s 79(2).

Sub-s (2): word 'Commissioners' in italics in each place it occurs repealed and subsequent word in square brackets substituted by the Charities Act 2006, s 75(1), Sch 8, paras 96, 122(1), (3).

Date in force: to be appointed: see the Charities Act 2006, s 79(2).

Sub-s (3): words 'the Commissioners' in italics repealed and subsequent words in square brackets substituted by the Charities Act 2006, s 75(1), Sch 8, paras 96, 122(1), (4)(a).

Date in force: to be appointed: see the Charities Act 2006, s 79(2).

Sub-s (3): words 'with them' in italics repealed and subsequent words in square brackets substituted by the Charities Act 2006, s 75(1), Sch 8, paras 96, 122(1), (4)(b).

Date in force: to be appointed: see the Charities Act 2006, s 79(2).

Sub-s (3): words 'officer of the Commissioners generally or specially authorised by them' in italics repealed and subsequent words in square brackets substituted by the Charities Act 2006, s 75(1), Sch 8, paras 96, 122(1), (4)(c).

Date in force: to be appointed: see the Charities Act 2006, s 79(2).

Sub-s (4): word 'Minister' in square brackets substituted by SI 2006/2951, art 6, Schedule, para 4(n).

Date in force: 13 December 2006: see SI 2006/2951, art 1(2).

Sub-s (4): words 'the Commissioners' in italics repealed and subsequent words in square brackets substituted by the Charities Act 2006, s 75(1), Sch 8, paras 96, 122(1), (5).

Date in force: to be appointed: see the Charities Act 2006, s 79(2).

Sub-s (5): words 'the Commissioners' in italics repealed and subsequent words in square brackets substituted by the Charities Act 2006, s 75(1), Sch 8, paras 96, 122(1), (6)(a).

Date in force: to be appointed: see the Charities Act 2006, s 79(2).

Sub-s (5): words 'by them' in italics repealed and subsequent words in square brackets substituted by the Charities Act 2006, s 75(1), Sch 8, paras 96, 122(1), (6)(b).

Date in force: to be appointed: see the Charities Act 2006, s 79(2).

Sub-s (5): words 'with them' in italics repealed and subsequent words in square brackets substituted by the Charities Act 2006, s 75(1), Sch 8, paras 96, 122(1), (6)(c).

Date in force: to be appointed: see the Charities Act 2006, s 79(2).

31 Power to order taxation of solicitor's bill

(1) *The Commissioners* [The Commission] may order that a solicitor's bill of costs for business done for a charity, or for charity trustees or trustees for a charity, shall be taxed, together with the costs of the taxation, by a taxing officer in such division of the High Court as may be specified in the order, or by the taxing officer of any other court having jurisdiction to order the taxation of the bill.

(2) On any order under this section for the taxation of a solicitor's bill the taxation shall proceed, and the taxing officer shall have the same powers and duties, and the costs of the taxation shall be borne, as if the order had been made, on the application of the person chargeable with the bill, by the court in which the costs are taxed.

(3) No order under this section for the taxation of a solicitor's bill shall be made after payment of the bill unless *the Commissioners are* [the Commission is] of opinion that it contains exorbitant charges; and no such order shall in any case be made where the solicitor's costs are not subject to taxation on an order of the High Court by reason either of an agreement as to his remuneration or the lapse of time since payment of the bill.

NOTES

Derivation

This section derived from the Charities Act 1960, s 26.

Initial Commencement

Specified date: 1 August 1993: see s 99(1).

Extent

This section does not extend to Scotland.

Amendment

Sub-s (1): words 'The Commissioners' in italics repealed and subsequent words in square brackets substituted by the Charities Act 2006, s 75(1), Sch 8, paras 96, 123(1), (2).

Date in force: to be appointed: see the Charities Act 2006, s 79(2).

Sub-s (3): words 'the Commissioners are' in italics repealed and subsequent words in square brackets substituted by the Charities Act 2006, s 75(1), Sch 8, paras 96, 123(1), (3).

Date in force: to be appointed: see the Charities Act 2006, s 79(2).

[31A Power to enter premises]

[(1) A justice of the peace may issue a warrant under this section if satisfied, on information given on oath by a member of the Commission's staff, that there are reasonable grounds for believing that each of the conditions in subsection (2) below is satisfied.

(2) The conditions are—

(a) that an inquiry has been instituted under section 8 above;
(b) that there is on the premises to be specified in the warrant any document or information relevant to that inquiry which the Commission could require to be produced or furnished under section 9(1) above; and
(c) that, if the Commission were to make an order requiring the document or information to be so produced or furnished—
  (i) the order would not be complied with, or
  (ii) the document or information would be removed, tampered with, concealed or destroyed.

(3) A warrant under this section is a warrant authorising the member of the Commission's staff who is named in it—

(a) to enter and search the premises specified in it;
(b) to take such other persons with him as the Commission considers are needed to assist him in doing anything that he is authorised to do under the warrant;
(c) to take possession of any documents which appear to fall within subsection (2)(b) above, or to take any other steps which appear to be necessary for preserving, or preventing interference with, any such documents;
(d) to take possession of any computer disk or other electronic storage device which appears to contain information falling within subsection (2)(b), or information contained in a document so falling, or to take any other steps which appear to be necessary for preserving, or preventing interference with, any such information;
(e) to take copies of, or extracts from, any documents or information falling within paragraph (c) or (d);
(f) to require any person on the premises to provide an explanation of any such document or information or to state where any such documents or information may be found;
(g) to require any such person to give him such assistance as he may reasonably require for the taking of copies or extracts as mentioned in paragraph (e) above.

(4) Entry and search under such a warrant must be at a reasonable hour and within one month of the date of its issue.

(5) The member of the Commission's staff who is authorised under such a warrant ('the authorised person') must, if required to do so, produce—

(a) the warrant, and
(b) documentary evidence that he is a member of the Commission's staff,

for inspection by the occupier of the premises or anyone acting on his behalf.

(6) The authorised person must make a written record of—

(a) the date and time of his entry on the premises;
(b) the number of persons (if any) who accompanied him onto the premises, and the names of any such persons;
(c) the period for which he (and any such persons) remained on the premises;
(d) what he (and any such persons) did while on the premises; and
(e) any document or device of which he took possession while there.

(7) If required to do so, the authorised person must give a copy of the record to the occupier of the premises or someone acting on his behalf.

(8) Unless it is not reasonably practicable to do so, the authorised person must comply with the following requirements before leaving the premises, namely—

(a) the requirements of subsection (6), and
(b) any requirement made under subsection (7) before he leaves the premises.

(9) Where possession of any document or device is taken under this section—

(a) the document may be retained for so long as the Commission considers that it is necessary to retain it (rather than a copy of it) for the purposes of the relevant inquiry under section 8 above, or
(b) the device may be retained for so long as the Commission considers that it is necessary to retain it for the purposes of that inquiry,

as the case may be.

(10) Once it appears to the Commission that the retention of any document or device has ceased to be so necessary, it shall arrange for the document or device to be returned as soon as is reasonably practicable—

(a) to the person from whose possession it was taken, or
(b) to any of the charity trustees of the charity to which it belonged or related.

(11) A person who intentionally obstructs the exercise of any rights conferred by a warrant under this section is guilty of an offence and liable on summary conviction—

(a) to imprisonment for a term not exceeding 51 weeks, or
(b) to a fine not exceeding level 5 on the standard scale,

or to both.]

NOTES

Amendment

Inserted by the Charities Act 2006, s 26(1).

Legal proceedings relating to charities

32 Proceedings by Commissioners [Commission]

(1) Subject to subsection (2) below, *the Commissioners* [the Commission] may exercise the same powers with respect to—

(a) the taking of legal proceedings with reference to charities or the property or affairs of charities, or
(b) the compromise of claims with a view to avoiding or ending such proceedings,

as are exercisable by the Attorney General acting ex officio.

(2) Subsection (1) above does not apply to the power of the Attorney General under section 63(1) below to present a petition for the winding up of a charity.

(3) The practice and procedure to be followed in relation to any proceedings taken by *the Commissioners* [the Commission] under subsection (1) above shall be the same in all respects (and in particular as regards costs) as if they were proceedings taken by the Attorney General acting ex officio.

(4) No rule of law or practice shall be taken to require the Attorney General to be a party to any such proceedings.

(5) The powers exercisable by *the Commissioners* [the Commission] by virtue of this section shall be exercisable *by them of their own* [by the Commission of its own] motion, but shall be exercisable only with the agreement of the Attorney General on each occasion.

NOTES

Derivation

This section derived from the Charities Act 1960, s 26A, as added by the Charities Act 1992, s 28.

Initial Commencement

Specified date: 1 August 1993: see s 99(1).

Extent

This section does not extend to Scotland.

Amendment

Section heading: word 'Commissioners' repealed and subsequent word in square brackets substituted by the Charities Act 2006, s 75(1), Sch 8, paras 96, 124(1), (4).

Date in force: to be appointed: see the Charities Act 2006, s 79(2).

Sub-s (1): words 'the Commissioners' in italics repealed and subsequent words in square brackets substituted by the Charities Act 2006, s 75(1), Sch 8, paras 96, 124(1), (2).

Date in force: to be appointed: see the Charities Act 2006, s 79(2).

Sub-s (3): words 'the Commissioners' in italics repealed and subsequent words in square brackets substituted by the Charities Act 2006, s 75(1), Sch 8, paras 96, 124(1), (2).

Date in force: to be appointed: see the Charities Act 2006, s 79(2).

Sub-s (5): words 'the Commissioners' in italics repealed and subsequent words in square brackets substituted by the Charities Act 2006, s 75(1), Sch 8, paras 96, 124(1), (3)(a).

Date in force: to be appointed: see the Charities Act 2006, s 79(2).

Sub-s (5): words 'by them of their own' in italics repealed and subsequent words in square brackets substituted by the Charities Act 2006, s 75(1), Sch 8, paras 96, 124(1), (3)(b).

Date in force: to be appointed: see the Charities Act 2006, s 79(2).

33 Proceedings by other persons

(1) Charity proceedings may be taken with reference to a charity either by the charity, or by any of the charity trustees, or by any person interested in the charity, or by any two or more inhabitants of the area of the charity if it is a local charity, but not by any other person.

(2) Subject to the following provisions of this section, no charity proceedings relating to a charity *(other than an exempt charity)* shall be entertained or proceeded with in any court unless the taking of the proceedings is authorised by order of *the Commissioners* [the Commission].

(3) *The Commissioners* [The Commission] shall not, without special reasons, authorise the taking of charity proceedings where in *their opinion* [its opinion] the case can be dealt with *by them* [by the Commission] under the powers of this Act other than those conferred by section 32 above.

(4) This section shall not require any order for the taking of proceedings in a pending cause or matter or for the bringing of any appeal.

(5) Where the foregoing provisions of this section require the taking of charity proceedings to be authorised by an order of *the Commissioners* [the Commission], the proceedings may nevertheless be entertained or proceeded with if, after the order had been applied for and refused, leave to take the proceedings was obtained from one of the judges of the High Court attached to the Chancery Division.

(6) Nothing in the foregoing subsections shall apply to the taking of proceedings by the Attorney General, with or without a relator, or to the taking of proceedings by *the Commissioners* [the Commission] in accordance with section 32 above.

(7) Where it appears to *the Commissioners* [the Commission], on an application for an order under this section or otherwise, that it is desirable for legal proceedings to be taken with reference to any charity *(other than an exempt charity)* or its property or affairs, and for the proceedings to be taken by the Attorney General, *the Commissioners* [the Commission] shall so inform the Attorney General, and send him such statements and particulars as *they think* [the Commission thinks] necessary to explain the matter.

(8) In this section 'charity proceedings' means proceedings in any court in England or Wales brought under the court's jurisdiction with respect to charities, or brought under the court's jurisdiction with respect to trusts in relation to the administration of a trust for charitable purposes.

NOTES

Derivation

Sub-ss (1), (2), (4), (5), (7), (8) derived from the Charities Act 1960, s 28(1), (2), (4), (5), (7), (8); sub-ss (3), (6) derived from the Charities Act 1960, s 28(3), (6), as amended by the Charities Act 1992, s 47, Sch 3, para 10.

Initial Commencement

Specified date: 1 August 1993: see s 99(1).

Extent

This section does not extend to Scotland.

Amendment

Sub-s (2): words '(other than an exempt charity)' in italics repealed by the Charities Act 2006, ss 12, 75(2), Sch 5, para 8(1), (2), Sch 9.

Date in force: to be appointed: see the Charities Act 2006, s 79(2).

Sub-s (2): words 'the Commissioners' in italics repealed and subsequent words in square brackets substituted by the Charities Act 2006, s 75(1), Sch 8, paras 96, 125(1), (2).

Date in force: to be appointed: see the Charities Act 2006, s 79(2).

Sub-s (3): words 'The Commissioners' in italics repealed and subsequent words in square brackets substituted by the Charities Act 2006, s 75(1), Sch 8, paras 96, 125(1), (3)(a).

Date in force: to be appointed: see the Charities Act 2006, s 79(2).

Sub-s (3): words 'their opinion' in italics repealed and subsequent words in square brackets substituted by the Charities Act 2006, s 75(1), Sch 8, paras 96, 125(1), (3)(b).

Date in force: to be appointed: see the Charities Act 2006, s 79(2).

Sub-s (3): words 'by them' in italics repealed and subsequent words in square brackets substituted by the Charities Act 2006, s 75(1), Sch 8, paras 96, 125(1), (3)(c).

Date in force: to be appointed: see the Charities Act 2006, s 79(2).

Sub-s (5): words 'the Commissioners' in italics repealed and subsequent words in square brackets substituted by the Charities Act 2006, s 75(1), Sch 8, paras 96, 125(1), (4).

Date in force: to be appointed: see the Charities Act 2006, s 79(2).

Sub-s (6): words 'the Commissioners' in italics repealed and subsequent words in square brackets substituted by the Charities Act 2006, s 75(1), Sch 8, paras 96, 125(1), (4).

Date in force: to be appointed: see the Charities Act 2006, s 79(2).

Sub-s (7): words 'the Commissioners' in italics in both places they occur repealed and subsequent words in square brackets substituted by the Charities Act 2006, s 75(1), Sch 8, paras 96, 125(1), (5)(a).

Date in force: to be appointed: see the Charities Act 2006, s 79(2).

Sub-s (7): words '(other than an exempt charity)' in italics repealed by the Charities Act 2006, ss 12, 75(2), Sch 5, para 8(1), (3), Sch 9.

Date in force: to be appointed: see the Charities Act 2006, s 79(2).

Sub-s (7): words 'they think' in italics repealed and subsequent words in square brackets substituted by the Charities Act 2006, s 75(1), Sch 8, paras 96, 125(1), (5)(b).

Date in force: to be appointed: see the Charities Act 2006, s 79(2).

34 Report of s 8 inquiry to be evidence in certain proceedings

(1) A copy of the report of the person conducting an inquiry under section 8 above shall, if certified by *the Commissioners* [the Commission] to be a true copy, be admissible in any proceedings to which this section applies—

(a) as evidence of any fact stated in the report; and
(b) as evidence of the opinion of that person as to any matter referred to in it.

(2) This section applies to—

(a) any legal proceedings instituted by *the Commissioners* [the Commission] under this Part of this Act; and
(b) any legal proceedings instituted by the Attorney General in respect of a charity.

(3) A document purporting to be a certificate issued for the purposes of subsection (1) above shall be received in evidence and be deemed to be such a certificate, unless the contrary is proved.

NOTES

Derivation

This section derived from the Charities Act 1960, s 28A, as added by the Charities Act 1992, s 11.

Initial Commencement

Specified date: 1 August 1993: see s 99(1).

Extent

This section does not extend to Scotland.

Amendment

Sub-s (1): words 'the Commissioners' in italics repealed and subsequent words in square brackets substituted by the Charities Act 2006, s 75(1), Sch 8, paras 96, 126.

Date in force: to be appointed: see the Charities Act 2006, s 79(2).

Sub-s (2): in para (a) words 'the Commissioners' in italics repealed and subsequent words in square brackets substituted by the Charities Act 2006, s 75(1), Sch 8, paras 96, 126.

Date in force: to be appointed: see the Charities Act 2006, s 79(2).

Meaning of 'trust corporation'

35 Application of provisions to trust corporations appointed under s 16 or 18

(1) In the definition of 'trust corporation' contained in the following provisions—

(a) section 117(xxx) of the Settled Land Act 1925,
(b) section 68(18) of the Trustee Act 1925,
(c) section 205(xxviii) of the Law of Property Act 1925,
(d) section 55(xxvi) of the Administration of Estates Act 1925, and
(e) section 128 of the *Supreme Court Act 1981* [Senior Courts Act 1981],

the reference to a corporation appointed by the court in any particular case to be a trustee includes a reference to a corporation appointed by *the Commissioners* [the Commission] under this Act to be a trustee.

(2) This section shall be deemed always to have had effect; but the reference to section 128 of the *Supreme Court Act 1981* [Senior Courts Act 1981] shall, in relation to any time before 1st January 1982, be construed as a reference to section 175(1) of the Supreme Court of Judicature (Consolidation) Act 1925.

NOTES

Derivation

Sub-s (1) derived from the Charities Act 1960, s 21A, as added by the Charities Act 1992, s 14(1); sub-s (2) derived from the Charities Act 1992, s 14(2).

Initial Commencement

Specified date: 1 August 1993: see s 99(1).

Extent

This section does not extend to Scotland.

Amendment

Sub-s (1): in para (e) words 'Supreme Court Act 1981' in italics repealed and subsequent words in square brackets substituted by the Constitutional Reform Act 2005, s 59(5), Sch 11, Pt 1, para 1(2).

Date in force: to be appointed: see the Constitutional Reform Act 2005, s 148(1).

Sub-s (1): words 'the Commissioners' in italics repealed and subsequent words in square brackets substituted by the Charities Act 2006, s 75(1), Sch 8, paras 96, 127.

Date in force: to be appointed: see the Charities Act 2006, s 79(2).

Sub-s (2): words 'Supreme Court Act 1981' in italics repealed and subsequent words in square brackets substituted by the Constitutional Reform Act 2005, s 59(5), Sch 11, Pt 1, para 1(2).

Date in force: to be appointed: see the Constitutional Reform Act 2005, s 148(1).

Part V
Charity Land

36 Restrictions on dispositions

(1) Subject to the following provisions of this section and section 40 below, no land held by or in trust for a charity shall be *sold* [conveyed, transferred], leased or otherwise disposed of without an order of the court or of *the Commissioners* [the Commission].

(2) Subsection (1) above shall not apply to a disposition of such land if—

(a) the disposition is made to a person who is not—
 (i) a connected person (as defined in Schedule 5 to this Act), or
 (ii) a trustee for, or nominee of, a connected person; and
(b) the requirements of subsection (3) or (5) below have been complied with in relation to it.

(3) Except where the proposed disposition is the granting of such a lease as is mentioned in subsection (5) below, [the requirements mentioned in subsection (2)(b) above are that] the charity trustees must, before entering into an agreement for the sale, or (as the case may be) for a lease or other disposition, of the land—

(a) obtain and consider a written report on the proposed disposition from a qualified surveyor instructed by the trustees and acting exclusively for the charity;
(b) advertise the proposed disposition for such period and in such manner as the surveyor has advised in his report (unless he has there advised that it would not be in the best interests of the charity to advertise the proposed disposition); and
(c) decide that they are satisfied, having considered the surveyor's report, that the terms on which the disposition is proposed to be made are the best that can reasonably be obtained for the charity.

(4) For the purposes of subsection (3) above a person is a qualified surveyor if—

(a) he is a fellow or professional associate of the Royal Institution of Chartered Surveyors or of the Incorporated Society of Valuers and Auctioneers or satisfies such other requirement or requirements as may be prescribed by regulations made by the [Minister]; and
(b) he is reasonably believed by the charity trustees to have ability in, and experience of, the valuation of land of the particular kind, and in the particular area, in question;

and any report prepared for the purposes of that subsection shall contain such information, and deal with such matters, as may be prescribed by regulations so made.

(5) Where the proposed disposition is the granting of a lease for a term ending not more than seven years after it is granted (other than one granted wholly or partly in consideration of a fine), [the requirements mentioned in subsection (2)(b) above are that] the charity trustees must, before entering into an agreement for the lease—

(a) obtain and consider the advice on the proposed disposition of a person who is reasonably believed by the trustees to have the requisite ability and practical experience to provide them with competent advice on the proposed disposition; and
(b) decide that they are satisfied, having considered that person's advice, that the terms on which the disposition is proposed to be made are the best that can reasonably be obtained for the charity.

(6) Where—

(a) any land is held by or in trust for a charity, and
(b) the trusts on which it is so held stipulate that it is to be used for the purposes, or any particular purposes, of the charity,

then (subject to subsections (7) and (8) below and without prejudice to the operation of the preceding provisions of this section) the land shall not be *sold* [conveyed, transferred], leased or otherwise disposed of unless the charity trustees have *previously* [before the relevant time]—

- (i) given public notice of the proposed disposition, inviting representations to be made to them within a time specified in the notice, being not less than one month from the date of the notice; and
- (ii) taken into consideration any representations made to them within that time about the proposed disposition.

[(6A) In subsection (6) above 'the relevant time' means—

- (a) where the charity trustees enter into an agreement for the sale, or (as the case may be) for the lease or other disposition, the time when they enter into that agreement, and
- (b) in any other case, the time of the disposition.]

(7) Subsection (6) above shall not apply to any such disposition of land as is there mentioned if—

- (a) the disposition is to be effected with a view to acquiring by way of replacement other property which is to be held on the trusts referred to in paragraph (b) of that subsection; or
- (b) the disposition is the granting of a lease for a term ending not more than two years after it is granted (other than one granted wholly or partly in consideration of a fine).

(8) *The Commissioners* [The Commission] may direct—

- (a) that subsection (6) above shall not apply to dispositions of land held by or in trust for a charity or class of charities (whether generally or only in the case of a specified class of dispositions or land, or otherwise as may be provided in the direction), or
- (b) that that subsection shall not apply to a particular disposition of land held by or in trust for a charity,

if, on an application made to them in writing by or on behalf of the charity or charities in question, *the Commissioners are satisfied* [the Commission is satisfied] that it would be in the interests of the charity or charities *for them* [for the Commission] to give the direction.

(9) The restrictions on disposition imposed by this section apply notwithstanding anything in the trusts of a charity; but nothing in this section applies—

- (a) to any disposition for which general or special authority is expressly given (without the authority being made subject to the sanction of an order of the court) by any statutory provision contained in or having effect under an Act of Parliament or by any scheme legally established; or
- (b) to any disposition of land held by or in trust for a charity which—
  - (i) is made to another charity otherwise than for the best price that can reasonably be obtained, and
  - (ii) is authorised to be so made by the trusts of the first-mentioned charity; or
- (c) to the granting, by or on behalf of a charity and in accordance with its trusts, of a lease to any beneficiary under those trusts where the lease—
  - (i) is granted otherwise than for the best rent that can reasonably be obtained; and
  - (ii) is intended to enable the demised premises to be occupied for the purposes, or any particular purposes, of the charity.

(10) Nothing in this section applies—

- (a) to any disposition of land held by or in trust for an exempt charity;
- (b) to any disposition of land by way of mortgage or other security; or
- (c) to any disposition of an advowson.

(11) In this section 'land' means land in England or Wales.

NOTES

Derivation

This section derived from the Charities Act 1992, s 32.

Initial Commencement

Specified date: 1 August 1993: see s 99(1).

Extent

This section does not extend to Scotland.

Amendment

Sub-s (1): word 'sold' in italics repealed and subsequent words in square brackets substituted by the Charities Act 2006, s 75(1), Sch 8, paras 96, 128(1), (2)(a).

Date in force: to be appointed: see the Charities Act 2006, s 79(2).

Sub-s (1): words 'the Commissioners' in italics repealed and subsequent words in square brackets substituted by the Charities Act 2006, s 75(1), Sch 8, paras 96, 128(1), (2)(b).

Date in force: to be appointed: see the Charities Act 2006, s 79(2).

Sub-s (3): words 'the requirements mentioned in subsection (2)(b) above are that' in square brackets inserted by the Charities Act 2006, s 75(1), Sch 8, paras 96, 128(1), (3).

Date in force: to be appointed: see the Charities Act 2006, s 79(2).

Sub-s (4): in para (a) word 'Minister' in square brackets substituted by SI 2006/2951, art 6, Schedule, para 4(o).

Date in force: 13 December 2006: see SI 2006/2951, art 1(2).

Sub-s (5): words 'the requirements mentioned in subsection (2)(b) above are that' in square brackets inserted by the Charities Act 2006, s 75(1), Sch 8, paras 96, 128(1), (4).

Date in force: to be appointed: see the Charities Act 2006, s 79(2).

Sub-s (6): word 'sold' in italics repealed and subsequent words in square brackets substituted by the Charities Act 2006, s 75(1), Sch 8, paras 96, 128(1), (5)(a).

Date in force: to be appointed: see the Charities Act 2006, s 79(2).

Sub-s (6): word 'previously' in italics repealed and subsequent words in square brackets substituted by the Charities Act 2006, s 75(1), Sch 8, paras 96, 128(1), (5)(b).

Date in force: to be appointed: see the Charities Act 2006, s 79(2).

Sub-s (6A): inserted by the Charities Act 2006, s 75(1), Sch 8, paras 96, 128(1), (6).

Date in force: to be appointed: see the Charities Act 2006, s 79(2).

Sub-s (8): words 'The Commissioners' in italics repealed and subsequent words in square brackets substituted by the Charities Act 2006, s 75(1), Sch 8, paras 96, 128(1), (7)(a).

Date in force: to be appointed: see the Charities Act 2006, s 79(2).

Sub-s (8): words 'the Commissioners are satisfied' in italics repealed and subsequent words in square brackets substituted by the Charities Act 2006, s 75(1), Sch 8, paras 96, 128(1), (7)(b).

Date in force: to be appointed: see the Charities Act 2006, s 79(2).

Sub-s (8): words 'for them' in italics repealed and subsequent words in square brackets substituted by the Charities Act 2006, s 75(1), Sch 8, paras 96, 128(1), (7)(c).

Date in force: to be appointed: see the Charities Act 2006, s 79(2).

37 Supplementary provisions relating to dispositions

(1) Any of the following instruments, namely—

(a) any contract for the sale, or for a lease or other disposition, of land which is held by or in trust for a charity, and
(b) any conveyance, transfer, lease or other instrument effecting a disposition of such land,

shall state—

(i) that the land is held by or in trust for a charity,
(ii) whether the charity is an exempt charity and whether the disposition is one falling within paragraph (a), (b) or (c) of subsection (9) of section 36 above, and
(iii) if it is not an exempt charity and the disposition is not one falling within any of those paragraphs, that the land is land to which the restrictions on disposition imposed by that section apply.

(2) Where any land held by or in trust for a charity is *sold* [conveyed, transferred], leased or otherwise disposed of by a disposition to which subsection (1) or (2) of section 36 above applies, the charity trustees shall certify in the instrument by which the disposition is effected—

(a) (where subsection (1) of that section applies) that the disposition has been sanctioned by an order of the court or of *the Commissioners* [the Commission] (as the case may be), or
(b) (where subsection (2) of that section applies) that the charity trustees have power under the trusts of the charity to effect the disposition, and that they have complied with the provisions of that section so far as applicable to it.

(3) Where subsection (2) above has been complied with in relation to any disposition of land, then in favour of a person who (whether under the disposition or afterwards) acquires an interest in the land for money or money's worth, it shall be conclusively presumed that the facts were as stated in the certificate.

(4) Where—

(a) any land held by or in trust for a charity is *sold* [conveyed, transferred], leased or otherwise disposed of by a disposition to which subsection (1) or (2) of section 36 above applies, but
(b) subsection (2) above has not been complied with in relation to the disposition,

then in favour of a person who (whether under the disposition or afterwards) in good faith acquires an interest in the land for money or money's worth, the disposition shall be valid whether or not—

(i) the disposition has been sanctioned by an order of the court or of *the Commissioners* [the Commission], or
(ii) the charity trustees have power under the trusts of the charity to effect the disposition and have complied with the provisions of that section so far as applicable to it.

(5) Any of the following instruments, namely—

(a) any contract for the sale, or for a lease or other disposition, of land which will, as a result of the disposition, be held by or in trust for a charity, and
(b) any conveyance, transfer, lease or other instrument effecting a disposition of such land,

shall state—

(i) that the land will, as a result of the disposition, be held by or in trust for a charity,
(ii) whether the charity is an exempt charity, and
(iii) if it is not an exempt charity, that the restrictions on disposition imposed by section 36 above will apply to the land (subject to subsection (9) of that section).

(6) ...

[(7) Where the disposition to be effected by any such instrument as is mentioned in subsection (1)(b) or (5)(b) above will be—

(a) a registrable disposition, or
(b) a disposition which triggers the requirement of registration,

the statement which, by virtue of subsection (1) or (5) above, is to be contained in the instrument shall be in such form as may be prescribed by land registration rules.

(8) Where the registrar approves an application for registration of—

(a) a disposition of registered land, or
(b) a person's title under a disposition of unregistered land,

and the instrument effecting the disposition contains a statement complying with subsections (5) and (7) above, he shall enter in the register a restriction reflecting the limitation under section 36 above on subsequent disposal.]

(9) Where—

(a) any such restriction is entered in the register in respect of any land, and
(b) the charity by or in trust for which the land is held becomes an exempt charity,

the charity trustees shall apply to the registrar for [the removal of the entry]; and on receiving any application duly made under this subsection the registrar shall [remove the entry].

(10) Where—

(a) any registered land is held by or in trust for an exempt charity and the charity ceases to be an exempt charity, or
(b) any registered land becomes, as a result of a declaration of trust by the registered proprietor, land held in trust for a charity (other than an exempt charity),

the charity trustees shall apply to the registrar for such a restriction as is mentioned in subsection (8) above to be entered in the register in respect of the land; and on receiving any application duly made under this subsection the registrar shall enter such a restriction in the register in respect of the land.

(11) In this section—

(a) references to a disposition of land do not include references to—
 (i) a disposition of land by way of mortgage or other security,
 (ii) any disposition of an advowson, or
 (iii) any release of a rentcharge failing within section 40(1) below; and
(b) 'land' means land in England or Wales;

and subsections (7) to (10) above shall be construed as one with the [Land Registration Act 2002].

NOTES

Derivation

This section derived from the Charities Act 1992, s 33.

Initial Commencement

Specified date: 1 August 1993: see s 99(1).

Extent

This section does not extend to Scotland.

Amendment

Sub-s (2): word 'sold' in italics repealed and subsequent words in square brackets substituted by the Charities Act 2006, s 75(1), Sch 8, paras 96, 129(a).

Date in force: to be appointed: see the Charities Act 2006, s 79(2).

Sub-s (2): in para (a) words 'the Commissioners' in italics repealed and subsequent words in square brackets substituted by the Charities Act 2006, s 75(1), Sch 8, paras 96, 129(b).

Date in force: to be appointed: see the Charities Act 2006, s 79(2).

Sub-s (4): word 'sold' in italics repealed and subsequent words in square brackets substituted by the Charities Act 2006, s 75(1), Sch 8, paras 96, 129(a).

Date in force: to be appointed: see the Charities Act 2006, s 79(2).

Sub-s (4): words 'the Commissioners' in italics repealed and subsequent words in square brackets substituted by the Charities Act 2006, s 75(1), Sch 8, paras 96, 129(b).

Date in force: to be appointed: see the Charities Act 2006, s 79(2).

Sub-s (6): repealed by the Trusts of Land and Appointment of Trustees Act 1996, s 25(2), Sch 4; for savings in relation to entailed interests created before the commencement of that Act, and savings consequential upon the abolition of the doctrine of conversion, see s 25(4), (5) thereof.

Sub-ss (7), (8): substituted by the Land Registration Act 2002, s 133, Sch 11, para 29(1), (2).

Date in force: 13 October 2003: see SI 2003/1725, art 2(1).

Sub-s (9): words 'the removal of the entry' in square brackets substituted by the Land Registration Act 2002, s 133, Sch 11, para 29(1), (3)(a).

Date in force: 13 October 2003: see SI 2003/1725, art 2(1).

Sub-s (9): words 'remove the entry' in square brackets substituted by the Land Registration Act 2002, s 133, Sch 11, para 29(1), (3)(b).

Date in force: 13 October 2003: see SI 2003/1725, art 2(1).

Sub-s (11): words 'Land Registration Act 2002' in square brackets substituted by the Land Registration Act 2002, s 133, Sch 11, para 29(1), (4).

Date in force: 13 October 2003: see SI 2003/1725, art 2(1).

Subordinate Legislation

Land Registration Rules 2003, SI 2003/1417 (made under sub-s (7)).

38 Restrictions on mortgaging

(1) Subject to subsection (2) below, no mortgage of land held by or in trust for a charity shall be granted without an order of the court or of *the Commissioners* [the Commission].

(2) Subsection (1) above shall not apply to a mortgage of any such land by way of security for the repayment of a loan where the charity trustees have, before executing the mortgage, obtained and considered proper advice, given to them in writing, on the matters mentioned in subsection (3) below.

(3) Those matters are—

(a) *whether the proposed loan is necessary in order for the charity trustees to be able to pursue the particular course of action in connection with which the loan is sought by them;*

(b) *whether the terms of the proposed loan are reasonable having regard to the status of the charity as a prospective borrower; and*

(c) *the ability of the charity to repay on those terms the sum proposed to be borrowed.*

[(2) Subsection (1) above shall not apply to a mortgage of any such land if the charity trustees have, before executing the mortgage, obtained and considered proper advice, given to them in writing, on the relevant matters or matter mentioned in subsection (3) or (3A) below (as the case may be).

(3) In the case of a mortgage to secure the repayment of a proposed loan or grant, the relevant matters are—

(a) whether the loan or grant is necessary in order for the charity trustees to be able to pursue the particular course of action in connection with which they are seeking the loan or grant;
(b) whether the terms of the loan or grant are reasonable having regard to the status of the charity as the prospective recipient of the loan or grant; and
(c) the ability of the charity to repay on those terms the sum proposed to be paid by way of loan or grant.

(3A) In the case of a mortgage to secure the discharge of any other proposed obligation, the relevant matter is whether it is reasonable for the charity trustees to undertake to discharge the obligation, having regard to the charity's purposes.

(3B) Subsection (3) or (as the case may be) subsection (3A) above applies in relation to such a mortgage as is mentioned in that subsection whether the mortgage—

(a) would only have effect to secure the repayment of the proposed loan or grant or the discharge of the proposed obligation, or
(b) would also have effect to secure the repayment of sums paid by way of loan or grant, or the discharge of other obligations undertaken, after the date of its execution.

(3C) Subsection (3D) below applies where—

(a) the charity trustees of a charity have executed a mortgage of land held by or in trust for a charity in accordance with subsection (2) above, and
(b) the mortgage has effect to secure the repayment of sums paid by way of loan or grant, or the discharge of other obligations undertaken, after the date of its execution.

(3D) In such a case, the charity trustees must not after that date enter into any transaction involving—

(a) the payment of any such sums, or
(b) the undertaking of any such obligations,

unless they have, before entering into the transaction, obtained and considered proper advice, given to them in writing, on the matters or matter mentioned in subsection (3)(a) to (c) or (3A) above (as the case may be).]

(4) For the purposes of *subsection (2) above* [this section] proper advice is the advice of a person—

(a) who is reasonably believed by the charity trustees to be qualified by his ability in and practical experience of financial matters; and
(b) who has no financial interest in *the making of the loan in question* [relation to the loan, grant or other transaction in connection with which his advice is given];

and such advice may constitute proper advice for those purposes notwithstanding that the person giving it does so in the course of his employment as an officer or employee of the charity or of the charity trustees.

(5) This section applies notwithstanding anything in the trusts of a charity; but nothing in this section applies to any mortgage for which general or special authority is given as mentioned in section 36(9)(a) above.

(6) In this section—

'land' means land in England or Wales;
'mortgage' includes a charge.

(7) Nothing in this section applies to an exempt charity.

NOTES

Derivation

This section derived from the Charities Act 1992, s 34.

Initial Commencement

Specified date: 1 August 1993: see s 99(1).

Extent

This section does not extend to Scotland.

Amendment

Sub-s (1): words 'the Commissioners' in italics repealed and subsequent words in square brackets substituted by the Charities Act 2006, s 75(1), Sch 8, paras 96, 130.

Date in force: to be appointed: see the Charities Act 2006, s 79(2).

Sub-ss (2), (3), (3A)–(3D): substituted, for sub-ss (2), (3) as originally enacted, by the Charities Act 2006, s 27(1), (2).

Sub-s (4): words 'this section' in square brackets substituted by the Charities Act 2006, s 27(1), (3)(a).

Sub-s (4): in para (b) words from 'relation to the' to 'advice is given' in square brackets substituted by the Charities Act 2006, s 27(1), (3)(b).

39 Supplementary provisions relating to mortgaging

(1) Any mortgage of land held by or in trust for a charity shall state—

(a) that the land is held by or in trust for a charity,
(b) whether the charity is an exempt charity and whether the mortgage is one falling within subsection (5) of section 38 above, and
(c) if it is not an exempt charity and the mortgage is not one falling within that subsection, that the mortgage is one to which the restrictions imposed by that section apply;

and where the mortgage will be a registered disposition any such statement shall be in such form as may be prescribed [by land registration rules].

[(1A) Where any such mortgage will be one to which section 4(1)(g) of the Land Registration Act 2002 applies—

(a) the statement required by subsection (1) above shall be in such form as may be prescribed by land registration rules; and
(b) if the charity is not an exempt charity, the mortgage shall also contain a statement, in such form as may be prescribed by land registration rules, that the restrictions on disposition imposed by section 36 above apply to the land (subject to subsection (9) of that section).

(1B) Where—

(a) the registrar approves an application for registration of a person's title to land in connection with such a mortgage as is mentioned in subsection (1A) above,
(b) the mortgage contains statements complying with subsections (1) and (1A) above, and
(c) the charity is not an exempt charity,

the registrar shall enter in the register a restriction reflecting the limitation under section 36 above on subsequent disposal.

(1C) Section 37(9) above shall apply in relation to any restriction entered under subsection (1B) as it applies in relation to any restriction entered under section 37(8).]

(2) Where subsection (1) or (2) of section 38 above applies to any mortgage of land held by or in trust for a charity, the charity trustees shall certify in the mortgage—

(a) (where subsection (1) of that section applies) that the mortgage has been sanctioned by an order of the court or of *the Commissioners* [the Commission] (as the case may be), or
(b) (where subsection (2) of that section applies) that the charity trustees have power under the trusts of the charity to grant the mortgage, and that they have obtained and considered such advice as is mentioned in that subsection.

(3) Where subsection (2) above has been complied with in relation to any mortgage, then in favour of a person who (whether under the mortgage or afterwards) acquires an interest in the land in question for money or money's worth, it shall be conclusively presumed that the facts were as stated in the certificate.

(4) Where—

(a) subsection (1) or (2) of section 38 above applies to any mortgage of land held by or in trust for a charity, but
(b) subsection (2) above has not been complied with in relation to the mortgage,

then in favour of a person who (whether under the mortgage or afterwards) in good faith acquires an interest in the land for money or money's worth, the mortgage shall be valid whether or not—

(i) the mortgage has been sanctioned by an order of the court or of *the Commissioners* [the Commission], or
(ii) the charity trustees have power under the trusts of the charity to grant the mortgage and have obtained and considered such advice as is mentioned in subsection (2) of that section.

[(4A) Where subsection (3D) of section 38 above applies to any mortgage of land held by or in trust for a charity, the charity trustees shall certify in relation to any transaction falling within that subsection that they have obtained and considered such advice as is mentioned in that subsection.

(4B) Where subsection (4A) above has been complied with in relation to any transaction, then, in favour of a person who (whether under the mortgage or afterwards) has acquired or acquires an interest in the land for money or money's worth, it shall be conclusively presumed that the facts were as stated in the certificate.]

(5) ...

(6) In this section—

'mortgage' includes a charge, and 'mortgagee' shall be construed accordingly;
'land' means land in England or Wales;

[and subsections (1) to (1B) above shall be construed as one with the Land Registration Act 2002].

NOTES

Derivation

This section derived from the Charities Act 1992, s 35.

Initial Commencement

Specified date: 1 August 1993: see s 99(1).

Extent

This section does not extend to Scotland.

Amendment

Sub-s (1): words 'by land registration rules' in square brackets inserted by the Land Registration Act 2002, s 133, Sch 11, para 29(1), (5).

Date in force: 13 October 2003: see SI 2003/1725, art 2(1).

Sub-ss (1A)–(1C): substituted, for sub-ss (1A), (1B) (as inserted by the Land Registration Act 1997, s 4(1), Sch 1, para 6(2)), by the Land Registration Act 2002, s 133, Sch 11, para 29(1), (6).

Date in force: 13 October 2003: see SI 2003/1725, art 2(1).

Sub-s (2): in para (a) words 'the Commissioners' in italics repealed and subsequent words in square brackets substituted by the Charities Act 2006, s 75(1), Sch 8, paras 96, 131(1), (2).

Date in force: to be appointed: see the Charities Act 2006, s 79(2).

Sub-s (4): in para (i) words 'the Commissioners' in italics repealed and subsequent words in square brackets substituted by the Charities Act 2006, s 75(1), Sch 8, paras 96, 131(1), (2).

Date in force: to be appointed: see the Charities Act 2006, s 79(2).

Sub-ss (4A), (4B): inserted by the Charities Act 2006, s 75(1), Sch 8, paras 96, 131(1), (3).

Date in force: to be appointed: see the Charities Act 2006, s 79(2).

Sub-s (5): repealed by the Trusts of Land and Appointment of Trustees Act 1996, s 25(2), Sch 4; for savings in relation to entailed interests created before the commencement of that Act, and savings consequential upon the abolition of the doctrine of conversion, see s 25(4), (5) thereof.

Sub-s (6): words from 'and subsections' to 'Land Registration Act 2002' in square brackets substituted by the Land Registration Act 2002, s 133, Sch 11, para 29(1), (7).

Date in force: 13 October 2003: see SI 2003/1725, art 2(1).

Subordinate Legislation

Land Registration Rules 2003, SI 2003/1417 (made under sub-ss (1), (1A)).

40 Release of charity rentcharges

(1) Section 36(1) above shall not apply to the release by a charity of a rentcharge which it is entitled to receive if the release is given in consideration of the payment of an amount which is not less than ten times the annual amount of the rentcharge.

(2) Where a charity which is entitled to receive a rentcharge releases it in consideration of the payment of an amount not exceeding £500, any costs incurred by the charity in connection with proving its title to the rentcharge shall be recoverable by the charity from the person or persons in whose favour the rentcharge is being released.

(3) Neither section 36(1) nor subsection (2) above applies where a rentcharge which a charity is entitled to receive is redeemed under sections 8 to 10 of the Rentcharges Act 1977.

(4) The [Minister] may by order amend subsection (2) above by substituting a different sum for the sum for the time being specified there.

NOTES

Derivation

This section derived from the Charities Act 1992, s 37.

Initial Commencement

Specified date: 1 August 1993: see s 99(1).

Extent

This section does not extend to Scotland.

Amendment

Sub-s (4): word 'Minister' in square brackets substituted by SI 2006/2951, art 6, Schedule, para 4(p).

Date in force: 13 December 2006: see SI 2006/2951, art 1(2).

Part VI
Charity Accounts, Reports and Returns

41 Duty to keep accounting records

(1) The charity trustees of a charity shall ensure that accounting records are kept in respect of the charity which are sufficient to show and explain all the charity's transactions, and which are such as to—

(a) disclose at any time, with reasonable accuracy, the financial position of the charity at that time, and
(b) enable the trustees to ensure that, where any statements of accounts are prepared by them under section 42(1) below, those statements of accounts comply with the requirements of regulations under that provision.

(2) The accounting records shall in particular contain—

(a) entries showing from day to day all sums of money received and expended by the charity, and the matters in respect of which the receipt and expenditure takes place; and
(b) a record of the assets and liabilities of the charity.

(3) The charity trustees of a charity shall preserve any accounting records made for the purposes of this section in respect of the charity for at least six years from the end of the financial year of the charity in which they are made.

(4) Where a charity ceases to exist within the period of six years mentioned in subsection (3) above as it applies to any accounting records, the obligation to preserve those records in accordance with that subsection shall continue to be discharged by the last charity trustees of the charity, unless *the Commissioners consent* [the Commission consents] in writing to the records being destroyed or otherwise disposed of.

(5) Nothing in this section applies to a charity which is a company.

NOTES

Derivation

This section derived from the Charities Act 1992, s 19.

Initial Commencement

To be appointed: see s 99(2).

Appointment

Appointment (for the purposes of making orders or regulations): 15 October 1995: see SI 1995/2695, art 3.

Appointment (for remaining purposes): 1 March 1996: see SI 1995/2695, art 2.

Extent

This section does not extend to Scotland.

Amendment

Sub-s (4): words 'the Commissioners consent' in square brackets substituted by the Charities Act 2006, s 75(1), Sch 8, paras 96, 132.

Date in force: to be appointed: see the Charities Act 2006, s 79(2).

42 Annual statements of accounts

(1) The charity trustees of a charity shall (subject to subsection (3) below) prepare in respect of each financial year of the charity a statement of accounts complying with such requirements as to its form and contents as may be prescribed by regulations made by the [Minister].

(2) Without prejudice to the generality of subsection (1) above, regulations under that subsection may make provision—

(a) for any such statement to be prepared in accordance with such methods and principles as are specified or referred to in the regulations;
(b) as to any information to be provided by way of notes to the accounts;

and regulations under that subsection may also make provision for determining the financial years of a charity for the purposes of this Act and any regulations made under it.

[(2A) Such regulations may, however, not impose on the charity trustees of a charity that is a charitable trust created by any person ('the settlor') any requirement to disclose, in any statement of accounts prepared by them under subsection (1)—

(a) the identities of recipients of grants made out of the funds of the charity, or
(b) the amounts of any individual grants so made,

if the disclosure would fall to be made at a time when the settlor or any spouse or civil partner of his was still alive.]

(3) Where a charity's gross income in any financial year does not exceed [£100,000], the charity trustees may, in respect of that year, elect to prepare the following, namely—

(a) a receipts and payments account, and
(b) a statement of assets and liabilities,

instead of a statement of accounts under subsection (1) above.

(4) The charity trustees of a charity shall preserve—

(a) any statement of accounts prepared by them under subsection (1) above, or
(b) any account and statement prepared by them under subsection (3) above,

for at least six years from the end of the financial year to which any such statement relates or (as the case may be) to which any such account and statement relate.

(5) Subsection (4) of section 41 above shall apply in relation to the preservation of any such statement or account and statement as it applies in relation to the preservation of any accounting records (the references to subsection (3) of that section being read as references to subsection (4) above).

(6) The [Minister] may by order amend subsection (3) above by substituting a different sum for the sum for the time being specified there.

(7) Nothing in this section applies to a charity which is a company.

[(8) Provisions about the preparation of accounts in respect of groups consisting of certain charities and their subsidiary undertakings, and about other matters relating to such groups, are contained in Schedule 5A to this Act (see section 49A below).]

NOTES

Derivation

This section derived from the Charities Act 1992, s 20.

Initial Commencement

To be appointed: see s 99(2).

Appointment

Appointment (for the purposes of making orders or regulations): 15 October 1995: see SI 1995/2695, art 3.

Appointment (for remaining purposes): 1 March 1996: see SI 1995/2695, art 2.

Extent

This section does not extend to Scotland.

Amendment

Sub-s (1): word 'Minister' in square brackets substituted by SI 2006/2951, art 6, Schedule, para 4(q).

Date in force: 13 December 2006: see SI 2006/2951, art 1(2).

Sub-s (2A): inserted by the Charities Act 2006, s 75(1), Sch 8, paras 96, 133(1), (2).

Date in force: to be appointed: see the Charities Act 2006, s 79(2).

Sub-s (3): sum in square brackets substituted by SI 1995/2696, art 2(3).

Sub-s (6): word 'Minister' in square brackets substituted by SI 2006/2951, art 6, Schedule, para 4(q).

Date in force: 13 December 2006: see SI 2006/2951, art 1(2).

Sub-s (8): inserted by the Charities Act 2006, s 75(1), Sch 8, paras 96, 133(1), (3).

Date in force: to be appointed: see the Charities Act 2006, s 79(2).

See Further

See further, in relation to the requirements imposed by this section only applying in respect of a financial year beginning on or after 1 March 1996: the Charities Act 1993 (Commencement and Transitional Provisions) Order 1995, SI 1995/2695, art 4.

Subordinate Legislation

Charities Act 1993 (Substitution of Sums) Order 1995, SI 1995/2696 (made under sub-s (6)).

Charities (Accounts and Reports) Regulations 2005, SI 2005/572.

43 Annual audit or examination of charity accounts

(1) Subsection (2) below applies to a financial year of a charity ('the relevant year') if the charity's gross income or total expenditure in any of the following, namely—

(a) the relevant year,
(b) the financial year of the charity immediately preceding the relevant year (if any), and
(c) the financial year of the charity immediately preceding the year specified in paragraph (b) above (if any),

exceeds [£250,000].

[(1) Subsection (2) below applies to a financial year of a charity if—

(a) the charity's gross income in that year exceeds £500,000; or
(b) the charity's gross income in that year exceeds the accounts threshold and at the end of the year the aggregate value of its assets (before deduction of liabilities) exceeds £2.8 million.

'The accounts threshold' means £100,000 or such other sum as is for the time being specified in section 42(3) above.]

(2) If this subsection applies to a financial year of a charity, the accounts of the charity for that year shall be audited by a person who—

(a) is, in accordance with section 25 of the Companies Act 1989 (eligibility for appointment), eligible for appointment as a company auditor, or
[(a) would be eligible for appointment as auditor of the charity under Part 2 of the Companies Act 1989 if the charity were a company, or]
(b) is a member of a body for the time being specified in regulations under section 44 below and is under the rules of that body eligible for appointment as auditor of the charity.

(3) If subsection (2) above does not apply to a financial year of a charity *[and its gross income or total expenditure in that year exceeds £10,000], then (subject to subsection (4) below)* [but its gross income in that year exceeds £10,000,] the accounts of the charity for that year shall, at the election of the charity trustees, either—

(a) be examined by an independent examiner, that is to say an independent person who is reasonably believed by the trustees to have the requisite ability and practical experience to carry out a competent examination of the accounts, or
(b) be audited by such a person as is mentioned in subsection (2) above.

[This is subject to the requirements of subsection (3A) below where the gross income exceeds £250,000, and to any order under subsection (4) below.]

[(3A) If subsection (3) above applies to the accounts of a charity for a year and the charity's gross income in that year exceeds £250,000, a person qualifies as an independent examiner for the purposes of paragraph (a) of that subsection if (and only if) he is an independent person who is—

(a) a member of a body for the time being specified in section 249D(3) of the Companies Act 1985 (reporting accountants);
(b) a member of the Chartered Institute of Public Finance and Accountancy; or
(c) a Fellow of the Association of Charity Independent Examiners.]

(4) Where it appears to *the Commissioners* [the Commission]—

(a) that subsection (2), or (as the case may be) subsection (3) above, has not been complied with in relation to a financial year of a charity within ten months from the end of that year, or
(b) that, although subsection (2) above does not apply to a financial year of a charity, it would nevertheless be desirable for the accounts of the charity for that year to be audited by such a person as is mentioned in that subsection,

the Commissioners [the Commission] may by order require the accounts of the charity for that year to be audited by such a person as is mentioned in that subsection.

(5) If *the Commissioners make* [the Commission makes] an order under subsection (4) above with respect to a charity, then unless—

(a) the order is made by virtue of paragraph (b) of that subsection, and
(b) the charity trustees themselves appoint an auditor in accordance with the order,

the auditor shall be a person appointed by *the Commissioners* [the Commission].

(6) The expenses of any audit carried out by an auditor appointed by *the Commissioners* [the Commission] under subsection (5) above, including the auditor's remuneration, shall be recoverable by *the Commissioners* [the Commission]—

(a) from the charity trustees of the charity concerned, who shall be personally liable, jointly and severally, for those expenses; or
(b) to the extent that it appears to *the Commissioners* [the Commission] not to be practical to seek recovery of those expenses in accordance with paragraph (a) above, from the funds of the charity.

(7) *The Commissioners* [The Commission] may—

(a) give guidance to charity trustees in connection with the selection of a person for appointment as an independent examiner;
(b) give such directions as *they think* [it thinks] appropriate with respect to the carrying out of an examination in pursuance of subsection (3)(a) above;

and any such guidance or directions may either be of general application or apply to a particular charity only.

(8) The [Minister] may by order amend subsection (1) [or (3)] above by substituting a different sum for the sum for the time being specified there.

[(8) The Minister may by order—

(a) amend subsection (1)(a) or (b), (3) or (3A) above by substituting a different sum for any sum for the time being specified there;
(b) amend subsection (3A) by adding or removing a description of person to or from the list in that subsection or by varying any entry for the time being included in that list.]

(9) Nothing in this section applies to a charity which is a company.

[(10) Nothing in this section applies in relation to a financial year of a charity where, at any time in the year, a charity is an English National Health Service charity or Welsh National Health Service charity (as defined in sections 43A and 43B respectively).]

NOTES

Derivation

This section derived from the Charities Act 1992, s 21.

Initial Commencement

To be appointed: see s 99(2).

Appointment

Appointment (for the purposes of making orders or regulations): 15 October 1995: see SI 1995/2695, art 3.

Appointment (for remaining purposes): 1 March 1996: see SI 1995/2695, art 2.

Extent

This section does not extend to Scotland.

Amendment

Sub-s (1): substituted by the Charities Act 2006, s 28(1), (2).

Sub-s (2): in para (a) substituted by the Charities Act 2006, s 28(1), (3).

Sub-s (3): in para (a) words 'but its gross income in that year exceeds £10,000,' in square brackets substituted by the Charities Act 2006, s 28(1), (4)(a).

Sub-s (3): words from 'This is subject' to 'subsection (4) below.' in square brackets inserted by the Charities Act 2006, s 28(1), (4)(b).

Sub-s (3A): inserted by the Charities Act 2006, s 28(1), (5).

Sub-s (4): words 'the Commissioners' in italics in both places they occur repealed and subsequent words in square brackets substituted by the Charities Act 2006, s 75(1), Sch 8, paras 96, 134(1), (2).

Date in force: to be appointed: see the Charities Act 2006, s 79(2).

Sub-s (5): words 'the Commissioners make' in italics repealed and subsequent words in square brackets substituted by the Charities Act 2006, s 75(1), Sch 8, paras 96, 134(1), (3)(a).

Date in force: to be appointed: see the Charities Act 2006, s 79(2).

Sub-s (5): words 'the Commissioners' in italics repealed and subsequent words in square brackets substituted by the Charities Act 2006, s 75(1), Sch 8, paras 96, 134(1), (3)(b).

Date in force: to be appointed: see the Charities Act 2006, s 79(2).

Sub-s (6): words 'the Commissioners' in italics in each place they occur repealed and subsequent words in square brackets substituted by the Charities Act 2006, s 75(1), Sch 8, paras 96, 134(1), (4).

Date in force: to be appointed: see the Charities Act 2006, s 79(2).

Sub-s (7): words 'The Commissioners' in italics repealed and subsequent words in square brackets substituted by the Charities Act 2006, s 75(1), Sch 8, paras 96, 134(1), (5)(a).

Date in force: to be appointed: see the Charities Act 2006, s 79(2).

Sub-s (7): in para (b) words 'they think' in italics repealed and subsequent words in square brackets substituted by the Charities Act 2006, s 75(1), Sch 8, paras 96, 134(1), (5)(b).

Date in force: to be appointed: see the Charities Act 2006, s 79(2).

Sub-s (8): substituted by the Charities Act 2006, s 28(1), (6).

Sub-s (8): word 'Minister' in square brackets substituted by SI 2006/2951, art 6, Schedule, para 4(r).

Date in force: 13 December 2006: see SI 2006/2951, art 1(2).

Sub-s (10): inserted by SI 2005/1074, art 3(1), (2).

Date in force: this amendment has effect in relation to the financial year of a trust starting on or after 1 April 2004: see SI 2005/1074, art 1(2).

See Further

See further, in relation to the requirements imposed by this section only applying in respect of a financial year beginning on or after 1 March 1996: the Charities Act 1993 (Commencement and Transitional Provisions) Order 1995, SI 1995/2695, art 4.

Subordinate Legislation

Charities Act 1993 (Substitution of Sums) Order 1995, SI 1995/2696 (made under sub-s (8)).

[43A Annual audit or examination of English National Health Service charity accounts]

[(1) This section applies in relation to a financial year of a charity where, at any time in the year, the charity is an English National Health Service charity.

(2) In any case where *the criterion set out in subsection (1) of section 43 is met in respect of* [paragraph (a) or (b) of section 43(1) is satisfied in relation to] a financial year of an English National Health Service charity, the accounts of the charity for that financial year shall be audited by a person appointed by the Audit Commission.

(3) In any other case, the accounts of the charity for that financial year shall, at the election of the Audit Commission, be—

(a) audited by a person appointed by the Audit Commission; or
(b) examined by a person so appointed.

(4) Section 3 of the Audit Commission Act 1998 (c 18) applies in relation to any appointment under subsection (2) or (3)(a).

(5) *The Commissioners* [The Commission] may give such directions as *they think* [it thinks] appropriate with respect to the carrying out of an examination in pursuance of subsection (3)(b); and any such directions may either be of general application or apply to a particular charity only.

(6) The Comptroller and Auditor General may at any time examine and inspect—

(a) the accounts of the charity for the financial year;
(b) any records relating to those accounts; and
(c) any report of a person appointed under subsection (2) or (3) to audit or examine those accounts.

(7) In this section—

'Audit Commission' means the Audit Commission for Local Authorities and the National Health Service in England and Wales; and
'English National Health Service charity' means a charitable trust, the trustees of which are—

(a) a Strategic Health Authority;
(b) a Primary Care Trust;
(c) a National Health Service trust all or most of whose hospitals, establishments and facilities are situated in England;
[(d) trustees appointed in pursuance of paragraph 10 of Schedule 4 to the National Health Service Act 2006 for a National Health Service trust falling within paragraph (c);
(da) special trustees appointed in pursuance of section 29(1) of the National Health Service Reorganisation Act 1973, section 95(1) of the National Health Service Act 1977 and section 212(1) of the National Health Service Act 2006 for such a National Health Service trust, or]
(e) trustees for a Primary Care Trust appointed in pursuance of [paragraph 12 of Schedule 3 to the National Health Service Act 2006].]

NOTES

Amendment

Inserted by SI 2005/1074, art 3(1), (3).

Date in force: this amendment has effect in relation to the financial year of a trust starting on or after 1 April 2004: see SI 2005/1074, art 1(2).

Sub-s (2): words from 'the criterion set' to 'in respect of' in italics repealed and subsequent words in square brackets substituted by the Charities Act 2006, s 75(1), Sch 8, paras 96, 135(1), (2).

Date in force: to be appointed: see the Charities Act 2006, s 79(2).

Sub-s (5): words 'The Commissioners' in italics repealed and subsequent words in square brackets substituted by the Charities Act 2006, s 75(1), Sch 8, paras 96, 135(1), (3)(a).

Date in force: to be appointed: see the Charities Act 2006, s 79(2).

Sub-s (5): words 'they think' in italics repealed and subsequent words in square brackets substituted by the Charities Act 2006, s 75(1), Sch 8, paras 96, 135(1), (3)(b).

Date in force: to be appointed: see the Charities Act 2006, s 79(2).

Sub-s (7): in definition 'English National Health Service charity' paras (d), (da) substituted, for para (d) as originally enacted, by the National Health Service (Consequential Provisions) Act 2006, s 2, Sch 1, paras 160, 161(a).

Date in force: 1 March 2007: see the National Health Service (Consequential Provisions) Act 2006, s 8(2).

Sub-s (7): in definition 'English National Health Service charity' in para (e) words 'paragraph 12 of Schedule 3 to the National Health Service Act 2006' in square brackets substituted by the National Health Service (Consequential Provisions) Act 2006, s 2, Sch 1, paras 160, 161(b).

Date in force: 1 March 2007: see the National Health Service (Consequential Provisions) Act 2006, s 8(2).

[43B Annual audit or examination of Welsh National Health Service charity accounts]

[(1) This section applies in relation to a financial year of a charity where, at any time in the year, the charity is a Welsh National Health Service charity.

(2) In any case where *the criterion set out in subsection (1) of section 43 is met in respect of* [paragraph (a) or (b) of section 43(1) is satisfied in relation to] a financial year of a Welsh National Health Service charity, the accounts of the charity for that financial year shall be audited by the Auditor General for Wales.

(3) In any other case, the accounts of the charity for that financial year shall, at the election of the Auditor General for Wales, be audited or examined by the Auditor General for Wales.

(4) In this section—

'Welsh National Health Service charity' means a charitable trust, the trustees of which are—

(a) a Local Health Board;

(b) a National Health Service trust all or most of whose hospitals, establishments and facilities are situated in Wales;

[(c) trustees appointed in pursuance of paragraph 10 of Schedule 3 to the National Health Service (Wales) Act 2006 for a National Health Service trust falling within paragraph (b); or

(d) special trustees appointed in pursuance of section 29(1) of the National Health Service Reorganisation Act 1973, section 95(1) of the National Health Service Act 1977 and section 160(1) of the National Health Service (Wales) Act 2006 for such a National Health Service trust].]

[(5) References in this Act to an auditor or an examiner have effect in relation to this section as references to the Auditor General for Wales acting under this section as an auditor or examiner.]

NOTES

Amendment

Inserted by SI 2005/1074, art 3(1), (3).

Date in force: this amendment has effect in relation to the financial year of a trust starting on or after 1 April 2004: see SI 2005/1074, art 1(2).

Sub-s (2): words from 'the criterion set' to 'in respect of' in italics repealed and subsequent words in square brackets substituted by the Charities Act 2006, s 75(1), Sch 8, paras 96, 136(1), (2).

Date in force: to be appointed: see the Charities Act 2006, s 79(2).

Sub-s (4): in definition 'Welsh National Health Service charity' paras (c), (d) substituted, for para (c) as originally enacted, by the National Health Service (Consequential Provisions) Act 2006, s 2, Sch 1, paras 160, 162.

Date in force: 1 March 2007: see the National Health Service (Consequential Provisions) Act 2006, s 8(2).

Sub-s (5): inserted by the Charities Act 2006, s 75(1), Sch 8, paras 96, 136(1), (3).

Date in force: to be appointed: see the Charities Act 2006, s 79(2).

44 Supplementary provisions relating to audits etc

(1) The Secretary of State may by regulations make provision—

(a) specifying one or more bodies for the purposes of section 43(2)(b) above;
(b) with respect to the duties of an auditor carrying out an audit under section 43[, 43A or 43B] above, including provision with respect to the making by him of a report on—
  (i) the statement of accounts prepared for the financial year in question under section 42(1) above, or
  (ii) the account and statement so prepared under section 42(3) above,
  as the case may be;
(c) with respect to the making by an independent examiner of a report in respect of an examination carried out by him under section 43 above;
[(c) with respect to the making of a report—
  (i) by an independent examiner in respect of an examination carried out by him under section 43 above; or
  (ii) by an examiner in respect of an examination carried out by him under section 43A or 43B above;]
(d) conferring on such an auditor or on an independent examiner [or examiner] a right of access with respect to books, documents and other records (however kept) which relate to the charity concerned;
(e) entitling such an auditor or an independent examiner [or examiner] to require, in the case of a charity, information and explanations from past or present charity trustees or trustees for the charity, or from past or present officers or employees of the charity;
(f) enabling *the Commissioners* [the Commission], in circumstances specified in the regulations, to dispense with the requirements of section 43(2) or (3) above in the case of a particular charity or in the case of any particular financial year of a charity.

(2) If any person fails to afford an auditor or an independent examiner [or examiner] any facility to which he is entitled by virtue of subsection (1)(d) or (e) above, *the Commissioners* [the Commission] may by order give—

(a) to that person, or
(b) to the charity trustees for the time being of the charity concerned,

such directions as *the Commissioners think* [the Commission thinks] appropriate for securing that the default is made good.

(3) *Section 727 of the Companies Act 1985 (power of court to grant relief in certain cases) shall have effect in relation to an auditor or independent examiner appointed by a charity in pursuance of section 43 above as it has effect in relation to a person employed as auditor by a company within the meaning of that Act.*

NOTES

Derivation

This section derived from the Charities Act 1992, s 22.

Initial Commencement

To be appointed: see s 99(2).

Appointment

Appointment (for the purposes of making orders or regulations): 15 October 1995: see SI 1995/2695, art 3.

Appointment (for remaining purposes): 1 March 1996: see SI 1995/2695, art 2.

Extent

This section does not extend to Scotland.

Amendment

Sub-s (1): in para (b) words ', 43A or 43B' in square brackets inserted by the Charities Act 2006, s 75(1), Sch 8, paras 96, 137(1), (2)(a).

Date in force: to be appointed: see the Charities Act 2006, s 79(2).

Sub-s (1): para (c) substituted by the Charities Act 2006, s 75(1), Sch 8, paras 96, 137(1), (2)(b).

Date in force: to be appointed: see the Charities Act 2006, s 79(2).

Sub-s (1): in para (d) words 'or examiner' in square brackets inserted by the Charities Act 2006, s 75(1), Sch 8, paras 96, 137(1), (2)(c).

Date in force: to be appointed: see the Charities Act 2006, s 79(2).

Sub-s (1): in para (e) words 'or examiner' in square brackets inserted by the Charities Act 2006, s 75(1), Sch 8, paras 96, 137(1), (2)(c).

Date in force: to be appointed: see the Charities Act 2006, s 79(2).

Sub-s (1): in para (f) words 'the Commissioners' in italics repealed and subsequent words in square brackets substituted by the Charities Act 2006, s 75(1), Sch 8, paras 96, 137(1), (2)(d).

Date in force: to be appointed: see the Charities Act 2006, s 79(2).

Sub-s (2): words 'or examiner' in square brackets inserted by the Charities Act 2006, s 75(1), Sch 8, paras 96, 137(1), (3)(a).

Date in force: to be appointed: see the Charities Act 2006, s 79(2).

Sub-s (2): words 'the Commission' in italics repealed and subsequent words in square brackets substituted by the Charities Act 2006, s 75(1), Sch 8, paras 96, 137(1), (3)(b).

Date in force: to be appointed: see the Charities Act 2006, s 79(2).

Sub-s (2): words 'the Commissioners think' in italics repealed and subsequent words in square brackets substituted by the Charities Act 2006, s 75(1), Sch 8, paras 96, 137(1), (3)(c).

Date in force: to be appointed: see the Charities Act 2006, s 79(2).

Sub-s (3): repealed by the Charities Act 2006, s 75(1), (2), Sch 8, paras 96, 137(1), (4), Sch 9.

Subordinate Legislation

Charities (Accounts and Reports) Regulations 2005, SI 2005/572.

[44A Duty of auditors etc to report matters to Commission]

[(1) This section applies to—

(a) a person acting as an auditor or independent examiner appointed by or in relation to a charity under section 43 above,

(b) a person acting as an auditor or examiner appointed under section 43A(2) or (3) above, and
(c) the Auditor General for Wales acting under section 43B(2) or (3) above.

(2) If, in the course of acting in the capacity mentioned in subsection (1) above, a person to whom this section applies becomes aware of a matter—

(a) which relates to the activities or affairs of the charity or of any connected institution or body, and
(b) which he has reasonable cause to believe is likely to be of material significance for the purposes of the exercise by the Commission of its functions under section 8 or 18 above,

he must immediately make a written report on the matter to the Commission.

(3) If, in the course of acting in the capacity mentioned in subsection (1) above, a person to whom this section applies becomes aware of any matter—

(a) which does not appear to him to be one that he is required to report under subsection (2) above, but
(b) which he has reasonable cause to believe is likely to be relevant for the purposes of the exercise by the Commission of any of its functions,

he may make a report on the matter to the Commission.

(4) Where the duty or power under subsection (2) or (3) above has arisen in relation to a person acting in the capacity mentioned in subsection (1), the duty or power is not affected by his subsequently ceasing to act in that capacity.

(5) Where a person makes a report as required or authorised by subsection (2) or (3), no duty to which he is subject is to be regarded as contravened merely because of any information or opinion contained in the report.

(6) In this section 'connected institution or body', in relation to a charity, means—

(a) an institution which is controlled by, or
(b) a body corporate in which a substantial interest is held by,

the charity or any one or more of the charity trustees acting in his or their capacity as such.

(7) Paragraphs 3 and 4 of Schedule 5 to this Act apply for the purposes of subsection (6) above as they apply for the purposes of provisions of that Schedule.]

NOTES

Amendment

Inserted by the Charities Act 2006, s 29(1); for transitional provisions and savings see s 75(3), Sch 10, para 8 thereto.

Date in force: to be appointed: see the Charities Act 2006, s 79(2).

45 Annual reports

(1) The charity trustees of a charity shall prepare in respect of each financial year of the charity an annual report containing—

(a) such a report by the trustees on the activities of the charity during that year, and
(b) such other information relating to the charity or to its trustees or officers,

as may be prescribed by regulations made by the [Minister].

(2) Without prejudice to the generality of subsection (1) above, regulations under that subsection may make provision—

(a) for any such report as is mentioned in paragraph (a) of that subsection to be prepared in accordance with such principles as are specified or referred to in the regulations;
(b) enabling *the Commissioners* [the Commission] to dispense with any requirement prescribed by virtue of subsection (1)(b) above in the case of a particular charity or a particular class of charities, or in the case of a particular financial year of a charity or of any class of charities.

(3) [Where *in any financial year of a charity its gross income or total expenditure* [a charity's gross income in any financial year] exceeds £10,000, [a copy of] the annual report required to be prepared under this section in respect of that year] shall be transmitted to *the Commissioners* [the Commission] by the charity trustees—

(a) within ten months from the end of that year, or
(b) within such longer period as *the Commissioners* [the Commission] may for any special reason allow in the case of that report.

[(3A) Where *in any financial year of a charity neither its gross income nor its total expenditure exceeds* [a charity's gross income in any financial year does not exceed] £10,000, [a copy of] the annual report required to be prepared under this section in respect of that year shall, if *the Commissioners so request, be transmitted to them* [the Commission so requests, be transmitted to it] by the charity trustees—

(a) in the case of a request made before the end of seven months from the end of the financial year to which the report relates, within ten months from the end of that year, and
(b) in the case of a request not so made, within three months from the date of the request,

or, in either case, within such longer period as *the Commissioners* [the Commission] may for any special reason allow in the case of that report.]

[(3B) But in the case of a charity which is constituted as a CIO—

(a) the requirement imposed by subsection (3) applies whatever the charity's gross income is, and
(b) subsection (3A) does not apply.]

(4) Subject to subsection (5) below, [any *annual report transmitted to the Commissioners* [copy of an annual report transmitted to the Commission] under this section] shall have attached to it [a copy of] the statement of accounts prepared for the financial year in question under section 42(1) above or (as the case may be) [a copy of] the account and statement so prepared under section 42(3) above, together with—

(a) where the accounts of the charity for that year have been audited under section 43[, 43A or 43B] above, a copy of the report made by the auditor on that statement of accounts or (as the case may be) on that account and statement;
(b) where the accounts of the charity for that year have been examined under section 43[, 43A or 43B] above, a copy of the report made by the [person carrying out the examination].

(5) Subsection (4) above does not apply to a charity which is a company, and any [copy of an] annual report transmitted by the charity trustees of such a charity under [this section] shall instead have attached to it a copy of the charity's annual accounts prepared for the financial year in question under Part VII of the Companies Act 1985, together with a copy of [any auditors' report or report made for the purposes of section 249A(2) of that Act] on those accounts.

(6) Any [copy of an] annual report transmitted to *the Commissioners* [the Commission] under [this section], together with the documents attached to it, shall be kept by *the Commissioners* [the Commission] for such period as *they think fit* [it thinks fit].

[(7) The charity trustees of a charity shall preserve, for at least six years from the end of the financial year to which it relates, any annual report prepared by them under subsection (1) above *which they have not been required to transmit to the Commissioners* [of which they have not been required to transmit a copy to the Commission].

(8) Subsection (4) of section 41 above shall apply in relation to the preservation of any such annual report as it applies in relation to the preservation of any accounting records (the references *in subsection (3)* [to subsection (3)] of that section being read as references to subsection (7) above).

(9) The [Minister] may by order amend subsection (3) or (3A) above by substituting a different sum for the sum for the time being specified there.]

NOTES

Derivation

This section derived from the Charities Act 1992, s 23.

Initial Commencement

To be appointed: see s 99(2).

Appointment

Appointment (for the purposes of making orders or regulations): 15 October 1995: see SI 1995/2695, art 3.

Appointment (for remaining purposes): 1 March 1996: see SI 1995/2695, art 2.

Extent

This section does not extend to Scotland.

Amendment

Sub-s (1): word 'Minister' in square brackets substituted by SI 2006/2951, art 6, Schedule, para 4(t).

Date in force: 13 December 2006: see SI 2006/2951, art 1(2).

Sub-s (2): in para (b) words 'the Commissioners' in italics repealed and subsequent words in square brackets substituted by the Charities Act 2006, s 75(1), Sch 8, paras 96, 138(1), (2).

Date in force: to be appointed: see the Charities Act 2006, s 79(2).

Sub-s (3): words from 'Where in any' to 'of that year' in square brackets substituted by the Deregulation and Contracting Out Act 1994, s 29(1).

Sub-s (3): words from 'in any financial' to 'or total expenditure' in italics repealed and subsequent words in square brackets substituted by the Charities Act 2006, s 75(1), Sch 8, paras 96, 138(1), (3)(a).

Date in force: to be appointed: see the Charities Act 2006, s 79(2).

Sub-s (3): words 'a copy of' in square brackets inserted by the Charities Act 2006, s 75(1), Sch 8, paras 96, 138(1), (3)(b).

Date in force: to be appointed: see the Charities Act 2006, s 79(2).

Sub-s (3): words 'the Commissioners' in italics in both places they occur repealed and subsequent words in square brackets substituted by the Charities Act 2006, s 75(1), Sch 8, paras 96, 138(1), (3)(c).

Date in force: to be appointed: see the Charities Act 2006, s 79(2).

Sub-s (3A): inserted by the Deregulation and Contracting Out Act 1994, s 29(2).

Sub-s (3A): words from 'in any financial' to 'total expenditure exceeds' in italics repealed and subsequent words in square brackets substituted by the Charities Act 2006, s 75(1), Sch 8, paras 96, 138(1), (4)(a).

Date in force: to be appointed: see the Charities Act 2006, s 79(2).

Sub-s (3A): words 'a copy of' in square brackets inserted by the Charities Act 2006, s 75(1), Sch 8, paras 96, 138(1), (4)(b).

Date in force: to be appointed: see the Charities Act 2006, s 79(2).

Sub-s (3A): words 'the Commissioners so request, be transmitted to them' in italics repealed and subsequent words in square brackets substituted by the Charities Act 2006, s 75(1), Sch 8, paras 96, 138(1), (4)(c).

Date in force: to be appointed: see the Charities Act 2006, s 79(2).

Sub-s (3A): words 'the Commissioners' in italics repealed and subsequent words in square brackets substituted by the Charities Act 2006, s 75(1), Sch 8, paras 96, 138(1), (4)(d).

Date in force: to be appointed: see the Charities Act 2006, s 79(2).

Sub-s (3B): inserted by the Charities Act 2006, s 34, Sch 7, Pt 2, paras 3, 4

Date in force: to be appointed: see the Charities Act 2006, s 79(2).

Sub-s (4): words 'any annual report transmitted to the Commissioners under this section' in square brackets substituted by the Deregulation and Contracting Out Act 1994, s 29(3).

Sub-s (4): words 'annual report transmitted to the Commissioners' in italics repealed and subsequent words in square brackets substituted by the Charities Act 2006, s 75(1), Sch 8, paras 96, 138(1), (5)(a).

Date in force: to be appointed: see the Charities Act 2006, s 79(2).

Sub-s (4): words 'a copy of' in square brackets in both places they occur inserted by the Charities Act 2006, s 75(1), Sch 8, paras 96, 138(1), (5)(b).

Date in force: to be appointed: see the Charities Act 2006, s 79(2).

Sub-s (4): in paras (a), (b) words ', 43A or 43B' in square brackets inserted by SI 2005/1074, art 3(1), (4)(a).

Date in force: this amendment has effect in relation to the financial year of a trust starting on or after 1 April 2004: see SI 2005/1074, art 1(2).

Sub-s (4): in para (b) words 'person carrying out the examination' in square brackets substituted by SI 2005/1074, art 3(1), (4)(b).

Date in force: this amendment has effect in relation to the financial year of a trust starting on or after 1 April 2004: see SI 2005/1074, art 1(2).

Sub-s (5): words 'copy of an' in square brackets inserted by the Charities Act 2006, s 75(1), Sch 8, paras 96, 138(1), (6).

Date in force: to be appointed: see the Charities Act 2006, s 79(2).

Sub-s (5): first words in square brackets substituted by the Deregulation and Contracting Out Act 1994, s 29(4); final words in square brackets substituted by SI 1994/1935, reg 4, Sch 1, para 6.

Sub-s (6): words 'copy of an' in square brackets inserted by the Charities Act 2006, s 75(1), Sch 8, paras 96, 138(1), (7)(a).

Date in force: to be appointed: see the Charities Act 2006, s 79(2).

Sub-s (6): words 'the Commissioners' in italics in both places they occur repealed and subsequent words in square brackets substituted by the Charities Act 2006, s 75(1), Sch 8, paras 96, 138(1), (7)(b).

Date in force: to be appointed: see the Charities Act 2006, s 79(2).

Sub-s (6): words 'this section' in square brackets substituted by the Deregulation and Contracting Out Act 1994, s 29(5).

Sub-s (6): words 'they think fit' in italics repealed and subsequent words in square brackets substituted by the Charities Act 2006, s 75(1), Sch 8, paras 96, 138(1), (7)(c).

Date in force: to be appointed: see the Charities Act 2006, s 79(2).

Sub-ss (7)–(9): inserted by the Deregulation and Contracting Out Act 1994, s 29(6).

Sub-s (7): words from 'which they have' to the end repealed and subsequent words in square brackets substituted by the Charities Act 2006, s 75(1), Sch 8, paras 96, 138(1), (8).

Date in force: to be appointed: see the Charities Act 2006, s 79(2).

Sub-s (8): words 'in subsection (3)' in italics repealed and subsequent words in square brackets substituted by the Charities Act 2006, s 75(1), Sch 8, paras 96, 138(1), (9).

Date in force: to be appointed: see the Charities Act 2006, s 79(2).

Sub-s (9): word 'Minister' in square brackets substituted by SI 2006/2951, art 6, Schedule, para 4(t).

Date in force: 13 December 2006: see SI 2006/2951, art 1(2).

See Further

See further, in relation to the requirements imposed by this section only applying in respect of financial years beginning on or after 1 March 1996: the Charities Act 1993 (Commencement and Transitional Provisions) Order 1995, SI 1995/2695, art 4.

Subordinate Legislation

Charities (Accounts and Reports) Regulations 2005, SI 2005/572.

46 Special provision as respects accounts and annual reports of exempt and other excepted charities

(1) Nothing in *sections 41 to 45* [sections 41 to 44 or section 45] above applies to any exempt charity; but the charity trustees of an exempt charity shall keep proper books of account with respect to the affairs of the charity, and if not required by or under the authority of any other Act to prepare periodical statements of account shall prepare consecutive statements of account consisting on each occasion of an income and expenditure account relating to a period of not more than fifteen months and a balance sheet relating to the end of that period.

(2) The books of accounts and statements of account relating to an exempt charity shall be preserved for a period of six years at least unless the charity ceases to exist and *the Commissioners consent* [the Commission consents] in writing to their being destroyed or otherwise disposed of.

[(2A) Section 44A(2) to (7) above shall apply in relation to a person appointed to audit, or report on, the accounts of an exempt charity which is not a company as they apply in relation to a person such as is mentioned in section 44A(1).

(2B) But section 44A(2) to (7) so apply with the following modifications—

(a) any reference to a person acting in the capacity mentioned in section 44A(1) is to be read as a reference to his acting as a person appointed as mentioned in subsection (2A) above; and
(b) any reference to the Commission or to any of its functions is to be read as a reference to the charity's principal regulator or to any of that person's functions in relation to the charity as such.]

(3) Nothing in [*section 43, 44 or 45*] *above applies to any charity which—*

(a) falls within section 3(5)(c) above, and
(b) is not registered.

[(3) Except in accordance with subsections (3A) and (3B) below, nothing in section 43, 44, 44A or 45 applies to any charity which—

(a) falls within section 3A(2)(d) above (whether or not it also falls within section 3A(2)(b) or (c)), and
(b) is not registered.

(3A) Section 44A above applies in accordance with subsections (2A) and (2B) above to a charity mentioned in subsection (3) above which is also an exempt charity.

(3B) Sections 44 and 44A above apply to a charity mentioned in subsection (3) above which is also an English National Health Service charity or a Welsh National Health Service charity (as defined in sections 43A and 43B above).]

(4) Except in accordance with subsection (7) below, nothing in section 45 above applies to any charity *(other than an exempt charity or a charity which falls within section 3(5)(c) above) which—*

(a) *is excepted by section 3(5) above, and*
(b) *is not registered* [which—
(a) falls within section 3A(2)(b) or (c) above but does not fall within section 3A(2)(d), and
(b) is not registered].

(5) If requested to do so by *the Commissioners* [the Commission], the charity trustees of any such charity as is mentioned in subsection (4) above shall prepare an annual report in respect of such financial year of the charity as is specified in *the Commissioners' request* [the Commission's request].

(6) Any report prepared under subsection (5) above shall contain—

(a) such a report by the charity trustees on the activities of the charity during the year in question, and
(b) such other information relating to the charity or to its trustees or officers,

as may be prescribed by regulations made under section 45(1) above in relation to annual reports prepared under that provision.

(7) Subsections (3) to (6) of section 45 [(as originally enacted)] above shall apply to any report required to be prepared under subsection (5) above as if it were an annual report required to be prepared under subsection (1) of that section.

[(7) The following provisions of section 45 above shall apply in relation to any report required to be prepared under subsection (5) above as if it were an annual report required to be prepared under subsection (1) of that section—

(a) subsection (3), with the omission of the words preceding 'a copy of the annual report', and
(b) subsections (4) to (6).]

(8) *Any reference in this section to a charity which falls within section 3(5)(c) above includes a reference to a charity which falls within that provision but is also excepted from registration by section 3(5)(b) above.*

NOTES

Derivation

Sub-s (1) derived from the Charities Act 1960, s 32(1) and the Charities Act 1992, s 24(1); sub-s (2) derived from the Charities Act 1960, s 32(2), (3) as amended by the Charities Act 1992, s 47, Sch 3, para 13; sub-ss (3)–(8) derived from the Charities Act 1992, s 24(2)–(7).

Initial Commencement

To be appointed: see s 99(2).

Appointment

Appointment (for the purposes of making orders or regulations): 15 October 1995: see SI 1995/2695, art 3.

Appointment (for remaining purposes): 1 March 1996: see SI 1995/2695, art 2.

Extent

This section does not extend to Scotland.

Amendment

Sub-s (1): words 'sections 41 to 45' in italics repealed and subsequent words in square brackets substituted by the Charities Act 2006, s 29(2)(a); for transitional provisions and savings see s 75(3), Sch 10, para 8 thereto.

Date in force: to be appointed: see the Charities Act 2006, s 79(2).

Sub-s (2): words 'the Commissioners consent' in italics repealed and subsequent words in square brackets substituted by the Charities Act 2006, s 75(1), Sch 8, paras 96, 139(1), (2).

Date in force: to be appointed: see the Charities Act 2006, s 79(2).

Sub-ss (2A), (2B): inserted by the Charities Act 2006, s 29(2)(b); for transitional provisions and savings see s 75(3), Sch 10, para 8 thereto.

Date in force: to be appointed: see the Charities Act 2006, s 79(2).

Sub-s (3): substituted, by subsequent sub-ss (3), (3A), (3B), by the Charities Act 2006, s 75(1), Sch 8, paras 96, 139(1), (3).

Date in force: to be appointed: see the Charities Act 2006, s 79(2).

Sub-s (3): words 'section 43, 44 or 45' in square brackets substituted by SI 2005/1074, art 3(1), (5).

Date in force: this amendment has effect in relation to the financial year of a trust starting on or after 1 April 2004: see SI 2005/1074, art 1(2).

Sub-s (4): words from '(other than an' to the end repealed and subsequent words in square brackets substituted by the Charities Act 2006, s 75(1), Sch 8, paras 96, 139(1), (4).

Date in force: to be appointed: see the Charities Act 2006, s 79(2).

Sub-s (5): words 'the Commissioners' in italics repealed and subsequent words in square brackets substituted by the Charities Act 2006, s 75(1), Sch 8, paras 96, 139(1), (5)(a).

Date in force: to be appointed: see the Charities Act 2006, s 79(2).

Sub-s (5): words 'the Commissioners' request' in italics repealed and subsequent words in square brackets substituted by the Charities Act 2006, s 75(1), Sch 8, paras 96, 139(1), (5)(b).

Date in force: to be appointed: see the Charities Act 2006, s 79(2).

Sub-s (7): substituted by the Charities Act 2006, s 75(1), Sch 8, paras 96, 139(1), (6).

Date in force: to be appointed: see the Charities Act 2006, s 79(2).

Sub-s (7): words in square brackets inserted by the Deregulation and Contracting Out Act 1994, s 29(7).

Sub-s (8): repealed by the Charities Act 2006, s 75(1), (2), Sch 8, paras 96, 139(1), (7), Sch 9.

Date in force: to be appointed: see the Charities Act 2006, s 79(2).

See Further

See further, in relation to the requirements imposed by sub-s (5) above only applying in respect of financial years beginning on or after 1 March 1996: the Charities Act 1993 (Commencement and Transitional Provisions) Order 1995, SI 1995/2695, art 4.

47 Public inspection of annual reports etc

(1) *Any annual report or other document kept by the Commissioners* [Any document kept by the Commission] in pursuance of section 45(6) above shall be open to public inspection at all reasonable times—

(a) during the period for which it is so kept; or
(b) if *the Commissioners so determine* [the Commission so determines], during such lesser period as *they may* [it may] specify.

(2) Where any person—

(a) requests the charity trustees of a charity in writing to provide him with a copy of the charity's most recent accounts [or (if subsection (4) below applies) of its most recent annual report], and
(b) pays them such reasonable fee (if any) as they may require in respect of the costs of complying with the request,

those trustees shall comply with the request within the period of two months beginning with the date on which it is made.

(3) In subsection (2) above the reference to a charity's most recent accounts is—

(a) ...
(b) in the case of [a charity other than one falling within paragraph (c) or (d) below], a reference to the statement of accounts or account and statement prepared in pursuance of section 42(1) or (3) above in respect of the last financial year of the charity in respect of which a statement of accounts or account and statement has or have been so prepared;
[(c) in the case of a charity which is a company, a reference to the most recent annual accounts of the company prepared under Part VII of the Companies Act 1985 in relation to which any of the following conditions is satisfied—
  (i) they have been audited;
  (ii) a report required for the purposes of section 249A(2) of that Act has been made in respect of them; or
  (iii) they relate to a year in respect of which the company is exempt from audit by virtue of section 249A(1) of that Act; and]
(d) in the case of an exempt charity, a reference to the accounts of the charity most recently audited in pursuance of any statutory or other requirement or, if its accounts are not required to be audited, the accounts most recently prepared in respect of the charity.

[(4) This subsection applies if an annual report has been prepared in respect of any financial year of a charity in pursuance of section 45(1) or 46(5) above.

(5) In subsection (2) above the reference to a charity's most recent annual report is a reference to the annual report prepared in pursuance of section 45(1) or 46(5) in respect of the last financial year of the charity in respect of which an annual report has been so prepared.]

NOTES

Derivation

This section derived from the Charities Act 1992, s 25(1), (3), (4).

Initial Commencement

To be appointed: see s 99(2).

Appointment

Appointment (for the purposes of making orders or regulations): 15 October 1995: see SI 1995/2695, art 3.

Appointment (for remaining purposes): 1 March 1996: see SI 1995/2695, art 2.

Extent

This section does not extend to Scotland.

Amendment

Sub-s (1): words 'Any anuual report or other document kept by the Commissioners' in italics repealed and subsequent words in square brackets substituted by the Charities Act 2006, s 75(1), Sch 8, paras 96, 140(1), (2)(a).

Date in force: to be appointed: see the Charities Act 2006, s 79(2).

Sub-s (1): in para (b) words 'the Commissioners so determine' in italics repealed and subsequent words in square brackets substituted by the Charities Act 2006, s 75(1), Sch 8, paras 96, 140(1), (2)(b).

Date in force: to be appointed: see the Charities Act 2006, s 79(2).

Sub-s (1): in para (b) words 'they may' in italics repealed and subsequent words in square brackets substituted by the Charities Act 2006, s 75(1), Sch 8, paras 96, 140(1), (2)(c).

Date in force: to be appointed: see the Charities Act 2006, s 79(2).

Sub-s (2): in para (a) words from 'or (if subsection' to 'recent annual report' in square brackets inserted by the Charities Act 2006, s 75(1), Sch 8, paras 96, 140(1), (3).

Date in force: to be appointed: see the Charities Act 2006, s 79(2).

Sub-s (3): para (a) repealed, and in para (b) words in square brackets substituted, by the Deregulation and Contracting Out Act 1994, ss 39, 81(1), Sch 11, para 12, Sch 17; para (c) substituted by SI 1994/1935, reg 4, Sch 1, para 7.

Sub-ss (4), (5): inserted by the Charities Act 2006, s 75(1), Sch 8, paras 96, 140(1), (4).

Date in force: to be appointed: see the Charities Act 2006, s 79(2).

48 Annual returns by registered charities

(1) [Subject to subsection (1A) below,] every registered charity shall prepare in respect of each of its financial years an annual return in such form, and containing such information, as may be prescribed by regulations made by *the Commissioners* [the Commission].

[(1A) Subsection (1) above shall not apply in relation to any financial year of a charity in which *neither the gross income nor the total expenditure of the charity exceeds* [the charity's gross income does not exceed] £10,000 [(but this subsection does not apply if the charity is constituted as a CIO)].]

(2) Any such return shall be transmitted to *the Commissioners* [the Commission] by the date by which the charity trustees are, by virtue of section 45(3) above, required to transmit *to them* [to the Commission] the annual report required to be prepared in respect of the financial year in question.

(3) *The Commissioners* [The Commission] may dispense with the requirements of subsection (1) above in the case of a particular charity or a particular class of charities, or in the case of a particular financial year of a charity or of any class of charities.

[(4) The [Minister] may by order amend subsection (1A) above by substituting a different sum for the sum for the time being specified there.]

NOTES

Derivation

This section derived from the Charities Act 1992, s 26.

Initial Commencement

To be appointed: see s 99(2).

Appointment

Appointment (for the purposes of making orders or regulations): 15 October 1995: see SI 1995/2695, art 3.

Appointment (for remaining purposes): 1 March 1996: see SI 1995/2695, art 2.

Extent

This section does not extend to Scotland.

Amendment

Sub-s (1): words in square brackets inserted by the Deregulation and Contracting Out Act 1994, s 30(2).

Sub-s (1): words 'the Commissioners' in italics repealed and subsequent words in square brackets substituted by the Charities Act 2006, s 75(1), Sch 8, paras 96, 141(1), (2).

Date in force: to be appointed: see the Charities Act 2006, s 79(2).

Sub-s (1A): inserted by the Deregulation and Contracting Out Act 1994, s 30(3)).

Sub-s (1A): words from 'neither the gross' to 'the charity exceeds' in italics repealed and subsequent words in square brackets substituted by the Charities Act 2006, s 75(1), Sch 8, paras 96, 141(1), (3).

Date in force: to be appointed: see the Charities Act 2006, s 79(2).

Sub-s (1A): words from '(but this subsection' to 'as a CIO)' in square brackets inserted by the Charities Act 2006, s 34, Sch 7, Pt 2, paras 3, 5.

Date in force: to be appointed: see the Charities Act 2006, s 79(2).

Sub-s (2): words 'the Commissioners' in italics repealed and subsequent words in square brackets substituted by the Charities Act 2006, s 75(1), Sch 8, paras 96, 141(1), (4)(a).

Date in force: to be appointed: see the Charities Act 2006, s 79(2).

Sub-s (2): words 'to them' in italics repealed and subsequent words in square brackets substituted by the Charities Act 2006, s 75(1), Sch 8, paras 96, 141(1), (4)(b).

Date in force: to be appointed: see the Charities Act 2006, s 79(2).

Sub-s (3): words 'The Commissioners' in italics repealed and subsequent words in square brackets substituted by the Charities Act 2006, s 75(1), Sch 8, paras 96, 141(1), (5).

Date in force: to be appointed: see the Charities Act 2006, s 79(2).

Sub-s (4): inserted by the Deregulation and Contracting Out Act 1994, s 30(3)).

Sub-s (4): word 'Minister' in square brackets substituted by SI 2006/2951, art 6, Schedule, para 4(u).

Date in force: 13 December 2006: see SI 2006/2951, art 1(2).

See Further

See further, in relation to the requirements imposed by this section only applying in respect of financial years beginning on or after 1 March 1996: the Charities Act 1993 (Commencement and Transitional Provisions) Order 1995, SI 1995/2695, art 4.

49 Offences [49 Offences]

Any person who, without reasonable excuse, is persistently in default in relation to any requirement imposed—

(a) *by section 45(3) [or (3A)] above (taken with section 45(4) or (5), as the case may require), or*
(b) *by section 47(2) or 48(2) above,*

shall be guilty of an offence and liable on summary conviction to a fine not exceeding level 4 on the standard scale.

[(1) If any requirement imposed—

(a) by section 45(3) or (3A) above (taken with section 45(3B), (4) and (5), as applicable), or
(b) by section 47(2) or 48(2) above,

is not complied with, each person who immediately before the date for compliance specified in the section in question was a charity trustee of the charity shall be guilty of an offence and liable on summary conviction to the penalty mentioned in subsection (2).

(2) The penalty is—

(a) a fine not exceeding level 4 on the standard scale, and
(b) for continued contravention, a daily default fine not exceeding 10% of level 4 on the standard scale for so long as the person in question remains a charity trustee of the charity.

(3) It is a defence for a person charged with an offence under subsection (1) to prove that he took all reasonable steps for securing that the requirement in question would be complied with in time.]

NOTES

Derivation

This section derived from the Charities Act 1992, s 27.

Initial Commencement

To be appointed: see s 99(2).

Appointment

Appointment (for the purposes of making orders or regulations): 15 October 1995: see SI 1995/2695, art 3.

Appointment (for remaining purposes): 1 March 1996: see SI 1995/2695, art 2.

Extent

This section does not extend to Scotland.

Amendment

Substituted by the Charities Act 2006, s 75(1), Sch 8, paras 96, 142.

Date in force: to be appointed: see the Charities Act 2006, s 79(2).

Words in square brackets inserted by the Deregulation and Contracting Out Act 1994, s 29(8).

[49A Group accounts]

[The provisions of Schedule 5A to this Act shall have effect with respect to—

(a) the preparation and auditing of accounts in respect of groups consisting of parent charities and their subsidiary undertakings (within the meaning of that Schedule), and
(b) other matters relating to such groups.]

NOTES

Amendment

Inserted by the Charities Act 2006, s 30(1).

Date in force: to be appointed: see the Charities Act 2006, s 79(2).

Part VII
Incorporation of Charity Trustees

50 Incorporation of trustees of a charity

(1) Where—

(a) the trustees of a charity, in accordance with section 52 below, apply to *the Commissioners* [the Commission] for a certificate of incorporation of the trustees as a body corporate, and
(b) *the Commissioners consider* [the Commission considers] that the incorporation of the trustees would be in the interests of the charity,

the Commissioners [the Commission] may grant such a certificate, subject to such conditions or directions as *they think fit* [the Commission thinks fit] to insert in it.

(2) *The Commissioners* [The Commission] shall not, however, grant such a certificate in a case where the charity appears *to them* [to the Commission] to be required to be registered *under section 3* [in accordance with section 3A] above but is not so registered.

(3) On the grant of such a certificate—

(a) the trustees of the charity shall become a body corporate by such name as is specified in the certificate; and
(b) (without prejudice to the operation of section 54 below) any relevant rights or liabilities of those trustees shall become rights or liabilities of that body.

(4) After their incorporation the trustees—

(a) may sue and be sued in their corporate name; and
(b) shall have the same powers, and be subject to the same restrictions and limitations, as respects the holding, acquisition and disposal of property for or in connection with the purposes of the charity as they had or were subject to while unincorporated;

and any relevant legal proceedings that might have been continued or commenced by or against the trustees may be continued or commenced by or against them in their corporate name.

(5) A body incorporated under this section need not have a common seal.

(6) In this section—

'relevant rights or liabilities' means rights or liabilities in connection with any property vesting in the body in question under section 51 below; and 'relevant legal proceedings' means legal proceedings in connection with any such property.

NOTES

Derivation

This section derived from the Charitable Trustees Incorporation Act 1872, s 1, as substituted by the Charities Act 1992, s 48, Sch 4, para 1.

Initial Commencement

Specified date: 1 August 1993: see s 99(1).

Extent

This section does not extend to Scotland.

Amendment

Sub-s (1): in para (a) words 'the Commissioners' in italics repealed and subsequent words in square brackets substituted by the Charities Act 2006, s 75(1), Sch 8, paras 96, 143(1), (2)(a).

Date in force: to be appointed: see the Charities Act 2006, s 79(2).

Sub-s (1): in para (b) words 'the Commissioners consider' in italics repealed and subsequent words in square brackets substituted by the Charities Act 2006, s 75(1), Sch 8, paras 96, 143(1), (2)(b).

Date in force: to be appointed: see the Charities Act 2006, s 79(2).

Sub-s (1): words 'the Commissioners' in italics repealed and subsequent words in square brackets substituted by the Charities Act 2006, s 75(1), Sch 8, paras 96, 143(1), (2)(a).

Date in force: to be appointed: see the Charities Act 2006, s 79(2).

Sub-s (1): words 'they think fit' in italics repealed and subsequent words in square brackets substituted by the Charities Act 2006, s 75(1), Sch 8, paras 96, 143(1), (2)(c).

Date in force: to be appointed: see the Charities Act 2006, s 79(2).

Sub-s (2): words 'The Commissioners' in italics repealed and subsequent words in square brackets substituted by the Charities Act 2006, s 75(1), Sch 8, paras 96, 143(1), (3)(a).

Date in force: to be appointed: see the Charities Act 2006, s 79(2).

Sub-s (2): words 'to them' in italics repealed and subsequent words in square brackets substituted by the Charities Act 2006, s 75(1), Sch 8, paras 96, 143(1), (3)(b).

Date in force: to be appointed: see the Charities Act 2006, s 79(2).

Sub-s (2): words 'under section 3' in italics repealed and subsequent words in square brackets substituted by the Charities Act 2006, s 75(1), Sch 8, paras 96, 143(1), (3)(c).

Date in force: to be appointed: see the Charities Act 2006, s 79(2).

51 Estate to vest in body corporate

The certificate of incorporation shall vest in the body corporate all real and personal estate, of whatever nature or tenure, belonging to or held by any person or persons in trust for the charity, and thereupon any person or persons in whose name or names any stocks, funds or securities are standing in trust for the charity, shall transfer them into the name of the body corporate, except that the foregoing provisions shall not apply to property vested in the official custodian.

NOTES

Derivation

This section derived from the Charitable Trustees Incorporation Act 1872, s 2, as amended by the Charities Act 1960, s 48(1), (2), Sch 6, Sch 7, Part I, and the Charities Act 1992, ss 48, 78(2), Sch 4, para 2, Sch 7.

Initial Commencement

Specified date: 1 August 1993: see s 99(1).

Extent

This section does not extend to Scotland.

52 Applications for incorporation

(1) Every application to *the Commissioners* [the Commission] for a certificate of incorporation under this Part of this Act shall—

(a) be in writing and signed by the trustees of the charity concerned; and
(b) be accompanied by such documents or information as *the Commissioners* [the Commission] may require for the purpose of the application.

(2) *The Commissioners* [The Commission] may require—

(a) any statement contained in any such application, or
(b) any document or information supplied under subsection (1)(b) above,

to be verified in such manner as *they may specify* [it may specify].

NOTES

Derivation

This section derived from the Charitable Trustees Incorporation Act 1872, s 3, as substituted by the Charities Act 1992, s 48, Sch 4, para 3.

Initial Commencement

Specified date: 1 August 1993: see s 99(1).

Extent

This section does not extend to Scotland.

Amendment

Sub-s (1): words 'the Commissioners' in italics in both places they occur repealed and subsequent words in square brackets substituted by the Charities Act 2006, s 75(1), Sch 8, paras 96, 144(1), (2).

Date in force: to be appointed: see the Charities Act 2006, s 79(2).

Sub-s (2): words 'The Commissioners' in italics repealed and subsequent words in square brackets substituted by the Charities Act 2006, s 75(1), Sch 8, paras 96, 144(1), (3)(a).

Date in force: to be appointed: see the Charities Act 2006, s 79(2).

Sub-s (2): words 'they may specify' in italics repealed and subsequent words in square brackets substituted by the Charities Act 2006, s 75(1), Sch 8, paras 96, 144(1), (3)(b).

Date in force: to be appointed: see the Charities Act 2006, s 79(2).

53 Nomination of trustees, and filling up vacancies

(1) Before a certificate of incorporation is granted under this Part of this Act, trustees of the charity must have been effectually appointed to the satisfaction of *the Commissioners* [the Commission].

(2) Where a certificate of incorporation is granted vacancies in the number of the trustees of the charity shall from time to time be filled up so far as required by the constitution or settlement of the charity, or by any conditions or directions in the certificate, by such legal means as would have been available for the appointment of new trustees of the charity if no certificate of incorporation had been granted, or otherwise as required by such conditions or directions.

NOTES

Derivation

This section derived from the Charitable Trustees Incorporation Act 1872, s 4, as amended by the Charities Act 1992, ss 48, 78(2), Sch 4, para 4, Sch 7.

Initial Commencement

Specified date: 1 August 1993: see s 99(1).

Extent

This section does not extend to Scotland.

Amendment

Sub-s (1): words 'the Commissioners' in italics repealed and subsequent words in square brackets substituted by the Charities Act 2006, s 75(1), Sch 8, paras 96, 145.

Date in force: to be appointed: see the Charities Act 2006, s 79(2).

54 Liability of trustees and others, notwithstanding incorporation

After a certificate of incorporation has been granted under this Part of this Act all trustees of the charity, notwithstanding their incorporation, shall be chargeable for such property as shall come into their hands, and shall be answerable and accountable for their own acts, receipts, neglects, and defaults, and for the due administration of the charity and its property, in the same manner and to the same extent as if no such incorporation had been effected.

NOTES

Derivation

This section derived from the Charitable Trustees Incorporation Act 1872, s 5, as amended by the Charities Act 1992, ss 48, 78(2), Sch 4, para 5, Sch 7.

Initial Commencement

Specified date: 1 August 1993: see s 99(1).

Extent

This section does not extend to Scotland.

55 Certificate to be evidence of compliance with requirements for incorporation

A certificate of incorporation granted under this Part of this Act shall be conclusive evidence that all the preliminary requirements for incorporation under this Part of this Act have been complied with, and the date of incorporation mentioned in the certificate shall be deemed to be the date at which incorporation has taken place.

NOTES

Derivation

This section derived from the Charitable Trustees Incorporation Act 1872, s 6.

Initial Commencement

Specified date: 1 August 1993: see s 99(1).

Extent

This section does not extend to Scotland.

56 Power of Commissioners [Commission] to amend certificate of incorporation

(1) *The Commissioners* [The Commission] may amend a certificate of incorporation either on the application of the incorporated body to which it relates or *of their own motion* [of the Commission's own motion].

(2) Before making any such amendment *of their own motion, the Commissioners* [of its own motion, the Commission] shall by notice in writing—

(a) inform the trustees of the relevant charity of *their proposals* [its proposals], and
(b) invite those trustees to make representations *to them* [to it] within a time specified in the notice, being not less than one month from the date of the notice.

(3) *The Commissioners* [The Commission] shall take into consideration any representations made by those trustees within the time so specified, and may then (without further notice) proceed with *their proposals* [its proposals] either without modification or with such modifications as appear *to them* [to it] to be desirable.

(4) *The Commissioners* [The Commission] may amend a certificate of incorporation either—

(a) by making an order specifying the amendment; or
(b) by issuing a new certificate of incorporation taking account of the amendment.

NOTES

Derivation

This section derived from the Charitable Trustees Incorporation Act 1872, s 6A, as added by the Charities Act 1992, s 48, Sch 4, para 6.

Initial Commencement

Specified date: 1 August 1993: see s 99(1).

Extent

This section does not extend to Scotland.

Amendment

Section heading: word 'Commissioners' repealed and subsequent word in square brackets substituted by the Charities Act 2006, s 75(1), Sch 8, paras 96, 146(1), (6).

Date in force: to be appointed: see the Charities Act 2006, s 79(2).

Sub-s (1): words 'The Commissioners' in italics repealed and subsequent words in square brackets substituted by the Charities Act 2006, s 75(1), Sch 8, paras 96, 146(1), (2)(a).

Date in force: to be appointed: see the Charities Act 2006, s 79(2).

Sub-s (1): words 'of their own motion' in italics repealed and subsequent words in square brackets substituted by the Charities Act 2006, s 75(1), Sch 8, paras 96, 146(1), (2)(b).

Date in force: to be appointed: see the Charities Act 2006, s 79(2).

Sub-s (2): words 'of their own motion, the Commissioners' in italics repealed and subsequent words in square brackets substituted by the Charities Act 2006, s 75(1), Sch 8, paras 96, 146(1), (3)(a).

Date in force: to be appointed: see the Charities Act 2006, s 79(2).

Sub-s (2): in para (a) words 'their proposals' in italics repealed and subsequent words in square brackets substituted by the Charities Act 2006, s 75(1), Sch 8, paras 96, 146(1), (3)(b).

Date in force: to be appointed: see the Charities Act 2006, s 79(2).

Sub-s (2): in para (b) words 'to them' in italics repealed and subsequent words in square brackets substituted by the Charities Act 2006, s 75(1), Sch 8, paras 96, 146(1), (3)(c).

Date in force: to be appointed: see the Charities Act 2006, s 79(2).

Sub-s (3): words 'The Commissioners' in italics repealed and subsequent words in square brackets substituted by the Charities Act 2006, s 75(1), Sch 8, paras 96, 146(1), (4)(a).

Date in force: to be appointed: see the Charities Act 2006, s 79(2).

Sub-s (3): words 'their proposals' in italics repealed and subsequent words in square brackets substituted by the Charities Act 2006, s 75(1), Sch 8, paras 96, 146(1), (4)(b).

Date in force: to be appointed: see the Charities Act 2006, s 79(2).

Sub-s (3): words 'to them' in italics repealed and subsequent words in square brackets substituted by the Charities Act 2006, s 75(1), Sch 8, paras 96, 146(1), (4)(c).

Date in force: to be appointed: see the Charities Act 2006, s 79(2).

Sub-s (4): words 'The Commissioners' in italics repealed and subsequent words in square brackets substituted by the Charities Act 2006, s 75(1), Sch 8, paras 96, 146(1), (5).

Date in force: to be appointed: see the Charities Act 2006, s 79(2).

57 Records of applications and certificates

(1) *The Commissioners* [The Commission] shall keep a record of all applications for, and certificates of, incorporation under this Part of this Act and shall preserve all documents sent *to them* [to it] under this Part of this Act.

(2) Any person may inspect such documents, under the direction of *the Commissioners* [the Commission], and any person may require a copy or extract of any such document to be certified by a certificate signed by *the secretary of the Commissioners* [a member of the staff of the Commission].

NOTES

Derivation

This section derived from the Charitable Trustees Incorporation Act 1872, s 7, as amended by the Charities Act 1992, ss 48, 78(2), Sch 4, para 7, Sch 7.

Initial Commencement

Specified date: 1 August 1993: see s 99(1).

Extent

This section does not extend to Scotland.

Amendment

Sub-s (1): words 'The Commissioners' in italics repealed and subsequent words in square brackets substituted by the Charities Act 2006, s 75(1), Sch 8, paras 96, 147(1), (2)(a).

Date in force: to be appointed: see the Charities Act 2006, s 79(2).

Sub-s (1): words 'to them' in italics repealed and subsequent words in square brackets substituted by the Charities Act 2006, s 75(1), Sch 8, paras 96, 147(1), (2)(b).

Date in force: to be appointed: see the Charities Act 2006, s 79(2).

Sub-s (2): words 'the Commissioners' in italics repealed and subsequent words in square brackets substituted by the Charities Act 2006, s 75(1), Sch 8, paras 96, 147(1), (3)(a).

Date in force: to be appointed: see the Charities Act 2006, s 79(2).

Sub-s (3): words 'the secretary of the Commissioners' in italics repealed and subsequent words in square brackets substituted by the Charities Act 2006, s 75(1), Sch 8, paras 96, 147(1), (3)(b).

Date in force: to be appointed: see the Charities Act 2006, s 79(2).

58 Enforcement of orders and directions

All conditions and directions inserted in any certificate of incorporation shall be binding upon and performed or observed by the trustees as trusts of the charity, and section 88 below shall apply to any trustee who fails to perform or observe any such condition or direction as it applies to a person guilty of disobedience to any such order of *the Commissioners* [the Commission] as is mentioned in that section.

NOTES

Derivation

This section derived from the Charitable Trustees Incorporation Act 1872, s 8, as amended by the Charities Act 1992, s 48, Sch 4, para 8.

Initial Commencement

Specified date: 1 August 1993: see s 99(1).

Extent

This section does not extend to Scotland.

Amendment

Words 'the Commissioners' in italics repealed and subsequent words in square brackets substituted by the Charities Act 2006, s 75(1), Sch 8, paras 96, 148.

Date in force: to be appointed: see the Charities Act 2006, s 79(2).

59 Gifts to charity before incorporation to have same effect afterwards

After the incorporation of the trustees of any charity under this Part of this Act every donation, gift and disposition of property, real or personal, lawfully made before the incorporation but not having actually taken effect, or thereafter lawfully made, by deed, will or otherwise to or in favour of the charity, or the trustees of the charity, or otherwise for the purposes of the charity, shall take effect as if made to or in favour of the incorporated body or otherwise for the like purposes.

NOTES

Derivation

This section derived from the Charitable Trustees Incorporation Act 1872, s 10.

Initial Commencement

Specified date: 1 August 1993: see s 99(1).

Extent

This section does not extend to Scotland.

60 Execution of documents by incorporated body

(1) This section has effect as respects the execution of documents by an incorporated body.

(2) If an incorporated body has a common seal, a document may be executed by the body by the affixing of its common seal.

(3) Whether or not it has a common seal, a document may be executed by an incorporated body either—

(a) by being signed by a majority of the trustees of the relevant charity and expressed (in whatever form of words) to be executed by the body; or
(b) by being executed in pursuance of an authority given under subsection (4) below.

(4) For the purposes of subsection (3)(b) above the trustees of the relevant charity in the case of an incorporated body may, subject to the trusts of the charity, confer on any two or more of their number—

(a) a general authority, or
(b) an authority limited in such manner as the trustees think fit,

to execute in the name and on behalf of the body documents for giving effect to transactions to which the body is a party.

(5) An authority under subsection (4) above—

(a) shall suffice for any document if it is given in writing or by resolution of a meeting of the trustees of the relevant charity, notwithstanding the want of any formality that would be required in giving an authority apart from that subsection;
(b) may be given so as to make the powers conferred exercisable by any of the trustees, or may be restricted to named persons or in any other way;
(c) subject to any such restriction, and until it is revoked, shall, notwithstanding any change in the trustees of the relevant charity, have effect as a continuing authority given by the trustees from time to time of the charity and exercisable by such trustees.

(6) In any authority under subsection (4) above to execute a document in the name and on behalf of an incorporated body there shall, unless the contrary intention appears, be implied authority also to execute it for the body in the name and on behalf of the official custodian or of any other person, in any case in which the trustees could do so.

(7) A document duly executed by an incorporated body which makes it clear on its face that it is intended by the person or persons making it to be a deed has effect, upon delivery, as a deed; and it shall be presumed, unless a contrary intention is proved, to be delivered upon its being so executed.

(8) In favour of a purchaser a document shall be deemed to have been duly executed by such a body if it purports to be signed—

(a) by a majority of the trustees of the relevant charity, or
(b) by such of the trustees of the relevant charity as are authorised by the trustees of that charity to execute it in the name and on behalf of the body,

and, where the document makes it clear on its face that it is intended by the person or persons making it to be a deed, it shall be deemed to have been delivered upon its being executed.

For this purpose 'purchaser' means a purchaser in good faith for valuable consideration and includes a lessee, mortgagee or other person who for valuable consideration acquires an interest in property.

NOTES

Derivation

This section derived from the Charitable Trustees Incorporation Act 1872, s 12, as substituted by the Charities Act 1992, s 48, Sch 4, para 9.

Initial Commencement

Specified date: 1 August 1993: see s 99(1).

Extent

This section does not extend to Scotland.

61 Power of Commissioners [Commission] to dissolve incorporated body

(1) Where *the Commissioners are* [the Commission is] satisfied—

(a) that an incorporated body has no assets or does not operate, or
(b) that the relevant charity in the case of an incorporated body has ceased to exist, or
(c) that the institution previously constituting, or *treated by them* [treated by the Commission] as constituting, any such charity has ceased to be, or (as the case may be) was not at the time of the body's incorporation, a charity, or
(d) that the purposes of the relevant charity in the case of an incorporated body have been achieved so far as is possible or are in practice incapable of being achieved,

they may of their own motion [the Commission may of its own motion] make an order dissolving the body as from such date as is specified in the order.

(2) Where *the Commissioners are* [the Commission is] satisfied, on the application of the trustees of the relevant charity in the case of an incorporated body, that it would be in the interests of the charity for that body to be dissolved, *the Commissioners* [the Commission] may make an order dissolving the body as from such date as is specified in the order.

(3) Subject to subsection (4) below, an order made under this section with respect to an incorporated body shall have the effect of vesting in the trustees of the relevant charity, in trust for that charity, all property for the time being vested—

(a) in the body, or
(b) in any other person (apart from the official custodian),

in trust for that charity.

(4) If *the Commissioners so direct* [the Commission so directs] in the order—

(a) all or any specified part of that property shall, instead of vesting in the trustees of the relevant charity, vest—
 (i) in a specified person as trustee for, or nominee of, that charity, or
 (ii) in such persons (other than the trustees of the relevant charity) as may be specified;
(b) any specified investments, or any specified class or description of investments, held by any person in trust for the relevant charity shall be transferred—
 (i) to the trustees of that charity, or
 (ii) to any such person or persons as is or are mentioned in paragraph (a)(i) or (ii) above;

and for this purpose 'specified' means specified by *the Commissioners* [the Commission] in the order.

(5) Where an order to which this subsection applies is made with respect to an incorporated body—

(a) any rights or liabilities of the body shall become rights or liabilities of the trustees of the relevant charity; and
(b) any legal proceedings that might have been continued or commenced by or against the body may be continued or commenced by or against those trustees.

(6) Subsection (5) above applies to any order under this section by virtue of which—

(a) any property vested as mentioned in subsection (3) above is vested—
  (i) in the trustees of the relevant charity, or
  (ii) in any person as trustee for, or nominee of, that charity; or
(b) any investments held by any person in trust for the relevant charity are required to be transferred—
  (i) to the trustees of that charity, or
  (ii) to any person as trustee for, or nominee of, that charity.

(7) *Any order made by the Commissioners under this section may be varied or revoked by a further order so made.*

NOTES

Derivation

This section derived from the Charitable Trustees Incorporation Act 1872, s 12A, as substituted by the Charities Act 1992, s 48, Sch 4, para 9.

Initial Commencement

Specified date: 1 August 1993: see s 99(1).

Extent

This section does not extend to Scotland.

Amendment

Section heading: word 'Commissioners' repealed and subsequent words in square brackets substituted by the Charities Act 2006, s 75(1), Sch 8, paras 96, 149(1), (6).

Date in force: to be appointed: see the Charities Act 2006, s 79(2).

Sub-s (1): words 'the Commissioners are' in italics repealed and subsequent words in square brackets substituted by the Charities Act 2006, s 75(1), Sch 8, paras 96, 149(1), (2)(a).

Date in force: to be appointed: see the Charities Act 2006, s 79(2).

Sub-s (1): in para (c) words 'treated by them' in italics repealed and subsequent words in square brackets substituted by the Charities Act 2006, s 75(1), Sch 8, paras 96, 149(1), (2)(b).

Date in force: to be appointed: see the Charities Act 2006, s 79(2).

Sub-s (1): words 'they may of their own motion' in italics repealed and subsequent words in square brackets substituted by the Charities Act 2006, s 75(1), Sch 8, paras 96, 149(1), (2)(c).

Date in force: to be appointed: see the Charities Act 2006, s 79(2).

Sub-s (2): words 'the Commissioners are' in italics repealed and subsequent words in square brackets substituted by the Charities Act 2006, s 75(1), Sch 8, paras 96, 149(1), (3)(a).

Date in force: to be appointed: see the Charities Act 2006, s 79(2).

Sub-s (2): words 'the Commissioners' in italics repealed and subsequent words in square brackets substituted by the Charities Act 2006, s 75(1), Sch 8, paras 96, 149(1), (3)(b).

Date in force: to be appointed: see the Charities Act 2006, s 79(2).

Sub-s (4): words 'the Commissioners so direct' in italics repealed and subsequent words in square brackets substituted by the Charities Act 2006, s 75(1), Sch 8, paras 96, 149(1), (4)(a).

Date in force: to be appointed: see the Charities Act 2006, s 79(2).

Sub-s (4): words 'the Commissioners' in italics repealed and subsequent words in square brackets substituted by the Charities Act 2006, s 75(1), Sch 8, paras 96, 149(1), (4)(b).

Date in force: to be appointed: see the Charities Act 2006, s 79(2).

Sub-s (7): repealed by the Charities Act 2006, s 75(1), (2), Sch 8, paras 96, 149(1), (5), Sch 9.

62 Interpretation of Part VII

In this Part of this Act—

'incorporated body' means a body incorporated under section 50 above;
'the relevant charity', in relation to an incorporated body, means the charity the trustees of which have been incorporated as that body;
'the trustees', in relation to a charity, means the charity trustees.

NOTES

Derivation

This section derived from the Charitable Trustees Incorporation Act 1872, s 14, as substituted by the Charities Act 1992, s 48, Sch 4, para 10.

Initial Commencement

Specified date: 1 August 1993: see s 99(1).

Extent

This section does not extend to Scotland.

Part VIII
Charitable Companies

63 Winding up

(1) Where a charity may be wound up by the High Court under the Insolvency Act 1986, a petition for it to be wound up under that Act by any court in England or Wales having jurisdiction may be presented by the Attorney General, as well as by any person authorised by that Act.

(2) Where a charity may be so wound up by the High Court, such a petition may also be presented by *the Commissioners* [the Commission] if, at any time after *they have instituted* [it has instituted] an inquiry under section 8 above with respect to the charity, *they are satisfied* [it is satisfied] as mentioned in section 18(1)(a) or (b) above.

(3) Where a charitable company is dissolved, *the Commissioners* [the Commission] may make an application under section 651 of the Companies Act 1985 (power of court to declare dissolution of company void) for an order to be made under that section with respect to the company; and for this purpose subsection (1) of that section shall have effect in relation to a charitable company as if the reference to the liquidator of the company included a reference to *the Commissioners* [the Commission].

(4) Where a charitable company's name has been struck off the register of companies under section 652 of the Companies Act 1985 (power of registrar to strike defunct company off register), *the Commissioners* [the Commission] may make an application under section 653(2) of that Act (objection to striking off by person aggrieved) for an order restoring the company's name to that register; and for this purpose section 653(2) shall have effect in relation to a charitable company as if the reference to any such person aggrieved as is there mentioned included a reference to *the Commissioners* [the Commission].

(5) The powers exercisable by *the Commissioners* [the Commission] by virtue of this section shall be exercisable *by them of their own motion* [by the Commission of its own motion], but shall be exercisable only with the agreement of the Attorney General on each occasion.

(6) In this section 'charitable company' means a company which is a charity.

NOTES

Derivation

Sub-s (1) derived from the Charities Act 1960, s 30(1), as substituted by the Companies Act 1989, s 111(1), and as amended by the Charities Act 1992, s 10(2); sub-ss (2)–(6) derived from the Charities Act 1960, s 30(2)–(6), as added by the Charities Act 1992, s 10(1).

Initial Commencement

Specified date: 1 August 1993: see s 99(1).

Extent

This section does not extend to Scotland.

Amendment

Sub-s (2): words 'the Commissioners' in italics repealed and subsequent words in square brackets substituted by the Charities Act 2006, s 75(1), Sch 8, paras 96, 150(1), (2)(a).

Date in force: to be appointed: see the Charities Act 2006, s 79(2).

Sub-s (2): words 'they have instituted' in italics repealed and subsequent words in square brackets substituted by the Charities Act 2006, s 75(1), Sch 8, paras 96, 150(1), (2)(b).

Date in force: to be appointed: see the Charities Act 2006, s 79(2).

Sub-s (2): words 'they are satisfied' in italics repealed and subsequent words in square brackets substituted by the Charities Act 2006, s 75(1), Sch 8, paras 96, 150(1), (2)(c).

Date in force: to be appointed: see the Charities Act 2006, s 79(2).

Sub-s (3): words 'the Commissioners' in italics in both places they occur repealed and subsequent words in square brackets substituted by the Charities Act 2006, s 75(1), Sch 8, paras 96, 150(1), (3).

Date in force: to be appointed: see the Charities Act 2006, s 79(2).

Sub-s (4): words 'the Commissioners' in italics in both places they occur repealed and subsequent words in square brackets substituted by the Charities Act 2006, s 75(1), Sch 8, paras 96, 150(1), (4).

Date in force: to be appointed: see the Charities Act 2006, s 79(2).

Sub-s (5): words 'the Commissioners' in italics repealed and subsequent words in square brackets substituted by the Charities Act 2006, s 75(1), Sch 8, paras 96, 150(1), (5)(a).

Date in force: to be appointed: see the Charities Act 2006, s 79(2).

Sub-s (5): words 'by them of their own motion' in italics repealed and subsequent words in square brackets substituted by the Charities Act 2006, s 75(1), Sch 8, paras 96, 150(1), (5)(b).

Date in force: to be appointed: see the Charities Act 2006, s 79(2).

64 Alteration of objects clause

(1) Where a charity is a company or other body corporate having power to alter the instruments establishing or regulating it as a body corporate, no exercise of that power which has the effect of the body ceasing to be a charity shall be valid so as to affect the application of—

(a) any property acquired under any disposition or agreement previously made otherwise than for full consideration in money or money's worth, or any property representing property so acquired,
(b) any property representing income which has accrued before the alteration is made, or
(c) the income from any such property as aforesaid.

(2) Where a charity is a company, any alteration by it—

(a) of the objects clause in its memorandum of association, or
(b) of any other provision in its memorandum of association, or any provision in its articles of association, which is a provision directing or restricting the manner in which property of the company may be used or applied,

is ineffective without the prior written consent of the Commissioners.

[(2) Where a charity is a company, any regulated alteration by the company—

(a) requires the prior written consent of the Commission, and
(b) is ineffective if such consent has not been obtained.

(2A) The following are 'regulated alterations'—

(a) any alteration of the objects clause in the company's memorandum of association,
(b) any alteration of any provision of its memorandum or articles of association directing the application of property of the company on its dissolution, and
(c) any alteration of any provision of its memorandum or articles of association where the alteration would provide authorisation for any benefit to be obtained by directors or members of the company or persons connected with them.

(2B) For the purposes of subsection (2A) above—

(a) 'benefit' means a direct or indirect benefit of any nature, except that it does not include any remuneration (within the meaning of section 73A below) whose receipt may be authorised under that section; and
(b) the same rules apply for determining whether a person is connected with a director or member of the company as apply, in accordance with section 73B(5) and (6) below, for determining whether a person is connected with a charity trustee for the purposes of section 73A.]

(3) Where a company has made *any such alteration* [a regulated alteration] in accordance with subsection (2) above and—

(a) in connection with the alteration is required by virtue of—
    (i) section 6(1) of the Companies Act 1985 (delivery of documents following alteration of objects), or
    (ii) that provision as applied by section 17(3) of that Act (alteration of condition in memorandum which could have been contained in articles),

    to deliver to the registrar of companies a printed copy of its memorandum, as altered, or

(b) is required by virtue of section 380(1) of that Act (registration etc of resolutions and agreements) to forward to the registrar a printed or other copy of the special resolution effecting the alteration,

the copy so delivered or forwarded by the company shall be accompanied by a copy of *the Commissioner's consent* [the Commission's consent].

(4) Section 6(3) of that Act (offences) shall apply to any default by a company in complying with subsection (3) above as it applies to any such default as is mentioned in that provision.

NOTES

Derivation

Sub-s (1) derived from the Charities Act 1960, s 30A(1), as substituted by the Companies Act 1989, s 111(1); sub-ss (2)–(4) derived from the Charities Act 1960, s 30A(2)–(4), as substituted by the Companies Act 1989, s 111(1), and as further substituted by the Charities Act 1992, s 40.

Initial Commencement

Specified date: 1 August 1993: see s 99(1).

Extent

This section does not extend to Scotland.

Amendment

Sub-s (2): substituted, by subsequent sub-ss (2), (2A), (2B), by the Charities Act 2006, s 31(1), (2).

Date in force: to be appointed: see the Charities Act 2006, s 79(2).

Sub-s (3): words 'any such alteration' in italics repealed and subsequent words in square brackets substituted by the Charities Act 2006, s 31(1), (3).

Date in force: to be appointed: see the Charities Act 2006, s 79(2).

Sub-s (3): words 'the Commissioner's consent' in italics repealed and subsequent words in square brackets substituted by the Charities Act 2006, s 75(1), Sch 8, paras 96, 151.

Date in force: to be appointed: see the Charities Act 2006, s 79(2).

65 Invalidity of certain transactions

(1) Sections 35 and 35A of the Companies Act 1985 (capacity of company not limited by its memorandum; power of directors to bind company) do not apply to the acts of a company which is a charity except in favour of a person who—

(a) gives full consideration in money or money's worth in relation to the act in question, and
(b) does not know that the act is not permitted by the company's memorandum or, as the case may be, is beyond the powers of the directors,

or who does not know at the time the act is done that the company is a charity.

(2) However, where such a company purports to transfer or grant an interest in property, the fact that the act was not permitted by the company's memorandum or, as the case may be, that the directors in connection with the act exceeded any limitation on their powers under the company's constitution, does not affect the title of a person who subsequently acquires the property or any interest in it for full consideration without actual notice of any such circumstances affecting the validity of the company's act.

(3) In any proceedings arising out of subsection (1) above the burden of proving—

(a) that a person knew that an act was not permitted by the company's memorandum or was beyond the powers of the directors, or
(b) that a person knew that the company was a charity,

lies on the person making that allegation.

(4) Where a company is a charity, the ratification of an act under section 35(3) of the Companies Act 1985, or the ratification of a transaction to which section 322A of that Act applies (invalidity of certain transactions to which directors or their associates are parties), is ineffective without the prior written consent of *the Commissioners* [the Commission].

NOTES

Derivation

This section derived from the Charities Act 1960, s 30B, as substituted by the Companies Act 1989, s 111(1).

Initial Commencement

Specified date: 1 August 1993: see s 99(1).

Extent

This section does not extend to Scotland.

Amendment

Sub-s (4): words 'the Commissioners' in italics repealed and subsequent words in square brackets substituted by the Charities Act 2006, s 75(1), Sch 8, paras 96, 152.

Date in force: to be appointed: see the Charities Act 2006, s 79(2).

66 Requirement of consent of Commissioners [Commission] to certain acts [66 Consent of Commission required for approval etc by members of charitable companies]

(1) Where a company is a charity—

(a) any approval given by the company for the purposes of any of the provisions of the Companies Act 1985 specified in subsection (2) below, and
(b) any affirmation by it for the purposes of section 322(2)(c) of that Act (affirmation of voidable arrangements under which assets are acquired by or from a director or person connected with him),

is ineffective without the prior written consent of the Commissioners [*Commission*].

(2) The provisions of the Companies Act 1985 referred to in subsection (1)(a) above are—

(a) section 312 (payment to director in respect of loss of office or retirement);
(b) section 313(1) (payment to director in respect of loss of office or retirement made in connection with transfer of undertaking or property of company);
(c) section 319(3) (incorporation in director's service contract of term whereby his employment will or may continue for a period of more than five years);
(d) section 320(1) (arrangement whereby assets are acquired by or from director or person connected with him);
(e) section 337(3)(a) (provision of funds to meet certain expenses incurred by director).

[(1) Where a company is a charity—

(a) any approval given by the members of the company under any provision of Chapter 4 of Part 10 of the Companies Act 2006 (transactions with directors requiring approval by members) listed in subsection (2) below, and
(b) any affirmation given by members of the company under section 196 or 214 of that Act (affirmation of unapproved property transactions and loans),

is ineffective without the prior written consent of the Commission.

(2) The provisions are—

(a) section 188 (directors' long-term service contracts);
(b) section 190 (substantial property transactions with directors etc);
(c) section 197, 198 or 200 (loans and quasi-loans to directors etc);
(d) section 201 (credit transactions for benefit of directors etc);
(e) section 203 (related arrangements);
(f) section 217 (payments to directors for loss of office);
(g) section 218 (payments to directors for loss of office: transfer of undertaking etc).]

NOTES

Derivation

This section derived from the Charities Act 1960, s 30BA, as added by the Charities Act 1992, s 41.

Initial Commencement

Specified date: 1 August 1993: see s 99(1).

Extent

This section does not extend to Scotland.

Amendment

Substituted, together with s 66A, for this section as originally enacted, by the Companies Act 2006, s 226.

Date in force: to be appointed: see the Companies Act 2006, s 1300(2).

Section heading: word 'Commissioners' repealed and subsequent word in square brackets substituted by the Charities Act 2006, s 75(1), Sch 8, paras 96, 153.

Date in force: to be appointed: see the Charities Act 2006, s 79(2).

Sub-s (1): word 'Commissioners' repealed and subsequent word in square brackets substituted by the Charities Act 2006, s 75(1), Sch 8, paras 96, 153.

Date in force: to be appointed: see the Charities Act 2006, s 79(2).

[66A Consent of Commission required for certain acts of charitable company]

[(1) A company that is a charity may not do an act to which this section applies without the prior written consent of the Commission.

(2) This section applies to an act that—

(a) does not require approval under a listed provision of Chapter 4 of Part 10 of the Companies Act 2006 (transactions with directors) by the members of the company, but
(b) would require such approval but for an exemption in the provision in question that disapplies the need for approval on the part of the members of a body corporate which is a wholly- owned subsidiary of another body corporate.

(3) The reference to a listed provision is a reference to a provision listed in section 66(2) above.

(4) If a company acts in contravention of this section, the exemption referred to in subsection (2)(b) shall be treated as of no effect in relation to the act.]

NOTES

Amendment

Substituted, together with s 66, for s 66 as originally enacted, by the Companies Act 2006, s 226.

Date in force: to be appointed: see the Companies Act 2006, s 1300(2).

67 Name to appear on correspondence etc

Section 30(7) of the Companies Act 1985 (exemption from requirements relating to publication of name etc) shall not, in its application to any company which is a charity, have the effect of exempting the company from the requirements of section 349(1) of that Act (company's name to appear in its correspondence etc).

NOTES

Derivation

This section derived from the Charities Act 1960, s 30BB, as added by the Charities Act 1992, s 42.

Initial Commencement

Specified date: 1 August 1993: see s 99(1).

Extent

This section does not extend to Scotland.

68 Status to appear on correspondence etc

(1) Where a company is a charity and its name does not include the word 'charity' or the word 'charitable' [then, subject to subsection (1A)], the fact that the company is a charity shall be stated ... in legible characters—

(a) in all business letters of the company,
(b) in all its notices and other official publications,
(c) in all bills of exchange, promissory notes, endorsements, cheques and orders for money or goods purporting to be signed on behalf of the company,
(d) in all conveyances purporting to be executed by the company, and
(e) in all bills rendered by it and in all its invoices, receipts, and letters of credit.

[(1A) Where a company's name includes the word 'elusen' or the word 'elusennol' (the Welsh equivalents of the words 'charity' and 'charitable'), subsection (1) above shall not apply in relation to any document which is wholly in Welsh.

(1B) The statement required by subsection (1) above shall be in English, except that, in the case of a document which is otherwise wholly in Welsh, the statement may be in Welsh if it consists of or includes the word 'elusen' or the word 'elusennol'.]

(2) In subsection (1)(d) above 'conveyance' means any instrument creating, transferring, varying or extinguishing an interest in land.

(3) Subsections (2) to (4) of section 349 of the Companies Act 1985 (offences in connection with failure to include required particulars in business letters etc) shall apply in relation to a contravention of subsection (1) above, taking the reference in subsection (3)(b) of that section to a bill of parcels as a reference to any such bill as is mentioned in subsection (1)(e) above.

NOTES

Derivation

Sub-s (1) derived from the Charities Act 1960, s 30C(1), as substituted by the Companies Act 1989, s 111(1), and as amended by the Charities Act 1992, ss 47, 78(2), Sch 3, para 11, Sch 7; sub-s (2), (3) derived from the Charities Act 1960, s 30C(2), (3), as substituted by the Companies Act 1989, s 111(1).

Initial Commencement

Specified date: 1 August 1993: see s 99(1).

Extent

This section does not extend to Scotland.

Amendment

Sub-s (1): words in square brackets inserted, and words omitted repealed, by the Welsh Language Act 1993, ss 33(2), 35, Sch 2.

Sub-ss (1A), (1B): inserted by the Welsh Language Act 1993, s 33(3).

[68A Duty of charity's auditors etc to report matters to Commission]

[(1) Section 44A(2) to (7) above shall apply in relation to a person acting as—

(a) an auditor of a charitable company appointed under Chapter 5 of Part 11 of the Companies Act 1985 (auditors), or
(b) a reporting accountant appointed by a charitable company for the purposes of section 249C of that Act (report required instead of audit),

as they apply in relation to a person such as is mentioned in section 44A(1).

(2) For this purpose any reference in section 44A to a person acting in the capacity mentioned in section 44A(1) is to be read as a reference to his acting in the capacity mentioned in subsection (1) of this section.

(3) In this section 'charitable company' means a charity which is a company.]

NOTES

Amendment

Inserted by the Charities Act 2006, s 33; for transitional provisions and savings see s 75(3), Sch 10, para 10 thereto.

Date in force: to be appointed: see the Charities Act 2006, s 79(2).

69 Investigation of accounts

(1) In the case of a charity which is a company *the Commissioners* [the Commission] may by order require that the condition and accounts of the charity for such period as *they think fit* [the Commission thinks fit] shall be investigated and audited by an auditor appointed *by them* [by the Commission], being a person eligible for appointment as a company auditor under section 25 of the Companies Act 1989.

(2) An auditor acting under subsection (1) above—

(a) shall have a right of access to all books, accounts and documents relating to the charity which are in the possession or control of the charity trustees or to which the charity trustees have access;
(b) shall be entitled to require from any charity trustee, past or present, and from any past

or present officer or employee of the charity such information and explanation as he thinks necessary for the performance of his duties;

(c) shall at the conclusion or during the progress of the audit make such reports to *the Commissioners* [the Commission] about the audit or about the accounts or affairs of the charity as he thinks the case requires, and shall send a copy of any such report to the charity trustees.

(3) The expenses of any audit under subsection (1) above, including the remuneration of the auditor, shall be paid by *the Commissioners* [the Commission].

(4) If any person fails to afford an auditor any facility to which he is entitled under subsection (2) above *the Commissioners* [the Commission] may by order give to that person or to the charity trustees for the time being such directions as *the Commissioners think* [the Commission thinks] appropriate for securing that the default is made good.

NOTES

Derivation

Sub-s (1) derived from the Charities Act 1960, s 8(3), as amended by the Companies Act 1989 (Eligibility for Appointment as Company Auditor) (Consequential Amendments) Regulations 1991, SI 1991/1997, reg 2, Schedule, para 7, and the Charities Act 1992, s 47, Sch 3, para 2(b); sub-s (2) derived from the Charities Act 1960, s 8(4), as amended by the Charities Act 1992, s 47, Sch 3, para 2(c); sub-s (3) derived from the Charities Act 1960, s 8(5); sub-s (4) derived from the Charities Act 1960, s 8(6), as amended by the Charities Act 1992, ss 47, 78(2), Sch 3, para 2(d), Sch 7.

Initial Commencement

To be appointed: see s 99(2).

Appointment

Appointment: 1 March 1996: see SI 1995/2695, art 2.

Extent

This section does not extend to Scotland.

Amendment

Sub-s (1): words 'the Commissioners' in italics repealed and subsequent words in square brackets substituted by the Charities Act 2006, s 75(1), Sch 8, paras 96, 154(1), (2)(a).

Date in force: to be appointed: see the Charities Act 2006, s 79(2).

Sub-s (1): words 'they think fit' in italics repealed and subsequent words in square brackets substituted by the Charities Act 2006, s 75(1), Sch 8, paras 96, 154(1), (2)(b).

Date in force: to be appointed: see the Charities Act 2006, s 79(2).

Sub-s (1): words 'by them' in italics repealed and subsequent words in square brackets substituted by the Charities Act 2006, s 75(1), Sch 8, paras 96, 154(1), (2)(c).

Date in force: to be appointed: see the Charities Act 2006, s 79(2).

Sub-s (2): in para (c) words 'the Commissioners' in italics repealed and subsequent words in square brackets substituted by the Charities Act 2006, s 75(1), Sch 8, paras 96, 154(1), (3).

Date in force: to be appointed: see the Charities Act 2006, s 79(2).

Sub-s (3): words 'the Commissioners' in italics repealed and subsequent words in square brackets substituted by the Charities Act 2006, s 75(1), Sch 8, paras 96, 154(1), (3).

Date in force: to be appointed: see the Charities Act 2006, s 79(2).

Sub-s (4): words 'the Commissioners' in italics repealed and subsequent words in square brackets substituted by the Charities Act 2006, s 75(1), Sch 8, paras 96, 154(1), (4)(a).

Date in force: to be appointed: see the Charities Act 2006, s 79(2).

Sub-s (4): words 'the Commissioners think' in italics repealed and subsequent words in square brackets substituted by the Charities Act 2006, s 75(1), Sch 8, paras 96, 154(1), (4)(b).

Date in force: to be appointed: see the Charities Act 2006, s 79(2).

[Part VIIIA
Charitable Incorporated Organisations]

NOTES

Amendment

Inserted by the Charities Act 2006, s 34, Sch 7, Pt 1, para 1.

Date in force (for remaining purposes): to be appointed: see the Charities Act 2006, s 79(2).

[Nature and constitution]

NOTES

Amendment

Inserted by the Charities Act 2006, s 34, Sch 7, Pt 1, para 1.

Date in force (for remaining purposes): to be appointed: see the Charities Act 2006, s 79(2).

[69A Charitable incorporated organisations]

[(1) In this Act, a charitable incorporated organisation is referred to as a 'CIO'.

(2) A CIO shall be a body corporate.

(3) A CIO shall have a constitution.

(4) A CIO shall have a principal office, which shall be in England or in Wales.

(5) A CIO shall have one or more members.

(6) The members may be either—

(a) not liable to contribute to the assets of the CIO if it is wound up, or
(b) liable to do so up to a maximum amount each.]

NOTES

Amendment

Inserted by the Charities Act 2006, s 34, Sch 7, Pt 1, para 1.

Date in force: to be appointed: see the Charities Act 2006, s 79(2).

[69B Constitution]

[(1) A CIO's constitution shall state—

(a) its name,
(b) its purposes,
(c) whether its principal office is in England or in Wales, and

(d) whether or not its members are liable to contribute to its assets if it is wound up, and (if they are) up to what amount.

(2) A CIO's constitution shall make provision—

(a) about who is eligible for membership, and how a person becomes a member,
(b) about the appointment of one or more persons who are to be charity trustees of the CIO, and about any conditions of eligibility for appointment, and
(c) containing directions about the application of property of the CIO on its dissolution.

(3) A CIO's constitution shall also provide for such other matters, and comply with such requirements, as are specified in regulations made by the Minister.

(4) A CIO's constitution—

(a) shall be in English if its principal office is in England,
(b) may be in English or in Welsh if its principal office is in Wales.

(5) A CIO's constitution shall be in the form specified in regulations made by the Commission, or as near to that form as the circumstances admit.

(6) Subject to anything in a CIO's constitution: a charity trustee of the CIO may, but need not, be a member of it; a member of the CIO may, but need not, be one of its charity trustees; and those who are members of the CIO and those who are its charity trustees may, but need not, be identical.]

NOTES

Amendment

Inserted by the Charities Act 2006, s 34, Sch 7, Pt 1, para 1.

Date in force (for remaining purposes): to be appointed: see the Charities Act 2006, s 79(2).

[69C Name and status]

[(1) The name of a CIO shall appear in legible characters—

(a) in all business letters of the CIO,
(b) in all its notices and other official publications,
(c) in all bills of exchange, promissory notes, endorsements, cheques and orders for money or goods purporting to be signed on behalf of the CIO,
(d) in all conveyances purporting to be executed by the CIO, and
(e) in all bills rendered by it and in all its invoices, receipts, and letters of credit.

(2) In subsection (1)(d), 'conveyance' means any instrument creating, transferring, varying or extinguishing an interest in land.

(3) Subsection (5) applies if the name of a CIO does not include—

(a) 'charitable incorporated organisation', or
(b) 'CIO', with or without full stops after each letter, or
(c) a Welsh equivalent mentioned in subsection (4) (but this option applies only if the CIO's constitution is in Welsh),

and it is irrelevant, in any such case, whether or not capital letters are used.

(4) The Welsh equivalents referred to in subsection (3)(c) are—

(a) 'sefydliad elusennol corfforedig', or
(b) 'SEC', with or without full stops after each letter.

(5) If this subsection applies, the fact that a CIO is a CIO shall be stated in legible characters in all the documents mentioned in subsection (1).

(6) The statement required by subsection (5) shall be in English, except that in the case of a document which is otherwise wholly in Welsh, the statement may be in Welsh.]

NOTES

Amendment

Inserted by the Charities Act 2006, s 34, Sch 7, Pt 1, para 1.

Date in force: to be appointed: see the Charities Act 2006, s 79(2).

[69D Offences connected with name and status]

[(1) A charity trustee of a CIO or a person on the CIO's behalf who issues or authorises the issue of any document referred to in paragraph (a), (b), (d) or (e) of section 69C(1) above which fails to comply with the requirements of section 69C(1), (5) or (6) is liable on summary conviction to a fine not exceeding level 3 on the standard scale.

(2) A charity trustee of a CIO or a person on the CIO's behalf who signs or authorises to be signed on behalf of the CIO any document referred to in paragraph (c) of section 69C(1) above which fails to comply with the requirements of section 69C(1), (5) or (6)—

(a) is liable on summary conviction to a fine not exceeding level 3 on the standard scale, and
(b) is personally liable to the holder of the bill of exchange (etc) for the amount of it, unless it is duly paid by the CIO.

(3) A person who holds any body out as being a CIO when it is not (however he does this) is guilty of an offence and is liable on summary conviction to a fine not exceeding level 3 on the standard scale.

(4) It is a defence for a person charged with an offence under subsection (3) to prove that he believed on reasonable grounds that the body was a CIO.]

NOTES

Amendment

Inserted by the Charities Act 2006, s 34, Sch 7, Pt 1, para 1.

Date in force: to be appointed: see the Charities Act 2006, s 79(2).

[Registration]

NOTES

Amendment

Inserted by the Charities Act 2006, s 34, Sch 7, Pt 1, para 1.

Date in force (for remaining purposes): to be appointed: see the Charities Act 2006, s 79(2).

[69E Application for registration]

[(1) Any one or more persons ('the applicants') may apply to the Commission for a CIO to be constituted and for its registration as a charity.

(2) The applicants shall supply the Commission with—

(a) a copy of the proposed constitution of the CIO,
(b) such other documents or information as may be prescribed by regulations made by the Minister, and
(c) such other documents or information as the Commission may require for the purposes of the application.

(3) The Commission shall refuse such an application if—

(a) it is not satisfied that the CIO would be a charity at the time it would be registered, or
(b) the CIO's proposed constitution does not comply with one or more of the requirements of section 69B above and any regulations made under that section.

(4) The Commission may refuse such an application if—

(a) the proposed name of the CIO is the same as, or is in the opinion of the Commission too like, the name of any other charity (whether registered or not), or
(b) the Commission is of the opinion referred to in any of paragraphs (b) to (e) of section 6(2) above (power of Commission to require change in charity's name) in relation to the proposed name of the CIO (reading paragraph (b) as referring to the proposed purposes of the CIO and to the activities which it is proposed it should carry on).]

NOTES

Amendment

Inserted by the Charities Act 2006, s 34, Sch 7, Pt 1, para 1.

Date in force (for remaining purposes): to be appointed: see the Charities Act 2006, s 79(2).

[69F Effect of registration]

[(1) If the Commission grants an application under section 69E above it shall register the CIO to which the application relates as a charity in the register of charities.

(2) Upon the registration of the CIO in the register of charities, it becomes by virtue of the registration a body corporate—

(a) whose constitution is that proposed in the application,
(b) whose name is that specified in the constitution, and
(c) whose first member is, or first members are, the applicants referred to in section 69E above.

(3) All property for the time being vested in the applicants (or, if more than one, any of them) on trust for the charitable purposes of the CIO (when incorporated) shall by virtue of this subsection become vested in the CIO upon its registration.

(4) The entry relating to the charity's registration in the register of charities shall include—

(a) the date of the charity's registration, and
(b) a note saying that it is constituted as a CIO.

(5) A copy of the entry in the register shall be sent to the charity at the principal office of the CIO.]

NOTES

Amendment

Inserted by the Charities Act 2006, s 34, Sch 7, Pt 1, para 1.

Date in force: to be appointed: see the Charities Act 2006, s 79(2).

[Conversion, amalgamation and transfer]

NOTES

Amendment

Inserted by the Charities Act 2006, s 34, Sch 7, Pt 1, para 1.

Date in force (for remaining purposes): to be appointed: see the Charities Act 2006, s 79(2).

[69G Conversion of charitable company or registered industrial and provident society]

[(1) The following may apply to the Commission to be converted into a CIO, and for the CIO's registration as a charity, in accordance with this section—

(a) a charitable company,
(b) a charity which is a registered society within the meaning of the Industrial and Provident Societies Act 1965.

(2) But such an application may not be made by—

(a) a company or registered society having a share capital if any of the shares are not fully paid up, or
(b) an exempt charity.

(3) Such an application is referred to in this section and sections 69H and 69I below as an 'application for conversion'.

(4) The Commission shall notify the following of any application for conversion—

(a) the appropriate registrar, and
(b) such other persons (if any) as the Commission thinks appropriate in the particular case.

(5) The company or registered society shall supply the Commission with—

(a) a copy of a resolution of the company or registered society that it be converted into a CIO,
(b) a copy of the proposed constitution of the CIO,
(c) a copy of a resolution of the company or registered society adopting the proposed constitution of the CIO,
(d) such other documents or information as may be prescribed by regulations made by the Minister, and
(e) such other documents or information as the Commission may require for the purposes of the application.

(6) The resolution referred to in subsection (5)(a) shall be—

(a) a special resolution of the company or registered society, or
(b) a unanimous written resolution signed by or on behalf of all the members of the company or registered society who would be entitled to vote on a special resolution.

(7) In the case of a registered society, 'special resolution' has the meaning given in section 52(3) of the Industrial and Provident Societies Act 1965.

(8) In the case of a company limited by guarantee which makes an application for conversion (whether or not it also has a share capital), the proposed constitution of the CIO shall (unless subsection (10) applies) provide for the CIO's members to be liable to contribute to its assets if it is wound up, and for the amount up to which they are so liable.

(9) That amount shall not be less than the amount up to which they were liable to contribute to the assets of the company if it was wound up.

(10) If the amount each member of the company is liable to contribute to its assets on its winding up is £10 or less, the guarantee shall be extinguished on the conversion of the company into a CIO, and the requirements of subsections (8) and (9) do not apply.

(11) In subsection (4), and in sections 69H and 69I below, 'the appropriate registrar' means—

(a) in the case of an application for conversion by a charitable company, the registrar of companies,
(b) in the case of an application for conversion by a registered society, the Financial Services Authority.

(12) In this section, 'charitable company' means a company which is a charity.]

NOTES

Amendment

Inserted by the Charities Act 2006, s 34, Sch 7, Pt 1, para 1.

Date in force (for remaining purposes): to be appointed: see the Charities Act 2006, s 79(2).

[69H Conversion: consideration of application]

[(1) The Commission shall consult those to whom it has given notice of an application for conversion under section 69G(4) above about whether the application should be granted.

(2) The Commission shall refuse an application for conversion if—

(a) it is not satisfied that the CIO would be a charity at the time it would be registered,
(b) the CIO's proposed constitution does not comply with one or more of the requirements of section 69B above and any regulations made under that section, or
(c) in the case of an application for conversion made by a company limited by guarantee, the CIO's proposed constitution does not comply with the requirements of subsections (8) and (9) of section 69G above.

(3) The Commission may refuse an application for conversion if—

(a) the proposed name of the CIO is the same as, or is in the opinion of the Commission too like, the name of any other charity (whether registered or not),
(b) the Commission is of the opinion referred to in any of paragraphs (b) to (e) of section 6(2) above (power of Commission to require change in charity's name) in relation to the proposed name of the CIO (reading paragraph (b) as referring to the proposed purposes of the CIO and to the activities which it is proposed it should carry on), or
(c) having considered any representations received from those whom it has consulted under subsection (1), the Commission considers (having regard to any regulations made under subsection (4)) that it would not be appropriate to grant the application.

(4) The Minister may make provision in regulations about circumstances in which it would not be appropriate to grant an application for conversion.

(5) If the Commission refuses an application for conversion, it shall so notify the appropriate registrar (see section 69G(11) above).]

NOTES

Amendment

Inserted by the Charities Act 2006, s 34, Sch 7, Pt 1, para 1.

Date in force (for remaining purposes): to be appointed: see the Charities Act 2006, s 79(2).

[69I Conversion: supplementary]

[(1) If the Commission grants an application for conversion, it shall—

(a) register the CIO to which the application related in the register of charities, and
(b) send to the appropriate registrar (see section 69G(11) above) a copy of each of the resolutions of the converting company or registered society referred to in section 69G(5)(a) and (c) above, and a copy of the entry in the register relating to the CIO.

(2) The registration of the CIO in the register shall be provisional only until the appropriate registrar cancels the registration of the company or registered society as required by subsection (3)(b).

(3) The appropriate registrar shall—

(a) register the documents sent to him under subsection (1)(b), and
(b) cancel the registration of the company in the register of companies, or of the society in the register of friendly societies,

and shall notify the Commission that he has done so.

(4) When the appropriate registrar cancels the registration of the company or of the registered society, the company or registered society is thereupon converted into a CIO, being a body corporate—

(a) whose constitution is that proposed in the application for conversion,
(b) whose name is that specified in the constitution, and
(c) whose first members are the members of the converting company or society immediately before the moment of conversion.

(5) If the converting company or registered society had a share capital, upon the conversion of the company or registered society all the shares shall by virtue of this subsection be cancelled, and no former holder of any cancelled share shall have any right in respect of it after its cancellation.

(6) Subsection (5) does not affect any right which accrued in respect of a share before its cancellation.

(7) The entry relating to the charity's registration in the register shall include—

(a) a note that it is constituted as a CIO,
(b) the date on which it became so constituted, and
(c) a note of the name of the company or society which was converted into the CIO,

but the matters mentioned in paragraphs (a) and (b) are to be included only when the appropriate registrar has notified the Commission as required by subsection (3).

(8) A copy of the entry in the register shall be sent to the charity at the principal office of the CIO.

(9) The conversion of a charitable company or of a registered society into a CIO does not affect, in particular, any liability to which the company or registered society was subject by virtue of its being a charitable company or registered society.]

NOTES

Amendment

Inserted by the Charities Act 2006, s 34, Sch 7, Pt 1, para 1.

Date in force: to be appointed: see the Charities Act 2006, s 79(2).

[69J Conversion of community interest company]

[(1) The Minister may by regulations make provision for the conversion of a community interest company into a CIO, and for the CIO's registration as a charity.

(2) The regulations may, in particular, apply, or apply with modifications specified in the regulations, or disapply, anything in sections 53 to 55 of the Companies (Audit, Investigations and Community Enterprise) Act 2004 or in sections 69G to 69I above.]

NOTES

Amendment

Inserted by the Charities Act 2006, s 34, Sch 7, Pt 1, para 1.

Date in force (for remaining purposes): to be appointed: see the Charities Act 2006, s 79(2).

[69K Amalgamation of CIOs]

[(1) Any two or more CIOs ('the old CIOs') may, in accordance with this section, apply to the Commission to be amalgamated, and for the incorporation and registration as a charity of a new CIO ('the new CIO') as their successor.

(2) Such an application is referred to in this section and section 69L below as an 'application for amalgamation'.

(3) Subsections (2) to (4) of section 69E above apply in relation to an application for amalgamation as they apply to an application for a CIO to be constituted, but in those subsections—

(a) 'the applicants' shall be construed as meaning the old CIOs, and
(b) references to the CIO are to the new CIO.

(4) In addition to the documents and information referred to in section 69E(2) above, the old CIOs shall supply the Commission with—

(a) a copy of a resolution of each of the old CIOs approving the proposed amalgamation, and
(b) a copy of a resolution of each of the old CIOs adopting the proposed constitution of the new CIO.

(5) The resolutions referred to in subsection (4) must have been passed—

(a) by a 75% majority of those voting at a general meeting of the CIO (including those voting by proxy or by post, if voting that way is permitted), or
(b) unanimously by the CIO's members, otherwise than at a general meeting.

(6) The date of passing of such a resolution is—

(a) the date of the general meeting at which it was passed, or
(b) if it was passed otherwise than at a general meeting, the date on which provision in the CIO's constitution or in regulations made under paragraph 13 of Schedule 5B to this Act deems it to have been passed (but that date may not be earlier than that on which the last member agreed to it).

(7) Each old CIO shall—

(a) give notice of the proposed amalgamation in the way (or ways) that in the opinion of its charity trustees will make it most likely to come to the attention of those who would be affected by the amalgamation, and
(b) send a copy of the notice to the Commission.

(8) The notice shall invite any person who considers that he would be affected by the proposed amalgamation to make written representations to the Commission not later than a date determined by the Commission and specified in the notice.

(9) In addition to being required to refuse it on one of the grounds mentioned in section 69E(3) above as applied by subsection (3) of this section, the Commission shall refuse an application for amalgamation if it considers that there is a serious risk that the new CIO would be unable properly to pursue its purposes.

(10) The Commission may refuse an application for amalgamation if it is not satisfied that the provision in the constitution of the new CIO about the matters mentioned in subsection (11) is the same, or substantially the same, as the provision about those matters in the constitutions of each of the old CIOs.

(11) The matters are—

(a) the purposes of the CIO,
(b) the application of property of the CIO on its dissolution, and
(c) authorisation for any benefit to be obtained by charity trustees or members of the CIO or persons connected with them.

(12) For the purposes of subsection (11)(c)—

(a) 'benefit' means a direct or indirect benefit of any nature, except that it does not include any remuneration (within the meaning of section 73A below) whose receipt may be authorised under that section, and
(b) the same rules apply for determining whether a person is connected with a charity trustee or member of the CIO as apply, in accordance with section 73B(5) and (6) below, for determining whether a person is connected with a charity trustee for the purposes of section 73A.]

NOTES

Amendment

Inserted by the Charities Act 2006, s 34, Sch 7, Pt 1, para 1.

Date in force: to be appointed: see the Charities Act 2006, s 79(2).

[69L Amalgamation: supplementary]

[(1) If the Commission grants an application for amalgamation, it shall register the new CIO in the register of charities.

(2) Upon the registration of the new CIO it thereupon becomes by virtue of the registration a body corporate—

(a) whose constitution is that proposed in the application for amalgamation,
(b) whose name is that specified in the constitution, and
(c) whose first members are the members of the old CIOs immediately before the new CIO was registered.

(3) Upon the registration of the new CIO—

(a) all the property, rights and liabilities of each of the old CIOs shall become by virtue of this subsection the property, rights and liabilities of the new CIO, and
(b) each of the old CIOs shall be dissolved.

(4) Any gift which—

(a) is expressed as a gift to one of the old CIOs, and
(b) takes effect on or after the date of registration of the new CIO,

takes effect as a gift to the new CIO.

(5) The entry relating to the registration in the register of the charity constituted as the new CIO shall include—

(a) a note that it is constituted as a CIO,
(b) the date of the charity's registration, and
(c) a note that the CIO was formed following amalgamation, and of the name of each of the old CIOs.

(6) A copy of the entry in the register shall be sent to the charity at the principal office of the new CIO.]

NOTES

Amendment

Inserted by the Charities Act 2006, s 34, Sch 7, Pt 1, para 1.

Date in force: to be appointed: see the Charities Act 2006, s 79(2).

[69M Transfer of CIO's undertaking]

[(1) A CIO may resolve that all its property, rights and liabilities should be transferred to another CIO specified in the resolution.

(2) Where a CIO has passed such a resolution, it shall send to the Commission—

(a) a copy of the resolution, and
(b) a copy of a resolution of the transferee CIO agreeing to the transfer to it.

(3) Subsections (5) and (6) of section 69K above apply to the resolutions referred to in subsections (1) and (2)(b) as they apply to the resolutions referred to in section 69K(4).

(4) Having received the copy resolutions referred to in subsection (2), the Commission—

(a) may direct the transferor CIO to give public notice of its resolution in such manner as is specified in the direction, and
(b) if it gives such a direction, must take into account any representations made to it by persons appearing to it to be interested in the transferor CIO, where those representations are made to it within the period of 28 days beginning with the date when public notice of the resolution is given by the transferor CIO.

(5) The resolution shall not take effect until confirmed by the Commission.

(6) The Commission shall refuse to confirm the resolution if it considers that there is a serious risk that the transferee CIO would be unable properly to pursue the purposes of the transferor CIO.

(7) The Commission may refuse to confirm the resolution if it is not satisfied that the provision in the constitution of the transferee CIO about the matters mentioned in section 69K(11) above is the same, or substantially the same, as the provision about those matters in the constitution of the transferor CIO.

(8) If the Commission does not notify the transferor CIO within the relevant period that it is either confirming or refusing to confirm the resolution, the resolution is to be treated as confirmed by the Commission on the day after the end of that period.

(9) Subject to subsection (10), 'the relevant period' means—

(a) in a case where the Commission directs the transferor CIO under subsection (4) to give public notice of its resolution, the period of six months beginning with the date when that notice is given, or
(b) in any other case, the period of six months beginning with the date when both of the copy resolutions referred to in subsection (2) have been received by the Commission.

(10) The Commission may at any time within the period of six months mentioned in subsection (9)(a) or (b) give the transferor CIO a notice extending the relevant period by such period (not exceeding six months) as is specified in the notice.

(11) A notice under subsection (10) must set out the Commission's reasons for the extension.

(12) If the resolution is confirmed (or treated as confirmed) by the Commission—

(a) all the property, rights and liabilities of the transferor CIO shall become by virtue of this subsection the property, rights and liabilities of the transferee CIO in accordance with the resolution, and
(b) the transferor CIO shall be dissolved.

(13) Any gift which—

(a) is expressed as a gift to the transferor CIO, and
(b) takes effect on or after the date on which the resolution is confirmed (or treated as confirmed),

takes effect as a gift to the transferee CIO.]

NOTES

Amendment

Inserted by the Charities Act 2006, s 34, Sch 7, Pt 1, para 1.

Date in force: to be appointed: see the Charities Act 2006, s 79(2).

[Winding up, insolvency and dissolution]

NOTES

Amendment

Inserted by the Charities Act 2006, s 34, Sch 7, Pt 1, para 1.

Date in force (for remaining purposes): to be appointed: see the Charities Act 2006, s 79(2).

[69N Regulations about winding up, insolvency and dissolution]

[(1) The Minister may by regulations make provision about—

(a) the winding up of CIOs,
(b) their insolvency,
(c) their dissolution, and
(d) their revival and restoration to the register following dissolution.

(2) The regulations may, in particular, make provision—

(a) about the transfer on the dissolution of a CIO of its property and rights (including property and rights held on trust for the CIO) to the official custodian or another person or body,
(b) requiring any person in whose name any stocks, funds or securities are standing in trust for a CIO to transfer them into the name of the official custodian or another person or body,
(c) about the disclaiming, by the official custodian or other transferee of a CIO's property, of title to any of that property,
(d) about the application of a CIO's property cy-près,
(e) about circumstances in which charity trustees may be personally liable for contributions to the assets of a CIO or for its debts,
(f) about the reversal on a CIO's revival of anything done on its dissolution.

(3) The regulations may—

(a) apply any enactment which would not otherwise apply, either without modification or with modifications specified in the regulations,
(b) disapply, or modify (in ways specified in the regulations) the application of, any enactment which would otherwise apply.

(4) In subsection (3), 'enactment' includes a provision of subordinate legislation within the meaning of the Interpretation Act 1978.]

NOTES

Amendment

Inserted by the Charities Act 2006, s 34, Sch 7, Pt 1, para 1.

Date in force (for remaining purposes): to be appointed: see the Charities Act 2006, s 79(2).

[Miscellaneous]

NOTES

Amendment

Inserted by the Charities Act 2006, s 34, Sch 7, Pt 1, para 1.

Date in force (for remaining purposes): to be appointed: see the Charities Act 2006, s 79(2).

[69O Power to transfer all property of unincorporated charity to one or more CIOs]

[Section 74 below (power to transfer all property of unincorporated charity) applies with the omission of paragraph (a) of subsection (1) in relation to a resolution by the charity trustees of a charity to transfer all its property to a CIO or to divide its property between two or more CIOs.]

NOTES

Amendment

Inserted by the Charities Act 2006, s 34, Sch 7, Pt 1, para 1.

Date in force: to be appointed: see the Charities Act 2006, s 79(2).

[69P Further provision about CIOs]

[The provisions of Schedule 5B to this Act shall have effect with respect to CIOs.]

NOTES

Amendment

Inserted by the Charities Act 2006, s 34, Sch 7, Pt 1, para 1.

Date in force: to be appointed: see the Charities Act 2006, s 79(2).

[69Q Regulations]

[(1) The Minister may by regulations make further provision about applications for registration of CIOs, the administration of CIOs, the conversion of charitable companies, registered societies and community interest companies into CIOs, the amalgamation of CIOs, and in relation to CIOs generally.

(2) The regulations may, in particular, make provision about—

(a) the execution of deeds and documents,
(b) the electronic communication of messages or documents relevant to a CIO or to any dealing with the Commission in relation to one,
(c) the maintenance of registers of members and of charity trustees,
(d) the maintenance of other registers (for example, a register of charges over the CIO's assets).

(3) The regulations may, in relation to charities constituted as CIOs—

(a) disapply any of sections 3 to 4 above,
(b) modify the application of any of those sections in ways specified in the regulations.

(4) Subsections (3) and (4) of section 69N above apply for the purposes of this section as they apply for the purposes of that.]

NOTES

Amendment

Inserted by the Charities Act 2006, s 34, Sch 7, Pt 1, para 1.

Date in force (for remaining purposes): to be appointed: see the Charities Act 2006, s 79(2).

Part IX
Miscellaneous

...

NOTES

Amendment

Repealed by virtue of the Trustee Act 2000, s 40(1), (3), Sch 2, Pt I, para 2, Sch 4, Pt I and by the Charities and Trustee Investment (Scotland) Act 2005, s 95, Sch 3, para 9.

Date in force (in relation to England and Wales): 1 February 2001: see SI 2001/49, art 2.

Date in force (in relation to Scotland): 1 January 2006: see SSI 2005/644, art 2(1), Schedule.

70 ...

...

NOTES

Amendment

Repealed by virtue of the Trustee Act 2000, s 40(1), (3), Sch 2, Pt I, para 2, Sch 4, Pt I and by the Charities and Trustee Investment (Scotland) Act 2005, s 95, Sch 3, para 9.

Date in force (in relation to England and Wales): 1 February 2001: see SI 2001/49, art 2.

Date in force (in relation to Scotland): 1 January 2006: see SSI 2005/644, art 2(1), Schedule.

71 ...

...

NOTES

Amendment

Repealed by virtue of the Trustee Act 2000, s 40(1), (3), Sch 2, Pt I, para 2, Sch 4, Pt I and by the Charities and Trustee Investment (Scotland) Act 2005, s 95, Sch 3, para 9.

Date in force (in relation to England and Wales): 1 February 2001: see SI 2001/49, art 2.

Date in force (in relation to Scotland): 1 January 2006: see SSI 2005/644, art 2(1), Schedule.

Disqualification for acting as charity trustee [Charity trustees]

NOTES

Amendment

Substituted by the Charities Act 2006, s 75(1), Sch 8, paras 96, 155.

Date in force: to be appointed: see the Charities Act 2006, s 79(2).

72 Persons disqualified for being trustees of a charity

(1) Subject to the following provisions of this section, a person shall be disqualified for being a charity trustee or trustee for a charity if—

(a) he has been convicted of any offence involving dishonesty or deception;
(b) he has been adjudged bankrupt or sequestration of his estate has been awarded and (in either case) he has not been discharged [or he is the subject of a bankruptcy restrictions order or an interim order];
(c) he has made a composition or arrangement with, or granted a trust deed for, his creditors and has not been discharged in respect of it;
(d) he has been removed from the office of charity trustee or trustee for a charity by an order made—
  (i) by the [Commission or] Commissioners under section 18(2)(i) above, or
  (ii) by the Commissioners under section 20(1A)(i) of the Charities Act 1960 (power to act for protection of charities) or under section 20(1)(i) of that Act (as in force before the commencement of section 8 of the Charities Act 1992), or
  (iii) by the High Court,
  on the grounds of any misconduct or mismanagement in the administration of the charity for which he was responsible or to which he was privy, or which he by his conduct contributed to or facilitated;
(e) he has been removed, under section 7 of the Law Reform (Miscellaneous Provisions) (Scotland) Act 1990 (powers of Court of Session to deal with management of charities) [or section 34(5)(e) of the Charities and Trustee Investment (Scotland) Act 2005 (powers of the Court of Session)], from being concerned in the management or control of any body;
(f) he is subject to a disqualification order [or disqualification undertaking] under the Company Directors Disqualification Act 1986 [to a disqualification order under Part II of the Companies (Northern Ireland) Order 1989] [or disqualification undertaking under the Company Directors Disqualification (Northern Ireland) Order 2002] or to an order made under section 429(2)(b) of the Insolvency Act 1986 (failure to pay under county court administration order).

(2) In subsection (1) above—

(a) paragraph (a) applies whether the conviction occurred before or after the commencement of that subsection, but does not apply in relation to any conviction which is a spent conviction for the purposes of the Rehabilitation of Offenders Act 1974;
(b) paragraph (b) applies whether the adjudication of bankruptcy or the sequestration [or the making of a bankruptcy restrictions order or an interim order] occurred before or after the commencement of that subsection;
(c) paragraph (c) applies whether the composition or arrangement was made, or the trust deed was granted, before or after the commencement of that subsection; and
(d) paragraphs (d) to (f) apply in relation to orders made and removals effected before or after the commencement of that subsection.

(3) Where (apart from this subsection) a person is disqualified under subsection (1)(b) above for being a charity trustee or trustee for any charity which is a company, he shall not be so disqualified if leave has been granted under section 11 of the Company Directors Disqualification Act 1986 (undischarged bankrupts) for him to act as director of the charity; and similarly a person shall not be disqualified under subsection (1)(f) above for being a charity trustee or trustee for such a charity if—

[(a) in the case of a person subject to a disqualification order or disqualification undertaking under the Company Directors Disqualification Act 1986, leave for the purposes of section 1(1)(a) or 1A(1)(a) of that Act has been granted for him to act as director of the charity,
(aa) in the case of a person subject to a disqualification order under Part II of the Companies (Northern Ireland) Order 1989 [or disqualification undertaking under the Company Directors Disqualification (Northern Ireland) Order 2002], leave has been granted by the High Court in Northern Ireland for him to act as director of the charity]

(b) in the case of a person subject to an order under section 429(2)(b) of the Insolvency Act 1986, leave has been granted by the court which made the order for him to so act.

(4) *The Commissioners* [The Commission] may, on the application of any person disqualified under subsection (1) above, waive his disqualification either generally or in relation to a particular charity or a particular class of charities; but no such waiver may be granted in relation to any charity which is a company if—

(a) the person concerned is for the time being prohibited, by virtue of—
  (i) a disqualification order [or disqualification undertaking] under the Company Directors Disqualification Act 1986, or
  (ii) section 11(1)[, 12(2)[, 12A or 12B]] of that Act (undischarged bankrupts; failure to pay under county court administration order[; Northern Irish disqualification orders][; Northern Irish disqualification undertakings]),

  from acting as director of the charity; and
(b) leave has not been granted for him to act as director of any other company.

[(4A) If—

(a) a person disqualified under subsection (1)(d) or (e) makes an application under subsection (4) above five years or more after the date on which his disqualification took effect, and
(b) the Commission is not prevented from granting the application by virtue of paragraphs (a) and (b) of subsection (4),

the Commission must grant the application unless satisfied that, by reason of any special circumstances, it should be refused.]

(5) Any waiver under subsection (4) above shall be notified in writing to the person concerned.

(6) For the purposes of this section *the Commissioners* [the Commission] shall keep, in such manner as *they think fit* [it thinks fit], a register of all persons who have been removed from office as mentioned in subsection (1)(d) above either—

(a) by an order of [the Commission or] the Commissioners made before or after the commencement of subsection (1) above, or
(b) by an order of the High Court made after the commencement of section 45(1) of the Charities Act 1992;

and, where any person is so removed from office by an order of the High Court, the court shall notify *the Commissioners* [the Commission] of his removal.

(7) The entries in the register kept under subsection (6) above shall be available for public inspection in legible form at all reasonable times.

[(8) In this section 'the Commissioners' means the Charity Commissioners for England and Wales.]

NOTES

Derivation

This section derived from the Charities Act 1992, s 45(1)–(4), (6)–(8).

Initial Commencement

Specified date: 1 August 1993: see s 99(1).

Extent

This section does not extend to Scotland.

Amendment

Sub-s (1): in para (b) words 'or he is the subject of a bankruptcy restrictions order or an interim order' in square brackets inserted by SI 2006/1722, art 2(2), Sch 2, Pt 1, para 4(a).

Date in force: 29 June 2006: see SI 2006/1722, art 1(1).

Sub-s (1): in para (d)(i) words 'Commission or' in square brackets inserted by the Charities Act 2006, s 75(1), Sch 8, paras 96, 156(1), (2).

Date in force: to be appointed: see the Charities Act 2006, s 79(2).

Sub-s (1): in para (e) words 'or section 34(5)(e) of the Charities and Trustee Investment (Scotland) Act 2005 (powers of the Court of Session)' in square brackets inserted by SI 2006/242, art 5, Schedule, Pt 1, para 6(1), (2).

Date in force: 1 April 2006: see SI 2006/242, art 1(3).

Sub-s (1): in para (f) words 'or disqualification undertaking' in square brackets inserted by the Insolvency Act 2000, s 8, Sch 4, Pt II, para 18(a).

Date in force: 2 April 2001: see SI 2001/766, art 2(1)(a).

Sub-s (1): in para (f) words 'to a disqualification order under Part II of the Companies (Northern Ireland) Order 1989' in square brackets inserted by the Insolvency Act 2000, s 8, Sch 4, Pt II, para 18(a).

Date in force: 2 April 2001: see SI 2001/766, art 2(1)(a).

Sub-s (1): in para (f) words 'or disqualification undertaking under the Company Directors Disqualification (Northern Ireland) Order 2002' in square brackets inserted by SI 2004/1941, art 3, Schedule, para 5(a).

Date in force: 1 September 2004 (in relation to disqualification undertakings under the Company Directors Disqualification (Northern Ireland) Order 2002, SI 2002/3150 (NI 4) accepted on or after that date): see SI 2004/1941, art 1(2).

Sub-s (2): in para (b) words 'or the making of a bankruptcy restrictions order or an interim order' in square brackets inserted by SI 2006/1722, art 2(2), Sch 2, Pt 1, para 4(b).

Date in force: 29 June 2006: see SI 2006/1722, art 1(1).

Sub-s (3): paras (a), (aa) substituted, for para (a) as originally enacted, by the Insolvency Act 2000, s 8, Sch 4, Pt II, para 18(b).

Date in force: 2 April 2001: see SI 2001/766, art 2(1)(a).

Sub-s (3): in para (aa) words 'or disqualification undertaking under the Company Directors Disqualification (Northern Ireland) Order 2002' in square brackets inserted by SI 2004/1941, art 3, Schedule, para 5(b).

Date in force: 1 September 2004 (in relation to disqualification undertakings under the Company Directors Disqualification (Northern Ireland) Order 2002, SI 2002/3150 (NI 4) accepted on or after that date): see SI 2004/1941, art 1(2).

Sub-s (4): words 'The Commissioners' in italics repealed and subsequent words in square brackets substituted by the Charities Act 2006, s 75(1), Sch 8, paras 96, 156(1), (3).

Date in force: to be appointed: see the Charities Act 2006, s 79(2).

Sub-s (4): in para (a)(i) words 'or disqualification undertaking' in square brackets inserted by the Insolvency Act 2000, s 8, Sch 4, Pt II, para 18(c)(i).

Date in force: 2 April 2001: see SI 2001/766, art 2(1)(a).

Sub-s (4): in para (a)(ii) words in square brackets beginning with the reference to ', 12(2)' substituted by the Insolvency Act 2000, s 8, Sch 4, Pt II, para 18(c)(ii).

Date in force: 2 April 2001: see SI 2001/766, art 2(1)(a).

Sub-s (4): in para (a)(ii) words ', 12A or 12B' in square brackets substituted by SI 2004/1941, art 3, Schedule, para 5(c).

Date in force: 1 September 2004 (in relation to disqualification undertakings under the Company Directors Disqualification (Northern Ireland) Order 2002, SI 2002/3150 (NI 4) accepted on or after that date): see SI 2004/1941, art 1(2).

Sub-s (4): in para (a)(ii) words '; Northern Irish disqualification orders' in square brackets inserted by the Insolvency Act 2000, s 8, Sch 4, Pt II, para 18(c)(ii).

Date in force: 2 April 2001: see SI 2001/766, art 2(1)(a).

Sub-s (4): in para (a)(ii) words '; Northern Irish disqualification undertakings' in square brackets inserted by SI 2004/1941, art 3, Schedule, para 5(c).

Date in force: 1 September 2004 (in relation to disqualification undertakings under the Company Directors Disqualification (Northern Ireland) Order 2002, SI 2002/3150 (NI 4) accepted on or after that date): see SI 2004/1941, art 1(2).

Sub-s (4A): inserted by the Charities Act 2006, s 35.

Sub-s (6): words 'the Commissioners' in italics repealed and subsequent words in square brackets substituted by the Charities Act 2006, s 75(1), Sch 8, paras 96, 156(1), (4)(a).

Date in force: to be appointed: see the Charities Act 2006, s 79(2).

Sub-s (6): words 'they think fit' in italics repealed and subsequent words in square brackets substituted by the Charities Act 2006, s 75(1), Sch 8, paras 96, 156(1), (4)(b).

Date in force: to be appointed: see the Charities Act 2006, s 79(2).

Sub-s (6): in para (a) words 'the Commission or' in square brackets inserted by the Charities Act 2006, s 75(1), Sch 8, paras 96, 156(1), (4)(c).

Date in force: to be appointed: see the Charities Act 2006, s 79(2).

Sub-s (6): words 'the Commissioners' in italics repealed and subsequent words in square brackets substituted by the Charities Act 2006, s 75(1), Sch 8, paras 96, 156(1), (4)(d).

Date in force: to be appointed: see the Charities Act 2006, s 79(2).

Sub-s (8): inserted by the Charities Act 2006, s 75(1), Sch 8, paras 96, 156(1), (5).

Date in force: to be appointed: see the Charities Act 2006, s 79(2).

73 Persons acting as charity trustee while disqualified

(1) Subject to subsection (2) below, any person who acts as a charity trustee or trustee for a charity while he is disqualified for being such a trustee by virtue of section 72 above shall be guilty of an offence and liable—

(a) on summary conviction, to imprisonment for a term not exceeding six months or to a fine not exceeding the statutory maximum, or both;
(b) on conviction on indictment, to imprisonment for a term not exceeding two years or to a fine, or both.

(2) Subsection (1) above shall not apply where—

(a) the charity concerned is a company; and
(b) the disqualified person is disqualified by virtue only of paragraph (b) or (f) of section 72(1) above.

(3) Any acts done as charity trustee or trustee for a charity by a person disqualified for being such a trustee by virtue of section 72 above shall not be invalid by reason only of that disqualification.

(4) Where *the Commissioners are* [the Commission is] satisfied—

(a) that any person has acted as charity trustee or trustee for a charity *(other than an exempt charity)* while disqualified for being such a trustee by virtue of section 72 above, and
(b) that, while so acting, he has received from the charity any sums by way of remuneration or expenses, or any benefit in kind, in connection with his acting as charity trustee or trustee for the charity,

they may by order [the Commission may by order] direct him to repay to the charity the whole or part of any such sums, or (as the case may be) to pay to the charity the whole or part of the monetary value *(as determined by them)* [(as determined by the Commission)] of any such benefit.

(5) Subsection (4) above does not apply to any sums received by way of remuneration or expenses in respect of any time when the person concerned was not disqualified for being a charity trustee or trustee for the charity.

NOTES

Derivation

This section derived from the Charities Act 1992, s 46.

Initial Commencement

Specified date: 1 August 1993: see s 99(1).

Extent

This section does not extend to Scotland.

Amendment

Sub-s (4): words 'the Commissioners are' in italics repealed and subsequent words in square brackets substituted by the Charities Act 2006, s 75(1), Sch 8, paras 96, 157(a).

Date in force: to be appointed: see the Charities Act 2006, s 79(2).

Sub-s (4): in para (a) words '(other than an exempt charity)' in italics repealed by the Charities Act 2006, ss 12, 75(2), Sch 5, para 9, Sch 9.

Date in force: to be appointed: see the Charities Act 2006, s 79(2).

Sub-s (4): words 'they may by order' in italics repealed and subsequent words in square brackets substituted by the Charities Act 2006, s 75(1), Sch 8, paras 96, 157(b).

Date in force: to be appointed: see the Charities Act 2006, s 79(2).

Sub-s (4): words '(as determined by them)' in italics repealed and subsequent words in square brackets substituted by the Charities Act 2006, s 75(1), Sch 8, paras 96, 157(c).

Date in force: to be appointed: see the Charities Act 2006, s 79(2).

[73A Remuneration of trustees etc providing services to charity]

[(1) This section applies to remuneration for services provided by a person to or on behalf of a charity where—

(a) he is a charity trustee or trustee for the charity, or
(b) he is connected with a charity trustee or trustee for the charity and the remuneration might result in that trustee obtaining any benefit.

This is subject to subsection (7) below.

(2) If conditions A to D are met in relation to remuneration within subsection (1), the person providing the services ('the relevant person') is entitled to receive the remuneration out of the funds of the charity.

(3) Condition A is that the amount or maximum amount of the remuneration—

(a) is set out in an agreement in writing between—
  (i) the charity or its charity trustees (as the case may be), and
  (ii) the relevant person,
  under which the relevant person is to provide the services in question to or on behalf of the charity, and
(b) does not exceed what is reasonable in the circumstances for the provision by that person of the services in question.

(4) Condition B is that, before entering into that agreement, the charity trustees decided that they were satisfied that it would be in the best interests of the charity for the services to be provided by the relevant person to or on behalf of the charity for the amount or maximum amount of remuneration set out in the agreement.

(5) Condition C is that if immediately after the agreement is entered into there is, in the case of the charity, more than one person who is a charity trustee and is—

(a) a person in respect of whom an agreement within subsection (3) above is in force, or
(b) a person who is entitled to receive remuneration out of the funds of the charity otherwise than by virtue of such an agreement, or
(c) a person connected with a person falling within paragraph (a) or (b) above,

the total number of them constitute a minority of the persons for the time being holding office as charity trustees of the charity.

(6) Condition D is that the trusts of the charity do not contain any express provision that prohibits the relevant person from receiving the remuneration.

(7) Nothing in this section applies to—

(a) any remuneration for services provided by a person in his capacity as a charity trustee or trustee for a charity or under a contract of employment, or
(b) any remuneration not within paragraph (a) which a person is entitled to receive out of the funds of a charity by virtue of any provision or order within subsection (8).

(8) The provisions or orders within this subsection are—

(a) any provision contained in the trusts of the charity,
(b) any order of the court or the Commission,
(c) any statutory provision contained in or having effect under an Act of Parliament other than this section.

(9) Section 73B below applies for the purposes of this section.]

NOTES

Amendment

Inserted by the Charities Act 2006, s 36; for transitional provisions and savings see s 75(3), Sch 10, para 12 thereto.

Date in force: to be appointed: see the Charities Act 2006, s 79(2).

[73B Supplementary provisions for purposes of section 73A]

[(1) Before entering into an agreement within section 73A(3) the charity trustees must have regard to any guidance given by the Commission concerning the making of such agreements.

(2) The duty of care in section 1(1) of the Trustee Act 2000 applies to a charity trustee when making such a decision as is mentioned in section 73A(4).

(3) For the purposes of section 73A(5) an agreement within section 73A(3) is in force so long as any obligations under the agreement have not been fully discharged by a party to it.

(4) In section 73A—

'benefit' means a direct or indirect benefit of any nature;
'maximum amount', in relation to remuneration, means the maximum amount of the remuneration whether specified in or ascertainable under the terms of the agreement in question;
'remuneration' includes any benefit in kind (and 'amount' accordingly includes monetary value);
'services', in the context of remuneration for services, includes goods that are supplied in connection with the provision of services.

(5) For the purposes of section 73A the following persons are 'connected' with a charity trustee or trustee for a charity—

(a) a child, parent, grandchild, grandparent, brother or sister of the trustee;
(b) the spouse or civil partner of the trustee or of any person falling within paragraph (a);
(c) a person carrying on business in partnership with the trustee or with any person falling within paragraph (a) or (b);
(d) an institution which is controlled—
  (i) by the trustee or by any person falling within paragraph (a), (b) or (c), or
  (ii) by two or more persons falling within sub-paragraph (i), when taken together;
(e) a body corporate in which—
  (i) the trustee or any connected person falling within any of paragraphs (a) to (c) has a substantial interest, or
  (ii) two or more persons falling within sub-paragraph (i), when taken together, have a substantial interest.

(6) Paragraphs 2 to 4 of Schedule 5 to this Act apply for the purposes of subsection (5) above as they apply for the purposes of provisions of that Schedule.]

NOTES

Amendment

Inserted by the Charities Act 2006, s 36; for transitional provisions and savings see s 75(3), Sch 10, para 12 thereto.

Date in force: to be appointed: see the Charities Act 2006, s 79(2).

[73C Disqualification of trustee receiving remuneration under section 73A]

[(1) This section applies to any charity trustee or trustee for a charity—

(a) who is or would be entitled to remuneration under an agreement or proposed agreement within section 73A(3) above, or
(b) who is connected with a person who is or would be so entitled.

(2) The charity trustee or trustee for a charity is disqualified from acting as such in relation to any decision or other matter connected with the agreement.

(3) But any act done by such a person which he is disqualified from doing by virtue of subsection (2) above shall not be invalid by reason only of that disqualification.

(4) Where the Commission is satisfied—

(a) that a person ('the disqualified trustee') has done any act which he was disqualified from doing by virtue of subsection (2) above, and

(b) that the disqualified trustee or a person connected with him has received or is to receive from the charity any remuneration under the agreement in question,

it may make an order under subsection (5) or (6) below (as appropriate).

(5) An order under this subsection is one requiring the disqualified trustee—

(a) to reimburse to the charity the whole or part of the remuneration received as mentioned in subsection (4)(b) above;
(b) to the extent that the remuneration consists of a benefit in kind, to reimburse to the charity the whole or part of the monetary value (as determined by the Commission) of the benefit in kind.

(6) An order under this subsection is one directing that the disqualified trustee or (as the case may be) connected person is not to be paid the whole or part of the remuneration mentioned in subsection (4)(b) above.

(7) If the Commission makes an order under subsection (5) or (6) above, the disqualified trustee or (as the case may be) connected person accordingly ceases to have any entitlement under the agreement to so much of the remuneration (or its monetary value) as the order requires him to reimburse to the charity or (as the case may be) as it directs is not to be paid to him.

(8) Subsections (4) to (6) of section 73B above apply for the purposes of this section as they apply for the purposes of section 73A above.]

NOTES

Amendment

Inserted by the Charities Act 2006, s 37.

Date in force: to be appointed: see the Charities Act 2006, s 79(2).

[73D Power to relieve trustees, auditors etc from liability for breach of trust or duty]

[(1) This section applies to a person who is or has been—

(a) a charity trustee or trustee for a charity,
(b) a person appointed to audit a charity's accounts (whether appointed under an enactment or otherwise), or
(c) an independent examiner, reporting accountant or other person appointed to examine or report on a charity's accounts (whether appointed under an enactment or otherwise).

(2) If the Commission considers—

(a) that a person to whom this section applies is or may be personally liable for a breach of trust or breach of duty committed in his capacity as a person within paragraph (a), (b) or (c) of subsection (1) above, but
(b) that he has acted honestly and reasonably and ought fairly to be excused for the breach of trust or duty,

the Commission may make an order relieving him wholly or partly from any such liability.

(3) An order under subsection (2) above may grant the relief on such terms as the Commission thinks fit.

(4) Subsection (2) does not apply in relation to any personal contractual liability of a charity trustee or trustee for a charity.

(5) For the purposes of this section and section 73E below—

(a) subsection (1)(b) above is to be read as including a reference to the Auditor General for Wales acting as auditor under section 43B above, and
(b) subsection (1)(c) above is to be read as including a reference to the Auditor General for Wales acting as examiner under that section;

and in subsection (1)(b) and (c) any reference to a charity's accounts is to be read as including any group accounts prepared by the charity trustees of a charity.

(6) This section does not affect the operation of—

(a) section 61 of the Trustee Act 1925 (power of court to grant relief to trustees),
(b) section 727 of the Companies Act 1985 (power of court to grant relief to officers or auditors of companies), or
(c) section 73E below (which extends section 727 to auditors etc of charities which are not companies).]

NOTES

Amendment

Inserted by the Charities Act 2006, s 38; for transitional provisions and savings see s 75(3), Sch 10, para 13 thereto.

Date in force (for remaining purposes): to be appointed: see the Charities Act 2006, s 79(2).

[73E Court's power to grant relief to apply to all auditors etc of charities which are not companies]

[(1) Section 727 of the Companies Act 1985 (power of court to grant relief to officers or auditors of companies) shall have effect in relation to a person to whom this section applies as it has effect in relation to a person employed as an auditor by a company.

(2) This section applies to—

(a) a person acting in a capacity within section 73D(1)(b) or (c) above in a case where, apart from this section, section 727 would not apply in relation to him as a person so acting, and
(b) a charity trustee of a CIO.]

NOTES

Amendment

Inserted by the Charities Act 2006, s 38; for transitional provisions and savings see s 75(3), Sch 10, para 13 thereto.

Date in force (for remaining purposes): to be appointed: see the Charities Act 2006, s 79(2).

[73F Trustees' indemnity insurance]

[(1) The charity trustees of a charity may arrange for the purchase, out of the funds of the charity, of insurance designed to indemnify the charity trustees or any trustees for the charity against any personal liability in respect of—

(a) any breach of trust or breach of duty committed by them in their capacity as charity trustees or trustees for the charity, or
(b) any negligence, default, breach of duty or breach of trust committed by them in their capacity as directors or officers of the charity (if it is a body corporate) or of any body corporate carrying on any activities on behalf of the charity.

(2) The terms of such insurance must, however, be so framed as to exclude the provision of any indemnity for a person in respect of—

(a) any liability incurred by him to pay—

(i) a fine imposed in criminal proceedings, or
(ii) a sum payable to a regulatory authority by way of a penalty in respect of non-compliance with any requirement of a regulatory nature (however arising);

(b) any liability incurred by him in defending any criminal proceedings in which he is convicted of an offence arising out of any fraud or dishonesty, or wilful or reckless misconduct, by him; or

(c) any liability incurred by him to the charity that arises out of any conduct which he knew (or must reasonably be assumed to have known) was not in the interests of the charity or in the case of which he did not care whether it was in the best interests of the charity or not.

(3) For the purposes of subsection (2)(b) above—

(a) the reference to any such conviction is a reference to one that has become final;
(b) a conviction becomes final—
(i) if not appealed against, at the end of the period for bringing an appeal, or
(ii) if appealed against, at the time when the appeal (or any further appeal) is disposed of; and
(c) an appeal is disposed of—
(i) if it is determined and the period for bringing any further appeal has ended, or
(ii) if it is abandoned or otherwise ceases to have effect.

(4) The charity trustees of a charity may not purchase insurance under this section unless they decide that they are satisfied that it is in the best interests of the charity for them to do so.

(5) The duty of care in section 1(1) of the Trustee Act 2000 applies to a charity trustee when making such a decision.

(6) The Minister may by order make such amendments of subsections (2) and (3) above as he considers appropriate.

(7) No order may be made under subsection (6) above unless a draft of the order has been laid before and approved by a resolution of each House of Parliament.

(8) This section—

(a) does not authorise the purchase of any insurance whose purchase is expressly prohibited by the trusts of the charity, but
(b) has effect despite any provision prohibiting the charity trustees or trustees for the charity receiving any personal benefit out of the funds of the charity.]

NOTES

Amendment

Inserted by the Charities Act 2006, s 39.

Small charities [Miscellaneous powers of charities]

NOTES

Amendment

Substituted by the Charities Act 2006, s 75(1), Sch 8, paras 96, 158.

Date in force: to be appointed: see the Charities Act 2006, s 79(2).

74 Power to transfer all property, modify objects etc [74 Power to transfer all property of unincorporated charity]

(1) This section applies to a charity if—

(a) its gross income in its last financial year did not exceed £5,000, and

(b) *it does not hold any land on trusts which stipulate that the land is to be used for the purposes, or any particular purposes, of the charity,*

and it is neither an exempt charity nor a charitable company.

(2) Subject to the following provisions of this section, the charity trustees of a charity to which this section applies may resolve for the purposes of this section—

(a) *that all the property of the charity should be transferred to such other charity as is specified in the resolution, being either a registered charity or a charity which is not required to be registered;*
(b) *that all the property of the charity should be divided, in such manner as is specified in the resolution, between such two or more other charities as are so specified, being in each case either a registered charity or a charity which is not required to be registered;*
(c) *that the trusts of the charity should be modified by replacing all or any of the purposes of the charity with such other purposes, being in law charitable, as are specified in the resolution;*
(d) *that any provision of the trusts of the charity—*
  (i) *relating to any of the powers exercisable by the charity trustees in the administration of the charity, or*
  (ii) *regulating the procedure to be followed in any respect in connection with its administration,*
  should be modified in such manner as is specified in the resolution.

(3) Any resolution passed under subsection (2) above must be passed by a majority of not less than two-thirds of such charity trustees as vote on the resolution.

(4) The charity trustees of a charity to which this section applies ('the transferor charity') shall not have power to pass a resolution under subsection (2)(a) or (b) above unless they are satisfied—

(a) *that the existing purposes of the transferor charity have ceased to be conducive to a suitable and effective application of the charity's resources; and*
(b) *that the purposes of the charity or charities specified in the resolution are as similar in character to the purposes of the transferor charity as is reasonably practicable;*

and before passing the resolution they must have received from the charity trustees of the charity, or (as the case may be) of each of the charities, specified in the resolution written confirmation that those trustees are willing to accept a transfer of property under this section.

(5) The charity trustees of any such charity shall not have power to pass a resolution under subsection (2)(c) above unless they are satisfied—

(a) *that the existing purposes of the charity (or, as the case may be, such of them as it is proposed to replace) have ceased to be conducive to a suitable and effective application of the charity's resources; and*
(b) *that the purposes specified in the resolution are as similar in character to those existing purposes as is practical in the circumstances.*

(6) Where charity trustees have passed a resolution under subsection (2) above, they shall—

(a) *give public notice of the resolution in such manner as they think reasonable in the circumstances; and*
(b) *send a copy of the resolution to the Commissioners, together with a statement of their reasons for passing it.*

(7) The Commissioners may, when considering the resolution, require the charity trustees to provide additional information or explanation—

(a) *as to the circumstances in and by reference to which they have determined to act under this section, or*
(b) *relating to their compliance with this section in connection with the resolution;*

and the Commissioners shall take into account any representations made to them by persons appearing to them to be interested in the charity where those representations are made within the period of six weeks beginning with the date when the Commissioners receive a copy of the resolution by virtue of subsection (6)(b) above.

(8) Where the Commissioners have so received a copy of a resolution from any charity trustees and it appears to them that the trustees have complied with this section in connection with the resolution, the Commissioners shall, within the period of three months beginning with the date when they receive the copy of the resolution, notify the trustees in writing either—

(a) that the Commissioners concur with the resolution; or
(b) that they do not concur with it.

(9) Where the Commissioners so notify their concurrence with the resolution, then—

(a) if the resolution was passed under subsection (2)(a) or (b) above, the charity trustees shall arrange for all the property of the transferor charity to be transferred in accordance with the resolution and on terms that any property so transferred—
  (i) shall be held and applied by the charity to which it is transferred ('the transferee charity') for the purposes of that charity, but
  (ii) shall, as property of the transferee charity, nevertheless be subject to any restrictions on expenditure to which it is subject as property of the transferor charity,

  and those trustees shall arrange for it to be so transferred by such date as may be specified in the notification; and
(b) if the resolution was passed under subsection (2)(c) or (d) above, the trusts of the charity shall be deemed, as from such date as may be specified in the notification, to have been modified in accordance with the terms of the resolution.

(10) For the purpose of enabling any property to be transferred to a charity under this section, the Commissioners shall have power, at the request of the charity trustees of that charity, to make orders vesting any property of the transferor charity—

(a) in the charity trustees of the first-mentioned charity or in any trustee for that charity, or
(b) in any other person nominated by those charity trustees to hold the property in trust for that charity.

(11) The [Minister] may by order amend subsection (1) above by substituting a different sum for the sum for the time being specified there.

(12) In this section—

(a) 'charitable company' means a charity which is a company or other body corporate; and
(b) references to the transfer of property to a charity are references to its transfer—
  (i) to the charity trustees, or
  (ii) to any trustee for the charity, or
  (iii) to a person nominated by the charity trustees to hold it in trust for the charity,

  as the charity trustees may determine.

[(1) This section applies to a charity if—

(a) its gross income in its last financial year did not exceed £10,000,
(b) it does not hold any designated land, and
(c) it is not a company or other body corporate.

'Designated land' means land held on trusts which stipulate that it is to be used for the purposes, or any particular purposes, of the charity.

(2) The charity trustees of such a charity may resolve for the purposes of this section—

(a) that all the property of the charity should be transferred to another charity specified in the resolution, or

(b) that all the property of the charity should be transferred to two or more charities specified in the resolution in accordance with such division of the property between them as is so specified.

(3) Any charity so specified may be either a registered charity or a charity which is not required to be registered.

(4) But the charity trustees of a charity ('the transferor charity') do not have power to pass a resolution under subsection (2) above unless they are satisfied—

(a) that it is expedient in the interests of furthering the purposes for which the property is held by the transferor charity for the property to be transferred in accordance with the resolution, and

(b) that the purposes (or any of the purposes) of any charity to which property is to be transferred under the resolution are substantially similar to the purposes (or any of the purposes) of the transferor charity.

(5) Any resolution under subsection (2) above must be passed by a majority of not less than two-thirds of the charity trustees who vote on the resolution.

(6) Where charity trustees have passed a resolution under subsection (2), they must send a copy of it to the Commission, together with a statement of their reasons for passing it.

(7) Having received the copy of the resolution, the Commission—

(a) may direct the charity trustees to give public notice of the resolution in such manner as is specified in the direction, and

(b) if it gives such a direction, must take into account any representations made to it by persons appearing to it to be interested in the charity, where those representations are made to it within the period of 28 days beginning with the date when public notice of the resolution is given by the charity trustees.

(8) The Commission may also direct the charity trustees to provide the Commission with additional information or explanations relating to—

(a) the circumstances in and by reference to which they have decided to act under this section, or

(b) their compliance with any obligation imposed on them by or under this section in connection with the resolution.

(9) Subject to the provisions of section 74A below, a resolution under subsection (2) above takes effect at the end of the period of 60 days beginning with the date on which the copy of it was received by the Commission.

(10) Where such a resolution has taken effect, the charity trustees must arrange for all the property of the transferor charity to be transferred in accordance with the resolution, and on terms that any property so transferred—

(a) is to be held by the charity to which it is transferred ('the transferee charity') in accordance with subsection (11) below, but

(b) when so held is nevertheless to be subject to any restrictions on expenditure to which it was subject as property of the transferor charity;

and the charity trustees must arrange for the property to be so transferred by such date after the resolution takes effect as they agree with the charity trustees of the transferee charity or charities concerned.

(11) The charity trustees of any charity to which property is transferred under this section must secure, so far as is reasonably practicable, that the property is applied for such of its purposes as are substantially similar to those of the transferor charity.

But this requirement does not apply if those charity trustees consider that complying with it would not result in a suitable and effective method of applying the property.

(12) For the purpose of enabling any property to be transferred to a charity under this section, the Commission may, at the request of the charity trustees of that charity, make orders vesting any property of the transferor charity—

(a) in the transferee charity, in its charity trustees or in any trustee for that charity, or
(b) in any other person nominated by those charity trustees to hold property in trust for that charity.

(13) The Minister may by order amend subsection (1) above by substituting a different sum for the sum for the time being specified there.

(14) In this section references to the transfer of property to a charity are references to its transfer—

(a) to the charity, or
(b) to the charity trustees, or
(c) to any trustee for the charity, or
(d) to a person nominated by the charity trustees to hold it in trust for the charity,

as the charity trustees may determine.

(15) Where a charity has a permanent endowment, this section has effect in accordance with section 74B.]

NOTES

Derivation

This section derived from the Charities Act 1992, s 43.

Initial Commencement

Specified date: 1 August 1993: see s 99(1).

Extent

This section does not extend to Scotland.

Amendment

Substituted, together with ss 74A, 74B for this section as originally enacted, by the Charities Act 2006, s 40.

Date in force: to be appointed: see the Charities Act 2006, s 79(2).

Sub-s (11): word 'Minister' in square brackets substituted by SI 2006/2951, art 6, Schedule, para 4(v).

Date in force: 13 December 2006: see SI 2006/2951, art 1(2).

[74A Resolution not to take effect or to take effect at later date]

[(1) This section deals with circumstances in which a resolution under section 74(2) above either—

(a) does not take effect under section 74(9) above, or
(b) takes effect at a time later than that mentioned in section 74(9).

(2) A resolution does not take effect under section 74(9) above if before the end of—

(a) the period of 60 days mentioned in section 74(9) ('the 60-day period'), or
(b) that period as modified by subsection (3) or (4) below,

the Commission notifies the charity trustees in writing that it objects to the resolution, either on procedural grounds or on the merits of the proposals contained in the resolution.

'On procedural grounds' means on the grounds that any obligation imposed on the charity trustees by or under section 74 above has not been complied with in connection with the resolution.

(3) If under section 74(7) above the Commission directs the charity trustees to give public notice of a resolution, the running of the 60-day period is suspended by virtue of this subsection—

(a) as from the date on which the direction is given to the charity trustees, and
(b) until the end of the period of 42 days beginning with the date on which public notice of the resolution is given by the charity trustees.

(4) If under section 74(8) above the Commission directs the charity trustees to provide any information or explanations, the running of the 60-day period is suspended by virtue of this subsection—

(a) as from the date on which the direction is given to the charity trustees, and
(b) until the date on which the information or explanations is or are provided to the Commission.

(5) Subsection (6) below applies once the period of time, or the total period of time, during which the 60-day period is suspended by virtue of either or both of subsections (3) and (4) above exceeds 120 days.

(6) At that point the resolution (if not previously objected to by the Commission) is to be treated as if it had never been passed.]

NOTES

Amendment

Substituted, together with ss 74, 74B for s 74 as originally enacted, by the Charities Act 2006, s 40.

Date in force: to be appointed: see the Charities Act 2006, s 79(2).

[74B Transfer where charity has permanent endowment]

[(1) This section provides for the operation of section 74 above where a charity within section 74(1) has a permanent endowment (whether or not the charity's trusts contain provision for the termination of the charity).

(2) In such a case section 74 applies as follows—

(a) if the charity has both a permanent endowment and other property ('unrestricted property')—
   (i) a resolution under section 74(2) must relate to both its permanent endowment and its unrestricted property, and
   (ii) that section applies in relation to its unrestricted property in accordance with subsection (3) below and in relation to its permanent endowment in accordance with subsections (4) to (11) below;
(b) if all of the property of the charity is comprised in its permanent endowment, that section applies in relation to its permanent endowment in accordance with subsections (4) to (11) below.

(3) Section 74 applies in relation to unrestricted property of the charity as if references in that section to all or any of the property of the charity were references to all or any of its unrestricted property.

(4) Section 74 applies in relation to the permanent endowment of the charity with the following modifications.

(5) References in that section to all or any of the property of the charity are references to all or any of the property comprised in its permanent endowment.

(6) If the property comprised in its permanent endowment is to be transferred to a single charity, the charity trustees must (instead of being satisfied as mentioned in section 74(4)(b)) be satisfied that the proposed transferee charity has purposes which are substantially similar to all of the purposes of the transferor charity.

(7) If the property comprised in its permanent endowment is to be transferred to two or more charities, the charity trustees must (instead of being satisfied as mentioned in section 74(4)(b)) be satisfied—

(a) that the proposed transferee charities, taken together, have purposes which are substantially similar to all of the purposes of the transferor charity, and
(b) that each of the proposed transferee charities has purposes which are substantially similar to one or more of the purposes of the transferor charity.

(8) In the case of a transfer to which subsection (7) above applies, the resolution under section 74(2) must provide for the property comprised in the permanent endowment of the charity to be divided between the transferee charities in such a way as to take account of such guidance as may be given by the Commission for the purposes of this section.

(9) The requirement in section 74(11) shall apply in the case of every such transfer, and in complying with that requirement the charity trustees of a transferee charity must secure that the application of property transferred to the charity takes account of any such guidance.

(10) Any guidance given by the Commission for the purposes of this section may take such form and be given in such manner as the Commission considers appropriate.

(11) For the purposes of sections 74 and 74A above, any reference to any obligation imposed on the charity trustees by or under section 74 includes a reference to any obligation imposed on them by virtue of any of subsections (6) to (8) above.

(12) Section 74(14) applies for the purposes of this section as it applies for the purposes of section 74.]

NOTES

Amendment

Substituted, together with ss 74, 74A for s 74 as originally enacted, by the Charities Act 2006, s 40.

Date in force: to be appointed: see the Charities Act 2006, s 79(2).

[74C Power to replace purposes of unincorporated charity]

[(1) This section applies to a charity if—

(a) its gross income in its last financial year did not exceed £10,000,
(b) it does not hold any designated land, and
(c) it is not a company or other body corporate.

'Designated land' means land held on trusts which stipulate that it is to be used for the purposes, or any particular purposes, of the charity.

(2) The charity trustees of such a charity may resolve for the purposes of this section that the trusts of the charity should be modified by replacing all or any of the purposes of the charity with other purposes specified in the resolution.

(3) The other purposes so specified must be charitable purposes.

(4) But the charity trustees of a charity do not have power to pass a resolution under subsection (2) above unless they are satisfied—

(a) that it is expedient in the interests of the charity for the purposes in question to be replaced, and

(b) that, so far as is reasonably practicable, the new purposes consist of or include purposes that are similar in character to those that are to be replaced.

(5) Any resolution under subsection (2) above must be passed by a majority of not less than two-thirds of the charity trustees who vote on the resolution.

(6) Where charity trustees have passed a resolution under subsection (2), they must send a copy of it to the Commission, together with a statement of their reasons for passing it.

(7) Having received the copy of the resolution, the Commission—

(a) may direct the charity trustees to give public notice of the resolution in such manner as is specified in the direction, and
(b) if it gives such a direction, must take into account any representations made to it by persons appearing to it to be interested in the charity, where those representations are made to it within the period of 28 days beginning with the date when public notice of the resolution is given by the charity trustees.

(8) The Commission may also direct the charity trustees to provide the Commission with additional information or explanations relating to—

(a) the circumstances in and by reference to which they have decided to act under this section, or
(b) their compliance with any obligation imposed on them by or under this section in connection with the resolution.

(9) Subject to the provisions of section 74A above (as they apply in accordance with subsection (10) below), a resolution under subsection (2) above takes effect at the end of the period of 60 days beginning with the date on which the copy of it was received by the Commission.

(10) Section 74A above applies to a resolution under subsection (2) of this section as it applies to a resolution under subsection (2) of section 74 above, except that any reference to section 74(7), (8) or (9) is to be read as a reference to subsection (7), (8) or (9) above.

(11) As from the time when a resolution takes effect under subsection (9) above, the trusts of the charity concerned are to be taken to have been modified in accordance with the terms of the resolution.

(12) The Minister may by order amend subsection (1) above by substituting a different sum for the sum for the time being specified there.]

NOTES

Amendment

Inserted by the Charities Act 2006, s 41.

Date in force: to be appointed: see the Charities Act 2006, s 79(2).

[74D Power to modify powers or procedures of unincorporated charity]

[(1) This section applies to any charity which is not a company or other body corporate.

(2) The charity trustees of such a charity may resolve for the purposes of this section that any provision of the trusts of the charity—

(a) relating to any of the powers exercisable by the charity trustees in the administration of the charity, or
(b) regulating the procedure to be followed in any respect in connection with its administration,

should be modified in such manner as is specified in the resolution.

(3) Subsection (4) applies if the charity is an unincorporated association with a body of members distinct from the charity trustees.

(4) Any resolution of the charity trustees under subsection (2) must be approved by a further resolution which is passed at a general meeting of the body either—

(a) by a majority of not less than two-thirds of the members entitled to attend and vote at the meeting who vote on the resolution, or
(b) by a decision taken without a vote and without any expression of dissent in response to the question put to the meeting.

(5) Where—

(a) the charity trustees have passed a resolution under subsection (2), and
(b) (if subsection (4) applies) a further resolution has been passed under that subsection,

the trusts of the charity are to be taken to have been modified in accordance with the terms of the resolution.

(6) The trusts are to be taken to have been so modified as from such date as is specified for this purpose in the resolution under subsection (2), or (if later) the date when any such further resolution was passed under subsection (4).]

NOTES

Amendment

Inserted by the Charities Act 2006, s 42.

75 Power to spend capital [75 Power of unincorporated charities to spend capital: general]

(1) This section applies to a charity if—

(a) it has a permanent endowment which does not consist of or comprise any land, and
(b) its gross income in its last financial year did not exceed £1,000,

and it is neither an exempt charity nor a charitable company.

(2) Where the charity trustees of a charity to which this section applies are of the opinion that the property of the charity is too small, in relation to its purposes, for any useful purpose to be achieved by the expenditure of income alone, they may resolve for the purposes of this section that the charity ought to be freed from the restrictions with respect to expenditure of capital to which its permanent endowment is subject.

(3) Any resolution passed under subsection (2) above must be passed by a majority of not less than two-thirds of such charity trustees as vote on the resolution.

(4) Before passing such a resolution the charity trustees must consider whether any reasonable possibility exists of effecting a transfer or division of all the charity's property under section 74 above (disregarding any such transfer or division as would, in their opinion, impose on the charity an unacceptable burden of costs).

(5) Where charity trustees have passed a resolution under subsection (2) above, they shall—

(a) give public notice of the resolution in such manner as they think reasonable in the circumstances; and
(b) send a copy of the resolution to the Commissioners, together with a statement of their reasons for passing it.

(6) The Commissioners may, when considering the resolution, require the charity trustees to provide additional information or explanation—

(a) as to the circumstances in and by reference to which they have determined to act under this section, or

(b) relating to their compliance with this section in connection with the resolution;

and the Commissioners shall take into account any representations made to them by persons appearing to them to be interested in the charity where those representations are made within the period of six weeks beginning with the date when the Commissioners receive a copy of the resolution by virtue of subsection (5)(b) above.

(7) Where the Commissioners have so received a copy of a resolution from any charity trustees and it appears to them that the trustees have complied with this section in connection with the resolution, the Commissioners shall, within the period of three months beginning with the date when they receive the copy of the resolution, notify the trustees in writing either—

(a) that the Commissioners concur with the resolution; or
(b) that they do not concur with it.

(8) Where the Commissioners so notify their concurrence with the resolution, the charity trustees shall have, as from such date as may be specified in the notification, power by virtue of this section to expend any property of the charity without regard to any such restrictions as are mentioned in subsection (2) above.

(9) The [Minister] may by order amend subsection (1) above by substituting a different sum for the sum for the time being specified there.

(10) In this section 'charitable company' means a charity which is a company or other body corporate.

[(1) This section applies to any available endowment fund of a charity which is not a company or other body corporate.

(2) But this section does not apply to a fund if section 75A below (power of larger charities to spend capital given for particular purpose) applies to it.

(3) Where the condition in subsection (4) below is met in relation to the charity, the charity trustees may resolve for the purposes of this section that the fund, or a portion of it, ought to be freed from the restrictions with respect to expenditure of capital that apply to it.

(4) The condition in this subsection is that the charity trustees are satisfied that the purposes set out in the trusts to which the fund is subject could be carried out more effectively if the capital of the fund, or the relevant portion of the capital, could be expended as well as income accruing to it, rather than just such income.

(5) Once the charity trustees have passed a resolution under subsection (3) above, the fund or portion may by virtue of this section be expended in carrying out the purposes set out in the trusts to which the fund is subject without regard to the restrictions mentioned in that subsection.

(6) The fund or portion may be so expended as from such date as is specified for this purpose in the resolution.

(7) In this section 'available endowment fund', in relation to a charity, means—

(a) the whole of the charity's permanent endowment if it is all subject to the same trusts, or

(b) any part of its permanent endowment which is subject to any particular trusts that are different from those to which any other part is subject.]

NOTES

Derivation

This section derived from the Charities Act 1992, s 44.

Initial Commencement

Specified date: 1 August 1993: see s 99(1).

Extent

This section does not extend to Scotland.

Amendment

Substituted, together with ss 75A, 75B for this section as originally enacted, by the Charities Act 2006, s 43.

Date in force: to be appointed: see the Charities Act 2006, s 79(2).

Sub-s (9): word 'Minister' in square brackets substituted by SI 2006/2951, art 6, Schedule, para 4(w).

Date in force: 13 December 2006: see SI 2006/2951, art 1(2).

[75A Power of larger unincorporated charities to spend capital given for particular purpose]

[(1) This section applies to any available endowment fund of a charity which is not a company or other body corporate if—

(a) the capital of the fund consists entirely of property given—
  (i) by a particular individual,
  (ii) by a particular institution (by way of grant or otherwise), or
  (iii) by two or more individuals or institutions in pursuit of a common purpose, and
(b) the financial condition in subsection (2) below is met.

(2) The financial condition in this subsection is met if—

(a) the relevant charity's gross income in its last financial year exceeded £1,000, and
(b) the market value of the endowment fund exceeds £10,000.

(3) Where the condition in subsection (4) below is met in relation to the charity, the charity trustees may resolve for the purposes of this section that the fund, or a portion of it, ought to be freed from the restrictions with respect to expenditure of capital that apply to it.

(4) The condition in this subsection is that the charity trustees are satisfied that the purposes set out in the trusts to which the fund is subject could be carried out more effectively if the capital of the fund, or the relevant portion of the capital, could be expended as well as income accruing to it, rather than just such income.

(5) The charity trustees—

(a) must send a copy of any resolution under subsection (3) above to the Commission, together with a statement of their reasons for passing it, and
(b) may not implement the resolution except in accordance with the following provisions of this section.

(6) Having received the copy of the resolution the Commission may—

(a) direct the charity trustees to give public notice of the resolution in such manner as is specified in the direction, and
(b) if it gives such a direction, must take into account any representations made to it by persons appearing to it to be interested in the charity, where those representations are made to it within the period of 28 days beginning with the date when public notice of the resolution is given by the charity trustees.

(7) The Commission may also direct the charity trustees to provide the Commission with additional information or explanations relating to—

(a) the circumstances in and by reference to which they have decided to act under this section, or
(b) their compliance with any obligation imposed on them by or under this section in connection with the resolution.

(8) When considering whether to concur with the resolution the Commission must take into account—

(a) any evidence available to it as to the wishes of the donor or donors mentioned in subsection (1)(a) above, and
(b) any changes in the circumstances relating to the charity since the making of the gift or gifts (including, in particular, its financial position, the needs of its beneficiaries, and the social, economic and legal environment in which it operates).

(9) The Commission must not concur with the resolution unless it is satisfied—

(a) that its implementation would accord with the spirit of the gift or gifts mentioned in subsection (1)(a) above (even though it would be inconsistent with the restrictions mentioned in subsection (3) above), and
(b) that the charity trustees have complied with the obligations imposed on them by or under this section in connection with the resolution.

(10) Before the end of the period of three months beginning with the relevant date, the Commission must notify the charity trustees in writing either—

(a) that the Commission concurs with the resolution, or
(b) that it does not concur with it.

(11) In subsection (10) 'the relevant date' means—

(a) in a case where the Commission directs the charity trustees under subsection (6) above to give public notice of the resolution, the date when that notice is given, and
(b) in any other case, the date on which the Commission receives the copy of the resolution in accordance with subsection (5) above.

(12) Where—

(a) the charity trustees are notified by the Commission that it concurs with the resolution, or
(b) the period of three months mentioned in subsection (10) above has elapsed without the Commission notifying them that it does not concur with the resolution,

the fund or portion may, by virtue of this section, be expended in carrying out the purposes set out in the trusts to which the fund is subject without regard to the restrictions mentioned in subsection (3).

(13) The Minister may by order amend subsection (2) above by substituting a different sum for any sum specified there.

(14) In this section—

(a) 'available endowment fund' has the same meaning as in section 75 above,
(b) 'market value', in relation to an endowment fund, means—
   (i) the market value of the fund as recorded in the accounts for the last financial year of the relevant charity, or
   (ii) if no such value was so recorded, the current market value of the fund as determined on a valuation carried out for the purpose, and
(c) the reference in subsection (1) to the giving of property by an individual includes his giving it under his will.]

NOTES

Amendment

Substituted, together with ss 75, 75B for s 75 as originally enacted, by the Charities Act 2006, s 43.

Date in force: to be appointed: see the Charities Act 2006, s 79(2).

[75B Power to spend capital subject to special trusts]

[(1) This section applies to any available endowment fund of a special trust which, as the result of a direction under section 96(5) below, is to be treated as a separate charity ('the relevant charity') for the purposes of this section.

(2) Where the condition in subsection (3) below is met in relation to the relevant charity, the charity trustees may resolve for the purposes of this section that the fund, or a portion of it, ought to be freed from the restrictions with respect to expenditure of capital that apply to it.

(3) The condition in this subsection is that the charity trustees are satisfied that the purposes set out in the trusts to which the fund is subject could be carried out more effectively if the capital of the fund, or the relevant portion of the capital, could be expended as well as income accruing to it, rather than just such income.

(4) Where the market value of the fund exceeds £10,000 and the capital of the fund consists entirely of property given—

(a) by a particular individual,
(b) by a particular institution (by way of grant or otherwise), or
(c) by two or more individuals or institutions in pursuit of a common purpose,

subsections (5) to (11) of section 75A above apply in relation to the resolution and that gift or gifts as they apply in relation to a resolution under section 75A(3) and the gift or gifts mentioned in section 75A(1)(a).

(5) Where—

(a) the charity trustees have passed a resolution under subsection (2) above, and
(b) (in a case where section 75A(5) to (11) above apply in accordance with subsection (4) above) either—
  (i) the charity trustees are notified by the Commission that it concurs with the resolution, or
  (ii) the period of three months mentioned in section 75A(10) has elapsed without the Commission notifying them that it does not concur with the resolution,

the fund or portion may, by virtue of this section, be expended in carrying out the purposes set out in the trusts to which the fund is subject without regard to the restrictions mentioned in subsection (2).

(6) The fund or portion may be so expended as from such date as is specified for this purpose in the resolution.

(7) The Minister may by order amend subsection (4) above by substituting a different sum for the sum specified there.

(8) In this section—

(a) 'available endowment fund' has the same meaning as in section 75 above,
(b) 'market value' has the same meaning as in section 75A above, and
(c) the reference in subsection (4) to the giving of property by an individual includes his giving it under his will.]

NOTES

Amendment

Substituted, together with ss 75, 75A for s 75 as originally enacted, by the Charities Act 2006, s 43.

Date in force: to be appointed: see the Charities Act 2006, s 79(2).

[Mergers]

NOTES

Amendment

Inserted by the Charities Act 2006, ss 44, 75(3), Sch 10, para 14.

Date in force: to be appointed: see the Charities Act 2006, s 79(2).

[75C Register of charity mergers]

[(1) The Commission shall establish and maintain a register of charity mergers.

(2) The register shall be kept by the Commission in such manner as it thinks fit.

(3) The register shall contain an entry in respect of every relevant charity merger which is notified to the Commission in accordance with subsections (6) to (9) and such procedures as it may determine.

(4) In this section 'relevant charity merger' means—

(a) a merger of two or more charities in connection with which one of them ('the transferee') has transferred to it all the property of the other or others, each of which (a 'transferor') ceases to exist, or is to cease to exist, on or after the transfer of its property to the transferee, or

(b) a merger of two or more charities ('transferors') in connection with which both or all of them cease to exist, or are to cease to exist, on or after the transfer of all of their property to a new charity ('the transferee').

(5) In the case of a merger involving the transfer of property of any charity which has both a permanent endowment and other property ('unrestricted property') and whose trusts do not contain provision for the termination of the charity, subsection (4)(a) or (b) applies in relation to any such charity as if—

(a) the reference to all of its property were a reference to all of its unrestricted property, and

(b) any reference to its ceasing to exist were omitted.

(6) A notification under subsection (3) above may be given in respect of a relevant charity merger at any time after—

(a) the transfer of property involved in the merger has taken place, or

(b) (if more than one transfer of property is so involved) the last of those transfers has taken place.

(7) If a vesting declaration is made in connection with a relevant charity merger, a notification under subsection (3) above must be given in respect of the merger once the transfer, or the last of the transfers, mentioned in subsection (6) above has taken place.

(8) A notification under subsection (3) is to be given by the charity trustees of the transferee and must—

(a) specify the transfer or transfers of property involved in the merger and the date or dates on which it or they took place;

(b) include a statement that appropriate arrangements have been made with respect to the discharge of any liabilities of the transferor charity or charities; and

(c) in the case of a notification required by subsection (7), set out the matters mentioned in subsection (9).

(9) The matters are—

(a) the fact that the vesting declaration in question has been made;

(b) the date when the declaration was made; and

(c) the date on which the vesting of title under the declaration took place by virtue of section 75E(2) below.

(10) In this section and section 75D—

(a) any reference to a transfer of property includes a transfer effected by a vesting declaration; and
(b) 'vesting declaration' means a declaration to which section 75E(2) below applies.

(11) Nothing in this section or section 75E or 75F applies in a case where section 69K (amalgamation of CIOs) or 69M (transfer of CIO's undertaking) applies.]

NOTES

Amendment

Inserted by the Charities Act 2006, s 44; for transitional provisions and savings see s 75(3), Sch 10, para 14 thereto.

Date in force: to be appointed: see the Charities Act 2006, s 79(2).

[75D Register of charity mergers: supplementary]

[(1) Subsection (2) applies to the entry to be made in the register in respect of a relevant charity merger, as required by section 75C(3) above.

(2) The entry must—

(a) specify the date when the transfer or transfers of property involved in the merger took place,
(b) if a vesting declaration was made in connection with the merger, set out the matters mentioned in section 75C(9) above, and
(c) contain such other particulars of the merger as the Commission thinks fit.

(3) The register shall be open to public inspection at all reasonable times.

(4) Where any information contained in the register is not in documentary form, subsection (3) above shall be construed as requiring the information to be available for public inspection in legible form at all reasonable times.

(5) In this section—

'the register' means the register of charity mergers;
'relevant charity merger' has the same meaning as in section 75C.]

NOTES

Amendment

Inserted by the Charities Act 2006, s 44.

Date in force: to be appointed: see the Charities Act 2006, s 79(2).

[75E Pre-merger vesting declarations]

[(1) Subsection (2) below applies to a declaration which—

(a) is made by deed for the purposes of this section by the charity trustees of the transferor,
(b) is made in connection with a relevant charity merger, and
(c) is to the effect that (subject to subsections (3) and (4)) all of the transferor's property is to vest in the transferee on such date as is specified in the declaration ('the specified date').

(2) The declaration operates on the specified date to vest the legal title to all of the transferor's property in the transferee, without the need for any further document transferring it.

This is subject to subsections (3) and (4).

(3) Subsection (2) does not apply to—

(a) any land held by the transferor as security for money subject to the trusts of the transferor (other than land held on trust for securing debentures or debenture stock);
(b) any land held by the transferor under a lease or agreement which contains any covenant (however described) against assignment of the transferor's interest without the consent of some other person, unless that consent has been obtained before the specified date; or
(c) any shares, stock, annuity or other property which is only transferable in books kept by a company or other body or in a manner directed by or under any enactment.

(4) In its application to registered land within the meaning of the Land Registration Act 2002, subsection (2) has effect subject to section 27 of that Act (dispositions required to be registered).

(5) In this section 'relevant charity merger' has the same meaning as in section 75C.

(6) In this section—

(a) any reference to the transferor, in relation to a relevant charity merger, is a reference to the transferor (or one of the transferors) within the meaning of section 75C above, and
(b) any reference to all of the transferor's property, where the transferor is a charity within section 75C(5), is a reference to all of the transferor's unrestricted property (within the meaning of that provision).

(7) In this section any reference to the transferee, in relation to a relevant charity merger, is a reference to—

(a) the transferee (within the meaning of section 75C above), if it is a company or other body corporate, and
(b) otherwise, to the charity trustees of the transferee (within the meaning of that section).]

NOTES

Amendment

Inserted by the Charities Act 2006, s 44.

Date in force: to be appointed: see the Charities Act 2006, s 79(2).

[75F Effect of registering charity merger on gifts to transferor]

[(1) This section applies where a relevant charity merger is registered in the register of charity mergers.

(2) Any gift which—

(a) is expressed as a gift to the transferor, and
(b) takes effect on or after the date of registration of the merger,

takes effect as a gift to the transferee, unless it is an excluded gift.

(3) A gift is an 'excluded gift' if—

(a) the transferor is a charity within section 75C(5), and
(b) the gift is intended to be held subject to the trusts on which the whole or part of the charity's permanent endowment is held.

(4) In this section—

'relevant charity merger' has the same meaning as in section 75C; and
'transferor' and 'transferee' have the same meanings as in section 75E.]

NOTES

Amendment

Inserted by the Charities Act 2006, s 44.

Date in force: to be appointed: see the Charities Act 2006, s 79(2).

Local charities

76 Local authority's index of local charities

(1) The council of a county [or county borough] or of a district or London borough and the Common Council of the City of London may maintain an index of local charities or of any class of local charities in the council's area, and may publish information contained in the index, or summaries or extracts taken from it.

(2) A council proposing to establish or maintaining under this section an index of local charities or of any class of local charities shall, on request, be supplied by *the Commissioners* [the Commission] free of charge with copies of such entries in the register of charities as are relevant to the index or with particulars of any changes in the entries of which copies have been supplied before; and *the Commissioners* [the Commission] may arrange that *they will* [it will] without further request supply a council with particulars of any such changes.

(3) An index maintained under this section shall be open to public inspection at all reasonable times.

(4) A council may employ any voluntary organisation as their agent for the purposes of this section, on such terms and within such limits (if any) or in such cases as they may agree; and for this purpose 'voluntary organisation' means any body of which the activities are carried on otherwise than for profit, not being a public or local authority.

(5) A joint board discharging any of a council's functions shall have the same powers under this section as the council as respects local charities in the council's area which are established for purposes similar or complementary to any services provided by the board.

NOTES

Derivation

Sub-ss (1), (4) derived from the Charities Act 1960, s 10(1), (4), as read with the London Government Act 1963, s 81(9)(b), and as amended by the Local Government Act 1972, ss 210(9), (10), 272(1), Sch 30; sub-ss (2), (3), (5) derived from the Charities Act 1960, s 10(2), (3), (5), as read with the London Government Act 1963, s 81(9)(b).

Initial Commencement

Specified date: 1 August 1993: see s 99(1).

Extent

This section does not extend to Scotland.

Amendment

Sub-s (1): words in square brackets inserted by the Local Government (Wales) Act 1994, s 66(6), Sch 16, para 101(1).

Sub-s (2): words 'the Commissioners' in italics in both places they occur repealed and subsequent words in square brackets substituted by the Charities Act 2006, s 75(1), Sch 8, paras 96, 159(a).

Date in force: to be appointed: see the Charities Act 2006, s 79(2).

Sub-s (2): words 'they will' in italics repealed and subsequent words in square brackets substituted by the Charities Act 2006, s 75(1), Sch 8, paras 96, 159(b).

Date in force: to be appointed: see the Charities Act 2006, s 79(2).

Modification

Modification: by virtue of the Environment Act 1995, s 70, Sch 9, para 15, this section has effect as if references to a council for any area included references to a National Park authority and as if the relevant Park were the authority's area.

77 Reviews of local charities by local authority

(1) The council of a county [or county borough] or of a district or London borough and the Common Council of the City of London may, subject to the following provisions of this section, initiate, and carry out in co-operation with the charity trustees, a review of the working of any group of local charities with the same or similar purposes in the council's area, and may make to *the Commissioners* [the Commission] such report on the review and such recommendations arising from it as the council after consultation with the trustees think fit.

(2) A council having power to initiate reviews under this section may co-operate with other persons in any review by them of the working of local charities in the council's area (with or without other charities), or may join with other persons in initiating and carrying out such a review.

(3) No review initiated by a council under this section shall extend to any charity without the consent of the charity trustees, nor to any ecclesiastical charity.

(4) No review initiated under this section by the council of a district shall extend to the working in any county of a local charity established for purposes similar or complementary to any services provided by county councils unless the review so extends with the consent of the council of that county.

[(4A) Subsection (4) above does not apply in relation to Wales.]

(5) Subsections (4) and (5) of section 76 above shall apply for the purposes of this section as they apply for the purposes of that section.

NOTES

Derivation

Sub-ss (1), (5) derived from the Charities Act 1960, s 11(1), (5), as amended by the Local Government Act 1972, s 210(9)(b), (10), and as read with the London Government Act 1963, s 81(9)(b); sub-ss (2), (3) derived from the Charities Act 1960, s 11(2), (3), as read with the London Government Act 1963, s 81(9)(b); sub-s (4) derived from the Charities Act 1960, s 11(4), as amended by the Local Government Act 1972, ss 210(9)(b), (10), 272(1), Sch 30, and as read with the London Government Act 1963, s 81(9)(b).

Initial Commencement

Specified date: 1 August 1993: see s 99(1).

Extent

This section does not extend to Scotland.

Amendment

Sub-s (1): words 'or county borough' in square brackets inserted by the Local Government (Wales) Act 1994, s 66(6), Sch 16, para 101(2).

Sub-s (1): words 'the Commissioners' in italics repealed and subsequent words in square brackets substituted by the Charities Act 2006, s 75(1), Sch 8, paras 96, 160.

Date in force: to be appointed: see the Charities Act 2006, s 79(2).

Sub-s (4A): inserted by the Local Government (Wales) Act 1994, s 66(6), Sch 16, para 101(2).

Modification

Modification: by virtue of the Environment Act 1995, s 70, Sch 9, para 15, this section has effect as if references to a council for any area included references to a National Park authority and as if the relevant Park were the authority's area.

78 Co-operation between charities, and between charities and local authorities

(1) Any local council and any joint board discharging any functions of such a council—

(a) may make, with any charity established for purposes similar or complementary to services provided by the council or board, arrangements for co-ordinating the activities of the council or board and those of the charity in the interests of persons who may benefit from those services or from the charity; and
(b) shall be at liberty to disclose to any such charity in the interests of those persons any information obtained in connection with the services provided by the council or board, whether or not arrangements have been made with the charity under this subsection.

In this subsection 'local council' means[, in relation to England,] the council of a county, or of a district, London borough, [or parish], and includes also the Common Council of the City of London and the Council of the Isles of Scilly [and, in relation to Wales, the council of a county, county borough or community].

(2) Charity trustees shall, notwithstanding anything in the trusts of the charity, have power by virtue of this subsection to do all or any of the following things, where it appears to them likely to promote or make more effective the work of the charity, and may defray the expense of so doing out of any income or money applicable as income of the charity, that is to say—

(a) they may co-operate in any review undertaken under section 77 above or otherwise of the working of charities or any class of charities;
(b) they may make arrangements with an authority acting under subsection (1) above or with another charity for co-ordinating their activities and those of the authority or of the other charity;
(c) they may publish information of other charities with a view to bringing them to the notice of those for whose benefit they are intended.

NOTES

Derivation

Sub-s (1) derived from the Charities Act 1960, s 12(1), as amended by the Local Government Act 1972, ss 210(9)(c), (10), 272(1), Sch 30, and as read with the London Government Act 1963, s 81(9)(a), and the Local Government Act 1972, ss 1(9), (10), 20(6), 179(1), (3), (4); sub-s (2) derived from the Charities Act 1960, s 12(2), as read with the London Government Act 1963, s 81(9)(a), and the Local Government Act 1972, ss 1(9), (10), 20(6), 179(1), (3), (4).

Initial Commencement

Specified date: 1 August 1993: see s 99(1).

Extent

This section does not extend to Scotland.

Amendment

Sub-s (1): first and final words in square brackets inserted, and second words in square brackets substituted, by the Local Government (Wales) Act 1994, s 66(6), Sch 16, para 101(3).

Modification

Modification: by virtue of the Environment Act 1995, s 70, Sch 9, para 15, this section has effect as if references to a council for any area included references to a National Park authority and as if the relevant Park were the authority's area.

79 Parochial charities

(1) Where trustees hold any property for the purposes of a public recreation ground, or of allotments (whether under inclosure Acts or otherwise), for the benefit of inhabitants of a parish having a parish council, or for other charitable purposes connected with such a parish, except for an ecclesiastical charity, they may with the approval of *the Commissioners* [the Commission] and with the consent of the parish council transfer the property to the parish council or to persons appointed by the parish council; and the council or their appointees shall hold the property on the same trusts and subject to the same conditions as the trustees did.

This subsection shall apply to property held for any public purposes as it applies to property held for charitable purposes.

(2) Where the charity trustees of a parochial charity in a parish, not being an ecclesiastical charity nor a charity founded within the preceding forty years, do not include persons elected by the local government electors, ratepayers or inhabitants of the parish or appointed by the parish council or parish meeting, the parish council or parish meeting may appoint additional charity trustees, to such number as *the Commissioners* [the Commission] may allow; and if there is a sole charity trustee not elected or appointed as aforesaid of any such charity, the number of the charity trustees may, with the approval of *the Commissioners* [the Commission], be increased to three of whom one may be nominated by the person holding the office of the sole trustee and one by the parish council or parish meeting.

(3) Where, under the trusts of a charity other than an ecclesiastical charity, the inhabitants of a rural parish (whether in vestry or not) or a select vestry were formerly (in 1894) entitled to appoint charity trustees for, or trustees or beneficiaries of, the charity, then—

(a) in a parish having a parish council, the appointment shall be made by the parish council or, in the case of beneficiaries, by persons appointed by the parish council; and
(b) in a parish not having a parish council, the appointment shall be made by the parish meeting.

(4) Where overseers as such or, except in the case of an ecclesiastical charity, churchwardens as such were formerly (in 1894) charity trustees of or trustees for a parochial charity in a rural parish, either alone or jointly with other persons, then instead of the former overseer or church warden trustees there shall be trustees (to a number not greater than that of the former overseer or churchwarden trustees) appointed by the parish council or, if there is no parish council, by the parish meeting.

(5) Where, outside Greater London (other than the outer London boroughs), overseers of a parish as such were formerly (in 1927) charity trustees of or trustees for any charity, either alone or jointly with other persons, then instead of the former overseer trustees there shall be trustees (to a number not greater than that of the former overseer trustees) appointed by the parish council or, if there is no parish council, by the parish meeting.

(6) In the case of an urban parish existing immediately before the passing of the Local Government Act 1972 which after 1st April 1974 is not comprised in a parish, the power of appointment under subsection (5) above shall be exercisable by the district council.

(7) In the application of the foregoing provisions of this section to Wales—

(a) for references in subsections (1) and (2) to a parish or a parish council there shall be substituted respectively references to a community or a community council;

(b) for references in subsections (3)(a) and (b) to a parish, a parish council or a parish meeting there shall be substituted respectively references to a community, a community council or the [council of the county or (as the case may be) county borough];

(c) for references in subsections (4) and (5) to a parish council or a parish meeting there shall be substituted respectively references to a community council or the [council of the county or (as the case may be) county borough].

(8) Any appointment of a charity trustee or trustee for a charity which is made by virtue of this section shall be for a term of four years, and a retiring trustee shall be eligible for re-appointment but—

(a) on an appointment under subsection (2) above, where no previous appointments have been made by virtue of that subsection or of the corresponding provision of the Local Government Act 1894 or the Charities Act 1960, and more than one trustee is appointed, half of those appointed (or as nearly as may be) shall be appointed for a term of two years; and

(b) an appointment made to fill a casual vacancy shall be for the remainder of the term of the previous appointment.

[(9) This section shall not affect the trusteeship, control or management of any [foundation or voluntary school within the meaning of the School Standards and Framework Act 1998.]]

(10) The provisions of this section shall not extend to the Isles of Scilly, and shall have effect subject to any order (including any future order) made under any enactment relating to local government with respect to local government areas or the powers of local authorities.

(11) In this section the expression 'formerly (in 1894)' relates to the period immediately before the passing of the Local Government Act 1894, and the expression 'formerly (in 1927)' to the period immediately before 1st April 1927; and the word 'former' shall be construed accordingly.

NOTES

Derivation

Sub-ss (1), (2) derived from the Charities Act 1960, s 37(1), (2), as amended by the Local Government Act 1972, s 272(1), Sch 30, and as read with s 179(1), (4) thereof; sub-ss (3), (4), (8), (10), (11) derived from the Charities Act 1960, s 37(3), (4), (6), (8), (9); sub-s (5) derived from the Charities Act 1960, s 37(5), as amended by the Local Government Act 1972, s 272(1), Sch 30, and as read with s 179(1), (4) thereof and with the London Government Act 1963, s 4(4); sub-s (6) derived from the Local Government Act 1972, s 210(9)(e); sub-s (7) derived in part from the Local Government Act 1972, s 210(9)(e), and is partly a drafting provision; sub-s (9) derived from the Charities Act 1960, s 37(7), as amended by the Education Reform Act 1988, s 237, Sch 12, para 9.

Initial Commencement

Specified date: 1 August 1993: see s 99(1).

Extent

This section does not extend to Scotland.

Amendment

Sub-s (1): words 'the Commissioners' in italics repealed and subsequent words in square brackets substituted by the Charities Act 2006, s 75(1), Sch 8, paras 96, 161(1), (2).

Date in force: to be appointed: see the Charities Act 2006, s 79(2).

Sub-s (2): words 'the Commissioners' in italics in both places they occur repealed and subsequent words in square brackets substituted by the Charities Act 2006, s 75(1), Sch 8, paras 96, 161(1), (3).

Date in force: to be appointed: see the Charities Act 2006, s 79(2).

Sub-s (7): in paras (b), (c) words in square brackets substituted by the Local Government (Wales) Act 1994, s 66(6), Sch 16, para 101(4).

Sub-s (9): substituted by the Education Act 1996, s 582(1), Sch 37, para 119.

Sub-s (9): words 'foundation or voluntary school within the meaning of the School Standards and Framework Act 1998.' in square brackets substituted by the School Standards and Framework Act 1998, s 140(1), Sch 30, para 49.

Date in force: 1 September 1999: see SI 1999/2323, art 2(1), Sch 1.

Scottish charities

80 Supervision by Commissioners [Commission] of certain Scottish charities

(1) The following provisions of this Act, namely—

(a) sections 8 and 9,
(b) section 18 (except subsection (2)(ii)), *and*
(c) section 19,
[(c) sections 19 to 19C, and
(d) section 31A,]

shall have effect in relation to any recognised body which is managed or controlled wholly or mainly in or from England or Wales as they have effect in relation to a charity.

(2) Where—

(a) a recognised body is managed or controlled wholly or mainly in or from Scotland, but
(b) any person in England and Wales holds any property on behalf of the body or of any person concerned in its management or control,

then, if *the Commissioners are satisfied* [the Commission is satisfied] as to the matters mentioned in subsection (3) below, *they may make* [it may make] an order requiring the person holding the property not to part with it without *their approval* [the Commission's approval].

(3) The matters referred to in subsection (2) above are—

(a) that there has been any misconduct or mismanagement in the administration of the body; and
(b) that it is necessary or desirable to make an order under that subsection for the purpose of protecting the property of the body or securing a proper application of such property for the purposes of the body;

and the reference in that subsection to *the Commissioners* [the Commission] being satisfied as to those matters is a reference to *their being* [the Commission being] so satisfied on the basis of such information as may be *supplied to them* [supplied to it] by the [Scottish Charity Regulator].

(4) Where—

(a) any person in England and Wales holds any property on behalf of a recognised body or of any person concerned in the management or control of such a body, and
(b) *the Commissioners are satisfied* [the Commission is satisfied] (whether on the basis of such information as may be *supplied to them* [supplied to it] by the [Scottish Charity Regulator] or otherwise)—
   (i) that there has been any misconduct or mismanagement in the administration of the body, and
   (ii) that it is necessary or desirable to make an order under this subsection for the

purpose of protecting the property of the body or securing a proper application of such property for the purposes of the body,

the Commissioners [the Commission] may by order vest the property in such recognised body or charity as is specified in the order in accordance with subsection (5) below, or require any persons in whom the property is vested to transfer it to any such body or charity, or appoint any person to transfer the property to any such body or charity.

(5) The *Commissioners* [Commission] may specify in an order under subsection (4) above such other recognised body or such charity as *they consider* [it considers] appropriate, being a body or charity whose purposes are, in the opinion of the *Commissioners* [Commission], as similar in character to those of the body referred to in paragraph (a) of that subsection as is reasonably practicable; but the *Commissioners* [Commission] shall not so specify any body or charity unless *they have received* [it has received]—

(a) from the persons concerned in the management or control of the body, or
(b) from the charity trustees of the charity,

as the case may be, written confirmation that they are willing to accept the property.

(6) In this section 'recognised body' [means a body entered in the Scottish Charity Register].

NOTES

Derivation

This section derived from the Charities Act 1992, s 12.

Initial Commencement

Specified date: 1 August 1993: see s 99(1).

Extent

This section does not extend to Scotland.

Amendment

Section heading: word 'Commissioners' repealed and subsequent word in square brackets substituted by the Charities Act 2006, s 75(1), Sch 8, paras 96, 162(1), (7).

Date in force: to be appointed: see the Charities Act 2006, s 79(2).

Sub-s (1): para (c) substituted, by subsequent paras (c), (d), by the Charities Act 2006, s 75(1), Sch 8, paras 96, 162(1), (2).

Date in force: to be appointed: see the Charities Act 2006, s 79(2).

Sub-s (2): words 'the Commissioners are satisfied' in italics repealed and subsequent words in square brackets substituted by the Charities Act 2006, s 75(1), Sch 8, paras 96, 162(1), (3)(a).

Date in force: to be appointed: see the Charities Act 2006, s 79(2).

Sub-s (2): words 'they may make' in italics repealed and subsequent words in square brackets substituted by the Charities Act 2006, s 75(1), Sch 8, paras 96, 162(1), (3)(b).

Date in force: to be appointed: see the Charities Act 2006, s 79(2).

Sub-s (2): words 'their approval' in italics repealed and subsequent words in square brackets substituted by the Charities Act 2006, s 75(1), Sch 8, paras 96, 162(1), (3)(c).

Date in force: to be appointed: see the Charities Act 2006, s 79(2).

Sub-s (3): words 'the Commissioners' in italics repealed and subsequent words in square brackets substituted by the Charities Act 2006, s 75(1), Sch 8, paras 96, 162(1), (4)(a).

Date in force: to be appointed: see the Charities Act 2006, s 79(2).

Sub-s (3): words 'their being' in italics repealed and subsequent words in square brackets substituted by the Charities Act 2006, s 75(1), Sch 8, paras 96, 162(1), (4)(b).

Date in force: to be appointed: see the Charities Act 2006, s 79(2).

Sub-s (3): words 'supplied to them' in italics repealed and subsequent words in square brackets substituted by the Charities Act 2006, s 75(1), Sch 8, paras 96, 162(1), (4)(c).

Date in force: to be appointed: see the Charities Act 2006, s 79(2).

Sub-s (3): words 'Scottish Charity Regulator' in square brackets substituted by SI 2006/242, art 5, Schedule, Pt 1, para 6(1), (3)(a).

Date in force: 1 April 2006: see SI 2006/242, art 1(3).

Sub-s (4): in para (b) words 'the Commissioners are satisfied' in italics repealed and subsequent words in square brackets substituted by the Charities Act 2006, s 75(1), Sch 8, paras 96, 162(1), (5)(a).

Date in force: to be appointed: see the Charities Act 2006, s 79(2).

Sub-s (4): in para (b) words 'supplied to them' in italics repealed and subsequent words in square brackets substituted by the Charities Act 2006, s 75(1), Sch 8, paras 96, 162(1), (5)(b).

Date in force: to be appointed: see the Charities Act 2006, s 79(2).

Sub-s (4): in para (b) words 'Scottish Charity Regulator' in square brackets substituted by SI 2006/242, art 5, Schedule, Pt 1, para 6(1), (3)(a).

Date in force: 1 April 2006: see SI 2006/242, art 1(3).

Sub-s (4): words 'the Commissioners' in italics repealed and subsequent words in square brackets substituted by the Charities Act 2006, s 75(1), Sch 8, paras 96, 162(1), (5)(c).

Date in force: to be appointed: see the Charities Act 2006, s 79(2).

Sub-s (5): word 'Commissioners' in italics in each place it occurs repealed and subsequent word in square brackets substituted by the Charities Act 2006, s 75(1), Sch 8, paras 96, 162(1), (6)(a).

Date in force: to be appointed: see the Charities Act 2006, s 79(2).

Sub-s (5): words 'they consider' in italics repealed and subsequent words in square brackets substituted by the Charities Act 2006, s 75(1), Sch 8, paras 96, 162(1), (6)(b).

Date in force: to be appointed: see the Charities Act 2006, s 79(2).

Sub-s (5): words 'they have received' in italics repealed and subsequent words in square brackets substituted by the Charities Act 2006, s 75(1), Sch 8, paras 96, 162(1), (6)(c).

Date in force: to be appointed: see the Charities Act 2006, s 79(2).

Sub-s (6): words 'means a body entered in the Scottish Charity Register' in square brackets substituted by SI 2006/242, art 5, Schedule, Pt 1, para 6(1), (3)(b).

Date in force: 1 April 2006: see SI 2006/242, art 1(3).

Administrative provisions about charities

81 Manner of giving notice of charity meetings, etc

(1) All notices which are required or authorised by the trusts of a charity to be given to a charity trustee, member or subscriber may be sent by post, and, if sent by post, may be addressed to any address given as his in the list of charity trustees, members or subscribers for the time being in use at the office or principal office of the charity.

(2) Where any such notice required to be given as aforesaid is given by post, it shall be deemed to have been given by the time at which the letter containing it would be delivered in the ordinary course of post.

(3) No notice required to be given as aforesaid of any meeting or election need be given to any charity trustee, member or subscriber, if in the list above mentioned he has no address in the United Kingdom.

NOTES

Derivation

This section derived from the Charities Act 1960, s 33.

Initial Commencement

Specified date: 1 August 1993: see s 99(1).

Extent

This section does not extend to Scotland.

82 Manner of executing instruments

(1) Charity trustees may, subject to the trusts of the charity, confer on any of their body (not being less than two in number) a general authority, or an authority limited in such manner as the trustees think fit, to execute in the names and on behalf of the trustees assurances or other deeds or instruments for giving effect to transactions to which the trustees are a party; and any deed or instrument executed in pursuance of an authority so given shall be of the same effect as if executed by the whole body.

(2) An authority under subsection (1) above—

(a) shall suffice for any deed or instrument if it is given in writing or by resolution of a meeting of the trustees, notwithstanding the want of any formality that would be required in giving an authority apart from that subsection;
(b) may be given so as to make the powers conferred exercisable by any of the trustees, or may be restricted to named persons or in any other way;
(c) subject to any such restriction, and until it is revoked, shall, notwithstanding any change in the charity trustees, have effect as a continuing authority given by the charity trustees from time to time of the charity and exercisable by such trustees.

(3) In any authority under this section to execute a deed or instrument in the names and on behalf of charity trustees there shall, unless the contrary intention appears, be implied authority also to execute it for them in the name and on behalf of the official custodian or of any other person, in any case in which the charity trustees could do so.

(4) Where a deed or instrument purports to be executed in pursuance of this section, then in favour of a person who (then or afterwards) in good faith acquires for money or money's worth an interest in or charge on property or the benefit of any covenant or agreement expressed to be entered into by the charity trustees, it shall be conclusively presumed to have been duly executed by virtue of this section.

(5) The powers conferred by this section shall be in addition to and not in derogation of any other powers.

NOTES

Derivation

Sub-ss (1), (3)–(5) derived from the Charities Act 1960, s 34(1), (3)–(5); sub-s (2) derived from the Charities Act 1960, s 34(2), as amended by the Charities Act 1992, s 47, Sch 3, para 14.

Initial Commencement

Specified date: 1 August 1993: see s 99(1).

Extent

This section does not extend to Scotland.

83 Transfer and evidence of title to property vested in trustees

(1) Where, under the trusts of a charity, trustees of property held for the purposes of the charity may be appointed or discharged by resolution of a meeting of the charity trustees, members or other persons, a memorandum declaring a trustee to have been so appointed or discharged shall be sufficient evidence of that fact if the memorandum is signed either at the meeting by the person presiding or in some other manner directed by the meeting and is attested by two persons present at the meeting.

(2) A memorandum evidencing the appointment or discharge of a trustee under subsection (1) above, if executed as a deed, shall have the like operation under section 40 of the Trustee Act 1925 (which relates to vesting declarations as respects trust property in deeds appointing or discharging trustees) as if the appointment or discharge were effected by the deed.

(3) For the purposes of this section, where a document purports to have been signed and attested as mentioned in subsection (1) above, then on proof (whether by evidence or as a matter of presumption) of the signature the document shall be presumed to have been so signed and attested, unless the contrary is shown.

(4) This section shall apply to a memorandum made at any time, except that subsection (2) shall apply only to those made after the commencement of the Charities Act 1960.

(5) This section shall apply in relation to any institution to which the Literary and Scientific Institutions Act 1854 applies as it applies in relation to a charity.

NOTES

Derivation

This section derived from the Charities Act 1960, s 35.

Initial Commencement

Specified date: 1 August 1993: see s 99(1).

Extent

This section does not extend to Scotland.

Part X
Supplementary

84 Supply by Commissioners [Commission] of copies of documents open to public inspection

The Commissioners [The Commission] shall, at the request of any person, furnish him with copies of, or extracts from, any document in *their possession* [the Commission's possession] which is for the time being open to inspection under Parts II to VI of this Act [or section 75D].

NOTES

Derivation

This section derived from the Charities Act 1960, s 9, as substituted by the Charities Act 1992, s 47, Sch 3, para 3, and from the Charities Act 1992, s 25(2).

Initial Commencement

Specified date: 1 August 1993: see s 99(1).

Extent

This section does not extend to Scotland.

Amendment

Section heading: word 'Commissioners' repealed and subsequent words in square brackets substituted by the Charities Act 2006, s 75(1), Sch 8, paras 96, 163(1), (5).

Date in force: to be appointed: see the Charities Act 2006, s 79(2).

Words 'The Commissioners' in italics repealed and subsequent words in square brackets substituted by the Charities Act 2006, s 75(1), Sch 8, paras 96, 163(1), (2).

Date in force: to be appointed: see the Charities Act 2006, s 79(2).

Words 'their possession' in italics repealed and subsequent words in square brackets substituted by the Charities Act 2006, s 75(1), Sch 8, paras 96, 163(1), (3).

Date in force: to be appointed: see the Charities Act 2006, s 79(2).

Words 'or section 75D' in square brackets inserted by the Charities Act 2006, s 75(1), Sch 8, paras 96, 163(1), (4).

Date in force: to be appointed: see the Charities Act 2006, s 79(2).

85 Fees and other amounts payable to Commissioners [Commission]

(1) The [Minister] may by regulations require the payment to *the Commissioners* [the Commission] of such fees as may be prescribed by the regulations in respect of—

(a) the discharge by *the Commissioners* [the Commission] of such functions under the enactments relating to charities as may be so prescribed;

(b) the inspection of the register of charities or of other material *kept by them* [kept by the Commission] under those enactments, or the furnishing of copies of or extracts from documents so kept.

(2) Regulations under this section may—

(a) confer, or provide for the conferring of, exemptions from liability to pay a prescribed fee;

(b) provide for the remission or refunding of a prescribed fee (in whole or in part) in circumstances prescribed by the regulations.

(3) Any regulations under this section which require the payment of a fee in respect of any matter for which no fee was previously payable shall not be made unless a draft of the regulations has been laid before and approved by a resolution of each House of Parliament.

(4) *The Commissioners* [The Commission] may impose charges of such amounts as *they consider* [it considers] reasonable in respect of the supply of any publications produced *by them* [by it].

(5) Any fees and other payments received by *the Commissioners* [the Commission] by virtue of this section shall be paid into the Consolidated Fund.

NOTES

Derivation

This section derived from the Charities Act 1992, s 51.

Initial Commencement

Specified date: 1 August 1993: see s 99(1).

Extent

This section does not extend to Scotland.

Amendment

Section heading: word 'Commissioners' repealed and subsequent word in square brackets substituted by the Charities Act 2006, s 75(1), Sch 8, paras 96, 164(1), (5).

Date in force: to be appointed: see the Charities Act 2006, s 79(2).

Sub-s (1): word 'Minister' in square brackets substituted by SI 2006/2951, art 6, Schedule, para 4(x).

Date in force: 13 December 2006: see SI 2006/2951, art 1(2).

Sub-s (1): words 'the Commissioners' in italics in both places they occur repealed and subsequent words in square brackets substituted by the Charities Act 2006, s 75(1), Sch 8, paras 96, 164(1), (2)(a).

Date in force: to be appointed: see the Charities Act 2006, s 79(2).

Sub-s (1): in para (b) words 'kept by them' in italics repealed and subsequent words in square brackets substituted by the Charities Act 2006, s 75(1), Sch 8, paras 96, 164(1), (2)(b).

Date in force: to be appointed: see the Charities Act 2006, s 79(2).

Sub-s (4): words 'The Commissioners' in italics repealed and subsequent words in square brackets substituted by the Charities Act 2006, s 75(1), Sch 8, paras 96, 164(1), (3)(a).

Date in force: to be appointed: see the Charities Act 2006, s 79(2).

Sub-s (4): words 'they consider' in italics repealed and subsequent words in square brackets substituted by the Charities Act 2006, s 75(1), Sch 8, paras 96, 164(1), (3)(b).

Date in force: to be appointed: see the Charities Act 2006, s 79(2).

Sub-s (4): words 'by them' in italics repealed and subsequent words in square brackets substituted by the Charities Act 2006, s 75(1), Sch 8, paras 96, 164(1), (3)(c).

Date in force: to be appointed: see the Charities Act 2006, s 79(2).

Sub-s (5): words 'the Commissioners' in italics repealed and subsequent words in square brackets substituted by the Charities Act 2006, s 75(1), Sch 8, paras 96, 164(1), (4).

Date in force: to be appointed: see the Charities Act 2006, s 79(2).

86 Regulations and orders

(1) Any regulations or order of the [Minister] under this Act—

(a) shall be made by statutory instrument; and
(b) (subject to subsection (2) below) shall be subject to annulment in pursuance of a resolution of either House of Parliament.

(2) Subsection (1)(b) above does not apply—

(a) to an order under section 17(2), [73F(6)] ... or 99(2) [or paragraph 6 of Schedule 1C]; [or]

[(aa) to regulations under section 69N above; and no regulations shall be made under that section unless a draft of the regulations has been laid before and approved by a resolution of each House of Parliament; or]

(b) ...

(c) to any regulations to which section 85(3) applies.

(3) Any regulations of the [Minister] or *the Commissioners* [the Commission] and any order of the [Minister] under this Act may make—

(a) different provision for different cases; and

(b) such supplemental, incidental, consequential or transitional provision or savings as the [Minister] or, as the case may be, *the Commissioners consider* [the Commission considers] appropriate.

(4) Before making any regulations under section 42, 44 *or 45* [, 45, 69N or 69Q] above [or Schedule 5A,] the [Minister] shall consult such persons or bodies of persons as he considers appropriate.

NOTES

Derivation

Sub-s (1) derived from the Charities Act 1960, ss 4(8B), 18(14), as added by the Charities Act 1992, ss 2(1), (7), 13(6), respectively and from the Charities Act 1960, s 43(3), as amended by the Education Act 1973, s 1(3), Sch 1, para 1(1), and from the Charities Act 1992, s 77(1); sub-s (2) derived in part from the Charities Act 1992, s 77(2), and is partly a drafting provision; sub-s (3) derived from the Charities Act 1960, s 43(2A), as added by the Charities Act 1992, s 47, Sch 3, para 17, and from the Charities Act 1992, s 77(3); sub-s (4) derived from the Charities Act 1992, s 77(4).

Initial Commencement

Specified date: 1 August 1993: see s 99(1).

Amendment

Sub-s (1): word 'Minister' in square brackets substituted by SI 2006/2951, art 6, Schedule, para 4(y).

Date in force: 13 December 2006: see SI 2006/2951, art 1(2).

Sub-s (2): in para (a) reference to '73F(6)' in square brackets inserted by the Charities Act 2006, s 75(1), Sch 8, paras 96, 165(1), (2)(a).

Date in force: to be appointed: see the Charities Act 2006, s 79(2).

Sub-s (2): in para (a) word omitted repealed by the Trustee Act 2000, s 40(1), (3), Sch 2, Pt I, para 2(2)(a), Sch 4, Pt I and by the Charities and Trustee Investment (Scotland) Act 2005, s 95, Sch 3, para 9.

Date in force (in relation to England and Wales): 1 February 2001: see SI 2001/49, art 2.

Date in force (in relation to Scotland): 1 January 2006: see SSI 2005/644, art 2(1), Schedule.

Sub-s (2): in para (a) words 'or paragraph 6 of Schedule 1C' in square brackets inserted by the Charities Act 2006, s 75(1), Sch 8, paras 96, 165(1), (2)(b).

Date in force: to be appointed: see the Charities Act 2006, s 79(2).

Sub-s (2): in para (a) word 'or' in square brackets inserted by the Trustee Act 2000, s 40(1), Sch 2, Pt I, para 2(2)(b).

Date in force: 1 February 2001: see SI 2001/49, art 2.

Sub-s (2): para (aa) inserted by the Charities Act 2006, s 34, Sch 7, Pt 2, paras 3, 6(a).

Sub-s (2): para (b) repealed by the Trustee Act 2000, s 40(1), (3), Sch 2, Pt I, para 2(3), Sch 4, Pt I and by the Charities and Trustee Investment (Scotland) Act 2005, s 95, Sch 3, para 9.

Date in force (in relation to England and Wales): 1 February 2001: see SI 2001/49, art 2.

Date in force (in relation to Scotland): 1 January 2006: see SSI 2005/644, art 2(1), Schedule.

Sub-s (3): word 'Minister' in square brackets in each place it occurs substituted by SI 2006/2951, art 6, Schedule, para 4(y).

Date in force: 13 December 2006: see SI 2006/2951, art 1(2).

Sub-s (3): words 'the Commissioners' in italics repealed and subsequent words in square brackets substituted by the Charities Act 2006, s 75(1), Sch 8, paras 96, 165(1), (3)(a).

Date in force: to be appointed: see the Charities Act 2006, s 79(2).

Sub-s (3): in para (b) words 'the Commissioners consider' in italics repealed and subsequent words in square brackets substituted by the Charities Act 2006, s 75(1), Sch 8, paras 96, 165(1), (3)(b).

Date in force: to be appointed: see the Charities Act 2006, s 79(2).

Sub-s (4): words ', 45, 69N or 69Q' in square brackets substituted by the Charities Act 2006, s 34, Sch 7, Pt 2, paras 3, 6(b).

Sub-s (4): words 'or Schedule 5A,' in square brackets inserted by the Charities Act 2006, s 75(1), Sch 8, paras 96, 165(1), (4).

Date in force: to be appointed: see the Charities Act 2006, s 79(2).

Sub-s (4): word 'Minister' in square brackets substituted by SI 2006/2951, art 6, Schedule, para 4(y).

Date in force: 13 December 2006: see SI 2006/2951, art 1(2).

Subordinate Legislation

Charities Act 1993 (Commencement and Transitional Provisions) Order 1995, SI 1995/2695 (made under sub-s (3)(b)).

[86A Consultation by Commission before exercising powers in relation to exempt charity]

[Before exercising in relation to an exempt charity any specific power exercisable by it in relation to the charity, the Commission must consult the charity's principal regulator.]

NOTES

Amendment

Inserted by the Charities Act 2006, s 14.

Date in force: to be appointed: see the Charities Act 2006, s 79(2).

87 Enforcement of requirements by order of Commissioners [Commission]

(1) If a person fails to comply with any requirement imposed by or under this Act then (subject to subsection (2) below) *the Commissioners* [the Commission] may by order give him such directions as *they consider* [it considers] appropriate for securing that the default is made good.

(2) Subsection (1) above does not apply to any such requirement if—

(a) a person who fails to comply with, or is persistently in default in relation to, the requirement is liable to any criminal penalty; or
(b) the requirement is imposed—
  (i) by an order of *the Commissioners* [the Commission] to which section 88 below applies, or
  (ii) by a direction of *the Commissioners* [the Commission] to which that section applies by virtue of section 90(2) below.

NOTES

Derivation

Sub-s (1) derived from the Charities Act 1992, s 56(1), (6); sub-s (2) derived from the Charities Act 1992, s 56(2).

Initial Commencement

Specified date: 1 August 1993: see s 99(1).

Extent

This section does not extend to Scotland.

Amendment

Section heading: word 'Commissioners' repealed and subsequent word in square brackets substituted by the Charities Act 2006, s 75(1), Sch 8, paras 96, 166(1), (4).

Date in force: to be appointed: see the Charities Act 2006, s 79(2).

Sub-s (1): words 'the Commissioners' in italics repealed and subsequent words in square brackets substituted by the Charities Act 2006, s 75(1), Sch 8, paras 96, 166(1), (2)(a).

Date in force: to be appointed: see the Charities Act 2006, s 79(2).

Sub-s (1): words 'they consider' in italics repealed and subsequent words in square brackets substituted by the Charities Act 2006, s 75(1), Sch 8, paras 96, 166(1), (2)(b).

Date in force: to be appointed: see the Charities Act 2006, s 79(2).

Sub-s (2): in para (b) words 'the Commissioners' in italics in both places they occur repealed and subsequent words in square brackets substituted by the Charities Act 2006, s 75(1), Sch 8, paras 96, 166(1), (3).

Date in force: to be appointed: see the Charities Act 2006, s 79(2).

88 Enforcement of orders of Commissioners [Commission]

A person guilty of disobedience—

(a) to an order of the Commissioners under section 9(1), 44(2), 61, 73 or 80 above; or
[(a) to an order of the Commission under section 9(1), 19A, 19B, 44(2), 61, 73, 73C or 80 above; or]
(b) to an order of *the Commissioners* [the Commission] under section 16 or 18 above requiring a transfer of property or payment to be called for or made; or
(c) to an order of *the Commissioners* [the Commission] requiring a default under this Act to be made good;

may on the application of *the Commissioners to* [the Commission to] the High Court be dealt with as for disobedience to an order of the High Court.

NOTES

Derivation

This section derived from the Charities Act 1960, s 41, as amended by the Charities Act 1992, s 47, Sch 3, para 16, and from the Charities Act 1992, s 56(3), (6).

Initial Commencement

Specified date: 1 August 1993: see s 99(1).

Extent

This section does not extend to Scotland.

Amendment

Section heading: word 'Commissioners' repealed and subsequent word in square brackets substituted by the Charities Act 2006, s 75(1), Sch 8, paras 96, 167(1), (5).

Date in force: to be appointed: see the Charities Act 2006, s 79(2).

Sub-s (a) substituted by the Charities Act 2006, s 75(1), Sch 8, paras 96, 167(1), (2).

Date in force: to be appointed: see the Charities Act 2006, s 79(2).

In sub-s (b) words 'the Commissioners' in italics repealed and subsequent words in square brackets substituted by the Charities Act 2006, s 75(1), Sch 8, paras 96, 167(1), (3).

Date in force: to be appointed: see the Charities Act 2006, s 79(2).

In sub-s (c) words 'the Commissioners' in italics repealed and subsequent words in square brackets substituted by the Charities Act 2006, s 75(1), Sch 8, paras 96, 167(1), (3).

Date in force: to be appointed: see the Charities Act 2006, s 79(2).

Words 'the Commissioners to' in italics repealed and subsequent words in square brackets substituted by the Charities Act 2006, s 75(1), Sch 8, paras 96, 167(1), (4).

Date in force: to be appointed: see the Charities Act 2006, s 79(2).

89 Other provisions as to orders of Commissioners [Commission]

(1) Any order made by *the Commissioners* [the Commission] under this Act may include such incidental or supplementary provisions as *the Commissioners think* [the Commission thinks] expedient for carrying into effect the objects of the order, and where *the Commissioners exercise* [the Commission exercises] any jurisdiction to make such an order on an application or reference *to them, they may* [to it, it may] insert any such provisions in the order notwithstanding that the application or reference does not propose their insertion.

(2) Where *the Commissioners make* [the Commission makes] an order under this Act, then (without prejudice to the requirements of this Act where the order is subject to appeal) *they may themselves* [the Commission may itself] give such public notice as *they think fit* [it thinks fit] of the making or contents of the order, or may require it to be given by any person on whose application the order is made or by any charity affected by the order.

(3) *The Commissioners* [The Commission] at any time within twelve months after *they have* [it has] made an order under any provision of this Act other than section 61 if *they are* [it is] satisfied that the order was made by mistake or on misrepresentation or otherwise than in conformity with this Act, may with or without any application or reference *to them* [to it] discharge the order in whole or in part, and subject or not to any savings or other transitional provisions.

(4) Except for the purposes of subsection (3) above or of an appeal under this Act, an order made by *the Commissioners* [the Commission] under this Act shall be deemed to have been duly and formally made and not be called in question on the ground only of irregularity or informality, but (subject to any further order) have effect according to its tenor.

[(5) Any order made by the Commission under any provision of this Act may be varied or revoked by a subsequent order so made.]

NOTES

Derivation

This section derived from the Charities Act 1960, s 40(1)–(4), and from the Charities Act 1992, s 56(4), (5), (6).

Initial Commencement

Specified date: 1 August 1993: see s 99(1).

Extent

This section does not extend to Scotland.

Amendment

Section heading: word 'Commissioners' repealed and subsequent words in square brackets substituted by the Charities Act 2006, s 75(1), Sch 8, paras 96, 168(1), (7).

Date in force: to be appointed: see the Charities Act 2006, s 79(2).

Sub-s (1): words 'the Commissioners' in italics repealed and subsequent words in square brackets substituted by the Charities Act 2006, s 75(1), Sch 8, paras 96, 168(1), (2)(a).

Date in force: to be appointed: see the Charities Act 2006, s 79(2).

Sub-s (1): words 'the Commissioners think' in italics repealed and subsequent words in square brackets substituted by the Charities Act 2006, s 75(1), Sch 8, paras 96, 168(1), (2)(b).

Date in force: to be appointed: see the Charities Act 2006, s 79(2).

Sub-s (1): words 'the Commissioners exercise' in italics repealed and subsequent words in square brackets substituted by the Charities Act 2006, s 75(1), Sch 8, paras 96, 168(1), (2)(c).

Date in force: to be appointed: see the Charities Act 2006, s 79(2).

Sub-s (1): words 'to them, they may' in italics repealed and subsequent words in square brackets substituted by the Charities Act 2006, s 75(1), Sch 8, paras 96, 168(1), (2)(d).

Date in force: to be appointed: see the Charities Act 2006, s 79(2).

Sub-s (2): words 'the Commissioners make' in italics repealed and subsequent words in square brackets substituted by the Charities Act 2006, s 75(1), Sch 8, paras 96, 168(1), (3)(a).

Date in force: to be appointed: see the Charities Act 2006, s 79(2).

Sub-s (2): words 'they may themselves' in italics repealed and subsequent words in square brackets substituted by the Charities Act 2006, s 75(1), Sch 8, paras 96, 168(1), (3)(b).

Date in force: to be appointed: see the Charities Act 2006, s 79(2).

Sub-s (2): words 'they think fit' in italics repealed and subsequent words in square brackets substituted by the Charities Act 2006, s 75(1), Sch 8, paras 96, 168(1), (3)(c).

Date in force: to be appointed: see the Charities Act 2006, s 79(2).

Sub-s (3): words 'The Commissioners' in italics repealed and subsequent words in square brackets substituted by the Charities Act 2006, s 75(1), Sch 8, paras 96, 168(1), (4)(a).

Date in force: to be appointed: see the Charities Act 2006, s 79(2).

Sub-s (3): words 'they have' in italics repealed and subsequent words in square brackets substituted by the Charities Act 2006, s 75(1), Sch 8, paras 96, 168(1), (4)(b).

Date in force: to be appointed: see the Charities Act 2006, s 79(2).

Sub-s (3): words 'they are' in italics repealed and subsequent words in square brackets substituted by the Charities Act 2006, s 75(1), Sch 8, paras 96, 168(1), (4)(c).

Date in force: to be appointed: see the Charities Act 2006, s 79(2).

Sub-s (3): words 'to them' in italics repealed and subsequent words in square brackets substituted by the Charities Act 2006, s 75(1), Sch 8, paras 96, 168(1), (4)(d).

Date in force: to be appointed: see the Charities Act 2006, s 79(2).

Sub-s (4): words 'the Commissioners' in italics repealed and subsequent words in square brackets substituted by the Charities Act 2006, s 75(1), Sch 8, paras 96, 168(1), (5).

Date in force: to be appointed: see the Charities Act 2006, s 79(2).

Sub-s (5): inserted by the Charities Act 2006, s 75(1), Sch 8, paras 96, 168(1), (6).

Date in force: to be appointed: see the Charities Act 2006, s 79(2).

90 Directions of the Commissioners [the Commission]

(1) Any direction given by *the Commissioners* [the Commission] under any provision contained in this Act—

(a) may be varied or revoked by a further direction given under that provision; and
(b) shall be given in writing.

(2) Sections 88 and 89(1), (2) and (4) above shall apply to any such directions as they apply to an order of *the Commissioners* [the Commission].

(3) In subsection (1) above the reference to *the Commissioners* [the Commission] includes, in relation to a direction under subsection (3) of section 8 above, a reference to any person conducting an inquiry under that section.

(4) Nothing in this section shall be read as applying to any directions contained in an order made by *the Commissioners* [the Commission] under section 87(1) above.

NOTES

Derivation

This section derived from the Charities Act 1992, s 57.

Initial Commencement

Specified date: 1 August 1993: see s 99(1).

Extent

This section does not extend to Scotland.

Amendment

Section Heading: words 'the Commissioners' repealed and subsequent words in square brackets substituted by the Charities Act 2006, s 75(1), Sch 8, paras 96, 169.

Date in force: to be appointed: see the Charities Act 2006, s 79(2).

Words 'the Commissioners' in italics in each place it occurs repealed and subsequent words in square brackets substituted by the Charities Act 2006, s 75(1), Sch 8, paras 96, 169.

Date in force: to be appointed: see the Charities Act 2006, s 79(2).

91 Service of orders and directions

(1) This section applies to any order or direction made or given by *the Commissioners* [the Commission] under this Act.

(2) An order or direction to which this section applies may be served on a person (other than a body corporate)—

(a) by delivering it to that person;
(b) by leaving it at his last known address in the United Kingdom; or
(c) by sending it by post to him at that address.

(3) An order or direction to which this section applies may be served on a body corporate by delivering it or sending it by post—

(a) to the registered or principal office of the body in the United Kingdom, or
(b) if it has no such office in the United Kingdom, to any place in the United Kingdom where it caries on business or conducts its activities (as the case may be).

(4) Any such order or direction may also be served on a person (including a body corporate) by sending it by post to that person at an address notified by that person to *the Commissioners* [the Commission] for the purposes of this subsection.

(5) In this section any reference to *the Commissioners* [the Commission] includes, in relation to a direction given under subsection (3) of section 8 above, a reference to any person conducting an inquiry under that section.

NOTES

Derivation

Sub-s (1) derived from the Charities Act 1960, s 40A(1), as added by the Charities Act 1992, s 47, Sch 3, para 15, and from the Charities Act 1992, s 76(1)(a); sub-ss (2)–(5) derived from the Charities Act 1960, s 40A(2)–(5), as added by the Charities Act 1992, s 47, Sch 3, para 15.

Initial Commencement

Specified date: 1 August 1993: see s 99(1).

Extent

This section does not extend to Scotland.

Amendment

Sub-ss (1), (4), (5): words 'the Commissioners' in italics repealed and subsequent words in square brackets substituted by the Charities Act 2006, s 75(1), Sch 8, paras 96, 170.

Date in force: to be appointed: see the Charities Act 2006, s 79(2).

92 Appeals from Commissioners

(1) Provision shall be made by rules of court for regulating appeals to the High Court under this Act against orders or decisions of the Commissioners.

(2) On such an appeal the Attorney General shall be entitled to appear and be heard, and such other persons as the rules allow or as the court may direct.

NOTES

Derivation

This section derived from the Charities Act 1960, s 42(1), (2).

Initial Commencement

Specified date: 1 August 1993: see s 99(1).

Extent

This section does not extend to Scotland.

Amendment

Repealed by the Charities Act 2006, s 75(1), (2), Sch 8, paras 96, 171, Sch 9; for transitional provisions and savings see s 75(3), Sch 10, para 18.

Date in force: to be appointed: see the Charities Act 2006, s 79(2).

93 Miscellaneous provisions as to evidence

(1) Where, in any proceedings to recover or compel payment of any rentcharge or other periodical payment claimed by or on behalf of a charity out of land or of the rents, profits or other income of land, otherwise than as rent incident to a reversion, it is shown that the rentcharge or other periodical payment has at any time been paid for twelve consecutive years to or for the benefit of the charity, that shall be prima facie evidence of the perpetual liability to it of the land or income, and no proof of its origin shall be necessary.

(2) In any proceedings, the following documents, that is to say,—

(a) the printed copies of the reports of the Commissioners for enquiring concerning charities, 1818 to 1837, who were appointed under the Act 58 Geo 3 c 91 and subsequent Acts; and
(b) the printed copies of the reports which were made for various counties and county boroughs to the Charity Commissioners by their assistant commissioners and presented to the House of Commons as returns to orders of various dates beginning with 8th December 1890, and ending with 9th September 1909,

shall be admissible as evidence of the documents and facts stated in them.

(3) Evidence of any order, certificate or other document issued by the Commissioners may be given by means of a copy retained by them, or taken from a copy so retained, and certified to be a true copy by any officer of the Commissioners generally or specially authorised by them to act for this purpose; and a document purporting to be such a copy shall be received in evidence without proof of the official position, authority or handwriting of the person certifying it.

[(3) Evidence of any order, certificate or other document issued by the Commission may be given by means of a copy which it retained, or which is taken from a copy so retained, and evidence of an entry in any register kept by it may be given by means of a copy of the entry, if (in each case) the copy is certified in accordance with subsection (4).

(4) The copy shall be certified to be a true copy by any member of the staff of the Commission generally or specially authorised by the Commission to act for that purpose.

(5) A document purporting to be such a copy shall be received in evidence without proof of the official position, authority or handwriting of the person certifying it.

(6) In subsection (3) above 'the Commission' includes the Charity Commissioners for England and Wales.]

NOTES

Derivation

This section derived from the Charities Act 1960, s 36.

Initial Commencement

Specified date: 1 August 1993: see s 99(1).

Extent

This section does not extend to Scotland.

Amendment

Sub-s (3): substituted, by subsequent sub-ss (3)–(6), by the Charities Act 2006, s 75(1), Sch 8, paras 96, 172.

Date in force: to be appointed: see the Charities Act 2006, s 79(2).

94 Restriction on institution of proceedings for certain offences

(1) No proceedings for an offence under this Act to which this section applies shall be instituted except by or with the consent of the Director of Public Prosecutions.

(2) This section applies to any offence under—

(a) section 5;
(b) section 11;
(c) section 18(14);
(d) section 49; or
(e) section 73(1).

NOTES

Derivation

This section derived from the Charities Act 1992, s 55.

Initial Commencement

Specified date: 1 August 1993: see s 99(1).

Extent

This section does not extend to Scotland.

95 Offences by bodies corporate

Where any offence under this Act is committed by a body corporate and is proved to have been committed with the consent or connivance of, or to be attributable to any neglect on the part of, any director, manager, secretary or other similar officer of the body corporate, or any person who was purporting to act in any such capacity, he as well as the body corporate shall be guilty of that offence and shall be liable to be proceeded against and punished accordingly.

In relation to a body corporate whose affairs are managed by its members, 'director' means a member of the body corporate.

NOTES

Derivation

This section derived from the Charities Act 1992, s 75(b).

Initial Commencement

Specified date: 1 August 1993: see s 99(1).

Extent

This section does not extend to Scotland.

96 Construction of references to a 'charity' or to particular classes of charity

(1) In this Act, except in so far as the context otherwise requires—

'charity' means any institution, corporate or not, which is established for charitable purposes and is subject to the control of the High Court in the exercise of the court's jurisdiction with respect to charities;
['charity' has the meaning given by section 1(1) of the Charities Act 2006;]
'ecclesiastical charity' has the same meaning as in the Local Government Act 1894;
'exempt charity' means *(subject to section 24(8) above)* a charity comprised in Schedule 2 to this Act;
'local charity' means, in relation to any area, a charity established for purposes which are by their nature or by the trusts of the charity directed wholly or mainly to the benefit of that area or of part of it;
'parochial charity' means, in relation to any parish or (in Wales) community, a charity the benefits of which are, or the separate distribution of the benefits of which is, confined to inhabitants of the parish or community, or of a single ancient ecclesiastical parish which included that parish or community or part of it, or of an area consisting of that parish or community with not more than four neighbouring parishes or communities.

(2) The expression 'charity' is not in this Act applicable—

(a) to any ecclesiastical corporation (that is to say, any corporation in the Church of England, whether sole or aggregate, which is established for spiritual purposes) in respect of the corporate property of the corporation, except to a corporation aggregate having some purposes which are not ecclesiastical in respect of its corporate property held for those purposes; or
(b) to any Diocesan Board of Finance [(or any subsidiary thereof)] within the meaning of the Endowments and Glebe Measure 1976 for any diocese in respect of the diocesan glebe land of that diocese within the meaning of that Measure; or
(c) to any trust of property for purposes for which the property has been consecrated.

(3) A charity shall be deemed for the purposes of this Act to have a permanent endowment unless all property held for the purposes of the charity may be expended for those purposes without distinction between capital and income, and in this Act 'permanent endowment' means, in relation to any charity, property held subject to a restriction on its being expended for the purposes of the charity.

(4) *References in this Act to a charity whose income from all sources does not in aggregate amount to more than a specified amount shall be construed—*

(a) by reference to the gross revenues of the charity, or
(b) if the Commissioners so determine, by reference to the amount which they estimate to be the likely amount of those revenues,

but without (in either case) bringing into account anything for the yearly value of land occupied by the charity apart from the pecuniary income (if any) received from that land; and any question as to the application of any such reference to a charity shall be determined by the Commissioners, whose decision shall be final.

(5) *The Commissioners* [The Commission] may direct that for all or any of the purposes of this Act an institution established for any special purposes of or in connection with a charity (being charitable purposes) shall be treated as forming part of that charity or as forming a distinct charity.

[(6) *The Commissioners* [The Commission] may direct that for all or any of the purposes of this Act two or more charities having the same charity trustees shall be treated as a single charity.]

NOTES

Derivation

Sub-s (1) derived from the Charities Act 1960, s 45(1), as read with the Local Government Act 1972, s 179(1), (4), and from the Charities Act 1992, s 1(2); sub-s (2) derived from the Charities Act 1960, s 45(2), as amended by the Endowments and Glebe Measure 1976, s 44, and from the Charities Act 1992, s 1(2); sub-ss (3), (4) derived from the Charities Act 1960, s 45(3), (4), as amended by the Charities Act 1992, ss 47, 48, 78(2), Sch 3, para 18(a), (b), Sch 7, and from the Charities Act 1992, s 1(2); sub-s (5) derived from the Charities Act 1960, s 45(5), and from the Charities Act 1992, s 1(2).

Initial Commencement

Specified date: 1 August 1993: see s 99(1).

Extent

This section does not extend to Scotland.

Amendment

Sub-s (1): definition 'charity' substituted by the Charities Act 2006, s 75(1), Sch 8, paras 96, 173(1), (2).

Date in force: to be appointed: see the Charities Act 2006, s 79(2).

Sub-s (1): in definition 'exempt charity' words '(subject to section 24(8) above)' in italics repealed by the Charities Act 2006, s 75(1), (2), Sch 8, paras 96, 173(1), (3)(a), Sch 9.

Date in force: to be appointed: see the Charities Act 2006, s 79(2).

Sub-s (2): in para (b) words '(or any subsidiary thereof)' in square brackets inserted by the Church of England (Miscellaneous Provisions) Measure 2000, s 11.

Date in force: 1 January 2001: see s 22(2) thereof and the Instrument made by the Archbishops of Canterbury and York dated 14 December 2000; for transitional provisions see s 19, Sch 7 thereto.

Sub-s (4): repealed by the Charities Act 2006, s 75(1), (2), Sch 8, paras 96, 173(1), (3)(b), Sch 9.

Date in force: to be appointed: see the Charities Act 2006, s 79(2).

Sub-s (5): words 'The Commissioners' in italics repealed and subsequent words in square brackets substituted by the Charities Act 2006, s 75(1), Sch 8, paras 96, 173(1), (4).

Date in force: to be appointed: see the Charities Act 2006, s 79(2).

Sub-s (6): inserted by the Charities (Amendment) Act 1995, s 1.

Sub-s (6): words 'The Commissioners' in italics repealed and subsequent words in square brackets substituted by the Charities Act 2006, s 75(1), Sch 8, paras 96, 173(1), (4).

Date in force: to be appointed: see the Charities Act 2006, s 79(2).

97 General interpretation

(1) In this Act, except in so far as the context otherwise requires—

'charitable purposes' means purposes which are exclusively *charitable according to the law of England and Wales* [charitable purposes as defined by section 2(1) of the Charities Act 2006];
'charity trustees' means the persons having the general control and management of the administration of a charity;
['CIO' means charitable incorporated organisation;]

'the Commissioners' means the Charity Commissioners for England and Wales;
['the Commission' means the Charity Commission;]
'company' means a company formed and registered under the Companies Act 1985 or to which the provisions of that Act apply as they apply to such a company;
'the court' means the High Court and, within the limits of its jurisdiction, any other court in England and Wales having a jurisdiction in respect of charities concurrent (within any limit of area or amount) with that of the High Court, and includes any judge or officer of the court exercising the jurisdiction of the court;
'financial year'—

(a) in relation to a charity which is a company, shall be construed in accordance with section 223 of the Companies Act 1985; and
(b) in relation to any other charity, shall be construed in accordance with regulations made by virtue of section 42(2) above;

but this definition is subject to the transitional provisions in section 99(4) below and Part II of Schedule 8 to this Act;

'gross income', in relation to charity, means its gross recorded income from all sources including special trusts;
'independent examiner', in relation to a charity, means such a person as is mentioned in section 43(3)(a) above;
'institution' [means an institution whether incorporated or not, and] includes any trust or undertaking;
['members', in relation to a charity with a body of members distinct from the charity trustees, means any of those members;]
['the Minister' means the Minister for the Cabinet Office;]
'the official custodian' means the official custodian for charities;
'permanent endowment' shall be construed in accordance with section 96(3) above;
['principal regulator', in relation to an exempt charity, means the charity's principal regulator within the meaning of section 13 of the Charities Act 2006;]
'the register' means the register of charities kept under section 3 above and 'registered' shall be construed accordingly;
'special trust' means property which is held and administered by or on behalf of a charity for any special purposes of the charity, and is so held and administered on separate trusts relating only to that property but a special trust shall not, by itself, constitute a charity for the purposes of Part VI of this Act;
['the Tribunal' means the Charity Tribunal;]
'trusts' in relation to a charity, means the provisions establishing it as a charity and regulating its purposes and administration, whether those provisions take effect by way of trust or not, and in relation to other institutions has a corresponding meaning.

(2) In this Act, except in so far as the context otherwise requires, 'document' includes information recorded in any form, and, in relation to information recorded otherwise than in legible form—

(a) any reference to its production shall be construed as a reference to the furnishing of a copy of it in legible form; and
(b) any reference to the furnishing of a copy of, or extract from, it shall accordingly be construed as a reference to the furnishing of a copy of, or extract from, it in legible form.

(3) No vesting or transfer of any property in pursuance of any provision of *Part IV or IX* [Part 4, 7, 8A or 9] of this Act shall operate as a breach of a covenant or condition against alienation or give rise to a forfeiture.

NOTES

Derivation

Sub-s (1) derived from the Charities Act 1960, s 46(1), as amended by the Companies Act 1989, s 111(2), the Courts Act 1971, s 56(4), Sch 11, Part II, and the Charities Act 1992, ss 47, 78(2), Sch 3, para 19(a), (b), Sch 7, and from the Charities Act 1992, s 1(1)–(3), and contains a drafting provision; sub-s (2) derived from the Charities Act 1960, s 46(2), as added by the Charities Act 1992, s 47, Sch 3, para 19(b), and from the Charities Act 1992, s 1(3); sub-s (3) derived from the Charities Act 1960, s 16(5), and from the Charities Act 1992, s 1(4).

Initial Commencement

Specified date: 1 August 1993: see s 99(1).

Extent

This section does not extend to Scotland.

Amendment

Sub-s (1): in definition 'charitable purposes' words 'charitable according to the law of England and Wales' in italics repealed and subsequent words in square brackets substituted by the Charities Act 2006, s 75(1), Sch 8, paras 96, 174(a).

Date in force: to be appointed: see the Charities Act 2006, s 79(2).

Sub-s (1): definition 'CIO' inserted by the Charities Act 2006, s 34, Sch 7, Pt 2, paras 3, 7.

Date in force: to be appointed: see the Charities Act 2006, s 79(2).

Sub-s (1): definition 'the Commissioners' substituted, by subsequent definition 'the Commission', by the Charities Act 2006, s 75(1), Sch 8, paras 96, 174(b).

Date in force: to be appointed: see the Charities Act 2006, s 79(2).

Sub-s (1): in definition 'institution' words 'means an institution whether incorporated or not, and' in square brackets inserted by the Charities Act 2006, s 75(1), Sch 8, paras 96, 174(c).

Date in force: to be appointed: see the Charities Act 2006, s 79(2).

Sub-s (1): definition 'members' inserted by the Charities Act 2006, s 75(1), Sch 8, paras 96, 174(d).

Date in force: 8 November 2006: see the Charities Act 2006, s 79(1)(g).

Sub-s (1): definition 'the Minister' inserted by the Charities Act 2006, s 75(1), Sch 8, paras 96, 174(d).

Date in force: 8 November 2006: see the Charities Act 2006, s 79(1)(g).

Sub-s (1): definition 'principal regulator' inserted by the Charities Act 2006, s 75(1), Sch 8, paras 96, 174(d).

Date in force: 8 November 2006: see the Charities Act 2006, s 79(1)(g).

Sub-s (1): definition 'the Tribunal' inserted by the Charities Act 2006, s 75(1), Sch 8, paras 96, 174(d).

Date in force: 8 November 2006: see the Charities Act 2006, s 79(1)(g).

Sub-s (3): words 'Part IV or IX' in italics repealed and subsequent words in square bracekts substituted by the Charities Act 2006, s 75(1), Sch 8, paras 96, 175.

Date in force: to be appointed: see the Charities Act 2006, s 79(2).

98 Consequential amendments and repeals

(1) The enactments mentioned in Schedule 6 to this Act shall be amended as provided in that Schedule.

(2) The enactments mentioned in Schedule 7 to this Act are hereby repealed to the extent specified in the third column of the Schedule.

NOTES

Derivation

This section is a drafting provision.

Initial Commencement

Sub-s (1): Specified date (for certain purposes): 1 August 1993: see s 99(1).

Sub-s (2): Specified date: 1 August 1993: see s 99(1).

Sub-s (1): To be appointed (for remaining purposes): see s 99(2).

Appointment

Sub-s (1): Appointment: 1 March 1996: see SI 1995/2695, art 2.

99 ...

...

NOTES

Amendment

Repealed by the Statute Law (Repeals) Act 2004.

Date in force: 22 July 2004: (no specific commencement provision).

Miscellaneous

Sub-s (1) stated that, subject to sub-s (2), this Act would come into force on 1 August 1993. Sub-s (2) stated that Pt VI, s 69 and Sch 6, para 21(3) would not come into force until such day as the Secretary of State may by order appoint and that different days could be appointed for different provisions or different purposes. Sub-s (3) stated that until the coming into force of all the provisions mentioned in sub-s (2), the provisions mentioned in Sch 8, Pt I would continue in force notwithstanding their repeal. Sub-s (4) stated that Sch 8, Pt II would have effect until the coming into force of the first regulations made by virtue of s 42(2) for determining the financial year of a charity for the purposes of the provisions mentioned in that Pt.

100 Short title and extent

(1) This Act may be cited as the Charities Act 1993.

(2) Subject to subsection (3) to (6) below, this Act extends only to England and Wales.

(3) *Section 10* [Sections 10 to 10C] above and this section extend to the whole of the United Kingdom.

(4) Section 15(2) *extends* [and sections 24 to 25A extend] also to Northern Ireland.

(5) ...

(6) The amendments in Schedule 6 and the repeals in Schedule 7 have the same extent as the enactments to which they refer and section 98 above extends accordingly.

NOTES

Derivation

Sub-ss (1), (6) are drafting provisions; sub-s (2) derived from the Charities Act 1960, s 49(2), as amended by the Statute Law (Repeals) Act 1978, s 1, Sch 1, Part II, and from the Charities Act 1992, s 79(3), and contains drafting provisions; sub-ss (3), (5) derived from the Charities Act 1992, s 79(4), (5); sub-s (4) derived from the Charities Act 1960, s 49(2)(c).

Initial Commencement

Specified date: 1 August 1993: see s 99(1).

Amendment

Sub-s (3): words 'Section 10' in italics repealed and subsequent words in square brackets substituted by the Charities Act 2006, s 75(1), Sch 8, paras 96, 176.

Date in force: to be appointed: see the Charities Act 2006, s 79(2).

Sub-s (4): words 'and sections 24 to 25A extend' in square brackets substituted by the Charities Act 2006, s 23(5).

Sub-s (5): repealed by the Charities and Trustee Investment (Scotland) Act 2005, s 95, Sch 3, para 9.

Date in force: 1 January 2006: see SSI 2005/644, art 2(1), Schedule.

Schedule 1
Constitution etc of Charity Commissioners

NOTES

Amendment

Repealed by the Charities Act 2006, ss 6(6), 75(2), Sch 9.

1

(1) There shall be a Chief Charity Commissioner and two other commissioners.

(2) Two at least of the commissioners shall be persons who have a seven year general qualification within the meaning of section 71 of the Courts and Legal Services Act 1990.

(3) The chief commissioner and the other commissioners shall be appointed by the [Minister], and shall be deemed for all purposes to be employed in the civil service of the Crown.

(4) There may be paid to each of the commissioners such salary and allowances as the [Minister] may with the approval of the Treasury determine.

(5) If at any time it appears to the [Minister] that there should be more than three commissioners, he may with the approval of the Treasury appoint not more than two additional commissioners.

2

(1) The chief commissioner may, with the approval of the Treasury as to number and conditions of service, appoint such assistant commissioners and other officers and such employees as he thinks necessary for the proper discharge of the functions of the Commissioners and of the official custodian.

(2) There may be paid to officers and employees so appointed such salaries or remuneration as the Treasury may determine.

3

(1) The Commissioners may use an official seal for the authentication of documents, and their seal shall be officially and judicially noticed.

(2) The Documentary Evidence Act 1868, as amended by the Documentary Evidence Act 1882, shall have effect as if in the Schedule to the Act of 1868 the Commissioners were

included in the first column and any commissioner or assistant commissioner and any officer authorised to act on behalf of the Commissioners were mentioned in the second column.

(3) The Commissioners shall have power to regulate their own procedure and, subject to any such regulations and to any directions of the chief commissioner, any one commissioner or any assistant commissioner may act for and in the name of the Commissioners.

(4) Where the Commissioners act as a board, then—

(a) if not more than four commissioners hold office for the time being, the quorum shall be two commissioners (of whom at least one must be a person having a qualification such as is mentioned in paragraph 1(2) above); and

(b) if five commissioners so hold office, the quorum shall be three commissioners (of whom at least one must be a person having such a qualification);

and in the case of an equality of votes the chief commissioner or in his absence the commissioner presiding shall have a second or casting vote.

(5) The Commissioners shall have power to act notwithstanding any vacancy in their number.

(6) It is hereby declared that the power of a commissioner or assistant commissioner to act for and in the name of the Commissioners in accordance with sub-paragraph (3) above may, in particular, be exercised in relation to functions of the Commissioners under sections 8, 18, 19 and 63 of this Act, including functions under sections 8, 18 and 19 as applied by section 80(1).

4

Legal proceedings may be instituted by or against the Commissioners by the name of the Charity Commissioners for England and Wales, and shall not abate or be affected by any change in the persons who are the commissioners.

NOTES

Initial Commencement

Specified date: 1 August 1993: see s 99(1).

Amendment

Repealed by the Charities Act 2006, ss 6(6), 75(2), Sch 9.

Para 1: in sub-para (3) word 'Minister' in square brackets substituted by SI 2006/2951, art 6, Schedule, para 4(z).

Date in force: 13 December 2006: see SI 2006/2951, art 1(2).

Para 1: in sub-para (4) word 'Minister' in square brackets substituted by SI 2006/2951, art 6, Schedule, para 4(z).

Date in force: 13 December 2006: see SI 2006/2951, art 1(2).

Para 1: in sub-para (5) word 'Minister' in square brackets substituted by SI 2006/2951, art 6, Schedule, para 4(z).

Date in force: 13 December 2006: see SI 2006/2951, art 1(2).

[Schedule 1A
The Charity Commission]

NOTES

Amendment

Inserted by the Charities Act 2006, s 6(2), Sch 1; for effect see s 6(7), Sch 2, para 2(6) thereto.

[Membership

1

(1) The Commission shall consist of a chairman and at least four, but not more than eight, other members.

(2) The members shall be appointed by the Minister.

(3) The Minister shall exercise the power in sub-paragraph (2) so as to secure that—

(a) the knowledge and experience of the members of the Commission (taken together) includes knowledge and experience of the matters mentioned in sub-paragraph (4),
(b) at least two members have a seven year general qualification within the meaning of section 71 of the Courts and Legal Services Act 1990, and
(c) at least one member knows about conditions in Wales and has been appointed following consultation with the National Assembly for Wales.

(4) The matters mentioned in this sub-paragraph are—

(a) the law relating to charities,
(b) charity accounts and the financing of charities, and
(c) the operation and regulation of charities of different sizes and descriptions.

(5) In sub-paragraph (3)(c) 'member' does not include the chairman of the Commission.

Terms of appointment and remuneration

2

The members of the Commission shall hold and vacate office as such in accordance with the terms of their respective appointments.

3

(1) An appointment of a person to hold office as a member of the Commission shall be for a term not exceeding three years.

(2) A person holding office as a member of the Commission—

(a) may resign that office by giving notice in writing to the Minister, and
(b) may be removed from office by the Minister on the ground of incapacity or misbehaviour.

(3) Before removing a member of the Commission the Minister shall consult—

(a) the Commission, and
(b) if the member was appointed following consultation with the National Assembly for Wales, the Assembly.

(4) No person may hold office as a member of the Commission for more than ten years in total.

(5) For the purposes of sub-paragraph (4), time spent holding office as a Charity Commissioner for England and Wales shall be counted as time spent holding office as a member of the Commission.

4

(1) The Commission shall pay to its members such remuneration, and such other allowances, as may be determined by the Minister.

(2) The Commission shall, if required to do so by the Minister—

(a) pay such pension, allowances or gratuities as may be determined by the Minister to or in respect of a person who is or has been a member of the Commission, or
(b) make such payments as may be so determined towards provision for the payment of a pension, allowances or gratuities to or in respect of such a person.

(3) If the Minister determines that there are special circumstances which make it right for a person ceasing to hold office as a member of the Commission to receive compensation, the Commission shall pay to him a sum by way of compensation of such amount as may be determined by the Minister.

Staff

5

(1) The Commission—

(a) shall appoint a chief executive, and
(b) may appoint such other staff as it may determine.

(2) The terms and conditions of service of persons appointed under sub-paragraph (1) are to be such as the Commission may determine with the approval of the Minister for the Civil Service.

Committees

6

(1) The Commission may establish committees and any committee of the Commission may establish sub-committees.

(2) The members of a committee of the Commission may include persons who are not members of the Commission (and the members of a sub-committee may include persons who are not members of the committee or of the Commission).

Procedure etc

7

(1) The Commission may regulate its own procedure (including quorum).

(2) The validity of anything done by the Commission is not affected by a vacancy among its members or by a defect in the appointment of a member.

Performance of functions

8

Anything authorised or required to be done by the Commission may be done by—

(a) any member or member of staff of the Commission who is authorised for that purpose by the Commission, whether generally or specially;
(b) any committee of the Commission which has been so authorised.

Evidence

9

The Documentary Evidence Act 1868 shall have effect as if—

(a) the Commission were mentioned in the first column of the Schedule to that Act,
(b) any member or member of staff of the Commission authorised to act on behalf of the Commission were specified in the second column of that Schedule in connection with the Commission, and
(c) the regulations referred to in that Act included any document issued by or under the authority of the Commission.

Execution of documents

10

(1) A document is executed by the Commission by the fixing of its common seal to the document.

(2) But the fixing of that seal to a document must be authenticated by the signature of—

(a) any member of the Commission, or
(b) any member of its staff,

who is authorised for the purpose by the Commission.

(3) A document which is expressed (in whatever form of words) to be executed by the Commission and is signed by—

(a) any member of the Commission, or
(b) any member of its staff,

who is authorised for the purpose by the Commission has the same effect as if executed in accordance with sub-paragraphs (1) and (2).

(4) A document executed by the Commission which makes it clear on its face that it is intended to be a deed has effect, upon delivery, as a deed; and it is to be presumed (unless a contrary intention is proved) to be delivered upon its being executed.

(5) In favour of a purchaser a document is to be deemed to have been duly executed by the Commission if it purports to be signed on its behalf by—

(a) any member of the Commission, or
(b) any member of its staff;

and, where it makes it clear on its face that it is intended to be a deed, it is to be deemed to have been delivered upon its being executed.

(6) For the purposes of this paragraph—

'authorised' means authorised whether generally or specially; and
'purchaser' means a purchaser in good faith for valuable consideration and includes a lessee, mortgagee or other person who for valuable consideration acquired an interest in property.

Annual report

11

(1) As soon as practicable after the end of each financial year the Commission shall publish a report on—

(a) the discharge of its functions,
(b) the extent to which, in its opinion, its objectives (see section 1B of this Act) have been met,
(c) the performance of its general duties (see section 1D of this Act), and
(d) the management of its affairs,

during that year.

(2) The Commission shall lay a copy of each such report before Parliament.

(3) In sub-paragraph (1) above, 'financial year' means—

(a) the period beginning with the date on which the Commission is established and ending with the next 31st March following that date, and
(b) each successive period of 12 months ending with 31st March.

Annual public meeting

12

(1) The Commission shall hold a public meeting ('the annual meeting') for the purpose of enabling a report under paragraph 11 above to be considered.

(2) The annual meeting shall be held within the period of three months beginning with the day on which the report is published.

(3) The Commission shall organise the annual meeting so as to allow—

(a) a general discussion of the contents of the report which is being considered, and
(b) a reasonable opportunity for those attending the meeting to put questions to the Commission about matters to which the report relates.

(4) But subject to sub-paragraph (3) above the annual meeting is to be organised and conducted in such a way as the Commission considers appropriate.

(5) The Commission shall—

(a) take such steps as are reasonable in the circumstances to ensure that notice of the annual meeting is given to every registered charity, and
(b) publish notice of the annual meeting in the way appearing to it to be best calculated to bring it to the attention of members of the public.

(6) Each such notice shall—

(a) give details of the time and place at which the meeting is to be held,
(b) set out the proposed agenda for the meeting,
(c) indicate the proposed duration of the meeting, and
(d) give details of the Commission's arrangements for enabling persons to attend.

(7) If the Commission proposes to alter any of the arrangements which have been included in notices given or published under sub-paragraph (5) above it shall—

(a) give reasonable notice of the alteration, and
(b) publish the notice in the way appearing to it to be best calculated to bring it to the attention of registered charities and members of the public.]

[Schedule 1B The Charity Tribunal]

NOTES

Amendment

Inserted by the Charities Act 2006, s 8(2), Sch 3.

Date in force: to be appointed: see the Charities Act 2006, s 79(2).

[Membership

1

(1) The Tribunal shall consist of the President and its other members.

(2) The Lord Chancellor shall appoint—

(a) a President of the Tribunal,
(b) legal members of the Tribunal, and
(c) ordinary members of the Tribunal.

(3) A person may be appointed as the President or a legal member of the Tribunal only if he has a seven year general qualification within the meaning of section 71 of the Courts and Legal Services Act 1990.

(4) A person may be appointed as an ordinary member of the Tribunal only if he appears to the Lord Chancellor to have appropriate knowledge or experience relating to charities.

Deputy President

2

(1) The Lord Chancellor may appoint a legal member as deputy President of the Tribunal.

(2) The deputy President—

(a) may act for the President when he is unable to act or unavailable, and
(b) shall perform such other functions as the President may delegate or assign to him.

Terms of appointment

3

(1) The members of the Tribunal shall hold and vacate office as such in accordance with the terms of their respective appointments.

(2) A person holding office as a member of the Tribunal—

(a) may resign that office by giving notice in writing to the Lord Chancellor, and
(b) may be removed from office by the Lord Chancellor on the ground of incapacity or misbehaviour.

(3) A previous appointment of a person as a member of the Tribunal does not affect his eligibility for re-appointment as a member of the Tribunal.

Retirement etc

4

(1) A person shall not hold office as a member of the Tribunal after reaching the age of 70.

(2) Section 26(5) and (6) of the Judicial Pensions and Retirement Act 1993 (extension to age 75) apply in relation to a member of the Tribunal as they apply in relation to a holder of a relevant office.

Remuneration etc

5

(1) The Lord Chancellor may pay to the members of the Tribunal such remuneration, and such other allowances, as he may determine.

(2) The Lord Chancellor may—

(a) pay such pension, allowances or gratuities as he may determine to or in respect of a person who is or has been a member of the Tribunal, or
(b) make such payments as he may determine towards provision for the payment of a pension, allowances or gratuities to or in respect of such a person.

(3) If the Lord Chancellor determines that there are special circumstances which make it right for a person ceasing to hold office as a member of the Tribunal to receive compensation, the Lord Chancellor may pay to him a sum by way of compensation of such amount as may be determined by the Lord Chancellor.

Staff and facilities

6

The Lord Chancellor may make staff and facilities available to the Tribunal.

Panels

7

(1) The functions of the Tribunal shall be exercised by panels of the Tribunal.

(2) Panels of the Tribunal shall sit at such times and in such places as the President may direct.

(3) Before giving a direction under sub-paragraph (2) above the President shall consult the Lord Chancellor.

(4) More than one panel may sit at a time.

8

(1) The President shall make arrangements for determining which of the members of the Tribunal are to constitute a panel of the Tribunal in relation to the exercise of any function.

(2) Those arrangements shall, in particular, ensure that each panel is constituted in one of the following ways—

(a) as the President sitting alone,
(b) as a legal member sitting alone,
(c) as the President sitting with two other members,
(d) as a legal member sitting with two other members,
(e) as the President sitting with one other member,
(f) as a legal member sitting with one other member,

(and references in paragraphs (d) and (f) to other members do not include the President).

(3) The President shall publish arrangements made under this paragraph.

Practice and procedure

9

(1) Decisions of the Tribunal may be taken by majority vote.

(2) In the case of a panel constituted in accordance with paragraph 8(2)(e), the President shall have a casting vote.

(3) In the case of a panel constituted in accordance with paragraph 8(2)(f) which consists of a legal member and an ordinary member, the legal member shall have a casting vote.

(4) The President shall make and publish arrangements as to who is to have a casting vote in the case of a panel constituted in accordance with paragraph 8(2)(f) which consists of two legal members.

10

The President may, subject to rules under section 2B of this Act, give directions about the practice and procedure of the Tribunal.]

NOTES

Amendment

Inserted by the Charities Act 2006, s 8(2), Sch 3.

Date in force: to be appointed: see the Charities Act 2006, s 79(2).

[Schedule 1C Appeals and Applications to Charity Tribunal]

NOTES

Amendment

Inserted by the Charities Act 2006, s 8(3), Sch 4.

Date in force (for remaining purposes): to be appointed: see the Charities Act 2006, s 79(2).

[Appeals: general

1

(1) Except in the case of a reviewable matter (see paragraph 3) an appeal may be brought to the Tribunal against any decision, direction or order mentioned in column 1 of the Table.

(2) Such an appeal may be brought by—

(a) the Attorney General, or
(b) any person specified in the corresponding entry in column 2 of the Table.

(3) The Commission shall be the respondent to such an appeal.

(4) In determining such an appeal the Tribunal—

(a) shall consider afresh the decision, direction or order appealed against, and
(b) may take into account evidence which was not available to the Commission.

(5) The Tribunal may—

(a) dismiss the appeal, or
(b) if it allows the appeal, exercise any power specified in the corresponding entry in column 3 of the Table.

Appeals: orders under section 9

2

(1) Paragraph 1(4)(a) above does not apply in relation to an appeal against an order made under section 9 of this Act.

(2) On such an appeal the Tribunal shall consider whether the information or document in question—

(a) relates to a charity;
(b) is relevant to the discharge of the functions of the Commission or the official custodian.

(3) The Tribunal may allow such an appeal only if it is satisfied that the information or document in question does not fall within either paragraph (a) or paragraph (b) of sub-paragraph (2) above.

Reviewable matters

3

(1) In this Schedule references to 'reviewable matters' are to—

(a) decisions to which sub-paragraph (2) applies, and
(b) orders to which sub-paragraph (3) applies.

(2) This sub-paragraph applies to decisions of the Commission—

(a) to institute an inquiry under section 8 of this Act with regard to a particular institution,
(b) to institute an inquiry under section 8 of this Act with regard to a class of institutions,
(c) not to make a common investment scheme under section 24 of this Act,
(d) not to make a common deposit scheme under section 25 of this Act,
(e) not to make an order under section 26 of this Act in relation to a charity,
(f) not to make an order under section 36 of this Act in relation to land held by or in trust for a charity,
(g) not to make an order under section 38 of this Act in relation to a mortgage of land held by or in trust for a charity.

(3) This sub-paragraph applies to an order made by the Commission under section 69(1) of this Act in relation to a company which is a charity.

Reviews

4

(1) An application may be made to the Tribunal for the review of a reviewable matter.

(2) Such an application may be made by—

(a) the Attorney General, or
(b) any person mentioned in the entry in column 2 of the Table which corresponds to the entry in column 1 which relates to the reviewable matter.

(3) The Commission shall be the respondent to such an application.

(4) In determining such an application the Tribunal shall apply the principles which would be applied by the High Court on an application for judicial review.

(5) The Tribunal may—

(a) dismiss the application, or
(b) if it allows the application, exercise any power mentioned in the entry in column 3 of the Table which corresponds to the entry in column 1 which relates to the reviewable matter.

Interpretation: remission of matters to Commission

5

References in column 3 of the Table to the power to remit a matter to the Commission are to the power to remit the matter either—

(a) generally, or
(b) for determination in accordance with a finding made or direction given by the Tribunal.

TABLE

1	*2*	*3*
Decision of the Commission under section 3 or 3A of this Act— (a) to enter or not to enter an institution in the register of charities, or (b) to remove or not to remove an institution from the register.	The persons are— (a) the persons who are or claim to be the charity trustees of the institution, (b) (if a body corporate) the institution itself, and (c) any other person who is or may be affected by the decision.	Power to quash the decision and (if appropriate)— (a) remit the matter to the Commission, (b) direct the Commission to rectify the register.
Decision of the Commission not to make a determination under section 3(9) of this Act in relation to particular information contained in the register.	The persons are— (a) the charity trustees of the charity to which the information relates, (b) (if a body corporate) the charity itself, and (c) any other person who is or may be affected by the decision.	Power to quash the decision and (if appropriate) remit the matter to the Commission.
Direction given by the Commission under section 6 of this Act requiring the name of a charity to be changed.	The persons are— (a) the charity trustees of the charity to which the direction relates, (b) (if a body corporate) the charity itself, and (c) any other person who is or may be affected by the direction.	Power to— (a) quash the direction and (if appropriate) remit the matter to the Commission, (b) substitute for the direction any other direction which could have been given by the Commission.

TABLE

1	*2*	*3*
Decision of the Commission to institute an inquiry under section 8 of this Act with regard to a particular institution.	The persons are— (a) the persons who have control or management of the institution, and (b) (if a body corporate) the institution itself.	Power to direct the Commission to end the inquiry.
Decision of the Commission to institute an inquiry under section 8 of this Act with regard to a class of institutions.	The persons are— (a) the persons who have control or management of any institution which is a member of the class of institutions, and (b) (if a body corporate) any such institution.	Power to— (a) direct the Commission that the inquiry should not consider a particular institution, (b) direct the Commission to end the inquiry.
Order made by the Commission under section 9 of this Act requiring a person to supply information or a document.	The persons are any person who is required to supply the information or document.	Power to— (a) quash the order, (b) substitute for all or part of the order any other order which could have been made by the Commission.
Order made by the Commission under section 16(1) of this Act (including such an order made by virtue of section 23(1)).	The persons are— (a) in a section 16(1)(a) case, the charity trustees of the charity to which the order relates or (if a body corporate) the charity itself, (b) in a section 16(1)(b) case, any person discharged or removed by the order, and (c) any other person who is or may be affected by the order.	Power to— (a) quash the order in whole or in part and (if appropriate) remit the matter to the Commission, (b) substitute for all or part of the order any other order which could have been made by the Commission, (c) add to the order anything which could have been contained in an order made by the Commission.
Order made by the Commission under section 18(1) of this Act in relation to a charity.	The persons are— (a) the charity trustees of the charity, (b) (if a body corporate) the charity itself, (c) in a section 18(1)(i) case, any person suspended by the order, and (d) any other person who is or may be affected by the order.	Power to— (a) quash the order in whole or in part and (if appropriate) remit the matter to the Commission, (b) substitute for all or part of the order any other order which could have been made by the Commission, (c) add to the order anything which could have been contained in an order made by the Commission.

TABLE

1	*2*	*3*
Order made by the Commission under section 18(2) of this Act in relation to a charity.	The persons are— (a) the charity trustees of the charity, (b) (if a body corporate) the charity itself, (c) in a section 18(2)(i) case, any person removed by the order, and (d) any other person who is or may be affected by the order.	Power to— (a) quash the order in whole or in part and (if appropriate) remit the matter to the Commission, (b) substitute for all or part of the order any other order which could have been made by the Commission, (c) add to the order anything which could have been contained in an order made by the Commission.
Order made by the Commission under section 18(4) of this Act removing a charity trustee.	The persons are— (a) the charity trustee, (b) the remaining charity trustees of the charity of which he was a charity trustee, (c) (if a body corporate) the charity itself, and (d) any other person who is or may be affected by the order.	Power to— (a) quash the order in whole or in part and (if appropriate) remit the matter to the Commission, (b) substitute for all or part of the order any other order which could have been made by the Commission, (c) add to the order anything which could have been contained in an order made by the Commission.
Order made by the Commission under section 18(5) of this Act appointing a charity trustee.	The persons are— (a) the other charity trustees of the charity, (b) (if a body corporate) the charity itself, and (c) any other person who is or may be affected by the order.	Power to— (a) quash the order in whole or in part and (if appropriate) remit the matter to the Commission, (b) substitute for all or part of the order any other order which could have been made by the Commission, (c) add to the order anything which could have been contained in an order made by the Commission.

TABLE

1	*2*	*3*
Decision of the Commission— (a) to discharge an order following a review under section 18(13) of this Act, or (b) not to discharge an order following such a review.	The persons are— (a) the charity trustees of the charity to which the order relates, (b) (if a body corporate) the charity itself, (c) if the order in question was made under section 18(1)(i), any person suspended by it, and (d) any other person who is or may be affected by the order.	Power to— (a) quash the decision and (if appropriate) remit the matter to the Commission, (b) make the discharge of the order subject to savings or other transitional provisions, (c) remove any savings or other transitional provisions to which the discharge of the order was subject, (d) discharge the order in whole or in part (whether subject to any savings or other transitional provisions or not).
Order made by the Commission under section 18A(2) of this Act which suspends a person's membership of a charity	The persons are— (a) the person whose membership is suspended by the order, and (b) any other person who is or may be affected by the order.	Power to quash the order and (if appropriate) remit the matter to the Commission.
Order made by the Commission under section 19A(2) of this Act which directs a person to take action specified in the order.	The persons are any person who is directed by the order to take the specified action.	Power to quash the order and (if appropriate) remit the matter to the Commission.
Order made by the Commission under section 19B(2) of this Act which directs a person to apply property in a specified manner.	The persons are any person who is directed by the order to apply the property in the specified manner.	Power to quash the order and (if appropriate) remit the matter to the Commission.
Order made by the Commission under section 23(2) of this Act in relation to any land vested in the official custodian in trust for a charity.	The persons are— (a) the charity trustees of the charity, (b) (if a body corporate) the charity itself, and (c) any other person who is or may be affected by the order.	Power to— (a) quash the order and (if appropriate) remit the matter to the Commission, (b) substitute for the order any other order which could have been made by the Commission, (c) add to the order anything which could have been contained in an order made by the Commission.

TABLE

1	*2*	*3*
Decision of the Commission not to make a common investment scheme under section 24 of this Act.	The persons are— (a) the charity trustees of a charity which applied to the Commission for the scheme, (b) (if a body corporate) the charity itself, and (c) any other person who is or may be affected by the decision.	Power to quash the decision and (if appropriate) remit the matter to the Commission.
Decision of the Commission not to make a common deposit scheme under section 25 of this Act.	The persons are— (a) the charity trustees of a charity which applied to the Commission for the scheme, (b) (if a body corporate) the charity itself, and (c) any other person who is or may be affected by the decision.	Power to quash the decision and (if appropriate) remit the matter to the Commission.
Decision by the Commission not to make an order under section 26 of this Act in relation to a charity.	The persons are— (a) the charity trustees of the charity, and (b) (if a body corporate) the charity itself.	Power to quash the decision and (if appropriate) remit the matter to the Commission.
Direction given by the Commission under section 28 of this Act in relation to an account held in the name of or on behalf of a charity.	The persons are— (a) the charity trustees of the charity, (b) (if a body corporate) the charity itself, and (c) any other person who is or may be affected by the order.	Power to— (a) quash the direction and (if appropriate) remit the matter to the Commission, (b) substitute for the direction any other direction which could have been given by the Commission, (c) add to the direction anything which could have been contained in a direction given by the Commission.
Order made by the Commission under section 31 of this Act for the taxation of a solicitor's bill.	The persons are— (a) the solicitor, (b) any person for whom the work was done by the solicitor, and (c) any other person who is or may be affected by the order.	Power to— (a) quash the order, (b) substitute for the order any other order which could have been made by the Commission, (c) add to the order anything which could have been contained in an order made by the Commission.

TABLE

1	*2*	*3*
Decision of the Commission not to make an order under section 36 of this Act in relation to land held by or in trust for a charity.	The persons are— (a) the charity trustees of the charity, (b) (if a body corporate) the charity itself, and (c) any other person who is or may be affected by the decision.	Power to quash the decision and (if appropriate) remit the matter to the Commission.
Decision of the Commission not to make an order under section 38 of this Act in relation to a mortgage of land held by or in trust for a charity.	The persons are— (a) the charity trustees of the charity, (b) (if a body corporate) the charity itself, and (c) any other person who is or may be affected by the decision.	Power to quash the decision and (if appropriate) remit the matter to the Commission.
Order made by the Commission under section 43(4) of this Act requiring the accounts of a charity to be audited.	The persons are— (a) the charity trustees of the charity, (b) (if a body corporate) the charity itself, and (c) any other person who is or may be affected by the order.	Power to— (a) quash the order, (b) substitute for the order any other order which could have been made by the Commission, (c) add to the order anything which could have been contained in an order made by the Commission.
Order made by the Commission under section 44(2) of this Act in relation to a charity, or a decision of the Commission not to make such an order in relation to a charity.	The persons are— (a) the charity trustees of the charity, (b) (if a body corporate) the charity itself, (c) in the case of a decision not to make an order, the auditor, independent examiner or examiner, and (d) any other person who is or may be affected by the order or the decision.	Power to— (a) quash the order or decision and (if appropriate) remit the matter to the Commission, (b) substitute for the order any other order of a kind the Commission could have made, (c) make any order which the Commission could have made.
Decision of the Commission under section 46(5) of this Act to request charity trustees to prepare an annual report for a charity.	The persons are— (a) the charity trustees, and (b) (if a body corporate) the charity itself.	Power to quash the decision and (if appropriate) remit the matter to the Commission.
Decision of the Commission not to dispense with the requirements of section 48(1) in relation to a charity or class of charities.	The persons are the charity trustees of any charity affected by the decision.	Power to quash the decision and (if appropriate) remit the matter to the Commission.

TABLE

1	*2*	*3*
Decision of the Commission— (a) to grant a certificate of incorporation under section 50(1) of this Act to the trustees of a charity, or (b) not to grant such a certificate.	The persons are— (a) the trustees of the charity, and (b) any other person who is or may be affected by the decision.	Power to quash— (a) the decision, (b) any conditions or directions inserted in the certificate, and (if appropriate) remit the matter to the Commission.
Decision of the Commission to amend a certificate of incorporation of a charity under section 56(4) of this Act.	The persons are— (a) the trustees of the charity, and (b) any other person who is or may be affected by the amended certificate of incorporation.	Power to quash the decision and (if appropriate) remit the matter to the Commission.
Decision of the Commission not to amend a certificate of incorporation under section 56(4) of this Act.	The persons are— (a) the trustees of the charity, and (b) any other person who is or may be affected by the decision not to amend the certificate of incorporation.	Power to— (a) quash the decision and (if appropriate) remit the matter to the Commission, (b) make any order the Commission could have made under section 56(4).
Order of the Commission under section 61(1) or (2) of this Act which dissolves a charity which is an incorporated body.	The persons are— (a) the trustees of the charity, (b) the charity itself, and (c) any other person who is or may be affected by the order.	Power to— (a) quash the order and (if appropriate) remit the matter to the Commission, (b) substitute for the order any other order which could have been made by the Commission, (c) add to the order anything which could have been contained in an order made by the Commission.
Decision of the Commission to give, or withhold, consent under section 64(2), 65(4) or 66(1) of this Act in relation to a body corporate which is a charity.	The persons are— (a) the charity trustees of the charity, (b) the body corporate itself, and (c) any other person who is or may be affected by the decision.	Power to quash the decision and (if appropriate) remit the matter to the Commission.

TABLE

1	*2*	*3*
Order made by the Commission under section 69(1) of this Act in relation to a company which is a charity.	The persons are— (a) the directors of the company, (b) the company itself, and (c) any other person who is or may be affected by the order.	Power to— (a) quash the order and (if appropriate) remit the matter to the Commission, (b) substitute for the order any other order which could have been made by the Commission, (c) add to the order anything which could have been contained in an order made by the Commission.
Order made by the Commission under section 69(4) of this Act which gives directions to a person or to charity trustees.	The persons are— (a) in the case of directions given to a person, that person, (b) in the case of directions given to charity trustees, those charity trustees and (if a body corporate) the charity of which they are charity trustees, and (c) any other person who is or may be affected by the directions.	Power to— (a) quash the order, (b) substitute for the order any other order which could have been made by the Commission, (c) add to the order anything which could have been contained in an order made by the Commission.
Decision of the Commission under section 69E of this Act to grant an application for the constitution of a CIO and its registration as a charity.	The persons are any person (other than the persons who made the application) who is or may be affected by the decision.	Power to quash the decision and (if appropriate)— (a) remit the matter to the Commission, (b) direct the Commission to rectify the register of charities.
Decision of the Commission under section 69E of this Act not to grant an application for the constitution of a CIO and its registration as a charity.	The persons are— (a) the persons who made the application, and (b) any other person who is or may be affected by the decision.	Power to— (a) quash the decision and (if appropriate) remit the matter to the Commission, (b) direct the Commission to grant the application.
Decision of the Commission under section 69H of this Act not to grant an application for the conversion of a charitable company or a registered society into a CIO and the CIO's registration as a charity.	The persons are— (a) the charity which made the application, (b) the charity trustees of the charity, and (c) any other person who is or may be affected by the decision.	Power to— (a) quash the decision and (if appropriate) remit the matter to the Commission, (b) direct the Commission to grant the application.

TABLE

1	*2*	*3*
Decision of the Commission under section 69K of this Act to grant an application for the amalgamation of two or more CIOs and the incorporation and registration as a charity of a new CIO as their successor.	The persons are any creditor of any of the CIOs being amalgamated.	Power to quash the decision and (if appropriate) remit the matter to the Commission.
Decision of the Commission under section 69K of this Act not to grant an application for the amalgamation of two or more CIOs and the incorporation and registration as a charity of a new CIO as their successor.	The persons are— (a) the CIOs which applied for the amalgamation, (b) the charity trustees of the CIOs, and (c) any other person who is or may be affected by the decision.	Power to— (a) quash the decision and (if appropriate) remit the matter to the Commission, (b) direct the Commission to grant the application.
Decision of the Commission to confirm a resolution passed by a CIO under section 69M(1) of this Act.	The persons are any creditor of the CIO.	Power to quash the decision and (if appropriate) remit the matter to the Commission.
Decision of the Commission not to confirm a resolution passed by a CIO under section 69M(1) of this Act.	The persons are— (a) the CIO, (b) the charity trustees of the CIO, and (c) any other person who is or may be affected by the decision.	Power to— (a) quash the decision and (if appropriate) remit the matter to the Commission, (b) direct the Commission to confirm the resolution.
Decision of the Commission under section 72(4) of this Act to waive, or not to waive, a person's disqualification.	The persons are— (a) the person who applied for the waiver, and (b) any other person who is or may be affected by the decision.	Power to— (a) quash the decision and (if appropriate) remit the matter to the Commission, (b) substitute for the decision any other decision of a kind which could have been made by the Commission.
Order made by the Commission under section 73(4) of this Act in relation to a person who has acted as charity trustee or trustee for a charity.	The persons are— (a) the person subject to the order, and (b) any other person who is or may be affected by the order.	Power to— (a) quash the order and (if appropriate) remit the matter to the Commission, (b) substitute for the order any other order which could have been made by the Commission.

TABLE

1	*2*	*3*
Order made by the Commission under section 73C(5) or (6) of this Act requiring a trustee or connected person to repay, or not to receive, remuneration.	The persons are— (a) the trustee or connected person, (b the other charity trustees of the charity concerned, and (c) any other person who is or may be affected by the order.	Power to— (a) quash the order and (if appropriate) remit the matter to the Commission, (b) substitute for the order any other order which could have been made by the Commission.
Decision of the Commission to notify charity trustees under section 74A(2) of this Act that it objects to a resolution of the charity trustees under section 74(2) or 74C(2).	The persons are— (a) the charity trustees, and (b any other person who is or may be affected by the decision.	Power to quash the decision.
Decision of the Commission not to concur under section 75A of this Act with a resolution of charity trustees under section 75A(3) or 75B(2).	The persons are— (a) the charity trustees, (b (if a body corporate) the charity itself, and (c) any other person who is or may be affected by the decision.	Power to quash the decision and (if appropriate) remit the matter to the Commission.
Decision of the Commission to withhold approval for the transfer of property from trustees to a parish council under section 79(1) of this Act.	The persons are— (a) the trustees, (b the parish council, and (c) any other person who is or may be affected by the decision.	Power to quash the decision and (if appropriate) remit the matter to the Commission.
Order made by the Commission under section 80(2) of this Act in relation to a person holding property on behalf of a recognised body or of any person concerned in its management or control.	The persons are— (a) the person holding the property in question, and (b) any other person who is or may be affected by the order.	Power to quash the order and (if appropriate) remit the matter to the Commission.
Decision of the Commission not to give a direction under section 96(5) or (6) of this Act in relation to an institution or a charity.	The persons are the trustees of the institution or charity concerned.	Power to quash the decision and (if appropriate) remit the matter to the Commission.
Decision of the Commission under paragraph 15 of Schedule 5B to this Act to refuse to register an amendment to the constitution of a CIO.	The persons are— (a) the CIO, (b) the charity trustees of the CIO, and (c) any other person who is or may be affected by the decision.	Power to quash the decision and (if appropriate)— (a) remit the matter to the Commission, (b) direct the Commission to register the amendment.

Power to amend Table etc

6

(1) The Minister may by order—

(a) amend or otherwise modify an entry in the Table,
(b) add an entry to the Table, or
(c) remove an entry from the Table.

(2) An order under sub-paragraph (1) may make such amendments, repeals or other modifications of paragraphs 1 to 5 of this Schedule, or of an enactment which applies this Schedule, as the Minister considers appropriate in consequence of any change in the Table made by the order.

(3) No order shall be made under this paragraph unless a draft of the order has been laid before and approved by a resolution of each House of Parliament.

7

Paragraph 6 above applies (with the necessary modifications) in relation to section 57 of the Charities Act 2006 as if—

(a) the provisions of that section were contained in this Schedule, and
(b) the reference in that paragraph to paragraphs 1 to 5 of this Schedule included a reference to any other provision relating to appeals to the Tribunal which is contained in Chapter 1 of Part 3 of the Charities Act 2006.]

NOTES

Amendment

Inserted by the Charities Act 2006, s 8(3), Sch 4.

Date in force (for remaining purposes): to be appointed: see the Charities Act 2006, s 79(2).

[Schedule 1D References to Charity Tribunal]

NOTES

Amendment

Inserted by the Charities Act 2006, s 8(3), Sch 4.

Date in force: to be appointed: see the Charities Act 2006, s 79(2).

[References by Commission

1

(1) A question which—

(a) has arisen in connection with the exercise by the Commission of any of its functions, and
(b) involves either the operation of charity law in any respect or its application to a particular state of affairs,

may be referred to the Tribunal by the Commission if the Commission considers it desirable to refer the question to the Tribunal.

(2) The Commission may make such a reference only with the consent of the Attorney General.

(3) The Commission shall be a party to proceedings before the Tribunal on the reference.

(4) The following shall be entitled to be parties to proceedings before the Tribunal on the reference—

(a) the Attorney General, and
(b) with the Tribunal's permission—
  (i) the charity trustees of any charity which is likely to be affected by the Tribunal's decision on the reference,
  (ii) any such charity which is a body corporate, and
  (iii) any other person who is likely to be so affected.

References by Attorney General

2

(1) A question which involves either—

(a) the operation of charity law in any respect, or
(b) the application of charity law to a particular state of affairs,

may be referred to the Tribunal by the Attorney General if the Attorney General considers it desirable to refer the question to the Tribunal.

(2) The Attorney General shall be a party to proceedings before the Tribunal on the reference.

(3) The following shall be entitled to be parties to proceedings before the Tribunal on the reference—

(a) the Commission, and
(b) with the Tribunal's permission—
  (i) the charity trustees of any charity which is likely to be affected by the Tribunal's decision on the reference,
  (ii) any such charity which is a body corporate, and
  (iii) any other person who is likely to be so affected.

Powers of Commission in relation to matters referred to Tribunal

3

(1) This paragraph applies where a question which involves the application of charity law to a particular state of affairs has been referred to the Tribunal under paragraph 1 or 2 above.

(2) The Commission shall not take any steps in reliance on any view as to the application of charity law to that state of affairs until—

(a) proceedings on the reference (including any proceedings on appeal) have been concluded, and
(b) any period during which an appeal (or further appeal) may ordinarily be made has ended.

(3) Where—

(a) paragraphs (a) and (b) of sub-paragraph (2) above are satisfied, and
(b) the question has been decided in proceedings on the reference,

the Commission shall give effect to that decision when dealing with the particular state of affairs to which the reference related.

Suspension of time limits while reference in progress

4

(1) Sub-paragraph (2) below applies if—

(a) paragraph 3(2) above prevents the Commission from taking any steps which it would otherwise be permitted or required to take, and
(b) the steps in question may be taken only during a period specified in an enactment ('the specified period').

(2) The running of the specified period is suspended for the period which—

(a) begins with the date on which the question is referred to the Tribunal, and
(b) ends with the date on which paragraphs (a) and (b) of paragraph 3(2) above are satisfied.

(3) Nothing in this paragraph or section 74A of this Act prevents the specified period being suspended concurrently by virtue of sub-paragraph (2) above and that section.

Agreement for Commission to act while reference in progress

5

(1) Paragraph 3(2) above does not apply in relation to any steps taken by the Commission with the agreement of—

(a) the persons who are parties to the proceedings on the reference at the time when those steps are taken, and
(b) (if not within paragraph (a) above) the charity trustees of any charity which—
  (i) is likely to be directly affected by the taking of those steps, and
  (ii) is not a party to the proceedings at that time.

(2) The Commission may take those steps despite the suspension in accordance with paragraph 4(2) above of any period during which it would otherwise be permitted or required to take them.

(3) Paragraph 3(3) above does not require the Commission to give effect to a decision as to the application of charity law to a particular state of affairs to the extent that the decision is inconsistent with any steps already taken by the Commission in relation to that state of affairs in accordance with this paragraph.

Appeals and applications in respect of matters determined on references

6

(1) No appeal or application may be made to the Tribunal by a person to whom sub-paragraph (2) below applies in respect of an order or decision made, or direction given, by the Commission in accordance with paragraph 3(3) above.

(2) This sub-paragraph applies to a person who was at any stage a party to the proceedings in which the question referred to the Tribunal was decided.

(3) Rules under section 2B(1) of this Act may include provision as to who is to be treated for the purposes of sub-paragraph (2) above as being (or not being) a party to the proceedings.

(4) Any enactment (including one contained in this Act) which provides for an appeal or application to be made to the Tribunal has effect subject to sub-paragraph (1) above.

Interpretation

7

(1) In this Schedule—

'charity law' means—

(a) any enactment contained in, or made under, this Act or the Charities Act 2006,
(b) any other enactment specified in regulations made by the Minister, and
(c) any rule of law which relates to charities, and

'enactment' includes an enactment comprised in subordinate legislation (within the meaning of the Interpretation Act 1978), and includes an enactment whenever passed or made.

(2) The exclusions contained in section 96(2) of this Act (ecclesiastical corporations etc) do not have effect for the purposes of this Schedule.]

NOTES

Amendment

Inserted by the Charities Act 2006, s 8(3), Sch 4.

Date in force: to be appointed: see the Charities Act 2006, s 79(2).

Schedule 2
Exempt Charities

The following institutions, so far as they are charities, are exempt charities within the meaning of this Act, that is to say—

(a) any institution which, if the Charities Act 1960 had not been passed, would be exempted from the powers and jurisdiction, under the Charitable Trusts Acts 1853 to 1939, of *the Commissioners* [the Charity Commissioners for England and Wales] or Minister of Education (apart from any power of the Commissioners or Minister to apply those Acts in whole or in part to charities otherwise exempt) by the terms of any enactment not contained in those Acts other than section 9 of the Places of Worship Registration Act 1855 [*(but see Note 1)*];
(b) the universities of Oxford, Cambridge, London, Durham and Newcastle, the colleges and halls in the universities of Oxford, Cambridge, Durham and Newcastle, [and] Queen Mary and Westfield College in the University of London *and the colleges of Winchester and Eton*;
(c) any university, university college, or institution connected with a university or university college, which Her Majesty declares by Order in Council to be an exempt charity for the purposes of this Act;
(d) ...
[(da) the Qualifications and Curriculum Authority;]
(e) ...
(f) ...
(g) ...
(h) ...
[(h) a higher education corporation;]
(i) a successor company to a higher education corporation (within the meaning of section 129(5) of the Education Reform Act 1988) at a time when an institution conducted by the company is for the time being designated under that section;
(j) ...
[(j) a further education corporation;]
(k) the Board of Trustees of the Victoria and Albert Museum;
(l) the Board of Trustees of the Science Museum;
(m) the Board of Trustees of the Armouries;
(n) the Board of Trustees of the Royal Botanic Gardens, Kew;

(o) the Board of Trustees of the National Museums and Galleries on Merseyside;
(p) the trustees of the British Museum and the trustees of the Natural History Museum;
(q) the Board of Trustees of the National Gallery;
(r) the Board of Trustees of the Tate Gallery;
(s) the Board of Trustees of the National Portrait Gallery;
(t) the Board of Trustees of the Wallace Collection;
(u) the Trustees of the Imperial War Museum;
(v) the Trustees of the National Maritime Museum;
(w) any institution which is administered by or on behalf of an institution included above and is established for the general purposes of, or for any special purpose of or in connection with, the last-mentioned institution [*(but see Note 2)*];
(x) *the Church Commissioners and any institution which is administered by them;*
(y) any registered society within the meaning of the Industrial and Provident Societies Act 1965 *and any registered society or branch within the meaning of the Friendly Societies Act 1974* [and which is also registered in the register of social landlords under Part 1 of the Housing Act 1996];
(z) the Board of Governors of the Museum of London;
(za) the British Library Board;
[(zb) ...].

[*NOTES*

1

Paragraph (a) above does not include—

(a) any Investment Fund or Deposit Fund within the meaning of the Church Funds Investment Measure 1958,
(b) any investment fund or deposit fund within the meaning of the Methodist Church Funds Act 1960, or
(c) the representative body of the Welsh Church or property administered by it.

2

Paragraph (w) above does not include any students' union.]

NOTES

Derivation

Paras (a), (c), (x) derived from the Charities Act 1960, Sch 2, paras (a), (c), (f); para (b) derived from the Charities Act 1960, Sch 2, para (b), as read with the Universities of Durham and Newcastle Act 1963, s 18, and the Queen Mary and Westfield College Act 1989, s 10; para (d) derived from the Education Reform Act 1988, Sch 12, Part I, para 10; paras (e)–(i) derived from the Education Reform Act 1988, Sch 12, Part III, paras 63, 64(1), (2); para (j) derived from the Further and Higher Education Act 1992, Sch 8, Part II, para 69(1); paras (k)–(n) derived from the Charities Act 1960, Sch 2, paras (ca)–(cd), as added by the National Heritage Act 1983, s 40(1), Sch 5, para 4; para (o) derived from the Charities Act 1960, Sch 2, para (ce), as added by the Local Government Reorganisation (Miscellaneous Provisions) Order, SI 1990/1765, art 3; para (p) derived from the Charities Act 1960, Sch 2, para (d), as substituted by the Museums and Galleries Act 1992, s 11(2), Sch 8, Part I, para 4; paras (q)–(t) derived from the Charities Act 1960, Sch 2, paras (ce)–(ch), as added by the Museums and Galleries Act 1992, s 11(2), Sch 8, Part II, para 10(1); para (u) derived from the Imperial War Museum Act 1920, s 5, as read with the Charities Act 1960, Sch 2, para (a); para (v) derived from the National Maritime Museum Act 1934, s 7, as read with the Charities Act 1960, Sch 2, para (a); para (w) derived from the Charities Act 1960, Sch 2, para (e), from the Education Reform Act 1988, Sch 12, Part I, para 10, Part III, paras 63, 64(3), and from the Further and Higher Education Act 1992, Sch 8, Part II, para 69(2); para (y) derived from the Charities Act 1960, Sch 2, para (g), as read with the Interpretation Act 1978, s 17(2)(a); para (z) derived from the Charities Act 1960, Sch 2, para (h), as added by the Museum of London Act 1965, s 11; para (za) derived from the Charities Act 1960, Sch 2, para (i), as added by the British Library Act 1972, s 4(2).

Initial Commencement

Specified date: 1 August 1993: see s 99(1).

Extent

This Schedule does not extend to Scotland.

Amendment

In para (a) words 'the Commissioners' in italics repealed and subsequent words in square brackets substituted by the Charities Act 2006, s 75(1), Sch 8, paras 96, 177.

Date in force: to be appointed: see the Charities Act 2006, s 79(2).

In para (a) words '(but see Note 1)' in square brackets inserted by the Charities Act 2006, s 11(1), (2).

Date in force: to be appointed: see the Charities Act 2006, s 79(2).

In para (b) word 'and' in square brackets inserted by the Charities Act 2006, s 11(1), (3)(a).

Date in force: to be appointed: see the Charities Act 2006, s 79(2).

In para (b) words 'and the colleges of Winchester and Eton' in italics repealed by the Charities Act 2006, ss 11(1), (3)(b), 75(2), Sch 9.

Date in force: to be appointed: see the Charities Act 2006, s 79(2).

Para (d) repealed by the School Standards and Framework Act 1998, s 140(3), Sch 31.

Date in force: 1 September 1999: see SI 1999/2323, art 2(1), Sch 1.

Para (da) inserted by the Education Act 1993, s 307(1), Sch 19, para 175 (repealed) and continued in force by the Education Act 1996, s 582(1), Sch 37, para 120(2), substituted with savings by the Education Act 1997, s 57(1), Sch 7, para 7(a), for savings see SI 1997/1468, Part II.

Paras (e), (g) repealed by the Education Act 1996, s 582(2), Sch 38, Pt I.

Para (f) repealed by SI 2005/3239, art 9(1), Sch 1, para 4.

Date in force: 1 April 2006: see SI 2005/3239, art 1(1); for transitional provisions see art 7(1)–(3) thereof.

First para (h) repealed by the Teaching and Higher Education Act 1998, s 44(2), Sch 4.

Date in force: 1 January 1999: see SI 1998/3237, art 2(2).

Second para (h) inserted by the Charities Act 2006, s 11(1), (4).

Date in force: to be appointed: see the Charities Act 2006, s 79(2).

First para (j) repealed by the Teaching and Higher Education Act 1998, s 44(2), Sch 4.

Date in force: 1 January 1999: see SI 1998/3237, art 2(2).

Second para (j) inserted by the Charities Act 2006, s 11(1), (5).

Date in force: to be appointed: see the Charities Act 2006, s 79(2).

In para (w) words '(but see Note 2)' in square brackets inserted by the Charities Act 2006, s 11(1), (6).

Date in force: to be appointed: see the Charities Act 2006, s 79(2).

Para (x) repealed by the Charities Act 2006, ss 11(1), (7), 75(2), Sch 9.

Date in force: to be appointed: see the Charities Act 2006, s 79(2).

In para (y) words from 'and any registered' to the end repealed and subsequent words in square brackets substituted by the Charities Act 2006, s 11(1), (8).

Date in force: to be appointed: see the Charities Act 2006, s 79(2).

Para (zb) inserted by the National Lottery etc Act 1993, s 37(2), Sch 5, para 12.

Para (zb) repealed by the National Lottery Act 2006, s 21, Sch 3.

Date in force: 1 December 2006: see SI 2006/3201, art 2(e).

Notes inserted by the Charities Act 2006, s 11(1), (9).

Date in force: to be appointed: see the Charities Act 2006, s 79(2).

Subordinate Legislation

Exempt Charities Order 1989, SI 1989/2394 (made under para (c)).

Exempt Charities Order 1993, SI 1993/2359 (made under para (c)).

Exempt Charities (No 2) Order 1994, SI 1994/2956 (made under para (c)).

Exempt Charities Order 1995, SI 1995/2998 (made under para (c)).

Exempt Charities Order 1996, SI 1996/1637 (made under para (c)).

Exempt Charities (No 2) Order 1996, SI 1996/1932 (made under para (c)).

Exempt Charities (No 3) Order 1996, SI 1996/1933 (made under para (c)).

Exempt Charities Order 1999, SI 1999/3139 (made under para (c)).

Exempt Charities Order 2000, SI 2000/1826 (made under para (c)).

Exempt Charities Order 2002, SI 2002/1626 (made under para (c)).

Exempt Charities Order 2003, SI 2003/1881 (made under para (c)).

Exempt Charities Order 2004, SI 2004/1995 (made under para (c)).

Exempt Charities Order 2006, SI 2006/1452 (made under para (c)).

Exempt Charities Order 2007, SI 2007/630 (made under para (c)).

Schedule 3
Enlargement of Areas of Local Charities

Existing area	*Permissible enlargement*
1. Greater London	Any area comprising Greater London.
2. Any area in Greater London and not in, or partly in, the City of London.	(i) Any area in Greater London and not in, or partly in, the City of London; (ii) the area of Greater London exclusive of the City of London; (iii) any area comprising the area of Greater London, exclusive of the City of London;

Existing area	*Permissible enlargement*
	(iv) any area partly in Greater London and partly in any adjacent parish or parishes (civil or ecclesiastical), and not partly in the City of London.
3. A district	Any area comprising the district
[3A. A Welsh county or county borough	Any area comprising that county or county borough.]
4. Any area in a district	(i) Any area in the district;
	(ii) the district;
	(iii) any area comprising the district;
	(iv) any area partly in the district and partly in any adjacent district [or in any adjacent Welsh county or county borough].
[4A. Any area in a Welsh county or county borough	(i) Any area in the county or county borough;
	(ii) the county or county borough;
	(iii) any area comprising the county or county borough;
	(iv) any area partly in the county or county borough and partly in any adjacent Welsh county or county borough or in any adjacent district.]
5. A parish (civil or ecclesiastical), or two or more parishes, or an area in a parish, or partly in each of two or more parishes	Any area not extending beyond the parish or parishes comprising or adjacent to the area in column 1.
6. In Wales, a community, or two or more communities, or an area in a community, or partly in each of two or more communities.	Any area not extending beyond the community or communities comprising or adjacent to the area in column 1.

NOTES

Derivation

This Schedule derived from the Charities Act 1960, Sch 3, as amended by virtue of the London Government Act 1963, s 81(9)(c), and the Local Government Act 1972, s 210(9)(f), (10), and as read with the Local Government Act 1972, s 179(1), (4).

Initial Commencement

Specified date: 1 August 1993: see s 99(1).

Extent

This Schedule does not extend to Scotland.

Amendment

Paras 3A, 4A: inserted by the Local Government (Wales) Act 1994, s 66(6), Sch 16, para 101(5), (6).

Para 4: in para (iv) words in square brackets inserted by the Local Government (Wales) Act 1994, s 66(6), Sch 16, para 101(6).

Schedule 4
Court's Jurisdiction Over Certain Charities Governed by or Under Statute

1

The court may by virtue of section 15(3) of this Act exercise its jurisdiction with respect to charities—

(a) in relation to charities established or regulated by any provision of the Seamen's Fund Winding-up Act 1851 which is repealed by the Charities Act 1960;
(b) in relation to charities established or regulated by schemes under the Endowed Schools Act 1869 to 1948, or section 75 of the Elementary Education Act 1870 or by schemes given effect under section 2 of the Education Act 1973 [or section 554 of the Education Act 1996];
(c) ...
(d) in relation to fuel allotments, that is to say, land which, by any enactment relating to inclosure or any instrument having effect under such an enactment, is vested in trustees upon trust that the land or the rents and profits of the land shall be used for the purpose of providing poor persons with fuel;
(e) in relation to charities established or regulated by any provision of the Municipal Corporations Act 1883 which is repealed by the Charities Act 1960 or by any scheme having effect under any such provision;
(f) in relation to charities regulated by schemes under the London Government Act 1899;
(g) in relation to charities established or regulated by orders or regulations under section 2 of the Regimental Charitable Funds Act 1935;
(h) in relation to charities regulated by section 79 of this Act, or by any such order as is mentioned in that section.

2

Notwithstanding anything in section 19 of the Commons Act 1876 a scheme for the administration of a fuel allotment (within the meaning of the foregoing paragraph) may provide—

(a) for the sale or letting of the allotment or any part thereof, for the discharge of the land sold or let from any restrictions as to the use thereof imposed by or under any enactment relating to inclosure and for the application of the sums payable to the trustees of the allotment in respect of the sale or lease; or
(b) for the exchange of the allotment or any part thereof for other land, for the discharge as aforesaid of the land given in exchange by the said trustees, and for the application of any money payable to the said trustees for equality of exchange; or
(c) for the use of the allotment or any part thereof for any purposes specified in the scheme.

NOTES

Derivation

Para 1 derived from the Charities Act 1960, Sch 4, para 1, as amended by virtue of the Education Act 1973, s 2(7); para 2 derived from the Charities Act 1960, Sch 4, para 2.

Initial Commencement

Specified date: 1 August 1993: see s 99(1).

Extent

This Schedule does not extend to Scotland.

Amendment

Para 1: in sub-para (b) words in square brackets inserted by the Education Act 1996, s 582(1), Sch 37, para 121; sub-para (c) repealed by the Statute Law (Repeals) Act 1993.

Schedule 5
Meaning of 'Connected Person' for Purposes of Section 36(2)

1

In section 36(2) of this Act 'connected person', in relation to a charity, means—

[(1) In section 36(2) of this Act 'connected person', in relation to a charity, means any person who falls within sub-paragraph (2)—

(a) at the time of the disposition in question, or
(b) at the time of any contract for the disposition in question.

(2) The persons falling within this sub-paragraph are—]

(a) a charity trustee or trustee for the charity;
(b) a person who is the donor of any land to the charity (whether the gift was made on or after the establishment of the charity);
(c) a child, parent, grandchild, grandparent, brother or sister of any such trustee or donor;
(d) an officer, agent or employee of the charity;
(e) the spouse [or civil partner] of any person falling within any of sub-paragraphs (a) to (d) above;
[(ea) a person carrying on business in partnership with any person falling within any of sub-paragraphs (a) to (e) above;]
(f) an institution which is controlled—
  (i) by any person failing within any of sub-paragraphs (a) to *(e)* [(ea)] above, or
  (ii) by two or more such persons taken together; or
(g) a body corporate in which—
  (i) any connected person falling within any of sub-paragraphs (a) to (f) above has a substantial interest, or
  (ii) two or more such persons, taken together, have a substantial interest.

2

(1) In paragraph *1(c)* [1(2)(c)] above 'child' includes a stepchild and an illegitimate child.

(2) For the purposes of paragraph *1(e)* [1(2)(e)] above a person living with another as that person's husband or wife shall be treated as that person's spouse.

[(3) Where two persons of the same sex are not civil partners but live together as if they were, each of them shall be treated for those purposes as the civil partner of the other.]

3

For the purposes of paragraph *1(f)* [1(2)(f)] above a person controls an institution if he is able to secure that the affairs of the institution are conducted in accordance with his wishes.

4

(1) For the purposes of paragraph *1(g)* [1(2)(g)] above any such connected person as is there mentioned has a substantial interest in a body corporate if the person or institution in question—

(a) is interested in shares comprised in the equity share capital of that body of a nominal value of more than one-fifth of that share capital, or
(b) is entitled to exercise, or control the exercise of, more than one-fifth of the voting power at any general meeting of that body.

(2) The rules set out in Part I of Schedule 13 to the Companies Act 1985 (rules for interpretation of certain provisions of that Act) shall apply for the purposes of sub-paragraph (1) above as they apply for the purposes of section 346(4) of that Act ('connected persons' etc).

(3) In this paragraph 'equity share capital' and 'share' have the same meaning as in that Act.

NOTES

Derivation

This Schedule derived from the Charities Act 1992, Sch 2.

Initial Commencement

Specified date: 1 August 1993: see s 99(1).

Extent

This Schedule does not extend to Scotland.

Amendment

Para 1: words from 'In section 36(2)' to 'a charity, means—' in italics repealed and subsequent words in square brackets substituted by the Charities Act 2006, s 75(1), Sch 8, paras 96, 178(1)–(3).

Date in force: to be appointed: see the Charities Act 2006, s 79(2).

Para 1: in sub-para (e) words 'or civil partner' in square brackets inserted by the Civil Partnership Act 2004, s 261(1), Sch 27, para 147.

Date in force: 5 December 2005: see SI 2005/3175, art 2(2).

Para 1: sub-para (2)(ea) inserted by the Charities Act 2006, s 75(1), Sch 8, paras 96, 178(1), (4).

Date in force: to be appointed: see the Charities Act 2006, s 79(2).

Para 1: in sub-para (f)(i) reference to '(e)' in italics repealed and subsequent reference '(ea)' in square brackets substituted by the Charities Act 2006, s 75(1), Sch 8, paras 96, 178(1), (4).

Date in force: to be appointed: see the Charities Act 2006, s 79(2).

Para 2: in sub-para (1) reference to '1(c)' in italics repealed and subsequent reference in square brackets substituted by the Charities Act 2006, s 75(1), Sch 8, paras 96, 178(1), (5)(a).

Date in force: to be appointed: see the Charities Act 2006, s 79(2).

Para 2: in sub-para (2) reference to '1(e)' in italics repealed and subsequent reference in square brackets substituted by the Charities Act 2006, s 75(1), Sch 8, paras 96, 178(1), (5)(b).

Date in force: to be appointed: see the Charities Act 2006, s 79(2).

Para 2: sub-para (3) inserted by the Charities Act 2006, s 75(1), Sch 8, paras 96, 178(1), (5)(c).

Date in force: to be appointed: see the Charities Act 2006, s 79(2).

Para 3: reference to '1(f)' in italics repealed and subsequent reference in suqare brackets substituted by the Charities Act 2006, s 75(1), Sch 8, paras 96, 178(1), (6).

Date in force: to be appointed: see the Charities Act 2006, s 79(2).

Para 4: in sub-para (1) reference to '1(g)' in italics repealed and subsequent reference in square brackets substituted by the Charities Act 2006, s 75(1), Sch 8, paras 96, 178(1), (7).

Date in force: to be appointed: see the Charities Act 2006, s 79(2).

[Schedule 5A Group Accounts]

NOTES

Amendment

Inserted by the Charities Act 2006, s 30(2); for transitional provisions and savings see s 75(1), Sch 6, Sch 10, para 17 thereto.

Date in force (for remaining purposes): to be appointed: see the Charities Act 2006, s 79(2).

[Interpretation

1

(1) This paragraph applies for the purposes of this Schedule.

(2) A charity is a 'parent charity' if—

(a) it is (or is to be treated as) a parent undertaking in relation to one or more other undertakings in accordance with the provisions of section 258 of, and Schedule 10A to, the Companies Act 1985, and
(b) it is not a company.

(3) Each undertaking in relation to which a parent charity is (or is to be treated as) a parent undertaking in accordance with those provisions is a 'subsidiary undertaking' in relation to the parent charity.

(4) But sub-paragraph (3) does not have the result that any of the following is a 'subsidiary undertaking'—

(a) any special trusts of a charity,
(b) any institution which, by virtue of a direction under section 96(5) of this Act, is to be treated as forming part of a charity for the purposes of this Part of this Act, or
(c) any charity to which a direction under section 96(6) of this Act applies for those purposes.

(5) 'The group', in relation to a parent charity, means that charity and its subsidiary undertaking or undertakings, and any reference to the members of the group is to be construed accordingly.

(6) For the purposes of—

(a) this paragraph, and
(b) the operation of the provisions mentioned in sub-paragraph (2) above for the purposes of this paragraph,

'undertaking' has the meaning given by sub-paragraph (7) below.

(7) For those purposes 'undertaking' means—

(a) an undertaking as defined by section 259(1) of the Companies Act 1985, or
(b) a charity which is not an undertaking as so defined.

Accounting records

2

(1) The charity trustees—

(a) of a parent charity, or
(b) of any charity which is a subsidiary undertaking,

must ensure that the accounting records kept in respect of the charity under section 41(1) of this Act not only comply with the requirements of that provision but also are such as to enable the charity trustees of the parent charity to ensure that, where any group accounts are prepared by them under paragraph 3(2), those accounts comply with the relevant requirements.

(2) If a parent charity has a subsidiary undertaking in relation to which the requirements of section 41(1) of this Act do not apply, the charity trustees of the parent charity must take reasonable steps to secure that the undertaking keeps such accounting records as to enable the trustees to ensure that, where any group accounts are prepared by them under paragraph 3(2), those accounts comply with the relevant requirements.

(3) In this paragraph 'the relevant requirements' means the requirements of regulations under paragraph 3.

Preparation of group accounts

3

(1) This paragraph applies in relation to a financial year of a charity if it is a parent charity at the end of that year.

(2) The charity trustees of the parent charity must prepare group accounts in respect of that year.

(3) 'Group accounts' means consolidated accounts—

(a) relating to the group, and
(b) complying with such requirements as to their form and contents as may be prescribed by regulations made by the Minister.

(4) Without prejudice to the generality of sub-paragraph (3), regulations under that sub-paragraph may make provision—

(a) for any such accounts to be prepared in accordance with such methods and principles as are specified or referred to in the regulations;
(b) for dealing with cases where the financial years of the members of the group do not all coincide;
(c) as to any information to be provided by way of notes to the accounts.

(5) Regulations under that sub-paragraph may also make provision—

(a) for determining the financial years of subsidiary undertakings for the purposes of this Schedule;
(b) for imposing on the charity trustees of a parent charity requirements with respect to securing that such financial years coincide with that of the charity.

(6) If the requirement in sub-paragraph (2) applies to the charity trustees of a parent charity in relation to a financial year—

(a) that requirement so applies in addition to the requirement in section 42(1) of this Act, and

(b) the option of preparing the documents mentioned in section 42(3) of this Act is not available in relation to that year (whatever the amount of the charity's gross income for that year).

(7) Sub-paragraph (2) has effect subject to paragraph 4.

Exceptions relating to requirement to prepare group accounts

4

(1) The requirement in paragraph 3(2) does not apply to the charity trustees of a parent charity in relation to a financial year if at the end of that year it is itself a subsidiary undertaking in relation to another charity.

(2) The requirement in paragraph 3(2) does not apply to the charity trustees of a parent charity in relation to a financial year if the aggregate gross income of the group for that year does not exceed such sum as is specified in regulations made by the Minister.

(3) Regulations made by the Minister may prescribe circumstances in which a subsidiary undertaking may or (as the case may be) must be excluded from group accounts required to be prepared under paragraph 3(2) for a financial year.

(4) Where, by virtue of such regulations, each of the subsidiary undertakings which are members of a group is either permitted or required to be excluded from any such group accounts for a financial year, the requirement in paragraph 3(2) does not apply to the charity trustees of the parent charity in relation to that year.

Preservation of group accounts

5

(1) The charity trustees of a charity shall preserve any group accounts prepared by them under paragraph 3(2) for at least six years from the end of the financial year to which the accounts relate.

(2) Subsection (4) of section 41 of this Act shall apply in relation to the preservation of any such accounts as it applies in relation to the preservation of any accounting records (the references to subsection (3) of that section being construed as references to sub-paragraph (1) above).

Audit of accounts of larger groups

6

(1) This paragraph applies where group accounts are prepared for a financial year of a parent charity under paragraph 3(2) and—

(a) the aggregate gross income of the group in that year exceeds the relevant income threshold, or

(b) the aggregate gross income of the group in that year exceeds the relevant income threshold and at the end of the year the aggregate value of the assets of the group (before deduction of liabilities) exceeds the relevant assets threshold.

(2) In sub-paragraph (1)—

(a) the reference in paragraph (a) or (b) to the relevant income threshold is a reference to the sum prescribed as the relevant income threshold for the purposes of that paragraph, and

(b) the reference in paragraph (b) to the relevant assets threshold is a reference to the sum prescribed as the relevant assets threshold for the purposes of that paragraph.

'Prescribed' means prescribed by regulations made by the Minister.

(3) This paragraph also applies where group accounts are prepared for a financial year of a parent charity under paragraph 3(2) and the appropriate audit provision applies in relation to the parent charity's own accounts for that year.

(4) If this paragraph applies in relation to a financial year of a parent charity by virtue of sub-paragraph (1) or (3), the group accounts for that year shall be audited—

(a) (subject to paragraph (b) or (c) below) by a person within section 43(2)(a) or (b) of this Act;
(b) if section 43A of this Act applies in relation to that year, by a person appointed by the Audit Commission (see section 43A(7));
(c) if section 43B of this Act applies in relation to that year, by the Auditor General for Wales.

(5) Where it appears to the Commission that sub-paragraph (4)(a) above has not been complied with in relation to that year within ten months from the end of that year—

(a) the Commission may by order require the group accounts for that year to be audited by a person within section 43(2)(a) or (b) of this Act, and
(b) if it so orders, the auditor shall be a person appointed by the Commission.

(6) Section 43(6) of this Act shall apply in relation to any such audit as it applies in relation to an audit carried out by an auditor appointed under section 43(5) (reading the reference to the funds of the charity as a reference to the funds of the parent charity).

(7) Section 43A(4) and (6) of this Act apply in relation to any appointment under sub-paragraph (4)(b) above as they apply in relation to an appointment under section 43A(2).

(8) If this paragraph applies in relation to a financial year of a parent charity by virtue of sub-paragraph (1), the appropriate audit provision shall apply in relation to the parent charity's own accounts for that year (whether or not it would otherwise so apply).

(9) In this paragraph 'the appropriate audit provision', in relation to a financial year of a parent charity, means—

(a) (subject to paragraph (b) or (c) below) section 43(2) of this Act;
(b) if section 43A of this Act applies in relation to that year, section 43A(2);
(c) if section 43B of this Act applies in relation to that year, section 43B(2).

Examination of accounts of smaller groups

7

(1) This paragraph applies where—

(a) group accounts are prepared for a financial year of a parent charity under paragraph 3(2), and
(b) paragraph 6 does not apply in relation to that year.

(2) If—

(a) this paragraph applies in relation to a financial year of a parent charity, and
(b) sub-paragraph (4) or (5) below does not apply in relation to it,

subsections (3) to (7) of section 43 of this Act shall apply in relation to the group accounts for that year as they apply in relation to the accounts of a charity for a financial year in relation to which subsection (2) of that section does not apply, but subject to the modifications in sub-paragraph (3) below.

(3) The modifications are—

(a) any reference to the charity trustees of the charity is to be construed as a reference to the charity trustees of the parent charity;
(b) any reference to the charity's gross income in the financial year in question is to be construed as a reference to the aggregate gross income of the group in that year; and
(c) any reference to the funds of the charity is to be construed as a reference to the funds of the parent charity.

(4) If—

(a) this paragraph applies in relation to a financial year of a parent charity, and
(b) section 43A of this Act also applies in relation to that year,

subsections (3) to (6) of that section shall apply in relation to the group accounts for that year as they apply in relation to the accounts of a charity for a financial year in relation to which subsection (2) of that section does not apply.

(5) If—

(a) this paragraph applies in relation to a financial year of a parent charity, and
(b) section 43B of this Act also applies in relation to that year,

subsection (3) of that section shall apply in relation to the group accounts for that year as they apply in relation to the accounts of a charity for a financial year in relation to which subsection (2) of that section does not apply.

(6) If the group accounts for a financial year of a parent charity are to be examined or audited in accordance with section 43(3) of this Act (as applied by sub-paragraph (2) above), section 43(3) shall apply in relation to the parent charity's own accounts for that year (whether or not it would otherwise so apply).

(7) Nothing in sub-paragraph (4) or (5) above affects the operation of section 43A(3) to (6) or (as the case may be) section 43B(3) in relation to the parent charity's own accounts for the financial year in question.

Supplementary provisions relating to audits etc

8

(1) Section 44(1) of this Act shall apply in relation to audits and examinations carried out under or by virtue of paragraph 6 or 7, but subject to the modifications in sub-paragraph (2) below.

(2) The modifications are—

(a) in paragraph (b), the reference to section 43, 43A or 43B of this Act is to be construed as a reference to paragraph 6 above or to any of those sections as applied by paragraph 7 above;
(b) also in paragraph (b), the reference to any such statement of accounts as is mentioned in sub-paragraph (i) of that paragraph is to be construed as a reference to group accounts prepared for a financial year under paragraph 3(2) above;
(c) in paragraph (c), any reference to section 43, 43A or 43B of this Act is to be construed as a reference to that section as applied by paragraph 7 above;
(d) in paragraphs (d) and (e), any reference to the charity concerned or a charity is to be construed as a reference to any member of the group; and
(e) in paragraph (f), the reference to the requirements of section 43(2) or (3) of this Act is to be construed as a reference to the requirements of paragraph 6(4)(a) or those applied by paragraph 7(2) above.

(3) Without prejudice to the generality of section 44(1)(e), as modified by sub-paragraph (2)(d) above, regulations made under that provision may make provision corresponding or similar to any provision made by section 389A of the Companies Act 1985 (c 6) in connection with the rights exercisable by an auditor of a company in relation to a subsidiary undertaking of the company.

(4) In section 44(2) of this Act the reference to section 44(1)(d) or (e) includes a reference to that provision as it applies in accordance with this paragraph.

Duty of auditors etc to report matters to Commission

9

(1) Section 44A(2) to (5) and (7) of this Act shall apply in relation to a person appointed to audit, or report on, any group accounts under or by virtue of paragraph 6 or 7 above as they apply in relation to a person such as is mentioned in section 44A(1).

(2) In section 44A(2)(a), as it applies in accordance with sub-paragraph (1) above, the reference to the charity or any connected institution or body is to be construed as a reference to the parent charity or any of its subsidiary undertakings.

Annual reports

10

(1) This paragraph applies where group accounts are prepared for a financial year of a parent charity under paragraph 3(2).

(2) The annual report prepared by the charity trustees of the parent charity in respect of that year under section 45 of this Act shall include—

(a) such a report by the trustees on the activities of the charity's subsidiary undertakings during that year, and
(b) such other information relating to any of those undertakings,

as may be prescribed by regulations made by the Minister.

(3) Without prejudice to the generality of sub-paragraph (2), regulations under that sub-paragraph may make provision—

(a) for any such report as is mentioned in paragraph (a) of that sub-paragraph to be prepared in accordance with such principles as are specified or referred to in the regulations;
(b) enabling the Commission to dispense with any requirement prescribed by virtue of sub-paragraph (2)(b) in the case of a particular subsidiary undertaking or a particular class of subsidiary undertaking.

(4) Section 45(3) to (3B) shall apply in relation to the annual report referred to in sub-paragraph (2) above as if any reference to the charity's gross income in the financial year in question were a reference to the aggregate gross income of the group in that year.

(5) When transmitted to the Commission in accordance with sub-paragraph (4) above, the copy of the annual report shall have attached to it both a copy of the group accounts prepared for that year under paragraph 3(2) and—

(a) a copy of the report made by the auditor on those accounts; or
(b) where those accounts have been examined under section 43, 43A or 43B of this Act (as applied by paragraph 7 above), a copy of the report made by the person carrying out the examination.

(6) The requirements in this paragraph are in addition to those in section 45 of this Act.

Excepted charities

11

(1) This paragraph applies where—

(a) a charity is required to prepare an annual report in respect of a financial year by virtue of section 46(5) of this Act,
(b) the charity is a parent charity at the end of the year, and
(c) group accounts are prepared for that year under paragraph 3(2) by the charity trustees of the charity.

(2) When transmitted to the Commission in accordance with section 46(7) of this Act, the copy of the annual report shall have attached to it both a copy of the group accounts and—

(a) a copy of the report made by the auditor on those accounts; or
(b) where those accounts have been examined under section 43, 43A or 43B of this Act (as applied by paragraph 7 above), a copy of the report made by the person carrying out the examination.

(3) The requirement in sub-paragraph (2) is in addition to that in section 46(6) of this Act.

Exempt charities

12

Nothing in the preceding provisions of this Schedule applies to an exempt charity.

Public inspection of annual reports etc

13

In section 47(2) of this Act, the reference to a charity's most recent accounts includes, in relation to a charity whose charity trustees have prepared any group accounts under paragraph 3(2), the group accounts most recently prepared by them.

Offences

14

(1) Section 49(1) of this Act applies in relation to a requirement within sub-paragraph (2) as it applies in relation to a requirement within section 49(1)(a).

(2) A requirement is within this sub-paragraph where it is imposed by section 45(3) or (3A) of this Act, taken with—

(a) section 45(3B), (4) and (5), and
(b) paragraph 10(5) or 11(2) above,

as applicable.

(3) In sub-paragraph (2) any reference to section 45(3), (3A) or (3B) of this Act is a reference to that provision as applied by paragraph 10(4) above.

(4) In section 49(1)(b) the reference to section 47(2) of this Act includes a reference to that provision as extended by paragraph 13 above.

Aggregate gross income

15

The Minister may by regulations make provision for determining for the purposes of this Schedule the amount of the aggregate gross income for a financial year of a group consisting of a parent charity and its subsidiary undertaking or undertakings.]

NOTES

Amendment

Inserted by the Charities Act 2006, s 30(2); for transitional provisions and savings see s 75(1), Sch 6, Sch 10, para 17 thereto.

Date in force: to be appointed: see the Charities Act 2006, s 79(2).

[Schedule 5B Further Provision about Charitable Incorporated Organisations]

NOTES

Amendment

Inserted by the Charities Act 2006, s 34, Sch 7, Pt 1, para 2.

Date in force (for remaining purposes): to be appointed: see the Charities Act 2006, s 79(2).

[Powers

1

(1) Subject to anything in its constitution, a CIO has power to do anything which is calculated to further its purposes or is conducive or incidental to doing so.

(2) The CIO's charity trustees shall manage the affairs of the CIO and may for that purpose exercise all the powers of the CIO.

Constitutional requirements

2

A CIO shall use and apply its property in furtherance of its purposes and in accordance with its constitution.

3

If the CIO is one whose members are liable to contribute to its assets if it is wound up, its constitution binds the CIO and its members for the time being to the same extent as if its provisions were contained in a contract—

(a) to which the CIO and each of its members was a party, and
(b) which contained obligations on the part of the CIO and each member to observe all the provisions of the constitution.

4

Money payable by a member to the CIO under the constitution is a debt due from him to the CIO, and is of the nature of a specialty debt.

Third parties

5

(1) Sub-paragraphs (2) and (3) are subject to sub-paragraph (4).

(2) The validity of an act done (or purportedly done) by a CIO shall not be called into question on the ground that it lacked constitutional capacity.

(3) The power of the charity trustees of a CIO to act so as to bind the CIO (or authorise others to do so) shall not be called into question on the ground of any constitutional limitations on their powers.

(4) But sub-paragraphs (2) and (3) apply only in favour of a person who gives full consideration in money or money's worth in relation to the act in question, and does not know—

(a) in a sub-paragraph (2) case, that the act is beyond the CIO's constitutional capacity, or
(b) in a sub-paragraph (3) case, that the act is beyond the constitutional powers of its charity trustees,

and (in addition) sub-paragraph (3) applies only if the person dealt with the CIO in good faith (which he shall be presumed to have done unless the contrary is proved).

(5) A party to an arrangement or transaction with a CIO is not bound to inquire—

(a) whether it is within the CIO's constitutional capacity, or
(b) as to any constitutional limitations on the powers of its charity trustees to bind the CIO or authorise others to do so.

(6) If a CIO purports to transfer or grant an interest in property, the fact that the act was beyond its constitutional capacity, or that its charity trustees in connection with the act exceeded their constitutional powers, does not affect the title of a person who subsequently acquires the property or any interest in it for full consideration without actual notice of any such circumstances affecting the validity of the CIO's act.

(7) In any proceedings arising out of sub-paragraphs (2) to (4), the burden of proving that a person knew that an act—

(a) was beyond the CIO's constitutional capacity, or
(b) was beyond the constitutional powers of its charity trustees,

lies on the person making that allegation.

(8) In this paragraph and paragraphs 6 to 8—

(a) references to a CIO's lack of 'constitutional capacity' are to lack of capacity because of anything in its constitution, and
(b) references to 'constitutional limitations' on the powers of a CIO's charity trustees are to limitations on their powers under its constitution, including limitations deriving from a resolution of the CIO in general meeting, or from an agreement between the CIO's members, and 'constitutional powers' is to be construed accordingly.

6

(1) Nothing in paragraph 5 prevents a person from bringing proceedings to restrain the doing of an act which would be—

(a) beyond the CIO's constitutional capacity, or
(b) beyond the constitutional powers of the CIO's charity trustees.

(2) But no such proceedings may be brought in respect of an act to be done in fulfilment of a legal obligation arising from a previous act of the CIO.

(3) Sub-paragraph (2) does not prevent the Commission from exercising any of its powers.

7

Nothing in paragraph 5(3) affects any liability incurred by the CIO's charity trustees (or any one of them) for acting beyond his or their constitutional powers.

8

Nothing in paragraph 5 absolves the CIO's charity trustees from their duty to act within the CIO's constitution and in accordance with any constitutional limitations on their powers.

Duties

9

It is the duty of—

(a) each member of a CIO, and
(b) each charity trustee of a CIO,

to exercise his powers, and (in the case of a charity trustee) to perform his functions, in his capacity as such, in the way he decides, in good faith, would be most likely to further the purposes of the CIO.

10

(1) Subject to any provision of a CIO's constitution permitted by virtue of regulations made under sub-paragraph (2), each charity trustee of a CIO shall in the performance of his functions in that capacity exercise such care and skill as is reasonable in the circumstances, having regard in particular—

(a) to any special knowledge or experience that he has or holds himself out as having, and
(b) if he acts as a charity trustee in the course of a business or profession, to any special knowledge or experience that it is reasonable to expect of a person acting in the course of that kind of business or profession.

(2) The Minister may make regulations permitting a CIO's constitution to provide that the duty in sub-paragraph (1) does not apply, or does not apply in so far as is specified in the constitution.

(3) Regulations under sub-paragraph (2) may provide for limits on the extent to which, or the cases in which, a CIO's constitution may disapply the duty in sub-paragraph (1).

Personal benefit and payments

11

(1) A charity trustee of a CIO may not benefit personally from any arrangement or transaction entered into by the CIO if, before the arrangement or transaction was entered into, he did not disclose to all the charity trustees of the CIO any material interest of his in it or in any other person or body party to it (whether that interest is direct or indirect).

(2) Nothing in sub-paragraph (1) confers authority for a charity trustee of a CIO to benefit personally from any arrangement or transaction entered into by the CIO.

12

A charity trustee of a CIO—

(a) is entitled to be reimbursed by the CIO, or
(b) may pay out of the CIO's funds,

expenses properly incurred by him in the performance of his functions as such.

Procedure

13

(1) The Minister may by regulations make provision about the procedure of CIOs.

(2) Subject to—

(a) any such regulations,
(b) any other requirement imposed by or by virtue of this Act or any other enactment, and
(c) anything in the CIO's constitution,

a CIO may regulate its own procedure.

(3) But a CIO's procedure shall include provision for the holding of a general meeting of its members, and the regulations referred to in sub-paragraph (1) may in particular make provision about such meetings.

Amendment of constitution

14

(1) A CIO may by resolution of its members amend its constitution (and a single resolution may provide for more than one amendment).

(2) Such a resolution must be passed—

(a) by a 75% majority of those voting at a general meeting of the CIO (including those voting by proxy or by post, if voting that way is permitted), or
(b) unanimously by the CIO's members, otherwise than at a general meeting.

(3) The date of passing of such a resolution is—

(a) the date of the general meeting at which it was passed, or
(b) if it was passed otherwise than at a general meeting, the date on which provision in the CIO's constitution or in regulations made under paragraph 13 deems it to have been passed (but that date may not be earlier than that on which the last member agreed to it).

(4) The power of a CIO to amend its constitution is not exercisable in any way which would result in the CIO's ceasing to be a charity.

(5) Subject to paragraph 15(5) below, a resolution containing an amendment which would make any regulated alteration is to that extent ineffective unless the prior written consent of the Commission has been obtained to the making of the amendment.

(6) The following are regulated alterations—

(a) any alteration of the CIO's purposes,

(b) any alteration of any provision of the CIO's constitution directing the application of property of the CIO on its dissolution,

(c) any alteration of any provision of the CIO's constitution where the alteration would provide authorisation for any benefit to be obtained by charity trustees or members of the CIO or persons connected with them.

(7) For the purposes of sub-paragraph (6)(c)—

(a) 'benefit' means a direct or indirect benefit of any nature, except that it does not include any remuneration (within the meaning of section 73A of this Act) whose receipt may be authorised under that section, and

(b) the same rules apply for determining whether a person is connected with a charity trustee or member of the CIO as apply, in accordance with section 73B(5) and (6) of this Act, for determining whether a person is connected with a charity trustee for the purposes of section 73A.

Registration and coming into effect of amendments

15

(1) A CIO shall send to the Commission a copy of a resolution containing an amendment to its constitution, together with—

(a) a copy of the constitution as amended, and

(b) such other documents and information as the Commission may require,

by the end of the period of 15 days beginning with the date of passing of the resolution (see paragraph 14(3)).

(2) An amendment to a CIO's constitution does not take effect until it has been registered.

(3) The Commission shall refuse to register an amendment if—

(a) in the opinion of the Commission the CIO had no power to make it (for example, because the effect of making it would be that the CIO ceased to be a charity, or that the CIO or its constitution did not comply with any requirement imposed by or by virtue of this Act or any other enactment), or

(b) the amendment would change the name of the CIO, and the Commission could have refused an application under section 69E of this Act for the constitution and registration of a CIO with the name specified in the amendment on a ground set out in subsection (4) of that section.

(4) The Commission may refuse to register an amendment if the amendment would make a regulated alteration and the consent referred to in paragraph 14(5) had not been obtained.

(5) But if the Commission does register such an amendment, paragraph 14(5) does not apply.]

NOTES

Amendment

Inserted by the Charities Act 2006, s 34, Sch 7, Pt 1, para 2.

Date in force (for remaining purposes): to be appointed: see the Charities Act 2006, s 79(2).

Schedule 6
Consequential Amendments

...

NOTES

Derivation

This Schedule derived from the Charities Act 1960, s 40(5), and from the Charities Act 1992, ss 54(1)(b), (3), 56(4), (5), and contains drafting provisions.

Initial Commencement

Specified date (in part): 1 August 1993: see s 99(1).

To be appointed (remainder): see s 99(2).

Appointment

Appointment: 1 March 1996: see SI 1995/2695, art 2.

Amendment

Repealed in part by the Reserve Forces Act 1996, s 131(2), Sch 11.

Repealed in part, in relation to England and Wales, by the Housing Act 1996, s 227, Sch 19, Part I.

Repealed in part, in relation to England and Wales, by SI 1996/2325, art 4(1), Sch 1, Part I.

Repealed in part by the Finance Act 1999, s 139, Sch 20, Pt V(5).

Date in force: this repeal has effect in relation to instruments executed on or after 6 February 2000: see the Finance Act 1999, Sch 20, Pt V(5).

Repealed in part by the Licensing Act 2003, s 199, Sch 7.

Date in force: 24 November 2005: see SI 2005/3056, arts 1(2), 2(2); for savings see art 4 thereof.

Repealed in part by the Companies Act 2006, s 1295, Sch 16.

Date in force: to be appointed: see the Companies Act 2006, s 1300(2).

Repealed in part by the Charities Act 2006, s 75(2), Sch 9.

Date in force: to be appointed: see the Charities Act 2006, s 79(2).

This Schedule amends the Places of Worship Registration Act 1855, s 9, the Open Spaces Act 1906, s 4, the New Parishes Measure 1943, ss 14, 31, the Clergy Pensions Measure 1961, s 33, the Cathedrals Measure 1963, ss 20, 51, the Incumbents and Churchwardens (Trusts) Measure 1964, s 1, the Leasehold Reform Act 1967, s 23, the Greater London Council (General Powers) Act 1968, s 43, the Redundant Churches and other Religious Buildings Act 1969, ss 4, 7, the Sharing of Church Buildings Act 1969, ss 2, 8, the Local Government Act 1972, ss 11, 29, 123, 127, 131, the Fire Precautions (Loans) Act 1973, s 1, the Theatres Trust Act 1976, s 2, the Interpretation Act 1978, Sch 1, the Disused Burial Grounds (Amendment) Act 1981, s 6, the Pastoral Measure 1983, ss 55, 63, 87, Sch 3, the Rates Act 1984, s 3, the Companies Act 1985, ss 35, 35A, 209, Sch 13, the Housing Associations Act 1985, ss 10, 35, 38, the Financial Services Act 1986, s 45, the Coal Industry Act 1987, s 5, the Reverter of Sites Act 1987, s 4, the Income and Corporation Taxes Act 1988, Sch 20, the Courts and Legal Services Act 1990, Sch 11, the London Local Authorities Act 1990, s 4, the Charities Act 1992, ss 29, 30, 58, 63, 72, 74, the National Health Service Reorganisation Act 1973, s 30, the Consumer Credit Act 1974, s 189, the Rent (Agriculture) Act 1976, s 5, the Rent Act 1977, s 15, the National Health Service

Act 1977, s 96, the Dioceses Measure 1978, s 19, the Ancient Monuments and Archaeological Areas Act 1979, s 49, the Greater London Council (General Powers) Act 1984, s 10, the Local Government Act 1985, s 90, the Housing Act 1985, ss 525, 622, the Landlord and Tenant Act 1987, s 60, the Education Reform Act 1988, ss 128, 192, the Copyright, Designs and Patents Act 1988, Sch 6, para 7, the Housing Act 1988, Sch 2, Part I, the University of Wales College of Cardiff Act 1988, s 9, the Imperial College Act 1988, s 10, the Local Government and Housing Act 1989, s 138.

Repealed in part by the Housing Grants, Construction and Regeneration Act 1996, s 147, Sch 3, Part I.

Schedule 7 Repeals

Chapter	*Short title*	*Extent of repeal*
35 & 36 Vic c 24	The Charitable Trustees Incorporation Act 1872	The whole Act so far as unrepealed.
10 & 11 Geo 5 c 16	The Imperial War Museum Act 1920	Section 5.
24 & 25 Geo 5 c 43	The National Maritime Museum Act 1934	Section 7.
8 & 9 Eliz 2 c 58	The Charities Act 1960	The whole Act so far as unrepealed except— section 28(9) section 35(6) section 38(3) to (5) section 39(2) sections 48 and 49 Schedule 6.
1963 c 33	The London Government Act 1963	Section 81(9)(b) and (c).
1963 c xi	The Universities of Durham and Newcastle-upon Tyne Act 1963	Section 10.
1965 c 17	The Museum of London Act 1965	Section 11.
1972 c 54	The British Library Act 1972	Section 4(2).
1972 c 70	The Local Government Act 1972	Section 210(9).
1973 c 16	The Education Act 1973	In section 2(7) the words from 'but' onwards. In Schedule 1, paragraph 1(1) and (3).
1976 No 4	The Endowments and Glebe Measure 1976	Section 44.
1983 c 47	The National Heritage Act 1983	In Schedule 5, paragraph 4.

Chapter	*Short title*	*Extent of repeal*
1985 c 9	The Companies Consolidation (Consequential Provisions) Act 1985	In Schedule 2 the entry relating to the Charities Act 1960.
1985 c 20	The Charities Act 1985	Section 1.
1986 c 60	The Financial Services Act 1986	In Schedule 16, paragraph 1.
1988 c 40	The Education Reform Act 1988	In Schedule 12, paragraphs 9, 10, 63 and 64.
1989 c 40	The Companies Act 1989	Section 111.
1989 c xiii	The Queen Mary and Westfield College Act 1989	Section 10.
1990 c 41	The Courts and Legal Services Act 1990	In Schedule 10, paragraph 14.
1992 c 13	The Further and Higher Education Act 1992	In Schedule 8, paragraph 69.
1992 c 41	The Charities Act 1992	The whole of Part I except—
		section 1(1) and (4)
		sections 29 and 30
		section 36
		sections 49 and 50
		Section 75(b).
		Section 76(1)(a).
		In section 77, subsections (2)(a), (b) and (c) and in subsection (4) the figures 20, 22 and 23.
		Section 79(4) and (5).
		Schedules 1 to 4.
		Schedule 6, paragraph 13(2).
		Schedule 7, the entries relating to section 8 of the Charities Act 1960 and (so far as not in force at the date specified in section 99(1) of this Act) the Charities Act 1985.
1992 c 44	The Museums and Galleries Act 1992	In Schedule 8, paragraphs 4 and 10.
		In Schedule 9, the entry relating to the Charities Act 1960.

NOTES

Initial Commencement

Specified date: 1 August 1993: see s 99(1).

Schedule 8

...

NOTES

Amendment

Repealed by the Statute Law (Repeals) Act 2004.

Date in force: 22 July 2004: (no specific commencement provision).

Part I

...

NOTES

Amendment

Repealed by the Statute Law (Repeals) Act 2004.

Date in force: 22 July 2004: (no specific commencement provision).

Part II

...

NOTES

Amendment

Repealed by the Statute Law (Repeals) Act 2004.

Date in force: 22 July 2004: (no specific commencement provision).

Appendix 3

Charities Act 2006

Charities Act 2006

2006 Chapter 50

An Act to provide for the establishment and functions of the Charity Commission for England and Wales and the Charity Tribunal; to make other amendments of the law about charities, including provision about charitable incorporated organisations; to make further provision about public charitable collections and other fund-raising carried on in connection with charities and other institutions; to make other provision about the funding of such institutions; and for connected purposes.

[8th November 2006]

Be it enacted by the Queen's most Excellent Majesty, by and with the advice and consent of the Lords Spiritual and Temporal, and Commons, in this present Parliament assembled, and by the authority of the same, as follows:

Arrangement

Exempt charities: registration and regulation

11 Changes in exempt charities
12 Increased regulation of exempt charities under 1993 Act
13 General duty of principal regulator in relation to exempt charity
14 Commission to consult principal regulator before exercising powers in relation to exempt charity

Chapter 4
Application of Property Cy-près

Cy-près occasions

15 Application cy-près by reference to current circumstances
16 Application cy-près of gifts by donors unknown or disclaiming
17 Application cy-près of gifts made in response to certain solicitations

Schemes

18 Cy-près schemes

Chapter 5
Assistance and Supervision of Charities by Court and Commission

Suspension or removal of trustees etc from membership

19 Power to suspend or remove trustees etc from membership of charity

Directions by Commission

20 Power to give specific directions for protection of charity
21 Power to direct application of charity property

Publicity relating to schemes

22 Relaxation of publicity requirements relating to schemes etc

Common investment schemes

23 Participation of Scottish and Northern Irish charities in common investment schemes etc

Advice or other assistance

24 Power to give advice and guidance
25 Power to determine membership of charity

Powers of entry etc

26 Power to enter premises and seize documents etc

Mortgages of charity land

27 Restrictions on mortgaging

Chapter 6
Audit or Examination of Accounts where Charity is not a Company

28 Annual audit or examination of accounts of charities which are not companies
29 Duty of auditor etc of charity which is not a company to report matters to Commission
30 Group accounts

Chapter 7
Charitable Companies

31 Relaxation of restriction on altering memorandum etc of charitable company
32 Annual audit or examination of accounts of charitable companies

33 Duty of auditor etc of charitable company to report matters to Commission

Chapter 8
Charitable Incorporated Organisations

34 Charitable incorporated organisations

Chapter 9
Charity Trustees etc

Waiver of disqualification

35 Waiver of trustee's disqualification

Remuneration of trustees etc

36 Remuneration of trustees etc providing services to charity
37 Disqualification of trustee receiving remuneration by virtue of section 36

Liability of trustees etc

38 Power of Commission to relieve trustees, auditors etc from liability for breach of trust or duty
39 Trustees' indemnity insurance

Chapter 10
Powers of Unincorporated Charities

40 Power to transfer all property
41 Power to replace purposes
42 Power to modify powers or procedures

Chapter 11
Powers to Spend Capital and Mergers

Spending of capital

43 Power to spend capital

Mergers

44 Merger of charities

Part 3
Funding for Charitable, Benevolent or Philanthropic Institutions

Chapter 1
Public Charitable Collections

Preliminary

45 Regulation of public charitable collections
46 Charitable appeals that are not public charitable collections
47 Other definitions for purposes of this Chapter

Restrictions on conducting collections

48 Restrictions on conducting collections in a public place
49 Restrictions on conducting door to door collections
50 Exemption for local, short-term collections

Public collections certificates

51 Applications for certificates
52 Determination of applications and issue of certificates
53 Grounds for refusing to issue a certificate
54 Power to call for information and documents
55 Transfer of certificate between trustees of unincorporated charity

Part 1
Meaning of 'Charity' and 'Charitable Purpose'

1 Meaning of 'charity'

(1) For the purposes of the law of England and Wales, 'charity' means an institution which—

(a) is established for charitable purposes only, and
(b) falls to be subject to the control of the High Court in the exercise of its jurisdiction with respect to charities.

(2) The definition of 'charity' in subsection (1) does not apply for the purposes of an enactment if a different definition of that term applies for those purposes by virtue of that or any other enactment.

(3) A reference in any enactment or document to a charity within the meaning of the Charitable Uses Act 1601 (c 4) or the preamble to it is to be construed as a reference to a charity as defined by subsection (1).

NOTES

Initial Commencement

To be appointed: see s 79(2).

2 Meaning of 'charitable purpose'

(1) For the purposes of the law of England and Wales, a charitable purpose is a purpose which—

(a) falls within subsection (2), and
(b) is for the public benefit (see section 3).

(2) A purpose falls within this subsection if it falls within any of the following descriptions of purposes—

(a) the prevention or relief of poverty;
(b) the advancement of education;
(c) the advancement of religion;
(d) the advancement of health or the saving of lives;
(e) the advancement of citizenship or community development;
(f) the advancement of the arts, culture, heritage or science;

(g) the advancement of amateur sport;
(h) the advancement of human rights, conflict resolution or reconciliation or the promotion of religious or racial harmony or equality and diversity;
(i) the advancement of environmental protection or improvement;
(j) the relief of those in need by reason of youth, age, ill-health, disability, financial hardship or other disadvantage;
(k) the advancement of animal welfare;
(l) the promotion of the efficiency of the armed forces of the Crown, or of the efficiency of the police, fire and rescue services or ambulance services;
(m) any other purposes within subsection (4).

(3) In subsection (2)—

(a) in paragraph (c) 'religion' includes—
  (i) a religion which involves belief in more than one god, and
  (ii) a religion which does not involve belief in a god;
(b) in paragraph (d) 'the advancement of health' includes the prevention or relief of sickness, disease or human suffering;
(c) paragraph (e) includes—
  (i) rural or urban regeneration, and
  (ii) the promotion of civic responsibility, volunteering, the voluntary sector or the effectiveness or efficiency of charities;
(d) in paragraph (g) 'sport' means sports or games which promote health by involving physical or mental skill or exertion;
(e) paragraph (j) includes relief given by the provision of accommodation or care to the persons mentioned in that paragraph; and
(f) in paragraph (l) 'fire and rescue services' means services provided by fire and rescue authorities under Part 2 of the Fire and Rescue Services Act 2004 (c 21).

(4) The purposes within this subsection (see subsection (2)(m)) are—

(a) any purposes not within paragraphs (a) to (l) of subsection (2) but recognised as charitable purposes under existing charity law or by virtue of section 1 of the Recreational Charities Act 1958 (c 17);
(b) any purposes that may reasonably be regarded as analogous to, or within the spirit of, any purposes falling within any of those paragraphs or paragraph (a) above; and
(c) any purposes that may reasonably be regarded as analogous to, or within the spirit of, any purposes which have been recognised under charity law as falling within paragraph (b) above or this paragraph.

(5) Where any of the terms used in any of paragraphs (a) to (l) of subsection (2), or in subsection (3), has a particular meaning under charity law, the term is to be taken as having the same meaning where it appears in that provision.

(6) Any reference in any enactment or document (in whatever terms)—

(a) to charitable purposes, or
(b) to institutions having purposes that are charitable under charity law,

is to be construed in accordance with subsection (1).

(7) Subsection (6)—

(a) applies whether the enactment or document was passed or made before or after the passing of this Act, but
(b) does not apply where the context otherwise requires.

(8) In this section—

'charity law' means the law relating to charities in England and Wales; and
'existing charity law' means charity law as in force immediately before the day on which this section comes into force.

NOTES

Initial Commencement

To be appointed: see s 79(2).

3 The 'public benefit' test

(1) This section applies in connection with the requirement in section 2(1)(b) that a purpose falling within section 2(2) must be for the public benefit if it is to be a charitable purpose.

(2) In determining whether that requirement is satisfied in relation to any such purpose, it is not to be presumed that a purpose of a particular description is for the public benefit.

(3) In this Part any reference to the public benefit is a reference to the public benefit as that term is understood for the purposes of the law relating to charities in England and Wales.

(4) Subsection (3) applies subject to subsection (2).

NOTES

Initial Commencement

To be appointed: see s 79(2).

4 Guidance as to operation of public benefit requirement

(1) The Charity Commission for England and Wales (see section 6 of this Act) must issue guidance in pursuance of its public benefit objective.

(2) That objective is to promote awareness and understanding of the operation of the requirement mentioned in section 3(1) (see section 1B(3) and (4) of the Charities Act 1993 (c 10), as inserted by section 7 of this Act).

(3) The Commission may from time to time revise any guidance issued under this section.

(4) The Commission must carry out such public and other consultation as it considers appropriate—

(a) before issuing any guidance under this section, or
(b) (unless it considers that it is unnecessary to do so) before revising any such guidance.

(5) The Commission must publish any guidance issued or revised under this section in such manner as it considers appropriate.

(6) The charity trustees of a charity must have regard to any such guidance when exercising any powers or duties to which the guidance is relevant.

NOTES

Initial Commencement

To be appointed: see s 79(2).

Extent

This section does not extend to Scotland: see s 80(2).

5 Special provisions about recreational charities, sports clubs etc

(1) The Recreational Charities Act 1958 (c 17) is amended in accordance with subsections (2) and (3).

(2) In section 1 (certain recreational and similar purposes deemed to be charitable) for subsection (2) substitute—

'(2) The requirement in subsection (1) that the facilities are provided in the interests of social welfare cannot be satisfied if the basic conditions are not met.

(2A) The basic conditions are—

(a) that the facilities are provided with the object of improving the conditions of life for the persons for whom the facilities are primarily intended; and
(b) that either—
  (i) those persons have need of the facilities by reason of their youth, age, infirmity or disability, poverty, or social and economic circumstances, or
  (ii) the facilities are to be available to members of the public at large or to male, or to female, members of the public at large.'

(3) Section 2 (miners' welfare trusts) is omitted.

(4) A registered sports club established for charitable purposes is to be treated as not being so established, and accordingly cannot be a charity.

(5) In subsection (4) a 'registered sports club' means a club for the time being registered under Schedule 18 to the Finance Act 2002 (c 23) (relief for community amateur sports club).

NOTES

Initial Commencement

To be appointed: see s 79(2).

Part 2
Regulation of Charities

Chapter 1
The Charity Commission

Establishment of Charity Commission

6 The Charity Commission

(1) After section 1 of the 1993 Act insert—

'1A The Charity Commission

(1) There shall be a body corporate to be known as the Charity Commission for England and Wales (in this Act referred to as 'the Commission').

(2) In Welsh the Commission shall be known as 'Comisiwn Elusennau Cymru a Lloegr'.

(3) The functions of the Commission shall be performed on behalf of the Crown.

(4) In the exercise of its functions the Commission shall not be subject to the direction or control of any Minister of the Crown or other government department.

(5) But subsection (4) above does not affect—

(a) any provision made by or under any enactment;
(b) any administrative controls exercised over the Commission's expenditure by the Treasury.

(6) The provisions of Schedule 1A to this Act shall have effect with respect to the Commission.'

(2) Schedule 1 (which inserts the new Schedule 1A into the 1993 Act) has effect.

(3) The office of Charity Commissioner for England and Wales is abolished.

(4) The functions of the Charity Commissioners for England and Wales and their property, rights and liabilities are by virtue of this subsection transferred to the Charity Commission for England and Wales.

(5) Any enactment or document has effect, so far as necessary for the purposes of or in consequence of the transfer effected by subsection (4), as if any reference to the Charity Commissioners for England and Wales or to any Charity Commissioner for England and Wales were a reference to the Charity Commission for England and Wales.

(6) Section 1 of, and Schedule 1 to, the 1993 Act cease to have effect.

(7) Schedule 2 (which contains supplementary provision relating to the establishment of the Charity Commission for England and Wales) has effect.

NOTES

Initial Commencement

To be appointed: see s 79(2).

Extent

Sub-ss (1)–(4), (6), (7) do not extend to Scotland: see s 80(2).

Commission's objectives, general functions etc

7 The Commission's objectives, general functions and duties

After section 1A of the 1993 Act (inserted by section 6 above) insert—

'1B The Commission's objectives

(1) The Commission has the objectives set out in subsection (2).

(2) The objectives are—

1 The public confidence objective.
2 The public benefit objective.
3 The compliance objective.
4 The charitable resources objective.
5 The accountability objective.

(3) Those objectives are defined as follows—

1 The public confidence objective is to increase public trust and confidence in charities.
2 The public benefit objective is to promote awareness and understanding of the operation of the public benefit requirement.
3 The compliance objective is to promote compliance by charity trustees with their legal obligations in exercising control and management of the administration of their charities.
4 The charitable resources objective is to promote the effective use of charitable resources.
5 The accountability objective is to enhance the accountability of charities to donors, beneficiaries and the general public.

(4) In this section 'the public benefit requirement' means the requirement in section 2(1)(b) of the Charities Act 2006 that a purpose falling within section 2(2) of that Act must be for the public benefit if it is to be a charitable purpose.

1C The Commission's general functions

(1) The Commission has the general functions set out in subsection (2).

(2) The general functions are—

1 Determining whether institutions are or are not charities.
2 Encouraging and facilitating the better administration of charities.
3 Identifying and investigating apparent misconduct or mismanagement in the administration of charities and taking remedial or protective action in connection with misconduct or mismanagement therein.
4 Determining whether public collections certificates should be issued, and remain in force, in respect of public charitable collections.
5 Obtaining, evaluating and disseminating information in connection with the performance of any of the Commission's functions or meeting any of its objectives.
6 Giving information or advice, or making proposals, to any Minister of the Crown on matters relating to any of the Commission's functions or meeting any of its objectives.

(3) The Commission's fifth general function includes (among other things) the maintenance of an accurate and up-to-date register of charities under section 3 below.

(4) The Commission's sixth general function includes (among other things) complying, so far as is reasonably practicable, with any request made by a Minister of the Crown for information or advice on any matter relating to any of its functions.

(5) In this section 'public charitable collection' and 'public collections certificate' have the same meanings as in Chapter 1 of Part 3 of the Charities Act 2006.

1D The Commission's general duties

(1) The Commission has the general duties set out in subsection (2).

(2) The general duties are—

1 So far as is reasonably practicable the Commission must, in performing its functions, act in a way—
 (a) which is compatible with its objectives, and
 (b) which it considers most appropriate for the purpose of meeting those objectives.
2 So far as is reasonably practicable the Commission must, in performing its functions, act in a way which is compatible with the encouragement of—
 (a) all forms of charitable giving, and
 (b) voluntary participation in charity work.
3 In performing its functions the Commission must have regard to the need to use its resources in the most efficient, effective and economic way.
4 In performing its functions the Commission must, so far as relevant, have regard to the principles of best regulatory practice (including the principles under which regulatory activities should be proportionate, accountable, consistent, transparent and targeted only at cases in which action is needed).
5 In performing its functions the Commission must, in appropriate cases, have regard to the desirability of facilitating innovation by or on behalf of charities.
6 In managing its affairs the Commission must have regard to such generally accepted principles of good corporate governance as it is reasonable to regard as applicable to it.

1E The Commission's incidental powers

(1) The Commission has power to do anything which is calculated to facilitate, or is conducive or incidental to, the performance of any of its functions or general duties.

(2) However, nothing in this Act authorises the Commission—

(a) to exercise functions corresponding to those of a charity trustee in relation to a charity, or
(b) otherwise to be directly involved in the administration of a charity.

(3) Subsection (2) does not affect the operation of section 19A or 19B below (power of Commission to give directions as to action to be taken or as to application of charity property).'

NOTES

Initial Commencement

To be appointed: see s 79(2).

Extent

This section does not extend to Scotland: see s 80(2).

Chapter 2
The Charity Tribunal

8 The Charity Tribunal

(1) After section 2 of the 1993 Act insert—

'Part 1A
The Charity Tribunal

2A The Charity Tribunal

(1) There shall be a tribunal to be known as the Charity Tribunal (in this Act referred to as 'the Tribunal').

(2) In Welsh the Tribunal shall be known as 'Tribiwnlys Elusennau'.

(3) The provisions of Schedule 1B to this Act shall have effect with respect to the constitution of the Tribunal and other matters relating to it.

(4) The Tribunal shall have jurisdiction to hear and determine—

(a) such appeals and applications as may be made to the Tribunal in accordance with Schedule 1C to this Act, or any other enactment, in respect of decisions, orders or directions of the Commission, and
(b) such matters as may be referred to the Tribunal in accordance with Schedule 1D to this Act by the Commission or the Attorney General.

(5) Such appeals, applications and matters shall be heard and determined by the Tribunal in accordance with those Schedules, or any such enactment, taken with section 2B below and rules made under that section.

2B Practice and procedure

(1) The Lord Chancellor may make rules—

(a) regulating the exercise of rights to appeal or to apply to the Tribunal and matters relating to the making of references to it;
(b) about the practice and procedure to be followed in relation to proceedings before the Tribunal.

(2) Rules under subsection (1)(a) above may, in particular, make provision—

(a) specifying steps which must be taken before appeals, applications or references are made to the Tribunal (and the period within which any such steps must be taken);
(b) specifying the period following the Commission's final decision, direction or order within which such appeals or applications may be made;
(c) requiring the Commission to inform persons of their right to appeal or apply to the Tribunal following a final decision, direction or order of the Commission;
(d) specifying the manner in which appeals, applications or references to the Tribunal are to be made.

(3) Rules under subsection (1)(b) above may, in particular, make provision—

(a) for the President or a legal member of the Tribunal (see paragraph 1(2)(b) of Schedule 1B to this Act) to determine preliminary, interlocutory or ancillary matters;

(b) for matters to be determined without an oral hearing in specified circumstances;
(c) for the Tribunal to deal with urgent cases expeditiously;
(d) about the disclosure of documents;
(e) about evidence;
(f) about the admission of members of the public to proceedings;
(g) about the representation of parties to proceedings;
(h) about the withdrawal of appeals, applications or references;
(i) about the recording and promulgation of decisions;
(j) about the award of costs.

(4) Rules under subsection (1)(a) or (b) above may confer a discretion on—

(a) the Tribunal,
(b) a member of the Tribunal, or
(c) any other person.

(5) The Tribunal may award costs only in accordance with subsections (6) and (7) below.

(6) If the Tribunal considers that any party to proceedings before it has acted vexatiously, frivolously or unreasonably, the Tribunal may order that party to pay to any other party to the proceedings the whole or part of the costs incurred by that other party in connection with the proceedings.

(7) If the Tribunal considers that a decision, direction or order of the Commission which is the subject of proceedings before it was unreasonable, the Tribunal may order the Commission to pay to any other party to the proceedings the whole or part of the costs incurred by that other party in connection with the proceedings.

(8) Rules of the Lord Chancellor under this section—

(a) shall be made by statutory instrument, and
(b) shall be subject to annulment in pursuance of a resolution of either House of Parliament.

(9) Section 86(3) below applies in relation to rules of the Lord Chancellor under this section as it applies in relation to regulations and orders of the Minister under this Act.

2C Appeal from Tribunal

(1) A party to proceedings before the Tribunal may appeal to the High Court against a decision of the Tribunal.

(2) Subject to subsection (3) below, an appeal may be brought under this section against a decision of the Tribunal only on a point of law.

(3) In the case of an appeal under this section against a decision of the Tribunal which determines a question referred to it by the Commission or the Attorney General, the High Court—

(a) shall consider afresh the question referred to the Tribunal, and
(b) may take into account evidence which was not available to the Tribunal.

(4) An appeal under this section may be brought only with the permission of—

(a) the Tribunal, or
(b) if the Tribunal refuses permission, the High Court.

(5) For the purposes of subsection (1) above—

(a) the Commission and the Attorney General are to be treated as parties to all proceedings before the Tribunal, and
(b) rules under section 2B(1) above may include provision as to who else is to be treated as being (or not being) a party to proceedings before the Tribunal.

2D Intervention by Attorney General

(1) This section applies to any proceedings—

(a) before the Tribunal, or
(b) on an appeal from the Tribunal,

to which the Attorney General is not a party.

(2) The Tribunal or, in the case of an appeal from the Tribunal, the court may at any stage of the proceedings direct that all the necessary papers in the proceedings be sent to the Attorney General.

(3) A direction under subsection (2) may be made by the Tribunal or court—

(a) of its own motion, or
(b) on the application of any party to the proceedings.

(4) The Attorney General may—

(a) intervene in the proceedings in such manner as he thinks necessary or expedient, and
(b) argue before the Tribunal or court any question in relation to the proceedings which the Tribunal or court considers it necessary to have fully argued.

(5) Subsection (4) applies whether or not the Tribunal or court has given a direction under subsection (2).'

(2) Schedule 3 (which inserts the new Schedule 1B into the 1993 Act) has effect.

(3) Schedule 4 (which inserts the new Schedules 1C and 1D into the 1993 Act) has effect.

NOTES

Initial Commencement

To be appointed: see s 79(2).

Extent

This section does not extend to Scotland: see s 80(2).

Chapter 3
Registration of Charities

General

9 Registration of charities

For section 3 of the 1993 Act substitute—

'3 Register of charities

(1) There shall continue to be a register of charities, which shall be kept by the Commission.

(2) The register shall be kept by the Commission in such manner as it thinks fit.

(3) The register shall contain—

(a) the name of every charity registered in accordance with section 3A below (registration), and
(b) such other particulars of, and such other information relating to, every such charity as the Commission thinks fit.

(4) The Commission shall remove from the register—

(a) any institution which it no longer considers is a charity, and

(b) any charity which has ceased to exist or does not operate.

(5) If the removal of an institution under subsection (4)(a) above is due to any change in its trusts, the removal shall take effect from the date of that change.

(6) A charity which is for the time being registered under section 3A(6) below (voluntary registration) shall be removed from the register if it so requests.

(7) The register (including the entries cancelled when institutions are removed from the register) shall be open to public inspection at all reasonable times.

(8) Where any information contained in the register is not in documentary form, subsection (7) above shall be construed as requiring the information to be available for public inspection in legible form at all reasonable times.

(9) If the Commission so determines, subsection (7) shall not apply to any particular information contained in the register that is specified in the determination.

(10) Copies (or particulars) of the trusts of any registered charity as supplied to the Commission under section 3B below (applications for registration etc) shall, so long as the charity remains on the register—

(a) be kept by the Commission, and
(b) be open to public inspection at all reasonable times.

3A Registration of charities

(1) Every charity must be registered in the register of charities unless subsection (2) below applies to it.

(2) The following are not required to be registered—

(a) any exempt charity (see Schedule 2 to this Act);
(b) any charity which for the time being—
  (i) is permanently or temporarily excepted by order of the Commission, and
  (ii) complies with any conditions of the exception,
  and whose gross income does not exceed £100,000;
(c) any charity which for the time being—
  (i) is, or is of a description, permanently or temporarily excepted by regulations made by the Secretary of State, and
  (ii) complies with any conditions of the exception,
  and whose gross income does not exceed £100,000; and
(d) any charity whose gross income does not exceed £5,000.

(3) For the purposes of subsection (2)(b) above—

(a) any order made or having effect as if made under section 3(5)(b) of this Act (as originally enacted) and in force immediately before the appointed day has effect as from that day as if made under subsection (2)(b) (and may be varied or revoked accordingly); and
(b) no order may be made under subsection (2)(b) so as to except on or after the appointed day any charity that was not excepted immediately before that day.

(4) For the purposes of subsection (2)(c) above—

(a) any regulations made or having effect as if made under section 3(5)(b) of this Act (as originally enacted) and in force immediately before the appointed day have effect as from that day as if made under subsection (2)(c) (and may be varied or revoked accordingly);
(b) such regulations shall be made under subsection (2)(c) as are necessary to secure that all of the formerly specified institutions are excepted under that provision (subject to compliance with any conditions of the exception and the financial limit mentioned in that provision); but

(c) otherwise no regulations may be made under subsection (2)(c) so as to except on or after the appointed day any description of charities that was not excepted immediately before that day.

(5) In subsection (4)(b) above 'formerly specified institutions' means—

(a) any institution falling within section 3(5B)(a) or (b) of this Act as in force immediately before the appointed day (certain educational institutions); or
(b) any institution ceasing to be an exempt charity by virtue of section 11 of the Charities Act 2006 or any order made under that section.

(6) A charity within—

(a) subsection (2)(b) or (c) above, or
(b) subsection (2)(d) above,

must, if it so requests, be registered in the register of charities.

(7) The Minister may by order amend—

(a) subsection (2)(b) and (c) above, or
(b) subsection (2)(d) above,

by substituting a different sum for the sum for the time being specified there.

(8) The Minister may only make an order under subsection (7) above—

(a) so far as it amends subsection (2)(b) and (c), if he considers it expedient to so with a view to reducing the scope of the exception provided by those provisions;
(b) so far as it amends subsection (2)(d), if he considers it expedient to do so in consequence of changes in the value of money or with a view to extending the scope of the exception provided by that provision,

and no order may be made by him under subsection (7)(a) unless a copy of a report under section 73 of the Charities Act 2006 (report on operation of that Act) has been laid before Parliament in accordance with that section.

(9) In this section 'the appointed day' means the day on which subsections (1) to (5) above come into force by virtue of an order under section 79 of the Charities Act 2006 relating to section 9 of that Act (registration of charities).

(10) In this section any reference to a charity's 'gross income' shall be construed, in relation to a particular time—

(a) as a reference to the charity's gross income in its financial year immediately preceding that time, or
(b) if the Commission so determines, as a reference to the amount which the Commission estimates to be the likely amount of the charity's gross income in such financial year of the charity as is specified in the determination.

(11) The following provisions of this section—

(a) subsection (2)(b) and (c),
(b) subsections (3) to (5), and
(c) subsections (6)(a), (7)(a), (8)(a) and (9),

shall cease to have effect on such day as the Minister may by order appoint for the purposes of this subsection.

3B Duties of trustees in connection with registration

(1) Where a charity required to be registered by virtue of section 3A(1) above is not registered, it is the duty of the charity trustees—

(a) to apply to the Commission for the charity to be registered, and
(b) to supply the Commission with the required documents and information.

(2) The 'required documents and information' are—

(a) copies of the charity's trusts or (if they are not set out in any extant document) particulars of them,
(b) such other documents or information as may be prescribed by regulations made by the Minister, and
(c) such other documents or information as the Commission may require for the purposes of the application.

(3) Where an institution is for the time being registered, it is the duty of the charity trustees (or the last charity trustees)—

(a) to notify the Commission if the institution ceases to exist, or if there is any change in its trusts or in the particulars of it entered in the register, and
(b) (so far as appropriate), to supply the Commission with particulars of any such change and copies of any new trusts or alterations of the trusts.

(4) Nothing in subsection (3) above requires a person—

(a) to supply the Commission with copies of schemes for the administration of a charity made otherwise than by the court,
(b) to notify the Commission of any change made with respect to a registered charity by such a scheme, or
(c) if he refers the Commission to a document or copy already in the possession of the Commission, to supply a further copy of the document.

(5) Where a copy of a document relating to a registered charity—

(a) is not required to be supplied to the Commission as the result of subsection (4) above, but
(b) is in the possession of the Commission,

a copy of the document shall be open to inspection under section 3(10) above as if supplied to the Commission under this section.'

NOTES

Initial Commencement

To be appointed: see s 79(2).

Extent

This section does not extend to Scotland: see s 80(2).

10 Interim changes in threshold for registration of small charities

(1) At any time before the appointed day, the Minister may by order amend section 3 of the 1993 Act (the register of charities) so as to—

(a) replace section 3(5)(c) (threshold for registration of small charities) with a provision referring to a charity whose gross income does not exceed such sum as is prescribed in the order, and
(b) define 'gross income' for the purposes of that provision.

(2) Subsection (1) does not affect the existing power under section 3(12) of that Act to increase the financial limit specified in section 3(5)(c).

(3) This section ceases to have effect on the appointed day.

(4) In this section 'the appointed day' means the day on which section 3A(1) to (5) of the 1993 Act (as substituted by section 9 of this Act) come into force by virtue of an order under section 79 of this Act.

NOTES

Initial Commencement

To be appointed: see s 79(2).

Extent

This section does not extend to Scotland: see s 80(2).

Subordinate Legislation

Charities Act 2006 (Interim changes in threshold for registration of small charities) Order 2007, SI 2007/789 (made under sub-s (1)).

Exempt charities: registration and regulation

11 Changes in exempt charities

(1) Schedule 2 to the 1993 Act (exempt charities) is amended as follows.

(2) In paragraph (a) (general exemption by reference to law existing prior to Charities Act 1960 (c 58)) after '1855' insert '*(but see Note 1)*'.

(3) In paragraph (b) (certain specified universities, colleges and schools)—

(a) before 'Queen Mary and Westfield College' insert 'and'; and
(b) omit 'and the colleges of Winchester and Eton'.

(4) Before paragraph (i) insert—

'(h) a higher education corporation;'.

(5) After paragraph (i) insert—

'(j) a further education corporation;'.

(6) In paragraph (w) (exemption for institutions administered by or on behalf of institutions exempted under preceding provisions) after 'last-mentioned institution' insert '*(but see Note 2)*'.

(7) Omit paragraph (x) (Church Commissioners and institutions administered by them).

(8) In paragraph (y) (industrial and provident societies etc) for the words from 'and any' onwards substitute 'and which is also registered in the register of social landlords under Part 1 of the Housing Act 1996;'.

(9) At the end insert—

'*Notes*

1

Paragraph (a) above does not include—

(a) any Investment Fund or Deposit Fund within the meaning of the Church Funds Investment Measure 1958,
(b) any investment fund or deposit fund within the meaning of the Methodist Church Funds Act 1960, or
(c) the representative body of the Welsh Church or property administered by it.

2

Paragraph (w) above does not include any students' union.'

(10) In section 24 of the 1993 Act (schemes to establish common investment funds), in subsection (8) (fund is to be a charity and, if the scheme admits only exempt charities, an exempt charity) omit the words from '; and if the scheme' onwards.

(11) The Minister may by order make such further amendments of Schedule 2 to the 1993 Act as he considers appropriate for securing—

(a) that (so far as they are charities) institutions of a particular description become or (as the case may be) cease to be exempt charities, or
(b) that (so far as it is a charity) a particular institution becomes or (as the case may be) ceases to be an exempt charity,

or for removing from that Schedule an institution that has ceased to exist.

(12) An order under subsection (11) may only be made for the purpose mentioned in paragraph (a) or (b) of that subsection if the Minister is satisfied that the order is desirable in the interests of ensuring appropriate or effective regulation of the charities or charity concerned in connection with compliance by the charity trustees of the charities or charity with their legal obligations in exercising control and management of the administration of the charities or charity.

(13) The Minister may by order make such amendments or other modifications of any enactment as he considers appropriate in connection with—

(a) charities of a particular description becoming, or ceasing to be, exempt charities, or
(b) a particular charity becoming, or ceasing to be, an exempt charity,

by virtue of any provision made by or under this section.

(14) In this section 'exempt charity' has the same meaning as in the 1993 Act.

NOTES

Initial Commencement

To be appointed: see s 79(2).

Extent

This section does not extend to Scotland: see s 80(2).

12 Increased regulation of exempt charities under 1993 Act

The 1993 Act is amended in accordance with Schedule 5 (which has effect for increasing the extent to which exempt charities are subject to regulation under that Act).

NOTES

Initial Commencement

To be appointed: see s 79(2).

Extent

This section does not extend to Scotland: see s 80(2).

13 General duty of principal regulator in relation to exempt charity

(1) This section applies to any body or Minister of the Crown who is the principal regulator in relation to an exempt charity.

(2) The body or Minister must do all that it or he reasonably can to meet the compliance objective in relation to the charity.

(3) The compliance objective is to promote compliance by the charity trustees with their legal obligations in exercising control and management of the administration of the charity.

(4) In this section—

(a) 'exempt charity' has the same meaning as in the 1993 Act; and
(b) 'principal regulator', in relation to an exempt charity, means such body or Minister of the Crown as is prescribed as its principal regulator by regulations made by the Minister.

(5) Regulations under subsection (4)(b) may make such amendments or other modifications of any enactment as the Minister considers appropriate for the purpose of facilitating, or otherwise in connection with, the discharge by a principal regulator of the duty under subsection (2).

NOTES

Initial Commencement

Sub-ss (4), (5): Royal Assent: 8 November 2006: see s 79(1)(a).

Sub-ss (1)–(3): To be appointed: see s 79(2).

Extent

This section does not extend to Scotland: see s 80(2).

14 Commission to consult principal regulator before exercising powers in relation to exempt charity

After section 86 of the 1993 Act insert—

'86A Consultation by Commission before exercising powers in relation to exempt charity

Before exercising in relation to an exempt charity any specific power exercisable by it in relation to the charity, the Commission must consult the charity's principal regulator.'

NOTES

Initial Commencement

To be appointed: see s 79(2).

Extent

This section does not extend to Scotland: see s 80(2).

Chapter 4
Application of Property Cy-près

Cy-près occasions

15 Application cy-près by reference to current circumstances

(1) Section 13 of the 1993 Act (occasions for applying property cy-près) is amended as follows.

(2) In subsection (1)(c), (d) and (e)(iii), for 'the spirit of the gift' substitute 'the appropriate considerations'.

(3) After subsection (1) insert—

'(1A) In subsection (1) above 'the appropriate considerations' means—

(a) (on the one hand) the spirit of the gift concerned, and
(b) (on the other) the social and economic circumstances prevailing at the time of the proposed alteration of the original purposes.'

NOTES

Initial Commencement

To be appointed: see s 79(2).

Extent

This section does not extend to Scotland: see s 80(2).

16 Application cy-près of gifts by donors unknown or disclaiming

(1) Section 14 of the 1993 Act (application cy-près of gifts of donors unknown or disclaiming) is amended as follows.

(2) In subsection (4) (power of court to direct that property is to be treated as belonging to donors who cannot be identified) after 'court', in both places, insert 'or the Commission'.

NOTES

Initial Commencement

To be appointed: see s 79(2).

Extent

This section does not extend to Scotland: see s 80(2).

17 Application cy-près of gifts made in response to certain solicitations

After section 14 of the 1993 Act insert—

'14A Application cy-près of gifts made in response to certain solicitations

(1) This section applies to property given—

(a) for specific charitable purposes, and
(b) in response to a solicitation within subsection (2) below.

(2) A solicitation is within this subsection if—

(a) it is made for specific charitable purposes, and
(b) it is accompanied by a statement to the effect that property given in response to it will, in the event of those purposes failing, be applicable cy-près as if given for charitable purposes generally, unless the donor makes a relevant declaration at the time of making the gift.

(3) A 'relevant declaration' is a declaration in writing by the donor to the effect that, in the event of the specific charitable purposes failing, he wishes the trustees holding the property to give him the opportunity to request the return of the property in question (or a sum equal to its value at the time of the making of the gift).

(4) Subsections (5) and (6) below apply if—

(a) a person has given property as mentioned in subsection (1) above,
(b) the specific charitable purposes fail, and
(c) the donor has made a relevant declaration.

(5) The trustees holding the property must take the prescribed steps for the purpose of—

(a) informing the donor of the failure of the purposes,
(b) enquiring whether he wishes to request the return of the property (or a sum equal to its value), and
(c) if within the prescribed period he makes such a request, returning the property (or such a sum) to him.

(6) If those trustees have taken all appropriate prescribed steps but—

(a) they have failed to find the donor, or
(b) the donor does not within the prescribed period request the return of the property (or a sum equal to its value),

section 14(1) above shall apply to the property as if it belonged to a donor within paragraph (b) of that subsection (application of property where donor has disclaimed right to return of property).

(7) If—

(a) a person has given property as mentioned in subsection (1) above,
(b) the specific charitable purposes fail, and
(c) the donor has not made a relevant declaration,

section 14(1) above shall similarly apply to the property as if it belonged to a donor within paragraph (b) of that subsection.

(8) For the purposes of this section—

(a) 'solicitation' means a solicitation made in any manner and however communicated to the persons to whom it is addressed,
(b) it is irrelevant whether any consideration is or is to be given in return for the property in question, and
(c) where any appeal consists of both solicitations that are accompanied by statements within subsection (2)(b) and solicitations that are not so accompanied, a person giving property as a result of the appeal is to be taken to have responded to the former solicitations and not the latter, unless he proves otherwise.

(9) In this section 'prescribed' means prescribed by regulations made by the Commission, and any such regulations shall be published by the Commission in such manner as it thinks fit.

(10) Subsections (7) and (10) of section 14 shall apply for the purposes of this section as they apply for the purposes of section 14.'

NOTES

Initial Commencement

To be appointed: see s 79(2).

Extent

This section does not extend to Scotland: see s 80(2).

Schemes

18 Cy-près schemes

After section 14A of the 1993 Act (inserted by section 17 above) insert—

'14B Cy-près schemes

(1) The power of the court or the Commission to make schemes for the application of property cy-près shall be exercised in accordance with this section.

(2) Where any property given for charitable purposes is applicable cy-près, the court or the Commission may make a scheme providing for the property to be applied—

(a) for such charitable purposes, and
(b) (if the scheme provides for the property to be transferred to another charity) by or on trust for such other charity,

as it considers appropriate, having regard to the matters set out in subsection (3).

(3) The matters are—

(a) the spirit of the original gift,
(b) the desirability of securing that the property is applied for charitable purposes which are close to the original purposes, and
(c) the need for the relevant charity to have purposes which are suitable and effective in the light of current social and economic circumstances.

The 'relevant charity' means the charity by or on behalf of which the property is to be applied under the scheme.

(4) If a scheme provides for the property to be transferred to another charity, the scheme may impose on the charity trustees of that charity a duty to secure that the property is applied for purposes which are, so far as is reasonably practicable, similar in character to the original purposes.

(5) In this section references to property given include the property for the time being representing the property originally given or property derived from it.

(6) In this section references to the transfer of property to a charity are references to its transfer—

(a) to the charity, or
(b) to the charity trustees, or
(c) to any trustee for the charity, or
(d) to a person nominated by the charity trustees to hold it in trust for the charity,

as the scheme may provide.'

NOTES

Initial Commencement

To be appointed: see s 79(2).

Extent

This section does not extend to Scotland: see s 80(2).

Chapter 5
Assistance and Supervision of Charities by Court and Commission

Suspension or removal of trustees etc from membership

19 Power to suspend or remove trustees etc from membership of charity

After section 18 of the 1993 Act insert—

'18A Power to suspend or remove trustees etc from membership of charity

(1) This section applies where the Commission makes—

(a) an order under section 18(1) above suspending from his office or employment any trustee, charity trustee, officer, agent or employee of a charity, or
(b) an order under section 18(2) above removing from his office or employment any officer, agent or employee of a charity,

and the trustee, charity trustee, officer, agent or employee (as the case may be) is a member of the charity.

(2) If the order suspends the person in question from his office or employment, the Commission may also make an order suspending his membership of the charity for the period for which he is suspended from his office or employment.

(3) If the order removes the person in question from his office or employment, the Commission may also make an order—

(a) terminating his membership of the charity, and
(b) prohibiting him from resuming his membership of the charity without the Commission's consent.

(4) If an application for the Commission's consent under subsection (3)(b) above is made five years or more after the order was made, the Commission must grant the application unless satisfied that, by reason of any special circumstances, it should be refused.'

NOTES

Initial Commencement

To be appointed: see s 79(2).

Extent

This section does not extend to Scotland: see s 80(2).

Directions by Commission

20 Power to give specific directions for protection of charity

After section 19 of the 1993 Act insert—

'19A Power to give specific directions for protection of charity

(1) This section applies where, at any time after the Commission has instituted an inquiry under section 8 above with respect to any charity, it is satisfied as mentioned in section 18(1)(a) or (b) above.

(2) The Commission may by order direct—

(a) the charity trustees,
(b) any trustee for the charity,
(c) any officer or employee of the charity, or
(d) (if a body corporate) the charity itself,

to take any action specified in the order which the Commission considers to be expedient in the interests of the charity.

(3) An order under this section—

(a) may require action to be taken whether or not it would otherwise be within the powers exercisable by the person or persons concerned, or by the charity, in relation to the administration of the charity or to its property, but
(b) may not require any action to be taken which is prohibited by any Act of Parliament or expressly prohibited by the trusts of the charity or is inconsistent with its purposes.

(4) Anything done by a person or body under the authority of an order under this section shall be deemed to be properly done in the exercise of the powers mentioned in subsection (3)(a) above.

(5) Subsection (4) does not affect any contractual or other rights arising in connection with anything which has been done under the authority of such an order.'

NOTES

Initial Commencement

To be appointed: see s 79(2).

Extent

This section does not extend to Scotland: see s 80(2).

21 Power to direct application of charity property

After section 19A of the 1993 Act (inserted by section 20 above) insert—

'19B Power to direct application of charity property

(1) This section applies where the Commission is satisfied—

(a) that a person or persons in possession or control of any property held by or on trust for a charity is or are unwilling to apply it properly for the purposes of the charity, and
(b) that it is necessary or desirable to make an order under this section for the purpose of securing a proper application of that property for the purposes of the charity.

(2) The Commission may by order direct the person or persons concerned to apply the property in such manner as is specified in the order.

(3) An order under this section—

(a) may require action to be taken whether or not it would otherwise be within the powers exercisable by the person or persons concerned in relation to the property, but
(b) may not require any action to be taken which is prohibited by any Act of Parliament or expressly prohibited by the trusts of the charity.

(4) Anything done by a person under the authority of an order under this section shall be deemed to be properly done in the exercise of the powers mentioned in subsection (3)(a) above.

(5) Subsection (4) does not affect any contractual or other rights arising in connection with anything which has been done under the authority of such an order.'

NOTES

Initial Commencement

To be appointed: see s 79(2).

Extent

This section does not extend to Scotland: see s 80(2).

Publicity relating to schemes

22 Relaxation of publicity requirements relating to schemes etc

For section 20 of the 1993 Act substitute—

'20 Publicity relating to schemes

(1) The Commission may not—

(a) make any order under this Act to establish a scheme for the administration of a charity, or
(b) submit such a scheme to the court or the Minister for an order giving it effect,

unless, before doing so, the Commission has complied with the publicity requirements in subsection (2) below.

This is subject to any disapplication of those requirements under subsection (4) below.

(2) The publicity requirements are—

(a) that the Commission must give public notice of its proposals, inviting representations to be made to it within a period specified in the notice; and
(b) that, in the case of a scheme relating to a local charity (other than an ecclesiastical charity) in a parish or in a community in Wales, the Commission must communicate a draft of the scheme to the parish or community council (or, where a parish has no council, to the chairman of the parish meeting).

(3) The time when any such notice is given or any such communication takes place is to be decided by the Commission.

(4) The Commission may determine that either or both of the publicity requirements is or are not to apply in relation to a particular scheme if it is satisfied that—

(a) by reason of the nature of the scheme, or
(b) for any other reason,

compliance with the requirement or requirements is unnecessary.

(5) Where the Commission gives public notice of any proposals under this section, the Commission—

(a) must take into account any representations made to it within the period specified in the notice, and
(b) may (without further notice) proceed with the proposals either without modifications or with such modifications as it thinks desirable.

(6) Where the Commission makes an order under this Act to establish a scheme for the administration of a charity, a copy of the order must be available, for at least a month after the order is published, for public inspection at all reasonable times—

(a) at the Commission's office, and
(b) if the charity is a local charity, at some convenient place in the area of the charity.

Paragraph (b) does not apply if the Commission is satisfied that for any reason it is unnecessary for a copy of the scheme to be available locally.

(7) Any public notice of any proposals which is to be given under this section—

(a) is to contain such particulars of the proposals, or such directions for obtaining information about them, as the Commission thinks sufficient and appropriate, and
(b) is to be given in such manner as the Commission thinks sufficient and appropriate.

20A Publicity for orders relating to trustees or other individuals

(1) The Commission may not make any order under this Act to appoint, discharge or remove a charity trustee or trustee for a charity, other than—

(a) an order relating to the official custodian, or
(b) an order under section 18(1)(ii) above,

unless, before doing so, the Commission has complied with the publicity requirement in subsection (2) below.

This is subject to any disapplication of that requirement under subsection (4) below.

(2) The publicity requirement is that the Commission must give public notice of its proposals, inviting representations to be made to it within a period specified in the notice.

(3) The time when any such notice is given is to be decided by the Commission.

(4) The Commission may determine that the publicity requirement is not to apply in relation to a particular order if it is satisfied that for any reason compliance with the requirement is unnecessary.

(5) Before the Commission makes an order under this Act to remove without his consent—

(a) a charity trustee or trustee for a charity, or

(b) an officer, agent or employee of a charity,

the Commission must give him not less than one month's notice of its proposals, inviting representations to be made to it within a period specified in the notice.

This does not apply if the person cannot be found or has no known address in the United Kingdom.

(6) Where the Commission gives notice of any proposals under this section, the Commission—

(a) must take into account any representations made to it within the period specified in the notice, and
(b) may (without further notice) proceed with the proposals either without modifications or with such modifications as it thinks desirable.

(7) Any notice of any proposals which is to be given under this section—

(a) is to contain such particulars of the proposals, or such directions for obtaining information about them, as the Commission thinks sufficient and appropriate, and
(b) (in the case of a public notice) is to be given in such manner as the Commission thinks sufficient and appropriate.

(8) Any notice to be given under subsection (5)—

(a) may be given by post, and
(b) if given by post, may be addressed to the recipient's last known address in the United Kingdom.'

NOTES

Initial Commencement

To be appointed: see s 79(2).

Extent

This section does not extend to Scotland: see s 80(2).

Common investment schemes

23 Participation of Scottish and Northern Irish charities in common investment schemes etc

(1) After section 24(3) of the 1993 Act (common investment schemes) insert—

'(3A) A common investment scheme may provide for appropriate bodies to be admitted to participate in the scheme (in addition to the participating charities) to such extent as the trustees appointed to manage the fund may determine.

(3B) In this section 'appropriate body' means—

(a) a Scottish recognised body, or
(b) a Northern Ireland charity,

and, in the application of the relevant provisions in relation to a scheme which contains provisions authorised by subsection (3A) above, 'charity' includes an appropriate body.

'The relevant provisions' are subsections (1) and (4) to (6) and (in relation only to a charity within paragraph (b)) subsection (7).'

(2) In section 25(2) of that Act (application of provisions of section 24 to common deposit funds) for 'subsections (2) to (4)' substitute 'subsections (2), (3) and (4)'.

(3) At the end of section 25 add—

'(4) A common deposit scheme may provide for appropriate bodies to be admitted to participate in the scheme (in addition to the participating charities) to such extent as the trustees appointed to manage the fund may determine.

(5) In this section 'appropriate body' means—

(a) a Scottish recognised body, or
(b) a Northern Ireland charity,

and, in the application of the relevant provisions in relation to a scheme which contains provisions authorised by subsection (4) above, 'charity' includes an appropriate body.

(6) 'The relevant provisions' are—

(a) subsection (1) above, and
(b) subsections (4) and (6) of section 24 above, as they apply in accordance with subsections (2) and (3) above, and
(c) (in relation only to a charity within subsection (5)(b) above) subsection (7) of that section, as it so applies.'

(4) After section 25 insert—

'25A Meaning of 'Scottish recognised body' and 'Northern Ireland charity' in sections 24 and 25

(1) In sections 24 and 25 above 'Scottish recognised body' means a body—

(a) established under the law of Scotland, or
(b) managed or controlled wholly or mainly in or from Scotland,

to which the Commissioners for Her Majesty's Revenue and Customs have given intimation, which has not subsequently been withdrawn, that relief is due under section 505 of the Income and Corporation Taxes Act 1988 in respect of income of the body which is applicable and applied to charitable purposes only.

(2) In those sections 'Northern Ireland charity' means an institution—

(a) which is a charity under the law of Northern Ireland, and
(b) to which the Commissioners for Her Majesty's Revenue and Customs have given intimation, which has not subsequently been withdrawn, that relief is due under section 505 of the Income and Corporation Taxes Act 1988 in respect of income of the institution which is applicable and applied to charitable purposes only.'

(5) In section 100(4) of the 1993 Act (provisions extending to Northern Ireland) for 'extends' substitute 'and sections 24 to 25A extend'.

NOTES

Initial Commencement

To be appointed: see s 79(2).

Extent

This section does not extend to Scotland: see s 80(2), (5)(c).

Advice or other assistance

24 Power to give advice and guidance

For section 29 of the 1993 Act substitute—

'29 Power to give advice and guidance

(1) The Commission may, on the written application of any charity trustee or trustee for a charity, give that person its opinion or advice in relation to any matter—

(a) relating to the performance of any duties of his, as such a trustee, in relation to the charity concerned, or
(b) otherwise relating to the proper administration of the charity.

(2) A charity trustee or trustee for a charity who acts in accordance with any opinion or advice given by the Commission under subsection (1) above (whether to him or to another trustee) is to be taken, as regards his responsibility for so acting, to have acted in accordance with his trust.

(3) But subsection (2) above does not apply to a person if, when so acting, either—

(a) he knows or has reasonable cause to suspect that the opinion or advice was given in ignorance of material facts, or
(b) a decision of the court or the Tribunal has been obtained on the matter or proceedings are pending to obtain one.

(4) The Commission may, in connection with its second general function mentioned in section 1C(2) above, give such advice or guidance with respect to the administration of charities as it considers appropriate.

(5) Any advice or guidance so given may relate to—

(a) charities generally,
(b) any class of charities, or
(c) any particular charity,

and may take such form, and be given in such manner, as the Commission considers appropriate.'

NOTES

Initial Commencement

To be appointed: see s 79(2).

Extent

This section does not extend to Scotland: see s 80(2).

25 Power to determine membership of charity

After section 29 of the 1993 Act (as substituted by section 24 of this Act) insert—

'29A Power to determine membership of charity

(1) The Commission may—

(a) on the application of a charity, or
(b) at any time after the institution of an inquiry under section 8 above with respect to a charity,

determine who are the members of the charity.

(2) The Commission's power under subsection (1) may also be exercised by a person appointed by the Commission for the purpose.

(3) In a case within subsection (1)(b) the Commission may, if it thinks fit, so appoint the person appointed to conduct the inquiry.'

NOTES

Initial Commencement

To be appointed: see s 79(2).

Extent

This section does not extend to Scotland: see s 80(2).

Powers of entry etc

26 Power to enter premises and seize documents etc

(1) After section 31 of the 1993 Act insert—

'31A Power to enter premises

(1) A justice of the peace may issue a warrant under this section if satisfied, on information given on oath by a member of the Commission's staff, that there are reasonable grounds for believing that each of the conditions in subsection (2) below is satisfied.

(2) The conditions are—

(a) that an inquiry has been instituted under section 8 above;
(b) that there is on the premises to be specified in the warrant any document or information relevant to that inquiry which the Commission could require to be produced or furnished under section 9(1) above; and
(c) that, if the Commission were to make an order requiring the document or information to be so produced or furnished—
  (i) the order would not be complied with, or
  (ii) the document or information would be removed, tampered with, concealed or destroyed.

(3) A warrant under this section is a warrant authorising the member of the Commission's staff who is named in it—

(a) to enter and search the premises specified in it;
(b) to take such other persons with him as the Commission considers are needed to assist him in doing anything that he is authorised to do under the warrant;
(c) to take possession of any documents which appear to fall within subsection (2)(b) above, or to take any other steps which appear to be necessary for preserving, or preventing interference with, any such documents;
(d) to take possession of any computer disk or other electronic storage device which appears to contain information falling within subsection (2)(b), or information contained in a document so falling, or to take any other steps which appear to be necessary for preserving, or preventing interference with, any such information;
(e) to take copies of, or extracts from, any documents or information falling within paragraph (c) or (d);
(f) to require any person on the premises to provide an explanation of any such document or information or to state where any such documents or information may be found;
(g) to require any such person to give him such assistance as he may reasonably require for the taking of copies or extracts as mentioned in paragraph (e) above.

(4) Entry and search under such a warrant must be at a reasonable hour and within one month of the date of its issue.

(5) The member of the Commission's staff who is authorised under such a warrant ('the authorised person') must, if required to do so, produce—

(a) the warrant, and
(b) documentary evidence that he is a member of the Commission's staff,

for inspection by the occupier of the premises or anyone acting on his behalf.

(6) The authorised person must make a written record of—

(a) the date and time of his entry on the premises;
(b) the number of persons (if any) who accompanied him onto the premises, and the names of any such persons;

(c) the period for which he (and any such persons) remained on the premises;
(d) what he (and any such persons) did while on the premises; and
(e) any document or device of which he took possession while there.

(7) If required to do so, the authorised person must give a copy of the record to the occupier of the premises or someone acting on his behalf.

(8) Unless it is not reasonably practicable to do so, the authorised person must comply with the following requirements before leaving the premises, namely—

(a) the requirements of subsection (6), and
(b) any requirement made under subsection (7) before he leaves the premises.

(9) Where possession of any document or device is taken under this section—

(a) the document may be retained for so long as the Commission considers that it is necessary to retain it (rather than a copy of it) for the purposes of the relevant inquiry under section 8 above, or
(b) the device may be retained for so long as the Commission considers that it is necessary to retain it for the purposes of that inquiry,

as the case may be.

(10) Once it appears to the Commission that the retention of any document or device has ceased to be so necessary, it shall arrange for the document or device to be returned as soon as is reasonably practicable—

(a) to the person from whose possession it was taken, or
(b) to any of the charity trustees of the charity to which it belonged or related.

(11) A person who intentionally obstructs the exercise of any rights conferred by a warrant under this section is guilty of an offence and liable on summary conviction—

(a) to imprisonment for a term not exceeding 51 weeks, or
(b) to a fine not exceeding level 5 on the standard scale,

or to both.'

(2) In Part 1 of Schedule 1 to the Criminal Justice and Police Act 2001 (c 16) (powers of seizure to which section 50 applies), after paragraph 56 insert—

'56A Charities Act 1993 (c 10)

The power of seizure conferred by section 31A(3) of the Charities Act 1993 (seizure of material for the purposes of an inquiry under section 8 of that Act).'

NOTES

Initial Commencement

To be appointed: see s 79(2).

Extent

This section does not extend to Scotland: see s 80(2).

Mortgages of charity land

27 Restrictions on mortgaging

(1) Section 38 of the 1993 Act (restrictions on mortgaging) is amended as follows.

(2) For subsections (2) and (3) substitute—

'(2) Subsection (1) above shall not apply to a mortgage of any such land if the charity trustees have, before executing the mortgage, obtained and considered proper advice, given to them in writing, on the relevant matters or matter mentioned in subsection (3) or (3A) below (as the case may be).

(3) In the case of a mortgage to secure the repayment of a proposed loan or grant, the relevant matters are—

(a) whether the loan or grant is necessary in order for the charity trustees to be able to pursue the particular course of action in connection with which they are seeking the loan or grant;
(b) whether the terms of the loan or grant are reasonable having regard to the status of the charity as the prospective recipient of the loan or grant; and
(c) the ability of the charity to repay on those terms the sum proposed to be paid by way of loan or grant.

(3A) In the case of a mortgage to secure the discharge of any other proposed obligation, the relevant matter is whether it is reasonable for the charity trustees to undertake to discharge the obligation, having regard to the charity's purposes.

(3B) Subsection (3) or (as the case may be) subsection (3A) above applies in relation to such a mortgage as is mentioned in that subsection whether the mortgage—

(a) would only have effect to secure the repayment of the proposed loan or grant or the discharge of the proposed obligation, or
(b) would also have effect to secure the repayment of sums paid by way of loan or grant, or the discharge of other obligations undertaken, after the date of its execution.

(3C) Subsection (3D) below applies where—

(a) the charity trustees of a charity have executed a mortgage of land held by or in trust for a charity in accordance with subsection (2) above, and
(b) the mortgage has effect to secure the repayment of sums paid by way of loan or grant, or the discharge of other obligations undertaken, after the date of its execution.

(3D) In such a case, the charity trustees must not after that date enter into any transaction involving—

(a) the payment of any such sums, or
(b) the undertaking of any such obligations,

unless they have, before entering into the transaction, obtained and considered proper advice, given to them in writing, on the matters or matter mentioned in subsection (3)(a) to (c) or (3A) above (as the case may be).'

(3) In subsection (4) (meaning of 'proper advice')—

(a) for 'subsection (2) above' substitute 'this section'; and
(b) for 'the making of the loan in question' substitute 'relation to the loan, grant or other transaction in connection with which his advice is given'.

NOTES

Initial Commencement

To be appointed: see s 79(2).

Extent

This section does not extend to Scotland: see s 80(2).

Chapter 6
Audit or Examination of Accounts where Charity is not a Company

28 Annual audit or examination of accounts of charities which are not companies

(1) Section 43 of the 1993 Act (annual audit or examination of accounts of charities which are not companies) is amended as follows.

(2) For subsection (1) substitute—

'(1) Subsection (2) below applies to a financial year of a charity if—

(a) the charity's gross income in that year exceeds £500,000; or
(b) the charity's gross income in that year exceeds the accounts threshold and at the end of the year the aggregate value of its assets (before deduction of liabilities) exceeds £2.8 million.

'The accounts threshold' means £100,000 or such other sum as is for the time being specified in section 42(3) above.'

(3) In subsection (2) (accounts required to be audited) for paragraph (a) substitute—

'(a) would be eligible for appointment as auditor of the charity under Part 2 of the Companies Act 1989 if the charity were a company, or'.

(4) In subsection (3) (independent examinations instead of audits)—

(a) for the words from 'and its gross income' to 'subsection (4) below)' substitute 'but its gross income in that year exceeds £10,000,'; and
(b) at the end insert—

"This is subject to the requirements of subsection (3A) below where the gross income exceeds £250,000, and to any order under subsection (4) below.'

(5) After subsection (3) insert—

'(3A) If subsection (3) above applies to the accounts of a charity for a year and the charity's gross income in that year exceeds £250,000, a person qualifies as an independent examiner for the purposes of paragraph (a) of that subsection if (and only if) he is an independent person who is—

(a) a member of a body for the time being specified in section 249D(3) of the Companies Act 1985 (reporting accountants);
(b) a member of the Chartered Institute of Public Finance and Accountancy; or
(c) a Fellow of the Association of Charity Independent Examiners.'

(6) For subsection (8) substitute—

'(8) The Minister may by order—

(a) amend subsection (1)(a) or (b), (3) or (3A) above by substituting a different sum for any sum for the time being specified there;
(b) amend subsection (3A) by adding or removing a description of person to or from the list in that subsection or by varying any entry for the time being included in that list.'

NOTES

Initial Commencement

To be appointed: see s 79(2).

Extent

This section does not extend to Scotland: see s 80(2).

29 Duty of auditor etc of charity which is not a company to report matters to Commission

(1) After section 44 of the 1993 Act insert—

'44A Duty of auditors etc to report matters to Commission

(1) This section applies to—

(a) a person acting as an auditor or independent examiner appointed by or in relation to a charity under section 43 above,
(b) a person acting as an auditor or examiner appointed under section 43A(2) or (3) above, and
(c) the Auditor General for Wales acting under section 43B(2) or (3) above.

(2) If, in the course of acting in the capacity mentioned in subsection (1) above, a person to whom this section applies becomes aware of a matter—

(a) which relates to the activities or affairs of the charity or of any connected institution or body, and
(b) which he has reasonable cause to believe is likely to be of material significance for the purposes of the exercise by the Commission of its functions under section 8 or 18 above,

he must immediately make a written report on the matter to the Commission.

(3) If, in the course of acting in the capacity mentioned in subsection (1) above, a person to whom this section applies becomes aware of any matter—

(a) which does not appear to him to be one that he is required to report under subsection (2) above, but
(b) which he has reasonable cause to believe is likely to be relevant for the purposes of the exercise by the Commission of any of its functions,

he may make a report on the matter to the Commission.

(4) Where the duty or power under subsection (2) or (3) above has arisen in relation to a person acting in the capacity mentioned in subsection (1), the duty or power is not affected by his subsequently ceasing to act in that capacity.

(5) Where a person makes a report as required or authorised by subsection (2) or (3), no duty to which he is subject is to be regarded as contravened merely because of any information or opinion contained in the report.

(6) In this section 'connected institution or body', in relation to a charity, means—

(a) an institution which is controlled by, or
(b) a body corporate in which a substantial interest is held by,

the charity or any one or more of the charity trustees acting in his or their capacity as such.

(7) Paragraphs 3 and 4 of Schedule 5 to this Act apply for the purposes of subsection (6) above as they apply for the purposes of provisions of that Schedule.'

(2) In section 46 of the 1993 Act (special provisions as respects accounts and annual reports of exempt and excepted charities)—

(a) in subsection (1) for 'sections 41 to 45' substitute 'sections 41 to 44 or section 45'; and
(b) after subsection (2) insert—

'(2A) Section 44A(2) to (7) above shall apply in relation to a person appointed to audit, or report on, the accounts of an exempt charity which is not a company as they apply in relation to a person such as is mentioned in section 44A(1).

(2B) But section 44A(2) to (7) so apply with the following modifications—

(a) any reference to a person acting in the capacity mentioned in section 44A(1) is to be read as a reference to his acting as a person appointed as mentioned in subsection (2A) above; and
(b) any reference to the Commission or to any of its functions is to be read as a reference to the charity's principal regulator or to any of that person's functions in relation to the charity as such.'

NOTES

Initial Commencement

To be appointed: see s 79(2).

Extent

This section does not extend to Scotland: see s 80(2).

30 Group accounts

(1) After section 49 of the 1993 Act insert—

'49A Group accounts

The provisions of Schedule 5A to this Act shall have effect with respect to—

(a) the preparation and auditing of accounts in respect of groups consisting of parent charities and their subsidiary undertakings (within the meaning of that Schedule), and
(b) other matters relating to such groups.'

(2) Schedule 6 (which inserts the new Schedule 5A into the 1993 Act) has effect.

NOTES

Initial Commencement

To be appointed: see s 79(2).

Extent

This section does not extend to Scotland: see s 80(2).

Chapter 7 Charitable Companies

31 Relaxation of restriction on altering memorandum etc of charitable company

(1) Section 64 of the 1993 Act (alteration of objects clause etc) is amended as follows.

(2) For subsection (2) substitute—

'(2) Where a charity is a company, any regulated alteration by the company—

(a) requires the prior written consent of the Commission, and
(b) is ineffective if such consent has not been obtained.

(2A) The following are 'regulated alterations'—

(a) any alteration of the objects clause in the company's memorandum of association,
(b) any alteration of any provision of its memorandum or articles of association directing the application of property of the company on its dissolution, and
(c) any alteration of any provision of its memorandum or articles of association where the alteration would provide authorisation for any benefit to be obtained by directors or members of the company or persons connected with them.

(2B) For the purposes of subsection (2A) above—

(a) 'benefit' means a direct or indirect benefit of any nature, except that it does not include any remuneration (within the meaning of section 73A below) whose receipt may be authorised under that section; and
(b) the same rules apply for determining whether a person is connected with a director or member of the company as apply, in accordance with section 73B(5) and (6) below, for determining whether a person is connected with a charity trustee for the purposes of section 73A.'

(3) In subsection (3) (documents required to be delivered to registrar of companies), for 'any such alteration' substitute 'a regulated alteration'.

NOTES

Initial Commencement

To be appointed: see s 79(2).

Extent

This section does not extend to Scotland: see s 80(2).

32 Annual audit or examination of accounts of charitable companies

(1) In section 249A(4) of the Companies Act 1985 (c 6) (circumstances in which charitable company's accounts may be subject to an accountant's report instead of an audit)—

(a) in paragraph (b) (gross income between £90,000 and £250,000) for '£250,000' substitute '£500,000'; and
(b) in paragraph (c) (balance sheet total not more than £1.4 million) for '£1.4 million' substitute '£2.8 million'.

(2) In section 249B(1C) of that Act (circumstances in which parent company or subsidiary not disqualified for exemption from auditing requirement), in paragraph (b) (group's aggregate turnover not more than £350,000 net or £420,000 gross in case of charity), for '£350,000 net (or £420,000 gross)' substitute '£700,000 net (or £840,000 gross)'.

NOTES

Initial Commencement

To be appointed: see s 79(2).

Extent

This section does not extend to Scotland: see s 80(2).

33 Duty of auditor etc of charitable company to report matters to Commission

After section 68 of the 1993 Act insert—

'68A Duty of charity's auditors etc to report matters to Commission

(1) Section 44A(2) to (7) above shall apply in relation to a person acting as—

(a) an auditor of a charitable company appointed under Chapter 5 of Part 11 of the Companies Act 1985 (auditors), or
(b) a reporting accountant appointed by a charitable company for the purposes of section 249C of that Act (report required instead of audit),

as they apply in relation to a person such as is mentioned in section 44A(1).

(2) For this purpose any reference in section 44A to a person acting in the capacity mentioned in section 44A(1) is to be read as a reference to his acting in the capacity mentioned in subsection (1) of this section.

(3) In this section 'charitable company' means a charity which is a company.'

NOTES

Initial Commencement

To be appointed: see s 79(2).

Extent

This section does not extend to Scotland: see s 80(2).

Chapter 8
Charitable Incorporated Organisations

34 Charitable incorporated organisations

Schedule 7, which makes provision about charitable incorporated organisations, has effect.

NOTES

Initial Commencement

To be appointed: see s 79(2).

Extent

This section does not extend to Scotland: see s 80(2).

Chapter 9
Charity Trustees etc

Waiver of disqualification

35 Waiver of trustee's disqualification

In section 72 of the 1993 Act (disqualification for being trustee of a charity) after subsection (4) insert—

'(4A) If—

(a) a person disqualified under subsection (1)(d) or (e) makes an application under subsection (4) above five years or more after the date on which his disqualification took effect, and

(b) the Commission is not prevented from granting the application by virtue of paragraphs (a) and (b) of subsection (4),

the Commission must grant the application unless satisfied that, by reason of any special circumstances, it should be refused.'

NOTES

Initial Commencement

To be appointed: see s 79(2).

Extent

This section does not extend to Scotland: see s 80(2).

Remuneration of trustees etc

36 Remuneration of trustees etc providing services to charity

After section 73 of the 1993 Act insert—

'73A Remuneration of trustees etc providing services to charity

(1) This section applies to remuneration for services provided by a person to or on behalf of a charity where—

(a) he is a charity trustee or trustee for the charity, or
(b) he is connected with a charity trustee or trustee for the charity and the remuneration might result in that trustee obtaining any benefit.

This is subject to subsection (7) below.

(2) If conditions A to D are met in relation to remuneration within subsection (1), the person providing the services ('the relevant person') is entitled to receive the remuneration out of the funds of the charity.

(3) Condition A is that the amount or maximum amount of the remuneration—

(a) is set out in an agreement in writing between—
  (i) the charity or its charity trustees (as the case may be), and
  (ii) the relevant person,
 under which the relevant person is to provide the services in question to or on behalf of the charity, and
(b) does not exceed what is reasonable in the circumstances for the provision by that person of the services in question.

(4) Condition B is that, before entering into that agreement, the charity trustees decided that they were satisfied that it would be in the best interests of the charity for the services to be provided by the relevant person to or on behalf of the charity for the amount or maximum amount of remuneration set out in the agreement.

(5) Condition C is that if immediately after the agreement is entered into there is, in the case of the charity, more than one person who is a charity trustee and is—

(a) a person in respect of whom an agreement within subsection (3) above is in force, or
(b) a person who is entitled to receive remuneration out of the funds of the charity otherwise than by virtue of such an agreement, or
(c) a person connected with a person falling within paragraph (a) or (b) above,

the total number of them constitute a minority of the persons for the time being holding office as charity trustees of the charity.

(6) Condition D is that the trusts of the charity do not contain any express provision that prohibits the relevant person from receiving the remuneration.

(7) Nothing in this section applies to—

(a) any remuneration for services provided by a person in his capacity as a charity trustee or trustee for a charity or under a contract of employment, or
(b) any remuneration not within paragraph (a) which a person is entitled to receive out of the funds of a charity by virtue of any provision or order within subsection (8).

(8) The provisions or orders within this subsection are—

(a) any provision contained in the trusts of the charity,
(b) any order of the court or the Commission,
(c) any statutory provision contained in or having effect under an Act of Parliament other than this section.

(9) Section 73B below applies for the purposes of this section.

73B Supplementary provisions for purposes of section 73A

(1) Before entering into an agreement within section 73A(3) the charity trustees must have regard to any guidance given by the Commission concerning the making of such agreements.

(2) The duty of care in section 1(1) of the Trustee Act 2000 applies to a charity trustee when making such a decision as is mentioned in section 73A(4).

(3) For the purposes of section 73A(5) an agreement within section 73A(3) is in force so long as any obligations under the agreement have not been fully discharged by a party to it.

(4) In section 73A—

'benefit' means a direct or indirect benefit of any nature;
'maximum amount', in relation to remuneration, means the maximum amount of the remuneration whether specified in or ascertainable under the terms of the agreement in question;
'remuneration' includes any benefit in kind (and 'amount' accordingly includes monetary value);
'services', in the context of remuneration for services, includes goods that are supplied in connection with the provision of services.

(5) For the purposes of section 73A the following persons are 'connected' with a charity trustee or trustee for a charity—

(a) a child, parent, grandchild, grandparent, brother or sister of the trustee;
(b) the spouse or civil partner of the trustee or of any person falling within paragraph (a);
(c) a person carrying on business in partnership with the trustee or with any person falling within paragraph (a) or (b);
(d) an institution which is controlled—
  (i) by the trustee or by any person falling within paragraph (a), (b) or (c), or
  (ii) by two or more persons falling within sub-paragraph (i), when taken together;
(e) a body corporate in which—
  (i) the trustee or any connected person falling within any of paragraphs (a) to (c) has a substantial interest, or
  (ii) two or more persons falling within sub-paragraph (i), when taken together, have a substantial interest.

(6) Paragraphs 2 to 4 of Schedule 5 to this Act apply for the purposes of subsection (5) above as they apply for the purposes of provisions of that Schedule.'

NOTES

Initial Commencement

To be appointed: see s 79(2).

Extent

This section does not extend to Scotland: see s 80(2).

37 Disqualification of trustee receiving remuneration by virtue of section 36

After section 73B of the 1993 Act (inserted by section 36 above) insert—

'73C Disqualification of trustee receiving remuneration under section 73A

(1) This section applies to any charity trustee or trustee for a charity—

(a) who is or would be entitled to remuneration under an agreement or proposed agreement within section 73A(3) above, or
(b) who is connected with a person who is or would be so entitled.

(2) The charity trustee or trustee for a charity is disqualified from acting as such in relation to any decision or other matter connected with the agreement.

(3) But any act done by such a person which he is disqualified from doing by virtue of subsection (2) above shall not be invalid by reason only of that disqualification.

(4) Where the Commission is satisfied—

(a) that a person ('the disqualified trustee') has done any act which he was disqualified from doing by virtue of subsection (2) above, and
(b) that the disqualified trustee or a person connected with him has received or is to receive from the charity any remuneration under the agreement in question,

it may make an order under subsection (5) or (6) below (as appropriate).

(5) An order under this subsection is one requiring the disqualified trustee—

(a) to reimburse to the charity the whole or part of the remuneration received as mentioned in subsection (4)(b) above;
(b) to the extent that the remuneration consists of a benefit in kind, to reimburse to the charity the whole or part of the monetary value (as determined by the Commission) of the benefit in kind.

(6) An order under this subsection is one directing that the disqualified trustee or (as the case may be) connected person is not to be paid the whole or part of the remuneration mentioned in subsection (4)(b) above.

(7) If the Commission makes an order under subsection (5) or (6) above, the disqualified trustee or (as the case may be) connected person accordingly ceases to have any entitlement under the agreement to so much of the remuneration (or its monetary value) as the order requires him to reimburse to the charity or (as the case may be) as it directs is not to be paid to him.

(8) Subsections (4) to (6) of section 73B above apply for the purposes of this section as they apply for the purposes of section 73A above.'

NOTES

Initial Commencement

To be appointed: see s 79(2).

Extent

This section does not extend to Scotland: see s 80(2).

Liability of trustees etc

38 Power of Commission to relieve trustees, auditors etc from liability for breach of trust or duty

After section 73C of the 1993 Act (inserted by section 37 above) insert—

'73D Power to relieve trustees, auditors etc from liability for breach of trust or duty

(1) This section applies to a person who is or has been—

(a) a charity trustee or trustee for a charity,
(b) a person appointed to audit a charity's accounts (whether appointed under an enactment or otherwise), or
(c) an independent examiner, reporting accountant or other person appointed to examine or report on a charity's accounts (whether appointed under an enactment or otherwise).

(2) If the Commission considers—

(a) that a person to whom this section applies is or may be personally liable for a breach of trust or breach of duty committed in his capacity as a person within paragraph (a), (b) or (c) of subsection (1) above, but
(b) that he has acted honestly and reasonably and ought fairly to be excused for the breach of trust or duty,

the Commission may make an order relieving him wholly or partly from any such liability.

(3) An order under subsection (2) above may grant the relief on such terms as the Commission thinks fit.

(4) Subsection (2) does not apply in relation to any personal contractual liability of a charity trustee or trustee for a charity.

(5) For the purposes of this section and section 73E below—

(a) subsection (1)(b) above is to be read as including a reference to the Auditor General for Wales acting as auditor under section 43B above, and
(b) subsection (1)(c) above is to be read as including a reference to the Auditor General for Wales acting as examiner under that section;

and in subsection (1)(b) and (c) any reference to a charity's accounts is to be read as including any group accounts prepared by the charity trustees of a charity.

(6) This section does not affect the operation of—

(a) section 61 of the Trustee Act 1925 (power of court to grant relief to trustees),
(b) section 727 of the Companies Act 1985 (power of court to grant relief to officers or auditors of companies), or
(c) section 73E below (which extends section 727 to auditors etc of charities which are not companies).

73E Court's power to grant relief to apply to all auditors etc of charities which are not companies

(1) Section 727 of the Companies Act 1985 (power of court to grant relief to officers or auditors of companies) shall have effect in relation to a person to whom this section applies as it has effect in relation to a person employed as an auditor by a company.

(2) This section applies to—

(a) a person acting in a capacity within section 73D(1)(b) or (c) above in a case where, apart from this section, section 727 would not apply in relation to him as a person so acting, and
(b) a charity trustee of a CIO.'

NOTES

Initial Commencement

To be appointed: see s 79(2).

Extent

This section does not extend to Scotland: see s 80(2).

39 Trustees' indemnity insurance

After section 73E of the 1993 Act (inserted by section 38 above) insert—

'73F Trustees' indemnity insurance

(1) The charity trustees of a charity may arrange for the purchase, out of the funds of the charity, of insurance designed to indemnify the charity trustees or any trustees for the charity against any personal liability in respect of—

(a) any breach of trust or breach of duty committed by them in their capacity as charity trustees or trustees for the charity, or
(b) any negligence, default, breach of duty or breach of trust committed by them in their capacity as directors or officers of the charity (if it is a body corporate) or of any body corporate carrying on any activities on behalf of the charity.

(2) The terms of such insurance must, however, be so framed as to exclude the provision of any indemnity for a person in respect of—

(a) any liability incurred by him to pay—
  (i) a fine imposed in criminal proceedings, or
  (ii) a sum payable to a regulatory authority by way of a penalty in respect of non-compliance with any requirement of a regulatory nature (however arising);
(b) any liability incurred by him in defending any criminal proceedings in which he is convicted of an offence arising out of any fraud or dishonesty, or wilful or reckless misconduct, by him; or
(c) any liability incurred by him to the charity that arises out of any conduct which he knew (or must reasonably be assumed to have known) was not in the interests of the charity or in the case of which he did not care whether it was in the best interests of the charity or not.

(3) For the purposes of subsection (2)(b) above—

(a) the reference to any such conviction is a reference to one that has become final;
(b) a conviction becomes final—
  (i) if not appealed against, at the end of the period for bringing an appeal, or
  (ii) if appealed against, at the time when the appeal (or any further appeal) is disposed of; and
(c) an appeal is disposed of—
  (i) if it is determined and the period for bringing any further appeal has ended, or
  (ii) if it is abandoned or otherwise ceases to have effect.

(4) The charity trustees of a charity may not purchase insurance under this section unless they decide that they are satisfied that it is in the best interests of the charity for them to do so.

(5) The duty of care in section 1(1) of the Trustee Act 2000 applies to a charity trustee when making such a decision.

(6) The Minister may by order make such amendments of subsections (2) and (3) above as he considers appropriate.

(7) No order may be made under subsection (6) above unless a draft of the order has been laid before and approved by a resolution of each House of Parliament.

(8) This section—

(a) does not authorise the purchase of any insurance whose purchase is expressly prohibited by the trusts of the charity, but
(b) has effect despite any provision prohibiting the charity trustees or trustees for the charity receiving any personal benefit out of the funds of the charity.'

NOTES

Initial Commencement

To be appointed: see s 79(2).

Extent

This section does not extend to Scotland: see s 80(2).

Chapter 10
Powers of Unincorporated Charities

40 Power to transfer all property

For section 74 of the 1993 Act substitute—

'74 Power to transfer all property of unincorporated charity

(1) This section applies to a charity if—

(a) its gross income in its last financial year did not exceed £10,000,
(b) it does not hold any designated land, and
(c) it is not a company or other body corporate.

'Designated land' means land held on trusts which stipulate that it is to be used for the purposes, or any particular purposes, of the charity.

(2) The charity trustees of such a charity may resolve for the purposes of this section—

(a) that all the property of the charity should be transferred to another charity specified in the resolution, or
(b) that all the property of the charity should be transferred to two or more charities specified in the resolution in accordance with such division of the property between them as is so specified.

(3) Any charity so specified may be either a registered charity or a charity which is not required to be registered.

(4) But the charity trustees of a charity ('the transferor charity') do not have power to pass a resolution under subsection (2) above unless they are satisfied—

(a) that it is expedient in the interests of furthering the purposes for which the property is held by the transferor charity for the property to be transferred in accordance with the resolution, and
(b) that the purposes (or any of the purposes) of any charity to which property is to be transferred under the resolution are substantially similar to the purposes (or any of the purposes) of the transferor charity.

(5) Any resolution under subsection (2) above must be passed by a majority of not less than two-thirds of the charity trustees who vote on the resolution.

(6) Where charity trustees have passed a resolution under subsection (2), they must send a copy of it to the Commission, together with a statement of their reasons for passing it.

(7) Having received the copy of the resolution, the Commission—

(a) may direct the charity trustees to give public notice of the resolution in such manner as is specified in the direction, and
(b) if it gives such a direction, must take into account any representations made to it by persons appearing to it to be interested in the charity, where those representations are made to it within the period of 28 days beginning with the date when public notice of the resolution is given by the charity trustees.

(8) The Commission may also direct the charity trustees to provide the Commission with additional information or explanations relating to—

(a) the circumstances in and by reference to which they have decided to act under this section, or
(b) their compliance with any obligation imposed on them by or under this section in connection with the resolution.

(9) Subject to the provisions of section 74A below, a resolution under subsection (2) above takes effect at the end of the period of 60 days beginning with the date on which the copy of it was received by the Commission.

(10) Where such a resolution has taken effect, the charity trustees must arrange for all the property of the transferor charity to be transferred in accordance with the resolution, and on terms that any property so transferred—

(a) is to be held by the charity to which it is transferred ('the transferee charity') in accordance with subsection (11) below, but
(b) when so held is nevertheless to be subject to any restrictions on expenditure to which it was subject as property of the transferor charity;

and the charity trustees must arrange for the property to be so transferred by such date after the resolution takes effect as they agree with the charity trustees of the transferee charity or charities concerned.

(11) The charity trustees of any charity to which property is transferred under this section must secure, so far as is reasonably practicable, that the property is applied for such of its purposes as are substantially similar to those of the transferor charity.

But this requirement does not apply if those charity trustees consider that complying with it would not result in a suitable and effective method of applying the property.

(12) For the purpose of enabling any property to be transferred to a charity under this section, the Commission may, at the request of the charity trustees of that charity, make orders vesting any property of the transferor charity—

(a) in the transferee charity, in its charity trustees or in any trustee for that charity, or
(b) in any other person nominated by those charity trustees to hold property in trust for that charity.

(13) The Minister may by order amend subsection (1) above by substituting a different sum for the sum for the time being specified there.

(14) In this section references to the transfer of property to a charity are references to its transfer—

(a) to the charity, or
(b) to the charity trustees, or
(c) to any trustee for the charity, or
(d) to a person nominated by the charity trustees to hold it in trust for the charity,

as the charity trustees may determine.

(15) Where a charity has a permanent endowment, this section has effect in accordance with section 74B.

74A Resolution not to take effect or to take effect at later date

(1) This section deals with circumstances in which a resolution under section 74(2) above either—

(a) does not take effect under section 74(9) above, or
(b) takes effect at a time later than that mentioned in section 74(9).

(2) A resolution does not take effect under section 74(9) above if before the end of—

(a) the period of 60 days mentioned in section 74(9) ('the 60-day period'), or
(b) that period as modified by subsection (3) or (4) below,

the Commission notifies the charity trustees in writing that it objects to the resolution, either on procedural grounds or on the merits of the proposals contained in the resolution.

'On procedural grounds' means on the grounds that any obligation imposed on the charity trustees by or under section 74 above has not been complied with in connection with the resolution.

(3) If under section 74(7) above the Commission directs the charity trustees to give public notice of a resolution, the running of the 60-day period is suspended by virtue of this subsection—

(a) as from the date on which the direction is given to the charity trustees, and
(b) until the end of the period of 42 days beginning with the date on which public notice of the resolution is given by the charity trustees.

(4) If under section 74(8) above the Commission directs the charity trustees to provide any information or explanations, the running of the 60-day period is suspended by virtue of this subsection—

(a) as from the date on which the direction is given to the charity trustees, and
(b) until the date on which the information or explanations is or are provided to the Commission.

(5) Subsection (6) below applies once the period of time, or the total period of time, during which the 60-day period is suspended by virtue of either or both of subsections (3) and (4) above exceeds 120 days.

(6) At that point the resolution (if not previously objected to by the Commission) is to be treated as if it had never been passed.

74B Transfer where charity has permanent endowment

(1) This section provides for the operation of section 74 above where a charity within section 74(1) has a permanent endowment (whether or not the charity's trusts contain provision for the termination of the charity).

(2) In such a case section 74 applies as follows—

(a) if the charity has both a permanent endowment and other property ('unrestricted property')—
  (i) a resolution under section 74(2) must relate to both its permanent endowment and its unrestricted property, and
  (ii) that section applies in relation to its unrestricted property in accordance with subsection (3) below and in relation to its permanent endowment in accordance with subsections (4) to (11) below;
(b) if all of the property of the charity is comprised in its permanent endowment, that section applies in relation to its permanent endowment in accordance with subsections (4) to (11) below.

(3) Section 74 applies in relation to unrestricted property of the charity as if references in that section to all or any of the property of the charity were references to all or any of its unrestricted property.

(4) Section 74 applies in relation to the permanent endowment of the charity with the following modifications.

(5) References in that section to all or any of the property of the charity are references to all or any of the property comprised in its permanent endowment.

(6) If the property comprised in its permanent endowment is to be transferred to a single charity, the charity trustees must (instead of being satisfied as mentioned in section 74(4)(b)) be satisfied that the proposed transferee charity has purposes which are substantially similar to all of the purposes of the transferor charity.

(7) If the property comprised in its permanent endowment is to be transferred to two or more charities, the charity trustees must (instead of being satisfied as mentioned in section 74(4)(b)) be satisfied—

(a) that the proposed transferee charities, taken together, have purposes which are substantially similar to all of the purposes of the transferor charity, and
(b) that each of the proposed transferee charities has purposes which are substantially similar to one or more of the purposes of the transferor charity.

(8) In the case of a transfer to which subsection (7) above applies, the resolution under section 74(2) must provide for the property comprised in the permanent endowment of the charity to be divided between the transferee charities in such a way as to take account of such guidance as may be given by the Commission for the purposes of this section.

(9) The requirement in section 74(11) shall apply in the case of every such transfer, and in complying with that requirement the charity trustees of a transferee charity must secure that the application of property transferred to the charity takes account of any such guidance.

(10) Any guidance given by the Commission for the purposes of this section may take such form and be given in such manner as the Commission considers appropriate.

(11) For the purposes of sections 74 and 74A above, any reference to any obligation imposed on the charity trustees by or under section 74 includes a reference to any obligation imposed on them by virtue of any of subsections (6) to (8) above.

(12) Section 74(14) applies for the purposes of this section as it applies for the purposes of section 74.'

NOTES

Initial Commencement

To be appointed: see s 79(2).

Extent

This section does not extend to Scotland: see s 80(2).

41 Power to replace purposes

After section 74B of the 1993 Act (inserted by section 40 above) insert—

'74C Power to replace purposes of unincorporated charity

(1) This section applies to a charity if—

(a) its gross income in its last financial year did not exceed £10,000,
(b) it does not hold any designated land, and
(c) it is not a company or other body corporate.

'Designated land' means land held on trusts which stipulate that it is to be used for the purposes, or any particular purposes, of the charity.

(2) The charity trustees of such a charity may resolve for the purposes of this section that the trusts of the charity should be modified by replacing all or any of the purposes of the charity with other purposes specified in the resolution.

(3) The other purposes so specified must be charitable purposes.

(4) But the charity trustees of a charity do not have power to pass a resolution under subsection (2) above unless they are satisfied—

(a) that it is expedient in the interests of the charity for the purposes in question to be replaced, and
(b) that, so far as is reasonably practicable, the new purposes consist of or include purposes that are similar in character to those that are to be replaced.

(5) Any resolution under subsection (2) above must be passed by a majority of not less than two-thirds of the charity trustees who vote on the resolution.

(6) Where charity trustees have passed a resolution under subsection (2), they must send a copy of it to the Commission, together with a statement of their reasons for passing it.

(7) Having received the copy of the resolution, the Commission—

(a) may direct the charity trustees to give public notice of the resolution in such manner as is specified in the direction, and
(b) if it gives such a direction, must take into account any representations made to it by persons appearing to it to be interested in the charity, where those representations are made to it within the period of 28 days beginning with the date when public notice of the resolution is given by the charity trustees.

(8) The Commission may also direct the charity trustees to provide the Commission with additional information or explanations relating to—

(a) the circumstances in and by reference to which they have decided to act under this section, or
(b) their compliance with any obligation imposed on them by or under this section in connection with the resolution.

(9) Subject to the provisions of section 74A above (as they apply in accordance with subsection (10) below), a resolution under subsection (2) above takes effect at the end of the period of 60 days beginning with the date on which the copy of it was received by the Commission.

(10) Section 74A above applies to a resolution under subsection (2) of this section as it applies to a resolution under subsection (2) of section 74 above, except that any reference to section 74(7), (8) or (9) is to be read as a reference to subsection (7), (8) or (9) above.

(11) As from the time when a resolution takes effect under subsection (9) above, the trusts of the charity concerned are to be taken to have been modified in accordance with the terms of the resolution.

(12) The Minister may by order amend subsection (1) above by substituting a different sum for the sum for the time being specified there.'

NOTES

Initial Commencement

To be appointed: see s 79(2).

Extent

This section does not extend to Scotland: see s 80(2).

42 Power to modify powers or procedures

After section 74C of the 1993 Act (inserted by section 41 above) insert—

'74D Power to modify powers or procedures of unincorporated charity

(1) This section applies to any charity which is not a company or other body corporate.

(2) The charity trustees of such a charity may resolve for the purposes of this section that any provision of the trusts of the charity—

(a) relating to any of the powers exercisable by the charity trustees in the administration of the charity, or
(b) regulating the procedure to be followed in any respect in connection with its administration,

should be modified in such manner as is specified in the resolution.

(3) Subsection (4) applies if the charity is an unincorporated association with a body of members distinct from the charity trustees.

(4) Any resolution of the charity trustees under subsection (2) must be approved by a further resolution which is passed at a general meeting of the body either—

(a) by a majority of not less than two-thirds of the members entitled to attend and vote at the meeting who vote on the resolution, or
(b) by a decision taken without a vote and without any expression of dissent in response to the question put to the meeting.

(5) Where—

(a) the charity trustees have passed a resolution under subsection (2), and
(b) (if subsection (4) applies) a further resolution has been passed under that subsection,

the trusts of the charity are to be taken to have been modified in accordance with the terms of the resolution.

(6) The trusts are to be taken to have been so modified as from such date as is specified for this purpose in the resolution under subsection (2), or (if later) the date when any such further resolution was passed under subsection (4).'

NOTES

Initial Commencement

To be appointed: see s 79(2).

Extent

This section does not extend to Scotland: see s 80(2).

Chapter 11
Powers to Spend Capital and Mergers

Spending of capital

43 Power to spend capital

For section 75 of the 1993 Act substitute—

'75 Power of unincorporated charities to spend capital: general

(1) This section applies to any available endowment fund of a charity which is not a company or other body corporate.

(2) But this section does not apply to a fund if section 75A below (power of larger charities to spend capital given for particular purpose) applies to it.

(3) Where the condition in subsection (4) below is met in relation to the charity, the charity trustees may resolve for the purposes of this section that the fund, or a portion of it, ought to be freed from the restrictions with respect to expenditure of capital that apply to it.

(4) The condition in this subsection is that the charity trustees are satisfied that the purposes set out in the trusts to which the fund is subject could be carried out more effectively if the capital of the fund, or the relevant portion of the capital, could be expended as well as income accruing to it, rather than just such income.

(5) Once the charity trustees have passed a resolution under subsection (3) above, the fund or portion may by virtue of this section be expended in carrying out the purposes set out in the trusts to which the fund is subject without regard to the restrictions mentioned in that subsection.

(6) The fund or portion may be so expended as from such date as is specified for this purpose in the resolution.

(7) In this section 'available endowment fund', in relation to a charity, means—

(a) the whole of the charity's permanent endowment if it is all subject to the same trusts, or
(b) any part of its permanent endowment which is subject to any particular trusts that are different from those to which any other part is subject.

75A Power of larger unincorporated charities to spend capital given for particular purpose

(1) This section applies to any available endowment fund of a charity which is not a company or other body corporate if—

(a) the capital of the fund consists entirely of property given—
  (i) by a particular individual,
  (ii) by a particular institution (by way of grant or otherwise), or
  (iii) by two or more individuals or institutions in pursuit of a common purpose, and
(b) the financial condition in subsection (2) below is met.

(2) The financial condition in this subsection is met if—

(a) the relevant charity's gross income in its last financial year exceeded £1,000, and
(b) the market value of the endowment fund exceeds £10,000.

(3) Where the condition in subsection (4) below is met in relation to the charity, the charity trustees may resolve for the purposes of this section that the fund, or a portion of it, ought to be freed from the restrictions with respect to expenditure of capital that apply to it.

(4) The condition in this subsection is that the charity trustees are satisfied that the purposes set out in the trusts to which the fund is subject could be carried out more effectively if the capital of the fund, or the relevant portion of the capital, could be expended as well as income accruing to it, rather than just such income.

(5) The charity trustees—

(a) must send a copy of any resolution under subsection (3) above to the Commission, together with a statement of their reasons for passing it, and
(b) may not implement the resolution except in accordance with the following provisions of this section.

(6) Having received the copy of the resolution the Commission may—

(a) direct the charity trustees to give public notice of the resolution in such manner as is specified in the direction, and
(b) if it gives such a direction, must take into account any representations made to it by persons appearing to it to be interested in the charity, where those representations are made to it within the period of 28 days beginning with the date when public notice of the resolution is given by the charity trustees.

(7) The Commission may also direct the charity trustees to provide the Commission with additional information or explanations relating to—

(a) the circumstances in and by reference to which they have decided to act under this section, or
(b) their compliance with any obligation imposed on them by or under this section in connection with the resolution.

(8) When considering whether to concur with the resolution the Commission must take into account—

(a) any evidence available to it as to the wishes of the donor or donors mentioned in subsection (1)(a) above, and
(b) any changes in the circumstances relating to the charity since the making of the gift or gifts (including, in particular, its financial position, the needs of its beneficiaries, and the social, economic and legal environment in which it operates).

(9) The Commission must not concur with the resolution unless it is satisfied—

(a) that its implementation would accord with the spirit of the gift or gifts mentioned in subsection (1)(a) above (even though it would be inconsistent with the restrictions mentioned in subsection (3) above), and
(b) that the charity trustees have complied with the obligations imposed on them by or under this section in connection with the resolution.

(10) Before the end of the period of three months beginning with the relevant date, the Commission must notify the charity trustees in writing either—

(a) that the Commission concurs with the resolution, or
(b) that it does not concur with it.

(11) In subsection (10) 'the relevant date' means—

(a) in a case where the Commission directs the charity trustees under subsection (6) above to give public notice of the resolution, the date when that notice is given, and
(b) in any other case, the date on which the Commission receives the copy of the resolution in accordance with subsection (5) above.

(12) Where—

(a) the charity trustees are notified by the Commission that it concurs with the resolution, or
(b) the period of three months mentioned in subsection (10) above has elapsed without the Commission notifying them that it does not concur with the resolution,

the fund or portion may, by virtue of this section, be expended in carrying out the purposes set out in the trusts to which the fund is subject without regard to the restrictions mentioned in subsection (3).

(13) The Minister may by order amend subsection (2) above by substituting a different sum for any sum specified there.

(14) In this section—

(a) 'available endowment fund' has the same meaning as in section 75 above,
(b) 'market value', in relation to an endowment fund, means—
    (i) the market value of the fund as recorded in the accounts for the last financial year of the relevant charity, or
    (ii) if no such value was so recorded, the current market value of the fund as determined on a valuation carried out for the purpose, and
(c) the reference in subsection (1) to the giving of property by an individual includes his giving it under his will.

75B Power to spend capital subject to special trusts

(1) This section applies to any available endowment fund of a special trust which, as the result of a direction under section 96(5) below, is to be treated as a separate charity ('the relevant charity') for the purposes of this section.

(2) Where the condition in subsection (3) below is met in relation to the relevant charity, the charity trustees may resolve for the purposes of this section that the fund, or a portion of it, ought to be freed from the restrictions with respect to expenditure of capital that apply to it.

(3) The condition in this subsection is that the charity trustees are satisfied that the purposes set out in the trusts to which the fund is subject could be carried out more effectively if the capital of the fund, or the relevant portion of the capital, could be expended as well as income accruing to it, rather than just such income.

(4) Where the market value of the fund exceeds £10,000 and the capital of the fund consists entirely of property given—

(a) by a particular individual,
(b) by a particular institution (by way of grant or otherwise), or
(c) by two or more individuals or institutions in pursuit of a common purpose,

subsections (5) to (11) of section 75A above apply in relation to the resolution and that gift or gifts as they apply in relation to a resolution under section 75A(3) and the gift or gifts mentioned in section 75A(1)(a).

(5) Where—

(a) the charity trustees have passed a resolution under subsection (2) above, and
(b) (in a case where section 75A(5) to (11) above apply in accordance with subsection (4) above) either—
  (i) the charity trustees are notified by the Commission that it concurs with the resolution, or
  (ii) the period of three months mentioned in section 75A(10) has elapsed without the Commission notifying them that it does not concur with the resolution,

the fund or portion may, by virtue of this section, be expended in carrying out the purposes set out in the trusts to which the fund is subject without regard to the restrictions mentioned in subsection (2).

(6) The fund or portion may be so expended as from such date as is specified for this purpose in the resolution.

(7) The Minister may by order amend subsection (4) above by substituting a different sum for the sum specified there.

(8) In this section—

(a) 'available endowment fund' has the same meaning as in section 75 above,
(b) 'market value' has the same meaning as in section 75A above, and
(c) the reference in subsection (4) to the giving of property by an individual includes his giving it under his will.'

NOTES

Initial Commencement

To be appointed: see s 79(2).

Extent

This section does not extend to Scotland: see s 80(2).

Mergers

44 Merger of charities

After section 75B of the 1993 Act (inserted by section 43 above) insert—

'Mergers

75C Register of charity mergers

(1) The Commission shall establish and maintain a register of charity mergers.

(2) The register shall be kept by the Commission in such manner as it thinks fit.

(3) The register shall contain an entry in respect of every relevant charity merger which is notified to the Commission in accordance with subsections (6) to (9) and such procedures as it may determine.

(4) In this section 'relevant charity merger' means—

(a) a merger of two or more charities in connection with which one of them ('the transferee') has transferred to it all the property of the other or others, each of which (a 'transferor') ceases to exist, or is to cease to exist, on or after the transfer of its property to the transferee, or

(b) a merger of two or more charities ('transferors') in connection with which both or all of them cease to exist, or are to cease to exist, on or after the transfer of all of their property to a new charity ('the transferee').

(5) In the case of a merger involving the transfer of property of any charity which has both a permanent endowment and other property ('unrestricted property') and whose trusts do not contain provision for the termination of the charity, subsection (4)(a) or (b) applies in relation to any such charity as if—

(a) the reference to all of its property were a reference to all of its unrestricted property, and
(b) any reference to its ceasing to exist were omitted.

(6) A notification under subsection (3) above may be given in respect of a relevant charity merger at any time after—

(a) the transfer of property involved in the merger has taken place, or
(b) (if more than one transfer of property is so involved) the last of those transfers has taken place.

(7) If a vesting declaration is made in connection with a relevant charity merger, a notification under subsection (3) above must be given in respect of the merger once the transfer, or the last of the transfers, mentioned in subsection (6) above has taken place.

(8) A notification under subsection (3) is to be given by the charity trustees of the transferee and must—

(a) specify the transfer or transfers of property involved in the merger and the date or dates on which it or they took place;
(b) include a statement that appropriate arrangements have been made with respect to the discharge of any liabilities of the transferor charity or charities; and
(c) in the case of a notification required by subsection (7), set out the matters mentioned in subsection (9).

(9) The matters are—

(a) the fact that the vesting declaration in question has been made;
(b) the date when the declaration was made; and
(c) the date on which the vesting of title under the declaration took place by virtue of section 75E(2) below.

(10) In this section and section 75D—

(a) any reference to a transfer of property includes a transfer effected by a vesting declaration; and
(b) 'vesting declaration' means a declaration to which section 75E(2) below applies.

(11) Nothing in this section or section 75E or 75F applies in a case where section 69K (amalgamation of CIOs) or 69M (transfer of CIO's undertaking) applies.

75D Register of charity mergers: supplementary

(1) Subsection (2) applies to the entry to be made in the register in respect of a relevant charity merger, as required by section 75C(3) above.

(2) The entry must—

(a) specify the date when the transfer or transfers of property involved in the merger took place,
(b) if a vesting declaration was made in connection with the merger, set out the matters mentioned in section 75C(9) above, and
(c) contain such other particulars of the merger as the Commission thinks fit.

(3) The register shall be open to public inspection at all reasonable times.

(4) Where any information contained in the register is not in documentary form, subsection (3) above shall be construed as requiring the information to be available for public inspection in legible form at all reasonable times.

(5) In this section—

'the register' means the register of charity mergers;
'relevant charity merger' has the same meaning as in section 75C.

75E Pre-merger vesting declarations

(1) Subsection (2) below applies to a declaration which—

(a) is made by deed for the purposes of this section by the charity trustees of the transferor,
(b) is made in connection with a relevant charity merger, and
(c) is to the effect that (subject to subsections (3) and (4)) all of the transferor's property is to vest in the transferee on such date as is specified in the declaration ('the specified date').

(2) The declaration operates on the specified date to vest the legal title to all of the transferor's property in the transferee, without the need for any further document transferring it.

This is subject to subsections (3) and (4).

(3) Subsection (2) does not apply to—

(a) any land held by the transferor as security for money subject to the trusts of the transferor (other than land held on trust for securing debentures or debenture stock);
(b) any land held by the transferor under a lease or agreement which contains any covenant (however described) against assignment of the transferor's interest without the consent of some other person, unless that consent has been obtained before the specified date; or
(c) any shares, stock, annuity or other property which is only transferable in books kept by a company or other body or in a manner directed by or under any enactment.

(4) In its application to registered land within the meaning of the Land Registration Act 2002, subsection (2) has effect subject to section 27 of that Act (dispositions required to be registered).

(5) In this section 'relevant charity merger' has the same meaning as in section 75C.

(6) In this section—

(a) any reference to the transferor, in relation to a relevant charity merger, is a reference to the transferor (or one of the transferors) within the meaning of section 75C above, and
(b) any reference to all of the transferor's property, where the transferor is a charity within section 75C(5), is a reference to all of the transferor's unrestricted property (within the meaning of that provision).

(7) In this section any reference to the transferee, in relation to a relevant charity merger, is a reference to—

(a) the transferee (within the meaning of section 75C above), if it is a company or other body corporate, and
(b) otherwise, to the charity trustees of the transferee (within the meaning of that section).

75F Effect of registering charity merger on gifts to transferor

(1) This section applies where a relevant charity merger is registered in the register of charity mergers.

(2) Any gift which—

(a) is expressed as a gift to the transferor, and
(b) takes effect on or after the date of registration of the merger,

takes effect as a gift to the transferee, unless it is an excluded gift.

(3) A gift is an 'excluded gift' if—

(a) the transferor is a charity within section 75C(5), and
(b) the gift is intended to be held subject to the trusts on which the whole or part of the charity's permanent endowment is held.

(4) In this section—

'relevant charity merger' has the same meaning as in section 75C; and
'transferor' and 'transferee' have the same meanings as in section 75E.'

NOTES

Initial Commencement

To be appointed: see s 79(2).

Extent

This section does not extend to Scotland: see s 80(2).

Part 3
Funding for Charitable, Benevolent or Philanthropic Institutions

Chapter 1
Public Charitable Collections

Preliminary

45 Regulation of public charitable collections

(1) This Chapter regulates public charitable collections, which are of the following two types—

(a) collections in a public place; and
(b) door to door collections.

(2) For the purposes of this Chapter—

(a) 'public charitable collection' means (subject to section 46) a charitable appeal which is made—
 (i) in any public place, or
 (ii) by means of visits to houses or business premises (or both);
(b) 'charitable appeal' means an appeal to members of the public which is—
 (i) an appeal to them to give money or other property, or
 (ii) an appeal falling within subsection (4),
 (or both) and which is made in association with a representation that the whole or any part of its proceeds is to be applied for charitable, benevolent or philanthropic purposes;
(c) a 'collection in a public place' is a public charitable collection that is made in a public place, as mentioned in paragraph (a)(i);
(d) a 'door to door collection' is a public charitable collection that is made by means of visits to houses or business premises (or both), as mentioned in paragraph (a)(ii).

(3) For the purposes of subsection (2)(b)—

(a) the reference to the giving of money is to doing so by whatever means; and
(b) it does not matter whether the giving of money or other property is for consideration or otherwise.

(4) An appeal falls within this subsection if it consists in or includes—

(a) the making of an offer to sell goods or to supply services, or
(b) the exposing of goods for sale,

to members of the public.

(5) In this section—

'business premises' means any premises used for business or other commercial purposes;
'house' includes any part of a building constituting a separate dwelling;
'public place' means—
(a) any highway, and
(b) (subject to subsection (6)) any other place to which, at any time when the appeal is made, members of the public have or are permitted to have access and which either—
(i) is not within a building, or
(ii) if within a building, is a public area within any station, airport or shopping precinct or any other similar public area.

(6) In subsection (5), paragraph (b) of the definition of 'public place' does not include—

(a) any place to which members of the public are permitted to have access only if any payment or ticket required as a condition of access has been made or purchased; or
(b) any place to which members of the public are permitted to have access only by virtue of permission given for the purposes of the appeal in question.

NOTES

Initial Commencement

To be appointed: see s 79(2).

Extent

This section does not extend to Scotland: see s 80(2).

46 Charitable appeals that are not public charitable collections

(1) A charitable appeal is not a public charitable collection if the appeal—

(a) is made in the course of a public meeting; or
(b) is made—
(i) on land within a churchyard or burial ground contiguous or adjacent to a place of public worship, or
(ii) on other land occupied for the purposes of a place of public worship and contiguous or adjacent to it,
where the land is enclosed or substantially enclosed (whether by any wall or building or otherwise); or
(c) is made on land to which members of the public have access only—
(i) by virtue of the express or implied permission of the occupier of the land, or
(ii) by virtue of any enactment,
and the occupier is the promoter of the collection; or
(d) is an appeal to members of the public to give money or other property by placing it in an unattended receptacle.

(2) For the purposes of subsection (1)(c) 'the occupier', in relation to unoccupied land, means the person entitled to occupy it.

(3) For the purposes of subsection (1)(d) a receptacle is unattended if it is not in the possession or custody of a person acting as a collector.

NOTES

Initial Commencement

To be appointed: see s 79(2).

Extent

This section does not extend to Scotland: see s 80(2).

47 Other definitions for purposes of this Chapter

(1) In this Chapter—

'charitable, benevolent or philanthropic institution' means—
- (a) a charity, or
- (b) an institution (other than a charity) which is established for charitable, benevolent, or philanthropic purposes;

'collector', in relation to a public charitable collection, means any person by whom the appeal in question is made (whether made by him alone or with others and whether made by him for remuneration or otherwise);
'local authority' means a unitary authority, the council of a district so far as it is not a unitary authority, the council of a London borough or of a Welsh county or county borough, the Common Council of the City of London or the Council of the Isles of Scilly;
'prescribed' means prescribed by regulations under section 63;
'proceeds', in relation to a public charitable collection, means all money or other property given (whether for consideration or otherwise) in response to the charitable appeal in question;
'promoter', in relation to a public charitable collection, means—
- (a) a person who (whether alone or with others and whether for remuneration or otherwise) organises or controls the conduct of the charitable appeal in question, or
- (b) where there is no person acting as mentioned in paragraph (a), any person who acts as a collector in respect of the collection,

and associated expressions are to be construed accordingly;
'public collections certificate' means a certificate issued by the Commission under section 52.

(2) In subsection (1) 'unitary authority' means—

- (a) the council of a county so far as it is the council for an area for which there are no district councils;
- (b) the council of any district comprised in an area for which there is no county council.

(3) The functions exercisable under this Chapter by a local authority are to be exercisable—

- (a) as respects the Inner Temple, by its Sub-Treasurer, and
- (b) as respects the Middle Temple, by its Under Treasurer;

and references in this Chapter to a local authority or to the area of a local authority are to be construed accordingly.

NOTES

Initial Commencement

To be appointed: see s 79(2).

Extent

This section does not extend to Scotland: see s 80(2).

Restrictions on conducting collections

48 Restrictions on conducting collections in a public place

(1) A collection in a public place must not be conducted unless—

(a) the promoters of the collection hold a public collections certificate in force under section 52 in respect of the collection, and
(b) the collection is conducted in accordance with a permit issued under section 59 by the local authority in whose area it is conducted.

(2) Subsection (1) does not apply to a public charitable collection which is an exempt collection by virtue of section 50 (local, short-term collections).

(3) Where—

(a) a collection in a public place is conducted in contravention of subsection (1), and
(b) the circumstances of the case do not fall within section 50(6),

every promoter of the collection is guilty of an offence and liable on summary conviction to a fine not exceeding level 5 on the standard scale.

NOTES

Initial Commencement

To be appointed: see s 79(2).

Extent

This section does not extend to Scotland: see s 80(2).

49 Restrictions on conducting door to door collections

(1) A door to door collection must not be conducted unless the promoters of the collection—

(a) hold a public collections certificate in force under section 52 in respect of the collection, and
(b) have within the prescribed period falling before the day (or the first of the days) on which the collection takes place—
    (i) notified the local authority in whose area the collection is to be conducted of the matters mentioned in subsection (3), and
    (ii) provided that authority with a copy of the certificate mentioned in paragraph (a).

(2) Subsection (1) does not apply to a door to door collection which is an exempt collection by virtue of section 50 (local, short-term collections).

(3) The matters referred to in subsection (1)(b)(i) are—

(a) the purpose for which the proceeds of the appeal are to be applied;
(b) the prescribed particulars of when the collection is to be conducted;
(c) the locality within which the collection is to be conducted; and
(d) such other matters as may be prescribed.

(4) Where—

(a) a door to door collection is conducted in contravention of subsection (1), and
(b) the circumstances of the case do not fall within section 50(6),

every promoter of the collection is guilty of an offence and liable on summary conviction to a fine not exceeding level 5 on the standard scale.

This is subject to subsection (5).

(5) Where—

(a) a door to door collection is conducted in contravention of subsection (1),
(b) the appeal is for goods only, and
(c) the circumstances of the case do not fall within section 50(6),

every promoter of the collection is guilty of an offence and liable on summary conviction to a fine not exceeding level 3 on the standard scale.

(6) In subsection (5) 'goods' includes all personal chattels other than things in action and money.

NOTES

Initial Commencement

To be appointed: see s 79(2).

Extent

This section does not extend to Scotland: see s 80(2).

50 Exemption for local, short-term collections

(1) A public charitable collection is an exempt collection if—

(a) it is a local, short-term collection (see subsection (2)), and
(b) the promoters notify the local authority in whose area it is to be conducted of the matters mentioned in subsection (3) within the prescribed period falling before the day (or the first of the days) on which the collection takes place,

unless, within the prescribed period beginning with the date when they are so notified, the local authority serve a notice under subsection (4) on the promoters.

(2) A public charitable collection is a local, short term collection if—

(a) the appeal is local in character; and
(b) the duration of the appeal does not exceed the prescribed period of time.

(3) The matters referred to in subsection (1)(b) are—

(a) the purpose for which the proceeds of the appeal are to be applied;
(b) the date or dates on which the collection is to be conducted;
(c) the place at which, or the locality within which, the collection is to be conducted; and
(d) such other matters as may be prescribed.

(4) Where it appears to the local authority—

(a) that the collection is not a local, short-term collection, or
(b) that the promoters or any of them have or has on any occasion—
  (i) breached any provision of regulations made under section 63, or
  (ii) been convicted of an offence within section 53(2)(a)(i) to (v),

they must serve on the promoters written notice of their decision to that effect and the reasons for their decision.

(5) That notice must also state the right of appeal conferred by section 62(1) and the time within which such an appeal must be brought.

(6) Where—

(a) a collection in a public place is conducted otherwise than in accordance with section 48(1) or a door to door collection is conducted otherwise than in accordance with section 49(1), and
(b) the collection is a local, short term collection but the promoters do not notify the local authority as mentioned in subsection (1)(b),

every promoter of the collection is guilty of an offence and liable on summary conviction to a fine not exceeding level 3 on the standard scale.

NOTES

Initial Commencement

To be appointed: see s 79(2).

Extent

This section does not extend to Scotland: see s 80(2).

Public collections certificates

51 Applications for certificates

(1) A person or persons proposing to promote public charitable collections (other than exempt collections) may apply to the Charity Commission for a public collections certificate in respect of those collections.

(2) The application must be made—

(a) within the specified period falling before the first of the collections is to commence, or
(b) before such later date as the Commission may allow in the case of that application.

(3) The application must—

(a) be made in such form as may be specified,
(b) specify the period for which the certificate is sought (which must be no more than 5 years), and
(c) contain such other information as may be specified.

(4) An application under this section may be made for a public collections certificate in respect of a single collection; and the references in this Chapter, in the context of such certificates, to public charitable collections are to be read accordingly.

(5) In subsections (2) and (3) 'specified' means specified in regulations made by the Commission after consulting such persons or bodies of persons as it considers appropriate.

(6) Regulations under subsection (5)—

(a) must be published in such manner as the Commission considers appropriate,
(b) may make different provision for different cases or descriptions of case, and
(c) may make such incidental, supplementary, consequential or transitional provision as the Commission considers appropriate.

(7) In this section 'exempt collection' means a public charitable collection which is an exempt collection by virtue of section 50.

NOTES

Initial Commencement

To be appointed: see s 79(2).

Extent

This section does not extend to Scotland: see s 80(2).

52 Determination of applications and issue of certificates

(1) On receiving an application for a public collections certificate made in accordance with section 51, the Commission may make such inquiries (whether under section 54 or otherwise) as it thinks fit.

(2) The Commission must, after making any such inquiries, determine the application by either—

(a) issuing a public collections certificate in respect of the collections, or
(b) refusing the application on one or more of the grounds specified in section 53(1).

(3) A public collections certificate—

(a) must specify such matters as may be prescribed, and
(b) shall (subject to section 56) be in force for—
  (i) the period specified in the application in accordance with section 51(3)(b), or
  (ii) such shorter period as the Commission thinks fit.

(4) The Commission may, at the time of issuing a public collections certificate, attach to it such conditions as it thinks fit.

(5) Conditions attached under subsection (4) may include conditions prescribed for the purposes of that subsection.

(6) The Commission must secure that the terms of any conditions attached under subsection (4) are consistent with the provisions of any regulations under section 63 (whether or not prescribing conditions for the purposes of that subsection).

(7) Where the Commission—

(a) refuses to issue a certificate, or
(b) attaches any condition to it,

it must serve on the applicant written notice of its decision and the reasons for its decision.

(8) That notice must also state the right of appeal conferred by section 57(1) and the time within which such an appeal must be brought.

NOTES

Initial Commencement

To be appointed: see s 79(2).

Extent

This section does not extend to Scotland: see s 80(2).

53 Grounds for refusing to issue a certificate

(1) The grounds on which the Commission may refuse an application for a public collections certificate are—

(a) that the applicant has been convicted of a relevant offence;
(b) where the applicant is a person other than a charitable, benevolent or philanthropic institution for whose benefit the collections are proposed to be conducted, that the Commission is not satisfied that the applicant is authorised (whether by any such institution or by any person acting on behalf of any such institution) to promote the collections;
(c) that it appears to the Commission that the applicant, in promoting any other collection authorised under this Chapter or under section 119 of the 1982 Act, failed to exercise the required due diligence;
(d) that the Commission is not satisfied that the applicant will exercise the required due diligence in promoting the proposed collections;
(e) that it appears to the Commission that the amount likely to be applied for charitable, benevolent or philanthropic purposes in consequence of the proposed collections would be inadequate, having regard to the likely amount of the proceeds of the collections;
(f) that it appears to the Commission that the applicant or any other person would be

likely to receive an amount by way of remuneration in connection with the collections that would be excessive, having regard to all the circumstances;

(g) that the applicant has failed to provide information—
  (i) required for the purposes of the application for the certificate or a previous application, or
  (ii) in response to a request under section 54(1);

(h) that it appears to the Commission that information so provided to it by the applicant is false or misleading in a material particular;

(i) that it appears to the Commission that the applicant or any person authorised by him—
  (i) has breached any conditions attached to a previous public collections certificate, or
  (ii) has persistently breached any conditions attached to a permit issued under section 59;

(j) that it appears to the Commission that the applicant or any person authorised by him has on any occasion breached any provision of regulations made under section 63(1)(b).

(2) For the purposes of subsection (1)—

(a) a 'relevant offence' is—
  (i) an offence under section 5 of the 1916 Act;
  (ii) an offence under the 1939 Act;
  (iii) an offence under section 119 of the 1982 Act or regulations made under it;
  (iv) an offence under this Chapter;
  (v) an offence involving dishonesty; or
  (vi) an offence of a kind the commission of which would, in the opinion of the Commission, be likely to be facilitated by the issuing to the applicant of a public collections certificate; and

(b) the 'required due diligence' is due diligence—
  (i) to secure that persons authorised by the applicant to act as collectors for the purposes of the collection were (or will be) fit and proper persons;
  (ii) to secure that such persons complied (or will comply) with the provisions of regulations under section 63(1)(b) of this Act or (as the case may be) section 119 of the 1982 Act; or
  (iii) to prevent badges or certificates of authority being obtained by persons other than those the applicant had so authorised.

(3) Where an application for a certificate is made by more than one person, any reference to the applicant in subsection (1) or (2) is to be construed as a reference to any of the applicants.

(4) Subject to subsections (5) and (6), the reference in subsection (2)(b)(iii) to badges or certificates of authority is a reference to badges or certificates of authority in a form prescribed by regulations under section 63(1)(b) of this Act or (as the case may be) under section 119 of the 1982 Act.

(5) Subsection (2)(b) applies to the conduct of the applicant (or any of the applicants) in relation to any public charitable collection authorised—

(a) under regulations made under section 5 of the 1916 Act (collection of money or sale of articles in a street or other public place), or

(b) under the 1939 Act (collection of money or other property by means of visits from house to house),

as it applies to his conduct in relation to a collection authorised under this Chapter, but subject to the modifications set out in subsection (6).

(6) The modifications are—

(a) in the case of a collection authorised under regulations made under the 1916 Act—

(i) the reference in subsection (2)(b)(ii) to regulations under section 63(1)(b) of this Act is to be construed as a reference to the regulations under which the collection in question was authorised, and
(ii) the reference in subsection (2)(b)(iii) to badges or certificates of authority is to be construed as a reference to any written authority provided to a collector pursuant to those regulations; and

(b) in the case of a collection authorised under the 1939 Act—
(i) the reference in subsection (2)(b)(ii) to regulations under section 63(1)(b) of this Act is to be construed as a reference to regulations under section 4 of that Act, and
(ii) the reference in subsection (2)(b)(iii) to badges or certificates of authority is to be construed as a reference to badges or certificates of authority in a form prescribed by such regulations.

(7) In subsections (1)(c) and (5) a reference to a collection authorised under this Chapter is a reference to a public charitable collection that—

(a) is conducted in accordance with section 48 or section 49 (as the case may be), or
(b) is an exempt collection by virtue of section 50.

(8) In this section—

'the 1916 Act' means the Police, Factories, &c. (Miscellaneous Provisions) Act 1916 (c 31);
'the 1939 Act' means the House to House Collections Act 1939 (c 44); and
'the 1982 Act' means the Civic Government (Scotland) Act 1982 (c 45).

NOTES

Initial Commencement

To be appointed: see s 79(2).

Extent

This section does not extend to Scotland: see s 80(2).

54 Power to call for information and documents

(1) The Commission may request—

(a) any applicant for a public collections certificate, or
(b) any person to whom such a certificate has been issued,

to provide it with any information in his possession, or document in his custody or under this control, which is relevant to the exercise of any of its functions under this Chapter.

(2) Nothing in this section affects the power conferred on the Commission by section 9 of the 1993 Act.

NOTES

Initial Commencement

To be appointed: see s 79(2).

Extent

This section does not extend to Scotland: see s 80(2).

55 Transfer of certificate between trustees of unincorporated charity

(1) One or more individuals to whom a public collections certificate has been issued ('the holders') may apply to the Commission for a direction that the certificate be transferred to one or more other individuals ('the recipients').

(2) An application under subsection (1) must—

(a) be in such form as may be specified, and
(b) contain such information as may be specified.

(3) The Commission may direct that the certificate be transferred if it is satisfied that—

(a) each of the holders is or was a trustee of a charity which is not a body corporate;
(b) each of the recipients is a trustee of that charity and consents to the transfer; and
(c) the charity trustees consent to the transfer.

(4) Where the Commission refuses to direct that a certificate be transferred, it must serve on the holders written notice of—

(a) its decision, and
(b) the reasons for its decision.

(5) That notice must also state the right of appeal conferred by section 57(2) and the time within which such an appeal must be brought.

(6) Subsections (5) and (6) of section 51 apply for the purposes of subsection (2) of this section as they apply for the purposes of subsection (3) of that section.

(7) Except as provided by this section, a public collections certificate is not transferable.

NOTES

Initial Commencement

To be appointed: see s 79(2).

Extent

This section does not extend to Scotland: see s 80(2).

56 Withdrawal or variation etc of certificates

(1) Where subsection (2), (3) or (4) applies, the Commission may—

(a) withdraw a public collections certificate,
(b) suspend such a certificate,
(c) attach any condition (or further condition) to such a certificate, or
(d) vary any existing condition of such a certificate.

(2) This subsection applies where the Commission—

(a) has reason to believe there has been a change in the circumstances which prevailed at the time when it issued the certificate, and
(b) is of the opinion that, if the application for the certificate had been made in the new circumstances, it would not have issued the certificate or would have issued it subject to different or additional conditions.

(3) This subsection applies where—

(a) the holder of a certificate has unreasonably refused to provide any information or document in response to a request under section 54(1), or
(b) the Commission has reason to believe that information provided to it by the holder of a certificate (or, where there is more than one holder, by any of them) for the purposes of the application for the certificate, or in response to such a request, was false or misleading in a material particular.

(4) This subsection applies where the Commission has reason to believe that there has been or is likely to be a breach of any condition of a certificate, or that a breach of such a condition is continuing.

(5) Any condition imposed at any time by the Commission under subsection (1) (whether by attaching a new condition to the certificate or by varying an existing condition) must be one that it would be appropriate for the Commission to attach to the certificate under section 52(4) if the holder was applying for it in the circumstances prevailing at that time.

(6) The exercise by the Commission of the power conferred by paragraph (b), (c) or (d) of subsection (1) on one occasion does not prevent it from exercising any of the powers conferred by that subsection on a subsequent occasion; and on any subsequent occasion the reference in subsection (2)(a) to the time when the Commission issued the certificate is a reference to the time when it last exercised any of those powers.

(7) Where the Commission—

(a) withdraws or suspends a certificate,
(b) attaches a condition to a certificate, or
(c) varies an existing condition of a certificate,

it must serve on the holder written notice of its decision and the reasons for its decision.

(8) That notice must also state the right of appeal conferred by section 57(3) and the time within which such an appeal must be brought.

(9) If the Commission—

(a) considers that the interests of the public require a decision by it under this section to have immediate effect, and
(b) includes a statement to that effect and the reasons for it in the notice served under subsection (7),

the decision takes effect when that notice is served on the holder.

(10) In any other case the certificate shall continue to have effect as if it had not been withdrawn or suspended or (as the case may be) as if the condition had not been attached or varied—

(a) until the time for bringing an appeal under section 57(3) has expired, or
(b) if such an appeal is duly brought, until the determination or abandonment of the appeal.

(11) A certificate suspended under this section shall (subject to any appeal and any withdrawal of the certificate) remain suspended until—

(a) such time as the Commission may by notice direct that the certificate is again in force, or
(b) the end of the period of six months beginning with the date on which the suspension takes effect,

whichever is the sooner.

NOTES

Initial Commencement

To be appointed: see s 79(2).

Extent

This section does not extend to Scotland: see s 80(2).

57 Appeals against decisions of the Commission

(1) A person who has duly applied to the Commission for a public collections certificate may appeal to the Charity Tribunal ('the Tribunal') against a decision of the Commission under section 52—

(a) to refuse to issue the certificate, or
(b) to attach any condition to it.

(2) A person to whom a public collections certificate has been issued may appeal to the Tribunal against a decision of the Commission not to direct that the certificate be transferred under section 55.

(3) A person to whom a public collections certificate has been issued may appeal to the Tribunal against a decision of the Commission under section 56—

(a) to withdraw or suspend the certificate,
(b) to attach a condition to the certificate, or
(c) to vary an existing condition of the certificate.

(4) The Attorney General may appeal to the Tribunal against a decision of the Commission—

(a) to issue, or to refuse to issue, a certificate,
(b) to attach, or not to attach, any condition to a certificate (whether under section 52 or section 56),
(c) to direct, or not to direct, that a certificate be transferred under section 55,
(d) to withdraw or suspend, or not to withdraw or suspend, a certificate, or
(e) to vary, or not to vary, an existing condition of a certificate.

(5) In determining an appeal under this section, the Tribunal—

(a) must consider afresh the decision appealed against, and
(b) may take into account evidence which was not available to the Commission.

(6) On an appeal under this section, the Tribunal may—

(a) dismiss the appeal,
(b) quash the decision, or
(c) substitute for the decision another decision of a kind that the Commission could have made;

and in any case the Tribunal may give such directions as it thinks fit, having regard to the provisions of this Chapter and of regulations under section 63.

(7) If the Tribunal quashes the decision, it may remit the matter to the Commission (either generally or for determination in accordance with a finding made or direction given by the Tribunal).

NOTES

Initial Commencement

To be appointed: see s 79(2).

Extent

This section does not extend to Scotland: see s 80(2).

Permits

58 Applications for permits to conduct collections in public places

(1) A person or persons proposing to promote a collection in a public place (other than an exempt collection) in the area of a local authority may apply to the authority for a permit to conduct that collection.

(2) The application must be made within the prescribed period falling before the day (or the first of the days) on which the collection is to take place, except as provided in subsection (4).

(3) The application must—

(a) specify the date or dates in respect of which it is desired that the permit, if issued, should have effect (which, in the case of two or more dates, must not span a period of more than 12 months);
(b) be accompanied by a copy of the public collections certificate in force under section 52 in respect of the proposed collection; and
(c) contain such information as may be prescribed.

(4) Where an application ('the certificate application') has been made in accordance with section 51 for a public collections certificate in respect of the collection and either—

(a) the certificate application has not been determined by the end of the period mentioned in subsection (2) above, or
(b) the certificate application has been determined by the issue of such a certificate but at a time when there is insufficient time remaining for the application mentioned in subsection (2) ('the permit application') to be made by the end of that period,

the permit application must be made as early as practicable before the day (or the first of the days) on which the collection is to take place.

(5) In this section 'exempt collection' means a collection in a public place which is an exempt collection by virtue of section 50.

NOTES

Initial Commencement

To be appointed: see s 79(2).

Extent

This section does not extend to Scotland: see s 80(2).

59 Determination of applications and issue of permits

(1) On receiving an application made in accordance with section 58 for a permit in respect of a collection in a public place, a local authority must determine the application within the prescribed period by either—

(a) issuing a permit in respect of the collection, or
(b) refusing the application on the ground specified in section 60(1).

(2) Where a local authority issue such a permit, it shall (subject to section 61) have effect in respect of the date or dates specified in the application in accordance with section 58(3)(a).

(3) At the time of issuing a permit under this section, a local authority may attach to it such conditions within paragraphs (a) to (d) below as they think fit, having regard to the local circumstances of the collection—

(a) conditions specifying the day of the week, date, time or frequency of the collection;
(b) conditions specifying the locality or localities within their area in which the collection may be conducted;
(c) conditions regulating the manner in which the collection is to be conducted;
(d) such other conditions as may be prescribed for the purposes of this subsection.

(4) A local authority must secure that the terms of any conditions attached under subsection (3) are consistent with the provisions of any regulations under section 63 (whether or not prescribing conditions for the purposes of that subsection).

(5) Where a local authority—

(a) refuse to issue a permit, or
(b) attach any condition to it,

they must serve on the applicant written notice of their decision and the reasons for their decision.

(6) That notice must also state the right of appeal conferred by section 62(2) and the time within which such an appeal must be brought.

NOTES

Initial Commencement

To be appointed: see s 79(2).

Extent

This section does not extend to Scotland: see s 80(2).

60 Refusal of permits

(1) The only ground on which a local authority may refuse an application for a permit to conduct a collection in a public place is that it appears to them that the collection would cause undue inconvenience to members of the public by reason of—

(a) the day or the week or date on or in which,
(b) the time at which,
(c) the frequency with which, or
(d) the locality or localities in which,

it is proposed to be conducted.

(2) In making a decision under subsection (1), a local authority may have regard to the fact (where it is the case) that the collection is proposed to be conducted—

(a) wholly or partly in a locality in which another collection in a public place is already authorised to be conducted under this Chapter, and
(b) on a day on which that other collection is already so authorised, or on the day falling immediately before, or immediately after, any such day.

(3) A local authority must not, however, have regard to the matters mentioned in subsection (2) if it appears to them—

(a) that the proposed collection would be conducted only in one location, which is on land to which members of the public would have access only—
  (i) by virtue of the express or implied permission of the occupier of the land, or
  (ii) by virtue of any enactment, and
(b) that the occupier of the land consents to that collection being conducted there;

and for this purpose 'the occupier', in relation to unoccupied land, means the person entitled to occupy it.

(4) In this section a reference to a collection in a public place authorised under this Chapter is a reference to a collection in a public place that—

(a) is conducted in accordance with section 48, or
(b) is an exempt collection by virtue of section 50.

NOTES

Initial Commencement

To be appointed: see s 79(2).

Extent

This section does not extend to Scotland: see s 80(2).

61 Withdrawal or variation etc of permits

(1) Where subsection (2), (3) or (4) applies, a local authority who have issued a permit under section 59 may—

(a) withdraw the permit,
(b) attach any condition (or further condition) to the permit, or
(c) vary any existing condition of the permit.

(2) This subsection applies where the local authority—

(a) have reason to believe that there has been a change in the circumstances which prevailed at the time when they issued the permit, and
(b) are of the opinion that, if the application for the permit had been made in the new circumstances, they would not have issued the permit or would have issued it subject to different or additional conditions.

(3) This subsection applies where the local authority have reason to believe that any information provided to them by the holder of a permit (or, where there is more than one holder, by any of them) for the purposes of the application for the permit was false or misleading in a material particular.

(4) This subsection applies where the local authority have reason to believe that there has been or is likely to be a breach of any condition of a permit issued by them, or that a breach of such a condition is continuing.

(5) Any condition imposed at any time by a local authority under subsection (1) (whether by attaching a new condition to the permit or by varying an existing condition) must be one that it would be appropriate for the authority to attach to the permit under section 59(3) if the holder was applying for it in the circumstances prevailing at that time.

(6) The exercise by a local authority of the power conferred by paragraph (b) or (c) of subsection (1) on one occasion does not prevent them from exercising any of the powers conferred by that subsection on a subsequent occasion; and on any subsequent occasion the reference in subsection (2)(a) to the time when the local authority issued the permit is a reference to the time when they last exercised any of those powers.

(7) Where under this section a local authority—

(a) withdraw a permit,
(b) attach a condition to a permit, or
(c) vary an existing condition of a permit,

they must serve on the holder written notice of their decision and the reasons for their decision.

(8) That notice must also state the right of appeal conferred by section 62(3) and the time within which such an appeal must be brought.

(9) Where a local authority withdraw a permit under this section, they must send a copy of their decision and the reasons for it to the Commission.

(10) Where a local authority under this section withdraw a permit, attach any condition to a permit, or vary an existing condition of a permit, the permit shall continue to have effect as if it had not been withdrawn or (as the case may be) as if the condition had not been attached or varied—

(a) until the time for bringing an appeal under section 62(3) has expired, or
(b) if such an appeal is duly brought, until the determination or abandonment of the appeal.

NOTES

Initial Commencement

To be appointed: see s 79(2).

Extent

This section does not extend to Scotland: see s 80(2).

62 Appeals against decisions of local authority

(1) A person who, in relation to a public charitable collection, has duly notified a local authority of the matters mentioned in section 50(3) may appeal to a magistrates' court against a decision of the local authority under section 50(4)—

(a) that the collection is not a local, short-term collection, or
(b) that the promoters or any of them has breached any such provision, or been convicted of any such offence, as is mentioned in paragraph (b) of that subsection.

(2) A person who has duly applied to a local authority for a permit to conduct a collection in a public place in the authority's area may appeal to a magistrates' court against a decision of the authority under section 59—

(a) to refuse to issue a permit, or
(b) to attach any condition to it.

(3) A person to whom a permit has been issued may appeal to a magistrates' court against a decision of the local authority under section 61—

(a) to withdraw the permit,
(b) to attach a condition to the permit, or
(c) to vary an existing condition of the permit.

(4) An appeal under subsection (1), (2) or (3) shall be by way of complaint for an order, and the Magistrates' Courts Act 1980 (c 43) shall apply to the proceedings.

(5) Any such appeal shall be brought within 14 days of the date of service on the person in question of the relevant notice under section 50(4), section 59(5) or (as the case may be) section 61(7); and for the purposes of this section an appeal shall be taken to be brought when the complaint is made.

(6) An appeal against the decision of a magistrates' court on an appeal under subsection (1), (2) or (3) may be brought to the Crown Court.

(7) On an appeal to a magistrates' court or the Crown Court under this section, the court may confirm, vary or reverse the local authority's decision and generally give such directions as it thinks fit, having regard to the provisions of this Chapter and of any regulations under section 63.

(8) On an appeal against a decision of a local authority under section 50(4), directions under subsection (7) may include a direction that the collection may be conducted—

(a) on the date or dates notified in accordance with section 50(3)(b), or
(b) on such other date or dates as may be specified in the direction;

and if so conducted the collection is to be regarded as one that is an exempt collection by virtue of section 50.

(9) It shall be the duty of the local authority to comply with any directions given by the court under subsection (7); but the authority need not comply with any directions given by a magistrates' court—

(a) until the time for bringing an appeal under subsection (6) has expired, or
(b) if such an appeal is duly brought, until the determination or abandonment of the appeal.

NOTES

Initial Commencement

To be appointed: see s 79(2).

Extent

This section does not extend to Scotland: see s 80(2).

Supplementary

63 Regulations

(1) The Minister may make regulations—

(a) prescribing the matters which a local authority are to take into account in determining whether a collection is local in character for the purposes of section 50(2)(a);
(b) for the purpose of regulating the conduct of public charitable collections;
(c) prescribing anything falling to be prescribed by virtue of any provision of this Chapter.

(2) The matters which may be prescribed by regulations under subsection (1)(a) include—

(a) the extent of the area within which the appeal is to be conducted;
(b) whether the appeal forms part of a series of appeals;
(c) the number of collectors making the appeal and whether they are acting for remuneration or otherwise;
(d) the financial resources (of any description) of any charitable, benevolent or philanthropic institution for whose benefit the appeal is to be conducted;
(e) where the promoters live or have any place of business.

(3) Regulations under subsection (1)(b) may make provision—

(a) about the keeping and publication of accounts;
(b) for the prevention of annoyance to members of the public;
(c) with respect to the use by collectors of badges and certificates of authority, or badges incorporating such certificates, including, in particular, provision—
  (i) prescribing the form of such badges and certificates;
  (ii) requiring a collector, on request, to permit his badge, or any certificate of authority held by him of the purposes of the collection, to be inspected by a constable or a duly authorised officer of a local authority, or by an occupier of any premises visited by him in the course of the collection;
(d) for prohibiting persons under a prescribed age from acting as collectors, and prohibiting others from causing them so to act.

(4) Nothing in subsection (2) or (3) prejudices the generality of subsection (1)(a) or (b).

(5) Regulations under this section may provide that any failure to comply with a specified provision of the regulations is to be an offence punishable on summary conviction by a fine not exceeding level 2 on the standard scale.

(6) Before making regulations under this section the Minister must consult such persons or bodies of persons as he considers appropriate.

NOTES

Initial Commencement

To be appointed: see s 79(2).

Extent

This section does not extend to Scotland: see s 80(2).

64 Offences

(1) A person commits an offence if, in connection with any charitable appeal, he displays or uses—

(a) a prescribed badge or prescribed certificate of authority which is not for the time being held by him for the purposes of the appeal pursuant to regulations under section 63, or
(b) any badge or article, or any certificate or other document, so nearly resembling a prescribed badge or (as the case may be) a prescribed certificate of authority as to be likely to deceive a member of the public.

(2) A person commits an offence if—

(a) for the purposes of an application made under section 51 or section 58, or
(b) for the purposes of section 49 or section 50,

he knowingly or recklessly furnishes any information which is false or misleading in a material particular.

(3) A person guilty of an offence under this section is liable on summary conviction to a fine not exceeding level 5 on the standard scale.

(4) In subsection (1) 'prescribed badge' and 'prescribed certificate of authority' mean respectively a badge and a certificate of authority in such form as may be prescribed.

NOTES

Initial Commencement

To be appointed: see s 79(2).

Extent

This section does not extend to Scotland: see s 80(2).

65 Offences by bodies corporate

(1) Where any offence under this Chapter or any regulations made under it—

(a) is committed by a body corporate, and
(b) is proved to have been committed with the consent or connivance of, or to be attributable to any neglect on the part of, any director, manager, secretary or other similar officer of the body corporate, or any person who was purporting to act in any such capacity,

he as well as the body corporate shall be guilty of that offence and shall be liable to be proceeded against and punished accordingly.

(2) In subsection (1) 'director', in relation to a body corporate whose affairs are managed by its members, means a member of the body corporate.

NOTES

Initial Commencement

To be appointed: see s 79(2).

Extent

This section does not extend to Scotland: see s 80(2).

66 Service of documents

(1) This section applies to any notice required to be served under this Chapter.

(2) A notice to which this section applies may be served on a person (other than a body corporate)—

(a) by delivering it to that person;
(b) by leaving it at his last known address in the United Kingdom; or
(c) by sending it by post to him at that address.

(3) A notice to which this section applies may be served on a body corporate by delivering it or sending it by post—

(a) to the registered or principal office of the body in the United Kingdom, or
(b) if it has no such office in the United Kingdom, to any place in the United Kingdom where it carries on business or conducts its activities (as the case may be).

(4) A notice to which this section applies may also be served on a person (including a body corporate) by sending it by post to that person at an address notified by that person for the purposes of this subsection to the person or persons by whom it is required to be served.

NOTES

Initial Commencement

To be appointed: see s 79(2).

Extent

This section does not extend to Scotland: see s 80(2).

Chapter 2
Fund-raising

67 Statements indicating benefits for charitable institutions and fund-raisers

(1) Section 60 of the Charities Act 1992 (c 41) (fund-raisers required to indicate institutions benefiting and arrangements for remuneration) is amended as follows.

(2) In subsection (1) (statements by professional fund-raisers raising money for particular charitable institutions), for paragraph (c) substitute—

'(c) the method by which the fund-raiser's remuneration in connection with the appeal is to be determined and the notifiable amount of that remuneration.'

(3) In subsection (2) (statements by professional fund-raisers raising money for charitable purposes etc), for paragraph (c) substitute—

'(c) the method by which his remuneration in connection with the appeal is to be determined and the notifiable amount of that remuneration.'

(4) In subsection (3) (statements by commercial participators raising money for particular charitable institutions), for paragraph (c) substitute—

'(c) the notifiable amount of whichever of the following sums is applicable in the circumstances—
  (i) the sum representing so much of the consideration given for goods or services sold or supplied by him as is to be given to or applied for the benefit of the institution or institutions concerned,
  (ii) the sum representing so much of any other proceeds of a promotional venture undertaken by him as is to be so given or applied, or
  (iii) the sum of the donations by him in connection with the sale or supply of any such goods or services which are to be so given or supplied.'

(5) After subsection (3) insert—

'(3A) In subsections (1) to (3) a reference to the 'notifiable amount' of any remuneration or other sum is a reference—

(a) to the actual amount of the remuneration or sum, if that is known at the time when the statement is made; and
(b) otherwise to the estimated amount of the remuneration or sum, calculated as accurately as is reasonably possible in the circumstances.'

NOTES

Initial Commencement

To be appointed: see s 79(2).

Extent

This section does not extend to Scotland: see s 80(2).

68 Statements indicating benefits for charitable institutions and collectors

After section 60 of the 1992 Act insert—

'60A Other persons making appeals required to indicate institutions benefiting and arrangements for remuneration

(1) Subsections (1) and (2) of section 60 apply to a person acting for reward as a collector in respect of a public charitable collection as they apply to a professional fund-raiser.

(2) But those subsections do not so apply to a person excluded by virtue of—

(a) subsection (3) below, or
(b) section 60B(1) (exclusion of lower-paid collectors).

(3) Those subsections do not so apply to a person if—

(a) section 60(1) or (2) applies apart from subsection (1) (by virtue of the exception in section 58(2)(c) for persons treated as promoters), or
(b) subsection (4) or (5) applies,

in relation to his acting for reward as a collector in respect of the collection mentioned in subsection (1) above.

(4) Where a person within subsection (6) solicits money or other property for the benefit of one or more particular charitable institutions, the solicitation shall be accompanied by a statement clearly indicating—

(a) the name or names of the institution or institutions for whose benefit the solicitation is being made;
(b) if there is more than one such institution, the proportions in which the institutions are respectively to benefit;
(c) the fact that he is an officer, employee or trustee of the institution or company mentioned in subsection (6); and
(d) the fact that he is receiving remuneration as an officer, employee or trustee or (as the case may be) for acting as a collector.

(5) Where a person within subsection (6) solicits money or other property for charitable, benevolent or philanthropic purposes of any description (rather than for the benefit of one or more particular charitable institutions), the solicitation shall be accompanied by a statement clearly indicating—

(a) the fact that he is soliciting money or other property for those purposes and not for the benefit of any particular charitable institution or institutions;
(b) the method by which it is to be determined how the proceeds of the appeal are to be distributed between different charitable institutions;

(c) the fact that he is an officer, employee or trustee of the institution or company mentioned in subsection (6); and
(d) the fact that he is receiving remuneration as an officer, employee or trustee or (as the case may be) for acting as a collector.

(6) A person is within this subsection if—

(a) he is an officer or employee of a charitable institution or a company connected with any such institution, or a trustee of any such institution,
(b) he is acting as a collector in that capacity, and
(c) he receives remuneration either in his capacity as officer, employee or trustee or for acting as a collector.

(7) But a person is not within subsection (6) if he is excluded by virtue of section 60B(4).

(8) Where any requirement of—

(a) subsection (1) or (2) of section 60, as it applies by virtue of subsection (1) above, or
(b) subsection (4) or (5) above,

is not complied with in relation to any solicitation, the collector concerned shall be guilty of an offence and liable on summary conviction to a fine not exceeding level 5 on the standard scale.

(9) Section 60(8) and (9) apply in relation to an offence under subsection (8) above as they apply in relation to an offence under section 60(7).

(10) In this section—

'the appeal', in relation to any solicitation by a collector, means the campaign or other fund-raising venture in the course of which the solicitation is made;
'collector' has the meaning given by section 47(1) of the Charities Act 2006;
'public charitable collection' has the meaning given by section 45 of that Act.

60B Exclusion of lower-paid collectors from provisions of section 60A

(1) Section 60(1) and (2) do not apply (by virtue of section 60A(1)) to a person who is under the earnings limit in subsection (2) below.

(2) A person is under the earnings limit in this subsection if he does not receive—

(a) more than—
  (i) £5 per day, or
  (ii) £500 per year,

  by way of remuneration for acting as a collector in relation to relevant collections, or
(b) more than £500 by way of remuneration for acting as a collector in relation to the collection mentioned in section 60A(1).

(3) In subsection (2) 'relevant collections' means public charitable collections conducted for the benefit of—

(a) the charitable institution or institutions, or
(b) the charitable, benevolent or philanthropic purposes,

for whose benefit the collection mentioned in section 60A(1) is conducted.

(4) A person is not within section 60A(6) if he is under the earnings limit in subsection (5) below.

(5) A person is under the earnings limit in this subsection if the remuneration received by him as mentioned in section 60A(6)(c)—

(a) is not more than—
  (i) £5 per day, or
  (ii) £500 per year, or
(b) if a lump sum, is not more than £500.

(6) The Minister may by order amend subsections (2) and (5) by substituting a different sum for any sum for the time being specified there.'

NOTES

Initial Commencement

To be appointed: see s 79(2).

Extent

This section does not extend to Scotland: see s 80(2).

69 Reserve power to control fund-raising by charitable institutions

After section 64 of the 1992 Act insert—

'64A Reserve power to control fund-raising by charitable institutions

(1) The Minister may make such regulations as appear to him to be necessary or desirable for or in connection with regulating charity fund-raising.

(2) In this section 'charity fund-raising' means activities which are carried on by—

(a) charitable institutions,
(b) persons managing charitable institutions, or
(c) persons or companies connected with such institutions,

and involve soliciting or otherwise procuring funds for the benefit of such institutions or companies connected with them, or for general charitable, benevolent or philanthropic purposes.

But 'activities' does not include primary purpose trading.

(3) Regulations under this section may, in particular, impose a good practice requirement on the persons managing charitable institutions in circumstances where—

(a) those institutions,
(b) the persons managing them, or
(c) persons or companies connected with such institutions,

are engaged in charity fund-raising.

(4) A 'good practice requirement' is a requirement to take all reasonable steps to ensure that the fund-raising is carried out in such a way that—

(a) it does not unreasonably intrude on the privacy of those from whom funds are being solicited or procured;
(b) it does not involve the making of unreasonably persistent approaches to persons to donate funds;
(c) it does not result in undue pressure being placed on persons to donate funds;
(d) it does not involve the making of any false or misleading representation about any of the matters mentioned in subsection (5).

(5) The matters are—

(a) the extent or urgency of any need for funds on the part of any charitable institution or company connected with such an institution;
(b) any use to which funds donated in response to the fund-raising are to be put by such an institution or company;
(c) the activities, achievements or finances of such an institution or company.

(6) Regulations under this section may provide that a person who persistently fails, without reasonable excuse, to comply with any specified requirement of the regulations is to be guilty of an offence and liable on summary conviction to a fine not exceeding level 2 on the standard scale.

(7) For the purposes of this section—

(a) 'funds' means money or other property;
(b) 'general charitable, benevolent or philanthropic purposes' means charitable, benevolent or philanthropic purposes other than those associated with one or more particular institutions;
(c) the persons 'managing' a charitable institution are the charity trustees or other persons having the general control and management of the administration of the institution; and
(d) a person is 'connected' with a charitable institution if he is an employee or agent of—
    (i) the institution,
    (ii) the persons managing it, or
    (iii) a company connected with it,

    or he is a volunteer acting on behalf of the institution or such a company.

(8) In this section 'primary purpose trading', in relation to a charitable institution, means any trade carried on by the institution or a company connected with it where—

(a) the trade is carried on in the course of the actual carrying out of a primary purpose of the institution; or
(b) the work in connection with the trade is mainly carried out by beneficiaries of the institution.'

NOTES

Initial Commencement

To be appointed: see s 79(2).

Extent

This section does not extend to Scotland: see s 80(2).

Chapter 3
Financial Assistance

70 Power of relevant Minister to give financial assistance to charitable, benevolent or philanthropic institutions

(1) A relevant Minister may give financial assistance to any charitable, benevolent or philanthropic institution in respect of any of the institution's activities which directly or indirectly benefit the whole or any part of England (whether or not they also benefit any other area).

(2) Financial assistance under subsection (1) may be given in any form and, in particular, may be given by way of—

(a) grants,
(b) loans,
(c) guarantees, or
(d) incurring expenditure for the benefit of the person assisted.

(3) Financial assistance under subsection (1) may be given on such terms and conditions as the relevant Minister considers appropriate.

(4) Those terms and conditions may, in particular, include provision as to—

(a) the purposes for which the assistance may be used;
(b) circumstances in which the assistance is to be repaid, or otherwise made good, to the relevant Minister, and the manner in which that is to be done;
(c) the making of reports to the relevant Minister regarding the uses to which the assistance has been put;
(d) the keeping, and making available for inspection, of accounts and other records;

(e) the carrying out of examinations by the Comptroller and Auditor General into the economy, efficiency and effectiveness with which the assistance has been used;
(f) the giving by the institution of financial assistance in any form to other persons on such terms and conditions as the institution or the relevant Minister considers appropriate.

(5) A person receiving assistance under this section must comply with the terms and conditions on which it is given, and compliance may be enforced by the relevant Minister.

(6) A relevant Minister may make arrangements for—

(a) assistance under subsection (1) to be given, or
(b) any other of his functions under this section to be exercised,

by some other person.

(7) Arrangements under subsection (6) may make provision for the functions concerned to be so exercised—

(a) either wholly or to such extent as may be specified in the arrangements, and
(b) either generally or in such cases or circumstances as may be so specified,

but do not prevent the functions concerned from being exercised by a relevant Minister.

(8) As soon as possible after 31st March in each year, a relevant Minister must make a report on any exercise by him of any powers under this section during the period of 12 months ending on that day.

(9) The relevant Minister must lay a copy of the report before each House of Parliament.

(10) In this section 'charitable, benevolent or philanthropic institution' means—

(a) a charity, or
(b) an institution (other than a charity) which is established for charitable, benevolent or philanthropic purposes.

(11) In this section 'relevant Minister' means the Secretary of State or the Minister for the Cabinet Office.

NOTES

Initial Commencement

To be appointed: see s 79(2).

Extent

This section does not extend to Scotland: see s 80(2).

71 Power of National Assembly for Wales to give financial assistance to charitable, benevolent or philanthropic institutions

(1) The National Assembly for Wales may give financial assistance to any charitable, benevolent or philanthropic institution in respect of any of the institution's activities which directly or indirectly benefit the whole or any part of Wales (whether or not they also benefit any other area).

(2) Financial assistance under subsection (1) may be given in any form and, in particular, may be given by way of—

(a) grants,
(b) loans,
(c) guarantees, or
(d) incurring expenditure for the benefit of the person assisted.

(3) Financial assistance under subsection (1) may be given on such terms and conditions as the Assembly considers appropriate.

(4) Those terms and conditions may, in particular, include provision as to—

(a) the purposes for which the assistance may be used;
(b) circumstances in which the assistance is to be repaid, or otherwise made good, to the Assembly, and the manner in which that is to be done;
(c) the making of reports to the Assembly regarding the uses to which the assistance has been put;
(d) the keeping, and making available for inspection, of accounts and other records;
(e) the carrying out of examinations by the Auditor General for Wales into the economy, efficiency and effectiveness with which the assistance has been used;
(f) the giving by the institution of financial assistance in any form to other persons on such terms and conditions as the institution or the Assembly considers appropriate.

(5) A person receiving assistance under this section must comply with the terms and conditions on which it is given, and compliance may be enforced by the Assembly.

(6) The Assembly may make arrangements for—

(a) assistance under subsection (1) to be given, or
(b) any other of its functions under this section to be exercised,

by some other person.

(7) Arrangements under subsection (6) may make provision for the functions concerned to be so exercised—

(a) either wholly or to such extent as may be specified in the arrangements, and
(b) either generally or in such cases or circumstances as may be so specified,

but do not prevent the functions concerned from being exercised by the Assembly.

(8) After 31st March in each year, the Assembly must publish a report on the exercise of powers under this section during the period of 12 months ending on that day.

(9) In this section 'charitable, benevolent or philanthropic institution' means—

(a) a charity, or
(b) an institution (other than a charity) which is established for charitable, benevolent or philanthropic purposes.

NOTES

Initial Commencement

To be appointed: see s 79(2).

Extent

This section does not extend to Scotland: see s 80(2).

Part 4
Miscellaneous and General

Miscellaneous

72 Disclosure of information to and by Northern Ireland regulator

(1) This section applies if a body (referred to in this section as 'the Northern Ireland regulator') is established to exercise functions in Northern Ireland which are similar in nature to the functions exercised in England and Wales by the Charity Commission.

(2) The Minister may by regulations authorise relevant public authorities to disclose information to the Northern Ireland regulator for the purpose of enabling or assisting the Northern Ireland regulator to discharge any of its functions.

(3) If the regulations authorise the disclosure of Revenue and Customs information, they must contain provision in relation to that disclosure which corresponds to the provision made in relation to the disclosure of such information by section 10(2) to (4) of the 1993 Act (as substituted by paragraph 104 of Schedule 8 to this Act).

(4) In the case of information disclosed to the Northern Ireland regulator pursuant to regulations made under this section, any power of the Northern Ireland regulator to disclose the information is exercisable subject to any express restriction subject to which the information was disclosed to the Northern Ireland regulator.

(5) Subsection (4) does not apply in relation to Revenue and Customs information disclosed to the Northern Ireland regulator pursuant to regulations made under this section; but any such information may not be further disclosed except with the consent of the Commissioners for Her Majesty's Revenue and Customs.

(6) Any person specified, or of a description specified, in regulations made under this section who discloses information in contravention of subsection (5) is guilty of an offence and liable—

(a) on summary conviction, to imprisonment for a term not exceeding 12 months or to a fine not exceeding the statutory maximum, or both;
(b) on conviction on indictment, to imprisonment for a term not exceeding two years or to a fine, or both.

(7) It is a defence for a person charged with an offence under subsection (5) of disclosing information to prove that he reasonably believed—

(a) that the disclosure was lawful, or
(b) that the information had already and lawfully been made available to the public.

(8) In the application of this section to Scotland or Northern Ireland, the reference to 12 months in subsection (6) is to be read as a reference to 6 months.

(9) In this section—

'relevant public authority' means—
(a) any government department (other than a Northern Ireland department),
(b) any local authority in England, Wales or Scotland,
(c) any person who is a constable in England and Wales or Scotland,
(d) any other body or person discharging functions of a public nature (including a body or person discharging regulatory functions in relation to any description of activities), except a body or person whose functions are exercisable only or mainly in or as regards Northern Ireland and relate only or mainly to transferred matters;

'Revenue and Customs information' means information held as mentioned in section 18(1) of the Commissioners for Revenue and Customs Act 2005 (c 11);
'transferred matter' has the same meaning as in the Northern Ireland Act 1998 (c 47).

NOTES

Initial Commencement

To be appointed: see s 79(2).

73 Report on operation of this Act

(1) The Minister must, before the end of the period of five years beginning with the day on which this Act is passed, appoint a person to review generally the operation of this Act.

(2) The review must address, in particular, the following matters—

(a) the effect of the Act on—
  (i) excepted charities,
  (ii) public confidence in charities,
  (iii) the level of charitable donations, and
  (iv) the willingness of individuals to volunteer,
(b) the status of the Charity Commission as a government department, and
(c) any other matters the Minister considers appropriate.

(3) After the person appointed under subsection (1) has completed his review, he must compile a report of his conclusions.

(4) The Minister must lay before Parliament a copy of the report mentioned in subsection (3).

(5) For the purposes of this section a charity is an excepted charity if—

(a) it falls within paragraph (b) or (c) of section 3A(2) of the 1993 Act (as amended by section 9 of this Act), or
(b) it does not fall within either of those paragraphs but, immediately before the appointed day (within the meaning of section 10 of this Act), it fell within section 3(5)(b) or (5B)(b) of the 1993 Act.

NOTES

Initial Commencement

To be appointed: see s 79(2).

Extent

This section does not extend to Scotland: see s 80(2).

General

74 Orders and regulations

(1) Any power of a relevant Minister to make an order or regulations under this Act is exercisable by statutory instrument.

(2) Any such power—

(a) may be exercised so as to make different provision for different cases or descriptions of case or different purposes or areas, and
(b) includes power to make such incidental, supplementary, consequential, transitory, transitional or saving provision as the relevant Minister considers appropriate.

(3) Subject to subsection (4), orders or regulations made by a relevant Minister under this Act are to be subject to annulment in pursuance of a resolution of either House of Parliament.

(4) Subsection (3) does not apply to—

(a) any order under section 11,
(b) any regulations under section 13(4)(b) which amend any provision of an Act,
(c) any regulations under section 72,
(d) any order under section 75(4) which amends or repeals any provision of an Act or an Act of the Scottish Parliament,
(e) any order under section 76 or 77, or
(f) any order under section 79(2).

(5) No order or regulations within subsection (4)(a), (b), (c), (d) or (e) may be made by a relevant Minister (whether alone or with other provisions) unless a draft of the order or regulations has been laid before, and approved by resolution of, each House of Parliament.

(6) If a draft of an instrument containing an order under section 11 would, apart from this subsection, be treated for the purposes of the Standing Orders of either House of Parliament as a hybrid instrument, it is to proceed in that House as if it were not such an instrument.

(7) In this section 'relevant Minister' means the Secretary of State or the Minister for the Cabinet Office.

NOTES

Initial Commencement

Royal Assent: 8 November 2006: see s 79(1)(b).

75 Amendments, repeals, revocations and transitional provisions

(1) Schedule 8 contains minor and consequential amendments.

(2) Schedule 9 makes provision for the repeal and revocation of enactments (including enactments which are spent).

(3) Schedule 10 contains transitional provisions and savings.

(4) A relevant Minister may by order make—

(a) such supplementary, incidental or consequential provision, or
(b) such transitory, transitional or saving provision,

as he considers appropriate for the general purposes, or any particular purposes, of this Act or in consequence of, or for giving full effect to, any provision made by this Act.

(5) An order under subsection (4) may amend, repeal, revoke or otherwise modify any enactment (including an enactment restating, with or without modifications, an enactment amended by this Act).

(6) In this section 'relevant Minister' means the Secretary of State or the Minister for the Cabinet Office.

NOTES

Initial Commencement

Sub-s (1) (for certain purposes): Royal Assent: 8 November 2006: see s 79(1)(g).

Sub-ss (4), (5): Royal Assent: 8 November 2006: see s 79(1)(c).

Sub-s (1) (for remaining purposes): To be appointed: see s 79(2).

Sub-ss (2), (3), (6): To be appointed: see s 79(2).

76 Pre-consolidation amendments

(1) The Minister may by order make such amendments of the enactments relating to charities as in his opinion facilitate, or are otherwise desirable in connection with, the consolidation of the whole or part of those enactments.

(2) An order under this section shall not come into force unless—

(a) a single Act, or
(b) a group of two or more Acts,

is passed consolidating the whole or part of the enactments relating to charities (with or without any other enactments).

(3) If such an Act or group of Acts is passed, the order shall (by virtue of this subsection) come into force immediately before the Act or group of Acts comes into force.

(4) Once an order under this section has come into force, no further order may be made under this section.

(5) In this section—

'amendments' includes repeals, revocations and modifications, and
'the enactments relating to charities' means—

(a) the Charities Act 1992 (c 41), the Charities Act 1993 (c 10) and this Act,
(b) any other enactment relating to institutions which fall within section 1(1) of this Act, and
(c) any other enactment, so far as forming part of the law of England and Wales, which makes provision relating to bodies or other institutions which are charities under the law of Scotland or Northern Ireland,

and section 78(2)(a) (definition of 'charity') does not apply for the purposes of this section.

77 Amendments reflecting changes in company law audit provisions

(1) The Minister may by order make such amendments of the 1993 Act or this Act as he considers appropriate—

(a) in consequence of, or in connection with, any changes made or to be made by any enactment to the provisions of company law relating to the accounts of charitable companies or to the auditing of, or preparation of reports in respect of, such accounts;
(b) for the purposes of, or in connection with, applying provisions of Schedule 5A to the 1993 Act (group accounts) to charitable companies that are not required to produce group accounts under company law.

(2) In this section—

'accounts' includes group accounts;
'amendments' includes repeals and modifications;
'charitable companies' means companies which are charities;
'company law' means the enactments relating to companies.

NOTES

Initial Commencement

Royal Assent: 8 November 2006: see s 79(1)(e).

78 Interpretation

(1) In this Act—

'the 1992 Act' means the Charities Act 1992 (c 41);
'the 1993 Act' means the Charities Act 1993 (c 10).

(2) In this Act—

(a) 'charity' has the meaning given by section 1(1);
(b) 'charitable purposes' has (in accordance with section 2(6)) the meaning given by section 2(1); and
(c) 'charity trustees' has the same meaning as in the 1993 Act;

but (subject to subsection (3) below) the exclusions contained in section 96(2) of the 1993 Act (ecclesiastical corporations etc) have effect in relation to references to a charity in this Act as they have effect in relation to such references in that Act.

(3) Those exclusions do not have effect in relation to references in section 1 or any reference to the law relating to charities in England and Wales.

(4) In this Act 'enactment' includes—

(a) any provision of subordinate legislation (within the meaning of the Interpretation Act 1978 (c 30)),
(b) a provision of a Measure of the Church Assembly or of the General Synod of the Church of England, and
(c) (in the context of section 6(5) or 75(5)) any provision made by or under an Act of the Scottish Parliament or Northern Ireland legislation,

and references to enactments include enactments passed or made after the passing of this Act.

(5) In this Act 'institution' means an institution whether incorporated or not, and includes a trust or undertaking.

(6) In this Act 'the Minister' means the Minister for the Cabinet Office.

(7) Subsections (2) to (5) apply except where the context otherwise requires.

NOTES

Initial Commencement

Royal Assent: 8 November 2006: see s 79(1)(d).

79 Commencement

(1) The following provisions come into force on the day on which this Act is passed—

(a) section 13(4) and (5),
(b) section 74,
(c) section 75(4) and (5),
(d) section 78,
(e) section 77,
(f) this section and section 80, and
(g) the following provisions of Schedule 8—
paragraph 90(2),
paragraph 104 so far as it confers power to make regulations, and
paragraph 174(d),
and section 75(1) so far as relating to those provisions.

(2) Otherwise, this Act comes into force on such day as the Minister may by order appoint.

(3) An order under subsection (2)—

(a) may appoint different days for different purposes or different areas;
(b) make such provision as the Minister considers necessary or expedient for transitory, transitional or saving purposes in connection with the coming into force of any provision of this Act.

NOTES

Initial Commencement

Royal Assent: 8 November 2006: see para (1)(f) above.

80 Short title and extent

(1) This Act may be cited as the Charities Act 2006.

(2) Subject to subsections (3) to (7), this Act extends to England and Wales only.

(3) The following provisions extend also to Scotland—

(a) sections 1 to 3 and 5,
(b) section 6(5),
(c) sections 72 and 74,

(d) section 75(2) and (3) and Schedules 9 and 10 so far as relating to the Recreational Charities Act 1958 (c 17), and
(e) section 75(4) and (5), sections 76 to 79 and this section.

(4) But the provisions referred to in subsection (3)(a) and (d) affect the law of Scotland only so far as they affect the construction of references to charities or charitable purposes in enactments which relate to matters falling within Section A1 of Part 2 of Schedule 5 to the Scotland Act 1998 (c 46) (reserved matters: fiscal policy etc); and so far as they so affect the law of Scotland—

(a) references in sections 1(1) and 2(1) to the law of England and Wales are to be read as references to the law of Scotland, and
(b) the reference in section 1(1) to the High Court is to be read as a reference to the Court of Session.

(5) The following provisions extend also to Northern Ireland—

(a) sections 1 to 3 and 5,
(b) section 6(5),
(c) section 23,
(d) sections 72 and 74,
(e) section 75(2) and (3) and Schedules 9 and 10 so far as relating to the Recreational Charities Act 1958 (c 17), and
(f) section 75(4) and (5), sections 76 to 79 and this section.

(6) But the provisions referred to in subsection (5)(a) and (e) affect the law of Northern Ireland only so far as they affect the construction of references to charities or charitable purposes in enactments which relate to matters falling within paragraph 9 of Schedule 2 to the Northern Ireland Act 1998 (c 47) (excepted matters: taxes and duties); and so far as they so affect the law of Northern Ireland—

(a) references in sections 1(1) and 2(1) to the law of England and Wales are to be read as references to the law of Northern Ireland, and
(b) the reference in section 1(1) to the High Court is to be read as a reference to the High Court in Northern Ireland.

(7) Any amendment, repeal or revocation made by this Act has the same extent as the enactment to which it relates.

(8) But subsection (7) does not apply to any amendment or repeal made in the Recreational Charities Act 1958 by a provision referred to in subsection (3) or (5).

(9) Subsection (7) also does not apply to—

(a) the amendments made by section 32 in the Companies Act 1985 (c 6), or
(b) those made by Schedule 8 in the Police, Factories, &c. (Miscellaneous Provisions) Act 1916 (c 31), or
(c) the repeal made in that Act by Schedule 9,

which extend to England and Wales only.

NOTES

Initial Commencement

Royal Assent: 8 November 2006: see s 79(1)(f).

Schedule 1
The Charity Commission

1

After Schedule 1 to the 1993 Act insert—

'Schedule 1A
The Charity Commission

Membership

1

(1) The Commission shall consist of a chairman and at least four, but not more than eight, other members.

(2) The members shall be appointed by the Minister.

(3) The Minister shall exercise the power in sub-paragraph (2) so as to secure that—

(a) the knowledge and experience of the members of the Commission (taken together) includes knowledge and experience of the matters mentioned in sub-paragraph (4),
(b) at least two members have a seven year general qualification within the meaning of section 71 of the Courts and Legal Services Act 1990, and
(c) at least one member knows about conditions in Wales and has been appointed following consultation with the National Assembly for Wales.

(4) The matters mentioned in this sub-paragraph are—

(a) the law relating to charities,
(b) charity accounts and the financing of charities, and
(c) the operation and regulation of charities of different sizes and descriptions.

(5) In sub-paragraph (3)(c) 'member' does not include the chairman of the Commission.

Terms of appointment and remuneration

2

The members of the Commission shall hold and vacate office as such in accordance with the terms of their respective appointments.

3

(1) An appointment of a person to hold office as a member of the Commission shall be for a term not exceeding three years.

(2) A person holding office as a member of the Commission—

(a) may resign that office by giving notice in writing to the Minister, and
(b) may be removed from office by the Minister on the ground of incapacity or misbehaviour.

(3) Before removing a member of the Commission the Minister shall consult—

(a) the Commission, and
(b) if the member was appointed following consultation with the National Assembly for Wales, the Assembly.

(4) No person may hold office as a member of the Commission for more than ten years in total.

(5) For the purposes of sub-paragraph (4), time spent holding office as a Charity Commissioner for England and Wales shall be counted as time spent holding office as a member of the Commission.

4

(1) The Commission shall pay to its members such remuneration, and such other allowances, as may be determined by the Minister.

(2) The Commission shall, if required to do so by the Minister—

(a) pay such pension, allowances or gratuities as may be determined by the Minister to or in respect of a person who is or has been a member of the Commission, or
(b) make such payments as may be so determined towards provision for the payment of a pension, allowances or gratuities to or in respect of such a person.

(3) If the Minister determines that there are special circumstances which make it right for a person ceasing to hold office as a member of the Commission to receive compensation, the Commission shall pay to him a sum by way of compensation of such amount as may be determined by the Minister.

Staff

5

(1) The Commission—

(a) shall appoint a chief executive, and
(b) may appoint such other staff as it may determine.

(2) The terms and conditions of service of persons appointed under sub-paragraph (1) are to be such as the Commission may determine with the approval of the Minister for the Civil Service.

Committees

6

(1) The Commission may establish committees and any committee of the Commission may establish sub-committees.

(2) The members of a committee of the Commission may include persons who are not members of the Commission (and the members of a sub-committee may include persons who are not members of the committee or of the Commission).

Procedure etc

7

(1) The Commission may regulate its own procedure (including quorum).

(2) The validity of anything done by the Commission is not affected by a vacancy among its members or by a defect in the appointment of a member.

Performance of functions

8

Anything authorised or required to be done by the Commission may be done by—

(a) any member or member of staff of the Commission who is authorised for that purpose by the Commission, whether generally or specially;
(b) any committee of the Commission which has been so authorised.

Evidence

9

The Documentary Evidence Act 1868 shall have effect as if—

(a) the Commission were mentioned in the first column of the Schedule to that Act,
(b) any member or member of staff of the Commission authorised to act on behalf of the Commission were specified in the second column of that Schedule in connection with the Commission, and
(c) the regulations referred to in that Act included any document issued by or under the authority of the Commission.

Execution of documents

10

(1) A document is executed by the Commission by the fixing of its common seal to the document.

(2) But the fixing of that seal to a document must be authenticated by the signature of—

(a) any member of the Commission, or
(b) any member of its staff,

who is authorised for the purpose by the Commission.

(3) A document which is expressed (in whatever form of words) to be executed by the Commission and is signed by—

(a) any member of the Commission, or
(b) any member of its staff,

who is authorised for the purpose by the Commission has the same effect as if executed in accordance with sub-paragraphs (1) and (2).

(4) A document executed by the Commission which makes it clear on its face that it is intended to be a deed has effect, upon delivery, as a deed; and it is to be presumed (unless a contrary intention is proved) to be delivered upon its being executed.

(5) In favour of a purchaser a document is to be deemed to have been duly executed by the Commission if it purports to be signed on its behalf by—

(a) any member of the Commission, or
(b) any member of its staff;

and, where it makes it clear on its face that it is intended to be a deed, it is to be deemed to have been delivered upon its being executed.

(6) For the purposes of this paragraph—

'authorised' means authorised whether generally or specially; and
'purchaser' means a purchaser in good faith for valuable consideration and includes a lessee, mortgagee or other person who for valuable consideration acquired an interest in property.

Annual report

11

(1) As soon as practicable after the end of each financial year the Commission shall publish a report on—

(a) the discharge of its functions,
(b) the extent to which, in its opinion, its objectives (see section 1B of this Act) have been met,
(c) the performance of its general duties (see section 1D of this Act), and
(d) the management of its affairs,

during that year.

(2) The Commission shall lay a copy of each such report before Parliament.

(3) In sub-paragraph (1) above, 'financial year' means—

(a) the period beginning with the date on which the Commission is established and ending with the next 31st March following that date, and
(b) each successive period of 12 months ending with 31st March.

Annual public meeting

12

(1) The Commission shall hold a public meeting ('the annual meeting') for the purpose of enabling a report under paragraph 11 above to be considered.

(2) The annual meeting shall be held within the period of three months beginning with the day on which the report is published.

(3) The Commission shall organise the annual meeting so as to allow—

(a) a general discussion of the contents of the report which is being considered, and
(b) a reasonable opportunity for those attending the meeting to put questions to the Commission about matters to which the report relates.

(4) But subject to sub-paragraph (3) above the annual meeting is to be organised and conducted in such a way as the Commission considers appropriate.

(5) The Commission shall—

(a) take such steps as are reasonable in the circumstances to ensure that notice of the annual meeting is given to every registered charity, and
(b) publish notice of the annual meeting in the way appearing to it to be best calculated to bring it to the attention of members of the public.

(6) Each such notice shall—

(a) give details of the time and place at which the meeting is to be held,
(b) set out the proposed agenda for the meeting,
(c) indicate the proposed duration of the meeting, and
(d) give details of the Commission's arrangements for enabling persons to attend.

(7) If the Commission proposes to alter any of the arrangements which have been included in notices given or published under sub-paragraph (5) above it shall—

(a) give reasonable notice of the alteration, and
(b) publish the notice in the way appearing to it to be best calculated to bring it to the attention of registered charities and members of the public.'

House of Commons Disqualification Act 1975 (c 24)

2

In Part 2 of Schedule 1 to the House of Commons Disqualification Act 1975 (bodies of which all members are disqualified) insert at the appropriate place—

'The Charity Commission.'

Northern Ireland Assembly Disqualification Act 1975 (c 25)

3

In Part 2 of Schedule 1 to the Northern Ireland Assembly Disqualification Act 1975 (bodies of which all members are disqualified) insert at the appropriate place—

'The Charity Commission.'

NOTES

Initial Commencement

To be appointed: see s 79(2).

Extent

This Schedule does not extend to Scotland: see s 80(2).

Schedule 2
Establishment of the Charity Commission: Supplementary

1

In this Schedule—

'commencement' means the coming into force of section 6, and
'the Commission' means the Charity Commission.

Appointments to Commission

2

(1) The person who immediately before commencement was the Chief Charity Commissioner for England and Wales is on commencement to become the chairman of the Commission as if duly appointed under paragraph 1 of Schedule 1A to the 1993 Act.

(2) Any other person who immediately before commencement was a Charity Commissioner for England and Wales is on commencement to become a member of the Commission as if duly appointed under that paragraph.

(3) While a person holds office as a member of the Commission by virtue of this paragraph he shall—

(a) continue to be deemed to be employed in the civil service of the Crown, and
(b) hold that office on the terms on which he held office as a Charity Commissioner for England and Wales immediately before commencement.

(4) Sub-paragraph (3)(b) is subject to—

(a) sub-paragraph (5),
(b) paragraph 3(4) and (5) of Schedule 1A to the 1993 Act, and
(c) any necessary modifications to the terms in question.

(5) No person may hold office as a member of the Commission by virtue of this paragraph for a term exceeding three years from commencement.

(6) Paragraphs 2 and 3(1) to (3) of Schedule 1A to the 1993 Act, and paragraphs 2 and 3 of Schedule 1 to this Act, shall not apply in relation to a person while he holds office as a member of the Commission by virtue of this paragraph.

Effect of transfers under section 6

3

(1) Anything which—

(a) has been done (or has effect as if done) by or in relation to the Commissioners, and
(b) is in effect immediately before commencement,

is to be treated as if done by or in relation to the Commission.

(2) Anything (including legal proceedings) which—

(a) relates to anything transferred by section 6(4), and

(b) is in the process of being done by or in relation to the Commissioners,

may be continued by or in relation to the Commission.

(3) But nothing in section 6 or this paragraph affects the validity of anything done by or in relation to the Commissioners.

(4) In this paragraph 'the Commissioners' means the Charity Commissioners for England and Wales (and includes any person acting for them by virtue of paragraph 3(3) of Schedule 1 to the 1993 Act).

First annual report of Commission

4

(1) This paragraph applies if there is a period of one or more days which—

(a) began on the day after the end of the last year for which the Charity Commissioners for England and Wales made a report under section 1(5) of the 1993 Act, and
(b) ended on the day before commencement.

(2) The first report published by the Commission under paragraph 11 of Schedule 1A to the 1993 Act shall also be a report on the operations of the Charity Commissioners for England and Wales during the period mentioned in sub-paragraph (1).

Resource accounts of Commission

5

(1) The new Commission and the old Commission shall be treated as being the same government department for the purposes of section 5 of the Government Resources and Accounts Act 2000 (c 20).

(2) Resource accounts sent to the Comptroller and Auditor General by the new Commission in respect of any period before commencement shall be resource accounts in the name of the new Commission.

(3) In this paragraph—

'the new Commission' means the Charity Commission established by section 6, and
'the old Commission' means the government department known as the Charity Commission and existing immediately before commencement.

NOTES

Initial Commencement

To be appointed: see s 79(2).

Extent

This Schedule does not extend to Scotland: see s 80(2).

Schedule 3
The Charity Tribunal

1

After Schedule 1A to the 1993 Act (inserted by Schedule 1 to this Act) insert—

'Schedule 1B
The Charity Tribunal

Membership

1

(1) The Tribunal shall consist of the President and its other members.

(2) The Lord Chancellor shall appoint—

(a) a President of the Tribunal,
(b) legal members of the Tribunal, and
(c) ordinary members of the Tribunal.

(3) A person may be appointed as the President or a legal member of the Tribunal only if he has a seven year general qualification within the meaning of section 71 of the Courts and Legal Services Act 1990.

(4) A person may be appointed as an ordinary member of the Tribunal only if he appears to the Lord Chancellor to have appropriate knowledge or experience relating to charities.

Deputy President

2

(1) The Lord Chancellor may appoint a legal member as deputy President of the Tribunal.

(2) The deputy President—

(a) may act for the President when he is unable to act or unavailable, and
(b) shall perform such other functions as the President may delegate or assign to him.

Terms of appointment

3

(1) The members of the Tribunal shall hold and vacate office as such in accordance with the terms of their respective appointments.

(2) A person holding office as a member of the Tribunal—

(a) may resign that office by giving notice in writing to the Lord Chancellor, and
(b) may be removed from office by the Lord Chancellor on the ground of incapacity or misbehaviour.

(3) A previous appointment of a person as a member of the Tribunal does not affect his eligibility for re-appointment as a member of the Tribunal.

Retirement etc

4

(1) A person shall not hold office as a member of the Tribunal after reaching the age of 70.

(2) Section 26(5) and (6) of the Judicial Pensions and Retirement Act 1993 (extension to age 75) apply in relation to a member of the Tribunal as they apply in relation to a holder of a relevant office.

Remuneration etc

5

(1) The Lord Chancellor may pay to the members of the Tribunal such remuneration, and such other allowances, as he may determine.

(2) The Lord Chancellor may—

(a) pay such pension, allowances or gratuities as he may determine to or in respect of a person who is or has been a member of the Tribunal, or
(b) make such payments as he may determine towards provision for the payment of a pension, allowances or gratuities to or in respect of such a person.

(3) If the Lord Chancellor determines that there are special circumstances which make it right for a person ceasing to hold office as a member of the Tribunal to receive compensation, the Lord Chancellor may pay to him a sum by way of compensation of such amount as may be determined by the Lord Chancellor.

Staff and facilities

6

The Lord Chancellor may make staff and facilities available to the Tribunal.

Panels

7

(1) The functions of the Tribunal shall be exercised by panels of the Tribunal.

(2) Panels of the Tribunal shall sit at such times and in such places as the President may direct.

(3) Before giving a direction under sub-paragraph (2) above the President shall consult the Lord Chancellor.

(4) More than one panel may sit at a time.

8

(1) The President shall make arrangements for determining which of the members of the Tribunal are to constitute a panel of the Tribunal in relation to the exercise of any function.

(2) Those arrangements shall, in particular, ensure that each panel is constituted in one of the following ways—

(a) as the President sitting alone,
(b) as a legal member sitting alone,
(c) as the President sitting with two other members,
(d) as a legal member sitting with two other members,
(e) as the President sitting with one other member,
(f) as a legal member sitting with one other member,

(and references in paragraphs (d) and (f) to other members do not include the President).

(3) The President shall publish arrangements made under this paragraph.

Practice and procedure

9

(1) Decisions of the Tribunal may be taken by majority vote.

(2) In the case of a panel constituted in accordance with paragraph 8(2)(e), the President shall have a casting vote.

(3) In the case of a panel constituted in accordance with paragraph 8(2)(f) which consists of a legal member and an ordinary member, the legal member shall have a casting vote.

(4) The President shall make and publish arrangements as to who is to have a casting vote in the case of a panel constituted in accordance with paragraph 8(2)(f) which consists of two legal members.

10

The President may, subject to rules under section 2B of this Act, give directions about the practice and procedure of the Tribunal.'

House of Commons Disqualification Act 1975 (c 24)

2

In Part 2 of Schedule 1 to the House of Commons Disqualification Act 1975 (bodies of which all members are disqualified) insert at the appropriate place—

'The Charity Tribunal.'

Northern Ireland Assembly Disqualification Act 1975 (c 25)

3

In Part 2 of Schedule 1 to the Northern Ireland Assembly Disqualification Act 1975 (bodies of which all members are disqualified) insert at the appropriate place—

'The Charity Tribunal.'

Courts and Legal Services Act 1990 (c 41)

4

In Schedule 11 to the Courts and Legal Services Act 1990 (judges etc barred from legal practice) insert at the end—

'President or other member of the Charity Tribunal'.

Tribunals and Inquiries Act 1992 (c 53)

5

In Part 1 of Schedule 1 to the Tribunals and Inquiries Act 1992 (tribunals under general supervision of Council) before paragraph 7 insert—

'Charities	6A The Charity Tribunal constituted under section 2A of, and Schedule 1B to, the Charities Act 1993.'

NOTES

Initial Commencement

To be appointed: see s 79(2).

Extent

This Schedule does not extend to Scotland: see s 80(2).

Schedule 4
Appeals and Applications to Charity Tribunal

After Schedule 1B to the 1993 Act (inserted by Schedule 3 to this Act) insert—

'Schedule 1C
Appeals and Applications to Charity Tribunal

Appeals: general

1

(1) Except in the case of a reviewable matter (see paragraph 3) an appeal may be brought to the Tribunal against any decision, direction or order mentioned in column 1 of the Table.

(2) Such an appeal may be brought by—

(a) the Attorney General, or
(b) any person specified in the corresponding entry in column 2 of the Table.

(3) The Commission shall be the respondent to such an appeal.

(4) In determining such an appeal the Tribunal—

(a) shall consider afresh the decision, direction or order appealed against, and
(b) may take into account evidence which was not available to the Commission.

(5) The Tribunal may—

(a) dismiss the appeal, or
(b) if it allows the appeal, exercise any power specified in the corresponding entry in column 3 of the Table.

Appeals: orders under section 9

2

(1) Paragraph 1(4)(a) above does not apply in relation to an appeal against an order made under section 9 of this Act.

(2) On such an appeal the Tribunal shall consider whether the information or document in question—

(a) relates to a charity;
(b) is relevant to the discharge of the functions of the Commission or the official custodian.

(3) The Tribunal may allow such an appeal only if it is satisfied that the information or document in question does not fall within either paragraph (a) or paragraph (b) of sub-paragraph (2) above.

Reviewable matters

3

(1) In this Schedule references to 'reviewable matters' are to—

(a) decisions to which sub-paragraph (2) applies, and
(b) orders to which sub-paragraph (3) applies.

(2) This sub-paragraph applies to decisions of the Commission—

(a) to institute an inquiry under section 8 of this Act with regard to a particular institution,
(b) to institute an inquiry under section 8 of this Act with regard to a class of institutions,
(c) not to make a common investment scheme under section 24 of this Act,
(d) not to make a common deposit scheme under section 25 of this Act,
(e) not to make an order under section 26 of this Act in relation to a charity,
(f) not to make an order under section 36 of this Act in relation to land held by or in trust for a charity,
(g) not to make an order under section 38 of this Act in relation to a mortgage of land held by or in trust for a charity.

(3) This sub-paragraph applies to an order made by the Commission under section 69(1) of this Act in relation to a company which is a charity.

Reviews

4

(1) An application may be made to the Tribunal for the review of a reviewable matter.

(2) Such an application may be made by—

(a) the Attorney General, or
(b) any person mentioned in the entry in column 2 of the Table which corresponds to the entry in column 1 which relates to the reviewable matter.

(3) The Commission shall be the respondent to such an application.

(4) In determining such an application the Tribunal shall apply the principles which would be applied by the High Court on an application for judicial review.

(5) The Tribunal may—

(a) dismiss the application, or
(b) if it allows the application, exercise any power mentioned in the entry in column 3 of the Table which corresponds to the entry in column 1 which relates to the reviewable matter.

Interpretation: remission of matters to Commission

5

References in column 3 of the Table to the power to remit a matter to the Commission are to the power to remit the matter either—

(a) generally, or
(b) for determination in accordance with a finding made or direction given by the Tribunal.

TABLE

1	*2*	*3*
Decision of the Commission under section 3 or 3A of this Act— (a) to enter or not to enter an institution in the register of charities, or (b) to remove or not to remove an institution from the register.	The persons are— (a) the persons who are or claim to be the charity trustees of the institution, (b) (if a body corporate) the institution itself, and (c) any other person who is or may be affected by the decision.	Power to quash the decision and (if appropriate)— (a) remit the matter to the Commission, (b) direct the Commission to rectify the register.
Decision of the Commission not to make a determination under section 3(9) of this Act in relation to particular information contained in the register.	The persons are— (a) the charity trustees of the charity to which the information relates, (b) (if a body corporate) the charity itself, and (c) any other person who is or may be affected by the decision.	Power to quash the decision and (if appropriate) remit the matter to the Commission.

TABLE

1	*2*	*3*
Direction given by the Commission under section 6 of this Act requiring the name of a charity to be changed.	The persons are— (a) the charity trustees of the charity to which the direction relates, (b) (if a body corporate) the charity itself, and (c) any other person who is or may be affected by the direction.	Power to— (a) quash the direction and (if appropriate) remit the matter to the Commission, (b) substitute for the direction any other direction which could have been given by the Commission.
Decision of the Commission to institute an inquiry under section 8 of this Act with regard to a particular institution.	The persons are— (a) the persons who have control or management of the institution, and (b) (if a body corporate) the institution itself.	Power to direct the Commission to end the inquiry.
Decision of the Commission to institute an inquiry under section 8 of this Act with regard to a class of institutions.	The persons are— (a) the persons who have control or management of any institution which is a member of the class of institutions, and (b) (if a body corporate) any such institution.	Power to— (a) direct the Commission that the inquiry should not consider a particular institution, (b) direct the Commission to end the inquiry.
Order made by the Commission under section 9 of this Act requiring a person to supply information or a document.	The persons are any person who is required to supply the information or document.	Power to— (a) quash the order, (b) substitute for all or part of the order any other order which could have been made by the Commission.
Order made by the Commission under section 16(1) of this Act (including such an order made by virtue of section 23(1)).	The persons are— (a) in a section 16(1)(a) case, the charity trustees of the charity to which the order relates or (if a body corporate) the charity itself, (b) in a section 16(1)(b) case, any person discharged or removed by the order, and (c) any other person who is or may be affected by the order.	Power to— (a) quash the order in whole or in part and (if appropriate) remit the matter to the Commission, (b) substitute for all or part of the order any other order which could have been made by the Commission, (c) add to the order anything which could have been contained in an order made by the Commission.

TABLE

1	*2*	*3*
Order made by the Commission under section 18(1) of this Act in relation to a charity.	The persons are— (a) the charity trustees of the charity, (b) (if a body corporate) the charity itself, (c) in a section 18(1)(i) case, any person suspended by the order, and (d) any other person who is or may be affected by the order.	Power to— (a) quash the order in whole or in part and (if appropriate) remit the matter to the Commission, (b) substitute for all or part of the order any other order which could have been made by the Commission, (c) add to the order anything which could have been contained in an order made by the Commission.
Order made by the Commission under section 18(2) of this Act in relation to a charity.	The persons are— (a) the charity trustees of the charity, (b) (if a body corporate) the charity itself, (c) in a section 18(2)(i) case, any person removed by the order, and (d) any other person who is or may be affected by the order.	Power to— (a) quash the order in whole or in part and (if appropriate) remit the matter to the Commission, (b) substitute for all or part of the order any other order which could have been made by the Commission, (c) add to the order anything which could have been contained in an order made by the Commission.
Order made by the Commission under section 18(4) of this Act removing a charity trustee.	The persons are— (a) the charity trustee, (b) the remaining charity trustees of the charity of which he was a charity trustee, (c) (if a body corporate) the charity itself, and (d) any other person who is or may be affected by the order.	Power to— (a) quash the order in whole or in part and (if appropriate) remit the matter to the Commission, (b) substitute for all or part of the order any other order which could have been made by the Commission, (c) add to the order anything which could have been contained in an order made by the Commission.
Order made by the Commission under section 18(5) of this Act appointing a charity trustee.	The persons are— (a) the other charity trustees of the charity, (b) (if a body corporate) the charity itself, and (c) any other person who is or may be affected by the order.	Power to— (a) quash the order in whole or in part and (if appropriate) remit the matter to the Commission, (b) substitute for all or part of the order any other order which could have been made by the Commission, (c) add to the order anything which could have been contained in an order made by the Commission.

TABLE

1	*2*	*3*
Decision of the Commission— (a) to discharge an order following a review under section 18(13) of this Act, or (b) not to discharge an order following such a review.	The persons are— (a) the charity trustees of the charity to which the order relates, (b) (if a body corporate) the charity itself, (c) if the order in question was made under section 18(1)(i), any person suspended by it, and (d) any other person who is or may be affected by the order.	Power to— (a) quash the decision and (if appropriate) remit the matter to the Commission, (b) make the discharge of the order subject to savings or other transitional provisions, (c) remove any savings or other transitional provisions to which the discharge of the order was subject, (d) discharge the order in whole or in part (whether subject to any savings or other transitional provisions or not).
Order made by the Commission under section 18A(2) of this Act which suspends a person's membership of a charity	The persons are— (a) the person whose membership is suspended by the order, and (b) any other person who is or may be affected by the order.	Power to quash the order and (if appropriate) remit the matter to the Commission.
Order made by the Commission under section 19A(2) of this Act which directs a person to take action specified in the order.	The persons are any person who is directed by the order to take the specified action.	Power to quash the order and (if appropriate) remit the matter to the Commission.
Order made by the Commission under section 19B(2) of this Act which directs a person to apply property in a specified manner.	The persons are any person who is directed by the order to apply the property in the specified manner.	Power to quash the order and (if appropriate) remit the matter to the Commission.
Order made by the Commission under section 23(2) of this Act in relation to any land vested in the official custodian in trust for a charity.	The persons are— (a) the charity trustees of the charity, (b) (if a body corporate) the charity itself, and (c) any other person who is or may be affected by the order.	Power to— (a) quash the order and (if appropriate) remit the matter to the Commission, (b) substitute for the order any other order which could have been made by the Commission, (c) add to the order anything which could have been contained in an order made by the Commission.

TABLE

1	*2*	*3*
Decision of the Commission not to make a common investment scheme under section 24 of this Act.	The persons are— (a) the charity trustees of a charity which applied to the Commission for the scheme, (b) (if a body corporate) the charity itself, and (c) any other person who is or may be affected by the decision.	Power to quash the decision and (if appropriate) remit the matter to the Commission.
Decision of the Commission not to make a common deposit scheme under section 25 of this Act.	The persons are— (a) the charity trustees of a charity which applied to the Commission for the scheme, (b) (if a body corporate) the charity itself, and (c) any other person who is or may be affected by the decision.	Power to quash the decision and (if appropriate) remit the matter to the Commission.
Decision by the Commission not to make an order under section 26 of this Act in relation to a charity.	The persons are— (a) the charity trustees of the charity, and (b) (if a body corporate) the charity itself.	Power to quash the decision and (if appropriate) remit the matter to the Commission.
Direction given by the Commission under section 28 of this Act in relation to an account held in the name of or on behalf of a charity.	The persons are— (a) the charity trustees of the charity, (b) (if a body corporate) the charity itself, and (c) any other person who is or may be affected by the order.	Power to— (a) quash the direction and (if appropriate) remit the matter to the Commission, (b) substitute for the direction any other direction which could have been given by the Commission, (c) add to the direction anything which could have been contained in a direction given by the Commission.
Order made by the Commission under section 31 of this Act for the taxation of a solicitor's bill.	The persons are— (a) the solicitor, (b) any person for whom the work was done by the solicitor, and (c) any other person who is or may be affected by the order.	Power to— (a) quash the order, (b) substitute for the order any other order which could have been made by the Commission, (c) add to the order anything which could have been contained in an order made by the Commission.

TABLE

1	*2*	*3*
Decision of the Commission not to make an order under section 36 of this Act in relation to land held by or in trust for a charity.	The persons are— (a) the charity trustees of the charity, (b) (if a body corporate) the charity itself, and (c) any other person who is or may be affected by the decision.	Power to quash the decision and (if appropriate) remit the matter to the Commission.
Decision of the Commission not to make an order under section 38 of this Act in relation to a mortgage of land held by or in trust for a charity.	The persons are— (a) the charity trustees of the charity, (b) (if a body corporate) the charity itself, and (c) any other person who is or may be affected by the decision.	Power to quash the decision and (if appropriate) remit the matter to the Commission.
Order made by the Commission under section 43(4) of this Act requiring the accounts of a charity to be audited.	The persons are— (a) the charity trustees of the charity, (b) (if a body corporate) the charity itself, and (c) any other person who is or may be affected by the order.	Power to— (a) quash the order, (b) substitute for the order any other order which could have been made by the Commission, (c) add to the order anything which could have been contained in an order made by the Commission.
Order made by the Commission under section 44(2) of this Act in relation to a charity, or a decision of the Commission not to make such an order in relation to a charity.	The persons are— (a) the charity trustees of the charity, (b) (if a body corporate) the charity itself, (c) in the case of a decision not to make an order, the auditor, independent examiner or examiner, and (d) any other person who is or may be affected by the order or the decision.	Power to— (a) quash the order or decision and (if appropriate) remit the matter to the Commission, (b) substitute for the order any other order of a kind the Commission could have made, (c) make any order which the Commission could have made.
Decision of the Commission under section 46(5) of this Act to request charity trustees to prepare an annual report for a charity.	The persons are— (a) the charity trustees, and (b) (if a body corporate) the charity itself.	Power to quash the decision and (if appropriate) remit the matter to the Commission.
Decision of the Commission not to dispense with the requirements of section 48(1) in relation to a charity or class of charities.	The persons are the charity trustees of any charity affected by the decision.	Power to quash the decision and (if appropriate) remit the matter to the Commission.

TABLE

1	*2*	*3*
Decision of the Commission— (a) to grant a certificate of incorporation under section 50(1) of this Act to the trustees of a charity, or (b) not to grant such a certificate.	The persons are— (a) the trustees of the charity, and (b) any other person who is or may be affected by the decision.	Power to quash— (a) the decision, (b) any conditions or directions inserted in the certificate, and (if appropriate) remit the matter to the Commission.
Decision of the Commission to amend a certificate of incorporation of a charity under section 56(4) of this Act.	The persons are— (a) the trustees of the charity, and (b) any other person who is or may be affected by the amended certificate of incorporation.	Power to quash the decision and (if appropriate) remit the matter to the Commission.
Decision of the Commission not to amend a certificate of incorporation under section 56(4) of this Act.	The persons are— (a) the trustees of the charity, and (b) any other person who is or may be affected by the decision not to amend the certificate of incorporation.	Power to— (a) quash the decision and (if appropriate) remit the matter to the Commission, (b) make any order the Commission could have made under section 56(4).
Order of the Commission under section 61(1) or (2) of this Act which dissolves a charity which is an incorporated body.	The persons are— (a) the trustees of the charity, (b) the charity itself, and (c) any other person who is or may be affected by the order.	Power to— (a) quash the order and (if appropriate) remit the matter to the Commission, (b) substitute for the order any other order which could have been made by the Commission, (c) add to the order anything which could have been contained in an order made by the Commission.
Decision of the Commission to give, or withhold, consent under section 64(2), 65(4) or 66(1) of this Act in relation to a body corporate which is a charity.	The persons are— (a) the charity trustees of the charity, (b) the body corporate itself, and (c) any other person who is or may be affected by the decision.	Power to quash the decision and (if appropriate) remit the matter to the Commission.

TABLE

1	*2*	*3*
Order made by the Commission under section 69(1) of this Act in relation to a company which is a charity.	The persons are— (a) the directors of the company, (b) the company itself, and (c) any other person who is or may be affected by the order.	Power to— (a) quash the order and (if appropriate) remit the matter to the Commission, (b) substitute for the order any other order which could have been made by the Commission, (c) add to the order anything which could have been contained in an order made by the Commission.
Order made by the Commission under section 69(4) of this Act which gives directions to a person or to charity trustees.	The persons are— (a) in the case of directions given to a person, that person, (b) in the case of directions given to charity trustees, those charity trustees and (if a body corporate) the charity of which they are charity trustees, and (c) any other person who is or may be affected by the directions.	Power to— (a) quash the order, (b) substitute for the order any other order which could have been made by the Commission, (c) add to the order anything which could have been contained in an order made by the Commission.
Decision of the Commission under section 69E of this Act to grant an application for the constitution of a CIO and its registration as a charity.	The persons are any person (other than the persons who made the application) who is or may be affected by the decision.	Power to quash the decision and (if appropriate)— (a) remit the matter to the Commission, (b) direct the Commission to rectify the register of charities.
Decision of the Commission under section 69E of this Act not to grant an application for the constitution of a CIO and its registration as a charity.	The persons are— (a) the persons who made the application, and (b) any other person who is or may be affected by the decision.	Power to— (a) quash the decision and (if appropriate) remit the matter to the Commission, (b) direct the Commission to grant the application.
Decision of the Commission under section 69H of this Act not to grant an application for the conversion of a charitable company or a registered society into a CIO and the CIO's registration as a charity.	The persons are— (a) the charity which made the application, (b) the charity trustees of the charity, and (c) any other person who is or may be affected by the decision.	Power to— (a) quash the decision and (if appropriate) remit the matter to the Commission, (b) direct the Commission to grant the application.

TABLE

1	*2*	*3*
Decision of the Commission under section 69K of this Act to grant an application for the amalgamation of two or more CIOs and the incorporation and registration as a charity of a new CIO as their successor.	The persons are any creditor of any of the CIOs being amalgamated.	Power to quash the decision and (if appropriate) remit the matter to the Commission.
Decision of the Commission under section 69K of this Act not to grant an application for the amalgamation of two or more CIOs and the incorporation and registration as a charity of a new CIO as their successor.	The persons are— (a) the CIOs which applied for the amalgamation, (b) the charity trustees of the CIOs, and (c) any other person who is or may be affected by the decision.	Power to— (a) quash the decision and (if appropriate) remit the matter to the Commission, (b) direct the Commission to grant the application.
Decision of the Commission to confirm a resolution passed by a CIO under section 69M(1) of this Act.	The persons are any creditor of the CIO.	Power to quash the decision and (if appropriate) remit the matter to the Commission.
Decision of the Commission not to confirm a resolution passed by a CIO under section 69M(1) of this Act.	The persons are— (a) the CIO, (b) the charity trustees of the CIO, and (c) any other person who is or may be affected by the decision.	Power to— (a) quash the decision and (if appropriate) remit the matter to the Commission, (b) direct the Commission to confirm the resolution.
Decision of the Commission under section 72(4) of this Act to waive, or not to waive, a person's disqualification.	The persons are— (a) the person who applied for the waiver, and (b) any other person who is or may be affected by the decision.	Power to— (a) quash the decision and (if appropriate) remit the matter to the Commission, (b) substitute for the decision any other decision of a kind which could have been made by the Commission.
Order made by the Commission under section 73(4) of this Act in relation to a person who has acted as charity trustee or trustee for a charity.	The persons are— (a) the person subject to the order, and (b) any other person who is or may be affected by the order.	Power to— (a) quash the order and (if appropriate) remit the matter to the Commission, (b) substitute for the order any other order which could have been made by the Commission.

TABLE

1	*2*	*3*
Order made by the Commission under section 73C(5) or (6) of this Act requiring a trustee or connected person to repay, or not to receive, remuneration.	The persons are— (a) the trustee or connected person, (b the other charity trustees of the charity concerned, and (c) any other person who is or may be affected by the order.	Power to— (a) quash the order and (if appropriate) remit the matter to the Commission, (b) substitute for the order any other order which could have been made by the Commission.
Decision of the Commission to notify charity trustees under section 74A(2) of this Act that it objects to a resolution of the charity trustees under section 74(2) or 74C(2).	The persons are— (a) the charity trustees, and (b any other person who is or may be affected by the decision.	Power to quash the decision.
Decision of the Commission not to concur under section 75A of this Act with a resolution of charity trustees under section 75A(3) or 75B(2).	The persons are— (a) the charity trustees, (b (if a body corporate) the charity itself, and (c) any other person who is or may be affected by the decision.	Power to quash the decision and (if appropriate) remit the matter to the Commission.
Decision of the Commission to withhold approval for the transfer of property from trustees to a parish council under section 79(1) of this Act.	The persons are— (a) the trustees, (b the parish council, and (c) any other person who is or may be affected by the decision.	Power to quash the decision and (if appropriate) remit the matter to the Commission.
Order made by the Commission under section 80(2) of this Act in relation to a person holding property on behalf of a recognised body or of any person concerned in its management or control.	The persons are— (a) the person holding the property in question, and (b) any other person who is or may be affected by the order.	Power to quash the order and (if appropriate) remit the matter to the Commission.
Decision of the Commission not to give a direction under section 96(5) or (6) of this Act in relation to an institution or a charity.	The persons are the trustees of the institution or charity concerned.	Power to quash the decision and (if appropriate) remit the matter to the Commission.
Decision of the Commission under paragraph 15 of Schedule 5B to this Act to refuse to register an amendment to the constitution of a CIO.	The persons are— (a) the CIO, (b) the charity trustees of the CIO, and (c) any other person who is or may be affected by the decision.	Power to quash the decision and (if appropriate)— (a) remit the matter to the Commission, (b) direct the Commission to register the amendment.

Power to amend Table etc

6

(1) The Minister may by order—

(a) amend or otherwise modify an entry in the Table,
(b) add an entry to the Table, or
(c) remove an entry from the Table.

(2) An order under sub-paragraph (1) may make such amendments, repeals or other modifications of paragraphs 1 to 5 of this Schedule, or of an enactment which applies this Schedule, as the Minister considers appropriate in consequence of any change in the Table made by the order.

(3) No order shall be made under this paragraph unless a draft of the order has been laid before and approved by a resolution of each House of Parliament.

7

Paragraph 6 above applies (with the necessary modifications) in relation to section 57 of the Charities Act 2006 as if—

(a) the provisions of that section were contained in this Schedule, and
(b) the reference in that paragraph to paragraphs 1 to 5 of this Schedule included a reference to any other provision relating to appeals to the Tribunal which is contained in Chapter 1 of Part 3 of the Charities Act 2006.

Schedule 1D
References to Charity Tribunal

References by Commission

1

(1) A question which—

(a) has arisen in connection with the exercise by the Commission of any of its functions, and
(b) involves either the operation of charity law in any respect or its application to a particular state of affairs,

may be referred to the Tribunal by the Commission if the Commission considers it desirable to refer the question to the Tribunal.

(2) The Commission may make such a reference only with the consent of the Attorney General.

(3) The Commission shall be a party to proceedings before the Tribunal on the reference.

(4) The following shall be entitled to be parties to proceedings before the Tribunal on the reference—

(a) the Attorney General, and
(b) with the Tribunal's permission—
    (i) the charity trustees of any charity which is likely to be affected by the Tribunal's decision on the reference,
    (ii) any such charity which is a body corporate, and
    (iii) any other person who is likely to be so affected.

References by Attorney General

2

(1) A question which involves either—

(a) the operation of charity law in any respect, or

(b) the application of charity law to a particular state of affairs,

may be referred to the Tribunal by the Attorney General if the Attorney General considers it desirable to refer the question to the Tribunal.

(2) The Attorney General shall be a party to proceedings before the Tribunal on the reference.

(3) The following shall be entitled to be parties to proceedings before the Tribunal on the reference—

(a) the Commission, and
(b) with the Tribunal's permission—
  (i) the charity trustees of any charity which is likely to be affected by the Tribunal's decision on the reference,
  (ii) any such charity which is a body corporate, and
  (iii) any other person who is likely to be so affected.

Powers of Commission in relation to matters referred to Tribunal

3

(1) This paragraph applies where a question which involves the application of charity law to a particular state of affairs has been referred to the Tribunal under paragraph 1 or 2 above.

(2) The Commission shall not take any steps in reliance on any view as to the application of charity law to that state of affairs until—

(a) proceedings on the reference (including any proceedings on appeal) have been concluded, and
(b) any period during which an appeal (or further appeal) may ordinarily be made has ended.

(3) Where—

(a) paragraphs (a) and (b) of sub-paragraph (2) above are satisfied, and
(b) the question has been decided in proceedings on the reference,

the Commission shall give effect to that decision when dealing with the particular state of affairs to which the reference related.

Suspension of time limits while reference in progress

4

(1) Sub-paragraph (2) below applies if—

(a) paragraph 3(2) above prevents the Commission from taking any steps which it would otherwise be permitted or required to take, and
(b) the steps in question may be taken only during a period specified in an enactment ('the specified period').

(2) The running of the specified period is suspended for the period which—

(a) begins with the date on which the question is referred to the Tribunal, and
(b) ends with the date on which paragraphs (a) and (b) of paragraph 3(2) above are satisfied.

(3) Nothing in this paragraph or section 74A of this Act prevents the specified period being suspended concurrently by virtue of sub-paragraph (2) above and that section.

Agreement for Commission to act while reference in progress

5

(1) Paragraph 3(2) above does not apply in relation to any steps taken by the Commission with the agreement of—

(a) the persons who are parties to the proceedings on the reference at the time when those steps are taken, and
(b) (if not within paragraph (a) above) the charity trustees of any charity which—
  (i) is likely to be directly affected by the taking of those steps, and
  (ii) is not a party to the proceedings at that time.

(2) The Commission may take those steps despite the suspension in accordance with paragraph 4(2) above of any period during which it would otherwise be permitted or required to take them.

(3) Paragraph 3(3) above does not require the Commission to give effect to a decision as to the application of charity law to a particular state of affairs to the extent that the decision is inconsistent with any steps already taken by the Commission in relation to that state of affairs in accordance with this paragraph.

Appeals and applications in respect of matters determined on references

6

(1) No appeal or application may be made to the Tribunal by a person to whom sub-paragraph (2) below applies in respect of an order or decision made, or direction given, by the Commission in accordance with paragraph 3(3) above.

(2) This sub-paragraph applies to a person who was at any stage a party to the proceedings in which the question referred to the Tribunal was decided.

(3) Rules under section 2B(1) of this Act may include provision as to who is to be treated for the purposes of sub-paragraph (2) above as being (or not being) a party to the proceedings.

(4) Any enactment (including one contained in this Act) which provides for an appeal or application to be made to the Tribunal has effect subject to sub-paragraph (1) above.

Interpretation

7

(1) In this Schedule—

'charity law' means—
  (a) any enactment contained in, or made under, this Act or the Charities Act 2006,
  (b) any other enactment specified in regulations made by the Minister, and
  (c) any rule of law which relates to charities, and
'enactment' includes an enactment comprised in subordinate legislation (within the meaning of the Interpretation Act 1978), and includes an enactment whenever passed or made.

(2) The exclusions contained in section 96(2) of this Act (ecclesiastical corporations etc) do not have effect for the purposes of this Schedule.'

NOTES

Initial Commencement

To be appointed: see s 79(2).

Extent

This Schedule does not extend to Scotland: see s 80(2).

Schedule 5
Exempt Charities: Increased Regulation under 1993 Act

Power to require charity's name to be changed

1

In section 6 of the 1993 Act (power of Commission to require charity's name to be changed) omit subsection (9) (exclusion of exempt charities).

Power to institute inquiries

2

In section 8(1) of the 1993 Act (power of Commission to institute inquiries with regard to charities but not in relation to any exempt charity) after 'any exempt charity' insert 'except where this has been requested by its principal regulator.'

Power to call for documents etc

3

In section 9 of the 1993 Act (power of Commission to call for documents and search records) omit subsection (4) (exclusion of documents relating only to exempt charities).

Concurrent jurisdiction of Commission with High Court

4

(1) Section 16 of the 1993 Act (concurrent jurisdiction of Commission with High Court for certain purposes) is amended as follows.

(2) In subsection (4)(c) (application for Commission to exercise powers may be made by Attorney General except in case of exempt charity) omit 'in the case of a charity other than an exempt charity,'.

(3) In subsection (5) (jurisdiction exercisable in case of charity which is not an exempt charity and whose annual income does not exceed £500) omit 'which is not an exempt charity and'.

Further powers of Commission

5

In section 17(7) of the 1993 Act (expenditure by charity on promoting Parliamentary Bill needs consent of court or Commission except in case of exempt charity) omit the words from 'but this subsection' onwards.

Power to act for protection of charities

6

In section 18 of the 1993 Act (power of Commission to act for protection of charities) for subsection (16) substitute—

'(16) In this section—

(a) subsections (1) to (3) apply in relation to an exempt charity, and
(b) subsections (4) to (6) apply in relation to such a charity at any time after the Commission have instituted an inquiry under section 8 with respect to it,

and the other provisions of this section apply accordingly.'

Power to give directions about dormant bank accounts

7

In section 28 of the 1993 Act (power of Commission to give directions about dormant bank accounts of charities), omit subsection (10) (exclusion of accounts held by or on behalf of exempt charity).

Proceedings by persons other than Commission

8

(1) Section 33 of the 1993 Act (charity proceedings by persons other than Commission) is amended as follows.

(2) In subsection (2) (proceedings relating to a charity other than an exempt charity must be authorised by the Commission) omit '(other than an exempt charity)'.

(3) In subsection (7) (participation by Attorney General in proceedings relating to charity other than exempt charity) omit '(other than an exempt charity)'.

Power to order disqualified person to repay sums received from charity

9

In section 73 of the 1993 Act (consequences of person acting as charity trustee while disqualified), in subsection (4) (power of Commission to order disqualified person to repay sums received from a charity other than an exempt charity) omit '(other than an exempt charity)'.

NOTES

Initial Commencement

To be appointed: see s 79(2).

Extent

This Schedule does not extend to Scotland: see s 80(2).

Schedule 6
Group Accounts

After Schedule 5 to the 1993 Act insert—

'Schedule 5A
Group Accounts

Interpretation

1

(1) This paragraph applies for the purposes of this Schedule.

(2) A charity is a 'parent charity' if—

(a) it is (or is to be treated as) a parent undertaking in relation to one or more other undertakings in accordance with the provisions of section 258 of, and Schedule 10A to, the Companies Act 1985, and
(b) it is not a company.

(3) Each undertaking in relation to which a parent charity is (or is to be treated as) a parent undertaking in accordance with those provisions is a 'subsidiary undertaking' in relation to the parent charity.

(4) But sub-paragraph (3) does not have the result that any of the following is a 'subsidiary undertaking'—

(a) any special trusts of a charity,
(b) any institution which, by virtue of a direction under section 96(5) of this Act, is to be treated as forming part of a charity for the purposes of this Part of this Act, or
(c) any charity to which a direction under section 96(6) of this Act applies for those purposes.

(5) 'The group', in relation to a parent charity, means that charity and its subsidiary undertaking or undertakings, and any reference to the members of the group is to be construed accordingly.

(6) For the purposes of—

(a) this paragraph, and
(b) the operation of the provisions mentioned in sub-paragraph (2) above for the purposes of this paragraph,

'undertaking' has the meaning given by sub-paragraph (7) below.

(7) For those purposes 'undertaking' means—

(a) an undertaking as defined by section 259(1) of the Companies Act 1985, or
(b) a charity which is not an undertaking as so defined.

Accounting records

2

(1) The charity trustees—

(a) of a parent charity, or
(b) of any charity which is a subsidiary undertaking,

must ensure that the accounting records kept in respect of the charity under section 41(1) of this Act not only comply with the requirements of that provision but also are such as to enable the charity trustees of the parent charity to ensure that, where any group accounts are prepared by them under paragraph 3(2), those accounts comply with the relevant requirements.

(2) If a parent charity has a subsidiary undertaking in relation to which the requirements of section 41(1) of this Act do not apply, the charity trustees of the parent charity must take reasonable steps to secure that the undertaking keeps such accounting records as to enable the trustees to ensure that, where any group accounts are prepared by them under paragraph 3(2), those accounts comply with the relevant requirements.

(3) In this paragraph 'the relevant requirements' means the requirements of regulations under paragraph 3.

Preparation of group accounts

3

(1) This paragraph applies in relation to a financial year of a charity if it is a parent charity at the end of that year.

(2) The charity trustees of the parent charity must prepare group accounts in respect of that year.

(3) 'Group accounts' means consolidated accounts—

(a) relating to the group, and
(b) complying with such requirements as to their form and contents as may be prescribed by regulations made by the Minister.

(4) Without prejudice to the generality of sub-paragraph (3), regulations under that sub-paragraph may make provision—

(a) for any such accounts to be prepared in accordance with such methods and principles as are specified or referred to in the regulations;
(b) for dealing with cases where the financial years of the members of the group do not all coincide;
(c) as to any information to be provided by way of notes to the accounts.

(5) Regulations under that sub-paragraph may also make provision—

(a) for determining the financial years of subsidiary undertakings for the purposes of this Schedule;
(b) for imposing on the charity trustees of a parent charity requirements with respect to securing that such financial years coincide with that of the charity.

(6) If the requirement in sub-paragraph (2) applies to the charity trustees of a parent charity in relation to a financial year—

(a) that requirement so applies in addition to the requirement in section 42(1) of this Act, and
(b) the option of preparing the documents mentioned in section 42(3) of this Act is not available in relation to that year (whatever the amount of the charity's gross income for that year).

(7) Sub-paragraph (2) has effect subject to paragraph 4.

Exceptions relating to requirement to prepare group accounts

4

(1) The requirement in paragraph 3(2) does not apply to the charity trustees of a parent charity in relation to a financial year if at the end of that year it is itself a subsidiary undertaking in relation to another charity.

(2) The requirement in paragraph 3(2) does not apply to the charity trustees of a parent charity in relation to a financial year if the aggregate gross income of the group for that year does not exceed such sum as is specified in regulations made by the Minister.

(3) Regulations made by the Minister may prescribe circumstances in which a subsidiary undertaking may or (as the case may be) must be excluded from group accounts required to be prepared under paragraph 3(2) for a financial year.

(4) Where, by virtue of such regulations, each of the subsidiary undertakings which are members of a group is either permitted or required to be excluded from any such group accounts for a financial year, the requirement in paragraph 3(2) does not apply to the charity trustees of the parent charity in relation to that year.

Preservation of group accounts

5

(1) The charity trustees of a charity shall preserve any group accounts prepared by them under paragraph 3(2) for at least six years from the end of the financial year to which the accounts relate.

(2) Subsection (4) of section 41 of this Act shall apply in relation to the preservation of any such accounts as it applies in relation to the preservation of any accounting records (the references to subsection (3) of that section being construed as references to sub-paragraph (1) above).

Audit of accounts of larger groups

6

(1) This paragraph applies where group accounts are prepared for a financial year of a parent charity under paragraph 3(2) and—

(a) the aggregate gross income of the group in that year exceeds the relevant income threshold, or
(b) the aggregate gross income of the group in that year exceeds the relevant income threshold and at the end of the year the aggregate value of the assets of the group (before deduction of liabilities) exceeds the relevant assets threshold.

(2) In sub-paragraph (1)—

(a) the reference in paragraph (a) or (b) to the relevant income threshold is a reference to the sum prescribed as the relevant income threshold for the purposes of that paragraph, and
(b) the reference in paragraph (b) to the relevant assets threshold is a reference to the sum prescribed as the relevant assets threshold for the purposes of that paragraph.

'Prescribed' means prescribed by regulations made by the Minister.

(3) This paragraph also applies where group accounts are prepared for a financial year of a parent charity under paragraph 3(2) and the appropriate audit provision applies in relation to the parent charity's own accounts for that year.

(4) If this paragraph applies in relation to a financial year of a parent charity by virtue of sub-paragraph (1) or (3), the group accounts for that year shall be audited—

(a) (subject to paragraph (b) or (c) below) by a person within section 43(2)(a) or (b) of this Act;
(b) if section 43A of this Act applies in relation to that year, by a person appointed by the Audit Commission (see section 43A(7));
(c) if section 43B of this Act applies in relation to that year, by the Auditor General for Wales.

(5) Where it appears to the Commission that sub-paragraph (4)(a) above has not been complied with in relation to that year within ten months from the end of that year—

(a) the Commission may by order require the group accounts for that year to be audited by a person within section 43(2)(a) or (b) of this Act, and
(b) if it so orders, the auditor shall be a person appointed by the Commission.

(6) Section 43(6) of this Act shall apply in relation to any such audit as it applies in relation to an audit carried out by an auditor appointed under section 43(5) (reading the reference to the funds of the charity as a reference to the funds of the parent charity).

(7) Section 43A(4) and (6) of this Act apply in relation to any appointment under sub-paragraph (4)(b) above as they apply in relation to an appointment under section 43A(2).

(8) If this paragraph applies in relation to a financial year of a parent charity by virtue of sub-paragraph (1), the appropriate audit provision shall apply in relation to the parent charity's own accounts for that year (whether or not it would otherwise so apply).

(9) In this paragraph 'the appropriate audit provision', in relation to a financial year of a parent charity, means—

(a) (subject to paragraph (b) or (c) below) section 43(2) of this Act;
(b) if section 43A of this Act applies in relation to that year, section 43A(2);
(c) if section 43B of this Act applies in relation to that year, section 43B(2).

Examination of accounts of smaller groups

7

(1) This paragraph applies where—

(a) group accounts are prepared for a financial year of a parent charity under paragraph 3(2), and
(b) paragraph 6 does not apply in relation to that year.

(2) If—

(a) this paragraph applies in relation to a financial year of a parent charity, and
(b) sub-paragraph (4) or (5) below does not apply in relation to it,

subsections (3) to (7) of section 43 of this Act shall apply in relation to the group accounts for that year as they apply in relation to the accounts of a charity for a financial year in relation to which subsection (2) of that section does not apply, but subject to the modifications in sub-paragraph (3) below.

(3) The modifications are—

(a) any reference to the charity trustees of the charity is to be construed as a reference to the charity trustees of the parent charity;
(b) any reference to the charity's gross income in the financial year in question is to be construed as a reference to the aggregate gross income of the group in that year; and
(c) any reference to the funds of the charity is to be construed as a reference to the funds of the parent charity.

(4) If—

(a) this paragraph applies in relation to a financial year of a parent charity, and
(b) section 43A of this Act also applies in relation to that year,

subsections (3) to (6) of that section shall apply in relation to the group accounts for that year as they apply in relation to the accounts of a charity for a financial year in relation to which subsection (2) of that section does not apply.

(5) If—

(a) this paragraph applies in relation to a financial year of a parent charity, and
(b) section 43B of this Act also applies in relation to that year,

subsection (3) of that section shall apply in relation to the group accounts for that year as they apply in relation to the accounts of a charity for a financial year in relation to which subsection (2) of that section does not apply.

(6) If the group accounts for a financial year of a parent charity are to be examined or audited in accordance with section 43(3) of this Act (as applied by sub-paragraph (2) above), section 43(3) shall apply in relation to the parent charity's own accounts for that year (whether or not it would otherwise so apply).

(7) Nothing in sub-paragraph (4) or (5) above affects the operation of section 43A(3) to (6) or (as the case may be) section 43B(3) in relation to the parent charity's own accounts for the financial year in question.

Supplementary provisions relating to audits etc

8

(1) Section 44(1) of this Act shall apply in relation to audits and examinations carried out under or by virtue of paragraph 6 or 7, but subject to the modifications in sub-paragraph (2) below.

(2) The modifications are—

(a) in paragraph (b), the reference to section 43, 43A or 43B of this Act is to be construed as a reference to paragraph 6 above or to any of those sections as applied by paragraph 7 above;
(b) also in paragraph (b), the reference to any such statement of accounts as is mentioned in sub-paragraph (i) of that paragraph is to be construed as a reference to group accounts prepared for a financial year under paragraph 3(2) above;
(c) in paragraph (c), any reference to section 43, 43A or 43B of this Act is to be construed as a reference to that section as applied by paragraph 7 above;
(d) in paragraphs (d) and (e), any reference to the charity concerned or a charity is to be construed as a reference to any member of the group; and
(e) in paragraph (f), the reference to the requirements of section 43(2) or (3) of this Act is to be construed as a reference to the requirements of paragraph 6(4)(a) or those applied by paragraph 7(2) above.

(3) Without prejudice to the generality of section 44(1)(e), as modified by sub-paragraph (2)(d) above, regulations made under that provision may make provision corresponding or similar to any provision made by section 389A of the Companies Act 1985 (c 6) in connection with the rights exercisable by an auditor of a company in relation to a subsidiary undertaking of the company.

(4) In section 44(2) of this Act the reference to section 44(1)(d) or (e) includes a reference to that provision as it applies in accordance with this paragraph.

Duty of auditors etc to report matters to Commission

9

(1) Section 44A(2) to (5) and (7) of this Act shall apply in relation to a person appointed to audit, or report on, any group accounts under or by virtue of paragraph 6 or 7 above as they apply in relation to a person such as is mentioned in section 44A(1).

(2) In section 44A(2)(a), as it applies in accordance with sub-paragraph (1) above, the reference to the charity or any connected institution or body is to be construed as a reference to the parent charity or any of its subsidiary undertakings.

Annual reports

10

(1) This paragraph applies where group accounts are prepared for a financial year of a parent charity under paragraph 3(2).

(2) The annual report prepared by the charity trustees of the parent charity in respect of that year under section 45 of this Act shall include—

(a) such a report by the trustees on the activities of the charity's subsidiary undertakings during that year, and
(b) such other information relating to any of those undertakings,

as may be prescribed by regulations made by the Minister.

(3) Without prejudice to the generality of sub-paragraph (2), regulations under that sub-paragraph may make provision—

(a) for any such report as is mentioned in paragraph (a) of that sub-paragraph to be prepared in accordance with such principles as are specified or referred to in the regulations;
(b) enabling the Commission to dispense with any requirement prescribed by virtue of sub-paragraph (2)(b) in the case of a particular subsidiary undertaking or a particular class of subsidiary undertaking.

(4) Section 45(3) to (3B) shall apply in relation to the annual report referred to in sub-paragraph (2) above as if any reference to the charity's gross income in the financial year in question were a reference to the aggregate gross income of the group in that year.

(5) When transmitted to the Commission in accordance with sub-paragraph (4) above, the copy of the annual report shall have attached to it both a copy of the group accounts prepared for that year under paragraph 3(2) and—

(a) a copy of the report made by the auditor on those accounts; or
(b) where those accounts have been examined under section 43, 43A or 43B of this Act (as applied by paragraph 7 above), a copy of the report made by the person carrying out the examination.

(6) The requirements in this paragraph are in addition to those in section 45 of this Act.

Excepted charities

11

(1) This paragraph applies where—

(a) a charity is required to prepare an annual report in respect of a financial year by virtue of section 46(5) of this Act,
(b) the charity is a parent charity at the end of the year, and
(c) group accounts are prepared for that year under paragraph 3(2) by the charity trustees of the charity.

(2) When transmitted to the Commission in accordance with section 46(7) of this Act, the copy of the annual report shall have attached to it both a copy of the group accounts and—

(a) a copy of the report made by the auditor on those accounts; or
(b) where those accounts have been examined under section 43, 43A or 43B of this Act (as applied by paragraph 7 above), a copy of the report made by the person carrying out the examination.

(3) The requirement in sub-paragraph (2) is in addition to that in section 46(6) of this Act.

Exempt charities

12

Nothing in the preceding provisions of this Schedule applies to an exempt charity.

Public inspection of annual reports etc

13

In section 47(2) of this Act, the reference to a charity's most recent accounts includes, in relation to a charity whose charity trustees have prepared any group accounts under paragraph 3(2), the group accounts most recently prepared by them.

Offences

14

(1) Section 49(1) of this Act applies in relation to a requirement within sub-paragraph (2) as it applies in relation to a requirement within section 49(1)(a).

(2) A requirement is within this sub-paragraph where it is imposed by section 45(3) or (3A) of this Act, taken with—

(a) section 45(3B), (4) and (5), and
(b) paragraph 10(5) or 11(2) above,

as applicable.

(3) In sub-paragraph (2) any reference to section 45(3), (3A) or (3B) of this Act is a reference to that provision as applied by paragraph 10(4) above.

(4) In section 49(1)(b) the reference to section 47(2) of this Act includes a reference to that provision as extended by paragraph 13 above.

Aggregate gross income

15

The Minister may by regulations make provision for determining for the purposes of this Schedule the amount of the aggregate gross income for a financial year of a group consisting of a parent charity and its subsidiary undertaking or undertakings.'

NOTES

Initial Commencement

To be appointed: see s 79(2).

Extent

This Schedule does not extend to Scotland: see s 80(2).

Schedule 7
Charitable Incorporated Organisations

Part 1
New Part 8A of and Schedule 5B to 1993 Act

1

After Part 8 of the 1993 Act insert the following new Part—

'Part 8A
Charitable Incorporated Organisations

Nature and constitution

69A Charitable incorporated organisations

(1) In this Act, a charitable incorporated organisation is referred to as a 'CIO'.

(2) A CIO shall be a body corporate.

(3) A CIO shall have a constitution.

(4) A CIO shall have a principal office, which shall be in England or in Wales.

(5) A CIO shall have one or more members.

(6) The members may be either—

(a) not liable to contribute to the assets of the CIO if it is wound up, or
(b) liable to do so up to a maximum amount each.

69B Constitution

(1) A CIO's constitution shall state—

(a) its name,
(b) its purposes,
(c) whether its principal office is in England or in Wales, and
(d) whether or not its members are liable to contribute to its assets if it is wound up, and (if they are) up to what amount.

(2) A CIO's constitution shall make provision—

(a) about who is eligible for membership, and how a person becomes a member,
(b) about the appointment of one or more persons who are to be charity trustees of the CIO, and about any conditions of eligibility for appointment, and
(c) containing directions about the application of property of the CIO on its dissolution.

(3) A CIO's constitution shall also provide for such other matters, and comply with such requirements, as are specified in regulations made by the Minister.

(4) A CIO's constitution—

(a) shall be in English if its principal office is in England,
(b) may be in English or in Welsh if its principal office is in Wales.

(5) A CIO's constitution shall be in the form specified in regulations made by the Commission, or as near to that form as the circumstances admit.

(6) Subject to anything in a CIO's constitution: a charity trustee of the CIO may, but need not, be a member of it; a member of the CIO may, but need not, be one of its charity trustees; and those who are members of the CIO and those who are its charity trustees may, but need not, be identical.

69C Name and status

(1) The name of a CIO shall appear in legible characters—

(a) in all business letters of the CIO,
(b) in all its notices and other official publications,
(c) in all bills of exchange, promissory notes, endorsements, cheques and orders for money or goods purporting to be signed on behalf of the CIO,
(d) in all conveyances purporting to be executed by the CIO, and
(e) in all bills rendered by it and in all its invoices, receipts, and letters of credit.

(2) In subsection (1)(d), 'conveyance' means any instrument creating, transferring, varying or extinguishing an interest in land.

(3) Subsection (5) applies if the name of a CIO does not include—

(a) 'charitable incorporated organisation', or
(b) 'CIO', with or without full stops after each letter, or
(c) a Welsh equivalent mentioned in subsection (4) (but this option applies only if the CIO's constitution is in Welsh),

and it is irrelevant, in any such case, whether or not capital letters are used.

(4) The Welsh equivalents referred to in subsection (3)(c) are—

(a) 'sefydliad elusennol corfforedig', or
(b) 'SEC', with or without full stops after each letter.

(5) If this subsection applies, the fact that a CIO is a CIO shall be stated in legible characters in all the documents mentioned in subsection (1).

(6) The statement required by subsection (5) shall be in English, except that in the case of a document which is otherwise wholly in Welsh, the statement may be in Welsh.

69D Offences connected with name and status

(1) A charity trustee of a CIO or a person on the CIO's behalf who issues or authorises the issue of any document referred to in paragraph (a), (b), (d) or (e) of section 69C(1) above which fails to comply with the requirements of section 69C(1), (5) or (6) is liable on summary conviction to a fine not exceeding level 3 on the standard scale.

(2) A charity trustee of a CIO or a person on the CIO's behalf who signs or authorises to be signed on behalf of the CIO any document referred to in paragraph (c) of section 69C(1) above which fails to comply with the requirements of section 69C(1), (5) or (6)—

(a) is liable on summary conviction to a fine not exceeding level 3 on the standard scale, and
(b) is personally liable to the holder of the bill of exchange (etc) for the amount of it, unless it is duly paid by the CIO.

(3) A person who holds any body out as being a CIO when it is not (however he does this) is guilty of an offence and is liable on summary conviction to a fine not exceeding level 3 on the standard scale.

(4) It is a defence for a person charged with an offence under subsection (3) to prove that he believed on reasonable grounds that the body was a CIO.

Registration

69E Application for registration

(1) Any one or more persons ('the applicants') may apply to the Commission for a CIO to be constituted and for its registration as a charity.

(2) The applicants shall supply the Commission with—

(a) a copy of the proposed constitution of the CIO,
(b) such other documents or information as may be prescribed by regulations made by the Minister, and
(c) such other documents or information as the Commission may require for the purposes of the application.

(3) The Commission shall refuse such an application if—

(a) it is not satisfied that the CIO would be a charity at the time it would be registered, or
(b) the CIO's proposed constitution does not comply with one or more of the requirements of section 69B above and any regulations made under that section.

(4) The Commission may refuse such an application if—

(a) the proposed name of the CIO is the same as, or is in the opinion of the Commission too like, the name of any other charity (whether registered or not), or
(b) the Commission is of the opinion referred to in any of paragraphs (b) to (e) of section 6(2) above (power of Commission to require change in charity's name) in relation to the proposed name of the CIO (reading paragraph (b) as referring to the proposed purposes of the CIO and to the activities which it is proposed it should carry on).

69F Effect of registration

(1) If the Commission grants an application under section 69E above it shall register the CIO to which the application relates as a charity in the register of charities.

(2) Upon the registration of the CIO in the register of charities, it becomes by virtue of the registration a body corporate—

(a) whose constitution is that proposed in the application,
(b) whose name is that specified in the constitution, and
(c) whose first member is, or first members are, the applicants referred to in section 69E above.

(3) All property for the time being vested in the applicants (or, if more than one, any of them) on trust for the charitable purposes of the CIO (when incorporated) shall by virtue of this subsection become vested in the CIO upon its registration.

(4) The entry relating to the charity's registration in the register of charities shall include—

(a) the date of the charity's registration, and
(b) a note saying that it is constituted as a CIO.

(5) A copy of the entry in the register shall be sent to the charity at the principal office of the CIO.

Conversion, amalgamation and transfer

69G Conversion of charitable company or registered industrial and provident society

(1) The following may apply to the Commission to be converted into a CIO, and for the CIO's registration as a charity, in accordance with this section—

(a) a charitable company,
(b) a charity which is a registered society within the meaning of the Industrial and Provident Societies Act 1965.

(2) But such an application may not be made by—

(a) a company or registered society having a share capital if any of the shares are not fully paid up, or
(b) an exempt charity.

(3) Such an application is referred to in this section and sections 69H and 69I below as an 'application for conversion'.

(4) The Commission shall notify the following of any application for conversion—

(a) the appropriate registrar, and
(b) such other persons (if any) as the Commission thinks appropriate in the particular case.

(5) The company or registered society shall supply the Commission with—

(a) a copy of a resolution of the company or registered society that it be converted into a CIO,
(b) a copy of the proposed constitution of the CIO,
(c) a copy of a resolution of the company or registered society adopting the proposed constitution of the CIO,
(d) such other documents or information as may be prescribed by regulations made by the Minister, and
(e) such other documents or information as the Commission may require for the purposes of the application.

(6) The resolution referred to in subsection (5)(a) shall be—

(a) a special resolution of the company or registered society, or
(b) a unanimous written resolution signed by or on behalf of all the members of the company or registered society who would be entitled to vote on a special resolution.

(7) In the case of a registered society, 'special resolution' has the meaning given in section 52(3) of the Industrial and Provident Societies Act 1965.

(8) In the case of a company limited by guarantee which makes an application for conversion (whether or not it also has a share capital), the proposed constitution of the CIO shall (unless subsection (10) applies) provide for the CIO's members to be liable to contribute to its assets if it is wound up, and for the amount up to which they are so liable.

(9) That amount shall not be less than the amount up to which they were liable to contribute to the assets of the company if it was wound up.

(10) If the amount each member of the company is liable to contribute to its assets on its winding up is £10 or less, the guarantee shall be extinguished on the conversion of the company into a CIO, and the requirements of subsections (8) and (9) do not apply.

(11) In subsection (4), and in sections 69H and 69I below, 'the appropriate registrar' means—

(a) in the case of an application for conversion by a charitable company, the registrar of companies,
(b) in the case of an application for conversion by a registered society, the Financial Services Authority.

(12) In this section, 'charitable company' means a company which is a charity.

69H Conversion: consideration of application

(1) The Commission shall consult those to whom it has given notice of an application for conversion under section 69G(4) above about whether the application should be granted.

(2) The Commission shall refuse an application for conversion if—

(a) it is not satisfied that the CIO would be a charity at the time it would be registered,
(b) the CIO's proposed constitution does not comply with one or more of the requirements of section 69B above and any regulations made under that section, or
(c) in the case of an application for conversion made by a company limited by guarantee, the CIO's proposed constitution does not comply with the requirements of subsections (8) and (9) of section 69G above.

(3) The Commission may refuse an application for conversion if—

(a) the proposed name of the CIO is the same as, or is in the opinion of the Commission too like, the name of any other charity (whether registered or not),
(b) the Commission is of the opinion referred to in any of paragraphs (b) to (e) of section 6(2) above (power of Commission to require change in charity's name) in relation to the proposed name of the CIO (reading paragraph (b) as referring to the proposed purposes of the CIO and to the activities which it is proposed it should carry on), or
(c) having considered any representations received from those whom it has consulted under subsection (1), the Commission considers (having regard to any regulations made under subsection (4)) that it would not be appropriate to grant the application.

(4) The Minister may make provision in regulations about circumstances in which it would not be appropriate to grant an application for conversion.

(5) If the Commission refuses an application for conversion, it shall so notify the appropriate registrar (see section 69G(11) above).

69I Conversion: supplementary

(1) If the Commission grants an application for conversion, it shall—

(a) register the CIO to which the application related in the register of charities, and
(b) send to the appropriate registrar (see section 69G(11) above) a copy of each of the resolutions of the converting company or registered society referred to in section 69G(5)(a) and (c) above, and a copy of the entry in the register relating to the CIO.

(2) The registration of the CIO in the register shall be provisional only until the appropriate registrar cancels the registration of the company or registered society as required by subsection (3)(b).

(3) The appropriate registrar shall—

(a) register the documents sent to him under subsection (1)(b), and

(b) cancel the registration of the company in the register of companies, or of the society in the register of friendly societies,

and shall notify the Commission that he has done so.

(4) When the appropriate registrar cancels the registration of the company or of the registered society, the company or registered society is thereupon converted into a CIO, being a body corporate—

(a) whose constitution is that proposed in the application for conversion,
(b) whose name is that specified in the constitution, and
(c) whose first members are the members of the converting company or society immediately before the moment of conversion.

(5) If the converting company or registered society had a share capital, upon the conversion of the company or registered society all the shares shall by virtue of this subsection be cancelled, and no former holder of any cancelled share shall have any right in respect of it after its cancellation.

(6) Subsection (5) does not affect any right which accrued in respect of a share before its cancellation.

(7) The entry relating to the charity's registration in the register shall include—

(a) a note that it is constituted as a CIO,
(b) the date on which it became so constituted, and
(c) a note of the name of the company or society which was converted into the CIO,

but the matters mentioned in paragraphs (a) and (b) are to be included only when the appropriate registrar has notified the Commission as required by subsection (3).

(8) A copy of the entry in the register shall be sent to the charity at the principal office of the CIO.

(9) The conversion of a charitable company or of a registered society into a CIO does not affect, in particular, any liability to which the company or registered society was subject by virtue of its being a charitable company or registered society.

69J Conversion of community interest company

(1) The Minister may by regulations make provision for the conversion of a community interest company into a CIO, and for the CIO's registration as a charity.

(2) The regulations may, in particular, apply, or apply with modifications specified in the regulations, or disapply, anything in sections 53 to 55 of the Companies (Audit, Investigations and Community Enterprise) Act 2004 or in sections 69G to 69I above.

69K Amalgamation of CIOs

(1) Any two or more CIOs ('the old CIOs') may, in accordance with this section, apply to the Commission to be amalgamated, and for the incorporation and registration as a charity of a new CIO ('the new CIO') as their successor.

(2) Such an application is referred to in this section and section 69L below as an 'application for amalgamation'.

(3) Subsections (2) to (4) of section 69E above apply in relation to an application for amalgamation as they apply to an application for a CIO to be constituted, but in those subsections—

(a) 'the applicants' shall be construed as meaning the old CIOs, and
(b) references to the CIO are to the new CIO.

(4) In addition to the documents and information referred to in section 69E(2) above, the old CIOs shall supply the Commission with—

(a) a copy of a resolution of each of the old CIOs approving the proposed amalgamation, and
(b) a copy of a resolution of each of the old CIOs adopting the proposed constitution of the new CIO.

(5) The resolutions referred to in subsection (4) must have been passed—

(a) by a 75% majority of those voting at a general meeting of the CIO (including those voting by proxy or by post, if voting that way is permitted), or
(b) unanimously by the CIO's members, otherwise than at a general meeting.

(6) The date of passing of such a resolution is—

(a) the date of the general meeting at which it was passed, or
(b) if it was passed otherwise than at a general meeting, the date on which provision in the CIO's constitution or in regulations made under paragraph 13 of Schedule 5B to this Act deems it to have been passed (but that date may not be earlier than that on which the last member agreed to it).

(7) Each old CIO shall—

(a) give notice of the proposed amalgamation in the way (or ways) that in the opinion of its charity trustees will make it most likely to come to the attention of those who would be affected by the amalgamation, and
(b) send a copy of the notice to the Commission.

(8) The notice shall invite any person who considers that he would be affected by the proposed amalgamation to make written representations to the Commission not later than a date determined by the Commission and specified in the notice.

(9) In addition to being required to refuse it on one of the grounds mentioned in section 69E(3) above as applied by subsection (3) of this section, the Commission shall refuse an application for amalgamation if it considers that there is a serious risk that the new CIO would be unable properly to pursue its purposes.

(10) The Commission may refuse an application for amalgamation if it is not satisfied that the provision in the constitution of the new CIO about the matters mentioned in subsection (11) is the same, or substantially the same, as the provision about those matters in the constitutions of each of the old CIOs.

(11) The matters are—

(a) the purposes of the CIO,
(b) the application of property of the CIO on its dissolution, and
(c) authorisation for any benefit to be obtained by charity trustees or members of the CIO or persons connected with them.

(12) For the purposes of subsection (11)(c)—

(a) 'benefit' means a direct or indirect benefit of any nature, except that it does not include any remuneration (within the meaning of section 73A below) whose receipt may be authorised under that section, and
(b) the same rules apply for determining whether a person is connected with a charity trustee or member of the CIO as apply, in accordance with section 73B(5) and (6) below, for determining whether a person is connected with a charity trustee for the purposes of section 73A.

69L Amalgamation: supplementary

(1) If the Commission grants an application for amalgamation, it shall register the new CIO in the register of charities.

(2) Upon the registration of the new CIO it thereupon becomes by virtue of the registration a body corporate—

(a) whose constitution is that proposed in the application for amalgamation,
(b) whose name is that specified in the constitution, and
(c) whose first members are the members of the old CIOs immediately before the new CIO was registered.

(3) Upon the registration of the new CIO—

(a) all the property, rights and liabilities of each of the old CIOs shall become by virtue of this subsection the property, rights and liabilities of the new CIO, and
(b) each of the old CIOs shall be dissolved.

(4) Any gift which—

(a) is expressed as a gift to one of the old CIOs, and
(b) takes effect on or after the date of registration of the new CIO,

takes effect as a gift to the new CIO.

(5) The entry relating to the registration in the register of the charity constituted as the new CIO shall include—

(a) a note that it is constituted as a CIO,
(b) the date of the charity's registration, and
(c) a note that the CIO was formed following amalgamation, and of the name of each of the old CIOs.

(6) A copy of the entry in the register shall be sent to the charity at the principal office of the new CIO.

69M Transfer of CIO's undertaking

(1) A CIO may resolve that all its property, rights and liabilities should be transferred to another CIO specified in the resolution.

(2) Where a CIO has passed such a resolution, it shall send to the Commission—

(a) a copy of the resolution, and
(b) a copy of a resolution of the transferee CIO agreeing to the transfer to it.

(3) Subsections (5) and (6) of section 69K above apply to the resolutions referred to in subsections (1) and (2)(b) as they apply to the resolutions referred to in section 69K(4).

(4) Having received the copy resolutions referred to in subsection (2), the Commission—

(a) may direct the transferor CIO to give public notice of its resolution in such manner as is specified in the direction, and
(b) if it gives such a direction, must take into account any representations made to it by persons appearing to it to be interested in the transferor CIO, where those representations are made to it within the period of 28 days beginning with the date when public notice of the resolution is given by the transferor CIO.

(5) The resolution shall not take effect until confirmed by the Commission.

(6) The Commission shall refuse to confirm the resolution if it considers that there is a serious risk that the transferee CIO would be unable properly to pursue the purposes of the transferor CIO.

(7) The Commission may refuse to confirm the resolution if it is not satisfied that the provision in the constitution of the transferee CIO about the matters mentioned in section 69K(11) above is the same, or substantially the same, as the provision about those matters in the constitution of the transferor CIO.

(8) If the Commission does not notify the transferor CIO within the relevant period that it is either confirming or refusing to confirm the resolution, the resolution is to be treated as confirmed by the Commission on the day after the end of that period.

(9) Subject to subsection (10), 'the relevant period' means—

(a) in a case where the Commission directs the transferor CIO under subsection (4) to give public notice of its resolution, the period of six months beginning with the date when that notice is given, or
(b) in any other case, the period of six months beginning with the date when both of the copy resolutions referred to in subsection (2) have been received by the Commission.

(10) The Commission may at any time within the period of six months mentioned in subsection (9)(a) or (b) give the transferor CIO a notice extending the relevant period by such period (not exceeding six months) as is specified in the notice.

(11) A notice under subsection (10) must set out the Commission's reasons for the extension.

(12) If the resolution is confirmed (or treated as confirmed) by the Commission—

(a) all the property, rights and liabilities of the transferor CIO shall become by virtue of this subsection the property, rights and liabilities of the transferee CIO in accordance with the resolution, and
(b) the transferor CIO shall be dissolved.

(13) Any gift which—

(a) is expressed as a gift to the transferor CIO, and
(b) takes effect on or after the date on which the resolution is confirmed (or treated as confirmed),

takes effect as a gift to the transferee CIO.

Winding up, insolvency and dissolution

69N Regulations about winding up, insolvency and dissolution

(1) The Minister may by regulations make provision about—

(a) the winding up of CIOs,
(b) their insolvency,
(c) their dissolution, and
(d) their revival and restoration to the register following dissolution.

(2) The regulations may, in particular, make provision—

(a) about the transfer on the dissolution of a CIO of its property and rights (including property and rights held on trust for the CIO) to the official custodian or another person or body,
(b) requiring any person in whose name any stocks, funds or securities are standing in trust for a CIO to transfer them into the name of the official custodian or another person or body,
(c) about the disclaiming, by the official custodian or other transferee of a CIO's property, of title to any of that property,
(d) about the application of a CIO's property cy-près,
(e) about circumstances in which charity trustees may be personally liable for contributions to the assets of a CIO or for its debts,
(f) about the reversal on a CIO's revival of anything done on its dissolution.

(3) The regulations may—

(a) apply any enactment which would not otherwise apply, either without modification or with modifications specified in the regulations,
(b) disapply, or modify (in ways specified in the regulations) the application of, any enactment which would otherwise apply.

(4) In subsection (3), 'enactment' includes a provision of subordinate legislation within the meaning of the Interpretation Act 1978.

Miscellaneous

69O Power to transfer all property of unincorporated charity to one or more CIOs

Section 74 below (power to transfer all property of unincorporated charity) applies with the omission of paragraph (a) of subsection (1) in relation to a resolution by the charity trustees of a charity to transfer all its property to a CIO or to divide its property between two or more CIOs.

69P Further provision about CIOs

The provisions of Schedule 5B to this Act shall have effect with respect to CIOs.

69Q Regulations

(1) The Minister may by regulations make further provision about applications for registration of CIOs, the administration of CIOs, the conversion of charitable companies, registered societies and community interest companies into CIOs, the amalgamation of CIOs, and in relation to CIOs generally.

(2) The regulations may, in particular, make provision about—

(a) the execution of deeds and documents,
(b) the electronic communication of messages or documents relevant to a CIO or to any dealing with the Commission in relation to one,
(c) the maintenance of registers of members and of charity trustees,
(d) the maintenance of other registers (for example, a register of charges over the CIO's assets).

(3) The regulations may, in relation to charities constituted as CIOs—

(a) disapply any of sections 3 to 4 above,
(b) modify the application of any of those sections in ways specified in the regulations.

(4) Subsections (3) and (4) of section 69N above apply for the purposes of this section as they apply for the purposes of that.'

2

After the Schedule 5A inserted in the 1993 Act by Schedule 6 to this Act, insert the following Schedule—

'Schedule 5B
Further Provision about Charitable Incorporated Organisations

Powers

1

(1) Subject to anything in its constitution, a CIO has power to do anything which is calculated to further its purposes or is conducive or incidental to doing so.

(2) The CIO's charity trustees shall manage the affairs of the CIO and may for that purpose exercise all the powers of the CIO.

Constitutional requirements

2

A CIO shall use and apply its property in furtherance of its purposes and in accordance with its constitution.

3

If the CIO is one whose members are liable to contribute to its assets if it is wound up, its constitution binds the CIO and its members for the time being to the same extent as if its provisions were contained in a contract—

(a) to which the CIO and each of its members was a party, and
(b) which contained obligations on the part of the CIO and each member to observe all the provisions of the constitution.

4

Money payable by a member to the CIO under the constitution is a debt due from him to the CIO, and is of the nature of a specialty debt.

Third parties

5

(1) Sub-paragraphs (2) and (3) are subject to sub-paragraph (4).

(2) The validity of an act done (or purportedly done) by a CIO shall not be called into question on the ground that it lacked constitutional capacity.

(3) The power of the charity trustees of a CIO to act so as to bind the CIO (or authorise others to do so) shall not be called into question on the ground of any constitutional limitations on their powers.

(4) But sub-paragraphs (2) and (3) apply only in favour of a person who gives full consideration in money or money's worth in relation to the act in question, and does not know—

(a) in a sub-paragraph (2) case, that the act is beyond the CIO's constitutional capacity, or
(b) in a sub-paragraph (3) case, that the act is beyond the constitutional powers of its charity trustees,

and (in addition) sub-paragraph (3) applies only if the person dealt with the CIO in good faith (which he shall be presumed to have done unless the contrary is proved).

(5) A party to an arrangement or transaction with a CIO is not bound to inquire—

(a) whether it is within the CIO's constitutional capacity, or
(b) as to any constitutional limitations on the powers of its charity trustees to bind the CIO or authorise others to do so.

(6) If a CIO purports to transfer or grant an interest in property, the fact that the act was beyond its constitutional capacity, or that its charity trustees in connection with the act exceeded their constitutional powers, does not affect the title of a person who subsequently acquires the property or any interest in it for full consideration without actual notice of any such circumstances affecting the validity of the CIO's act.

(7) In any proceedings arising out of sub-paragraphs (2) to (4), the burden of proving that a person knew that an act—

(a) was beyond the CIO's constitutional capacity, or
(b) was beyond the constitutional powers of its charity trustees,

lies on the person making that allegation.

(8) In this paragraph and paragraphs 6 to 8—

(a) references to a CIO's lack of 'constitutional capacity' are to lack of capacity because of anything in its constitution, and
(b) references to 'constitutional limitations' on the powers of a CIO's charity trustees are to limitations on their powers under its constitution, including limitations deriving

from a resolution of the CIO in general meeting, or from an agreement between the CIO's members, and 'constitutional powers' is to be construed accordingly.

6

(1) Nothing in paragraph 5 prevents a person from bringing proceedings to restrain the doing of an act which would be—

(a) beyond the CIO's constitutional capacity, or
(b) beyond the constitutional powers of the CIO's charity trustees.

(2) But no such proceedings may be brought in respect of an act to be done in fulfilment of a legal obligation arising from a previous act of the CIO.

(3) Sub-paragraph (2) does not prevent the Commission from exercising any of its powers.

7

Nothing in paragraph 5(3) affects any liability incurred by the CIO's charity trustees (or any one of them) for acting beyond his or their constitutional powers.

8

Nothing in paragraph 5 absolves the CIO's charity trustees from their duty to act within the CIO's constitution and in accordance with any constitutional limitations on their powers.

Duties

9

It is the duty of—

(a) each member of a CIO, and
(b) each charity trustee of a CIO,

to exercise his powers, and (in the case of a charity trustee) to perform his functions, in his capacity as such, in the way he decides, in good faith, would be most likely to further the purposes of the CIO.

10

(1) Subject to any provision of a CIO's constitution permitted by virtue of regulations made under sub-paragraph (2), each charity trustee of a CIO shall in the performance of his functions in that capacity exercise such care and skill as is reasonable in the circumstances, having regard in particular—

(a) to any special knowledge or experience that he has or holds himself out as having, and
(b) if he acts as a charity trustee in the course of a business or profession, to any special knowledge or experience that it is reasonable to expect of a person acting in the course of that kind of business or profession.

(2) The Minister may make regulations permitting a CIO's constitution to provide that the duty in sub-paragraph (1) does not apply, or does not apply in so far as is specified in the constitution.

(3) Regulations under sub-paragraph (2) may provide for limits on the extent to which, or the cases in which, a CIO's constitution may disapply the duty in sub-paragraph (1).

Personal benefit and payments

11

(1) A charity trustee of a CIO may not benefit personally from any arrangement or transaction entered into by the CIO if, before the arrangement or transaction was entered into, he did not disclose to all the charity trustees of the CIO any material interest of his in it or in any other person or body party to it (whether that interest is direct or indirect).

(2) Nothing in sub-paragraph (1) confers authority for a charity trustee of a CIO to benefit personally from any arrangement or transaction entered into by the CIO.

12

A charity trustee of a CIO—

(a) is entitled to be reimbursed by the CIO, or
(b) may pay out of the CIO's funds,

expenses properly incurred by him in the performance of his functions as such.

Procedure

13

(1) The Minister may by regulations make provision about the procedure of CIOs.

(2) Subject to—

(a) any such regulations,
(b) any other requirement imposed by or by virtue of this Act or any other enactment, and
(c) anything in the CIO's constitution,

a CIO may regulate its own procedure.

(3) But a CIO's procedure shall include provision for the holding of a general meeting of its members, and the regulations referred to in sub-paragraph (1) may in particular make provision about such meetings.

Amendment of constitution

14

(1) A CIO may by resolution of its members amend its constitution (and a single resolution may provide for more than one amendment).

(2) Such a resolution must be passed—

(a) by a 75% majority of those voting at a general meeting of the CIO (including those voting by proxy or by post, if voting that way is permitted), or
(b) unanimously by the CIO's members, otherwise than at a general meeting.

(3) The date of passing of such a resolution is—

(a) the date of the general meeting at which it was passed, or
(b) if it was passed otherwise than at a general meeting, the date on which provision in the CIO's constitution or in regulations made under paragraph 13 deems it to have been passed (but that date may not be earlier than that on which the last member agreed to it).

(4) The power of a CIO to amend its constitution is not exercisable in any way which would result in the CIO's ceasing to be a charity.

(5) Subject to paragraph 15(5) below, a resolution containing an amendment which would make any regulated alteration is to that extent ineffective unless the prior written consent of the Commission has been obtained to the making of the amendment.

(6) The following are regulated alterations—

(a) any alteration of the CIO's purposes,
(b) any alteration of any provision of the CIO's constitution directing the application of property of the CIO on its dissolution,
(c) any alteration of any provision of the CIO's constitution where the alteration would provide authorisation for any benefit to be obtained by charity trustees or members of the CIO or persons connected with them.

(7) For the purposes of sub-paragraph (6)(c)—

(a) 'benefit' means a direct or indirect benefit of any nature, except that it does not include any remuneration (within the meaning of section 73A of this Act) whose receipt may be authorised under that section, and
(b) the same rules apply for determining whether a person is connected with a charity trustee or member of the CIO as apply, in accordance with section 73B(5) and (6) of this Act, for determining whether a person is connected with a charity trustee for the purposes of section 73A.

Registration and coming into effect of amendments

15

(1) A CIO shall send to the Commission a copy of a resolution containing an amendment to its constitution, together with—

(a) a copy of the constitution as amended, and
(b) such other documents and information as the Commission may require,

by the end of the period of 15 days beginning with the date of passing of the resolution (see paragraph 14(3)).

(2) An amendment to a CIO's constitution does not take effect until it has been registered.

(3) The Commission shall refuse to register an amendment if—

(a) in the opinion of the Commission the CIO had no power to make it (for example, because the effect of making it would be that the CIO ceased to be a charity, or that the CIO or its constitution did not comply with any requirement imposed by or by virtue of this Act or any other enactment), or
(b) the amendment would change the name of the CIO, and the Commission could have refused an application under section 69E of this Act for the constitution and registration of a CIO with the name specified in the amendment on a ground set out in subsection (4) of that section.

(4) The Commission may refuse to register an amendment if the amendment would make a regulated alteration and the consent referred to in paragraph 14(5) had not been obtained.

(5) But if the Commission does register such an amendment, paragraph 14(5) does not apply.'

NOTES

Initial Commencement

To be appointed: see s 79(2).

Extent

This Part of this Schedule does not extend to Scotland: see s 80(2).

Part 2
Other Amendments of 1993 Act

3

The 1993 Act is further amended as follows.

4

In section 45 (annual reports), after subsection (3A) insert—

'(3B) But in the case of a charity which is constituted as a CIO—

(a) the requirement imposed by subsection (3) applies whatever the charity's gross income is, and
(b) subsection (3A) does not apply.'

5

In section 48 (annual returns), in subsection (1A), at the end add '(but this subsection does not apply if the charity is constituted as a CIO)'.

6

In section 86 (regulations and orders)—

(a) in subsection (2), after paragraph (a) insert—
'(aa) to regulations under section 69N above; and no regulations shall be made under that section unless a draft of the regulations has been laid before and approved by a resolution of each House of Parliament; or',
(b) in subsection (4), for 'or 45' substitute ', 45, 69N or 69Q'.

7

In section 97 (general interpretation), in subsection (1), at the appropriate place insert—

"CIO' means charitable incorporated organisation;'.

NOTES

Initial Commencement

To be appointed: see s 79(2).

Extent

This Part of this Schedule does not extend to Scotland: see s 80(2).

Schedule 8
Minor and Consequential Amendments

Literary and Scientific Institutions Act 1854 (c 112)

1

In section 6 of the Literary and Scientific Institutions Act 1854 (power of corporations etc to convey land for the purposes of that Act) for 'without the consent of the Charity Commissioners' substitute 'except with the consent of the Charity Commission or in accordance with such provisions of section 36(2) to (8) of the Charities Act 1993 as are applicable'.

Places of Worship Registration Act 1855 (c 81)

2

In section 9(1) of the Places of Worship Registration Act 1855 (certified places exempt from requirement to register)—

(a) for 'shall be excepted under subsection (5) of section 3 of the Charities Act 1993, from registration under that section' substitute 'shall, so far as it is a charity, be treated for the purposes of section 3A(4)(b) of the Charities Act 1993 (institutions to be excepted from registration under that Act) as if that provision applied to it', and

(b) for 'Charity Commissioners' substitute 'Charity Commission'.

Bishops Trusts Substitution Act 1858 (c 71)

3

The Bishops Trusts Substitution Act 1858 has effect subject to the following amendments.

4

In section 1 (substitution of one bishop for another as trustee)—

(a) for 'Charity Commissioners' substitute 'Charity Commission', and
(b) for 'them' substitute 'it'.

5

In section 3 (how costs are to be defrayed) for 'said Charity Commissioners' (in both places) substitute 'Charity Commission'.

Places of Worship Sites Amendment Act 1882 (c 21)

6

In section 1(d) of the Places of Worship Sites Amendment Act 1882 (conveyance of lands by corporations and other public bodies) for 'without the consent of the Charity Commissioners' substitute 'except with the consent of the Charity Commission or in accordance with such provisions of section 36(2) to (8) of the Charities Act 1993 as are applicable'.

Municipal Corporations Act 1882 (c 50)

7

In section 133(2) of the Municipal Corporations Act 1882 (administration of charitable trusts and vesting of legal estate) for 'Charity Commissioners' substitute 'Charity Commission'.

Technical and Industrial Institutions Act 1892 (c 29)

8

In section 9(1) of the Technical and Industrial Institutions Act 1892 (site may be sold or exchanged) for 'with the consent of the Charity Commissioners' substitute 'with the consent of the Charity Commission or in accordance with such provisions of section 36(2) to (8) of the Charities Act 1993 as are applicable'.

Local Government Act 1894 (c 73)

9

(1) In section 75(2) of the Local Government Act 1894 (construction of that Act) the definition of 'ecclesiastical charity' is amended as follows.

(2) In the second paragraph (proviso)—

(a) for 'Charity Commissioners' substitute 'Charity Commission', and
(b) for 'them' substitute 'it'.

(3) In the third paragraph (inclusion of other buildings) for 'Charity Commissioners' substitute 'Charity Commission'.

Commons Act 1899 (c 30)

10

In section 18 of the Commons Act 1899 (power to modify provisions as to recreation grounds)—

(a) for 'Charity Commissioners' substitute 'Charity Commission', and
(b) for 'their' substitute 'its'.

Open Spaces Act 1906 (c 25)

11

The Open Spaces Act 1906 has effect subject to the following amendments.

12

In section 3(1) (transfer to local authority of spaces held by trustees for purposes of public recreation) for 'Charity Commissioners' substitute 'Charity Commission'.

13

(1) Section 4 (transfer by charity trustees of open space to local authority) is amended as follows.

(2) In subsection (1), for the words from 'and with the sanction' to 'as hereinafter provided' substitute 'and in accordance with subsection (1A)'.

(3) After subsection (1) insert—

'(1A) The trustees act in accordance with this subsection if they convey or demise the open space as mentioned in subsection (1)—

(a) with the sanction of an order of the Charity Commission or with that of an order of the court to be obtained as provided in the following provisions of this section, or
(b) in accordance with such provisions of section 36(2) to (8) of the Charities Act 1993 as are applicable.'

(4) In subsection (4)—

(a) for 'Charity Commissioners' substitute 'Charity Commission', and
(b) for 'them' substitute 'it'.

14

In section 21(1) (application to Ireland)—

(a) for 'Charity Commissioners' substitute 'Charity Commission', and
(b) for 'Commissioners of Charity Donations and Bequests for Ireland' substitute 'the Department for Social Development'.

Police, Factories, &c (Miscellaneous Provisions) Act 1916 (c 31)

15

(1) Section 5 of the Police, Factories, &c. (Miscellaneous Provisions) Act 1916 (regulation of street collections) is amended as follows.

(2) In subsection (1) for 'the benefit of charitable or other purposes,' substitute 'any purposes in circumstances not involving the making of a charitable appeal,'.

(3) In paragraph (b) of the proviso to subsection (1) omit the words from ', and no representation' onwards.

(4) In subsection (4) before the definition of 'street' insert—

"charitable appeal' has the same meaning as in Chapter 1 of Part 3 of the Charities Act 2006;'.

National Trust Charity Scheme Confirmation Act 1919 (c lxxxiv)

16

The National Trust Charity Scheme Confirmation Act 1919 has effect subject to the following amendments.

17

In section 1 (confirmation of the scheme) for 'Charity Commissioners' substitute 'Charity Commission'.

18

In paragraph 3 of the scheme set out in the Schedule, for 'Charity Commissioners upon such application made to them for the purpose as they think' substitute 'Charity Commission upon such application made to it for the purpose as it thinks'.

Settled Land Act 1925 (c 18)

19

In section 29(3) of the Settled Land Act 1925 (charitable and public trusts: saving) for 'Charity Commissioners' substitute 'Charity Commission'.

Landlord and Tenant Act 1927 (c 36)

20

In Part 2 of the Second Schedule to the Landlord and Tenant Act 1927 (application to ecclesiastical and charity land), in paragraph 2, for 'Charity Commissioners' substitute 'Charity Commission'.

Voluntary Hospitals (Paying Patients) Act 1936 (c 17)

21

The Voluntary Hospitals (Paying Patients) Act 1936 has effect subject to the following amendments.

22

In section 1 (definitions), in the definition of 'Order', for 'Charity Commissioners' substitute 'Charity Commission'.

23

(1) Section 2 (accommodation for and charges to paying patients) is amended as follows.

(2) In subsections (1), (3) and (4) for 'Charity Commissioners' substitute 'Charity Commission'.

(3) In subsection (4)—

(a) for 'the Commissioners' (in both places) substitute 'the Commission',
(b) for 'they' substitute 'it', and
(c) for 'their' substitute 'its'.

24

In section 3(1) (provision for patients able to make some, but not full, payment)—

(a) for 'Charity Commissioners are' substitute 'Charity Commission is', and
(b) for 'they' substitute 'it'.

25

In section 4 (provisions for protection of existing trusts)—

(a) for 'Charity Commissioners' substitute 'Charity Commission', and
(b) in paragraphs (a), (b) and (c) for 'they are' substitute 'it is'.

26

(1) Section 5 (power to make rules) is amended as follows.

(2) In subsection (1)—

(a) for 'Charity Commissioners' substitute 'Charity Commission', and
(b) for 'they' substitute 'it'.

(3) In subsection (3)—

(a) for 'Charity Commissioners' (in both places) substitute 'Charity Commission',
(b) for 'they' and 'them' (in each place) substitute 'it', and
(c) for 'an officer' substitute 'a member of staff'.

(4) In the sidenote, for 'Charity Commissioners' substitute 'Charity Commission'.

27

In section 6(2) (savings)—

(a) for 'Charity Commissioners' substitute 'Charity Commission', and
(b) for 'them' substitute 'it'.

Green Belt (London and Home Counties) Act 1938 (c xciii)

28

In section 20 of the Green Belt (London and Home Counties) Act 1938 (lands held on charitable trusts) for 'Charity Commissioners' substitute 'Charity Commission'.

New Parishes Measure 1943 (No 1)

29

The New Parishes Measure 1943 has effect subject to the following amendments.

30

In section 14(1)(b) (power of corporations etc to give or grant land for sites of churches, etc) for 'with the sanction of an order of the Charity Commissioners' substitute—

'(i) with the sanction of an order of the Charity Commission, or

(ii) in accordance with such provisions of section 36(2) to (8) of the Charities Act 1993 as are applicable;'.

31

In section 31 (charitable trusts)—

(a) for 'the Board of Charity Commissioners' substitute 'the Charity Commission', and
(b) for 'the Charity Commissioners' substitute 'the Charity Commission'.

Crown Proceedings Act 1947 (c 44)

32

In section 23(3) of the Crown Proceedings Act 1947 (proceedings with respect to which Part 2 of the Act does not apply) for 'Charity Commissioners' substitute 'Charity Commission'.

London County Council (General Powers) Act 1947 (c xlvi)

33

(1) Section 6 of the London County Council (General Powers) Act 1947 (saving for certain trusts) is amended as follows.

(2) In subsection (2)—

(a) for 'Charity Commissioners' substitute 'Charity Commission', and
(b) at the end add '; but this is subject to subsection (3)'.

(3) After subsection (2) add—

'(3) In relation to any disposition of land falling within section 36(1) of the Charities Act 1993, the Council or the borough council may, instead of acting with the sanction of an order of the court or of the Charity Commission, make the disposition in accordance with such provisions of section 36(2) to (8) of that Act as are applicable.'

London County Council (General Powers) Act 1951 (c xli)

34

In section 33(6) of the London County Council (General Powers) Act 1951 (improvement of roadside amenities: saving for certain land) for 'Charity Commissioners' substitute 'Charity Commission'.

City of London (Various Powers) Act 1952 (c vi)

35

In section 4(6) of the City of London (Various Powers) Act 1952 (improvement of amenities) for 'Charity Commissioners' substitute 'Charity Commission'.

City of London (Guild Churches) Act 1952 (c xxxviii)

36

In section 35 of the City of London (Guild Churches) Act 1952 (saving of rights of certain persons) for 'Charity Commissioners' substitute 'Charity Commission'.

London County Council (General Powers) Act 1955 (c xxix)

37

(1) Section 34 of the London County Council (General Powers) Act 1955 (powers as to erection of buildings: saving for certain land and buildings) is amended as follows.

(2) In subsection (2)—

(a) for 'Charity Commissioners' substitute 'Charity Commission', and
(b) at the end add '; but this is subject to subsection (3)'.

(3) After subsection (2) add—

'(3) In relation to any disposition of land falling within section 36(1) of the Charities Act 1993, the Council may, instead of acting with the sanction of an order of the court or of the Charity Commission, make the disposition in accordance with such provisions of section 36(2) to (8) of that Act as are applicable.'

Parochial Church Councils (Powers) Measure 1956 (No 3)

38

In section 6(5) of the Parochial Church Councils (Powers) Measure 1956 (consents required for transactions relating to certain property) for 'Charity Commissioners' substitute 'Charity Commission'.

Recreational Charities Act 1958 (c 17)

39

In section 6 of the Recreational Charities Act 1958 (short title and extent) for subsection (2) substitute—

'(2) Section 1 of this Act, as amended by section 5 of the Charities Act 2006, has the same effect in relation to the law of Scotland or Northern Ireland as section 5 of that Act has by virtue of section 80(3) to (6) of that Act.

(3) Sections 1 and 2 of this Act, as in force before the commencement of section 5 of that Act, continue to have effect in relation to the law of Scotland or Northern Ireland so far as they affect the construction of any references to charities or charitable purposes which—

(a) are to be construed in accordance with the law of England and Wales, but
(b) are not contained in enactments relating to matters of the kind mentioned in section 80(4) or (6) of that Act.'

Church Funds Investment Measure 1958 (No 1)

40

Section 5 of the Church Funds Investment Measure 1958 (jurisdiction of Charity Commissioners) is omitted.

Incumbents and Churchwardens (Trusts) Measure 1964 (No 2)

41

The Incumbents and Churchwardens (Trusts) Measure 1964 has effect subject to the following amendments.

42

In section 2(3) (property to which Measure applies) for 'Charity Commissioners' substitute 'Charity Commission'.

43

In section 3(6) (vesting of property in diocesan authority: saving) for 'Charity Commissioners' substitute 'Charity Commission'.

44

In section 5 (provisions as to property vested in the diocesan authority) for 'Charity Commissioners' substitute 'Charity Commission'.

45

(1) The Schedule (procedure where diocesan authority is of the opinion that Measure applies to an interest) is amended as follows.

(2) In paragraph 2 for 'Charity Commissioners' substitute 'Charity Commission'.

(3) In paragraph 3—

(a) for 'Charity Commissioners' substitute 'Charity Commission',
(b) for 'they think' (in both places) substitute 'it thinks', and
(c) for 'the Commissioners' substitute 'the Commission'.

(4) In paragraph 5—

(a) for 'Charity Commissioners have' substitute 'Charity Commission has', and
(b) for 'they' substitute 'it'.

Faculty Jurisdiction Measure 1964 (No 5)

46

In section 4(2) of the Faculty Jurisdiction Measure 1964 (sale of books in parochial libraries under a faculty) for 'Charity Commissioners' substitute 'Charity Commission'.

Industrial and Provident Societies Act 1965 (c 12)

47

In section 7D(4) of the Industrial and Provident Societies Act 1965 (application of sections 7A and 7B to charitable societies) for 'Charity Commissioners' substitute 'Charity Commission'.

Clergy Pensions (Amendment) Measure 1967 (No 1)

48

In section 4(5) of the Clergy Pensions (Amendment) Measure 1967 (amendments of powers of Board relating to provision of residences) for 'Charity Commissioners' and 'said Commissioners' substitute 'Charity Commission'.

Ministry of Housing and Local Government Provisional Order Confirmation (Greater London Parks and Open Spaces) Act 1967 (c xxix)

49

In article 11(3) of the order set out in the Schedule to the Ministry of Housing and Local Government Provisional Order Confirmation (Greater London Parks and Open Spaces) Act 1967 (exercise of powers under articles 7 to 10 of the order) for 'Charity Commissioners' substitute 'Charity Commission'.

Redundant Churches and other Religious Buildings Act 1969 (c 22)

50

The Redundant Churches and other Religious Buildings Act 1969 has effect subject to the following amendments.

51

(1) Section 4 (transfer of certain redundant places of worship) is amended as follows.

(2) In subsections (6), (7) and (8) for 'Charity Commissioners' substitute 'Charity Commission'.

(3) In subsection (6) for 'Commissioners'' substitute 'Commission's'.

(4) In subsection (8) for 'they have' substitute 'it has'.

(5) After subsection (8) insert—

'(8A) Schedule 1C to the Charities Act 1993 shall apply in relation to an order made by virtue of subsection (8) above as it applies in relation to an order made under section 16(1) of that Act.'

52

In section 7(2) (saving) for 'Charity Commissioners' (in both places) substitute 'Charity Commission'.

Children and Young Persons Act 1969 (c 54)

53

In Schedule 3 to the Children and Young Persons Act 1969 (approved schools and other institutions), in paragraph 6(3), for 'Charity Commissioners' substitute 'Charity Commission'.

Synodical Government Measure 1969 (No 2)

54

(1) Schedule 3 to the Synodical Government Measure 1969 (which sets out the Church Representation Rules) is amended as follows.

(2) In Rule 46A(a)—

(a) for 'Charity Commissioners' substitute 'Charity Commission', and
(b) for 'them' substitute 'it'.

(3) In Section 4 of Appendix I to those Rules (which sets out certain forms), in Note 3—

(a) for 'Charity Commissioners' substitute 'Charity Commission', and
(b) for 'them' substitute 'it'.

(4) In Section 6 of that Appendix, in the Note—

(a) for 'Charity Commissioners' substitute 'Charity Commission', and
(b) for 'them' substitute 'it'.

(5) In Appendix II to those Rules (general provisions relating to parochial church councils), in paragraph 16, for 'Charity Commissioners' substitute 'Charity Commission'.

Local Government Act 1972 (c 70)

55

In section 131(3) of the Local Government Act 1972 (savings in relation to charity land) for 'Charity Commissioners' substitute 'Charity Commission'.

Consumer Credit Act 1974 (c 39)

56

In section 16 of the Consumer Credit Act 1974 (exempt agreements), in the table in subsection (3A) and in subsections (8) and (9), for 'Charity Commissioners' substitute 'Charity Commission'.

Sex Discrimination Act 1975 (c 65)

57

In section 21A of the Sex Discrimination Act 1975 (public authorities) in paragraph 14 in the Table of Exceptions in subsection (9), for 'Charity Commissioners for England and Wales' substitute 'Charity Commission'.

Endowments and Glebe Measure 1976 (No 4)

58

The Endowments and Glebe Measure 1976 has effect subject to the following amendments.

59

In section 11(2) (extinguishment of certain trusts) for 'the Charity Commissioners' substitute 'the Charity Commission or in accordance with such provisions of section 36(2) to (8) of the Charities Act 1993 as are applicable'.

60

In section 18(2) (means by which land may become diocesan) for 'Charity Commissioners' substitute 'Charity Commission'.

Interpretation Act 1978 (c 30)

61

In Schedule 1 to the Interpretation Act 1978 (words and expressions defined) for the definition of 'Charity Commissioners' substitute—

"Charity Commission' means the Charity Commission for England and Wales established by section 1A of the Charities Act 1993.'

Dioceses Measure 1978 (No 1)

62

The Dioceses Measure 1978 has effect subject to the following amendments.

63

In section 5(1) (preparation of draft scheme: meaning of 'interested parties'), in paragraph (e), for 'the Charity Commissioners' substitute 'the Charity Commission'.

64

In section 19(4) (schemes with respect to discharge of functions of diocesan bodies corporate, etc) for 'Charity Commissioners' substitute 'Charity Commission'.

Disused Burial Grounds (Amendment) Act 1981 (c 18)

65

In section 6 of the Disused Burial Grounds (Amendment) Act 1981 (saving for Charity Commission) for 'Charity Commissioners' substitute 'Charity Commission'.

Local Government (Miscellaneous Provisions) Act 1982 (c 30)

66

In Schedule 4 to the Local Government (Miscellaneous Provisions) Act 1982 (street trading) for paragraph 1(2)(j) substitute—

'(j) conducting a public charitable collection that—
  (i) is conducted in accordance with section 48 or 49 of the Charities Act 2006, or
  (ii) is an exempt collection by virtue of section 50 of that Act.'

Administration of Justice Act 1982 (c 53)

67

In section 41(1) of the Administration of Justice Act 1982 (transfer of funds in court to official custodian for charities and Church Commissioners) for 'Charity Commissioners' substitute 'Charity Commission'.

Pastoral Measure 1983 (No 1)

68

The Pastoral Measure 1983 has effect subject to the following amendments.

69

In section 55(1) (schemes under the Charities Act 1993 for redundant chapels belonging to charities) for 'Charity Commissioners' substitute 'Charity Commission'.

70

In section 63(4) (trusts for the repair etc of redundant buildings and contents) for 'the Charity Commissioners given under the hand of an Assistant Commissioner' substitute 'the Charity Commission'.

71

In section 76(1) (grant of land for new churches etc and vesting of certain churches) for 'Charity Commissioners' substitute 'Charity Commission'.

72

In Schedule 3, in paragraph 11(1), (2), (6) and (7), for 'Charity Commissioners' substitute 'Charity Commission'.

Rates Act 1984 (c 33)

73

In section 3(9) of the Rates Act 1984 (expenditure levels) for ', or excepted from registration, under section 3 of the Charities Act 1993' substitute 'in accordance with section 3A of the Charities Act 1993 or not required to be registered (by virtue of subsection (2) of that section)'.

Companies Act 1985 (c 6)

74

The Companies Act 1985 has effect subject to the following amendments.

75

(1) Section 380 (registration of resolutions) is amended as follows.

(2) In subsection (4), at the beginning insert 'Except as mentioned in subsection (4ZB),'.

(3) After subsection (4ZA) insert—

'(4ZB) Paragraphs (a) and (c) of subsection (4) do not apply to the resolutions of a charitable company mentioned in paragraphs (a) and (b) respectively of section 69G(6) of the Charities Act 1993.'

76

In Schedule 15D (permitted disclosures of information), in paragraph 21, for 'Charity Commissioners to exercise their' substitute 'Charity Commission to exercise its'.

Housing Act 1985 (c 68)

77

(1) Section 6A of the Housing Act 1985 (definition of 'Relevant Authority') is amended as follows.

(2) In subsection (2) for 'Charity Commissioners' substitute 'Charity Commission'.

(3) In subsection (5)—

(a) for 'under section 3' substitute 'in accordance with section 3A', and
(b) omit the words from 'and is not' onwards.

Housing Associations Act 1985 (c 69)

78

In section 10(1) of the Housing Associations Act 1985 (dispositions excepted from section 9 of that Act) for 'Charity Commissioners' (in both places) substitute 'Charity Commission'.

Agricultural Holdings Act 1986 (c 5)

79

In section 86(4) of the Agricultural Holdings Act 1986 (power of landlord to obtain charge on holding) for 'Charity Commissioners' substitute 'Charity Commission'.

Coal Industry Act 1987 (c 3)

80

(1) Section 5 of the Coal Industry Act 1987 (coal industry trusts) is amended as follows.

(2) In subsection (1)—

(a) for 'Charity Commissioners' (in the first place) substitute 'Charity Commission ('the Commission')',
(b) for 'to them' substitute 'to the Commission',
(c) for 'Charity Commissioners' (in the second place) substitute 'Commission', and
(d) for 'they consider' substitute 'the Commission considers'.

(3) In subsection (2) for 'Charity Commissioners consider' (in both places) substitute 'Commission considers'.

(4) In subsections (4) and (6) for 'Charity Commissioners' substitute 'Commission'.

(5) In subsection (7)—

(a) for 'Charity Commissioners' substitute 'Commission',
(b) for 'their powers' substitute 'its powers',
(c) for 'they consider' substitute 'it considers', and
(d) for 'the Charities Act 1960' substitute 'the Charities Act 1993'.

(6) In subsection (8)—

(a) for '16(3), (9), (11) to (14)' substitute '16(3) and (9)',
(b) for 'and 20' substitute ', 20 and 20A',
(c) for 'Charity Commissioners' substitute 'Commission',
(d) for 'their powers' substitute 'its powers', and
(e) for '91 and 92' substitute 'and 91'.

(7) In subsection (8A)—

(a) for 'Commissioners' (in both places) substitute 'Commission',
(b) for 'they were proceeding' substitute 'the Commission was proceeding', and
(c) for 'to them' substitute 'to it'.

(8) After subsection (8A) insert—

'(8B) Schedule 1C to the Charities Act 1993 shall apply in relation to an order made under this section as it applies in relation to an order made under section 16(1) of that Act.'

(9) In subsection (9) for 'Charity Commissioners' substitute 'Commission'.

(10) In subsection (10)(b) for 'Charity Commissioners' substitute 'Commission'.

Reverter of Sites Act 1987 (c 15)

81

The Reverter of Sites Act 1987 has effect subject to the following amendments.

82

(1) Section 2 (Charity Commissioners' schemes) is amended as follows.

(2) In subsection (1) for 'Charity Commissioners' substitute 'Charity Commission'.

(3) For subsection (3) substitute—

'(3) The charitable purposes specified in an order made under this section on an application with respect to any trust shall be such as the Charity Commission consider appropriate, having regard to the matters set out in subsection (3A).

(3A) The matters are—

(a) the desirability of securing that the property is held for charitable purposes ('the new purposes') which are close to the purposes, whether charitable or not, for which the trustees held the relevant land before the cesser of use in consequence of which the trust arose ('the former purposes); and
(b) the need for the new purposes to be capable of having a significant social or economic effect.

(3B) In determining the character of the former purposes, the Commission may, if they think it appropriate to do so, give greater weight to the persons or locality benefited by those purposes than to the nature of the benefit.'

(4) In subsection (5)—

(a) for 'Charity Commissioners' substitute 'Charity Commission',
(b) in paragraph (c), for 'Commissioners'' and 'them' substitute 'Commission's' and 'it', and
(c) in paragraph (d), for 'Commissioners have' substitute 'Commission has'.

(5) In subsection (7) for 'Charity Commissioners' substitute 'Charity Commission'.

(6) In subsection (8)—

(a) for 'Commissioners'' substitute 'Commission's',
(b) for 'they think' substitute 'it thinks', and
(c) for 'Commissioners decide' substitute 'Commission decides'.

(7) In the sidenote, for 'Charity Commissioners'' substitute 'Charity Commission's'.

83

(1) Section 4 (provisions supplemental to sections 2 and 3) is amended as follows.

(2) In subsection (1)—

(a) for 'Charity Commissioners think' substitute 'Charity Commission thinks';
(b) for 'Commissioners'' substitute 'Commission's'; and
(c) for 'the Commissioners think' substitute 'the Commission thinks'.

(3) For subsections (2) and (3) substitute—

'(2) Schedule 1C to the Charities Act 1993 shall apply in relation to an order made under section 2 above as it applies in relation to an order made under section 16(1) of that Act, except that the persons who may bring an appeal against an order made under section 2 above are—

(a) the Attorney General;
(b) the trustees of the trust established under the order;
(c) a beneficiary of, or the trustees of, the trust in respect of which the application for the order had been made;
(d) any person interested in the purposes for which the last-mentioned trustees or any of their predecessors held the relevant land before the cesser of use in consequence of which the trust arose under section 1 above;
(e) any two or more inhabitants of the locality where that land is situated;
(f) any other person who is or may be affected by the order.'

(4) In subsection (4)—

(a) for 'Sections 89, 91 and 92' substitute 'Sections 89 and 91', and
(b) omit 'and appeals' and (in both places) ', and to appeals against,'.

84

In section 5(3) (orders under section 554 of the Education Act 1996)—

(a) for 'Charity Commissioners' (in both places) substitute 'Charity Commission';
(b) for 'the Commissioners' substitute 'the Commission'; and
(c) for 'them' substitute 'it'.

Education Reform Act 1988 (c 40)

85

For section 125A of the Education Reform Act 1988 substitute—

'**125A Charitable status of a higher education corporation**

A higher education corporation shall be a charity within the meaning of the Charities Act 1993 (and in accordance with Schedule 2 to that Act is an exempt charity for the purposes of that Act).'

Courts and Legal Services Act 1990 (c 41)

86

In Schedule 11 to the Courts and Legal Services Act 1990 (judges etc barred from legal practice) for the entry beginning 'Charity Commissioner' substitute 'Member of the Charity Commission appointed as provided in Schedule 1A to the Charities Act 1993'.

London Local Authorities Act 1991 (c xiii)

87

In section 4 of the London Local Authorities Act 1991 (interpretation of Part 2), in paragraph (d) of the definition of 'establishment for special treatment', for the words from 'under section 3' to 'that section' substitute 'in accordance with section 3A of the Charities Act 1993 or is not required to be registered (by virtue of subsection (2) of that section)'.

Further and Higher Education Act 1992 (c 13)

88

For section 22A of the Further and Higher Education Act 1992 substitute—

'**22A Charitable status of a further education corporation**

A further education corporation shall be a charity within the meaning of the Charities Act 1993 (and in accordance with Schedule 2 to that Act is an exempt charity for the purposes of that Act).'

Charities Act 1992 (c 41)

89

The 1992 Act has effect subject to the following amendments.

90

(1) Section 58 (interpretation of Part 2) is amended as follows.

(2) In subsection (1) after the definition of 'institution' insert—

"the Minister' means the Minister for the Cabinet Office;'.

(3) In subsection (2)—

(a) in paragraph (c) for 'to be treated as a promoter of such a collection by virtue of section 65(3)' substitute 'a promoter of such a collection as defined in section 47(1) of the Charities Act 2006', and
(b) for 'Part III of this Act' substitute 'Chapter 1 of Part 3 of the Charities Act 2006'.

(4) In subsection (4) for 'whether or not the purposes are charitable within the meaning of any rule of law' substitute 'as defined by section 2(1) of the Charities Act 2006'.

91

Omit Part 3 (public charitable collections).

92

In section 76(1) (service of documents) omit paragraph (c) and the 'and' preceding it.

93

(1) Section 77 (regulations and orders) is amended as follows.

(2) In subsection (1)(b) for 'subsection (2)' substitute 'subsections (2) and (2A)'.

(3) After subsection (2) insert—

'(2A) Subsection (1)(b) does not apply to regulations under section 64A, and no such regulations may be made unless a draft of the statutory instrument containing the regulations has been laid before, and approved by a resolution of, each House of Parliament.'

(4) In subsection (4)—

(a) after '64' insert 'or 64A'; and
(b) omit 'or 73'.

94

In section 79 (short title, commencement and extent) omit—

(a) in subsection (6), the words '(subject to subsection (7))', and
(b) subsection (7).

95

In Schedule 7 (repeals) omit the entry relating to the Police, Factories, &c. (Miscellaneous Provisions) Act 1916 (c 31).

Charities Act 1993 (c 10)

96

The 1993 Act has effect subject to the following amendments.

97

In the heading for Part 1, for 'CHARITY COMMISSIONERS' substitute 'CHARITY COMMISSION'.

98

(1) Section 2 (official custodian for charities) is amended as follows.

(2) For subsection (2) substitute—

'(2) Such individual as the Commission may from time to time designate shall be the official custodian.'

(3) In subsection (3), for 'Commissioners' (in both places) substitute 'Commission'.

(4) In subsection (4)—

(a) for 'officer of the Commissioners' substitute 'member of the staff of the Commission', and
(b) for 'by them' substitute 'by it'.

(5) In subsection (7) omit the words from ', and the report' onwards.

(6) After subsection (7) add—

'(8) The Comptroller and Auditor General shall send to the Commission a copy of the accounts as certified by him together with his report on them.

(9) The Commission shall publish and lay before Parliament a copy of the documents sent to it under subsection (8) above.'

99

(1) Section 4 (claims and objections to registration) is amended as follows.

(2) In subsection (2)—

(a) for 'the Commissioners' substitute 'the Commission', and
(b) for 'to them' substitute 'to the Commission'.

(3) Omit subsection (3).

(4) In subsection (4)—

(a) for 'High Court' substitute 'Tribunal',
(b) for 'the Commissioners' (in the first and third places) substitute 'the Commission', and
(c) for 'the Commissioners are' substitute 'the Commission is'.

(5) In subsection (5)—

(a) for 'subsection (3) above' substitute 'Schedule 1C to this Act',
(b) for 'the Commissioners' (in both places) substitute 'the Commission', and
(c) omit ', whether given on such an appeal or not'.

100

(1) Section 6 (power to require charity's name to be changed) is amended as follows.

(2) For 'Commissioners' (in each place including the sidenote) substitute 'Commission'.

(3) In subsection (5) for 'section 3(7)(b) above' substitute 'section 3B(3)'.

101

For the heading for Part 3 substitute 'INFORMATION POWERS'.

102

(1) Section 8 (power to institute inquiries) is amended as follows.

(2) In subsection (1) for 'The Commissioners' substitute 'The Commission'.

(3) In subsection (2)—

(a) for 'The Commissioners' substitute 'The Commission',

(b) for 'themselves' substitute 'itself', and
(c) for 'to them' substitute 'to the Commission'.

(4) In subsection (3) for 'the Commissioners, or a person appointed by them' substitute 'the Commission, or a person appointed by the Commission'.

(5) In subsection (5) for 'The Commissioners' substitute 'The Commission'.

(6) In subsection (6)—

(a) for 'the Commissioners' substitute 'the Commission',
(b) for 'they think' substitute 'the Commission thinks',
(c) for 'their opinion' substitute 'the Commission's opinion', and
(d) for 'to them' substitute 'to the Commission'.

(7) In subsection (7) for 'the Commissioners' substitute 'the Commission'.

103

(1) Section 9 (power to call for documents and search records) is amended as follows.

(2) In subsection (1)—

(a) for 'The Commissioners' substitute 'The Commission',
(b) for 'furnish them' (in both places) substitute 'furnish the Commission',
(c) for 'their functions' (in both places) substitute 'the Commission's functions', and
(d) for 'them for their' substitute 'the Commission for its'.

(3) In subsection (2)—

(a) for 'officer of the Commissioners, if so authorised by them' substitute 'member of the staff of the Commission, if so authorised by it', and
(b) for 'the Commissioners' (in the second place) substitute 'the Commission'.

(4) In subsection (3)—

(a) for 'The Commissioners' substitute 'The Commission',
(b) for 'to them' (in the first place) substitute 'to it',
(c) for 'to them' (in the second place) substitute 'to the Commission',
(d) for 'their inspection' substitute 'it to inspect', and
(e) for 'the Commissioners' substitute 'the Commission'.

(5) After subsection (5) add—

'(6) In subsection (2) the reference to a member of the staff of the Commission includes the official custodian even if he is not a member of the staff of the Commission.'

104

For section 10 substitute—

'10 Disclosure of information to Commission

(1) Any relevant public authority may disclose information to the Commission if the disclosure is made for the purpose of enabling or assisting the Commission to discharge any of its functions.

(2) But Revenue and Customs information may be disclosed under subsection (1) only if it relates to an institution, undertaking or body falling within one (or more) of the following paragraphs—

(a) a charity;
(b) an institution which is established for charitable, benevolent or philanthropic purposes;

(c) an institution by or in respect of which a claim for exemption has at any time been made under section 505(1) of the Income and Corporation Taxes Act 1988;
(d) a subsidiary undertaking of a charity;
(e) a body entered in the Scottish Charity Register which is managed or controlled wholly or mainly in or from England or Wales.

(3) In subsection (2)(d) above 'subsidiary undertaking of a charity' means an undertaking (as defined by section 259(1) of the Companies Act 1985) in relation to which—

(a) a charity is (or is to be treated as) a parent undertaking in accordance with the provisions of section 258 of, and Schedule 10A to, the Companies Act 1985, or
(b) two or more charities would, if they were a single charity, be (or be treated as) a parent undertaking in accordance with those provisions.

(4) For the purposes of the references to a parent undertaking—

(a) in subsection (3) above, and
(b) in section 258 of, and Schedule 10A to, the Companies Act 1985 as they apply for the purposes of that subsection,

'undertaking' includes a charity which is not an undertaking as defined by section 259(1) of that Act.

10A Disclosure of information by Commission

(1) Subject to subsections (2) and (3) below, the Commission may disclose to any relevant public authority any information received by the Commission in connection with any of the Commission's functions—

(a) if the disclosure is made for the purpose of enabling or assisting the relevant public authority to discharge any of its functions, or
(b) if the information so disclosed is otherwise relevant to the discharge of any of the functions of the relevant public authority.

(2) In the case of information disclosed to the Commission under section 10(1) above, the Commission's power to disclose the information under subsection (1) above is exercisable subject to any express restriction subject to which the information was disclosed to the Commission.

(3) Subsection (2) above does not apply in relation to Revenue and Customs information disclosed to the Commission under section 10(1) above; but any such information may not be further disclosed (whether under subsection (1) above or otherwise) except with the consent of the Commissioners for Her Majesty's Revenue and Customs.

(4) Any responsible person who discloses information in contravention of subsection (3) above is guilty of an offence and liable—

(a) on summary conviction, to imprisonment for a term not exceeding 12 months or to a fine not exceeding the statutory maximum, or both;
(b) on conviction on indictment, to imprisonment for a term not exceeding two years or to a fine, or both.

(5) It is a defence for a responsible person charged with an offence under subsection (4) above of disclosing information to prove that he reasonably believed—

(a) that the disclosure was lawful, or
(b) that the information had already and lawfully been made available to the public.

(6) In the application of this section to Scotland or Northern Ireland, the reference to 12 months in subsection (4) is to be read as a reference to 6 months.

(7) In this section 'responsible person' means a person who is or was—

(a) a member of the Commission,
(b) a member of the staff of the Commission,

(c) a person acting on behalf of the Commission or a member of the staff of the Commission, or
(d) a member of a committee established by the Commission.

10B Disclosure to and by principal regulators of exempt charities

(1) Sections 10 and 10A above apply with the modifications in subsections (2) to (4) below in relation to the disclosure of information to or by the principal regulator of an exempt charity.

(2) References in those sections to the Commission or to any of its functions are to be read as references to the principal regulator of an exempt charity or to any of the functions of that body or person as principal regulator in relation to the charity.

(3) Section 10 above has effect as if for subsections (2) and (3) there were substituted—

'(2) But Revenue and Customs information may be disclosed under subsection (1) only if it relates to—

(a) the exempt charity in relation to which the principal regulator has functions as such, or
(b) a subsidiary undertaking of the exempt charity.

(3) In subsection (2)(b) above 'subsidiary undertaking of the exempt charity' means an undertaking (as defined by section 259(1) of the Companies Act 1985) in relation to which—

(a) the exempt charity is (or is to be treated as) a parent undertaking in accordance with the provisions of section 258 of, and Schedule 10A to, the Companies Act 1985, or
(b) the exempt charity and one or more other charities would, if they were a single charity, be (or be treated as) a parent undertaking in accordance with those provisions.'

(4) Section 10A above has effect as if for the definition of 'responsible person' in subsection (7) there were substituted a definition specified by regulations under section 13(4)(b) of the Charities Act 2006 (regulations prescribing principal regulators).

(5) Regulations under section 13(4)(b) of that Act may also make such amendments or other modifications of any enactment as the Secretary of State considers appropriate for securing that any disclosure provisions that would otherwise apply in relation to the principal regulator of an exempt charity do not apply in relation to that body or person in its or his capacity as principal regulator.

(6) In subsection (5) above 'disclosure provisions' means provisions having effect for authorising, or otherwise in connection with, the disclosure of information by or to the principal regulator concerned.

10C Disclosure of information: supplementary

(1) In sections 10 and 10A above 'relevant public authority' means—

(a) any government department (including a Northern Ireland department),
(b) any local authority,
(c) any constable, and
(d) any other body or person discharging functions of a public nature (including a body or person discharging regulatory functions in relation to any description of activities).

(2) In section 10A above 'relevant public authority' also includes any body or person within subsection (1)(d) above in a country or territory outside the United Kingdom.

(3) In sections 10 to 10B above and this section—

'enactment' has the same meaning as in the Charities Act 2006;
'Revenue and Customs information' means information held as mentioned in section 18(1) of the Commissioners for Revenue and Customs Act 2005.

(4) Nothing in sections 10 and 10A above (or in those sections as applied by section 10B(1) to (4) above) authorises the making of a disclosure which—

(a) contravenes the Data Protection Act 1998, or
(b) is prohibited by Part 1 of the Regulation of Investigatory Powers Act 2000.'

105

(1) Section 11 (supply of false or misleading information) is amended as follows.

(2) For 'Commissioners' (in each place including the sidenote) substitute 'Commission'.

(3) In subsection (1)(b) for 'their functions' substitute 'its functions'.

106

In the heading for Part 4 for 'AND COMMISSIONERS' substitute 'AND COMMISSION'.

107

(1) Section 14 (application cy-près of gifts of donors unknown or disclaiming) is amended as follows.

(2) In subsection (6) for 'the Commissioners so direct' substitute 'the Commission so directs'.

(3) In subsection (8) for 'the Commissioners' substitute 'the Commission'.

(4) In subsection (9)—

(a) for 'the Commissioners' (in both places) substitute 'the Commission', and
(b) for 'they think fit' substitute 'it thinks fit'.

108

In the heading preceding section 16 for '*Powers of Commissioners*' substitute '*Powers of Commission*'.

109

(1) Section 16 (concurrent jurisdiction of Commissioners with High Court) is amended as follows.

(2) In subsection (1) for 'the Commissioners' substitute 'the Commission'.

(3) In subsection (2)—

(a) for 'the Commissioners for them' substitute 'the Commission for it', and
(b) for 'the Commissioners' (in the second place) substitute 'the Commission'.

(4) In subsection (3) for 'The Commissioners' substitute 'The Commission'.

(5) In subsection (4) for 'the Commissioners shall not exercise their' substitute 'the Commission shall not exercise its'.

(6) In subsection (5)—

(a) for 'income from all sources does not in aggregate' substitute 'gross income does not', and
(b) for 'the Commissioners may exercise their' substitute 'the Commission may exercise its'.

(7) In subsection (6)—

(a) for 'the Commissioners are' substitute 'the Commission is',
(b) for 'the Commissioners have' substitute 'the Commission has',

(c) for 'the Commissioners' (in the third and fourth places) substitute 'the Commission', and
(d) for 'they act' substitute 'it acts'.

(8) In subsection (7)—

(a) for 'the Commissioners' (in the first and third places) substitute 'the Commission', and
(b) for 'the Commissioners consider' substitute 'the Commission considers'.

(9) In subsection (8)—

(a) for 'The Commissioners' substitute 'The Commission', and
(b) for 'their jurisdiction' substitute 'its jurisdiction'.

(10) In subsection (9) for 'the Commissioners shall give notice of their' substitute 'the Commission shall give notice of its'.

(11) In subsection (10)—

(a) for 'The Commissioners shall not exercise their' substitute 'The Commission shall not exercise its', and
(b) for 'the Commissioners' (in the second place) substitute 'the Commission'.

(12) Omit subsections (11) to (14).

(13) In subsection (15)(b) for 'the Commissioners may exercise their' substitute 'the Commission may exercise its'.

110

(1) Section 17 (further power to make schemes or alter application of charitable property) is amended as follows.

(2) In subsection (1)—

(a) for 'the Commissioners' (in both places) substitute 'the Commission', and
(b) for 'by them' substitute 'by the Commission'.

(3) In subsection (2) for 'the Commissioners' substitute 'the Commission'.

(4) In subsection (4) for 'the Commissioners' (in both places) substitute 'the Commission'.

(5) In subsection (6)—

(a) for 'Commissioners' (in both places) substitute 'Commission',
(b) for 'if they were' substitute 'if the Commission was',
(c) for 'they act' substitute 'it acts', and
(d) for 'to them' substitute 'to it'.

(6) In subsection (7) for 'the Commissioners' substitute 'the Commission'.

(7) In subsection (8)—

(a) for 'the Commissioners are' substitute 'the Commission is', and
(b) for 'the Commissioners' (in the second place) substitute 'the Commission'.

111

(1) Section 18 (power to act for protection of charities) is amended as follows.

(2) In subsection (1)—

(a) for 'after they have' substitute 'after it has',
(b) for 'the Commissioners are' substitute 'the Commission is',
(c) for 'the Commissioners may of their' substitute 'the Commission may of its',
(d) for 'as they consider' substitute 'as it considers',

(e) for 'the Commissioners' (in the third, fourth and fifth places) substitute 'the Commission', and
(f) for 'a receiver' substitute 'an interim manager, who shall act as receiver'.

(3) In subsection (2)—

(a) for 'they have' substitute 'it has',
(b) for 'the Commissioners are' substitute 'the Commission is', and
(c) for 'the Commissioners may of their' substitute 'the Commission may of its'.

(4) In subsection (4)—

(a) for 'The Commissioners' substitute 'The Commission', and
(b) for 'their own motion' substitute 'its own motion'.

(5) In subsection (5)—

(a) for 'The Commissioners may by order made of their' substitute 'The Commission may by order made of its',
(b) for 'removed by them' substitute 'removed by the Commission', and
(c) for 'the Commissioners are of' (in both places) substitute 'the Commission is of'.

(6) In subsection (6)—

(a) for 'the Commissioners' (in both places) substitute 'the Commission',
(b) for 'their own motion' substitute 'its own motion', and
(c) for 'by them' substitute 'by it'.

(7) Omit subsections (8) to (10).

(8) In subsection (11) for 'the Commissioners' substitute 'the Commission'.

(9) In subsection (12)—

(a) for 'the Commissioners' substitute 'the Commission', and
(b) for 'their intention' substitute 'its intention'.

(10) In subsection (13)—

(a) for 'The Commissioners' substitute 'The Commission',
(b) for 'they think fit' substitute 'it thinks fit',
(c) for 'by them' substitute 'by it',
(d) for 'to them' substitute 'to the Commission', and
(e) for 'they shall' substitute 'the Commission shall'.

112

(1) Section 19 (supplementary provisions relating to receiver and manager appointed for a charity) is amended as follows.

(2) For subsection (1) substitute—

'(1) The Commission may under section 18(1)(vii) above appoint to be interim manager in respect of a charity such person (other than a member of its staff) as it thinks fit.'

(3) In subsection (2)—

(a) for 'the Commissioners' (in both places) substitute 'the Commission', and
(b) for 'receiver and manager' substitute 'interim manager'.

(4) In subsection (3) for 'receiver and manager' (in both places) substitute 'interim manager'.

(5) In subsection (4)—

(a) for 'receiver and manager' substitute 'interim manager', and
(b) for 'the Commissioners' substitute 'the Commission'.

(6) In subsections (6)(c) and (7) for 'the Commissioners' substitute 'the Commission'.

(7) In the sidenote for 'receiver and manager' substitute 'interim manager'.

113

After section 19B (inserted by section 21 of this Act) insert—

'19C Copy of order under section 18, 18A, 19A or 19B, and Commission's reasons, to be sent to charity

(1) Where the Commission makes an order under section 18, 18A, 19A or 19B, it must send the documents mentioned in subsection (2) below—

(a) to the charity concerned (if a body corporate), or
(b) (if not) to each of the charity trustees.

(2) The documents are—

(a) a copy of the order, and
(b) a statement of the Commission's reasons for making it.

(3) The documents must be sent to the charity or charity trustees as soon as practicable after the making of the order.

(4) The Commission need not, however, comply with subsection (3) above in relation to the documents, or (as the case may be) the statement of its reasons, if it considers that to do so—

(a) would prejudice any inquiry or investigation, or
(b) would not be in the interests of the charity;

but, once the Commission considers that this is no longer the case, it must send the documents, or (as the case may be) the statement, to the charity or charity trustees as soon as practicable.

(5) Nothing in this section requires any document to be sent to a person who cannot be found or who has no known address in the United Kingdom.

(6) Any documents required to be sent to a person under this section may be sent to, or otherwise served on, that person in the same way as an order made by the Commission under this Act could be served on him in accordance with section 91 below.'

114

In section 22(3) (property vested in official custodian) for 'the Commissioners' substitute 'the Commission'.

115

(1) Section 23 (divestment in case of land subject to Reverter of Sites Act 1987 (c 15)) is amended as follows.

(2) In subsection (1)—

(a) for 'the Commissioners' (in both places) substitute 'the Commission',
(b) for 'by them of their own' substitute 'by the Commission of its own', and
(c) for 'appear to them' substitute 'appear to the Commission'.

(3) In subsection (2)—

(a) for 'the Commissioners (of their own motion)' substitute 'the Commission (of its own motion)', and
(b) omit 'or them'.

(4) In subsection (3)—

(a) for 'the Commissioners' (in the first and second places) substitute 'the Commission', and
(b) for 'the Commissioners is or are' substitute 'the Commission is'.

116

In section 24 (schemes to establish common investment funds), in subsections (1) and (2), for 'the Commissioners' substitute 'the Commission'.

117

In section 25(1) (schemes to establish common deposit funds) for 'the Commissioners' substitute 'the Commission'.

118

For the heading preceding section 26 substitute '*Additional powers of Commission*'.

119

In section 26(1) (power to authorise dealings with charity property)—

(a) for 'the Commissioners' substitute 'the Commission', and
(b) for 'they may' substitute 'the Commission may'.

120

(1) Section 27 (power to authorise ex gratia payments) is amended as follows.

(2) In subsection (1) for 'the Commissioners' substitute 'the Commission'.

(3) In subsection (2)—

(a) for 'the Commissioners' (in both places) substitute 'the Commission', and
(b) for 'by them' substitute 'by the Commission'.

(4) In subsection (3)—

(a) for 'the Commissioners for them' substitute 'the Commission for it',
(b) for 'they are not' substitute 'it is not',
(c) for 'they consider' substitute 'the Commission considers',
(d) for 'by them' substitute 'by the Commission', and
(e) for 'they shall' substitute 'the Commission shall'.

(5) In subsection (4)—

(a) for 'to them' substitute 'to the Commission', and
(b) for 'the Commissioners determine' substitute 'the Commission determines'.

121

(1) Section 28 (power to give directions about dormant bank accounts) is amended as follows.

(2) In subsection (1)—

(a) for 'the Commissioners' substitute 'the Commission',
(b) for 'are informed' substitute 'is informed',
(c) for 'are unable' substitute 'is unable', and

(d) for 'they may give' substitute 'it may give'.

(3) In subsection (3)—

(a) for 'Commissioners' (in both places) substitute 'Commission',
(b) for 'they consider' substitute 'it considers',
(c) for 'to them' substitute 'to the Commission', and
(d) for 'they have received' substitute 'it has received'.

(4) In subsection (5)—

(a) for 'the Commissioners have been' substitute 'the Commission has been',
(b) for 'the Commissioners' (in the second and third places) substitute 'the Commission',
(c) for 'they shall revoke' substitute 'it shall revoke', and
(d) for 'by them' substitute 'by it'.

(5) In subsection (7)—

(a) for 'the Commissioners' substitute 'the Commission', and
(b) for 'them to discharge their functions' substitute 'the Commission to discharge its functions'.

(6) In subsection (8)(a) for 'the Commissioners are informed' substitute 'the Commission is informed'.

(7) In subsection (9)—

(a) for 'the Commissioners have' substitute 'the Commission has', and
(b) for 'the Commissioners' (in the second place) substitute 'the Commission'.

122

(1) Section 30 (powers for preservation of charity documents) is amended as follows.

(2) In subsection (1) for 'The Commissioners' substitute 'The Commission'.

(3) In subsection (2) for 'Commissioners' (in each place) substitute 'Commission'.

(4) In subsection (3)—

(a) for 'the Commissioners' (in the first place) substitute 'the Commission',
(b) for 'with them' substitute 'with the Commission',
(c) for 'officer of the Commissioners generally or specially authorised by them' substitute 'member of the staff of the Commission generally or specially authorised by the Commission'.

(5) In subsection (4) for 'the Commissioners' substitute 'the Commission'.

(6) In subsection (5)—

(a) for 'the Commissioners' substitute 'the Commission',
(b) for 'by them' substitute 'by the Commission', and
(c) for 'with them' substitute 'with the Commission'.

123

(1) Section 31 (power to order taxation of solicitor's bill) is amended as follows.

(2) In subsection (1) for 'The Commissioners' substitute 'The Commission'.

(3) In subsection (3) for 'the Commissioners are' substitute 'the Commission is'.

124

(1) Section 32 (proceedings by Commissioners) is amended as follows.

(2) In subsections (1) and (3) for 'the Commissioners' substitute 'the Commission'.

(3) In subsection (5)—

(a) for 'the Commissioners' substitute 'the Commission', and
(b) for 'by them of their own' substitute 'by the Commission of its own'.

(4) In the sidenote, for 'Commissioners' substitute 'Commission'.

125

(1) Section 33 (proceedings by other persons) is amended as follows.

(2) In subsection (2) for 'the Commissioners' substitute 'the Commission'.

(3) In subsection (3)—

(a) for 'The Commissioners' substitute 'The Commission',
(b) for 'their opinion' substitute 'its opinion', and
(c) for 'by them' substitute 'by the Commission'.

(4) In subsections (5) and (6) for 'the Commissioners' substitute 'the Commission'.

(5) In subsection (7)—

(a) for 'the Commissioners' (in both places) substitute 'the Commission', and
(b) for 'they think' substitute 'the Commission thinks'.

126

In section 34 (report of inquiry to be evidence in certain proceedings), in subsections (1) and (2), for 'the Commissioners' substitute 'the Commission'.

127

In section 35(1) (application of certain provisions to trust corporations) for 'the Commissioners' substitute 'the Commission'.

128

(1) Section 36 (restrictions on dispositions) is amended as follows.

(2) In subsection (1)—

(a) for 'sold' substitute 'conveyed, transferred', and
(b) for 'the Commissioners' substitute 'the Commission'.

(3) In subsection (3) after 'subsection (5) below,' insert 'the requirements mentioned in subsection (2)(b) above are that'.

(4) In subsection (5) after 'consideration of a fine),' insert 'the requirements mentioned in subsection (2)(b) above are that'.

(5) In subsection (6)—

(a) for 'sold' substitute 'conveyed, transferred', and
(b) for 'previously' substitute 'before the relevant time'.

(6) After subsection (6) insert—

'(6A) In subsection (6) above 'the relevant time' means—

(a) where the charity trustees enter into an agreement for the sale, or (as the case may be) for the lease or other disposition, the time when they enter into that agreement, and
(b) in any other case, the time of the disposition.'

(7) In subsection (8)—

(a) for 'The Commissioners' substitute 'The Commission',
(b) for 'the Commissioners are satisfied' substitute 'the Commission is satisfied', and
(c) for 'for them' substitute 'for the Commission'.

129

In section 37 (supplementary provisions relating to dispositions), in subsections (2) and (4)—

(a) for 'sold' substitute 'conveyed, transferred', and
(b) for 'the Commissioners' substitute 'the Commission'.

130

In section 38(1) (restrictions on mortgaging) for 'the Commissioners' substitute 'the Commission'.

131

(1) Section 39 (supplementary provisions relating to mortgaging) is amended as follows.

(2) In subsections (2)(a) and (4) for 'the Commissioners' substitute 'the Commission'.

(3) After subsection (4) insert—

'(4A) Where subsection (3D) of section 38 above applies to any mortgage of land held by or in trust for a charity, the charity trustees shall certify in relation to any transaction falling within that subsection that they have obtained and considered such advice as is mentioned in that subsection.

(4B) Where subsection (4A) above has been complied with in relation to any transaction, then, in favour of a person who (whether under the mortgage or afterwards) has acquired or acquires an interest in the land for money or money's worth, it shall be conclusively presumed that the facts were as stated in the certificate.'

132

In section 41(4) (obligation to preserve accounting records) for 'the Commissioners consent' substitute 'the Commission consents'.

133

(1) Section 42 (annual statements of accounts) is amended as follows.

(2) After subsection (2) insert—

'(2A) Such regulations may, however, not impose on the charity trustees of a charity that is a charitable trust created by any person ('the settlor') any requirement to disclose, in any statement of accounts prepared by them under subsection (1)—

(a) the identities of recipients of grants made out of the funds of the charity, or
(b) the amounts of any individual grants so made,

if the disclosure would fall to be made at a time when the settlor or any spouse or civil partner of his was still alive.'

(3) After subsection (7) add—

'(8) Provisions about the preparation of accounts in respect of groups consisting of certain charities and their subsidiary undertakings, and about other matters relating to such groups, are contained in Schedule 5A to this Act (see section 49A below).'

134

(1) Section 43 (annual audit or examination of charity accounts) is amended as follows.

(2) In subsection (4) for 'the Commissioners' (in both places) substitute 'the Commission'.

(3) In subsection (5)—

(a) for 'the Commissioners make' substitute 'the Commission makes', and
(b) for 'the Commissioners' (in the second place) substitute 'the Commission'.

(4) In subsection (6) for 'the Commissioners' (in each place) substitute 'the Commission'.

(5) In subsection (7)—

(a) for 'The Commissioners' substitute 'The Commission', and
(b) for 'they think' substitute 'it thinks'.

135

(1) Section 43A (annual audit or examination of English NHS charity accounts) is amended as follows.

(2) In subsection (2) for 'the criterion set out in subsection (1) of section 43 is met in respect of' substitute 'paragraph (a) or (b) of section 43(1) is satisfied in relation to'.

(3) In subsection (5)—

(a) for 'The Commissioners' substitute 'The Commission', and
(b) for 'they think' substitute 'it thinks'.

136

(1) Section 43B (annual audit or examination of Welsh NHS charity accounts) is amended as follows.

(2) In subsection (2) for 'the criterion set out in subsection (1) of section 43 is met in respect of' substitute 'paragraph (a) or (b) of section 43(1) is satisfied in relation to'.

(3) After subsection (4) add—

'(5) References in this Act to an auditor or an examiner have effect in relation to this section as references to the Auditor General for Wales acting under this section as an auditor or examiner.'

137

(1) Section 44 (supplementary provisions relating to audits) is amended as follows.

(2) In subsection (1)—

(a) in paragraph (b) after 'section 43' insert ', 43A or 43B',
(b) for paragraph (c) substitute—
'(c) with respect to the making of a report—
 (i) by an independent examiner in respect of an examination carried out by him under section 43 above; or

(ii) by an examiner in respect of an examination carried out by him under section 43A or 43B above;'

(c) in each of paragraphs (d) and (e) after 'independent examiner' insert 'or examiner', and

(d) in paragraph (f) for 'the Commissioners' substitute 'the Commission'.

(3) In subsection (2)—

(a) after 'independent examiner' insert 'or examiner',
(b) for 'the Commissioners' (in the first place) substitute 'the Commission', and
(c) for 'the Commissioners think' substitute 'the Commission thinks'.

(4) Omit subsection (3).

138

(1) Section 45 (annual reports) is amended as follows.

(2) In subsection (2)(b) for 'the Commissioners' substitute 'the Commission'.

(3) In subsection (3)—

(a) for the words from 'in any' to 'expenditure' substitute 'a charity's gross income in any financial year',
(b) before 'the annual report' insert 'a copy of', and
(c) for 'the Commissioners' (in both places) substitute 'the Commission'.

(4) In subsection (3A)—

(a) for the words from 'in any' to 'exceeds' substitute 'a charity's gross income in any financial year does not exceed',
(b) before 'the annual report' insert 'a copy of',
(c) for 'the Commissioners so request, be transmitted to them' substitute 'the Commission so requests, be transmitted to it', and
(d) for 'the Commissioners' (in the second place) substitute 'the Commission'.

(5) In subsection (4)—

(a) for 'annual report transmitted to the Commissioners' substitute 'copy of an annual report transmitted to the Commission', and
(b) before 'the statement', and before 'the account and statement', insert 'a copy of'.

(6) In subsection (5) before 'annual report' insert 'copy of an'.

(7) In subsection (6)—

(a) after 'Any' insert 'copy of an',
(b) for 'the Commissioners' (in both places) substitute 'the Commission', and
(c) for 'they think fit' substitute 'it thinks fit'.

(8) In subsection (7) for the words from 'which they have not' onwards substitute 'of which they have not been required to transmit a copy to the Commission.'

(9) In subsection (8) for 'in subsection (3)' substitute 'to subsection (3)'.

139

(1) Section 46 (special provisions as respects accounts etc of excepted charities) is amended as follows.

(2) In subsection (2) for 'the Commissioners consent' substitute 'the Commission consents'.

(3) For subsection (3) substitute—

'(3) Except in accordance with subsections (3A) and (3B) below, nothing in section 43, 44, 44A or 45 applies to any charity which—

(a) falls within section 3A(2)(d) above (whether or not it also falls within section 3A(2)(b) or (c)), and
(b) is not registered.

(3A) Section 44A above applies in accordance with subsections (2A) and (2B) above to a charity mentioned in subsection (3) above which is also an exempt charity.

(3B) Sections 44 and 44A above apply to a charity mentioned in subsection (3) above which is also an English National Health Service charity or a Welsh National Health Service charity (as defined in sections 43A and 43B above).'

(4) In subsection (4) for the words from '(other than' onwards substitute

'which—

(a) falls within section 3A(2)(b) or (c) above but does not fall within section 3A(2)(d), and
(b) is not registered.'

(5) In subsection (5)—

(a) for 'the Commissioners' (in the first place) substitute 'the Commission', and
(b) for 'the Commissioners' request' substitute 'the Commission's request'.

(6) For subsection (7) substitute—

'(7) The following provisions of section 45 above shall apply in relation to any report required to be prepared under subsection (5) above as if it were an annual report required to be prepared under subsection (1) of that section—

(a) subsection (3), with the omission of the words preceding 'a copy of the annual report', and
(b) subsections (4) to (6).'

(7) Omit subsection (8).

140

(1) Section 47 (public inspection of annual reports etc) is amended as follows.

(2) In subsection (1)—

(a) for 'Any annual report or other document kept by the Commissioners' substitute 'Any document kept by the Commission',
(b) for 'the Commissioners so determine' substitute 'the Commission so determines', and
(c) for 'they may' substitute 'it may'.

(3) In subsection (2)(a) after 'accounts' insert 'or (if subsection (4) below applies) of its most recent annual report'.

(4) After subsection (3) add—

'(4) This subsection applies if an annual report has been prepared in respect of any financial year of a charity in pursuance of section 45(1) or 46(5) above.

(5) In subsection (2) above the reference to a charity's most recent annual report is a reference to the annual report prepared in pursuance of section 45(1) or 46(5) in respect of the last financial year of the charity in respect of which an annual report has been so prepared.'

141

(1) Section 48 (annual returns by registered charities) is amended as follows.

(2) In subsection (1) for 'the Commissioners' substitute 'the Commission'.

(3) In subsection (1A) for the words from 'neither' to 'exceeds' substitute 'the charity's gross income does not exceed'.

(4) In subsection (2)—

(a) for 'the Commissioners' substitute 'the Commission', and
(b) for 'to them' substitute 'to the Commission'.

(5) In subsection (3) for 'The Commissioners' substitute 'The Commission'.

142

For section 49 (offences) substitute—

'49 Offences

(1) If any requirement imposed—

(a) by section 45(3) or (3A) above (taken with section 45(3B), (4) and (5), as applicable), or
(b) by section 47(2) or 48(2) above,

is not complied with, each person who immediately before the date for compliance specified in the section in question was a charity trustee of the charity shall be guilty of an offence and liable on summary conviction to the penalty mentioned in subsection (2).

(2) The penalty is—

(a) a fine not exceeding level 4 on the standard scale, and
(b) for continued contravention, a daily default fine not exceeding 10% of level 4 on the standard scale for so long as the person in question remains a charity trustee of the charity.

(3) It is a defence for a person charged with an offence under subsection (1) to prove that he took all reasonable steps for securing that the requirement in question would be complied with in time.'

143

(1) Section 50 (incorporation of trustees of charity) is amended as follows.

(2) In subsection (1)—

(a) for 'the Commissioners' (in the first and third places) substitute 'the Commission',
(b) for 'the Commissioners consider' substitute 'the Commission considers', and
(c) for 'they think fit' substitute 'the Commission thinks fit'.

(3) In subsection (2)—

(a) for 'The Commissioners' substitute 'The Commission',
(b) for 'to them' substitute 'to the Commission', and
(c) for 'under section 3' substitute 'in accordance with section 3A'.

144

(1) Section 52 (applications for incorporation) is amended as follows.

(2) In subsection (1) for 'the Commissioners' (in both places) substitute 'the Commission'.

(3) In subsection (2)—

(a) for 'The Commissioners' substitute 'The Commission', and
(b) for 'they may specify' substitute 'it may specify'.

145

In section 53(1) (nomination of trustees, and filling up vacancies) for 'the Commissioners' substitute 'the Commission'.

146

(1) Section 56 (power of Commissioners to amend certificate of incorporation) is amended as follows.

(2) In subsection (1)—

(a) for 'The Commissioners' substitute 'The Commission', and
(b) for 'of their own motion' substitute 'of the Commission's own motion'.

(3) In subsection (2)—

(a) for 'of their own motion, the Commissioners' substitute 'of its own motion, the Commission',
(b) for 'their proposals' substitute 'its proposals', and
(c) for 'to them' substitute 'to it'.

(4) In subsection (3)—

(a) for 'The Commissioners' substitute 'The Commission',
(b) for 'their proposals' substitute 'its proposals', and
(c) for 'to them' substitute 'to it'.

(5) In subsection (4) for 'The Commissioners' substitute 'The Commission'.

(6) In the sidenote, for 'Commissioners' substitute 'Commission'.

147

(1) Section 57 (records of applications and certificates) is amended as follows.

(2) In subsection (1)—

(a) for 'The Commissioners' substitute 'The Commission', and
(b) for 'to them' substitute 'to it'.

(3) In subsection (2)—

(a) for 'the Commissioners' (in the first place) substitute 'the Commission', and
(b) for 'the secretary of the Commissioners' substitute 'a member of the staff of the Commission'.

148

In section 58 (enforcement of orders and directions) for 'the Commissioners' substitute 'the Commission'.

149

(1) Section 61 (power of Commissioners to dissolve incorporated body) is amended as follows.

(2) In subsection (1)—

(a) for 'the Commissioners are' substitute 'the Commission is',
(b) for 'treated by them' substituted 'treated by the Commission', and
(c) for 'they may of their own motion' substitute 'the Commission may of its own motion'.

(3) In subsection (2)—

(a) for 'the Commissioners are' substitute 'the Commission is', and
(b) for 'the Commissioners' (in the second place) substitute 'the Commission'.

(4) In subsection (4)—

(a) for 'the Commissioners so direct' substitute 'the Commission so directs', and
(b) for 'the Commissioners' (in the second place) substitute 'the Commission'.

(5) Omit subsection (7).

(6) In the sidenote, for 'Commissioners' substitute 'Commission'.

150

(1) Section 63 (winding up) is amended as follows.

(2) In subsection (2)—

(a) for 'the Commissioners' substitute 'the Commission',
(b) for 'they have instituted' substitute 'it has instituted', and
(c) for 'they are satisfied' substitute 'it is satisfied'.

(3) In subsection (3) for 'the Commissioners' (in both places) substitute 'the Commission'.

(4) In subsection (4) for 'the Commissioners' (in both places) substitute 'the Commission'.

(5) In subsection (5)—

(a) for 'the Commissioners' substitute 'the Commission', and
(b) for 'by them of their own motion' substitute 'by the Commission of its own motion'.

151

In section 64(3) (alteration of objects clause) for 'the Commissioner's consent' substitute 'the Commission's consent'.

152

In section 65(4) (invalidity of certain transactions) for 'the Commissioners' substitute 'the Commission'.

153

In section 66 (requirement of consent of Commissioners to certain acts), in subsection (1) and the sidenote, for 'Commissioners' substitute 'Commission'.

154

(1) Section 69 (investigation of accounts) is amended as follows.

(2) In subsection (1)—

(a) for 'the Commissioners' substitute 'the Commission',
(b) for 'they think fit' substitute 'the Commission thinks fit', and
(c) for 'by them' substitute 'by the Commission'.

(3) In subsections (2)(c) and (3) for 'the Commissioners' substitute 'the Commission'.

(4) In subsection (4)—

(a) for 'the Commissioners' (in the first place) substitute 'the Commission', and
(b) for 'the Commissioners think' substitute 'the Commission thinks'.

155

For the heading preceding section 72 substitute '*Charity trustees*'.

156

(1) Section 72 (persons disqualified for being trustees of a charity) is amended as follows.

(2) In subsection (1)(d)(i) after 'by the' insert 'Commission or'.

(3) In subsection (4) for 'The Commissioners' substitute 'The Commission'.

(4) In subsection (6)—

(a) for 'the Commissioners' (in the first place) substitute 'the Commission',
(b) for 'they think fit' substitute 'it thinks fit',
(c) after 'order of' insert 'the Commission or', and
(d) for 'the Commissioners' (in the third place) substitute 'the Commission'.

(5) After subsection (7) add—

'(8) In this section 'the Commissioners' means the Charity Commissioners for England and Wales.'

157

In section 73(4) (person acting as charity trustee while disqualified)—

(a) for 'the Commissioners are' substitute 'the Commission is',
(b) for 'they may by order' substitute 'the Commission may by order', and
(c) for '(as determined by them)' substitute '(as determined by the Commission)'.

158

For the heading preceding section 74 substitute '*Miscellaneous powers of charities*'.

159

In section 76(2) (local authority's index of local charities)—

(a) for 'the Commissioners' (in both places) substitute 'the Commission', and
(b) for 'they will' substitute 'it will'.

160

In section 77(1) (reviews of local charities by local authority) for 'the Commissioners' substitute 'the Commission'.

161

(1) Section 79 (parochial charities) is amended as follows.

(2) In subsection (1) for 'the Commissioners' substitute 'the Commission'.

(3) In subsection (2) for 'the Commissioners' (in both places) substitute 'the Commission'.

162

(1) Section 80 (supervision by Commissioners of certain Scottish charities) is amended as follows.

(2) In subsection (1) for paragraph (c) and the 'and' preceding it substitute—

'(c) sections 19 to 19C, and
(d) section 31A,'.

(3) In subsection (2)—

(a) for 'the Commissioners are satisfied' substitute 'the Commission is satisfied',
(b) for 'they may make' substitute 'it may make', and
(c) for 'their approval' substitute 'the Commission's approval'.

(4) In subsection (3)—

(a) for 'the Commissioners' substitute 'the Commission',
(b) for 'their being' substitute 'the Commission being', and
(c) for 'supplied to them' substitute 'supplied to it'.

(5) In subsection (4)—

(a) for 'the Commissioners are satisfied' substitute 'the Commission is satisfied',
(b) for 'supplied to them' substitute 'supplied to it', and
(c) for 'the Commissioners' (in the second place) substitute 'the Commission'.

(6) In subsection (5)—

(a) for 'Commissioners' (in each place) substitute 'Commission',
(b) for 'they consider' substitute 'it considers', and
(c) for 'they have received' substitute 'it has received'.

(7) In the sidenote, for 'Commissioners' substitute 'Commission'.

163

(1) Section 84 (supply by Commissioners of copies of documents open to public inspection) is amended as follows.

(2) For 'The Commissioners' substitute 'The Commission'.

(3) For 'their possession' substitute 'the Commission's possession'.

(4) At the end add 'or section 75D'.

(5) In the sidenote, for 'Commissioners' substitute 'Commission'.

164

(1) Section 85 (fees and other amounts payable to Commissioners) is amended as follows.

(2) In subsection (1)—

(a) for 'the Commissioners' (in both places) substitute 'the Commission', and
(b) for 'kept by them' substitute 'kept by the Commission'.

(3) In subsection (4)—

(a) for 'The Commissioners' substitute 'The Commission',
(b) for 'they consider' substitute 'it considers', and
(c) for 'by them' substitute 'by it'.

(4) In subsection (5) for 'the Commissioners' substitute 'the Commission'.

(5) In the sidenote, for 'Commissioners' substitute 'Commission'.

165

(1) Section 86 (regulations and orders) is amended as follows.

(2) In subsection (2)(a)—

(a) after '17(2),' insert '73F(6)', and
(b) after '99(2)' insert 'or paragraph 6 of Schedule 1C'.

(3) In subsection (3)—

(a) for 'the Commissioners' (in the first place) substitute 'the Commission', and
(b) for 'the Commissioners consider' substitute 'the Commission considers'.

(4) In subsection (4) after 'above' insert 'or Schedule 5A,'.

166

(1) Section 87 (enforcement of requirement by order of Commissioners) is amended as follows.

(2) In subsection (1)—

(a) for 'the Commissioners' substitute 'the Commission', and
(b) for 'they consider' substitute 'it considers'.

(3) In subsection (2) for 'the Commissioners' (in both places) substitute 'the Commission'.

(4) In the sidenote, for 'Commissioners' substitute 'Commission'.

167

(1) Section 88 (enforcement of orders of Commissioners) is amended as follows.

(2) For paragraph (a) substitute—

'(a) to an order of the Commission under section 9(1), 19A, 19B, 44(2), 61, 73, 73C or 80 above; or'.

(3) In paragraphs (b) and (c) for 'the Commissioners' substitute 'the Commission'.

(4) For 'the Commissioners to' substitute 'the Commission to'.

(5) In the sidenote, for 'Commissioners' substitute 'Commission'.

168

(1) Section 89 (other provisions as to orders of Commissioners) is amended as follows.

(2) In subsection (1)—

(a) for 'the Commissioners' (in the first place) substitute 'the Commission',
(b) for 'the Commissioners think' substitute 'the Commission thinks',
(c) for 'the Commissioners exercise' substitute 'the Commission exercises', and
(d) for 'to them, they may' substitute 'to it, it may'.

(3) In subsection (2)—

(a) for 'the Commissioners make' substitute 'the Commission makes',
(b) for 'they may themselves' substitute 'the Commission may itself', and
(c) for 'they think fit' substitute 'it thinks fit'.

(4) In subsection (3)—

(a) for 'The Commissioners' substitute 'The Commission',
(b) for 'they have' substitute 'it has',
(c) for 'they are' substitute 'it is', and
(d) for 'to them' substitute 'to it'.

(5) In subsection (4) for 'the Commissioners' substitute 'the Commission'.

(6) At the end add—

'(5) Any order made by the Commission under any provision of this Act may be varied or revoked by a subsequent order so made.'

(7) In the sidenote, for 'Commissioners' substitute 'Commission'.

169

In section 90 (directions of the Commissioners) for 'the Commissioners' (in each place including the sidenote) substitute 'the Commission'.

170

In section 91 (service of orders and directions), in subsections (1), (4) and (5), for 'the Commissioners' (in each place) substitute 'the Commission'.

171

Omit section 92 (appeals from Commissioners).

172

In section 93 (miscellaneous provisions as to evidence), for subsection (3) substitute—

'(3) Evidence of any order, certificate or other document issued by the Commission may be given by means of a copy which it retained, or which is taken from a copy so retained, and evidence of an entry in any register kept by it may be given by means of a copy of the entry, if (in each case) the copy is certified in accordance with subsection (4).

(4) The copy shall be certified to be a true copy by any member of the staff of the Commission generally or specially authorised by the Commission to act for that purpose.

(5) A document purporting to be such a copy shall be received in evidence without proof of the official position, authority or handwriting of the person certifying it.

(6) In subsection (3) above 'the Commission' includes the Charity Commissioners for England and Wales.'

173

(1) Section 96 (construction of references to a 'charity' etc) is amended as follows.

(2) In subsection (1) for the definition of 'charity' substitute—

"charity' has the meaning given by section 1(1) of the Charities Act 2006;'.

(3) Omit—

(a) in the definition of 'exempt charity' in subsection (1), the words '(subject to section 24(8) above)', and
(b) subsection (4).

(4) In subsections (5) and (6) for 'The Commissioners' substitute 'The Commission'.

174

In section 97(1) (interpretation)—

(a) in the definition of 'charitable purposes', for 'charitable according to the law of England and Wales;' substitute 'charitable purposes as defined by section 2(1) of the Charities Act 2006;';
(b) for the definition of 'the Commissioners' substitute—
"the Commission' means the Charity Commission;';
(c) in the definition of 'institution', after "institution" insert 'means an institution whether incorporated or not, and'; and
(d) at the appropriate place insert—
"members', in relation to a charity with a body of members distinct from the charity trustees, means any of those members;'
"the Minister' means the Minister for the Cabinet Office;'
"principal regulator', in relation to an exempt charity, means the charity's principal regulator within the meaning of section 13 of the Charities Act 2006;'
"the Tribunal' means the Charity Tribunal;'.

175

In section 97(3) (general interpretation) for 'Part IV or IX' substitute 'Part 4, 7, 8A or 9'.

176

In section 100(3) (extent) for 'Section 10' substitute 'Sections 10 to 10C'.

177

In paragraph (a) of Schedule 2 (exempt charities) for 'the Commissioners' (in the first place) substitute 'the Charity Commissioners for England and Wales'.

178

(1) Schedule 5 (meaning of 'connected person' for the purposes of section 36(2)) is amended as follows.

(2) In paragraph 1 for the words preceding paragraphs (a) to (g) substitute—

'(1) In section 36(2) of this Act 'connected person', in relation to a charity, means any person who falls within sub-paragraph (2)—

(a) at the time of the disposition in question, or
(b) at the time of any contract for the disposition in question.

(2) The persons falling within this sub-paragraph are—'.

(3) Paragraphs (a) to (g) of paragraph 1 become paragraphs (a) to (g) of sub-paragraph (2) (as inserted by sub-paragraph (2) above).

(4) After paragraph (e) of sub-paragraph (2) (as so inserted) insert—

'(ea) a person carrying on business in partnership with any person falling within any of sub-paragraphs (a) to (e) above;';

and in paragraph (f)(i) of that sub-paragraph, for '(e)' substitute '(ea)'.

(5) In paragraph 2—

(a) in sub-paragraph (1), for '1(c)' substitute '1(2)(c)',
(b) in sub-paragraph (2), for '1(e)' substitute '1(2)(e)', and
(c) after that sub-paragraph add—

'(3) Where two persons of the same sex are not civil partners but live together as if they were, each of them shall be treated for those purposes as the civil partner of the other.'

(6) In paragraph 3 for '1(f)' substitute '1(2)(f)'.

(7) In paragraph 4(1) for '1(g)' substitute '1(2)(g)'.

Deregulation and Contracting Out Act 1994 (c 40)

179

(1) Section 79 of the Deregulation and Contracting Out Act 1994 (interpretation of Part 2) is amended as follows.

(2) For subsection (3)(a) substitute—

'(a) any reference to a Minister included a reference to the Forestry Commissioners or to the Charity Commission;
(b) any reference to an officer in relation to the Charity Commission were a reference to a member or member of staff of the Commission; and.'

(3) In subsection (4) after 'those Commissioners' insert 'or that Commission'.

Pensions Act 1995 (c 26)

180

In section 107(1) of the Pensions Act 1995 (disclosure for facilitating discharge of functions by other supervisory authorities), for the entry in the Table relating to the Charity Commissioners substitute—

'The Charity Commission.	Functions under the Charities Act 1993 or the Charities Act 2006.'

Reserve Forces Act 1996 (c 14)

181

(1) Schedule 5 to the Reserve Forces Act 1996 (charitable property on disbanding of units) is amended as follows.

(2) In paragraph 1(2) for 'the Charity Commissioners' substitute 'the Charity Commission'.

(3) In paragraph 4(1)—

(a) for 'Charity Commissioners consider' substitute 'Charity Commission considers', and
(b) for 'they' substitute 'it'.

(4) In paragraph 5(2)—

(a) for 'Charity Commissioners' substitute 'Charity Commission', and
(b) for 'the Commissioners' (in both places) substitute 'the Commission'.

(5) In paragraph 6—

(a) for 'Charity Commissioners' substitute 'Charity Commission',
(b) for 'the Commissioners' substitute 'the Commission', and
(c) for 'their' substitute 'its'.

Trusts of Land and Appointment of Trustees Act 1996 (c 47)

182

In section 6(7) of the Trusts of Land and Appointment of Trustees Act 1996 (limitation on general powers of trustees) for 'Charity Commissioners' substitute 'Charity Commission'.

Housing Act 1996 (c 52)

183

The Housing Act 1996 has effect subject to the following amendments.

184

In section 3(3) (registration as social landlord) for 'Charity Commissioners' substitute 'Charity Commission'.

185

In section 4(6) (removal from the register of social landlords) for 'Charity Commissioners' substitute 'Charity Commission'.

186

In section 6(3) (notice of appeal against decision on removal) for 'Charity Commissioners' substitute 'Charity Commission'.

187

In section 44(3) (consultation on proposals as to ownership and management of landlord's land) for 'Charity Commissioners' substitute 'Charity Commission'.

188

In section 45(4) (service of copy of agreed proposals) for 'Charity Commissioners' substitute 'Charity Commission'.

189

In section 46(2) (notice of appointment of manager to implement agreed proposals) for 'Charity Commissioners' substitute 'Charity Commission'.

190

In section 56(2) (meaning of 'the Relevant Authority') for 'Charity Commissioners' substitute 'Charity Commission'.

191

In section 58(1)(b) (definitions relating to charities)—

(a) for 'under section 3' substitute 'in accordance with section 3A', and
(b) omit the words from 'and is not' onwards.

192

(1) Schedule 1 (regulation of registered social landlords) is amended as follows.

(2) In paragraph 6(2) (exercise of power to appoint new director or trustee) for 'Charity Commissioners' substitute 'Charity Commission'.

(3) In paragraph 10 (change of objects by certain charities)—

(a) in sub-paragraphs (1) and (2) for 'Charity Commissioners' (in each place) substitute 'Charity Commission', and
(b) in sub-paragraph (2) for 'their' substitute 'its'.

(4) In paragraph 18(4), for paragraphs (a) and (b) and the words following them substitute—

'(a) the charity's gross income arising in connection with its housing activities exceeds the sum for the time being specified in section 43(1)(a) of the Charities Act 1993, or
(b) the charity's gross income arising in that connection exceeds the accounts threshold and at the end of that period the aggregate value of its assets (before deduction of liabilities) in respect of its housing activities exceeds the sum for the time being specified in section 43(1)(b) of that Act;

and in this sub-paragraph 'gross income' and 'accounts threshold' have the same meanings as in section 43 of the Charities Act 1993.'

(5) In paragraph 28(4) (notification upon exercise of certain powers in relation to registered charities) for 'Charity Commissioners' substitute 'Charity Commission'.

School Standards and Framework Act 1998 (c 31)

193

The School Standards and Framework Act 1998 has effect subject to the following amendments.

194

(1) Section 23 is amended as follows.

(2) In subsection (1) (certain school bodies to be charities that are exempt charities) omit 'which are exempt charities for the purposes of the Charities Act 1993'.

(3) After that subsection insert—

'(1A) Any body to which subsection (1)(a) or (b) applies is an institution to which section 3A(4)(b) of the Charities Act 1993 applies (institutions to be excepted from registration under that Act).'

(4) In subsection (2) (connected bodies that are to be exempt charities) for the words from 'also' onwards substitute 'be treated for the purposes of section 3A(4)(b) of the Charities Act 1993 as if it were an institution to which that provision applies.'

(5) In subsection (3) (status of certain foundations) for the words from 'which (subject' onwards substitute ', and is an institution to which section 3A(4)(b) of the Charities Act 1993 applies.'

195

In Schedule 1 (education action forums), in paragraph 10, for the words from 'which is' onwards substitute 'within the meaning of the Charities Act 1993, and is an institution to which section 3A(4)(b) of that Act applies (institutions to be excepted from registration under that Act).'

Cathedrals Measure 1999 (No 1)

196

In section 34 of the Cathedrals Measure 1999 (charities) for 'Charity Commissioners' substitute 'Charity Commission'.

Trustee Act 2000 (c 29)

197

In section 19(4) of the Trustee Act 2000 (guidance concerning persons who may be appointed as nominees or custodians) for 'Charity Commissioners' substitute 'Charity Commission'.

Churchwardens Measure 2001 (No 1)

198

In section 2(1) of the Churchwardens Measure 2001 (person disqualified from being churchwarden if disqualified from being a charity trustee)—

(a) for 'Charity Commissioners' substitute 'Charity Commission', and
(b) for 'them' substitute 'it'.

Licensing Act 2003 (c 17)

199

In Schedule 2 to the Licensing Act 2003 (provision of late night refreshment) in paragraph 5(4)—

(a) for 'under section 3' substitute 'in accordance with section 3A', and
(b) for 'subsection (5)' substitute 'subsection (2)'.

Companies (Audit, Investigations and Community Enterprise) Act 2004 (c 27)

200

The Companies (Audit, Investigations and Community Enterprise) Act 2004 has effect subject to the following amendments.

201

In section 39 (existing companies: charities), in subsections (1) and (2), for 'Charity Commissioners' substitute 'Charity Commission'.

202

In section 40 (existing companies: Scottish charities), in subsections (4)(b) and (6), for 'Charity Commissioners' substitute 'Charity Commission'.

203

In section 54(7) (requirements for becoming a charity or a Scottish charity)—

(a) for 'Charity Commissioners' substitute 'Charity Commission', and
(b) for 'their' substitute 'its'.

204

In paragraph 4 of Schedule 3 (regulator of community interest companies)—

(a) for 'Chief Charity Commissioner' substitute 'chairman of the Charity Commission', and
(b) for 'any officer or employee appointed under paragraph 2(1) of Schedule 1 to the Charities Act 1993 (c 10)' substitute 'any other member of the Commission appointed under paragraph 1(2) of Schedule 1A to the Charities Act 1993 or any member of staff of the Commission appointed under paragraph 5(1) of that Schedule'.

Pensions Act 2004 (c 35)

205

The Pensions Act 2004 has effect subject to the following amendments.

206

In Schedule 3 (certain permitted disclosures of restricted information held by the Regulator), for the entry relating to the Charity Commissioners substitute—

'The Charity Commission.	Functions under the Charities Act 1993 (c 10) or the Charities Act 2006.'

207

In Schedule 8 (certain permitted disclosures of restricted information held by the Board), for the entry relating to the Charity Commissioners substitute—

'The Charity Commission.	Functions under the Charities Act 1993 (c 10) or the Charities Act 2006.'

Constitutional Reform Act 2005 (c 4)

208

In Part 3 of Schedule 14 to the Constitutional Reform Act 2005 (the Judicial Appointments Commission: relevant offices etc) after the entries relating to section 6(5) of the Tribunals and Inquiries Act 1992 insert—

'President of the Charity Tribunal	Paragraph 1(2) of Schedule 1B to the Charities Act 1993 (c 10).'
Legal member of the Charity Tribunal	
Ordinary member of the Charity Tribunal	

Charities and Trustee Investment (Scotland) Act 2005 (asp 10)

209

The Charities and Trustee Investment (Scotland) Act 2005 has effect subject to the following amendments.

210

In section 36(1) (powers of OSCR in relation to English and Welsh charities)—

(a) for 'Charity Commissioners for England and Wales inform' substitute 'Charity Commission for England and Wales informs',
(b) for 'under section 3' substitute 'in accordance with section 3A', and
(c) for 'section 3(5) of that Act,' substitute 'subsection (2) of that section,'.

211

In section 69(2)(d)(i) (persons disqualified from being charity trustees)—

(a) at the beginning insert 'by the Charity Commission for England and Wales under section 18(2)(i) of the Charities Act 1993 or', and
(b) for 'under section 18(2)(i) of the Charities Act 1993 (c 10),' substitute ', whether under section 18(2)(i) of that Act or under'.

Equality Act 2006 (c 3)

212

(1) The Equality Act 2006 has effect subject to the following amendments.

(2) In section 58(2) (charities relating to religion or belief)—

(a) for 'Charity Commissioners for England and Wales' substitute 'Charity Commission', and
(b) for 'the Commissioners' substitute 'the Commission'.

(3) In section 79(1)(a) (interpretation) after 'given by' insert 'section 1(1) of'.

NOTES

Initial Commencement

Paras 90(2), 174(d): Royal Assent: 8 November 2006: see s 79(1)(g).

Para 104 (in so far as it confers power to make regulations): Royal Assent: 8 November 2006: see s 79(1)(g).

Paras 1–89, 90(1), 90(3), (4), 91–103, 105–173, 174(a)–(c), 175–212: to be appointed: see s 79(2).

Extent

This Schedule does not extend to Scotland: see s 80(2).

Schedule 9
Repeals and Revocations

Short title and chapter or title and number	*Extent of repeal or revocation*
Police, Factories, &c. (Miscellaneous Provisions) Act 1916 (c 31)	In section 5(1), in paragraph (b) of the proviso, the words from ', and no representation' onwards.
Recreational Charities Act 1958 (c 17)	Section 2.

Short title and chapter or title and number	*Extent of repeal or revocation*
Church Funds Investment Measure 1958 (No 1)	Section 5.
Charities Act 1960 (c 58)	The whole Act.
Housing Act 1985 (c 68)	In section 6A(5), the words from 'and is not' onwards.
Reverter of Sites Act 1987 (c 15)	In section 4(4), the words 'and appeals' and (in both places) ', and to appeals against,'.
Charities Act 1992 (c 41)	Part 1 (so far as unrepealed).
	Part 3.
	Section 76(1)(c) and the word 'and' preceding it.
	In section 77(4), 'or 73'.
	In section 79, in subsection (6) the words '(subject to subsection (7))', and subsection (7).
	Schedule 5.
	In Schedule 6, paragraph 9.
	In Schedule 7, the entry relating to the Police, Factories, &c. (Miscellaneous Provisions) Act 1916.
Charities Act 1993 (c 10)	Section 1.
	In section 2(7), the words from ', and the report' onwards.
	In section 4, subsection (3) and, in subsection (5), the words ', whether given on such an appeal or not'.
	Section 6(9).
	Section 9(4).
	In section 16, in subsection (4)(c) the words 'in the case of a charity other than an exempt charity,', in subsection (5) the words 'which is not an exempt charity and', and subsections (11) to (14).
	In section 17(7), the words from 'but this subsection' onwards.
	Section 18(8) to (10).
	In section 23(2), the words 'or them'.
	In section 24(8), the words from '; and if the scheme' onwards.
	Section 28(10).
	In section 33, in each of subsections (2) and (7) the words '(other than an exempt charity)'.
	Section 44(3).
	Section 46(8).

Short title and chapter or title and number	*Extent of repeal or revocation*
	Section 61(7).
	In section 73(4), the words '(other than an exempt charity)'.
	Section 92.
	In section 96, in the definition of 'exempt charity' in subsection (1) the words '(subject to section 24(8) above)', and subsection (4).
	Schedule 1.
	In Schedule 2, in paragraph (b) the words 'and the colleges of Winchester and Eton', and paragraph (x).
	In Schedule 6, paragraphs 1(2), 26, 28 and 29(2) to (4), (7) and (8).
National Lottery etc Act 1993 (c 39)	In Schedule 5, paragraph 12.
Local Government (Wales) Act 1994 (c 19)	In Schedule 16, paragraph 99.
Deregulation and Contracting Out Act 1994 (c 40)	Section 28.
	Section 29(7) and (8).
Housing Act 1996 (c 52)	In section 58(1)(b), the words from 'and is not' onwards.
Teaching and Higher Education Act 1998 (c 30)	Section 41.
	In Schedule 3, paragraph 9.
School Standards and Framework Act 1998 (c 31)	In section 23(1), the words 'which are exempt charities for the purposes of the Charities Act 1993'.
	In Schedule 30, paragraph 48.
Intervention Board for Agricultural Produce (Abolition) Regulations 2001 (SI 2001/3686)	Regulation 6(11)(a).
Regulatory Reform (National Health Service Charitable and Non-Charitable Trust Accounts and Audit) Order 2005 (SI 2005/1074)	Article 3(5).

NOTES

Initial Commencement

To be appointed: see s 79(2).

Schedule 10
Transitional Provisions and Savings

Section 4: guidance as to operation of public benefit requirement

1

Any consultation initiated by the Charity Commissioners for England and Wales before the day on which section 4 of this Act comes into force is to be as effective for the purposes of section 4(4)(a) as if it had been initiated by the Commission on or after that day.

Section 5: recreational charities etc

2

Where section 2 of the Recreational Charities Act 1958 (c 17) applies to any trusts immediately before the day on which subsection (3) of section 5 of this Act comes into force, that subsection does not prevent the trusts from continuing to be charitable if they constitute a charity in accordance with section 1(1) of this Act.

Section 18: cy-près schemes

3

The amendment made by section 18 applies to property given for charitable purposes whether before or on or after the day on which that section comes into force.

Section 19: suspension or removal of trustee etc from membership of charity

4

The amendment made by section 19 applies where the misconduct or other relevant conduct on the part of the person suspended or removed from his office or employment took place on or after the day on which section 19 comes into force.

Section 20: specific directions for protection of charity

5

The amendment made by section 20 applies whether the inquiry under section 8 of the 1993 Act was instituted before or on or after the day on which section 20 comes into force.

Section 26: offence of obstructing power of entry

6

In relation to an offence committed before the commencement of section 281(5) of the Criminal Justice Act 2003 (c 44) (alteration of penalties for summary offences), the reference to 51 weeks in section 31A(11) of the 1993 Act (as inserted by section 26 of this Act) is to be read as a reference to 3 months.

Section 28: audit or examination of accounts of charity which is not a company

7

The amendments made by section 28 apply in relation to any financial year of a charity which begins on or after the day on which that section comes into force.

Section 29: auditor etc of charity which is not a company to report matters to Commission

8

(1) The amendments made by section 29 apply in relation to matters ('pre-commencement matters') of which a person became aware at any time falling—

(a) before the day on which that section comes into force, and
(b) during a financial year ending on or after that day,

as well as in relation to matters of which he becomes aware on or after that day.

(2) Any duty imposed by or by virtue of the new section 44A(2) or 46(2A) of the 1993 Act inserted by section 29 must be complied with in relation to any such pre-commencement matters as soon as practicable after section 29 comes into force.

Section 32: audit or examination of accounts of charitable companies

9

The amendments made by section 32 apply in relation to any financial year of a charity which begins on or after the day on which that section comes into force.

Section 33: auditor etc of charitable company to report matters to Commission

10

(1) The amendment made by section 33 applies in relation to matters ('pre-commencement matters') of which a person became aware at any time falling—

(a) before the day on which that section comes into force, and
(b) during a financial year ending on or after that day,

as well as in relation to matters of which he becomes aware on or after that day.

(2) Any duty imposed by virtue of the new section 68A(1) of the 1993 Act inserted by section 33 must be complied with in relation to any such pre-commencement matters as soon as practicable after section 33 comes into force.

Section 35: waiver of trustee's disqualification

11

The amendment made by section 35 applies whether the disqualification took effect before, on or after the day on which that section comes into force.

Section 36: remuneration of trustees etc providing services to charity

12

The amendment made by section 36 does not affect the payment of remuneration or provision of services in accordance with an agreement made before the day on which that section comes into force.

Section 38: relief from liability for breach of trust or duty

13

Sections 73D and 73E of the 1993 Act (as inserted by section 38 of this Act) have effect in relation to acts or omissions occurring before the day on which section 38 comes into force as well as in relation to those occurring on or after that day.

Section 44: registration of charity mergers

14

Section 75C of the 1993 Act (as inserted by section 44 of this Act) applies to relevant charity mergers taking place before the day on which section 44 comes into force as well as to ones taking place on or after that day.

Section 67: statements relating to fund-raising

15

The amendments made by section 67 apply in relation to any solicitation or representation to which section 60(1), (2) or (3) of the 1992 Act applies and which is made on or after the day on which section 67 comes into force.

Section 72: Disclosure of information to and by Northern Ireland regulator

16

In relation to an offence committed in England and Wales before the commencement of section 154(1) of the Criminal Justice Act 2003 (c 44) (general limit on magistrates' court's power to impose imprisonment), the reference to 12 months in section 72(6) is to be read as a reference to 6 months.

Schedule 6: group accounts

17

Paragraph 3(2) of the new Schedule 5A inserted in the 1993 Act by Schedule 6 to this Act does not apply in relation to any financial year of a parent charity beginning before the day on which paragraph 3(2) comes into force.

Schedule 8: minor and consequential amendments

18

The following provisions, namely—

(a) paragraphs 80(6) and (8), 83(3) and (4), 99(3), (4)(a) and (5)(a) and (c), 109(12), 111(7) and 171 of Schedule 8, and
(b) the corresponding entries in Schedule 9,

do not affect the operation of the Coal Industry Act 1987 (c 3), the Reverter of Sites Act 1987 (c 15) or the 1993 Act in relation to any appeal brought in the High Court before the day on which those provisions come into force.

19

Paragraph 98(2) of Schedule 8 does not affect the validity of any designation made by the Charity Commissioners for England and Wales under section 2(2) of the 1993 Act which is in effect immediately before that paragraph comes into force.

20

In relation to an offence committed in England and Wales before the commencement of section 154(1) of the Criminal Justice Act 2003 (c 44) (general limit on magistrates' court's power to impose imprisonment), the reference to 12 months in section 10A(4) of the 1993 Act (as inserted by paragraph 104 of Schedule 8 to this Act) is to be read as a reference to 6 months.

Schedule 9: savings on repeal of provisions of Charities Act 1960

21

(1) This paragraph applies where, immediately before the coming into force of the repeal by this Act of section 35(6) of the Charities Act 1960 (c 58) (transfer and evidence of title to property vested in trustees), any relevant provision had effect, in accordance with that provision, as if contained in a conveyance or other document declaring the trusts on which land was held at the commencement of that Act.

(2) In such a case the relevant provision continues to have effect as if so contained despite the repeal of section 35(6) of that Act.

(3) A 'relevant provision' means a provision of any of the following Acts providing for the appointment of trustees—

(a) the Trustee Appointment Act 1850 (c 28),
(b) the Trustee Appointment Act 1869 (c 26),
(c) the Trustees Appointment Act 1890 (c 19), or
(d) the School Sites Act 1852 (c 49) so far as applying any of the above Acts,

as in force at the commencement of the Charities Act 1960.

22

The repeal by this Act of section 39(2) of the Charities Act 1960 (repeal of obsolete enactments) does not affect the continued operation of any trusts which, at the commencement of that Act, were wholly or partly comprised in an enactment specified in Schedule 5 to that Act (enactments repealed as obsolete).

23

The repeal by this Act of section 48(1) of, and Schedule 6 to, the Charities Act 1960 (consequential amendments etc) does not affect the amendments made by Schedule 6 in—

(a) section 9 of the Places of Worship Registration Act 1855 (c 81),
(b) section 4(1) of the Open Spaces Act 1906 (c 25),
(c) section 24(4) of the Landlord and Tenant Act 1927 (c 36), or
(d) section 14(1) or 31 of the New Parishes Measure 1943.

24

Despite the repeal by this Act of section 48(3) of the Charities Act 1960, section 30(3) to (5) of the 1993 Act continue to apply to documents enrolled by or deposited with the Charity Commissioners under the Charitable Trusts Acts 1853 to 1939.

25

Despite the repeal by this Act of section 48(4) of the Charities Act 1960—

(a) any scheme, order, certificate or other document issued under or for the purposes of the Charitable Trusts Acts 1853 to 1939 and having effect in accordance with section 48(4) immediately before the commencement of that repeal continues to have the same effect (and to be enforceable or liable to be discharged in the same way) as would have been the case if that repeal had not come into force, and
(b) any such document, and any document under the seal of the official trustees of charitable funds, may be proved as if the 1960 Act had not been passed.

26

(1) Despite the repeal by this Act of section 48(6) of the Charities Act 1960 (c 58), the official custodian for charities is to continue to be treated as the successor for all purposes both of the official trustee of charity lands and of the official trustees of charitable funds as if—

(a) the functions of the official trustee or trustees had been functions of the official custodian, and
(b) as if the official trustee or trustees had been, and had discharged his or their functions as, holder of the office of the official custodian.

(2) Despite the repeal of section 48(6) (and without affecting the generality of sub-paragraph (1))—

(a) any property which immediately before the commencement of that repeal was, by virtue of section 48(6), held by the official custodian as if vested in him under section 21 of the 1993 Act continues to be so held, and
(b) any enactment or document referring to the official trustee or trustees mentioned above continues to have effect, so far as the context permits, as if the official custodian had been mentioned instead.

27

The repeal by this Act of the Charities Act 1960 does not affect any transitional provision or saving contained in that Act which is capable of having continuing effect but whose effect is not preserved by any other provision of this Schedule.

Schedule 9: savings on repeal of provisions of Charities Act 1992

28

The repeal by this Act of section 49 of, and Schedule 5 to, the 1992 Act (amendments relating to redundant churches etc) does not affect the amendments made by that Schedule in the Redundant Churches and Other Religious Buildings Act 1969.

Schedule 9: repeal of certain repeals made by Charities Acts 1960 and 1992

29

(1) It is hereby declared that (in accordance with sections 15 and 16 of the Interpretation Act 1978 (c 30)) the repeal by this Act of any of the provisions mentioned in sub-paragraph (2) does not revive so much of any enactment or document as ceased to have effect by virtue of that provision.

(2) The provisions are—

(a) section 28(9) of the Charities Act 1960 (repeal of provisions regulating taking of charity proceedings),
(b) section 36 of the 1992 Act (repeal of provisions requiring Charity Commissioners' consent to dealings with charity land), and
(c) section 50 of that Act (repeal of provisions requiring amount of contributions towards maintenance etc of almshouses to be sanctioned by Charity Commissioners).

NOTES

Initial Commencement

To be appointed: see s 79(2).

Appendix 4

List of Primary Regulators for Exempt Charities

Proposed primary regulators

The following table is the list of the proposed primary regulators for exempt charities.

Provision	*Description*	*Proposed regulator*
Section 3 of the 1993 Act		
Section 3(5A)(a)	Higher education corporations	Higher Education Funding Council for England
Section 3(5A)(b)	Further education corporations	Learning and Skills Council
Section 3(5B)(a)(i)	Foundation and voluntary schools	Charity Commission
Section 3(5B)(a)(ii)	Education Action Forums	Charity Commission
Section 24(8)	Common investment funds	Charity Commission
Section 25(2)	Common deposit schemes	Charity Commission
	Common deposit funds	Charity Commission
Paragraph of Sch 2		
(a)	Several universities	Higher Education Funding Council for England
	Property falling within the Methodist Church Funds Act 1960	Charity Commission
	The representative body of the Welsh Church and property vested in or administered by it	Charity Commission
	Property within the Church Funds Investment Measure 1958	Charity Commission
(b)	Universities of Oxford, Cambridge, London, Durham and Newcastle	Higher Education Funding Council for England
	Colleges and halls in the universities of Oxford, Cambridge and Durham	Charity Commission
	Queen Mary and Westfield College in the University of London	Higher Education Funding Council for England
	The colleges of Winchester and Eton	Charity Commission

Provision	*Description*	*Proposed regulator*
(c)	Any university, university college or institution connected with a university or university college which Her Majesty declares by Order in Council to be an exempt charity for the purposes of the Charities Act 1993	Higher Education Funding Council for England (universities in England), Charity Commission (universities in Wales and university colleges and institutions connected with a university in England or Wales)
(d)	[Repealed]	
(da)	The Qualifications and Curriculum Authority	Department for Education and Skills
(e)	[Repealed]	
(f)	The Qualifications, Curriculum and Assessment Authority for Wales	Welsh Assembly Government
(g)	[Repealed]	
(h)	[Repealed]	
(i)	A successor company to a higher education corporation (within the meaning of section 129(5) of the Education Reform Act 1988) at a time when an institution conducted by the company is for the time being designated under that section	Higher Education Funding Council for England (organisations in England) and the Charity Commission (organisations in Wales)
(j)	[Repealed]	
(k)	Victoria and Albert Museum	Department for Culture, Media and Sport
(l)	Science Museum	Department for Culture, Media and Sport
(m)	Armouries	Department for Culture, Media and Sport
(n)	Royal Botanic Gardens, Kew	Department for Culture, Media and Sport
(o)	National Museums and Galleries on Merseyside	Department for Culture, Media and Sport
(p)	British Museum	Department for Culture, Media and Sport
	Natural History Museum	Department for Culture, Media and Sport
(q)	National Gallery	Department for Culture, Media and Sport
(r)	Tate Gallery	Department for Culture, Media and Sport
(s)	National Portrait Gallery	Department for Culture, Media and Sport
(t)	Wallace Collection	Department for Culture, Media and Sport

Provision	*Description*	*Proposed regulator*
(u)	Imperial War Museum	Department for Culture, Media and Sport
(v)	National Maritime Museum	Department for Culture, Media and Sport
(w)	Any institution which is administered by or on behalf of an institution included above and is established for the general purposes of, or for any special purpose of or in connection with, the last named institutions	As for the parent institution except students' unions who would be required to register with the Charity Commission
(x)	The Church Commissioners and any institution adminstered by them	Charity Commission
(y)	Any charitable registered society within the meaning of the Industrial and Provident Societies Act 1965	Housing Corporation for RSLs, Charity Commission for others
	Any charitable registered society or branch within the meaning of the Friendly Socities Act 1974	
(z)	Museum of London	Department for Culture, Media and Sport
(za)	British Library	Department for Culture, Media and Sport
(zb)	Community Fund	Department for Culture, Media and Sport

Table of Statutes

Paragraph references printed in **bold** type indicate where the Act is set out in part or in full.

Table of Statutory Instruments

Paragraph references printed in **bold** type indicate where the section of a Statutory Instrument is set out in part or in full.

Table of Cases

Index

References are to paragraph numbers.